Springer Proceedings in Mathematics & Statistics

Volume 66

For further volumes:
http://www.springer.com/series/10533

Springer Proceedings in Mathematics & Statistics

This book series features volumes composed of select contributions from workshops and conferences in all areas of current research in mathematics and statistics, including OR and optimization. In addition to an overall evaluation of the interest, scientific quality, and timeliness of each proposal at the hands of the publisher, individual contributions are all refereed to the high quality standards of leading journals in the field. Thus, this series provides the research community with well-edited, authoritative reports on developments in the most exciting areas of mathematical and statistical research today.

Roger E. Millsap • L. Andries van der Ark
Daniel M. Bolt • Carol M. Woods
Editors

New Developments in Quantitative Psychology

Presentations from the 77th Annual Psychometric Society Meeting

Springer

Editors
Roger E. Millsap
Department of Psychology
Arizona State University
Tempe, AZ, USA

L. Andries van der Ark
Department of Methodology and Statistics
Tilburg University
Tilburg, The Netherlands

Daniel M. Bolt
Department of Educational Psychology
University of Wisconsin
Madison, WI, USA

Carol M. Woods
Department of Psychology
University of Kansas
Lawrence, KS, USA

ISSN 2194-1009 ISSN 2194-1017 (electronic)
ISBN 978-1-4614-9347-1 ISBN 978-1-4614-9348-8 (eBook)
DOI 10.1007/978-1-4614-9348-8
Springer New York Heidelberg Dordrecht London

Library of Congress Control Number: 2014930294

Printed on acid-free paper

Springer is part of Springer Science+Business Media (www.springer.com)

Preface

This volume represents presentations given at the 77th annual meeting of the Psychometric Society, held at the Cornhusker Hotel in Lincoln, Nebraska, during July 9–12, 2012. The annual meeting of the Psychometric Society typically attracts participants from around the world, and the 2012 conference was no exception. Attendees came from more than 15 different countries, with 149 papers being presented, along with 50 poster presentations, three workshops, two keynote speakers, six state-of-the-art speakers, five invited presentations, and seven invited symposia. A full list of the conference presentation titles can be found in the January 2013 issue of *Psychometrika*, pp. 188–201. We thank the local organizer Ralph de Ayala, along with his staff and students, for hosting a successful conference.

The idea for the present volume began with the recognition that many of the useful ideas presented at the conference do not become available to a wider audience unless the authors decide to seek publication in one of the quantitative journals. This volume provides an opportunity for the presenters to make their ideas available to the wider research community more quickly, while still being thoroughly reviewed. The 31 chapters published here address a diverse set of topics, including item response theory, reliability, test design, test validation, response styles, factor analysis, structural equation modeling, categorical data analysis, longitudinal data analysis, test equating, and latent score estimation. For the published chapters, we asked the authors to include the ideas presented in their conference papers, and we also gave them the opportunity to expand on these ideas in the published chapters. Psychological measurement is playing a larger role internationally than ever before, not only in educational applications but also in medicine and neuroscience. It is important that this expanding role be supported by rigorous and thoughtful research. We thank all of the chapter authors for their fine contributions to this volume. We hope that the contents of this volume will stimulate wider interest in psychometric research, both theoretical and applied.

Tempe, AZ, USA — Roger E. Millsap
Madison, WI, USA — Daniel M. Bolt
Tilburg, The Netherlands — L. Andries van der Ark
Lawrence, KS, USA — Carol M. Woods

Preface

Lawrence, KS, USA

Contents

A Nonparametric Ability Measure

Nan L. Kong

1 Introduction

Before we define an ability measure, we need to make clear about the concept of measure. In this section, we look into several well-defined measures from which we try to find the property in common across these measures. We believe that the ability measure, which is the topic of this paper, should also be defined on the basis of this common property.

It is well known that the area of a rectangle is measured by the product of its length and width. For example, for a rectangle with length of 2 and width of 1, the area can be directly measured with $2 = 2 \times 1$. Actually, this rectangle can also be measured indirectly: (i) split this rectangle into two unit squares with both length and width equal to 1; (ii) the areas of these two unit squares are measured with $1 = 1 \times 1$; (iii) make summation of these two area measures in (ii) with $2 = 1 + 1$. The summation in (iii) is the "indirect" measure of the area of the rectangle with length of 2 and width of 1. As we can see, both "direct" and "indirect" area measures on this rectangle produce the same value which is 2 in this example. The relation between "direct" and "indirect" area measures is mathematically expressed by $2 \times 1 = 1 \times 1 + 1 \times 1$. The left-hand side of this equation corresponds to "direct" measure while the right-hand side corresponds to "indirect" measure. Generally, for the same area, both "direct" and "indirect" measures must produce the same value—this is called *additivity* according to the measure theory (Halmos 1974). In the same example, if we measure the area of the rectangle by summation of length and width, instead of product of its length and width, with the steps in (i)–(iii), we will receive two different values for the "direct" measure, which is $3 = 1 + 2$, and the "indirect" measures which is $4 = (1 + 1) + (1 + 1)$. Obviously, with summation of length and

N.L. Kong (✉)
Educational Testing Service, 270 Hampshire Dr., Plainsboro, NJ 08536, USA
e-mail: nankg@yahoo.com

R.E. Millsap et al. (eds.), *New Developments in Quantitative Psychology*, Springer Proceedings in Mathematics & Statistics 66, DOI 10.1007/978-1-4614-9348-8_1,

width, the area of the rectangle is measured in a wrong way—the way that has no additivity. Any measure without additivity is similar to measuring area of rectangle by summation of its length and width.

In measure theory (Halmos 1974), a set function is a function whose domain of definition is a class of sets. An extended real-valued set function $\mu(.)$ defined on a class S of sets is additive if, whenever $E \in S$, $F \in S$, $E \cup F \in S$, and $E \cap F = \emptyset$, then $\mu(E \cup F) = \mu(E) + \mu(F)$. For the measure of the rectangle area, the class S contains all rectangles (each rectangle is a set of points) and $\mu(.)$ is defined by the product of its length and width.

The next well-defined measure is called probability which measures randomness (Hays 1970). If two events A and B are exclusive, we have

$$Prob(A \cup B) = Prob(A) + Prob(B). \tag{1}$$

Equation (1) is called *additivity*.

In information theory, the entropy (Shannon 1948; Wiener 1948) is defined to measure the uncertainty in the random variables. One of the entropy fundamental properties is the following equation:

$$H(X,Y) = H(X) + H(Y) - I(X,Y), \tag{2}$$

where X and Y are two categorical random variables; $H(X)$ and $H(Y)$ are the entropies for X and Y, respectively; $H(X,Y)$ is the entropy of X and Y; $I(X,Y)$ is the mutual information among X and Y.

If X and Y are independent from each other, which implies $I(X,Y) = 0$, Eq. (2) becomes

$$H(X,Y) = H(X) + H(Y). \tag{3}$$

Equation (3) is called *additivity*.

Unlike Shannon's entropy, Fisher information (Fisher 1922 and 1925) is defined to measure the parameter(s)' information given random variable(s). If random variables X and Y are independent, we have

$$I_{X,Y}(\theta) = I_X(\theta) + I_Y(\theta), \tag{4}$$

where $I_{X,Y}(\theta)$ is the Fisher information given X and Y; $I_X(\theta)$ and $I_Y(\theta)$ are the Fisher information given X and Y, respectively. θ is the parameter(s).

Equation (4) is called *additivity*.

So far, we have looked into the theoretical structures for several well-defined measures. All of these structures reveal the same property—*additivity* as shown in (1), (3) and (4). We believe that the *additivity* is the general property for a measure. The purpose of this paper is to study a new ability measure and, therefore, it is requested that this ability measure be of the property of the additivity. In the next section, an ability measure is defined and studied according to the additivity.

2 A Nonparametric Ability Measure

In testing and psychometrics, the term ability means the knowledge, skills, or other characteristics of a test taker measured by the test. A test question, with any stimulus material provided with the test question, and the response choice or the scoring rules, is called an item. Items that are scored in two categories - right (R) or wrong (W) - are referred to as dichotomous items. In this section, the test taker's ability will be measured on the basis of a test consisting of a set of dichotomous items. For a test consisting of I items, let X_i be the item-score variable for the item i ($i = 1,\dots,I$), with realization $X_i \in \{W,R\}$. Also, we suppose that a respondent answers $L(0 \leq L \leq I)$ items correctly, then these correctly answered items are indicated by $i_1,\dots,i_l,\dots,i_L$. For example, suppose an item-response vector of RRWWWR, then $I = 6, L = 3, i_1 = 1, i_2 = 2$, and $i_3 = 6$. The probability of right response for i_1 is denoted by $P(X_{i_1} = R)$ and, the probability of right responses for both i_1 and i_2 is denoted by $P(X_{i_l} = R, X_{i_2} = R)$, etc.

Definition 1. The ability with right (R) response(s) for items i_l ($l = 1,\dots,L; L \geq 1$) is defined as

$$\theta(i_1,\dots,i_l,\dots,i_L) = -ln(P(X_{i_1} = R,\dots,X_{i_l} = R,\dots,X_{i_L} = R)).(L \geq 1) \quad (5)$$

In (5), $\theta(i_1,\dots,i_l,\dots,i_L)$ is called the measure of the ability with right (R) response(s) for the items $i_l(l = 1,\dots,L)$. We also request that the examinee's ability be measured as zero if this examinee does not respond to any item correctly, i.e. $L = 0$ in (5).

In Definition 1, only the probabilities on correctly responded items are used for measuring abilities, some probabilities such as those for incorrectly responded items are not shown in (5). Because the probabilities on any combinations of the correctly responded items and the incorrectly responded items can be fully expressed by the probabilities on those correctly responded items, the probabilities on correctly responded items have fully represented all of the information associated with the joint probabilities. Therefore, the ability measure in Definition 1 has lost nothing in terms of the information associated with the joint probabilities.

If items $i_1,\dots,i_L$ are (jointly) independent, the following equation can be obtained directly from Definition 1 and shows that the ability measure in Definition 1 is additive

$$\theta(i_1,\cdots,i_L) = \theta(i_1) + \cdots + \theta(i_L). \quad (6)$$

As we can see in Eq. (6) that, if the items are jointly independent, the measure of examinee's total ability with right responses on all these items is the summation of the measures of the examinee's abilities with right responses on each of these items. The additivity in Eq. (6) implies that the summation of the ability measures on subscales can be the total ability measure if and only if these subscales are jointly independent. For the case that the items are not jointly independent, not only the ability measure on each subscale but also the interactions among the items play the roles in total ability measure. In Sect. 4, the total ability measure will be studied in more detail.

Corollary 1.

$$0 \leq \theta(i_1,\cdots,i_L) \leq +\infty. \tag{7}$$

Proof. This is obvious from Definition 1.

Corollary 2.

$$\theta(i_1,\cdots,i_L) = 0 \iff P(X_{i_l} = R,\cdots,X_{i_L} = R) = 1 \tag{8}$$

Proof. This is obvious from Definition 1.

Corollary 3.

$$\theta(i_1,\cdots,i_L) = +\infty \iff P(X_{i_l} = R,\cdots,X_{i_L} = R) = 0 \tag{9}$$

Proof. This is obvious from Definition 1.

As shown in Corollary 1, the ability measure defined in (5) is nonnegative which implies the total ability measure is always greater than or equal to the ability measure on each subscale according to the additivity. Because the minus sign has no meaning in the ability measure, the additivity requests that the ability measure be nonnegative (generally, the measure theory always requests that a measure be nonnegative).

Now, assume that $0 < M \leq L$, there is

$$\begin{aligned}
\theta(i_1,\cdots,i_M) &= -ln(P(X_{i_l} = R,\cdots,X_{i_M} = R)) \\
&\leq -ln(P(X_{i_l} = R,\cdots,X_{i_M} = R) \\
&\quad \times P(X_{i_{M+1}} = R,\cdots,X_{i_L} = R|X_{i_l} = R,\cdots,X_{i_M} = R)) \\
&= -ln(P(X_{i_l} = R,\cdots,X_{i_L} = R)) = \theta(i_1,\cdots,i_L)
\end{aligned}$$

Therefore, the following theorem is obtained:

Theorem 1. *For* $0 < M \leq L$,

$$\theta(i_1,\cdots,i_M) \leq \theta(i_1,\cdots i_L) \tag{10}$$

Theorem 1 is another fundamental property of the ability measure: the measure of the ability associated with subset of all correctly responded items is no greater than the measure of the ability associated with all correctly responded items, i.e. the measure of the ability associated with subscale can not be greater than the measure of its total ability.

In summary, the ability measure defined in (5) has the following properties: (a) Additivity (if the items are independent) as shown in Eq. (6). (b) The ability measure is nonnegative. Therefore, the total ability measure is greater than or equal to the ability measure on each subscale. (c) The ability measures with the same response patterns are the same (this is obvious by Definition 1). (d) The ability measure on a response pattern is greater than or equal to the ability measure on the subset of its response pattern (Theorem 1). (e) The ability measure is determined by the difficulties of the items and the interactions among those items. The more difficult and more jointly independent items cause higher ability measure. (f) The ability measure in Definition 1 has no specific parametric structure. Therefore, the ability measure in Definition 1 has no those assumptions or limitations associated with the specific parametric structure. (g) The ability measure is defined with the joint probability of the items in a given test and all of the response vectors out of these items are utilized for measuring ability, therefore, the ability is measured with full information for given joint probabilities.

In the next two sections, the following properties of the ability measure defined in (5) will be studied: (h) With the additivity, it is possible to measure the shared ability and unique ability. Generally speaking, an examinee's ability consists of two parts: the unique part that belongs to the examinee and the part shared with others. (i) The total ability measure and the ability measures on subscales are related to the additivity. Therefore, the interactive structures of the total ability and those abilities associated with the subscales can be mathematically expressed.

3 Shared Ability Measure and Conditional Ability Measure

Because the ability measure in Definition 1 has the property of additivity, it is possible to measure the shared ability among the correctly responded items and unique ability of each correctly responded item.

Definition 2. The shared ability among correctly responded items i_1 and i_2 is measured with

$$\theta(i_1 * i_2) = \theta(i_1) + \theta(i_2) - \theta(i_1, i_2), \tag{11}$$

where $\theta(i_1)$, $\theta(i_2)$, and $\theta(i_1, i_2)$ are defined in Definition 1.

According to Definitions 1 and 2, the following equation can be obtained:

$$\theta(i_1 * i_2) = -ln\frac{P(X_{i_1} = R)P(X_{i_2} = R)}{P(X_{i_1} = R, X_{i_2} = R)} \tag{12}$$

By (12), it is obvious that $\theta(i_1 * i_2) = \theta(i_2 * i_1)$.

The following theorem offers a sufficient and necessary condition for no shared ability between two items i_1 and i_2.

Theorem 2.

$$\theta(i_1 * i_2) = 0 \iff i_1 \textit{ and } i_2 \textit{ are independent}.$$

Proof. Let X_{i_1} and X_{i_2} be the item-score variables of the items i_1 and i_2. By Definition 1,

$$\theta(i_1) = -ln(P(X_{i_1} = R), \tag{13}$$

$$\theta(i_2) = -ln(P(X_{i_2} = R), \tag{14}$$

$$\theta(i_1, i_2) = -ln(P(X_{i_1} = R, X_{i_2} = R)). \tag{15}$$

Therefore, X_{i_1} and X_{i_2} are independent if and only if

$$\theta(i_1, i_2) = \theta(i_1) + \theta(i_2)$$

By Eq. (11), we have

$$\theta(i_1 * i_2) = 0$$

This is the proof of Theorem 2.

In concept, the shared ability is closer to the concept of interaction between those items associated with different respondents or subscales. The stronger association between those items implies that the more abilities are shared. For example, if two items are identical, the shared ability is the same as the ability associated with each of those items. Another extreme case is that, if two items are independent, the shared ability is zero. The shared ability is also related to the redundant or overlapped information among the items, i.e. the items could be heavily similar to each other in which the scope for those items to cover for testing could be limited. Therefore, the shared ability among the different items should not be too big.

Unlike the ability measure in Definition 1 which is nonnegative, the shared ability measure in Definition 2 can be negative. If an examinee with correct response on one item tends to correctly respond to another item, this examinee has positive shared ability among these two items. If an examinee with correct response on one item tends to wrongly respond to another item, this examinee has negative shared ability among these two items. In practice, for most of cases, the shared ability is positive. The negative shared ability only happens for two items associated with the exclusive abilities.

Definition 3. The unique or conditional ability with i_1 given i_2 is measured with

$$\theta(i_1|i_2) = -lnP(X_{i_1} = R|X_{i_2} = R). \tag{16}$$

Corollary 4.

$$\theta(i_1, i_2) = \theta(i_2) + \theta(i_1|i_2) \tag{17}$$

Proof. The proof is obvious from Definitions 1 and 3 with noting that:

$$\theta(i_1|i_2) = -ln(P(X_{i_1} = R|X_{i_2} = R)) = -ln(P(X_{i_1} = R, X_{i_2} = R)) + ln(P(X_{i_2} = R))$$

Corollary 5.

$$\theta(i_1 * i_2) = \theta(i_1) - \theta(i_1|i_2) \tag{18}$$

Proof. The proof is obvious from Definition 2 and Corollary 4.

The unique or conditional ability $\theta(i_1|i_2)$ measures the part of the ability with i_1, but exclusive of i_2, that is, $\theta(i_1|i_2)$ measures the unique ability associated with i_1 out of the ability associated with i_1 and i_2. The following equation, which can be proved with Corollaries 4 and 5, describes the relation among total ability, shared ability, and unique ability:

$$\theta(i_1, i_2) = \theta(i_1 * i_2) + \theta(i_1|i_2) + \theta(i_2|i_1). \tag{19}$$

In (19), the $\theta(i_1, i_2)$ is decomposed into three parts—the shared ability associated with i_1 and i_2, the unique ability associated with i_1 with exclusive of the ability associated with i_2, and the unique ability associated with i_2 with exclusive of the ability associated with i_1. Equation (19) is also available in probability and entropy:

$$P(A \cup B) = P(A \cap B) + P(A \cap B^c) + P(B \cap A^c),$$
$$H(X, Y) = I(X, Y) + H(X|Y) + H(Y|X),$$

where A and B are events; A^c and B^c are the events "not A" and "not B". X and Y are two random variables; $H(X,Y)$ is the entropy of X and Y; $H(X)$ and $H(Y)$ are the entropies for X and Y, respectively; $H(X|Y)$ is the conditional entropy of X given Y; $I(X,Y)$ is the mutual information among X and Y.

Theorem 3.

$$\theta(i_1 * i_2) \leq \theta(i_1) \tag{20}$$

Proof.

$$P(X_{X_{i_2}} = R) \geq P(X_{i_1} = R, X_{i_2} = R) \iff ln\frac{P(X_{i_2} = R)}{P(X_{i_1} = R, X_{i_2} = R)} \geq 0$$
$$\iff -ln\frac{P(X_{i_1} = R, X_{i_2} = R)}{P(X_{i_1} = R)P(X_{i_2} = R)} \leq -lnP(X_{i_1} = R)$$
$$\iff \theta(i_1 * i_2) \leq \theta(i_1).$$

This is the proof of Theorem 3.

The measure of the shared ability associated with i_1 and i_2 in Definition 2 can be extended into the measure of the shared ability associated with $i_1, i_2, \cdots, i_L$ which is denoted by $\theta(i_1 * \cdots * i_L)$. Without loss of generality, $\theta(i * i_2 * i_3)$ can be defined by:

$$\begin{aligned}\theta(i_1 * i_2 * i_3) &= \theta(i_1) + \theta(i_2) + \theta(i_3) - \theta(i_1, i_2) \\ &\quad - \theta(i_1, i_3) - \theta(i_2, i_3) + \theta(i_1, i_2, i_3).\end{aligned} \tag{21}$$

Obviously, according to (21), (joint) independence among i_1, i_2, and i_3 implies that $\theta(i_1 * i_2 * i_3) = 0$. Similar to $\theta(i_1 * i_2)$, $\theta(i_1 * i_2 * i_3)$ can be negative, but the interpretation for this is more complicated. Roughly speaking, $\theta(i_1 * i_2 * i_3)$ is the interactive ability contribution by i_1, i_2, and i_3 to the total ability $\theta(i_1, i_2, i_3)$.

4 Total Ability and Abilities Associated with Subscales

Given the item responses $i_1 \dots i_L$ answered correctly by a respondent, the examinees' abilities can be measured according to (5). The ability measured by (5) is called the overall or total ability because it is measured by all correctly answered items. In case that those correctly answered item responses $i_1 \dots i_L$ contain several subscales in which each subscale is associated with a subset of $\{i_1 \dots i_L\}$, we need to measure the examinees' abilities on the basis of each subscale. First, let us look into the case of two subscales: S_1 and S_2 which S_1 is associated with the subset $\{i_{j_1}, \dots, i_{j_M}\}$ and S_2 is associated with the subset $\{i_{k_1}, \dots, i_{k_N}\}$ where $M \leq L$ and $N \leq L$. Here the intersection of $\{i_{j_1}, \dots, i_{j_M}\}$ and $\{i_{k_1}, \dots, i_{k_N}\}$ may not be empty set $\emptyset$, that is, some items may be associated with both S_1 and S_2. We also assume that $\{i_{j_1}, \dots, i_{j_M}\} \cup \{i_{k_1}, \dots, i_{k_N}\} = \{i_1 \dots i_L\}$.

Without loss of generality, the total ability and the abilities associated with the subscales S_1 and S_2 are measured with

$$\theta(Total) = -ln(P(X_{i_1} = R, \cdots, X_{i_L} = R)), \tag{22}$$

$$\theta(S_1) = -ln(P(X_{i_{j_1}} = R, \cdots, X_{i_{j_M}} = R)), \tag{23}$$

$$\theta(S_2) = -ln(P(X_{i_{k_1}} = R, \cdots, X_{i_{k_N}} = R)). \tag{24}$$

Here X_i is the item-score variable for the item i. Because $\theta(S_1)$ and $\theta(S_2)$ in (23) and (24) are defined with the subsets $\{i_{j_1}, \dots, i_{j_M}\}$ and $\{i_{k_1}, \dots, i_{k_N}\}$ out of total correctly answered items $\{i_1 \dots i_L\}$, the $\theta(S_1)$ and $\theta(S_2)$ are also called marginal measures of the abilities associated with S_1 and S_2.

Similar to Definition 2, we can define the measure for the shared ability associated with S_1 and S_2.

Definition 4. The shared ability associated with S_1 and S_2 is measured with

$$\theta(S_1 * S_2) = \theta(S_1) + \theta(S_2) - \theta(S_1, S_2), \tag{25}$$

where

$$\theta(S_1,S_2) = \theta(Total) = -ln(P(X_{i_1} = R, \cdots, X_{i_L} = R)). \tag{26}$$

Equivalently, by Definition 4

$$\theta(Total) = \theta(S_1) + \theta(S_2) - \theta(S_1 * S_2). \tag{27}$$

Equation (27) expresses the relation among the measures of the total ability and the abilities associated with the S_1 and S_2. From Definition 4, it is obvious that, if S_1 and S_2 are independent, the measure of the total ability is the summation of the measures of the abilities associated with S_1 and S_2, i.e. $\theta(Total) = \theta(S_1) + \theta(S_2)$. Also, similar to (12), $\theta(S_1 * S_2)$ can be negative in case that the abilities associated with S_1 and S_2 are exclusive from each other.

In Eq. (22), some items may be shared by both S_1 and S_2. Obviously, these shared items contribute the relation between S_1 and S_2 (the items which are not shared by S_1 and S_2 also contribute the relation between S_1 and S_2 because those not-shared items may be related across the different subscales) and relation between S_1 and S_2 determines $\theta(S_1 * S_2)$ in Eq. (27). Therefore, the total ability measure is affected by the shared items through their interactive ability measure $\theta(S_1 * S_2)$.

Definition 5. The conditional ability associated with S_1 given the ability associated with S_2 is measured with

$$\theta(S_1|S_2) = \theta(Total) - \theta(S_2), \tag{28}$$

where $\theta(Total) = \theta(S_1,S_2)$ which is defined in (22).

$\theta(S_1|S_2)$ in (28) measures the ability associated with S_1 with exclusion of S_2. If S_1 and S_2 are independent, $\theta(S_1|S_2)$ is equal to $\theta(S_1)$, i.e. $\theta(S_1|S_2) = \theta(S_1)$.

Similar to Eq. (19), the following theorem shows the same decomposition of the total ability in terms of the subscales.

Theorem 4.

$$\theta(Total) = \theta(S_1|S_2) + \theta(S_2|S_1) + \theta(S_1 * S_2) \tag{29}$$

Proof. By Definition 5, there is

$$\theta(S_1|S_2) = \theta(Total) - \theta(S_2), \tag{30}$$

$$\theta(S_2|S_1) = \theta(Total) - \theta(S_1). \tag{31}$$

By (30) + (31) and (27),

$$\theta(S_1|S_2) + \theta(S_2|S_1) = 2\theta(Total) - \theta(S_1) - \theta(S_2)$$

$$\Longleftrightarrow$$

$$\theta(S_1|S_2)+\theta(S_2|S_1)=\theta(\mathit{Total})-\theta(S_1*S_2)$$

$$\Longleftrightarrow$$

$$\theta(\mathit{Total})=\theta(S_1|S_2)+\theta(S_2|S_1)+\theta(S_1*S_2).$$

This is the proof of Theorem 4.

In Theorem 4, the measure of the total ability is the summation of the measure of the ability associated with S_1 with exclusion of S_2 and the measure of the ability associated with S_2 with exclusion of S_1 and the measure of the shared ability among S_1 and S_2. Obviously, if S_1 and S_2 are independent, the measure of the total ability is the summation of the measures of the ability associated with S_1 and the ability associated with S_2, i.e. $\theta(\mathit{Total})=\theta(S_1)+\theta(S_2)$.

So far, we have discussed the measures on the abilities associated with two subscales. In case of multiple subscales, the measures can be defined in the similar way. Without loss of generality, let us look into the case of three subscales S_1, S_2, and S_3 which their items are those items in $\mathscr{S}_1$, $\mathscr{S}_2$ and $\mathscr{S}_3$, the subsets of all correctly responded items, which is $\{i_1,\ldots,i_L\}$, respectively.

$$\begin{aligned}
S_1 &\sim \mathscr{S}_1 \subseteq \{i_1,\ldots,i_L\}\\
S_2 &\sim \mathscr{S}_2 \subseteq \{i_1,\ldots,i_L\}\\
S_3 &\sim \mathscr{S}_3 \subseteq \{i_1,\ldots,i_L\}\\
\mathit{Total} &\sim \{i_1,\ldots,i_L\},
\end{aligned}$$

where "$S_1 \sim \mathscr{S}_1$" means the items that belong to subscale S_1 are those in the set $\mathscr{S}_1$, which is a subset of all correctly responded items $\{i_1,\ldots,i_L\}$. Also, we assume $\mathscr{S}_1\cup\mathscr{S}_2\cup\mathscr{S}_3=\{i_1,\ldots,i_L\}$.

Definition 6. The measure of the shared abilities associated with S_1, S_2, and S_3 is defined by

$$\begin{aligned}
\theta(S_1*S_2*S_3) &= \theta(S_1)+\theta(S_2)+\theta(S_3)\\
&\quad -\theta(S_1,S_2)-\theta(S_1,S_3)-\theta(S_2,S_3)+\theta(S_1,S_2,S_3), \qquad (32)
\end{aligned}$$

where

$$\theta(S_1,S_2,S_3) = \theta(\mathit{Total}) = -ln(P(X_{i_1}=R,\ldots,X_{i_L}=R)), \qquad (33)$$

$$\theta(S_j,S_k) = -ln(P(X_{i_1}=R,\ldots,X_{i_{M_{j,k}}}=R)). \qquad (34)$$

In Eq. (34), the $M_{j,k}$ correctly responded items $i_1,\ldots,i_{M_{j,k}}$ are exactly those in $\mathscr{S}_j\cup\mathscr{S}_k$, i.e. $\{i_1,\ldots,i_{M_{j,k}}\}=\mathscr{S}_j\cup\mathscr{S}_k$ for $j,k=1,2,3$.

It is interesting to compare the similar structure between Eqs. (21) and (32) and, in fact, Eq. (21) is nothing but a special case of Eq. (32) if each subscale only contains a single item. Similar to $\theta(S_1 * S_2)$, $\theta(S_1 * S_2 * S_3)$ can be negative, but its interpretation is more complicated. Although $\theta(S_1 * S_2 * S_3)$ is called shared ability here, this concept is closer to the interaction among the abilities associated with S_1, S_2, and S_3.

Corollary 6. *If S_1, S_2 and S_3 are (jointly) independent, then*

$$\theta(Total) = \theta(S_1) + \theta(S_2) + \theta(S_3). \tag{35}$$

Proof. The proof is obvious by the definitions:

$\theta(S_i) = -ln(P(X_{i_1} = R, \ldots, X_{i_{M_i}} = R))$ where the M_i correctly responded items $i_1, \ldots, i_{M_i}$ are exactly those in $\mathcal{S}_i$, i.e. $\{i_1, \ldots, i_{M_i}\} = \mathcal{S}_i$ for $i = 1,2,3$.

$\theta(Total) = -ln(P(X_{i_1} = R, \ldots, X_{i_L} = R))$ where the L correctly responded items $i_1, \ldots, i_L$ are exactly those in $\mathcal{S}_1 \cup \mathcal{S}_2 \cup \mathcal{S}_3$, i.e. $\{i_1, \ldots, i_L\} = \mathcal{S}_1 \cup \mathcal{S}_2 \cup \mathcal{S}_3$.

Equation (35) in Corollary 6 is another example of additivity in terms of their subscales. Equation (6) can be thought as a special case of Eq. (35) for each subscale to associate with a single item. Although there are three subscales in Corollary 6, the property of additivity is also true for the case of multiple subscales.

Corollary 7. *If S_1, S_2 and S_3 are (jointly) independent, then*

$$\theta(S_1 * S_2 * S_3) = 0. \tag{36}$$

Proof. The proof is similar to that in Corollary 6.

Theorem 5.

$$\begin{aligned}\theta(Total) = \; & \theta(S_1) + \theta(S_2) + \theta(S_3) - \theta(S_1 * S_2) - \theta(S_1 * S_3) \\ & -\theta(S_2 * S_3) + \theta(S_1 * S_2 * S_3).\end{aligned} \tag{37}$$

Proof. First, similar to (25), there are

$$\theta(S_j, S_k) = \theta(S_j) + \theta(S_k) - \theta(S_j * S_k) \qquad for \;\; j,k = 1,2,3 \tag{38}$$

By Definition 6 and (38), there is

$$\begin{aligned}&\theta(S_1 * S_2 * S_3) \\ &\quad = \theta(S_1) + \theta(S_2) + \theta(S_3) - \theta(S_1, S_2) - \theta(S_1, S_3) - \theta(S_2, S_3) + \theta(S_1, S_2, S_3) \\ &\quad = \theta(S_1) + \theta(S_2) + \theta(S_3) - \theta(S_1) - \theta(S_2) + \theta(S_1 * S_2) - \theta(S_1) - \theta(S_3) \\ &\qquad + \theta(S_1 * S_3) - \theta(S_2) - \theta(S_3) + \theta(S_2 * S_3) + \theta(S_1, S_2, S_3) \\ &\quad = -\theta(S_1) - \theta(S_2) - \theta(S_3) + \theta(S_1, S_2) + \theta(S_1, S_3) \\ &\qquad + \theta(S_2, S_3) + \theta(S_1, S_2, S_3)\end{aligned}$$

Therefore,

$$\theta(S_1,S_2,S_3) = \theta(S_1)+\theta(S_2)+\theta(S_3)-\theta(S_1*S_2)-\theta(S_1*S_3) \\ -\theta(S_2*S_3)+\theta(S_1*S_2*S_3).$$

This is the proof of Theorem 5.

Theorem 5 shows that the measure of the total ability can be linearly expressed with the measures of the shared abilities. In fact, according to (32) and (37), $\theta(S_1,S_2,S_3)$ and $\theta(S_1*S_2*S_3)$ are two conjugate concepts.

Theorem 6.

$$\theta(Total) = \theta(S_1|S_2)+\theta(S_2|S_3)+\theta(S_3|S_1)+\theta(S_1*S_2*S_3). \tag{39}$$

Proof. First, by (38), there is

$$\theta(S_1*S_2) = \theta(S_1)+\theta(S_2)-\theta(S_1,S_2) \tag{40}$$

By Theorem 5 and (40), there is

$$\begin{aligned}\theta(Total) &= \theta(S_1)+\theta(S_2)+\theta(S_3)-\theta(S_1*S_2)-\theta(S_1*S_3) \\ &\quad -\theta(S_2*S_3)+\theta(S_1*S_2*S_3) \\ &= \theta(S_1,S_2)+\theta(S_3)-\theta(S_1*S_3)-\theta(S_2*S_3)+\theta(S_1*S_2*S_3)\end{aligned}$$

Equivalently, Eq. (28) can be rewritten as

$$\theta(S_1,S_2) = \theta(S_1|S_2)+\theta(S_2). \tag{41}$$

By applying (41), we have

$$\theta(Total) = \theta(S_1|S_2)+\theta(S_2)+\theta(S_3)-\theta(S_1*S_3)-\theta(S_2*S_3)+\theta(S_1*S_2*S_3)$$

In the same way, by applying the following equations,

$$\begin{aligned}\theta(S_1*S_3) &= \theta(S_1)+\theta(S_3)-\theta(S_1,S_3), \\ \theta(S_2*S_3) &= \theta(S_2)+\theta(S_3)-\theta(S_2,S_3), \\ \theta(S_1,S_3) &= \theta(S_1|S_3)+\theta(S_3), \\ \theta(S_2,S_3) &= \theta(S_2|S_3)+\theta(S_3).\end{aligned}$$

We finally have

$$\begin{aligned}\theta(\mathit{Total}) &= \theta(S_1|S_2) + \theta(S_2, S_3) - \theta(S_1 * S_3) + \theta(S_1 * S_2 * S_3)\\ &= \theta(S_1|S_2) + \theta(S_2|S_3) + \theta(S_3) - \theta(S_1 * S_3) + \theta(S_1 * S_2 * S_3)\\ &= \theta(S_1|S_2) + \theta(S_2|S_3) + \theta(S_3|S_1) + \theta(S_1 * S_2 * S_3).\end{aligned}$$

This is the proof of Theorem 6.

It is obvious that, if S_1, S_2, and S_3 are jointly independent, Eq. (39) becomes (6) and therefore, Eq. (39) in Theorem 6 can be thought as a general form of additivity. In Theorem 6, the total ability is decomposed into four parts which are $\theta(S_1|S_2)$, $\theta(S_1|S_3)$, $\theta(S_2|S_3)$ and $\theta(S_1 * S_2 * S_3)$. The decomposition in Theorem 6 is not unique. In similar way, the total ability can also be decomposed as follows:

$$\theta(\mathit{Total}) = \theta(S_1|S_3) + \theta(S_3|S_2) + \theta(S_2|S_1) + \theta(S_1 * S_2 * S_3). \tag{42}$$

Although the total ability is decomposed into four components in Theorem 6, each of these four decomposed components can still be further decomposed. In the remaining part of this section, a unique and complete decomposition for the total ability will be derived. First, the following concepts are introduced:

$$\theta(S_1, S_2, S_3) = \theta(\mathit{Total}) = -ln(P(X_{i_1} = R, \ldots, X_{i_L} = R)), \tag{43}$$

$$\theta(S_j, S_k) = -ln(P(X_{i_1} = R, \ldots, X_{i_{M_{j,k}}} = R)). \tag{44}$$

In Eq. (43), the L correctly responded items $i_1, \ldots, i_L$ are exactly those in $\mathcal{S}_1 \cup \mathcal{S}_2 \cup \mathcal{S}_3$, i.e. $\{i_1, \ldots, i_L\} = \mathcal{S}_1 \cup \mathcal{S}_2 \cup \mathcal{S}_3$. In Eq. (44), the $M_{j,k}$ correctly responded items $i_1, \ldots, i_{M_{j,k}}$ are exactly those in $\mathcal{S}_j \cup \mathcal{S}_k$, i.e. $\{i_1, \ldots, i_{M_{j,k}}\} = \mathcal{S}_j \cup \mathcal{S}_k$ for $j, k = 1, 2, 3$.

With $\theta(S_1, S_2, S_3)$ and $\theta(S_j, S_k)$ in (43) and (44), we can define the following ability measures conditioned on the subscale(s):

Definition 7.

$$\theta(S_1|S_2, S_3) = \theta(S_1, S_2, S_3) - \theta(S_2, S_3), \tag{45}$$

where $\theta(S_j, S_k)$ for $j, k = 1, 2, 3$ and $\theta(S_1, S_2, S_3)$ are defined in (44) and (43).

Definition 8.

$$\theta(S_1, S_2|S_3) = \theta(S_1, S_2, S_3) - \theta(S_3), \tag{46}$$

where $\theta(S_1, S_2, S_3)$ is defined in (44).

By Definition 7, there is

$$\begin{aligned}\theta(S_1,S_2,S_3) &= \theta(S_3|S_1,S_2)+\theta(S_1,S_2)\\ &= \theta(S_3|S_1,S_2)+\theta(S_2|S_1)+\theta(S_1).\end{aligned} \tag{47}$$

Equation (47) is also called additivity.

Definition 9.

$$\theta(S_1 * S_2|S_3) = \theta(S_1|S_3)+\theta(S_2|S_3)-\theta(S_1,S_2|S_3), \tag{48}$$

where $\theta(S_i|S_3)$ for $i=1,2$ is defined in (28).

Theorem 7.

$$\begin{aligned}\theta(\mathit{Total}) &= \theta(S_1|S_2,S_3)+\theta(S_2|S_1,S_3)+\theta(S_3|S_1,S_2)+\theta(S_1 * S_3|S_2)\\ &\quad +\theta(S_1 * S_2|S_3)+\theta(S_2 * S_3|S_1)+\theta(S_1 * S_2 * S_3).\end{aligned} \tag{49}$$

Proof. First, by Definitions 7 and 9,

$$\begin{aligned}\theta(S_1|S_2,S_3)+\theta(S_1 * S_2|S_3) &= \theta(S_1,S_2,S_3)-\theta(S_2,S_3)+\theta(S_1|S_3)\\ &\quad +\theta(S_2|S_3)-\theta(S_1,S_2|S_3).\end{aligned} \tag{50}$$

Second, by Definition 8 and Eq. (41),

$$\theta(S_1,S_2|S_3) = \theta(S_1,S_2,S_3)-\theta(S_1,S_2), \tag{51}$$

$$\theta(S_1|S_3) = \theta(S_1,S_3)-\theta(S_3), \tag{52}$$

$$\theta(S_2|S_3) = \theta(S_2,S_3)-\theta(S_3). \tag{53}$$

By substituting (51), (52), and (53) into (50) and rearranging the terms, we have

$$\begin{aligned}\theta(S_1|S_2,S_3)+\theta(S_1 * S_2|S_3) &= \theta(S_1,S_2,S_3)-\theta(S_2,S_3)\\ &\quad +\theta(S_1,S_3)-\theta(S_3)+\theta(S_2,S_3)\\ &\quad -\theta(S_3)-\theta(S_1,S_2,S_3)+\theta(S_3)\\ &= \theta(S_1,S_3)-\theta(S_3)=\theta(S_1|S_3).\end{aligned} \tag{54}$$

By (54) and in the same way as (54), we have

$$\theta(S_1|S_3) = \theta(S_1|S_2,S_3)+\theta(S_1 * S_2|S_3), \tag{55}$$

$$\theta(S_3|S_2) = \theta(S_3|S_1,S_2)+\theta(S_1 * S_3|S_2), \tag{56}$$

$$\theta(S_2|S_1) = \theta(S_2|S_1,S_3)+\theta(S_2 * S_3|S_1). \tag{57}$$

Finally, by substituting (55), (56), and (57) into (42), we have

$$\begin{aligned}\theta(\mathit{Total}) &= \theta(S_1|S_3)+\theta(S_3|S_2)+\theta(S_2|S_1)+\theta(S_1*S_2*S_3)\\ &= \theta(S_1|S_2,S_3)+\theta(S_2|S_1,S_3)+\theta(S_3|S_1,S_2)+\theta(S_1*S_3|S_2)\\ &\quad+\theta(S_1*S_2|S_3)+\theta(S_2*S_3|S_1)+\theta(S_1*S_2*S_3).\end{aligned}$$

This is the proof of Theorem 7.

In Theorem 7, the total ability of three subscales is decomposed into seven basic components. The interpretation of each component is different from one to another. With the decomposition in Theorem 7, we can look into the details of subscale structure of the total ability.

Although we have discussed the decomposition (49) for the case of three subscales in Theorem 7, the decomposition for the case of arbitrary number of subscales can also be derived in the similar way. Readers are encouraged to derive the decomposition for the cases of four subscales or more.

5 Discussion

In this paper, the measure of the ability defined in (5) shows (1) additivity; (2) nonnegativity; (3) the measure of the ability with incorrect responses for all items is equal to zero. Therefore, the definition in (5) conceptually can be called the measure of the ability according to Measure Theory (Halmos 1974). Here, we place emphasis on the concept of measure because, without additivity, an "ability measure" can cause unexpected results. For example, without additivity, the directly measured value and indirectly measured value for the same total ability are not the same for most of cases. This is similar to measuring the area of a rectangle by summation of its length and width (see *Introduction* of this paper).

In Sect. 3, the measure of the shared abilities is defined. We point out that the measure of the shared abilities does not make sense without additivity. Unlike the ability measure in Definition 1 which is nonnegative, measure of the shared abilities can be negative. The negative value of the measure of the shared abilities is interpreted as the conflicted or exclusive interaction among these two abilities. For two exclusive abilities, the higher for one ability, the lower will be for another ability. The positive value of the measure of the shared abilities implies that these two abilities are not conflicted which means that, the higher for one ability, the higher will be also for another ability. In practice, it is very rare for the measure of the shared ability to be negative although it is possible.

The marginal measure of the ability associated with the subscale is defined in Sect. 4. We also look into the relation between the measure of the total ability and the measures of those abilities associated with the subscales by decomposing the measure of the total ability in terms of the measures of those abilities associated with the subscales. Like the measure of the shared ability, without additivity, it is impossible to decompose the measure of the total ability in terms of the measures of those abilities associated with the subscales.

Although, throughout this paper, we assume all items are dichotomous, the definition in (5) can be expanded to include partial credits, i.e. the items can have more than two categories of right (R) and wrong (W). Under the case of partial credits, the property of additivity is still reserved, i.e. the ability measure with the partial credits is on the basis of measure theory. The nonparametric ability measure with partial credits currently is under organization and will meet with readers in the near future.

Finally, in this paper, most conclusions can be extended to more general form in the same way. Also, the ability measures defined in this paper may be parameterized with some reasonable constraints such as the log-linear model. In practice, the parameterized measures is possible to handle the datasets of small size. How to parameterize the ability measures defined in this paper could be the topic for the future work.

Acknowledgments Author would like to express his thanks to Prof. Andries van der Ark for his valuable comments with which this paper can be significantly improved for its readability. Author also thanks Gwen Exner for his assistances and helps.

References

Fisher, R. A. (1922). On the mathematical foundations of theoretical statistics. *Philosophical Transactions of the Royal Society of London, Series A*, *222*, 309–368.

Fisher, R. A. (1925). Theory of statistical estimation. *Proceedings of the Cambridge Philosophical Society*, *22*, 700–725.

Halmos, P. R. (1974). *Measure theory*. New York: Springer.

Hays, W. L. (1970). *Statistics (Volume 1) - Probability, Inference, and Decision*. New York: Holt, Rinehart and Winston.

Shannon, C. E. (1948). A mathematical theory of communications. *The Bell System Technical Journal*, *27*, 379–423.

Wiener, N. (1948). Cybernetics or Control and Communication in the Animal and the Machine. Cambridge, Mass.: The MIT Press.

An Alternative to Cronbach's Alpha: An L-Moment-Based Measure of Internal-Consistency Reliability

Todd Christopher Headrick and Yanyan Sheng

1 Introduction

Coefficient alpha (Cronbach 1951; Guttman 1945) is a commonly used index for measuring internal-consistency reliability. Consider alpha (α) in terms of a model that decomposes an observed score into the sum of two independent components: a true unobservable score t_i and a random error component e_{ij}. The model can be summarized as

$$X_{ij} = t_i + e_{ij} \tag{1}$$

where X_{ij} is the observed score associated with the i-th examinee on the j-th test item, and where $i = 1,\ldots,n$; $j = 1,\ldots,k$; and the error terms (e_{ij}) are independent with a mean of zero. Inspection of (1) indicates that this particular model restricts the true score t_i to be the same across all k test items. The reliability measure associated with the test items in (1) is a function of the true score variance and cannot be computed directly. Thus, estimates of reliability such as coefficient α have been derived and will be defined herein as (e.g., Christman and Van Aelst 2006)

$$\alpha = \frac{k}{k-1}\left(1 - \frac{\sum_j \sigma_j^2}{\sum_j \sigma_j^2 + \sum\sum_{j \neq j'} \sigma_{jj'}}\right). \tag{2}$$

A conventional estimate of α can be obtained by substituting the usual OLS sample estimates associated with σ_j^2 and $\sigma_{jj'}$ into (2) as

T.C. Headrick (✉) • Y. Sheng
Section of Statistics and Measurement, Department of EPSE,
Southern Illinois University Carbondale, Carbondale, IL 62901, USA
e-mail: headrick@siu.edu; ysheng@siu.edu

R.E. Millsap et al. (eds.), *New Developments in Quantitative Psychology*,
Springer Proceedings in Mathematics & Statistics 66, DOI 10.1007/978-1-4614-9348-8_2,

$$\hat{\alpha}_C = \frac{k}{k-1}\left(1 - \frac{\sum_j s_j^2}{\sum_j s_j^2 + \sum\sum_{j \neq j'} s_{jj'}}\right) \tag{3}$$

where s_j^2 and $s_{jj'}$ are the diagonal and off-diagonal elements from the variance–covariance matrix, respectively.

Although coefficient α is often used as an index for reliability, it is also well known that its use is limited when data are non-normal, in particular leptokurtic, or when sample sizes are small (e.g., Bay 1973; Christman and Van Aelst 2006; Sheng and Sheng 2012; Wilcox 1992). These limitations are of concern because data sets in the social and behavioral sciences can often possess heavy tails or consist of small sample sizes (e.g., Micceri 1989; Yuan et al. 2004). Specifically, it has been demonstrated that $\hat{\alpha}_C$ can substantially underestimate α when heavy-tailed distributions are encountered. For example, Sheng and Sheng (2012, Table 1) sampled from a symmetric leptokurtic distribution and found the empirical estimate of α to be approximately $\hat{\alpha}_C = 0.70$ when the true population parameter was $\alpha = 0.80$. Further, it is not uncommon that data sets consist of small sample sizes, e.g., $n = 10$ or 20. More specifically, small sample sizes are commonly encountered in the contexts of rehabilitation (e.g., alcohol treatment programs, group therapy, etc.) and special education as student–teacher ratios are often small. Furthermore, Monte Carlo evidence has demonstrated that $\hat{\alpha}_C$ can underestimate α—even when small samples are drawn from a normal distribution (see Sheng and Sheng 2012, Table 1).

L-moment estimators (e.g., Hosking 1990; Hosking and Wallis 1997) have demonstrated to be superior to the conventional product-moment estimators in terms of bias, efficiency, and their resistance to outliers (e.g., Headrick 2011; Hodis et al. 2012; Hosking 1992; Vogel and Fennessy 1993). Further, *L*-comoment estimators (Serfling and Xiao 2007) such as the *L*-correlation have demonstrated to be an attractive alternative to the conventional Pearson correlation in terms of relative bias when heavy-tailed distributions are of concern (Headrick and Pant 2012a,b,c,d,e).

In view of the above, the present aim here is to propose an *L*-comoment-based coefficient *L*-α, and its estimator denoted as $\hat{\alpha}_L$, as an alternative to conventional alpha $\hat{\alpha}_C$ in (3). Empirical results associated with the simulation study herein indicate that $\hat{\alpha}_L$ can be substantially superior to $\hat{\alpha}_C$ in terms of relative bias and relative standard error (RSE) when distributions are heavy-tailed and sample sizes are small.

The rest of the paper is organized as follows. In Sect. 2, summaries of univariate *L*-moments and *L*-comoments are first provided. Coefficient *L*-α ($\hat{\alpha}_L$) is then introduced and numerical examples are provided to illustrate the computation and sampling distribution associated with $\hat{\alpha}_L$. In Sect. 3, a Monte Carlo study is carried out to evaluate the performance of $\hat{\alpha}_C$ and $\hat{\alpha}_L$. The results of the study are discussed in Sect. 4.

2 *L*-Moments, *L*-Comoments, and Coefficient *L*-α

The system of univariate *L*-moments (Hosking 1990, 1992; Hosking and Wallis 1997) can be considered in terms of the expectations of linear combinations of order statistics associated with a random variable Y. Specifically, the first four L-moments are expressed as

$$\begin{aligned}
\lambda_1 &= E[Y_{1:1}] \\
\lambda_2 &= \frac{1}{2}E[Y_{2:2} - Y_{1:2}] \\
\lambda_3 &= \frac{1}{3}E[Y_{3:3} - 2Y_{2:3} + Y_{1:3}] \\
\lambda_4 &= \frac{1}{4}E[Y_{4:4} - 3Y_{3:4} + 3Y_{2:4} - Y_{1:4}]
\end{aligned}$$

where $Y_{\ell:m}$ denotes the ℓth smallest observation from a sample of size m. As such, $Y_{1:m} \leq Y_{2:m} \leq \ldots \leq Y_{m:m}$ are referred to as order statistics drawn from the random variable Y. The values of λ_1 and λ_2 are measures of location and scale and are the arithmetic mean and one-half of the coefficient of mean difference (or Gini's index of spread), respectively. Higher order L-moments are transformed to dimensionless quantities referred to as L-moment ratios defined as $\tau_r = \lambda_r/\lambda_2$ for $r \geq 3$, where τ_3 and τ_4 are the analogs to the conventional measures of skew and kurtosis. In general, L-moment ratios are bounded in the interval $-1 < \tau_r < 1$ as is the index of L-skew (τ_3) where a symmetric distribution implies that all L-moment ratios with odd subscripts are zero. Other smaller boundaries can be found for more specific cases. For example, the index of L-kurtosis (τ_4) has the boundary condition for continuous distributions of $(5\tau_3^2 - 1)/4 < \tau_4 < 1$.

L-comoments (Olkin and Yitzhuki 1992; Serfling and Xiao 2007) are introduced by considering two random variables Y_j and Y_k with distribution functions $F(Y_j)$ and $F(Y_k)$. The second L-moments associated with Y_j and Y_k can alternatively be expressed as

$$\begin{aligned}
\lambda_2(Y_j) &= 2\mathrm{Cov}(Y_j, F(Y_j)) \\
\lambda_2(Y_k) &= 2\mathrm{Cov}(Y_k, F(Y_k)).
\end{aligned} \tag{4}$$

The second L-comoments of Y_j toward Y_k and Y_k toward Y_j are

$$\begin{aligned}
\lambda_2(Y_j, Y_k) &= 2\mathrm{Cov}(Y_j, F(Y_k)) \\
\lambda_2(Y_k, Y_j) &= 2\mathrm{Cov}(Y_k, F(Y_j)).
\end{aligned} \tag{5}$$

The ratio $\eta_{jk} = \lambda_2(Y_j, Y_k)/\lambda_2(Y_j)$ is defined as the L-correlation of Y_j with respect to Y_k, which measures the monotonic relationship (not just linear) between two variables (Headrick and Pant 2012c). Note that in general, $\eta_{jk} \neq \eta_{kj}$. The estimators of (4) and (5) are U-statistics (Serfling 1980; Serfling and Xiao 2007) and their sampling distributions converge to a normal distribution when the sample size is sufficiently large.

In terms of coefficient L-α, an approach that can be taken to equate the conventional and L-moment (comoment) definitions of α is to express (2) as

Table 1 Data (Items) for computing the second *L*-moment–comoment matrix in Table 2

X_{i1}	X_{i2}	X_{i3}	$\hat{F}(X_{i1})$	$\hat{F}(X_{i2})$	$\hat{F}(X_{i3})$
2	4	3	0.15	0.45	0.15
5	7	7	0.75	0.95	1.00
3	5	5	0.35	0.65	0.40
6	6	6	0.90	0.80	0.75
7	7	6	1.00	0.95	0.75
5	2	6	0.75	0.10	0.75
2	3	3	0.15	0.25	0.15
4	3	6	0.55	0.25	0.75
3	5	5	0.35	0.65	0.40
4	4	5	0.55	0.45	0.40

The data are part of the "Satisfaction With Life Data" from McDonald (1999, p. 47)

Table 2 Second *L*-moment–comoment matrix for coefficient $\hat{\alpha}_L$ in Eq. (9)

Item	1	2	3
1	$\ell_{2(1)} = 0.989$	$\ell_{2(12)} = 0.500$	$\ell_{2(13)} = 0.789$
2	$\ell_{2(21)} = 0.500$	$\ell_{2(2)} = 1.022$	$\ell_{2(23)} = 0.411$
3	$\ell_{2(31)} = 0.667$	$\ell_{2(32)} = 0.333$	$\ell_{2(3)} = 0.733$

$$\alpha = \frac{1}{1+(R-1)/k} = \frac{k}{k-1}\left(1 - \frac{\sum_j \sigma_j^2}{\sum_j \sigma_j^2 + \sum\sum_{j \neq j'} \sigma_{jj'}}\right) \tag{6}$$

where $R > 1$ is the common ratio between the main and off-diagonal elements of the variance–covariance matrix, i.e. $R = \sigma_j^2 / \sigma_{jj'}$. (See the appendix for the derivation of Eq. (6)). As such, given a fixed value of R in (6) will allow for α to be defined in terms of the second *L*-moments and second *L*-comoments as

$$\alpha = \frac{1}{1+(R-1)/k} = \frac{k}{k-1}\left(1 - \frac{\sum_j \lambda_{2(j)}}{\sum_j \lambda_{2(j)} + \sum\sum_{j \neq j'} \lambda_{2(jj')}}\right) \tag{7}$$

where $R = \lambda_{2(j)}/\lambda_{2(jj')}$. Thus, the estimator of L-α is expressed as

$$\hat{\alpha}_L = \frac{k}{k-1}\left(1 - \frac{\sum_j \ell_{2(j)}}{\sum_j \ell_{2(j)} + \sum\sum_{j \neq j'} \ell_{2(jj')}}\right) \tag{8}$$

where $\ell_{2(j)}$ ($\ell_{2(jj')}$) denotes the sample estimate of the second *L*-moments (second *L*-comoment) in (4) and (5). An example demonstrating the computation of $\hat{\alpha}_L$ is provided below in Eq. (9). The computed estimate of $\hat{\alpha}_L = 0.807$ in (9) is based on the data in Table 1 and the second *L*-moment–comoment matrix in Table 2. The corresponding conventional estimate for the data in Table 1 is $\hat{\alpha}_C = 0.798$.

$$\begin{aligned}\hat{\alpha}_L = 0.807 = {} & (3/2)(1 - (\ell_{2(1)} + \ell_{2(2)} + \ell_{2(3)})/(\ell_{2(1)} + \ell_{2(2)} + \ell_{2(3)} \\ & + \ell_{2(21)} + \ell_{2(31)} + \ell_{2(32)} + \ell_{2(12)} + \ell_{2(13)} + \ell_{2(23)})).\end{aligned} \tag{9}$$

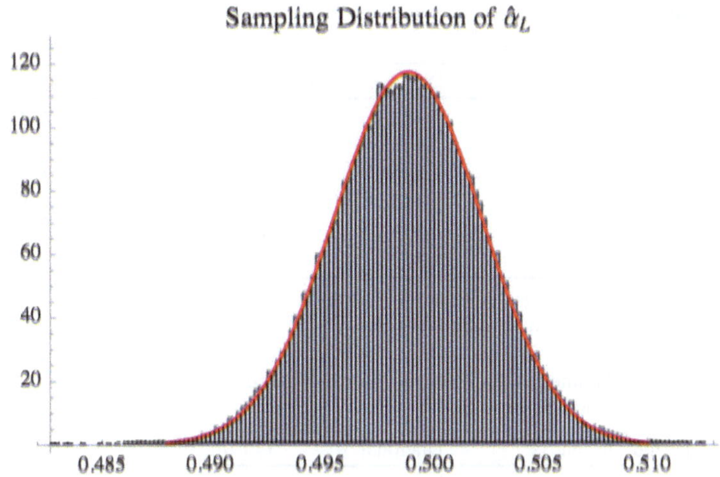

Fig. 1 Approximate normal sampling distribution of $\hat{\alpha}_L$ with $\alpha = 0.50$. The distribution consists of 25,000 statistics based on samples of size $n = 100{,}000$ and the heavy-tailed distribution (kurtosis of 25) in Fig. 2

The estimator $\hat{\alpha}_L$ in (8) and (9) is a ratio of the sums of U-statistics and thus a consistent estimator of α in (7) with a sampling distribution that converges, for large samples, to the normal distribution (e.g., Olkin and Yitzhuki 1992; Schechtman and Yitzhaki 1987; Serfling and Xiao 2007). For convenience to the reader, provided in Fig. 1 is the sampling distribution of $\hat{\alpha}_L$ that is approximately normal and based on $\alpha = 0.50$, $n = 100{,}000$, and a symmetric heavy-tailed distribution (kurtosis of 25, see Fig. 2) that would be associated with t_i in (1).

3 Monte Carlo Simulation

An algorithm was written in MATLAB (Mathworks 2010) to generate 25,000 independent sample estimates of conventional and L-comoment α. The estimators $\hat{\alpha}_C$ and $\hat{\alpha}_L$ were based on the parameters (α, k, R) given in Tables 3 and 4 and the distributions in Figs. 2–4. The parameters of α were selected because they represent commonly used references of various degrees of reliability, i.e. 0.50 (poor); 5/7 = 0.714 (acceptable); 0.80 (good); and 0.90 (excellent). Further, for each set of parameters in Tables 3 and 4, the empirical estimators $\hat{\alpha}_C$ and $\hat{\alpha}_L$ were generated based on sample sizes of $n = 10, 20, 1{,}000$. For all cases in the simulation, the error term e_{ij} in (1) was normally distributed with zero mean and with the variance parameters (σ_e^2) listed in Tables 3 and 4.

The three distributions depicted in Figs. 2–4 are associated with the true scores t_i in Eq. (1). These distributions are referred to as: Distribution 1 is symmetric and leptokurtic (skew = 0, kurtosis = 25; L-skew = 0, L-kurtosis = 0.4225);

Table 3 Parameters for the Conventional covariance (*L*-comoment) matrix and distributions in Figs. 2–4

Distribution-matrix	Diagonal	Off-diagonal	σ_e^2
1-C	3.420	1.710	1.710
1-L	0.848	0.424	1.000
2-C	3.224	1.612	1.612
2-L	0.842	0.421	1.000
3-C	2.000	1.000	1.000
3-L	0.798	0.399	1.000

Reliability is $\alpha = 0.80, 0.90$; number of items are $k = 4, 9$
Ratio of diagonal to off-diagonal is $R = 2$

Table 4 Parameters for the Conventional covariance (*L*-comoment) matrix and distributions in Figs. 2–4

Distribution-matrix	Diagonal	Off-diagonal	σ_e^2
1-C	8.550	1.710	6.840
1-L	1.470	0.294	5.313
2-C	8.060	1.612	6.448
2-L	1.443	0.2886	5.135
3-C	5.000	1.000	4.000
3-L	1.262	0.2524	4.000

Reliability is $\alpha = 0.50, 0.714$; number of items are $k = 4, 10$
Ratio of diagonal to off-diagonal is $R = 5$

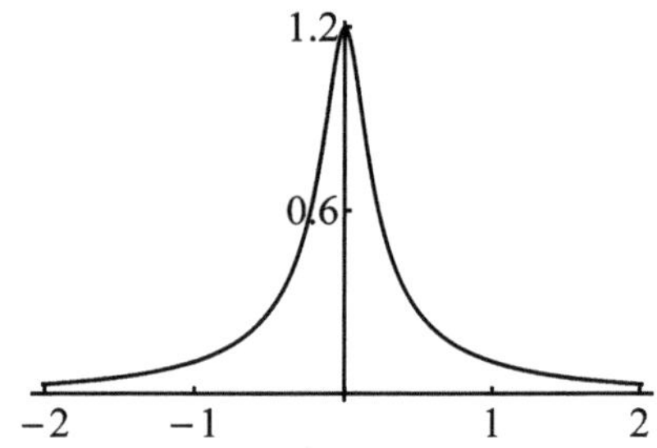

Fig. 2 Distribution 1 with skew (*L*-skew) of 0 (0) and kurtosis (*L*-kurtosis) of 25 (0.4225)

Distribution 2 is asymmetric and leptokurtic (skew = 3, kurtosis = 21; *L*-skew = 0.3130, *L*-kurtosis = 0.3335); and Distribution 3 is standard normal (skew = 0, kurtosis = 0; *L*-skew = 0, *L*-kurtosis = 0.1226). We would note that Distributions 1 and 2 have been used in several studies in the social and behavioral sciences (e.g., Berkovits et al. 2000; Enders 2001; Harwell and Serlin 1988; Headrick and Sawilowsky 1999, 2000; Olsson et al. 2003).

The pseudo-random deviates associated with the distributions in Figs. 2–4 were generated for this study using the *L*-moment-based power method transformation derived by Headrick (2011). Specifically, the true scores t_i in (1) were generated using the following (Fleishman 1978) type polynomial

$$t_i = c_1 + c_2 Z_i + c_3 Z_i^2 + c_4 Z_i^3 \tag{10}$$

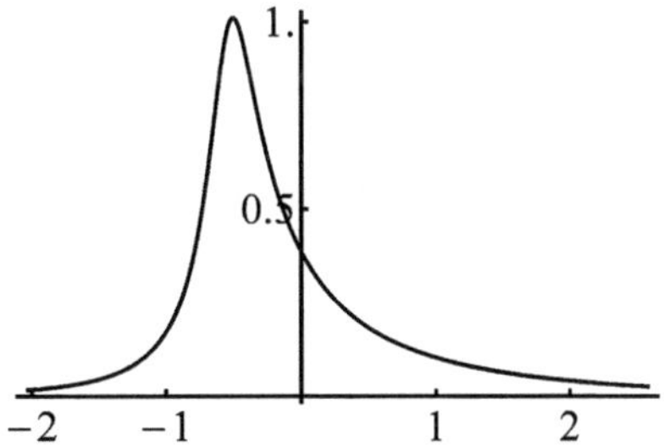

Fig. 3 Distribution 2 with skew (L-skew) of 3 (0.3130) and kurtosis (L-kurtosis) of 21 (0.3335)

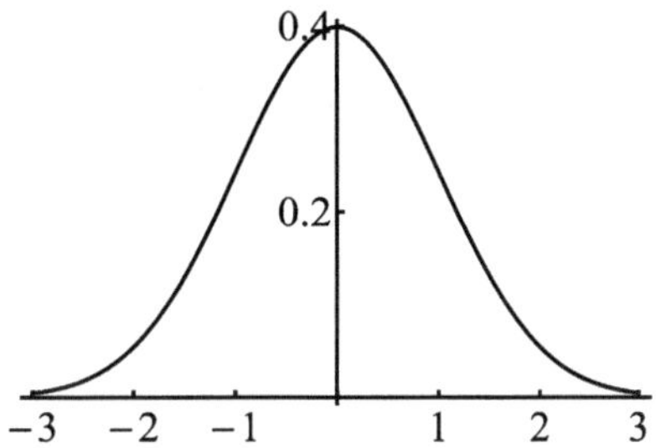

Fig. 4 Distribution 3 is standard normal with skew (L-skew) of 0 (0) and kurtosis (L-kurtosis) of 0 (0.1226)

where $Z_i \sim$ iid $N(0,1)$. The shape of the distribution of the true scores t_i in (10) is contingent on the values of the coefficients, which are computed based on Headrick's equations (2.14)–(2.17) in Headrick (2011) as

$$c_1 = -c_3 = -\tau_3\sqrt{\frac{\pi}{3}}$$
$$c_2 = \frac{-16\delta_2 + \sqrt{2}(3+2\tau_4)\pi}{8(5\delta_1 - 2\delta_2)}$$
$$c_4 = \frac{40\delta_1 - \sqrt{2}(3+2\tau_4)\pi}{20(5\delta_1 - 2\delta_2)}. \tag{11}$$

The three sets of coefficients for the distributions in Figs. 2–4 are (respectively): (1) $c_1 = 0.0$, $c_2 = 0.3338$, $c_3 = 0.0$, $c_4 = 0.2665$; (2) $c_1 = -0.3203$, $c_2 = 0.5315$, $c_3 = 0.3203$, $c_4 = 0.1874$; and (3) $c_1 = 0.0$, $c_2 = 1.0$, $c_3 = 0.0$, $c_4 = 0.0$. The values of the three sets of coefficients are based on the values of L-skew and L-kurtosis given in Figs. 2–4 and where $\delta_1 = 0.36045147$ and $\delta_2 = 1.15112868$ in (11) (see Headrick 2011, Eqs. A.1, A.2). The solutions to the coefficients in (11) ensure that $\lambda_1 = 0$ and $\lambda_2 = 1/\sqrt{\pi}$, which are associated with the unit normal distribution.

The estimator $\hat{\alpha}_C$ was computed using Eq. (3). The estimator $\hat{\alpha}_L$ was computed using Eqs. (4), (5), and (8) as was demonstrated in Tables 1 and 2. The estimators were both transformed to the form of an intraclass correlation as

$\bar{\rho}_{C,L} = \hat{\alpha}_{C,L}/(1-(k-1)\hat{\alpha}_{C,L})$ (e.g., Headrick 2010, p. 104) and were subsequently Fisher z' transformed, i.e. $z'_{\bar{\rho}_{C,L}}$. Bias-corrected accelerated bootstrapped average (mean) estimates, confidence intervals (C.I.s), and standard errors were subsequently obtained for $z'_{\bar{\rho}_{C,L}}$ using 10,000 resamples. The bootstrap results associated with the means and C.I.s were then transformed back to their original metrics (i.e., the estimators $\hat{\alpha}_C$ and $\hat{\alpha}_L$). Further, percentages of relative bias (RBias) and RSE were computed for $\hat{\alpha}_{C,L}$ as: RBias $= ((\hat{\alpha}_{C,L} - \alpha)/\alpha) \times 100$ and RSE $= (\text{standarderror}/\hat{\alpha}_{C,L}) \times 100$. The results of the simulation are reported in Tables 5–7 and are discussed in the next section.

4 Discussion and Conclusion

One of the advantages that L-moment ratios have over conventional product-moment estimators is that they can be far less biased when sampling is from distributions with more severe departures from normality (Hosking and Wallis 1997; Serfling and Xiao 2007). And, inspection of the simulation results in Tables 5

Table 5 Simulation results for α based on the Conventional (C) and L-moment (L) procedures (Proc) based on samples of size $n = 10$

Parameters	Dist–Proc	Estimate (α)	95 % C.I.	RSE (%)	RBias (%)
$\alpha = 0.50, k = 4$	1-C	0.4416	0.4367, 0.4465	0.5661	−11.68
$\alpha = 0.50, k = 4$	1-L	0.4847	0.4801, 0.4891	0.4725	−3.06
$\alpha = 0.50, k = 4$	2-C	0.4448	0.4400, 0.4495	0.3237	−11.04
$\alpha = 0.50, k = 4$	2-L	0.4839	0.4796, 0.4883	0.2583	−3.22
$\alpha = 0.50, k = 4$	3-C	0.4888	0.4852, 0.4922	0.3621	−2.24
$\alpha = 0.50, k = 4$	3-L	0.5003	0.4968, 0.5040	0.3698	0.06
$\alpha = 0.714, k = 10$	1-C	0.6617	0.6581, 0.6652	0.2720	−7.36
$\alpha = 0.714, k = 10$	1-L	0.6960	0.6931, 0.6989	0.2155	−2.56
$\alpha = 0.714, k = 10$	2-C	0.6662	0.6628, 0.6697	0.2612	−6.73
$\alpha = 0.714, k = 10$	2-L	0.6975	0.6946, 0.7003	0.2079	−2.35
$\alpha = 0.714, k = 10$	3-C	0.7069	0.7051, 0.7086	0.1273	−1.03
$\alpha = 0.714, k = 10$	3-L	0.7131	0.7113, 0.7149	0.1290	−0.17
$\alpha = 0.80, k = 4$	1-C	0.7306	0.7275, 0.7336	0.2053	−8.67
$\alpha = 0.80, k = 4$	1-L	0.7887	0.7866, 0.7908	0.1357	−1.41
$\alpha = 0.80, k = 4$	2-C	0.7398	0.7371, 0.7426	0.1906	−7.52
$\alpha = 0.80, k = 4$	2-L	0.7924	0.7904, 0.7944	0.1287	−0.95
$\alpha = 0.80, k = 4$	3-C	0.7908	0.7893, 0.7922	0.0923	−1.15
$\alpha = 0.80, k = 4$	3-L	0.8030	0.8016, 0.8044	0.0909	0.37
$\alpha = 0.90, k = 9$	1-C	0.8591	0.8575, 0.8609	0.0989	−4.54
$\alpha = 0.90, k = 9$	1-L	0.8924	0.8914, 0.8936	0.0628	−0.84
$\alpha = 0.90, k = 9$	2-C	0.8636	0.8620, 0.8651	0.0926	−4.04
$\alpha = 0.90, k = 9$	2-L	0.8933	0.8922, 0.8944	0.0605	−0.74
$\alpha = 0.90, k = 9$	3-C	0.8934	0.8927, 0.8941	0.0381	−0.73
$\alpha = 0.90, k = 9$	3-L	0.8991	0.8985, 0.8998	0.0378	−0.10

See Tables 3 and 4 for the parameters and Figs. 2–4 for the distributions (Dist)

Table 6 Simulation results for α based on the Conventional (C) and L-moment (L) procedures (Proc) based on samples of size $n = 20$

Parameters	Dist–Proc	Estimate (α)	95 % C.I.	RSE (%)	RBias (%)
$\alpha = 0.50, k = 4$	1-C	0.4643	0.4606, 0.4679	0.3977	−7.15
$\alpha = 0.50, k = 4$	1-L	0.4903	0.4870, 0.4933	0.3263	−1.94
$\alpha = 0.50, k = 4$	2-C	0.4697	0.4663, 0.4732	0.3732	−6.05
$\alpha = 0.50, k = 4$	2-L	0.4938	0.4909, 0.4967	0.306	−1.24
$\alpha = 0.50, k = 4$	3-C	0.4945	0.4921, 0.4968	0.2389	−1.11
$\alpha = 0.50, k = 4$	3-L	0.4995	0.4971, 0.5019	0.2456	−0.11
$\alpha = 0.714, k = 10$	1-C	0.6852	0.6826, 0.6878	0.1926	−4.07
$\alpha = 0.714, k = 10$	1-L	0.7056	0.7036, 0.7077	0.1485	−1.22
$\alpha = 0.714, k = 10$	2-C	0.6858	0.6834, 0.6882	0.1831	−3.98
$\alpha = 0.714, k = 10$	2-L	0.7047	0.7028, 0.7066	0.1414	−1.34
$\alpha = 0.714, k = 10$	3-C	0.7098	0.7086, 0.7111	0.0881	−0.62
$\alpha = 0.714, k = 10$	3-L	0.7130	0.7117, 0.7142	0.0882	−0.19
$\alpha = 0.80, k = 4$	1-C	0.7569	0.7549, 0.7591	0.1404	−5.39
$\alpha = 0.80, k = 4$	1-L	0.7937	0.7923, 0.7952	0.0917	−0.78
$\alpha = 0.80, k = 4$	2-C	0.7612	0.7592, 0.7631	0.1330	−4.85
$\alpha = 0.80, k = 4$	2-L	0.7940	0.7926, 0.7954	0.0893	−0.75
$\alpha = 0.80, k = 4$	3-C	0.7944	0.7935, 0.7954	0.0627	−0.7
$\alpha = 0.80, k = 4$	3-L	0.8000	0.7990, 0.8010	0.0613	−0.002
$\alpha = 0.90, k = 9$	1-C	0.8750	0.8737, 0.8761	0.0690	−2.79
$\alpha = 0.90, k = 9$	1-L	0.8958	0.8950, 0.8966	0.0431	−0.47
$\alpha = 0.90, k = 9$	2-C	0.8784	0.8773, 0.8795	0.0644	−2.4
$\alpha = 0.90, k = 9$	2-L	0.8965	0.8958, 0.8972	0.0411	−0.39
$\alpha = 0.90, k = 9$	3-C	0.8969	0.8965, 0.8974	0.0247	−0.34
$\alpha = 0.90, k = 9$	3-L	0.8998	0.8994, 0.9002	0.0250	−0.02

See Tables 3 and 4 for the parameters and Figs. 2–4 for the distributions (Dist)

and 6 clearly indicates that this is the case. That is, the superiority that the L-comoment-based estimator $\hat{\alpha}_L$ has over its corresponding conventional counterpart $\hat{\alpha}_C$ is obvious in the contexts of Distributions 1 and 2. For example, inspection of the first entry in Table 5 ($\alpha = 0.50$, $k = 4$, $n = 10$) indicates that the estimator $\hat{\alpha}_C$ associated with Distribution 1 was, on average, 88.32 % of its associated population parameter whereas the estimator $\hat{\alpha}_L$ was 96.94 % of its parameter. Further, and in the context of Distribution 1, it is also evident that $\hat{\alpha}_L$ is a more efficient estimator as its RSE is smaller than its corresponding conventional estimator (see Table 5, $\alpha = 0.50$, $k = 4$, $n = 10$). This demonstrates that $\hat{\alpha}_L$ has more precision because it has less variance around its estimate.

In summary, the L-comoment-based $\hat{\alpha}_L$ is an attractive alternative to the traditional Cronbach alpha $\hat{\alpha}_C$ when distributions with heavy tails and small samples sizes are encountered. It is also worthy to point out that $\hat{\alpha}_L$ had a slight advantage over $\hat{\alpha}_C$ when sampling was from normal populations (see Table 5; $\alpha = 0.50$, $k = 4$, $n = 10$, 3-C, 3-L). When sample sizes was large the performance of the two estimators $\hat{\alpha}_{C,L}$ were similar (see Table 7; $n = 1{,}000$).

Table 7 Simulation results for α based on the Conventional (C) and L-moment (L) procedures (Proc) based on samples of size $n = 1,000$

Parameters	Dist–Proc	Estimate (α)	95 % C.I.	RSE (%)	RBias (%)
$\alpha = 0.50, k = 4$	1-C	0.4988	0.4982, 0.4994	0.05814	−0.24
$\alpha = 0.50, k = 4$	1-L	0.4988	0.4984, 0.4992	0.04210	−0.24
$\alpha = 0.50, k = 4$	2-C	0.4993	0.4987, 0.4998	0.05613	−0.14
$\alpha = 0.50, k = 4$	2-L	0.5001	0.4997, 0.5005	0.04200	0.02
$\alpha = 0.50, k = 4$	3-C	0.5000	0.4997, 0.5003	0.03200	0.00
$\alpha = 0.50, k = 4$	3-L	0.5000	0.4997, 0.5004	0.03400	0.00
$\alpha = 0.714, k = 10$	1-C	0.7134	0.7129, 0.7138	0.03084	−0.12
$\alpha = 0.714, k = 10$	1-L	0.7132	0.7129, 0.7135	0.02103	−0.15
$\alpha = 0.714, k = 10$	2-C	0.7133	0.7129, 0.7137	0.02804	−0.14
$\alpha = 0.714, k = 10$	2-L	0.7140	0.7137, 0.7143	0.01961	−0.04
$\alpha = 0.714, k = 10$	3-C	0.7141	0.7140, 0.7143	0.01120	−0.03
$\alpha = 0.714, k = 10$	3-L	0.7142	0.7140, 0.7144	0.01260	−0.01
$\alpha = 0.80, k = 4$	1-C	0.7991	0.7987, 0.7994	0.02127	−0.11
$\alpha = 0.80, k = 4$	1-L	0.8017	0.8015, 0.8019	0.01247	0.21
$\alpha = 0.80, k = 4$	2-C	0.7990	0.7987, 0.7993	0.02003	−0.12
$\alpha = 0.80, k = 4$	2-L	0.8011	0.8009, 0.8013	0.01248	0.14
$\alpha = 0.80, k = 4$	3-C	0.7999	0.7998, 0.8000	0.00875	−0.01
$\alpha = 0.80, k = 4$	3-L	0.8000	0.7998, 0.8001	0.00875	0.00
$\alpha = 0.90, k = 9$	1-C	0.8992	0.8990, 0.8994	0.01001	−0.09
$\alpha = 0.90, k = 9$	1-L	0.9008	0.9007, 0.9009	0.00555	0.09
$\alpha = 0.90, k = 9$	2-C	0.8994	0.8992, 0.8995	0.01000	−0.07
$\alpha = 0.90, k = 9$	2-L	0.9005	0.9004, 0.9006	0.00556	0.06
$\alpha = 0.90, k = 9$	3-C	0.8999	0.8999, 0.9000	0.00333	−0.01
$\alpha = 0.90, k = 9$	3-L	0.9000	0.8999, 0.9000	0.00333	0.00

See Tables 3 and 4 for the parameters and Figs. 2–4 for the distributions (Dist)

Appendix

Under the assumption of parallel measures, the error term e_{ij} in Eq. (1) has constant variance σ_e^2, the variance–covariance matrix assumes compound-symmetry, and thus the main and off-diagonal elements are $\sigma_j^2 = \sigma_X^2$ and $\sigma_{jj'} = \sigma_t^2$, respectively. Hence, Eq. (2) can be expressed using the true score and observed score variances as

$$\alpha = \frac{k}{k-1}\left(1 - \frac{k\sigma_X^2}{k\sigma_X^2 + k(k-1)\sigma_t^2}\right),$$

which can be simplified to

$$\alpha = \frac{k}{k-1}\left(1 - \frac{\sigma_X^2}{\sigma_X^2 + (k-1)\sigma_t^2}\right)$$

$$= \frac{k}{k-1}\left(\frac{(k-1)\sigma_t^2}{\sigma_X^2+(k-1)\sigma_t^2}\right)$$

$$= \frac{k\sigma_t^2}{\sigma_X^2+(k-1)\sigma_t^2}.$$

If we let $R = \sigma_j^2/\sigma_{jj'} = \sigma_X^2/\sigma_t^2$, then it follows that

$$\alpha = \frac{k}{R+k-1} = \frac{1}{1+(R-1)/k},$$

which is given in Eq. (6).

References

Bay, K. S. (1973). The effect of non-normality on the sampling distribution and standard error of reliability coefficient estimates under an analysis of variance model. *British Journal of Mathematical and Statistical Psychology*, *26*(1), 45–57.

Berkovits, I., Hancock, G. R., & Nevitt J. (2000). Bootstrap resampling approaches for repeated measures designs: Relative robustness to sphericity and normality violations. *Educational and Psychological Measurement*, *60*(6), 877–892.

Christman, A., & Van Aelst, S. (2006). Robust estimation of Cronbach's alpha. *Journal of Multivariate Analysis*, *97*(7), 1660–1674.

Cronbach, L. J. (1951). Coefficient alpha and the internal structure of tests. *Psychometrika*, *16*(3), 297–334.

Enders, C. K. (2001). The impact of nonnormality on full information maximum likelihood estimation for structural equation models with missing data. *Psychological Methods*, *6*(3), 352–370.

Fleishman A. I. (1978). A method for simulating non-normal distributions. *Psychometrika*, *43*(4), 521–532.

Guttman, L. A. (1945). A basis for test-retest reliability. *Psychometrika*, *10*(4), 255–282.

Harwell, M. R., & Serlin, R. C. (1988). An empirical study of a proposed test of nonparametric analysis of covariance. *Psychological Bulletin*, *104*(2), 268–281.

Headrick, T. C. (2010). *Statistical simulation: Power method polynomials and other transformations*. Boca Raton: Chapman and Hall/CRC.

Headrick, T. C. (2011). A characterization of power method transformations through *L*-moments. *Journal of Probability and Statistics*, 22 pp. doi:10.1155/497463/2011.

Headrick, T. C., & Pant, M. D. (2012a). Characterizing Tukey *h* and *hh*-distributions through *L*-moments and the *L*-correlation. *ISRN Applied Mathematics*, 20 pp. doi:10.5402/980153/2012.

Headrick, T. C., & Pant, M. D. (2012b). A doubling method for the generalized lambda distribution. *ISRN Applied Mathematics*, 20 pp. doi:10.5402/725754/2012.

Headrick, T. C., & Pant, M. D. (2012c). Simulating non-normal distributions with specified *L*-moments and *L*-correlations. *Statistica Neerlandica*, *66*(4), 422–441. doi:10.1111/j.1467-9574.2012.00523.

Headrick, T. C., & Pant, M. D. (2012d). A method for simulating non-normal distributions with specified *L*-skew, *L*-kurtosis, and *L*-correlation. *ISRN Applied Mathematics*, 23 pp. doi:10.5402/980827/2012.

Headrick, T. C., & Pant, M. D. (2012e). A logistic L-moment based analog for the Tukey *g-h*, *g*, *h*, and *h-h* system of distributions. *ISRN Probability and Statistics*, 23 pp. doi:10.5402/245986/2012.

Headrick, T. C., & Sawilowsky, S. S. (1999) Simulating correlated multivariate non-normal distributions: Extending the Fleishman power method. *Psychometrika*, *64*(1), 25–35.

Headrick, T. C., & Sawilowsky, S. S. (2000). Properties of the rank transformation in factorial analysis of covariance. *Communications in Statistics: Simulation and Computation*, *29*(4), 1059–1088.

Hodis, F. A., Headrick, T. C., & Sheng Y. (2012). Power method distributions through conventional moments and *L*-moments. *Applied Mathematical Sciences*, *6*(44), 2159–2193.

Hosking, J. R. M. (1990). *L*-moments: Analysis and estimation of distributions using linear combinations of order statistics. *Journal of the Royal Statistical Society, Series B*, *52*(1), 105–124.

Hosking, J. R. M. (1992). Moments or L-moments? An example comparing two measures of distributional shape. *American Statistician*, *46*(3), 186–189.

Hosking, J. R. M., & Wallis, J. R. (1997). *Regional frequency analysis: An approach based on L-moments*. Cambridge: Cambridge University Press.

Mathworks (2010). *MATLAB, version 7.11 computer software*. Natick: Mathworks.

McDonald, R. P. (1999). *Test theory: A unified treatment*. Mahwah: Lawrence Erlbaum.

Micceri, T. (1989). The unicorn, the normal curve, and other improbable creatures. *Psychological Bulletin*, *105*(1), 156–166.

Olkin, I., & Yitzhuki, S. (1992). Gini regression analysis. *International Statistical Review*, *60*(2), 185–196.

Olsson, U. H., Foss, T., & Troye, S. V. (2003). Does ADF fit function decrease when the kurtosis increases. *British Journal of Mathematical and Statistical Psychology*, *56*(2), 289–303.

Schechtman, E., & Yitzhaki, S. (1987). A measure of association based on Gini's mean difference. *Communications in Statistics: Theory and Methods*, *16*(1), 207–231.

Serfling, R. (1980). *Aroximation theorems for mathematical statistics*. New York: Wiley.

Serfling, R., & Xiao, P. (2007). A contribution to multivariate *L*-moments: *L*-comoment matrices. *Journal of Multivariate Analysis*, *98*(9), 1765–1781.

Sheng, Y., & Sheng, Z. (2012). Is coefficient alpha robust to non-normal data? *Frontiers in Psychology*, *3*(34), 13 pp. doi:10.3389/fpsyg.2012.00034.

Vogel, R. M., & Fennessy, N. M. (1993). *L*-moment diagrams should replace product moment diagrams. *Water Resources Research*, *29*(6), 1745–1752.

Wilcox, R. R. (1992). Robust generalizations of classical test reliability and Cronbach's alpha. *British Journal of Mathematical and Statistical Psychology*, *45*(2), 239–254.

Yuan, K., Bentler, P. M., & Chan, W. (2004). Structural equation modeling with heavy tailed distributions. *Psychometrika*, *69*(3), 421–436.

Using the Testlet Response Model as a Shortcut to Multidimensional Item Response Theory Subscore Computation

David Thissen

1 Introduction

In many assessment contexts there may be perceived usefulness for diagnostic scores that describe a profile of performance, reflecting a more nuanced description of individual differences than is obtained with a single total score. Several ways to compute diagnostic scores have been proposed and used, but the use of classic *subscores* originated more than 70 years ago with tests like the Wechsler–Bellevue Intelligence Scale (WBIS) (Wechsler 1939). The WBIS provided eleven "subtest scores" in addition to verbal, performance, and full-scale IQ scores. Estes (1946) referred to the subtest scores as "subscores," possibly originating modern usage. A footnote to the score conversion table for the subtest scores on the WBIS noted that "one must recognize the relative unreliability of these subtest scores," anticipating modern concerns about the unreliability of subscores based on a few items that are a subset of a longer test.

In the past three decades, several systems have been proposed to calculate more reliable subscores for small subsets of test items by "borrowing strength" (Tukey 1973), using additional information such as the total score on the test, or the other subscores on the test. Yen (1987) described an *objective performance index* that used ideas from item response theory (IRT) to combine information from a subscore with the total score on the entire test into a more reliable score. Wainer et al. (2001) contained details on the computation of two kinds of *augmented subscores*: (1) those based on summed scores, as estimates of classical *true scores*, using the multivariate generalization of Kelley's (1927) regressed estimates, and (2) those arising from a multi-step procedure to mimic the multivariate Kelley

D. Thissen (✉)
Department of Psychology, The University of North Carolina at Chapel Hill,
Chapel Hill, NC 27599, USA
e-mail: dthissen@email.unc.edu

R.E. Millsap et al. (eds.), *New Developments in Quantitative Psychology*,
Springer Proceedings in Mathematics & Statistics 66, DOI 10.1007/978-1-4614-9348-8_3,

regressed estimates with multiple univariate IRT analyses. Wainer et al.'s (2001) augmented scores are estimates based on the regression of each true score on all of the subscores; for summed scores, Haberman (2008) proposed an alternative scheme to compute augmented subscores using only the subscore in question and the total score on the test.

Haberman (2008) also proposed evaluation of the value of subscores using the comparison of the proportional reduction in mean squared error (PRMSE) for each of several subscore estimates—for the subscore itself, for the total score as an estimate of the subscore, and for the augmented subscore. PRMSE is, in some senses, reliability, computed for a particular observed score as an estimate of a particular true score. Historically, there are many estimates denoted "reliability," and nearly as many meanings of the word, so it was wise to use "PRMSE" instead—it is semantically neutral, and it is accurate: how much the mean squared error in estimating the score is reduced by any observed score (relative to using the mean).

Procedures for computing augmented summed scores are well developed and computationally straightforward (Edwards and Vevea 2006; Haberman 2008; Sinharay et al. 2008). However, many assessment systems use IRT scale scores; the computation of augmented IRT subscores has been more challenging, and that is the subject of this presentation. Advances in computational equipment and algorithms in the past two decades have made direct use of multidimensional IRT (MIRT) models practical for the calculation of augmented subscores; this presentation draws together several threads from recent research to propose a useful system.

2 MIRT and Subscores

To provide a concrete setting for the ideas described here, we use one of the examples described by Wainer et al. (2001), involving responses to the late-1990s North Carolina Test of Computer Skills—an 8th Grade performance test with four parts: (1) Keyboarding (Kb), with three four-category items; (2) Editing (Ed), with ten dichotomous items; (3) Database (Db), with four dichotomous items and three three-category items; and (4) Spreadsheet (Ss) with five dichotomous items and one item scored in three-categories.

The multi-step IRT procedure to compute augmented scores described by Wainer et al. (2001) was developed at a time when it was not clear that MIRT models could be reliably fitted directly to data, so it made use of assembled univariate IRT analyses of each subscale. Nevertheless, the underlying idea was to fit a model like that shown in path-analytic form in the left panel of Fig. 1: The model includes four correlated latent variables, one for each subscale. Augmented MIRT subscores are the IRT trait estimates (e.g., the maximum a posteriori (MAP) or expected a posteriori (EAP) values) for the four latent variables, each of which depends on the item responses for its own subscale as well as those on the other subscales through the correlations.

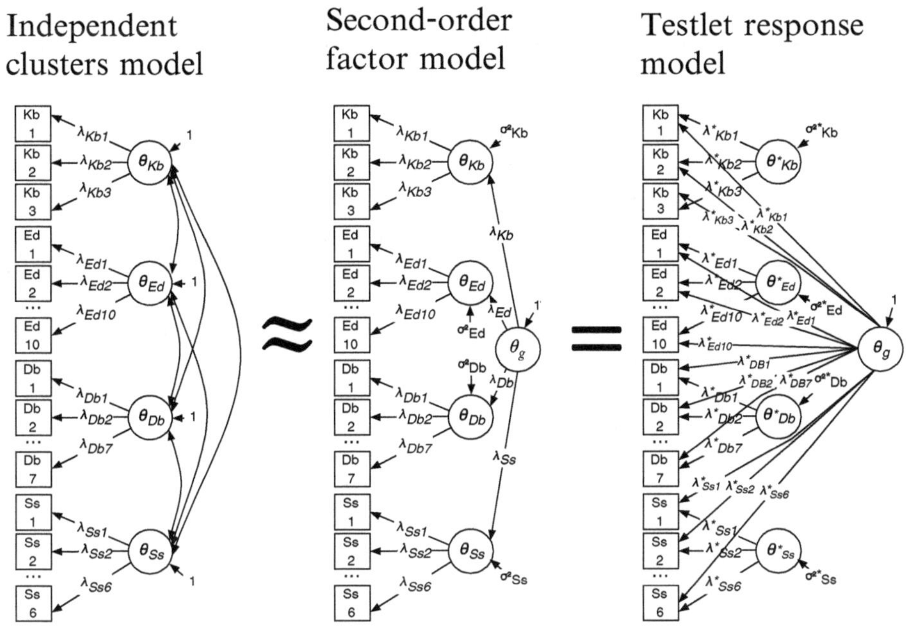

Fig. 1 Path diagrams illustrating the latent variable structures of a four-dimensional independent clusters model (*left panel*), a second-order factor model (*center panel*), and the testlet response model (*right panel*) for the four subscales of a North Carolina Test of Computer Skills

Since publication of the work by Wainer et al. (2001), there have been many advances in statistical estimation for MIRT models, so Wainer et al.'s (2001) multi-step procedure combining results obtained with parallel unidimensional IRT models can be abandoned. To show that MIRT models could be fitted to data, early efforts used Markov chain Monte Carlo (MCMC) algorithms (Béguin and Glas 2001; Bolt and Lall 2003; Yao and Schwarz 2006; Yao and Boughton 2009; Edwards 2010). Some of that work with MCMC algorithms has been focused on subscores, and even higher-order models, which will be a focus of this presentation (de la Torre and Hong 2009; de la Torre and Song 2009; de la Torre 2009; de la Torre and Patz 2005; Yao 2010; Yao and Boughton 2007). The use of more convenient, if less sophisticated or elegant, point estimation by maximum likelihood (ML) has lagged behind, but has become practical with contemporary software (Haberman and Sinharay 2010; Cai et al. 2011).

Even with the advent of modern MIRT software, parameter estimation remains challenging for models with more than two or three latent dimensions—in the context of subscores, that means more than two or three subscales, and that situation is common. It follows that the use of dimension-reduction techniques could be helpful; this presentation describes a way to recast item parameter estimation for a high-dimensional MIRT model into parameter estimation for a bifactor model, which can be done with more computational efficiency.

First, we note that it is often the case that the kind of *independent clusters* or *simple structure* MIRT model illustrated in the left panel of Fig. 1 can be approximated with the *second-order* or *higher-order* factor model shown in the center panel of the graphic. In a second-order factor model, as originally described by Tucker (1940), a second- or higher-order latent variable θ_g explains the correlation among the first-order latent variables—in this case those are the subscale θs. For four or more subscales, the relationship between the second-order factor model and the independent clusters model is one of the approximations: It is often the case, empirically, that the correlations among the subscores can be well approximated by a one-factor model, but counterexamples can be found. For three subscales, for some patterns of correlation the relationship is exact, while for others it is approximate; for two subscales, the relationship is tautological. de la Torre (2009), de la Torre and Hong (2009), and de la Torre and Song (2009) have suggested the direct use of a second-order factor model for subscore estimation.

In this presentation, we take advantage of the relationships among the second-order factor model, the Wainer et al. (2007) *testlet response model* (TRM), and the *bifactor* model (Holzinger and Swineford 1937), to simplify computation. The TRM can be expressed in path-diagram form as shown in the right panel of Fig. 1: There is a general factor, θ_g, that explains covariation among all the items, and a set of subscale-specific latent variables θ^* that explain residual covariation within each subscale. While the right panel of Fig. 1 shows two factor loadings (λs) relating each item's latent response to the subscale-specific and general latent variables, those two λs are constrained equal in the TRM. The estimated parameters are one (1) loading (or equivalently, IRT slope) for each item, and as many variances as there are subscales (Wainer et al. 2007; Bradlow et al. 1999; Wainer et al. 2000; Wang et al. 2002).

The original software by Wang et al. (2005) to estimate the parameters of the TRM used MCMC. However, when the model is expressed as in Fig. 1 to show that it is a constrained bifactor model, ML estimation using dimension-reduction techniques (Gibbons and Hedeker 1992; Gibbons et al. 2007; Cai 2010c; Rijmen 2010; Cai et al. 2011) as implemented in software such as IRTRPO (Cai et al. 2011) can also be used. That means that the parameters of TRMs like that shown in the right panel of Fig. 1 can be estimated efficiently using ML, with numerical integration over only two latent dimensions regardless of the number of subscores.

To relate this to the higher-order model in the center of Fig. 1, and then back to the original subscore problem, we note that the higher-order model in the center of Fig. 1 is a reparameterization of the TRM in the rightmost panel. Yung et al. (1999), based on pioneering work by Schmid and Leiman (1957), established this identity relation for the continuous-normal factor model. Rijmen (2010) extended these results to MIRT models; see also Li et al. (2006) and Thissen and Steinberg (2010).

Assembling these relationships among models yields the basis for an efficient three-step plan to estimate MIRT parameters, and subsequently compute IRT scale subscores, for the Computer Skills subscales: (1) Estimate the parameters for the TRM in the right panel of Fig. 1 by ML using dimension-reduction techniques

Table 1 Correlations among the four latent variables for the North Carolina Test of Computer Skills subscales

	4D Model					TRM			
	θ_{Kb}	θ_{Ed}	θ_{Db}	θ_{Ss}		θ_{Kb}	θ_{Ed}	θ_{Db}	θ_{Ss}
θ_{Kb}	1.00				θ_{Kb}	1.00			
θ_{Ed}	0.69	1.00			θ_{Ed}	0.60	1.00		
θ_{Db}	0.52	0.49	1.00		θ_{Db}	0.60	0.52	1.00	
θ_{Ss}	0.55	0.45	0.59	1.00	θ_{Ss}	0.58	0.50	0.50	1.00

that require numerical integration over only two dimensions (Gibbons and Hedeker 1992; Gibbons et al. 2007; Cai 2010c; Rijmen 2010; Cai et al. 2011). (2) Convert the parameter estimates for the TRM into those of the second-order model in the center of Fig. 1, using a simplification of the algorithm provided by Yung et al. (1999). (3) Convert the parameter estimates for the second-order model into those of the independent clusters model in the left panel of Fig. 1, and then compute the subscores from that model as either EAP estimates (which require four-dimensional integration) or MAP estimates (with no numerical integration).

Yung et al. (1999) provide an algorithm to convert the parameters of an unconstrained bifactor model into the factor loadings of a more general second-order factor model than illustrated in Fig. 1; the more general model also includes direct paths from θ_g to each observed variable. In the present case, however, with the equality constraints imposed on the bifactor model to yield the TRM, Yung et al.'s (1999) procedure can be simplified.

The second-order factor loadings, in terms of the TRM testlet variances, are

$$\lambda_g = \begin{bmatrix} \frac{1}{\sqrt{1+\sigma^{2*}_{Kb}}} \\ \frac{1}{\sqrt{1+\sigma^{2*}_{Ed}}} \\ \frac{1}{\sqrt{1+\sigma^{2*}_{Db}}} \\ \frac{1}{\sqrt{1+\sigma^{2*}_{Ss}}} \end{bmatrix} . \tag{1}$$

Then the implied correlation matrix among the factors of the original four-dimensional correlated independent clusters model is

$$\mathbf{R} = \lambda_g \lambda_g' + [\mathbf{I} - \text{diag}(\lambda_g \lambda_g')] . \tag{2}$$

Table 1 illustrates the results obtained with the data from the Computer Skills test; in the left side of the table are the correlations among the four latent variables as estimated using four-dimensional (4D) adaptive quadrature (Schilling and Bock 2005), and the right side of the table shows the similar correlation estimates obtained using Eqs. (1) and (2) after fitting the TRM. The correlations differ by as much as 0.09; however, that is probably due in part to their large standard errors—the sample size for this example is only 266, and the standard errors of the latent-variable correlations are 0.08–0.13. Because the sample size is so small, neither estimation problem requires much time to compute; however, the four-dimensional model required almost five times as long as the TRM to fit (165 s vs. 36 s) with the IRTPRO software (Cai et al. 2011).

To obtain scores, MIRT slope and intercept parameters are also required. In principle, the intercept parameters are the same for all three models shown in Fig. 1; in practice, they vary slightly between the 4D model and the two equivalent models on the right because the slopes are slightly different. We ignore that, and use the TRM intercept estimates in the approximation. To compute the implied slopes for the independent cluster model from the slopes for the TRM, we first convert the factor loadings using a simplification of Yung et al.'s (1999) algorithm. To do that, it is convenient to partition the loading matrix for the bifactor representation of the TRM as follows:

$$\Lambda^* = \left[\begin{array}{c|cccc} \lambda^* & \lambda^* & 0 & 0 & 0 \\ \lambda^* & \lambda^* & 0 & 0 & 0 \\ \lambda^* & \lambda^* & 0 & 0 & 0 \\ \lambda^* & 0 & \lambda^* & 0 & 0 \\ \vdots & \vdots & \vdots & \vdots & \vdots \\ \lambda^* & 0 & \lambda^* & 0 & 0 \\ \lambda^* & 0 & 0 & \lambda^* & 0 \\ \vdots & \vdots & \vdots & \vdots & \vdots \\ \lambda^* & 0 & 0 & \lambda^* & 0 \\ \lambda^* & 0 & 0 & 0 & \lambda^* \\ \vdots & \vdots & \vdots & \vdots & \vdots \\ \lambda^* & 0 & 0 & 0 & \lambda^* \end{array}\right] = \lambda_g^* | \Lambda_s^* . \tag{3}$$

Then loadings in the submatrix Λ_s^* are rescaled using the matrix $\mathbf{Y}$,

$$\Lambda = \Lambda^* \mathbf{Y}. \tag{4}$$

$\mathbf{Y}$ is a simplification of one of the matrices in Yung et al.'s (1999) "inverse Schmid–Leiman transformation":

$$\mathbf{Y} = \begin{bmatrix} \sqrt{1+\sigma_{Kb}^2} & 0 & 0 & 0 \\ 0 & \sqrt{1+\sigma_{Ed}^2} & 0 & 0 \\ 0 & 0 & \sqrt{1+\sigma_{Db}^2} & 0 \\ 0 & 0 & 0 & \sqrt{1+\sigma_{Ss}^2} \end{bmatrix} . \tag{5}$$

Table 2 PRMSE values for the North Carolina Test of Computer Skills

	Kb	Ed	Db	Ss
PRMSE($\theta_k\|\mathbf{u}_k$)	0.67	0.73	0.67	0.77
PRMSE($\theta_k\|\bar{\theta}_g$)	0.48	0.37	0.36	0.34
PRMSE($\theta_k\|\mathbf{u}$)[1]	0.65	0.77	0.71	0.79
PRMSE($\theta_k\|\mathbf{u}$)[2]	0.67	0.77	0.72	0.80

[1] Parameters from TRM/higher-order model
[2] Parameters from unconstrained 4D model

Direct 4D estimation produced one set of MIRT parameters for the model in the left panel of Fig. 1; the use of Eqs. (1)–(5) with parameters from the fitted TRM produced another very similar set of parameters. The precision of augmented subscore estimates computed with those two sets of parameters can be compared to each other, and to other score estimates, using PRMSE as proposed by Haberman (2008) and Haberman and Sinharay (2010). Two alternative subscore estimates that might be considered would be the EAP estimate for θ for subscale k computed from a unidimensional IRT model fitted to subscale k, and the EAP estimate for θ for subscale k computed from its regression on θ_g from the TRM/higher-order model (as an IRT analog to the replacement of all subscore estimates with the total score). PRMSE values for these score estimates are:

PRMSE($\theta_k|\mathbf{u}_k$): the PRMSE using the EAP estimate for θ for subscale k computed from a unidimensional IRT model fitted to subscale k as an estimate of θ_k.

PRMSE($\theta_k|\bar{\theta}_g$): the PRMSE using the EAP estimate for θ for subscale k computed from its regression on θ_g from the TRM/higher-order model as an estimate of θ_k.

PRMSE($\theta_k|\mathbf{u}$): the PRMSE using the augmented EAP estimate for θ for subscale k computed from a MIRT model fitted to the entire test as an estimate of θ_k. There are two of these, one for the independent clusters model and one for the TRM-derived version.

Table 2 shows the values of PRMSE for those four subscore estimates for the Computer Skills subscales. The most salient feature of the values in Table 2 is that all of the subscale estimates are much more precise than estimates derived from the total score $\bar{\theta}_g$. By comparison, 4D subscore augmentation increases precision only modestly, from 0.00 (for Kb) to 0.05 (for Db), as reflected in the difference between PRMSE($\theta_k|\mathbf{u}_k$) and PRMSE($\theta_k|\mathbf{u}$)^2. The pattern of results reflects the fact that the latent variables for these four subscales are only moderately correlated (0.5–0.6; see Table 1). The values of PRMSE($\theta_k|\mathbf{u}$)^1 for subscale scores computed with the TRM-derived approximation to the 4D model are only 0.00–0.02 lower than the values for the 4D model.

3 Additional Examples

The PROMIS pediatric emotional distress scales (Irwin et al. 2010, 2012) provide second example with a similar pattern of results. The PROMIS pediatric emotional distress scales were constructed as three distinct unidimensional IRT scales measuring Depressive Symptoms, Anxiety, and Anger. However, here we investigate the properties of the suggested short forms of the three scales as if they were subscales of a global *emotional distress* measure. Table 3 shows the correlations among the three latent variables as estimated using adaptive quadrature with a three-dimensional (3D) correlated independent clusters model, and as estimated with the TRM and then computed using Eqs. (1)–(5); the three correlations are essentially the same either way.

Table 4 shows the values of PRMSE for the subscore estimates for the PROMIS pediatric Anger (Ang), Anxiety (Anx), and Depressive Symptoms (Dep) scales. As was the case with the previous example, the most obvious feature of the values in Table 4 is that all of the subscale estimates are much more precise than estimates derived from a (hypothetical) total score, as reflected in the difference between PRMSE$(\theta_k|\mathbf{u}_k)$ and PRMSE$(\theta_k|\mathbf{u})^2$. Again, 3D subscore augmentation increases precision only modestly, from 0.02 (for Anger) to 0.05 (for Depressive Symptoms). This is the case even though these three latent variables are correlated 0.66–0.78 (see Table 3), and is probably due to the fact that these scales, comprising 6–8 five-category graded response items, already have relatively large PRMSE values when unidimensional models are used. The values of PRMSE$(\theta_k|\mathbf{u})^1$ for subscale scores computed with the TRM-derived approximation to the 3D model are essentially the same as the values for the 3D model, because the correlations are essentially the same.

Table 3 Correlations among the three latent variables for the PROMIS pediatric emotional distress scales

	3D Model				TRM		
	θ_{Ang}	θ_{Anx}	θ_{Dep}		θ_{Ang}	θ_{Anx}	θ_{Dep}
θ_{Ang}	1.00			θ_{Ang}	1.00		
θ_{Anx}	0.656	1.00		θ_{Anx}	0.656	1.00	
θ_{Dep}	0.778	0.770	1.00	θ_{Dep}	0.777	0.769	1.00

Table 4 PRMSE values for the PROMIS pediatric emotional distress scales

	Anger	Anxiety	Depr. Symp.
PRMSE$(\theta_k\|\mathbf{u}_k)$	0.86	0.86	0.84
PRMSE$(\theta_k\|\bar{\theta}_g)$	0.57	0.56	0.78
PRMSE$(\theta_k\|\mathbf{u})^1$	0.88	0.89	0.89
PRMSE$(\theta_k\|\mathbf{u})^2$	0.88	0.89	0.89

[1] Parameters from TRM/higher-order model
[2] Parameters from unconstrained 3D model

Table 5 Correlations among the six latent variables for the APICS certification examination

	6D Model							TRM					
	θ_{Con}	θ_{HR}	θ_{TQC}	θ_{Tech}	θ_{Int}	θ_{Impl}		θ_{Con}	θ_{HR}	θ_{TQC}	θ_{Tech}	θ_{Int}	θ_{Impl}
θ_{Con}	1.00						θ_{Con}	1.00					
θ_{HR}	0.93	1.00					θ_{HR}	0.91	1.00				
θ_{TQC}	0.92	0.89	1.00				θ_{TQC}	0.88	0.85	1.00			
θ_{Tech}	0.95	0.93	0.89	1.00			θ_{Tech}	0.94	0.90	0.87	1.00		
θ_{Int}	0.97	0.95	0.92	0.97	1.00		θ_{Int}	0.97	0.93	0.91	0.96	1.00	
θ_{Impl}	0.96	0.94	0.91	0.96	0.98	1.00	θ_{Impl}	0.96	0.92	0.89	0.95	0.98	1.00

Table 6 PRMSE values for the APICS certification examination

	Concepts	HR	TotalQC	Techniques	Integration	Implementation
$\text{PRMSE}(\theta_k \mid \mathbf{u}_k)$	0.47	0.54	0.66	0.67	0.55	0.71
$\text{PRMSE}(\theta_k \mid \tilde{\theta}_g)$	0.81	0.74	0.70	0.79	0.85	0.82
$\text{PRMSE}(\theta_k \mid \mathbf{u})^1$	0.84	0.80	0.80	0.84	0.87	0.86
$\text{PRMSE}(\theta_k \mid \mathbf{u})^2$	0.85	0.83	0.82	0.86	0.88	0.87

[1] Parameters from TRM/higher-order model
[2] Parameters from unconstrained 6D model

A third example is another described by Wainer et al. (2001) that involves a certification examination for the American Production and Inventory Control Society (APICS) administered in 1994. This 100-item multiple-choice test was designed to have six subscales, measuring Concepts (Con), Human Resources (HR), Total Quality Control (TQC), Techniques (Tech), Integration (Int), and Implementation (Impl). After various analyses, Wainer et al. (2001) found that this test was so nearly unidimensional that any computation of subscores produced values with poor reliability (for the subscales alone), or values that amounted to reproducing the total score six times (for augmented subscores). The correlations among the latent variables for the six subscales for the APICS exam shown in Table 5 make it clear why that is the case: Nearly all of the correlations exceed 0.9.

The values in the left half of Table 5 are very challenging to estimate; fitting a six-dimensional correlated independent clusters model is beyond the capacity of even modern MIRT software using quadrature. The estimates shown in the left half of Table 5 were obtained using Cai's (2010a, 2010b) Metropolis-Hastings Robbins-Monro (MH-RM) algorithm, with starting values derived from the TRM solution. On the other hand, the TRM solution was easy to obtain. Table 5 shows that the correlation estimates are not very much different.

Table 6 shows the values of PRMSE for the subscore estimates for the APICS certification examination subscales; the pattern is very different from that previously seen in Tables 2 and 4. In this case, all of the subscale estimates are much *less* precise than estimates derived from a total score, as reflected in the difference between $\text{PRMSE}(\theta_k \mid \mathbf{u}_k)$ and $\text{PRMSE}(\theta_k \mid \mathbf{u})^2$. 6D subscore augmentation increases precision a great deal, from 0.38 (for Concepts) down to 0.16 (for Total QC and

Implementation). However, the fact that the subscales scores are so highly correlated means that the augmented subscores, while reliable, are nearly the same as simply reporting the total score six times—all subscores regress to nearly the same value. The values of $\text{PRMSE}(\theta_k|\mathbf{u})^1$ for subscale scores computed with the TRM-derived approximation to the 6D model are similar to those obtained with the more complex model.

4 Conclusion

The conclusion that is unique to this presentation is that it may be effective to use the computational "shortcut" that involves fitting the TRM (as a constrained bifactor model) to multidimensional item response data, and then using Eqs. (1)–(5) to approximate the more difficult to estimate parameters of a correlated simple structure model to compute subscores.

However, the examples in this presentation, together with similar examples in the literature, suggest that subscore augmentation has a narrow window of usefulness: If the correlations among the latent variables for the subscores are relatively low (as in the Computer Skills example, in which they were 0.5–0.6), or if the subscales are already relatively reliable (as in the PROMIS emotional distress scales), augmentation is not necessarily very helpful. In those cases, separate unidimensional models for the individual subscales are simple and effective. On the other hand, if the correlation among the subscales are very high (as was the case with the APICS certification exam), subscore augmentation simply reproduces the total score; so it may be better to avoid reporting subscores entirely. It is useful to follow (Haberman's 2008) suggestion that comparison of relevant PRMSE values can be used to evaluate subscores.

There are cases in which subscore augmentation is clearly useful, but they appear to come from a narrowly defined window, in which subscale scores have relatively low reliability (PRMSE) when considered alone, and when they appear on tests with latent-variable correlations among the subscores between about 0.8 and the low 0.9 s. Haberman and Sinharay (2010) provide three examples of examinations in that window for which they found subscore augmentation to be unambigously helpful; they also reported results for two exams with higher correlations among the latent variables, for which the total score tended to be the better choice.

For tests with short subscales that do not produce sufficiently reliable scores on their own, but are intercorrelated moderately highly, perhaps between 0.75 and 0.95 for the latent variables, an MIRT approach to subscore augmentation may be effective if IRT scales are used for score reporting. In that context, the computational shortcut described in this presentation, using the TRM, is more efficient computationally and may be more numerically stable, and should be considered.

References

Béguin, A. A., & Glas, C. A. W. (2001). MCMC estimation and some model-fit analysis of multidimensional IRT models. *Psychometrika, 66*, 541–561.

Bolt, D. M., & Lall, V. F. (2003). Estimation of compensatory and noncompensatory multidimensional IRT models using Markov chain Monte Carlo. *Applied Psychological Measurement, 27*, 395–414.

Bradlow, E., Wainer, H., & Wang, X. (1999). A Bayesian random effects model for testlets. *Psychometrika, 64*, 153–168.

Cai, L. (2010a). High-dimensional exploratory item factor analysis by a Metropolis-Hastings Robbins-Monro algorithm. *Psychometrika, 75*, 33–57.

Cai, L. (2010b). Metropolis-Hastings Robbins-Monro algorithm for confirmatory item factor analysis. *Journal of Educational and Behavioral Statistics, 35*, 307–335.

Cai, L. (2010c). A two-tier full-information item factor analysis model with applications. *Psychometrika, 75*, 581–612.

Cai, L., Thissen, D., & du Toit, S. (2011). IRTPRO version 2: Flexible, multidimensional, multiple categorical IRT modeling [Computer software manual]. Chicago, IL.

Cai, L., Yang, J., & Hansen, M. (2011). Generalized full-information item bifactor analysis. *Psychological Methods, 16*, 221–248.

de la Torre, J. (2009). Improving the quality of ability estimates through multidimensional scoring and incorporation of ancillary variables. *Applied Psychological Measurement, 33*, 465–485.

de la Torre, J., & Hong, Y. (2009). Parameter estimation with small sample size: A higher-order IRT approach. *Applied Psychological Measurement, 34*, 267–285.

de la Torre, J., & Patz, R. J. (2005). Making the most of what we have: A practical application of multidimensional item response theory in test scoring. *Journal of Educational and Behavioral Statistics, 30*, 295–311.

de la Torre, J., & Song, H. (2009). Simultaneous estimation of overall and domain abilities: A higher-order IRT model approach. *Applied Psychological Measurement, 33*, 620–639.

Edwards, M. C. (2010). A Markov chain Monte Carlo approach to confirmatory item factor analysi. *Psychometrika, 75*, 474–497.

Edwards, M. C., & Vevea, J. L. (2006). An empirical bayes approach to subscore augmentation: How much strength can we borrow? *Journal of Educational and Behavioral Statistics, 31*, 241–259.

Estes, S. (1946). Deviations of Wechsler-Bellevue subtest scores from vocabulary level in superior adults. *Journal of Abnormal and Social Psychology, 41*, 226–228.

Gibbons, R., Bock, R., Hedeker, D., Weiss, D., Segawa, E., Bhaumik, D., et al. (2007). Full-information item bifactor analysis of graded response data. *Applied Psychological Measurement, 31*, 4–19.

Gibbons, R., & Hedeker, D. (1992). Full-information item bi-factor analysis. *Psychometrika, 57*, 423–436.

Haberman, S. J. (2008). When can subscores have value? *Journal of Educational and Behavioral Statistics, 22*, 204–229.

Haberman, S. J., & Sinharay, S. (2010). Reporting of subscores using multidimensional item response theory. *Psychometrika, 75*, 209–227.

Holzinger, K. J., & Swineford, F. (1937). The bi-factor method. *Psychometrika, 2*, 41–54.

Irwin, D., Stucky, B. D., Langer, M. M., Thissen, D., DeWitt, E. M., Lai, J. S., et al. (2010). An item response analysis of the Pediatric PROMIS Anxiety and Depressive Symptoms Scales. *Quality of Life Research, 19*, 595–607.

Irwin, D., Stucky, B. D., Langer, M. M., Thissen, D., DeWitt, E. M., Lai, J. S., et al. (2012). PROMIS Pediatric Anger Scale: An item response theory analysis. *Quality of Life Research, 21*, 697–706.

Kelley, T. L. (1927). *The interpretation of educational measurements*. New York: World Book.

Li, Y., Bolt, D. M., & Fu, J. (2006). A comparison of alternative models for testlets. *Applied Psychological Measurement, 30*, 3–21.

Rijmen, F. (2010). Formal relations and an empirical comparison between the bi-factor, the testlet, and a second-order multidimensional IRT model. *Journal of Educational Measurement, 47*, 361–372.

Schilling, S., & Bock, R. D. (2005). High-dimensional maximum marginal likelihood item factor analysis by adaptive quadrature. *Psychometrika, 70*, 533–555.

Schmid, J., & Leiman, J. M. (1957). The development of hierarchical factor solutions. *Psychometrika, 22*, 53–61.

Sinharay, S., Haberman, S. J., & Puhan, G. (2008). Subscores based on classical test theory: To report or not to report. *Educational Measurement: Issues and Practice, 26*, 21–28.

Thissen, D., & Steinberg, L. (2010). Using item response theory to disentangle constructs at different levels of generality. In S. Embretson (Ed.), *Measuring psychological constructs: Advances in model-based approaches* (pp. 123–144). Washington, DC: American Psychological Association.

Tucker, L. R. (1940). The role of correlated factors in factor analysis. *Psychometrika, 5*, 141–152.

Tukey, J. W. (1973). Exploratory data analysis as part of a large whole. In *Proceedings of the Eighteenth Conference on the Design of Experiments in Army Research, Development and Testing, Part I* (pp. 1–10), Durham, NC.

Wainer, H., Bradlow, E., & Du, Z. (2000). Testlet response theory: An analog for the 3-PL useful in testlet-based adaptive testing. In W. J. van der Linden & C. A. W. Glas (Eds.), *Computerized adaptive testing: Theory and practice* (pp. 245–270). Boston: Kluwer Academic.

Wainer, H., Bradlow, E., & Wang, X. (2007). *Testlet response theory and its applications*. New York: Cambridge University Press.

Wainer, H., Vevea, J. L., Camacho, F., Reeve, B. B., Rosa, K., Nelson, L., et al. (2001). Augmented scores: "Borrowing strength" to compute scores based on small numbers of items. In D. Thissen & H. Wainer (Eds.), *Test scoring* (pp. 343–387). Hillsdale: Lawrence Erlbaum Associates.

Wang, X., Bradlow, E., & Wainer, H. (2002). A general Bayesian model for testlets: Theory and applications. *Applied Psychological Measurement, 26*, 109–128.

Wang, X., Bradlow, E., & Wainer, H. (2005). *A user's guide for SCORIGHT version 3.0.* (ETS Technical Report RR-04-49). Princeton: Educational Testing Service.

Wechsler, D. (1939). *The measurement of adult intelligence*. Baltimore: Williams & Witkins.

Yao, L. (2010). Reporting valid and reliability overall score and domain scores. *Journal of Educational Measurement, 47*, 339–360.

Yao, L., & Boughton, K. A. (2007). A multidimensional item response modeling approach for improving subscale proficiency estimation and classification. *Applied Psychological Measurement, 31*, 1–23.

Yao, L., & Boughton, K. A. (2009). Multidimensional linking for tests containing polytomous items. *Journal of Educational Measurement, 46*, 177–197.

Yao, L., & Schwarz, R. D. (2006). A multidimensional partial credit model with associated item and test statistics: An application to mixed-format tests. *Applied Psychological Measurement, 30*, 469–492.

Yen, W. M. (1987, June). *A Bayesian/IRT Index of Objective Performance.* Paper presented at the annual meeting of the Psychometric Society, Montreal, Quebec, Canada.

Yung, Y. F., McLeod, L. D., & Thissen, D. (1999). The development of hierarchical factor solutions. *Psychometrika, 64*, 113–128.

Anatomy of Pearson's Chi-Square Statistic in Three-Way Contingency Tables

Yoshio Takane and Lixing Zhou

1 Introduction

Research in psychology and other social sciences often involves discrete multivariate data. Such data are conveniently summarized in the form of contingency tables. There have been two widely used classes of techniques for analysis of such tables. One is log linear models (e.g., Andersen 1980; Bishop et al. 1975) and the other is correspondence analysis (CA; e.g., Greenacre 1984; Nishisato 1980). The former allow ANOVA-like decompositions of the log likelihood ratio (LR) statistic (also known as the deviance statistic or the Kullback and Leibler 1951 divergence). This statistic measures the difference in log likelihood between the saturated and independence models. When the latter model is correct, it follows the asymptotic chi-square distribution with degrees of freedom (df) equal to the difference in the number of parameters in the two models.

In CA, on the other hand, an emphasis is placed on graphical representations of associations between rows and columns of contingency tables. This approach typically uses PCA-like (componentwise) decompositions of Pearson's (1900) chi-square statistic, measuring essentially the same thing as the log LR chi-square statistic. In this paper, we develop ANOVA-like decompositions of Pearson's chi-square statistic, similar to those for the log LR statistic.

These decompositions are useful in constrained CA, such as canonical correspondence analysis (CCA; ter Braak 1986) and canonical analysis with linear constraints

Y. Takane (✉)
Department of Psychology, University of Victoria, P.O. Box 3050 Victoria, BC, Canada, V8W 3P5
e-mail: takane@uvic.ca

L. Zhou
Department of Psychology, McGill University, 1205 Dr. Penfield Ave. Montreal, QC, Canada, H3A 1B1
e-mail: lixing.zhou@mail.mcgill.ca

R.E. Millsap et al. (eds.), *New Developments in Quantitative Psychology*, Springer Proceedings in Mathematics & Statistics 66, DOI 10.1007/978-1-4614-9348-8_4,

(CALC; Böckenholt and Böckenholt 1990), in which the total association between rows and columns of contingency tables is decomposed into what can and cannot be explained by the constraints. Different terms in the decompositions highlight different aspects of the total association. The terms in the proposed decompositions are mutually orthogonal and follow independent asymptotic chi-square distributions under suitable null hypotheses. This is in contrast to the decompositions suggested by Lancaster (1951), in which individual terms do not necessarily follow asymptotic chi-square distributions (Placket 1962). All terms in the proposed decompositions can be obtained in closed form unlike some of the terms in the decompositions of the log LR chi-square statistic.

Takane and Jung (2009b) proposed similar decompositions of the CATANOVA C-statistic (Light and Margolin 1971), which also follows an asymptotic chi-square distribution. This statistic, however, has been developed for situations in which rows and columns of contingency tables assume asymmetric roles, that is, one is the predictor, and the other is the criterion. It thus represents the overall predictability of, say, rows on columns. Pearson's chi-square statistic, on the other hand, represents a symmetric association. It may be argued, however, that a symmetric measure of association may still be useful in the predictive contexts. There are many cases in which symmetric analysis methods (those that do not distinguish between predictors and criterion variables) are used for prediction purposes. For example, canonical correlation analysis (Hotelling 1936) and its special cases, canonical discriminant analysis (Fisher 1936), CCA and CALC (cited above), reduced rank regression analysis (Anderson 1951; Izenman 1975), maximum likelihood reduced-rank GMANOVA (growth curve models; Reinsell and Velue 1998), and the curds and whey method (Breiman and Friedman 1997) all involve some kind of symmetric analysis. This suggests that decompositions of a symmetric measure of association, such as Pearson's chi-square statistic, may well be useful in predictive contexts.

This paper is organized as follows. Section 2 briefly reviews basic facts about Pearson's chi-square statistic and its historical development. Section 3 presents our main results, the proposed decompositions, starting from elementary two-term decompositions to full decompositions. It will be shown that the order in which various effects are taken into consideration plays a crucial role in deriving the decompositions. Section 4 compares the proposed decompositions to those for the log LR statistic recently proposed by Cheng et al. (2006). Section 5 draws conclusions.

2 Preliminaries

We use uppercase Roman alphabets (e.g., A, B, ...) to designate variable names and the corresponding characters in italic (e.g., A, B, ...) to denote the number of categories (levels) in the variables. Categories of a variable are indexed by the corresponding lowercase alphabets in italic (e.g., $a = 1, \cdots A$).

Let there be A mutually exclusive events with known probabilities of occurrence, p_a $(a = 1, \cdots, A)$, and let f_a $(a = 1, \cdots, A)$ denote the observed frequency of event a out of N replicated observations. Then the following statistic

$$\chi_A^2 = \sum_{a=1}^{A} \left(\frac{f_a - Np_a}{\sqrt{Np_a}} \right)^2 \tag{1}$$

asymptotically follows the chi-square distribution with A df (Pearson 1900). Here, Np_a is the expected value of f_a under the prescribed conditions. This is the generic form of Pearson's chi-square statistic, from which many special cases follow.

In one-way layouts (i.e., when there is only one categorical variable), we are typically interested in testing $\mathrm{H}_0 : p_a = p$ for all a $(a = 1, \cdots, A)$. We estimate p by $\hat{p} = 1/A$. If we insert this estimate in (1), we obtain

$$\chi_{A-1}^2 = \sum_{a=1}^{A} \left(\frac{f_a - N/A}{\sqrt{N/A}} \right)^2. \tag{2}$$

This statistic follows the asymptotic chi-square distribution with $A - 1$ df under H_0. Note that we lose 1 df for estimating p. When $A > 2$, the above statistic can be partitioned into the sum of $A - 1$ independent chi-square variables each with 1 df. Let $\mathbf{g}$ denote the A-component vector of $(f_a - N/A)/\sqrt{N/A}$ $(a = 1, \cdots, A)$. We may transform this vector by the Helmert type of contrasts for unequal cell sizes (Irwin 1949; Lancaster 1949). For $A = 3$, this contrast matrix looks like

$$\mathbf{T} = \begin{bmatrix} \sqrt{\frac{\hat{p}_2}{\hat{p}_1+\hat{p}_2}} & -\sqrt{\frac{\hat{p}_1}{\hat{p}_1+\hat{p}_2}} & 0 \\ \sqrt{\frac{\hat{p}_3\hat{p}_1}{(\hat{p}_1+\hat{p}_2)(\hat{p}_1+\hat{p}_2+\hat{p}_3)}} & \sqrt{\frac{\hat{p}_3\hat{p}_2}{(\hat{p}_1+\hat{p}_2)(\hat{p}_1+\hat{p}_2+\hat{p}_3)}} & -\sqrt{\frac{\hat{p}_1+\hat{p}_2}{\hat{p}_1+\hat{p}_2+\hat{p}_3}} \end{bmatrix}', \tag{3}$$

where $\hat{p}_a = f_a/N$. Define

$$\mathbf{h} = \mathbf{T}'\mathbf{g}. \tag{4}$$

Then each of the $A - 1$ elements of $\mathbf{h}$ asymptotically follows the independent standard normal distribution under H_0, whose sum of squares (i.e., $\mathbf{h}'\mathbf{h}$) asymptotically follows the chi-square distribution with $A - 1$ df under H_0. Note that $\mathbf{T}$ is not unique. It can be any columnwise orthogonal matrix with one additional requirement that it is also orthogonal to the vector with the square root of $\hat{p}_a$ as the a-th element for $a = 1, \cdots, A$. It can be easily verified that $\mathbf{T}'\mathbf{T} = \mathbf{I}_{A-1}$, and that $\mathbf{T}'\hat{\mathbf{p}} = \mathbf{0}$ for $\mathbf{T}$ defined in (3), where $\hat{\mathbf{p}} = (\sqrt{\hat{p}_1}, \cdots, \sqrt{\hat{p}_A})'$.

In two-way layouts, we assume that there is another variable B with B categories. Let f_{ba} denote the observed frequency of category b of variable B and category a of variable A. Let f_{ba} be arranged in a B by A contingency table $\mathbf{F}$. We are typically interested in testing the independence between the rows and columns of **F**, i.e., $\text{H}_0 : p_{ba} = p_b p_a$, where p_{ba} is the joint probability of row b and column a, and p_b and p_a are the marginal probabilities of row b and column a, respectively. Let $\hat{p}_b = \Sigma_a f_{ba}/N$ and $\hat{p}_a = \Sigma_b f_{ba}/N$ denote the estimates of p_b and p_a, and define

$$\chi^2_{(B-1)(A-1)} = \sum_{b=1}^{B} \sum_{a=1}^{A} \left(\frac{f_{ba} - N\hat{p}_b\hat{p}_a}{\sqrt{N\hat{p}_b\hat{p}_a}} \right)^2. \quad (5)$$

This statistic represents the total association (or the departure from independence) between the rows and columns of **F**. It is sometimes referred to as the A by B interaction and is denoted as $\chi^2(\text{AB})$. It follows the asymptotic chi-square distribution with $(B-1)(A-1)$ df under H_0. As before, it can be decomposed into the sum of $(B-1)(A-1)$ independent chi-square variables each with 1 df when $B > 2$ and/or $A > 2$. Let **G** represent the B by A matrix whose ba-th element is equal to $(f_{ba} - N\hat{p}_b\hat{p}_a)/\sqrt{N\hat{p}_b\hat{p}_a}$. We then pre- and postmultiply **G** by something analogous to $\mathbf{T}'$ and $\mathbf{T}$ defined in (3). The resultant matrix has $(B-1)(A-1)$ independent asymptotically standard normal variables under H_0, whose sum of squares follows the asymptotic chi-square distribution with $(B-1)(A-1)$ df.

It will be handy to have a matrix representation of the chi-square statistic given above. Let **K** and **L** denote the diagonal matrices whose diagonal elements are the row and the column totals of **F**, and let $\mathbf{Q}_{1/K} = \mathbf{I}_B - \mathbf{1}_B\mathbf{1}_B'\mathbf{K}/N$, where $\mathbf{1}_B$ is the B-element vector of ones. Then, **G** can be expressed in terms of **F** by

$$\mathbf{G} = \sqrt{N}\mathbf{K}^{-1}\mathbf{Q}_{1/K}'\mathbf{F}\mathbf{L}^{-1} = \sqrt{N}\mathbf{Q}_{1/K}\mathbf{K}^{-1}\mathbf{F}\mathbf{L}^{-1}. \quad (6)$$

The $\chi^2_{(B-1)(A-1)}$ can then be rewritten as

$$\chi^2_{(B-1)(A-1)} = \text{tr}(\mathbf{G}'\mathbf{K}\mathbf{G}\mathbf{L}) = \text{SS}(\mathbf{G})_{K,L}. \quad (7)$$

In three-way layouts, we take into account a third variable C with C categories. Let f_{cba} denote the observed frequency of category c of variable C, category b of variable B, and category a of variable A, and define

$$\chi^2_{CBA-C-B-A+2} = \sum_{c=1}^{C} \sum_{b=1}^{B} \sum_{a=1}^{A} \left(\frac{f_{cba} - N\hat{p}_c\hat{p}_b\hat{p}_a}{\sqrt{N\hat{p}_c\hat{p}_b\hat{p}_a}} \right)^2. \quad (8)$$

This statistic represents the departure from independence among the three categorical variables. Under the independence hypothesis (i.e., H_0: $p_{cba} = p_c p_b p_a$), this statistic follows the asymptotic chi-square distribution with $CBA - C - B - A + 2$ df, which are always larger than 1. Consequently it can always be decomposed into the sum of $CBA - C - B - A + 2$ independent chi-square variables each with 1 df.

As in the case of two-way layouts, we can express the above chi-square in matrix notation. We first arrange a three-way table into a two-way format by factorially combining two of the three variables. Suppose that variables B and C

Table 1 A three-way contingency table arranged in two-way format

		A_1	A_2	Total
C_1	B_1	79	177	256
	B_2	62	121	183
C_2	B_1	73	81	154
	B_2	168	75	243
Total		382	454	836

are combined to form row categories. (Which two variables we choose to combine makes no difference for our immediate purpose. Note, however, that this will have a rather grave impact on the decompositions of Pearson's chi-square statistic that follow.) We may then take categories of A as columns. Suppose further that the row categories are ordered in such a way that the index for B categories moves fastest. (See Table 1 below for an example.) Let $\mathbf{F}$ denote the two-way table thus constructed. Let $\mathbf{K} = \mathbf{D}_C \otimes \mathbf{D}_B$, where $\mathbf{D}_C$ and $\mathbf{D}_B$ are diagonal matrices with marginal frequencies of categories of variables C and B, and $\otimes$ indicates a Kronecker product. Let $\mathbf{L} = \mathbf{D}_A$ denote the diagonal matrix of column totals of $\mathbf{F}$, and define

$$\mathbf{G} = N\mathbf{K}^{-1}(\mathbf{F} - \mathbf{K}\mathbf{1}_{CB}\mathbf{1}'_A\mathbf{L}/N^2)\mathbf{L}^{-1}. \tag{9}$$

Then

$$\chi^2_{CBA-C-B-A+2} = \mathrm{tr}(\mathbf{G}'\mathbf{K}\mathbf{G}\mathbf{L}) = \mathrm{SS}(\mathbf{G})_{K,L}. \tag{10}$$

Consider, as an example, the three-way contingency table given in Table 1. This is a 2 by 2 by 2 table arranged in a 4 by 2 two-way format according to the prescription given above. This is a famous data set used by Snedecor (1958) to illustrate the differences in the notion of the three-way interaction effect in a three-way contingency table given by several prominent statisticians, including Bartlett (1935), Mood (1950), and Lancaster (1951). According to Cheng et al. (2006), however, all of them made crucial mistakes in conceptualizing the three-way interaction effect. We are going to use this same data set to demonstrate our proposed decompositions of Pearson's chi-square statistic (Sect. 3) and compare them with those of the log LR statistic (Sect. 4). For the moment, however, we are satisfied with only calculating χ^2_4 for this data set using the formula given in (8) or (10). This value turns out to be 131.99.

The χ^2_4 for this table reflects the joint effects of four sources, the A by B, A by C, B by C, and A by B by C interaction effects with the main effects of the three variables A, B, and C being eliminated by their marginal probabilities. Thus, χ^2_4 may also be written as χ^2(AB, AC, BC, ABC). Note, however, that these four effects are usually not mutually orthogonal due to unequal marginal frequencies, and consequently their joint effects cannot be obtained by their sum. In this paper, we develop systematic ways of orthogonalizing these effects to make them additive.

3 The Proposed Decompositions

In order to derive proper decompositions of Pearson's chi-square statistic for a three-way contingency table, its reduction to a two-way table seems essential. Table 1 shows one way of reduction. There are two other ways of reducing a three-way table into two, depending on which two of the three variables are combined to create a new variable. In Table 1, B and C were combined, but A and B, and A and C could likewise be combined. Generally, different decompositions result, depending on which reduction method is employed. In this section we start with the reduction method used in Table 1 and then expand our view to other situations.

If we look at Table 1 as purely a two-way table, we notice that the total association in this table excludes certain effects in the chi-square statistic for the original three-way table. The independence model for Table 1 implies that the expected cell frequency is estimated by $N\hat{p}_{cb}\hat{p}_a$, where $\hat{p}_{ba}$ is the estimate of the joint marginal probability of category c of variable C and category b of variable B. Following (5), Pearson's chi-square statistic representing the association between the rows and columns of Table 1 is given by

$$\chi^2_{(CB-1)(A-1)} = \sum_{cb=1}^{CB} \sum_{a=1}^{A} \left(\frac{f_{bca} - N\hat{p}_{cb}\hat{p}_a}{\sqrt{N\hat{p}_{cb}\hat{p}_a}} \right)^2. \tag{11}$$

This is obviously different from (8), which further assumes $\hat{p}_{cb} = \hat{p}_c\hat{p}_b$.

How can we account for the difference? As noted toward the end of the previous section, $\chi^2_{CBA-C-B-A+2}$ reflects the joint effects of the AB, AC, BC, and ABC interactions, and thus it may be written as χ^2(AB, AC, BC, ABC). The $\chi^2_{(CB-1)(A-1)}$, on the other hand, reflects the joint effects of the AB, AC, and ABC interactions (i.e., $\chi^2_{(CB-1)(A-1)} = \chi^2$(AB, AC, ABC)) with the BC interaction effect excluded as the marginal effect of the rows of the table. The difference then must be due to the BC interaction effect. More specifically, we call this effect the BC interaction eliminating the joint effects of the AB, AC, and ABC interactions because it represents the portion of the AB, AC, BC, ABC effects left unaccounted for by AB, AC, ABC. This effect is denoted by BC|AB, AC, ABC, where the variables listed on the right of "|" indicate those eliminated from the effect listed on the left. The size of this effect is found by the difference between the two chi-squares, i.e.,

$$\chi^2(\text{BC}|\text{AB, AC, ABC}) = \chi^2(\text{AB, AC, BC, ABC}) - \chi^2(\text{AB, AC, ABC}). \tag{12}$$

An equivalent way of looking at the above equation is that AB, AC, BC, ABC is decomposed into the sum of the effects of AB, AC, ABC and BC|AB, AC, ABC, that is,

$$\chi^2(\text{AB, AC, BC, ABC}) = \chi^2(\text{AB, AC, ABC}) + \chi^2(\text{AB}|\text{AC, BC, ABC}). \tag{13}$$

For Table 1, we find χ^2_3(AB, AC, ABC) $= 86.99$, so that χ^2_1(BC|AB, AC, ABC) $=$ $131.99 - 86.99 = 45.00$.

If χ^2(BC|AB, AC, ABC) has more than 1 df, it may be further decomposed into the sum of the effects each with 1 df. In the present case, it has only 1 df, so that no further decompositions are applicable. The χ^2(AB, AC, ABC), on the other hand, has 3 df, which invites further decompositions. There are a number of (in fact, infinitely many) possible decompositions. For example, we may use the Helmert type of contrasts, as before, to decompose this chi-square. However, then each component χ^2 may be empirically less meaningful. We therefore focus on the decompositions that reflect the factorial structure among the rows of Table 1. This means that we are decomposing χ^2(AB, AC, ABC) into separate effects of AB, AC, and ABC interactions. The problem is that these effects are usually not orthogonal to each other, and consequently must be orthogonalized to derive additive decompositions of the chi-square. As has been alluded to earlier, the order in which they are taken into account will have a crucial effect in this orthogonalization process. There are six possible ways of ordering three effects. We may, however, cut down this number by considering only those orderings in which lower-order interactions are always considered prior to higher-order interactions. We are then left with only two possibilities. One is in which AB is considered first, then AC, and then ABC, and the other is in which AC is considered first, then AB, and then ABC.

When we add a new effect, we only add its unique effect. For example, when we add AC in the first situation described above, we add only the portion of the AC not already explained by AB. This effect, called AC eliminating AB, is orthogonal to AB, and is denoted as AC|AB. The effect of AB considered first, on the other hand, ignores all other effects (AC and ABC), and is simply written as AB. The ABC effect considered last eliminates both AB and AC, and is written as ABC|AB, AC. In general, the effect taken into account first ignores all other effects, the effect considered last eliminates all other effects, and the effect taken into account in-between eliminates all the effects considered earlier, but ignores all the effects considered later. How to calculate the chi-square for these effects will be described shortly.

The two possible orderings of AB, AC, and ABC suggested above give rise to two orthogonal decompositions of the joint effects of AB, AC, and ABC. Symbolically, this is written as

$$\chi^2(\text{AB, AC, ABC}) = \chi^2(\text{AB}) + \chi^2(\text{AC}|\text{AB}) + \chi^2(\text{ABC}|\text{AB, AC}) \tag{14}$$

$$= \chi^2(\text{AC}) + \chi^2(\text{AB}|\text{AC}) + \chi^2(\text{ABC}|\text{AB, AC}). \tag{15}$$

Combining (13) and (14), we obtain the first decomposition of AB, AC, BC, ABC.

Decomposition (i):

$$\chi^2(\text{AB, AC, BC, ABC}) = \chi^2(\text{AB}) + \chi^2(\text{AC}|\text{AB}) + \chi^2(\text{ABC}|\text{AB, AC}) + \chi^2(\text{BC}|\text{AB, AC, ABC}). \tag{16}$$

Combining (13) and (15), we obtain the second decomposition of AB, AC, BC, ABC.

Decomposition (ii):

$$\chi^2(\text{AB, AC, BC, ABC}) = \chi^2(\text{AC}) + \chi^2(\text{AB}|\text{AC}) + \chi^2(\text{ABC}|\text{AB, AC}) + \chi^2(\text{BC}|\text{AB, AC, ABC}). \quad (17)$$

The $\chi^2(\text{AB})$, $\chi^2(\text{AC}|\text{AB})$, and $\chi^2(\text{ABC}|\text{AB, AC})$ are calculated as follows. We first set up contrast vectors,

$$\mathbf{t}_1 = \begin{pmatrix} 1 \\ -1 \\ 1 \\ -1 \end{pmatrix}, \quad \mathbf{t}_2 = \begin{pmatrix} 1 \\ 1 \\ -1 \\ -1 \end{pmatrix}, \text{ and } \mathbf{t}_3 = \begin{pmatrix} 1 \\ -1 \\ -1 \\ 1 \end{pmatrix}. \quad (18)$$

The $\mathbf{t}_1$ represents the main effect of B among the rows of Table 1. When it is used as a linear constraint on the rows, it captures the portion of the association between the rows and columns that can be explained by the main effect of B, which is called the AB interaction effect. Similarly, $\mathbf{t}_2$ captures the AC interaction effect, and $\mathbf{t}_3$ captures the ABC interaction effect. Note that these contrast vectors assume that there are only two categories in all three variables. We will need more than one contrast to represent each of these effects if there are more than two levels in some of the variables. For example, if $B = 3$, $\mathbf{t}_1$ will be a matrix like

$$\mathbf{t}_1 = \begin{bmatrix} 1 & 1 \\ -1 & 1 \\ 0 & -2 \\ 1 & 1 \\ -1 & 1 \\ 0 & -2 \end{bmatrix}. \quad (19)$$

Note also that if we want to decompose the effects of AB, AC, ABC differently, for example, if AB, AC, ABC is decomposed into AB within C_1, AB within C_2, and AC, $\mathbf{t}_1$, $\mathbf{t}_2$, and $\mathbf{t}_3$ would be:

$$\mathbf{t}_1 = \begin{pmatrix} 1 \\ -1 \\ 0 \\ 0 \end{pmatrix}, \quad \mathbf{t}_2 = \begin{pmatrix} 0 \\ 0 \\ 1 \\ -1 \end{pmatrix}, \text{ and } \mathbf{t}_3 = \begin{pmatrix} 1 \\ 1 \\ -1 \\ -1 \end{pmatrix}. \quad (20)$$

The following computations use $\mathbf{t}_1$, $\mathbf{t}_2$, and $\mathbf{t}_3$ defined in (18). The χ^2 due to the AB interaction ignoring all other effects (AC and ABC) is calculated by first defining

$$\mathbf{H} = \sqrt{N}\mathbf{P}_{Q_{1/K}t_1}\mathbf{K}^{-1}\mathbf{F}\mathbf{L}^{-1}, \tag{21}$$

where

$$\mathbf{P}_{Q_{1/K}t_1/K} = \mathbf{Q}_{1/K}\mathbf{t}_1(\mathbf{t}_1'\mathbf{Q}_{1/K}'\mathbf{K}\mathbf{t}_1)^{-1}\mathbf{t}_1'\mathbf{Q}_{1/K}'\mathbf{K} \tag{22}$$

is the projector onto $\mathrm{Sp}(\mathbf{Q}_{1/K}\mathbf{t}_1)$ (the space spanned by $\mathbf{Q}_{1/K}\mathbf{t}_1$) along $\mathrm{Ker}(\mathbf{t}_1'\mathbf{Q}_{1/K}'\mathbf{K})$ (the space spanned by all vectors $\mathbf{y}$ such that $\mathbf{y}'\mathbf{Q}_{1/K}\mathbf{t}_1 = 0$). Recall that N is the total sample size, $\mathbf{K}$ and $\mathbf{L}$ are diagonal matrices of row and column totals of $\mathbf{F}$, respectively, and $\mathbf{Q}_{1/K} = \mathbf{I} - \mathbf{1}\mathbf{1}'\mathbf{K}/N$, where $\mathbf{1}$ is the CB-element vector of ones. Note that $\mathbf{Q}_{1/K}'\mathbf{K} = \mathbf{Q}_{1/K}'\mathbf{K}\mathbf{Q}_{1/K}$. We then calculate

$$\chi^2(\mathbf{H}) = \mathrm{SS}(\mathbf{H})_{K,L}. \tag{23}$$

This value turns out to be 24.10(1) for the data in Table 1 (the value in parentheses indicates the df). The $\chi^2(\mathbf{H})$ is equal to the chi-square representing the total association in the marginal two-way table obtained by collapsing the three-way table across the levels of C.

The $\chi^2(\mathrm{AC}|\mathrm{AB})$ (the AC interaction eliminating AB, but ignoring ABC) is calculated as follows: Let $\mathbf{T}_1 = [\mathbf{1}, \mathbf{t}_1]$, and define $\mathbf{Q}_{T_1/K}$ similarly to $\mathbf{Q}_{1/K}$ above, that is,

$$\mathbf{Q}_{T_1/K} = \mathbf{I} - \mathbf{T}_1(\mathbf{T}_1'\mathbf{K}\mathbf{T}_1)^{-1}\mathbf{T}_1'\mathbf{K}. \tag{24}$$

Then, define

$$\mathbf{P}_{Q_{T_1/K}t_2/K} = \mathbf{Q}_{T_1/K}\mathbf{t}_2(\mathbf{t}_2'\mathbf{Q}_{T_1/K}'\mathbf{K}\mathbf{t}_2)^{-1}\mathbf{t}_2'\mathbf{Q}_{T_1/K}'\mathbf{K}, \tag{25}$$

and

$$\mathbf{E} = \sqrt{N}\mathbf{P}_{Q_{T_1/K}t_2/K}\mathbf{K}^{-1}\mathbf{F}\mathbf{L}^{-1}. \tag{26}$$

Again, note that $\mathbf{Q}_{T_1/K}'\mathbf{K} = \mathbf{Q}_{T_1/K}'\mathbf{K}\mathbf{Q}_{T_1/K}$, and that $\mathbf{P}_{Q_{T_1/K}t_2/K}$ is the projector onto $\mathrm{Sp}(\mathbf{Q}_{T_1/K}\mathbf{t}_2)$ along $\mathrm{Ker}(\mathbf{t}_2'\mathbf{Q}_{T_1/K}'\mathbf{K})$. Finally,

$$\chi^2(\mathbf{E}) = \mathrm{SS}(\mathbf{E})_{K,L}. \tag{27}$$

This value is found to be 55.83(1) for the data in Table 1. (There are other ways to calculate this quantity. See (37) and (38) in Takane and Jung 2009b.)

The $\chi^2(\mathrm{ABC}|\mathrm{AB, AC})$ (the ABC interaction eliminating both AB and AC) is calculated as follows: First let $\mathbf{T}_{12} = [\mathbf{1}, \mathbf{t}_1, \mathbf{t}_2]$, and define $\mathbf{Q}_{T_{12}/K} = \mathbf{I} - \mathbf{T}_{12}(\mathbf{T}_{12}'\mathbf{K}\mathbf{T}_{12})^{-1}\mathbf{T}_{12}'\mathbf{K}$. Then, define

$$\mathbf{P}_{Q_{T_{12}/K}t_3/K} = \mathbf{Q}_{T_{12}/K}\mathbf{t}_3(\mathbf{t}_3'\mathbf{Q}_{T_{12}/K}'\mathbf{K}\mathbf{t}_3)^{-1}\mathbf{t}_3'\mathbf{Q}_{T_{12}/K}'\mathbf{K}, \tag{28}$$

and

$$\mathbf{J} = \sqrt{N}\mathbf{P}_{Q_{T_{12}/K}t_3/K}\mathbf{K}^{-1}\mathbf{F}\mathbf{L}^{-1}. \tag{29}$$

Note that $\mathbf{Q}'_{T_{12}/K}\mathbf{K} = \mathbf{Q}'_{T_{12}/K}\mathbf{K}\mathbf{Q}_{T_{12}/K}$, and that $\mathbf{P}_{Q_{T_{12}/K}\mathbf{t}_3/K}$ is the projector onto $\mathrm{Sp}(\mathbf{Q}_{T_{12}/K}\mathbf{t}_3)$ along $\mathrm{Ker}(\mathbf{t}'_3\mathbf{Q}'_{T_{12}/K}\mathbf{K})$. Finally,

$$\chi^2(\mathbf{J}) = \mathrm{SS}(\mathbf{J})_{K,L}. \tag{30}$$

This value turns out to be 7.06(1) for the data in Table 1. Takane and Jung (2009b) showed that $\mathbf{J}$ above can also be calculated by

$$\mathbf{J} = \sqrt{N}\mathbf{K}^{-1}\mathbf{t}_3(\mathbf{t}'_3\mathbf{K}^{-1}\mathbf{t}_3)^{-1}\mathbf{t}'_3\mathbf{K}^{-1}\mathbf{F}\mathbf{L}^{-1}, \tag{31}$$

which is somewhat simpler.

It can be easily verified that 24.10(1), 55.83(1), and 7.06(1) add up to 86.99(3) calculated previously. The χ^2(AC) and χ^2(AB|AC) can be calculated similarly to the above. It turns out that the former is 68.66(1), and the latter is 11.27(1). These and 7.06(1) for the ABC interaction again add up to 86.99(3). So there are indeed two alternative decompositions of χ^2(AB, AC, ABC) depending on whether AB or AC is taken into account first. Corresponding to the two decompositions of AB, AC, ABC, there are two decompositions of χ^2(AB, AC, BC, ABC), as stated in (16) and (17).

As remarked earlier, there are two other possible arrangements of a three-way table into two. In Table 1, variables B and C were combined to form rows of the table. We may have also combined A and B, or A and C. In either case, the remaining variable constitutes the columns. Each of these two cases gives rise to two different decompositions of AB, AC, BC, ABC analogous to those given in (16) and (17).

Let us start with the case in which A and B are combined. In this case, (13) will become:

$$\chi^2(\mathrm{AB, AC, BC, ABC}) = \chi^2(\mathrm{AC, BC, ABC}) + \chi^2(\mathrm{AB|AC, BC, ABC}), \tag{32}$$

and (14) and (15) become

$$\chi^2(\mathrm{AC, BC, ABC}) = \chi^2(\mathrm{AC}) + \chi^2(\mathrm{BC|AC}) + \chi^2(\mathrm{ABC|AC, BC}) \tag{33}$$

$$= \chi^2(\mathrm{BC}) + \chi^2(\mathrm{AC|BC}) + \chi^2(\mathrm{ABC|AC, BC}). \tag{34}$$

The terms in these decompositions can be calculated similarly to the above. We find χ^2(AC, BC, ABC) $=$ 93.73(3) (the df in parentheses), so that χ^2(AB|AC, *BC*,*ABC*) $=$ 38.26(1) $=$ 131.99(4) $-$ 93.73(3) $= \chi^2$(AB, AC, BC, ABC) $- \chi^2$(AC, BC, *ABC*). We also find χ^2(AC) $=$ 68.66(1) (this is the same χ^2(AC) calculated previously), χ^2(BC|AC) $=$ 18.44, and χ^2(ABC|AC, BC) $=$ 6.63, so that 68.66(1) $+$ 18.44(1) $+$ 6.63(1) $=$ 93.77(3) $= \chi^2$(AC, BC, ABC), verifying (33). We also find χ^2(BC) $=$ 31.80(1), and χ^2(AC|BC) $=$ 55.30(1), so that 31.80(1) $+$ 55.30(1) $+$ 6.63(1) $=$ 93.77(3), verifying (34). Combining (32) with (33) and (34), we, respectively, obtain

Decomposition (iii):

$$\chi^2(\text{AB, AC, BC, ABC}) = \chi^2(\text{AC}) + \chi^2(\text{BC}|\text{AC}) + \chi^2(\text{ABC}|\text{AC, BC}) + \chi^2(\text{AB}|\text{AC, BC, ABC})), \quad (35)$$

and Decomposition (iv):

$$\chi^2(\text{AB, AC, BC, ABC}) = \chi^2(\text{BC}) + \chi^2(\text{AC}|\text{BC}) + \chi^2(\text{ABC}|\text{AC, BC}) + \chi^2(\text{AB}|\text{AC, BC, ABC}). \quad (36)$$

Similarly, when A and C are combined, we obtain

$$\chi^2(\text{AB, AC, BC, ABC}) = \chi^2(\text{AB, BC, ABC}) + \chi^2(\text{AC}|\text{AB, BC, ABC}), \quad (37)$$

and

$$\chi^2(\text{AB, BC, ABC}) = \chi^2(\text{AB}) + \chi^2(\text{BC}|\text{AB}) + \chi^2(\text{ABC}|\text{AB, BC}) \quad (38)$$

$$= \chi^2(\text{BC}) + \chi^2(\text{AB}|\text{BC}) + \chi^2(\text{ABC}|\text{AB, BC}). \quad (39)$$

For the illustrative data we have been using, we find $\chi^2(\text{AB, BC, ABC}) = 49.96(3)$, so that $\chi^2(\text{AC}|\text{AB, BC, ABC}) = 82.03(1) = 131.99(4) - 49.96(3) = \chi^2(\text{AB, AC, BC, ABC}) - \chi^2(\text{AB, BC, ABC})$. We also find $\chi^2(\text{AB}) = 24.10(1)$ (this is the same $\chi^2(\text{AB})$ calculated previously), $\chi^2(\text{BC}|\text{AB}) = 19.18(1)$, and $\chi^2(\text{ABC}|\text{AB, BC}) = 6.35(1)$, so that $24.10(1) + 19.51(1) + 6.35(1) = 49.96(3) = \chi^2(\text{AB, BC, ABC})$, verifying (38). We also find $\chi^2(\text{BC}) = 31.80(1)$ (this is the same $\chi^2(\text{BC})$ calculated before), and $\chi^2(\text{AB}|\text{BC}) = 1181(1)$, so that $31.80(1) + 11.81(1) + 6.35(1) = 49.96(3)$, verifying (39). Combining (37) with (38) and (39), we obtain the fifth and sixth decompositions of $\chi^2(\text{AB, AC, BC, ABC})$.

Decomposition (v):

$$\chi^2(\text{AB, AC, BC, ABC}) = \chi^2(\text{AB}) + \chi^2(\text{BC}|\text{AB}) + \chi^2(\text{ABC}|\text{AB, BC}) + \chi^2(\text{AC}|\text{AB, BC, ABC}), \quad (40)$$

and Decomposition (vi):

$$\chi^2(\text{AB, AC, BC, ABC}) = \chi^2(\text{BC}) + \chi^2(\text{AB}|\text{BC}) + \chi^2(\text{ABC}|\text{AB, BC}) + \chi^2(\text{AC}|\text{AB, BC, ABC}). \quad (41)$$

Altogether we obtain (at least) six fundamental decompositions of Pearson's chi-square statistic for a three-way contingency table. Lancaster (1951) defined $\chi^2(\text{ABC}|\text{AB, AC, BC})$ by

$$\chi^2(\text{ABC}|\text{AB, AC, BC}) \\ = \chi^2(\text{AB, AC, BC, ABC}) - \chi^2(\text{AB}) - \chi^2(\text{AC}) - \chi^2(\text{BC}). \quad (42)$$

Then, $\chi^2(\text{ABC}|\text{AB, AC, BC})$ is unique. However, as has been noted earlier, $\chi^2(\text{AB})$, $\chi^2(\text{AC})$, and $\chi^2(\text{BC})$ are usually not independent from each other, and consequently, $\chi^2(\text{ABC}|\text{AB, AC, BC})$ may not follow an asymptotic chi-square distribution (Placket 1962).

4 Analogous Decompositions of the Log LR Statistic

In this section, we discuss decompositions of the log LR chi-square statistic analogous to Decompositions (i) through (vi). The log LR statistic for a three-way contingency table is defined as

$$LR_{CBA-C-B-A+2} = -2\sum_{c=1}^{C}\sum_{b=1}^{B}\sum_{a=1}^{A} f_{cba}\log\frac{f_{cba}}{\hat{p}_c\hat{p}_b\hat{p}_a}. \quad (43)$$

This statistic, like Pearson's chi-square statistic, represents the departure from the three-way independence model and reflects the joint effects of AB, AC, BC, and ABC (i.e., AB, AC, BC, ABC). Similarly to the case of Pearson's chi-square statistic, these four effects are not mutually independent, and consequently their joint effects cannot be obtained by their sum. We find the effect of AB, AC, BC, ABC to be 120.59 for the data given in Table 1, using the above formula.

In this section, we first take a heuristic approach to get an intuitive idea about proper decompositions. We then present a theory due to Cheng et al. (2006) to back up our intuition. Our heuristic approach begins with analyzing the data in Table 1 by log linear models. In log linear analysis, no reduction of a three-way table into a two-way format is necessary in contrast to Pearson's statistic. The three variables are treated completely symmetrically.

We first ran the "Hiloglinear" procedure in SPSS. We obtained the three-way interaction effect of $LR(\text{ABC}|\text{AB, AC, BC}) = 6.82(1)$. We also obtained the joint effects of three two-way interactions of $LR(\text{AB, AC, BC}) = 113.77(3)$. The three individual two-way interaction effects (these were the two-way interactions eliminating all other two-way interactions) were found to be $LR(\text{AB}|\text{AC, BC}) = 12.22(1)$, $LR(\text{AC}|\text{AB, BC}) = 57.54(1)$, and $LR(\text{BC}|\text{AB, AC}) = 20.00(1)$. These effects do not add up to $LR(\text{AB, AC, BC})$, as $12.22 + 57.54 + 20.00 = 89.76 \neq 113.77$. Note that in log linear analysis, only the independence or conditional independence models can be fitted non-iteratively, which implies that none of the above quantities can be calculated in closed form.

In order to find proper constituents of the joint two-way interaction effects, we had to run another log linear analysis procedure in SPSS called "Loglinear," which provided individual two-way interaction effects ignoring the other two-way interaction effects. They were found to be $LR(\text{AB}) = 24.23(1)$, $LR(\text{AC}) = 69.54(1)$, and $LR(\text{BC}) = 32.04(1)$. These quantities can be calculated in closed form. They do not add up to LR(AB, AC, BC), either, as $24.23 + 69.54 + 32.02 = 125.79 \neq 113.77$. However, we find

$$\begin{aligned} &LR(\text{AB}) + LR(\text{AC}) + LR(\text{BC}|\text{AB, AC}) \\ &\quad = 24.23 + 69.54 + 20.00 = 113.77 = LR(\text{AB, AC, BC}), \end{aligned} \tag{44}$$

$$\begin{aligned} &LR(\text{AC}) + LR(\text{BC}) + LR(\text{AB}|\text{AC, BC}) \\ &\quad = 69.54 + 32.02 + 12.22 = 113.77 = LR(\text{AB, AC, BC}), \end{aligned} \tag{45}$$

and

$$\begin{aligned} &LR(\text{AB}) + LR(\text{BC}) + LR(\text{AC}|\text{AB, BC}) \\ &\quad = 32.02 + 24.23 + 57.54 = 113.77 = LR(\text{AB, AC, BC}). \end{aligned} \tag{46}$$

That is, we cannot add the three two-way interactions all ignoring the other two to obtain their joint effects. One of the three must be the two-way interaction eliminating the other two.

Adding one more term, $LR(\text{ABC}|\text{AB, AC, BC}) = 6.82$, to the above identities, we obtain three alternative decompositions of

$$\begin{aligned} &LR(\text{AB, AC, BC, ABC}) \\ &\quad = LR(\text{AB, AC, BC}) + LR(\text{ABC}|\text{AB, AC, BC}) = 113.77 + 6.82 = 120.59, \end{aligned} \tag{47}$$

namely, Decomposition (a):

$$\begin{aligned} &LR(\text{AB, AC, BC, ABC}) \\ &\quad = LR(\text{AB}) + LR(\text{AC}) + LR(\text{BC}|\text{AB, AC}) + LR(\text{ABC}|\text{AB, AC, BC}), \end{aligned} \tag{48}$$

Decomposition (b):

$$\begin{aligned} &LR(\text{AB, AC, BC, ABC}) \\ &\quad = LR(\text{AC}) + LR(\text{BC}) + LR(\text{AB}|\text{AC, BC}) + LR(\text{ABC}|\text{AB, AC, BC}), \end{aligned} \tag{49}$$

and Decomposition (c):

$$\begin{aligned} &LR(\text{AB, AC, BC, ABC}) \\ &\quad = LR(\text{AB}) + LR(\text{BC}) + LR(\text{AC}|\text{AB, BC}) + LR(\text{ABC}|\text{AB, AC, BC}). \end{aligned} \tag{50}$$

It is obvious that Decomposition (a) "corresponds" with Decompositions (i) and (ii), (b) with (iii) and (iv), and (c) with (v) and (vi) for Pearson's chi-square statistic.

These three decompositions are consistent with Cheng et al.'s (2006) decompositions derived rigorously through information identities. Cheng et al. however, arrived at these decompositions via a somewhat different route. They first derived the sum of the last two terms in each of the above three decompositions. For example, they first obtained $LR^*(\text{BC}|\text{A}) \equiv LR(\text{BC}|\text{AB, AC}) + LR(\text{ABC}|\text{AB, AC, BC})$ for Decomposition (a). This quantity can be calculated in closed form using the information identities, whereas neither of the two terms on the right-hand side can. Cheng et al. (2006) called the quantity on the left-hand side, i.e., $LR^*(\text{BC}|\text{A})$, the conditional dependence between B and C across levels of A (or the simple two-way interaction between B and C across levels of A). They then split this into two additive terms on the right-hand side, $LR(\text{BC}|\text{AB, AC})$ ($LR(\text{BC}||\text{A})$ in their notation) and $LR(\text{ABC}|\text{AB, AC, BC})$, by way of log linear analysis. The first term was interpreted as the uniform part, and the second as the nonuniform part, of the conditional dependence between B and C across levels of A (or equivalently, the homogeneous and heterogenous aspects of the simple two-way interactions between B and C across levels of A). In our framework, the former is interpreted as the BC interaction eliminating the effects of AB and AC. It is interesting to find that this effect is equivalent to the uniform part of the simple two-way interactions. The latter is nothing but the three-way interaction among A, B, and C eliminating the joint effects of AB, AC, and BC. Similar remarks can be made for Decompositions (b) and (c).

5 Discussion

As has been observed in the previous section, the order in which two two-way interactions ignoring the other two are accounted for makes no difference in the log LR statistic, while it does in Pearson's chi-square statistic. In fact, we have

$$LR(\text{AB}) = LR(\text{AB}|\text{AC}) = LR(\text{AB}|\text{BC}) \neq LR(\text{AB}|\text{AC, BC}), \tag{51}$$

$$LR(\text{AC}) = LR(\text{AC}|\text{AB}) = LR(\text{AC}|\text{BC}) \neq LR(\text{AC}|\text{AB, BC}), \tag{52}$$

and

$$LR(\text{BC}) = LR(\text{BC}|\text{AB}) = LR(\text{BC}|\text{AC}) \neq LR(\text{BC}|\text{AB, AC}), \tag{53}$$

while the four versions of the AB interaction effects for Pearson's chi-square, $\chi^2(\text{AB})$, $\chi^2(\text{AB}|\text{AC})$, $\chi^2(\text{AB}|\text{BC})$, and $\chi^2(\text{AB}|\text{AC, BC, ABC})$, are all distinct, and so are the four versions of AC and BC. Also, there is a single unique three-way interaction in the decompositions of the log LR statistic ($LR(\text{ABC}|\text{AB, AC, BC})$), while there are three distinct versions of the three-way interaction effect for Pearson's chi-square, ($\chi^2(\text{ABC}|\text{AB, AC})$, $\chi^2(\text{ABC}|\text{AB, BC})$, and $\chi^2(\text{ABC}|\text{AC, BC})$). These differences stem from the fact that there is no way to evaluate $\chi^2(\text{AB, AC, BC})$ in the latter, which in turn is more fundamentally caused by the fact that a three-way table must always be reduced to a two-way table to obtain the decompositions of Pearson's statistic. This prevents us from obtaining quantities such as $\chi^2(\text{AB}|\text{AC, BC})$, $\chi^2(\text{AC}|\text{AB, BC})$, $\chi^2(\text{BC}|\text{AB, AC})$, and $\chi^2(\text{ABC}|\text{AB, AC, BC})$.

Having fewer distinct terms in the decompositions of the log LR statistic may be a point in its favor over Pearson's statistic. However, there are still three alternative decompositions for the former. A choice among them may not be straightforward. This is particularly so because log linear analysis treats all variables symmetrically, yet the resultant decompositions are not symmetric.

The fact that Pearson's chi-square statistic has six alternative decompositions is surely a bit unwieldy. However, if one layout of a three-way table into a two-way format is in some sense more natural than the other two, this number is reduced to two, which differ from each other only in a minor way. Such is the case when analysis of contingency tables is conducted in predictive settings, and yet a symmetric measure of association such as Pearson's statistic is in order. In CCA, for example, one of the variables is typically taken as the criterion variable, while the others are used as predictor variables. There are also other considerations to be taken into account. Pearson's chi-square statistic is known to approach a chi-square distribution more quickly than the log LR statistic. It is also the case that all the terms in the decompositions of Pearson's chi-square can be calculated in closed form, whereas some of the terms in the log LR statistic must be obtained iteratively.

It may also be pointed out that there seems to be a "cultural" difference between log linear analysis (based on the log LR statistic) and CA (based on Pearson's statistic). The former tends to focus on residual effects (eliminating effects). If we fit the AB interaction effect, for example, we get the deviation chi-square of this model from the saturated model. It represents the effects of all variables not included in the model eliminating AB. To obtain the effect of AB ignoring all other variables we have to subtract this value from the independence chi-square representing the deviation of the independence model from the saturated model. To obtain the AB interaction effect eliminating some other effects, we have to fit the model with these "some other effects" only, and the model with the additional effect of AB, and take the difference in chi-square values between the two models. In CA, on the other hand, the chi-square value due to AB ignoring other effects is obtained directly by the difference between the fitted model and the independence model. We need an extra step to obtain a residual effect representing the effect of a variable not included in the fitted model, which amounts to taking the difference in chi-square between the saturated model (which is equal to Pearson's chi-square for the total association) and the fitted model. A notable exception is van der Heijden and Meijerink (1989), who attempted to analyze residual effects in constrained CA. In the present authors' view, both analyses (analyses of the fitted models and the residual effects) are equally important, as has been emphasized by Takane and Jung (2009a).

Cheng et al. (2007) attempt to extend their approach to higher-order designs, thereby generalizing their decompositions of the log LR statistic. Presumably, similar things could be done for Pearson's chi-square statistic.

Acknowledgments The work reported in this paper has been supported by the Social Sciences and Humanities Research Council of Canada (SSHRC) grant 36952, and by the Natural Sciences and Engineering Research Council of Canada (NSERC) discovery grant 10630 to the first author.

References

Andersen, E. B. (1980). *Discrete statistical models with social science applications*. Amsterdam: North Holland.

Anderson, T. W. (1951). Estimating linear restrictions on regression coefficients for multivariate normal distributions. *Annals of Mathematical Statistics*, *22*, 327–351.

Bartlett, M. S. (1935). Contingency table interactions. *Journal of the Royal Statistical Society, Series B*, *2*, 248–252.

Bishop, Y. M. M., Fienberg, S. E., & Holland, P. W. (1975). *Discrete multivariate analysis: Theory and practice*. Cambridge: MIT Press.

Böckenholt, U., & Böckenholt, I. (1990). Canonical analysis of contingency tables with linear constraints. *Psychometrika*, *55*, 633–639.

Breiman, L., & Friedman, J. H. (1997). Predicting multivariate responses in multiple linear regression. *Journal of the Royal Statistical Society, Series B*, *57*, 3–54.

Cheng, P. E., Liou, J. W., Liou, M., & Aston, J. A. D. (2006). Data information in contingency tables: A fallacy of hierarchical loglinear models. *Journal of Data Science*, *4*, 387–398.

Cheng, P. E., Liou, J. W., Liou, M., & Aston, J. A. D. (2007). Linear information models: An introduction. *Journal of Data Science*, *5*, 297–313.

Fisher, R. A. (1936). The use of multiple measurement in taxonomic problem. *Annals of Eugenics*, *7*, 179–188.

Greenacre, M. J. (1984). *Theory and applications of correspondence analysis*. London: Academic.

Hotelling, H. (1936). Relations between two sets of variables. *Biometrika*, *28*, 417–441.

Irwin, J. O. (1949). A note on the subdivision of χ^2 into components. *Biometrika*, *36*, 130–134.

Izenman, A. J. (1975). Reduced-rank regression for the multivariate linear model. *Journal of Multivariate Analysis*, *5*, 248–264.

Kullback, S., & Leibler, R. A. (1951). On information and sufficiency. *Annals of Mathematical Statistics*, *22*, 79–86.

Lancaster, H. O. (1949). The derivation and partition of χ^2 in certain discrete distributions. *Biometrika*, *36*, 117–129.

Lancaster, H. O. (1951). Complex contingency tables treated by the partition of chi-square. *Journal of the Royal Statistical Society, Series B*, *13*, 242–249.

Light, R. J., & Margolin, B. H. (1971). An analysis of variance for categorical data. *Journal of the American Statistical Association*, *66*, 534–544.

Mood, A. M. (1950). *Introduction to the theory of statistics*. New York: McGraw-Hill.

Nishisato, S. (1980). *Analysis of categorical data: Dual scaling and its applications*. Toronto: University of Toronto Press.

Pearson, K. (1900). On the criterion that a given system of deviation from the probable in the case of a correlated system of variables is such that it can be reasonably supposed to have arisen from random sampling. *Philosophy Magazine*, *50*, 157–172.

Placket, R. L. (1962). A note on interactions in contingency tables. *Journal of the Royal Statistical Society, Series B*, *24*, 162–166.

Reinsell, G. C., & Velue, R. P. (1998). *Multivariate reduced-rank regression*. New York: Springer.

Snedecor, G. W. (1958). Chi-squares of Bartlett, Mood and Lancaster in a 2^3 contingency table. *Biometrics*, *14*, 560–562.

Takane, Y., & Jung, S. (2009a). Regularized nonsymmetric correspondence analysis. *Computational Statistics and Data Analysis*, *53*, 3159–3170.

Takane, Y., & Jung, S. (2009b). Tests of ignoring and eliminating in nonsymmetric correspondence analysis. *Advances in Data Analysis and Classification*, *3*, 315–340.
ter Braak, C. J. F. (1986). Canonical correspondence analysis: A new eigenvector technique for multivariate direct gradient analysis. *Ecology*, *67*, 1167–1179.
van der Heijden, P. G. M., & Meijerink, F. (1989). Generalized correspondence analysis of multi-way contingency tables. In R. Coppi & S. Bolasco (Eds.), *Multiway data analysis* (pp. 185–202). Amsterdam: Elsevier.

Visualizing Uncertainty of Estimated Response Functions in Nonparametric Item Response Theory

L. Andries van der Ark

1 Introduction

Nonparametric item response theory (IRT) models are flexible models for ordinal measurement (for an overview, see, e.g., Sijtsma and Molenaar 2002). An important part of nonparametric IRT analysis, often referred to as Mokken scale analysis, consists of investigating model fit using the following rationale. A nonparametric IRT model implies certain observable properties. Each observable property is investigated in the test data. Not observing the property in the test data indicates that the model does not fit the data, whereas observing the property indicates that the model may fit the data. The observable properties can be investigated by means of specialized software packages such as MSP (Molenaar and Sijtsma 2000) and the R-package `mokken` (Van der Ark 2007, 2012). These software packages can graphically display the results from Mokken scale analysis to facilitate interpretation. However, the uncertainty of the results is not taken into account. As a result, a graph based on a very small sample, $N = 20$ say, may look exactly the same as a graph based on a large sample, $N = 10,000$ say. For small samples, interpreting the graphs may yield misleading results. In this paper we focus on visualizing the uncertainty in estimated response functions (RFs).

Suppose a test consists of J items, and each item has $m+1$ ordered answer categories, which are scored $0, 1, \ldots, m$. Let $X_1, \ldots, X_J$ denote the item-score variables. Let $X_+ = \sum_h X_h$, let $R_{(j)} = X_+ - X_j$, and let $R_{(ij)} = X_+ - X_i - X_j$. X_+ is called the *test score*; $R_{(j)}$ and $R_{(ij)}$ are called *rest scores*. Suppose that a latent variable Θ explains the associations between the item scores. Let θ be a realization of Θ.

L. Andries van der Ark (✉)
Tilburg University, P.O. Box 90153, 5000 LE, Tilburg, The Netherlands
e-mail: a.vdark@uvt.nl

R.E. Millsap et al. (eds.), *New Developments in Quantitative Psychology*, Springer Proceedings in Mathematics & Statistics 66, DOI 10.1007/978-1-4614-9348-8_5,

$\Pr(X_j \geq x|\theta)$ $(x = 1,\ldots,m)$ are called the *item-step RFs* of item j; $\mathrm{E}(X_j|\theta)$ is called the *item RFs* of item j. Both RFs are functions of θ. Note that for dichotomous items (i.e., $m = 1$), the item-step RF and the item RF are equivalent. Most assumptions of nonparametric IRT models pertain to RFs: For example, the monotone homogeneity model for dichotomous items (Mokken 1971) includes the assumption that the item RFs are nondecreasing in θ; the double monotonicity model for polytomous items (Molenaar 1997) includes the assumption that item-step RFs do not intersect (Sijtsma and Molenaar 2002).

For checking such assumptions, it is convenient to plot estimated RFs. To visualize the uncertainty, we propose plotting Wald confidence intervals around the estimated RFs. First, we briefly discuss the RFs in Mokken scale analysis. Second, we derive asymptotic standard errors (ASEs) for the RFs and the corresponding Wald confidence intervals. The approach taken here is similar to the approach for deriving ASEs for the scalability coefficients in Mokken scale analysis (Kuijpers et al. 2013). Third, we show how plotting confidence envelopes based on Wald 95 % confidence intervals around the estimated RFs helps interpreting the plot.

2 Plotting Estimated Response Functions

We discuss three assumptions of nonparametric IRT models that involve RFs. These assumptions can be investigated by inspecting plots of estimated RFs. We use the responses of 433 students to the 10 items of the Achievement scale of the Adjective Checklist (Gough and Heilbrun 1980) to provide examples of plotted RFs. Each item has five ordered answer categories ($m = 4$). The data and more details on the data are available from the R package `mokken`. The appendix contains the computer code for producing the graphs.

2.1 Monotonicity

Monotonicity is the assumption that the item-step RFs are nondecreasing in θ (e.g., Junker and Sijtsma 2000):

$$\Pr(X_j \geq x|\theta) \text{ nondecreasing in } \theta \text{ for } j = 1,\ldots,J; x = 1,\ldots,m. \tag{1}$$

Alternatively, monotonicity can be defined in terms of the item RF:

$$\mathrm{E}(X_j|\theta) \text{ nondecreasing in } \theta \text{ for } j = 1,\ldots,J. \tag{2}$$

For dichotomous items, Eqs. (1) and (2) are equivalent; for polytomous items ($m > 1$), Eq. (1) implies Eqs. (2). Monotonicity is assumed by all well-known IRT models.

Monotonicity can be investigated by an observable property called *manifest monotonicity* (Junker 1993), where Θ in Eqs. (1) and (2) is replaced by rest-score $R_{(j)}$. Junker (1993) showed that for dichotomous items, monotonicity implies manifest monotonicity. For polytomous items, monotonicity defined in terms of Eq. (1) does not imply manifest monotonicity, although violations are rare (Junker and Sijtsma 2000). However, using the same logic as Junker (1993), it can be shown that for polytomous items, monotonicity defined in terms of Eq. (2) implies manifest monotonicity. Because some values of $R_{(j)}$ may be empty or very sparse, estimates of $\Pr(X_j \geq x|R_{(j)} = r)$ may become very unstable, and it is recommended to combine adjacent rest scores until the sample size of a rest-score group is large enough (Molenaar and Sijtsma 2000). Combining rest-score groups does not affect the relationship between monotonicity and manifest monotonicity. Let $R^*_{(j)}$ denote the rest score with possibly some adjacent scores combined with realization r^*, then the estimate of the item-step RF (Eq. (1)) is

$$P(X_j \geq x|r^*_{(j)}), \tag{3}$$

and the estimate of the item RF (Eq. (2)) is

$$\overline{X}_j|r^*_{(j)}. \tag{4}$$

As an example, Fig. 1 shows a plot of $P(X_1 \geq x|r^*_{(1)})$ for $x = 1,\ldots,4$ (top left), and a plot of $\overline{X}_1|r^*_{(1)}$ (top right). Note that the $Jm+1 = 37$ possible rest scores have been clustered into four rest-score groups: $\{0,\ldots,18\}$, $\{19,20,21\}$, $\{22,23,24\}$, and $\{25,\ldots,36\}$. There is a slight decrease between $P(X_1 \geq 2|R_{(j)} \in \{19,20,21\})$, and $P(X_1 \geq 2|R_{(j)} \in \{22,23,24\})$, indicating a violation of monotonicity. However, it is unknown whether this is a relevant decrease.

2.2 Invariant Item Ordering

Invariant item ordering (IIO) (Sijtsma and Hemker 1998) is the assumption that the item RFs are non-intersecting. Let the items be ordered and numbered accordingly such that $\mathrm{E}(X_1) \leq \mathrm{E}(X_2) \leq \cdots \leq \mathrm{E}(X_J)$, then an IIO means that

$$\mathrm{E}(X_1|\theta) \leq \mathrm{E}(X_2|\theta) \leq \cdots \leq \mathrm{E}(X_J|\theta) \text{ for all } \theta. \tag{5}$$

Except for the Rasch model (Rasch 1960) and double monotonicity model for dichotomous items (Mokken 1971), IIO is typically not included in the set of IRT model assumptions and has to be investigated separately.

IIO can be investigated by an observable property called *manifest IIO* (Ligtvoet et al. 2010). In manifest IIO, Θ in Eq. (5) is replaced by a manifest variable independent from the item scores. Ligtvoet et al. (2010) suggested to make a

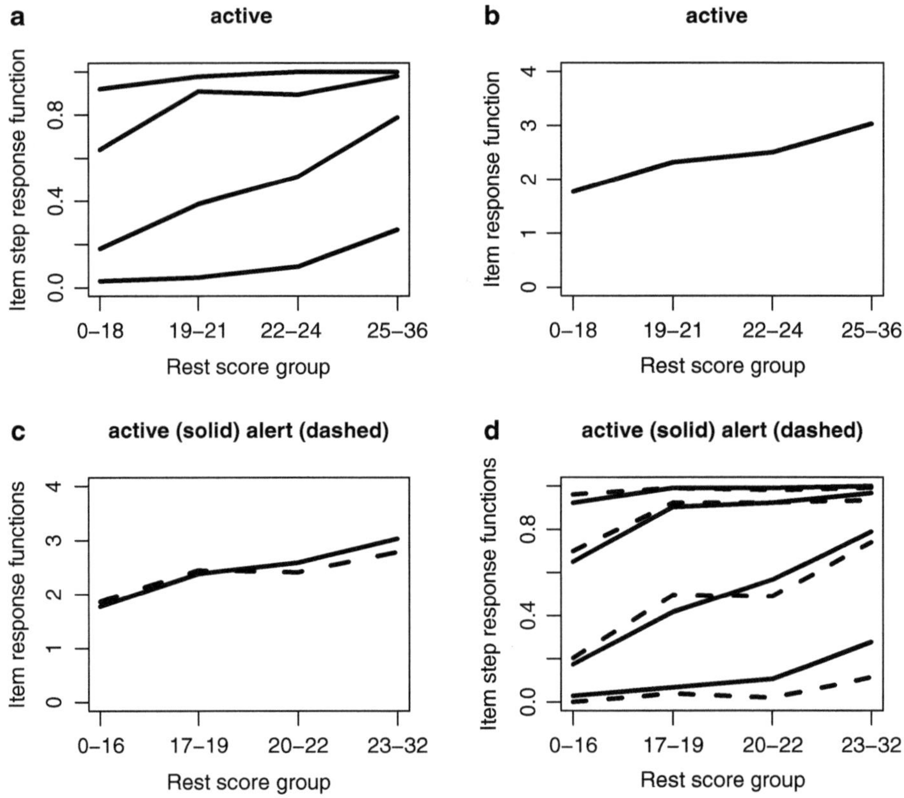

Fig. 1 Plots of item-step RFs for monotonicity (**a**), item RF for monotonicity (**b**), item RF for IIO (**c**), and item-step RFs for non-intersection (**d**)

pairwise comparison of item RFs on non-intersection, and for the comparison of item i and item j, replace Θ by $R^*_{(ij)}$. The asterisk indicates that adjacent rest groups may be joined. Hence the estimated RF is

$$\overline{X}_j | r^*_{(ij)} \tag{6}$$

As an example, Fig. 1 shows the plot of $\overline{X}_1 | r^*_{(1,2)}$ and $\overline{X}_2 | r^*_{(1,2)}$ (bottom left). The two estimated RFs are intersecting and almost overlapping, hence is no indication of an IIO.

2.3 Non-intersection of Item-Step Response Functions

The double monotonicity model includes the assumption of non-intersecting item-step RFs. Let θ^* be a value of Θ. Non-intersection of item-step RFs implies that if $\Pr(X_i \geq x | \theta^*) \leq \Pr(X_j \geq y | \theta^*)$ for $\Theta = \theta^*$, then

$$\Pr(X_i \geq x|\theta) \leq \Pr(X_j \geq y|\theta) \text{ for all } \theta \text{ and for all } i \neq j, x, y. \quad (7)$$

Three methods have been proposed to investigate non-intersection of item-step RFs. For one of these methods, *method rest score*, estimated RFs can be plotted. These estimated RFs take Eq. (7) as a starting point and replace θ by $r^*_{(ij)}$. Hence the estimated RF is

$$\Pr(X_j \geq x|r^*_{(ij)}). \quad (8)$$

If the double monotonicity model holds, then the estimated RFs in Eq. (8) are non-intersecting (Sijtsma and Molenaar 2002). For each item pair, the estimated RFs are plotted for visual inspection. As an example, Fig. 1 (bottom left) shows the plot of $P(X_1 \geq x|r^*_{(1,2)})$ and $P(X_2 \geq x|r^*_{(1,2)})$ for $x = 1,2,3,4$. The estimated RFs are intersecting, which indicates that the double monotonicity model does not hold.

3 Standard Errors of Estimated Response Functions

Let G be a general indicator for the grouping variable, with realization g. Each respondent belongs to one group and one group only, so the groups are independent samples. The estimated RFs can be classified into two types: *Conditional means* (Eqs. (4) and (6)) are denoted by $\overline{X}_j|g$ and *conditional cumulative proportions* (Eqs. (3) and (8)) are denoted by $P(X_j \geq x|g)$. For both types, ASEs must be derived.

For conditional means, the ASEs have the well-known form

$$ase(\overline{X}_j|g) = S(X_j|g)/\sqrt{N},$$

where $S(X_j|g)$ is the standard deviation of $X_j|g$.

To compute the ASEs for conditional cumulative proportions, we use a two-step method that takes into account possible dependencies between cumulative proportions pertaining to the same item. The first step is to write the RFs as a function of the observed item-score proportions. Let $\mathbf{p} = [P(X_j = 0|g), \ldots, P(X_j = m|g)]$ be the vector of observed item-score proportions in group g for item j; let $\mathbf{p}^* = [P(X_j \geq 1|g), \ldots, P(X_j \geq m|g)]$ be the vector of observed cumulative proportions; and let $\mathbf{U}_m$ be an $m \times (m+1)$ matrix: an $(m+1) \times (m+1)$ upper triangular matrix of ones with the first row deleted. For example,

$$\mathbf{U}_2 = \begin{bmatrix} 0 & 1 & 1 \\ 0 & 0 & 1 \end{bmatrix}.$$

Cumulative proportions $P(X_j \geq x|g)$ $(x = 1,2,\ldots,m)$ are a linear function of proportions $P(X_j = x|g)$ $x = 0,1,\ldots,m$:

$$\mathbf{p}^* = \mathbf{U}_m \cdot \mathbf{p}.$$

The second step is to use the delta method to obtain the ASEs for the cumulative proportions. Let $\mathbf{V_p}$ and $\mathbf{V_{p^*}}$ be the asymptotic variance–covariance matrix of $\mathbf{p}$ and $\mathbf{p}^*$, respectively; and let $\mathbf{D}(\mathbf{p})$ be a diagonal matrix with the elements of vector $\mathbf{p}$ on the diagonal. If $\mathbf{p}$ follows a multinomial distribution, then

$$\mathbf{V_p} = \frac{1}{N} * (\mathbf{D}(\mathbf{p}) - \mathbf{p} \cdot \mathbf{p}^{\mathrm{T}})$$

(e.g., Agresti 2007, p. 6). Now if, $\mathbf{F} = \mathbf{F}(\mathbf{p})$ is the Jacobian, the matrix of first partial derivatives of $\mathbf{p}^*$ to $\mathbf{p}$, then according to the delta method (e.g., Casella and Berger 2002)

$$\mathbf{V_{p^*}} = \mathbf{F}\mathbf{V_p}\mathbf{F}^{\mathrm{T}}. \tag{9}$$

Because $\mathbf{p}^*$ is a linear function of $\mathbf{p}$, the Jacobian simply equals $\mathbf{U}_m$. Let v_{xy} the element at the xth row and yth column of $\mathbf{V_{p^*}}$. Elaborating Eq. (9) using standard algebra yields

$$v_{xy} = \frac{1}{N}[P(X_j \geq x|g) - P(X_j \geq x|g)P(X_j \geq y|g)]$$

for $x \geq y$, and

$$v_{xy} = \frac{1}{N}[P(X_j \geq y|g) - P(X_j \geq x|g)P(X_j \geq y|g)]$$

for $x < y$. Taking the square root of the diagonal of $\mathbf{V_{p^*}}$ produces the required ASEs of $\mathbf{p}^*$:

$$ase[P(X_j \geq x|g)] = \sqrt{P(X_j \geq x|g) - P^2(X_j \geq x|g)}/\sqrt{N}.$$

4 Graphic Display of Wald Confidence Intervals

Let $f(p)$ be the element of interest of an estimated RF and let $z_{1-\alpha/2}$ be the $(1-\alpha/2) * 100$ percentile of the standard normal distribution, then the bounds of the $(1-\alpha) * 100\,\%$ Wald confidence interval are

$$f(p) \pm z_{1-\alpha/2} * ase[f(p)].$$

Figure 2 shows the estimated RFs from Fig. 1 with the Wald 95 % confidence intervals plotted as confidence envelopes around the estimated RFs. The appendix shows the computer code in R for these figures. Visual inspection of Fig. 2 (top left) indicates that the slight decrease in $P(X_j \geq 2|r^*)$ may be due to sample fluctuation. Visual inspection of Fig. 2 (bottom) shows that the current item scores are inconclusive with respect to non-intersection (bottom left) and IIO (bottom

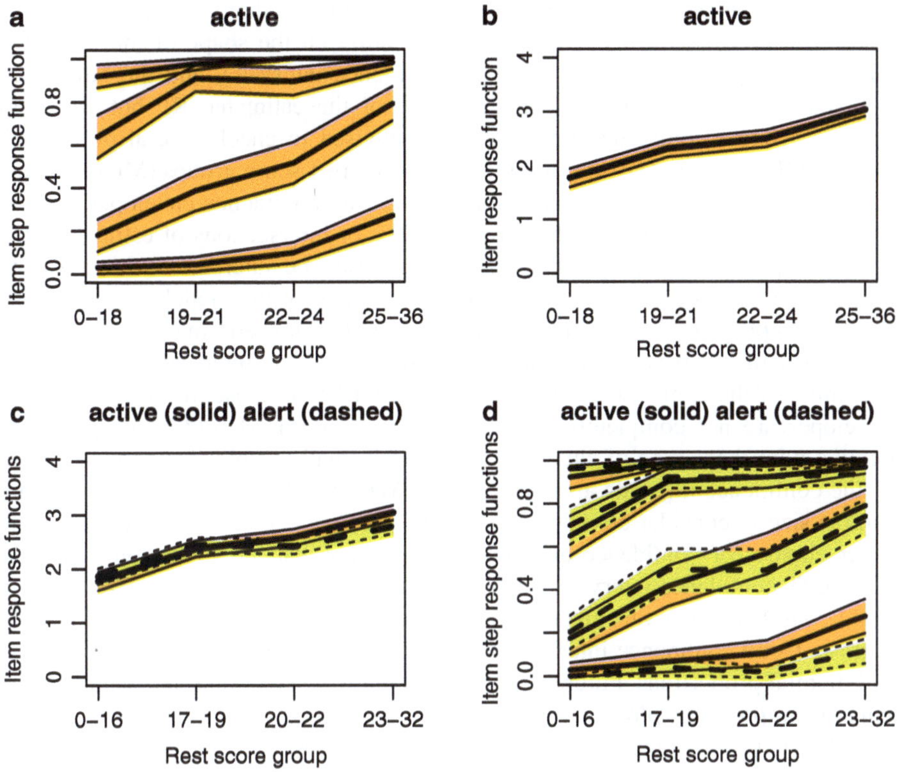

Fig. 2 Plots of item-step RFs for monotonicity (**a**), item RF for monotonicity (**b**), item RF for IIO (**c**), and item-step RFs for non-intersection (**d**) with confidence intervals

right) because the confidence intervals are overlapping. Note that the user can choose different percentages for the confidence intervals, different sample-size requirements the rest-groups, and different colors for the confidence envelopes. In Fig. 2, the default settings (Molenaar and Sijtsma 2000) were used.

5 Discussion

The ASEs and Wald confidence intervals are available in the R package `mokken` as of version 2.7.3. They allow the interpretation of the stability of the estimated RFs in Mokken scale analysis. The confidence intervals can be visualized, and inspecting the plots may help diagnosing violations of nonparametric IRT model. However, four considerations should be taken into account. First, the plot depends on the sample-size requirements for the rest-score groups. In Figs. 1 and 2, the default settings were used, but one can also choose to plot fewer rest-score groups that have larger sample sizes, or more rest-score groups that have smaller sample sizes. The first case will provide less information on the shape of the estimated RF but with greater accuracy (smaller confidence intervals), and the latter case will lead to more information on the shape of the estimated RF but with less accuracy (larger confidence intervals). It is advised to check several plots, each having different sample-size requirements for the rest-score groups (Molenaar and Sijtsma 2000). Second, for small sample sizes, the confidence envelopes may be so wide that all decreases in the estimated RFs or intersections of estimated RFs can be explained by sample fluctuation. This may be interpreted either as "no evidence against the model" or "no evidence in favor of the model." For example, the overlapping confidence envelopes in Fig. 2 (bottom left) may be interpreted as in favor of IIO because it is possible to draw two non-intersecting RFs within the limits of the confidence envelopes, or against IIO because the two confidence envelopes are not completely separated. New standards should be provided for dealing with these type of situations. Third, for small sample sizes, the precision of the confidence intervals also deteriorates. Whether there should be a minimum sample size to consider confidence intervals is a topic for future research. Fourth, other choices of confidence are possible that may also affect the plots. Rather than 95 % confidence intervals, other percentages may be chosen, and rather than Wald confidence intervals inverted chi-square confidence intervals (Lang 2008) or Agresti–Coull confidence intervals (Agresti and Coull 1998) may be used in case of binomial proportions. Future research may show whether alternative confidence intervals improve the plots.

Other methods for investigating non-intersection of RFs are the methods *p-matrix* and *rest-split* (Sijtsma and Molenaar 2002). Results for Method *p-matrix* can also be displayed (Van der Ark 2007) but deriving ASEs is more involved than deriving ASEs for estimated RFs due to a more complex dependencies. Results from Method *rest-split* have not yet been visualized. This is also a topic for future research.

Acknowledgments I would to thank Alberto Mayeu-Olivares and Marcel Croon for commenting on the derivation of ASEs.

Appendix: R Code for Plotting Estimated RFs Without and with Confidence Envelopes

```
# Activate 'mokken' package
library(mokken)
# Activate ACL data
data(acl)
# Select Achievement scale
X <- acl[,11:20]
# Investigate Monotonicity, IIO, and Non-intersection
cm <- check.monotonicity(X)
```

```
ci <- check.iio(X)
cr <- check.restscore(X)

# Plotting estimated RFs without confidence envelopes
# Figure 1 (top left)
plot(cm, items = 1, curve = "ISRF", plot.ci = FALSE,
  ask = FALSE)
# Figure 1 (top right)
plot(cm, items = 1, curve = "IRF", plot.ci = FALSE,
  ask = FALSE)
# Figure 1 (bottom left)
plot(ci, item.pairs = 27, plot.ci = FALSE, ask =
  FALSE)
# Figure 1 (bottom right)
plot(cr, item.pairs = 1, plot.ci = FALSE, ask =
  FALSE)

# Plotting estimated RFs with confidence envelopes
# Figure 2 (top left)
plot(cm, items = 1, curve = "ISRF", ask = FALSE)
# Figure 2 (top right)
plot(cm, items = 1, curve = "IRF", ask = FALSE)
# Figure 2 (bottom left)
plot(ci, item.pairs = 27, ask = FALSE)
# Figure 2 (bottom right)
plot(cr, item.pairs = 1, ask = FALSE)
```

References

Agresti, A. (2007). *An introduction to categorical data analysis*. New York: Wiley.

Agresti, A., & Coull, B.A. (1998). Approximate is better than "exact" for interval estimation of binomial proportions. *The American Statistician, 52*, 119–126.

Casella, G. & Berger, R. L. (2002). *Statistical inference* (2nd ed.). Pacific Grove: Duxburry/Thomson Learning.

Gough, H. G., & Heilbrun, A. B. (1980). *The Adjective Check List, manual 1980 edition*. Palo Alto: Consulting Psychologists Press.

Junker, B. W. (1993). Conditional association, essential independence and monotone unidimensional item response models. *The Annals of Statistics, 21*, 1359–1378.

Junker, B. W., & Sijtsma, K. (2000). Latent and manifest monotonicity. *Applied Psychological Measurement, 24*, 65–81.

Kuijpers, R. E., Van der Ark, L. A., & Croon, M. A. (2013). Computing standard errors and confidence intervals for scalability coefficients in Mokken scale analysis using marginal models. *Sociological Methodology, 43*, 42–69.

Lang, J. B. (2008). Score and profile likelihood confidence intervals for contingency table parameters. *Statistics in Medicine, 27*, 5975–5990.

Ligtvoet, R., Van der Ark, L. A., Te Marvelde, J. M., & Sijtsma, K. (2010). Investigating an invariant item ordering for polytomously scored items. *Educational and Psychological Measurement, 70,* 578–595.

Mokken, R. J. (1971). *A theory and procedure of scale analysis.* Berlin: De Gruyter.

Molenaar, I. W. (1997). Nonparametric models for polytomous responses. In W. J. van der Linden & R. K. Hambleton (Eds.), *Handbook of modern item response theory* (pp. 369–380). New York: Springer.

Molenaar, I. W., & Sijtsma, K. (2000). *User's Manual MSP5 for Windows.* Groningen: IEC ProGAMMA.

Rasch, G. (1960). *Probabilistic models for some intelligence and attainment tests.* Copenhagen: Denmarks Paedagogiske Institut.

Sijtsma, K., & Hemker, B. T. (1998). Nonparametric polytomous IRT models for invariant item ordering, with results for parametric models. *Psychometrika, 63,* 183–200.

Sijtsma, K., & Molenaar, I. W. (2002). *Introduction to nonparametric item response theory.* Thousand Oaks: Sage.

Van der Ark, L. A. (2007). Mokken Scale Analysis in R. *Journal of Statistical Software, 20*(11), 1–19.

Van der Ark, L. A. (2012). New developments in Mokken Scale Analysis in R. *Journal of Statistical Software, 48*(5), 1–27.

Bayesian Estimation of the Three-Parameter Multi-Unidimensional Model

Yanyan Sheng

1 Introduction

Multidimensional item response theory (IRT) models have been found useful for dealing with complex test situations where multiple traits are required in producing the manifest responses to an item (Reckase 2009). Often, however, a test involves several latent traits and each item measures exactly one of them. The multidimensional model specific for this scenario is referred to as the so-called multi-unidimensional IRT model (Sheng and Wikle 2007). In the literature, this model has been called the multidimensional model with a simple structure (McDonald 1999) or the between-items multidimensional model (Adams et al. 1997). The shorter term "multi-unidimensional" is adopted in this paper to account for the structure that the overall test involves multiple traits, whereas each subtest is unidimensional. Fully Bayesian estimation using Gibbs sampling (Casella and George 1992; Geman and Geman 1984) has been developed for such models with two item parameters (Lee 1995; Sheng 2008; Sheng and Wikle 2007). The model directly estimates the intertrait correlation and its advantages over the two-parameter unidimensional model have been demonstrated (Sheng 2008; Sheng and Wikle 2007). The extension of the algorithm to the three-parameter multi-unidimensional model is straightforward.

However, previous research on the Gibbs sampler of unidimensional models developed by Albert (1992) and Sahu (2002) indicates that with an additional pseudo-chance-level parameter, three-parameter models are more complicated than two-parameter models in that noninformative prior distributions for item slope and intercept parameters create problems in the convergence of the Markov chain

Y. Sheng (✉)
Department of Educational Psychology & Special Education, Southern Illinois University Carbondale, Carbondale, IL 62901, USA
e-mail: ysheng@siu.edu

R.E. Millsap et al. (eds.), *New Developments in Quantitative Psychology*,
Springer Proceedings in Mathematics & Statistics 66, DOI 10.1007/978-1-4614-9348-8_6,

(Sheng 2010). Specifically, studies have shown that improper noninformative prior densities for component (i.e., component of the mixture model) specific parameters (i.e., item slope and intercept parameters in this context) result in an undefined posterior distribution, which gives rise to unstable parameter estimates (Sheng 2008, 2010). Even with proper noninformative prior densities, the procedure either fails to converge or requires an enormous number of iterations for the Markov chain to reach convergence (Sheng 2010). On the other hand, priors for the non-component (i.e., the pseudo-chance-level) parameter can be chosen in a typical fashion, as its posterior estimates are not sensitive to informative or noninformative prior specifications (Sheng 2008, 2010).

In view of the above, it is believed that the three-parameter multi-unidimensional model is more complicated than its two-parameter counterpart and therefore requires attention in specifying prior distributions for item slope and intercept parameters. This study focuses on the prior specification of item parameters for the model while investigating its advantages over other IRT models.

The remainder of the paper is organized as follows. The multi-unidimensional model is briefly outlined in Sect. 2, with a description of the Gibbs sampling procedure and prior specifications for the model parameters. Section 3 presents a simulation study on the performance of the developed Gibbs sampler for the three-parameter model where sample sizes and choices of the prior distributions for item parameters are taken into consideration. In Sect. 4, another simulation study is presented to compare the three-parameter multi-unidimensional model with two existing IRT models. The comparison of these models is further illustrated in Sect. 5 using a real data example. Finally, a few summary remarks are provided in Sect. 6.

2 Model and the Gibbs Sampler

Multi-unidimensional models allow separate inferences to be made about a person for each distinct dimension being measured by a test item while taking into consideration the relationship between all latent traits measured by the overall test. The two-parameter normal ogive (2PNO) multi-unidimensional model generalizes the conventional 2PNO model to a multi-unidimensional structure so that each item measures exactly one of the multiple traits the test is designed to measure. Suppose a K-item test consists of m subtests, each containing k_v dichotomous (0–1) items, where $v = 1,2,\ldots,m$. Let y_{vij} denote the ith person's response to the jth item in the vth subtest, where $i = 1,2,\ldots,n$ and $j = 1,2,\ldots,k_v$. With a probit link, the 2PNO multi-unidimensional model is defined as

$$P(y_{vij} = 1) = \Phi(\alpha_{vj}\theta_{vi} - \beta_{vj}) = \int_{-\infty}^{\alpha_{vj}\theta_{vi}-\beta_{vj}} \frac{1}{\sqrt{2\pi}} e^{\frac{-t^2}{2}} dt \tag{1}$$

(e.g., Lee 1995; Sheng and Wikle 2007), where θ_{vi} is a scalar person trait parameter in the vth latent dimension, α_{vj} is a positive scalar slope parameter representing the item discrimination, and β_{vj} is a scalar intercept parameter that is related to the location in the vth dimension where the item provides maximum information.

Having an additional item pseudo-chance-level (or lower asymptote) parameter γ_{vj}, the three-parameter normal ogive (3PNO) multi-unidimensional model is defined as

$$P(y_{vij} = 1) = \gamma_{vj} + (1 - \gamma_{vj})\Phi(\alpha_{vj}\theta_{vi} - \beta_{vj}), 0 < \gamma_{vj} < 1 \tag{2}$$

so that the probability of correct response is greater than zero even for those with very low trait levels. Fully Bayesian estimation for this model is a straightforward extension of that for the two-parameter model as detailed in Sheng (2008). To implement the Gibbs sampler, two augmented latent variables, Z and W, are introduced such that $Z_{vij} \sim N(\eta_{vij}, 1)$, where $\eta_{vij} = \alpha_{vj}\theta_{vi} - \beta_{vj}$, and $W_{vij} = 1 (W_{vij} = 0)$ if person i knows (does not know) the correct answer to item j in subtest v, with a probability function

$$P(W_{vij} = w_{vij} | \eta_{vij}) = \Phi(\eta_{vij})^{w_{vij}} + (1 - \Phi(\eta_{vij}))^{1-w_{vij}}. \tag{3}$$

If we denote each person's latent traits as $\boldsymbol{\theta}_i = (\theta_{1i}, \ldots, \theta_{mi})'$ and specify a multivariate normal prior distribution for them so that $\boldsymbol{\theta}_i \sim N_m(\mathbf{0}, \mathbf{P})$, where $\mathbf{P}$ is a constrained covariance matrix (or a correlation matrix) with 1s on the diagonal. It is noted that the proper multivariate normal prior for θ_{vi} with their location and scale parameters specified to be 0 and 1, respectively, ensures unique scaling and hence is essential in resolving a particular identification problem for the model (see, e.g., Lee 1995 for a description of the problem). Further, it follows that the off-diagonal element of $\mathbf{P}$ is the correlation ρ_{st} between θ_{si} and θ_{ti}, $s \neq t$. One may note that when $\rho_{st} = 1$ for all s, t, the model reduces to the 3PNO unidimensional model, whose probability function is defined as

$$P(y_{ij} = 1) = \gamma_j + (1 - \gamma_j)\Phi(\alpha_j\theta_i - \beta_j), \qquad i = 1, \ldots, n, \quad j = 1, \ldots, K. \tag{4}$$

Moreover, we can introduce an unconstrained covariance matrix Σ, where $\Sigma = [\sigma_{vv'}]_{m \times m}$, so that the constrained covariance matrix $\mathbf{P}$ can be readily transformed from Σ using

$$\rho_{st} = \frac{\sigma_{st}}{\sqrt{\sigma_{ss}\sigma_{tt}}}, \qquad s \neq t. \tag{5}$$

A noninformative prior can be assumed for Σ so that $p(\Sigma) \propto |\Sigma|^{-\frac{m+1}{2}}$ (Lee 1995).

Hence, with prior distributions assumed for γ_{vj} and ξ_{vj}, where $\xi_{vj} = (\alpha_{vj}, \beta_{vj})'$, the joint posterior distribution of (θ, ξ, $\mathbf{W}$, $\mathbf{Z}$, γ, Σ) is

$$p(\theta, \xi, \mathbf{W}, \mathbf{Z}, \gamma, \Sigma | \mathbf{y}) \propto f(\mathbf{y} | \mathbf{W}, \gamma) p(\mathbf{W} | \mathbf{Z}) p(\mathbf{Z} | \theta, \xi) p(\xi) p(\gamma) p(\theta | \mathbf{P}) p(\Sigma), \tag{6}$$

where

$$f(\mathbf{y}|\mathbf{Z}) = \prod_{v=1}^{m}\prod_{i=1}^{n}\prod_{j=1}^{k_v} p_{vij}^{y_{vij}}(1-p_{vij})^{1-y_{vij}} \tag{7}$$

is the likelihood function, with p_{vij} being the probability function for the multi-unidimensional model as defined in (2).

Assuming a conjugate Beta prior for γ_{vj} so that $\gamma_{vj} \sim Beta(s_v, t_v)$, the implementation of the Gibbs sampling procedure thus involves six sampling processes, namely,

1. a sampling of the augmented W parameters from

$$W_{vij}|\bullet \sim \begin{cases} Bernoulli\left(\frac{\Phi(\eta_{vij})}{\gamma_{vj}+(1-\gamma_{vj})\Phi(\eta_{vij})}\right), \text{ if } & y_{vij}=1 \\ Bernoulli(0), & \text{if } \quad y_{vij}=0 \end{cases}, \tag{8}$$

2. a sampling of the augmented Z parameters from

$$Z_{vij}|\bullet \sim \begin{cases} N_{(0,\infty)}(\eta_{vij},1), \text{ if } & W_{vij}=1 \\ N_{(-\infty,0)}(\eta_{vij},1), \text{ if } & W_{vij}=0 \end{cases}; \tag{9}$$

3. a sampling of person traits θ from

$$\theta_i|\bullet \sim N_m((\mathbf{A}'\mathbf{A}+\mathbf{P})^{-1}\mathbf{A}'\mathbf{B}, (\mathbf{A}'\mathbf{A}+\mathbf{P})^{-1}), \tag{10}$$

where $\mathbf{A} = \begin{bmatrix} \alpha_1 & \mathbf{0} & \cdots & \mathbf{0} \\ \mathbf{0} & \alpha_2 & \cdots & \mathbf{0} \\ \vdots & \vdots & \cdots & \vdots \\ \mathbf{0} & \mathbf{0} & \ldots & \alpha_m \end{bmatrix}_{K\times m}$ and $\mathbf{B} = \begin{bmatrix} \mathbf{Z}_{1i}+\beta_1 \\ \mathbf{Z}_{2i}+\beta_2 \\ \vdots \\ \mathbf{Z}_{mi}+\beta_m \end{bmatrix}_{K\times 1}$, in which $\alpha_v = (\alpha_{v1},\ldots,\alpha_{vk_v})'$, $\mathbf{Z}_{vi} = (Z_{vi1},\ldots,Z_{vik_v})'$, $\beta_v = (\beta_{v1},\ldots,\beta_{vk_v})'$;

4. a sampling of the item slope and intercept parameters ξ from

$$\xi_{vj}|\bullet \sim N_2((\mathbf{x}_v'\mathbf{x}_v)^{-1}\mathbf{x}_v'\mathbf{Z}_{vj}, (\mathbf{x}_v'\mathbf{x}_v)^{-1})I(\alpha_{vj}>0), \tag{11}$$

where $\mathbf{x}_v = [\theta_v, -1]$, assuming noninformative uniform priors $\alpha_{vj} > 0$ and $p(\beta_{vj}) \propto 1$, or from

$$\xi_{vj}|\bullet \sim N_2((\mathbf{x}_v'\mathbf{x}_v+\Sigma_{\xi_v}^{-1})^{-1}(\mathbf{x}_v'\mathbf{Z}_{vj}+\Sigma_{\xi_v}^{-1}\mu_{\xi_v}), (\mathbf{x}_v'\mathbf{x}_v+\Sigma_{\xi_v}^{-1})^{-1})I(\alpha_{vj}>0), \tag{12}$$

where $\mu_{\xi_v} = (\mu_{\alpha_v}, \mu_{\beta_v})'$ and $\Sigma_{\xi_v} = \text{diag}(\sigma^2_{\alpha_v}, \sigma^2_{\beta_v})$ assuming conjugate normal priors $\alpha_{vj} \sim N_{(0,\infty)}(\mu_{\alpha_v}, \sigma^2_{\alpha_v})$, $\beta_{vj} \sim N(\mu_{\beta_v}, \sigma^2_{\beta_v})$;

5. a sampling of the pseudo-chance-level parameters γ from

$$\gamma_{vj}|\bullet \sim Beta(a_{vj}+s_v, b_{vj}-a_{vj}+t_v), \tag{13}$$

where b_{vj} denotes the number of persons who do not know the correct answer to item j in subtest v, and a_{vj} denotes the number of correct responses to this item obtained by guessing; and

6. a sampling of the unconstrained covariance matrix $\mathbf{\Sigma}$ from

$$\mathbf{\Sigma}|\bullet \sim W^{-1}(\mathbf{S}^{-1}, n) \tag{14}$$

(an inverse Wishart distribution), where $\mathbf{S} = \sum_{i=1}^{n}(\mathbf{C}\boldsymbol{\theta}_i)(\mathbf{C}\boldsymbol{\theta}_i)'$, in which $\mathbf{C} = \text{diag}\left(\left(\prod_{j=1}^{k_1}\alpha_{1j}\right)^{1/k_1}, \ldots, \left(\prod_{j=1}^{k_m}\alpha_{mj}\right)^{1/k_m}\right)$ (see Lee 1995 for a detailed derivation of the full conditional distribution for $\mathbf{\Sigma}$). From each sampled $\mathbf{\Sigma}$, the constrained covaraince matrix $\mathbf{P}$ can be obtained using (5). Hence, with starting values $\boldsymbol{\theta}^{(0)}$, $\boldsymbol{\xi}^{(0)}$, $\boldsymbol{\gamma}^{(0)}$, and $\mathbf{P}^{(0)}$, observations ($\mathbf{W}^{(\ell)}$, $\mathbf{Z}^{(\ell)}$, $\boldsymbol{\theta}^{(\ell)}$, $\boldsymbol{\xi}^{(\ell)}$, $\mathbf{\Sigma}^{(\ell)}$, $\mathbf{P}^{(\ell)}$) can be drawn or transformed iteratively from (8), (9), (10), (11), (13), (14), and (5) (or (12) in lieu of (11)), respectively.

3 Simulation Study 1

To investigate the performance of the developed Gibbs sampling procedure for the 3PNO multi-unidimensional model, a simulation study was conducted where three factors were manipulated, namely, sample size, intertrait correlation, and the specificity of the prior density for each item parameter involved in the model. In the simulation, tests that measure two latent traits were considered so that the first half of the items measured one latent trait and the second half measured another. As sample sizes play a more important role than test lengths in the Gibbs sampler for 3PNO unidimensional models (Sheng 2010, p.107), item responses for 18 items and n persons ($n = 1{,}000, 2{,}000, 5{,}000$) were generated according to the 3PNO multi-unidimensional model, as defined in (2). Ability parameters were generated as samples from a bivariate normal distribution with an intertrait correlation (ρ) of 0.2, 0.5, or 0.7. Item parameters were generated from uniform distributions such that $\alpha_{vj} \sim U(0,2)$, $\beta_{vj} \sim U(-2,2)$, and $\gamma_{vj} \sim U(0.05, 0.25)$, and were held constant across the investigated factors.

Four prior specifications were considered in this study for the item slope and intercept parameters ($prior_{\alpha\beta}$):

1. $\alpha_{vj} > 0$, $\beta_{vj} \propto 1$;
2. $\alpha_{vj} \sim N_{(0,\infty)}(0, 10^{10})$, $\beta_{vj} \sim N(0, 10^{10})$;
3. $\alpha_{vj} \sim N_{(0,\infty)}(0, 4)$, $\beta_{vj} \sim N(0, 4)$;
4. $\alpha_{vj} \sim N_{(0,\infty)}(0, 1)$, $\beta_{vj} \sim N(0, 1)$.

It is noted that the first specification was uniform noninformative and the second specification was conjugate noninformative, assuming a relatively flat prior on

α_{vj} or β_{vj}. With increasingly smaller prior variances, specifications 3 and 4 were increasingly more informative, constraining posterior values to be closer to their prior means. For each of these four prior specifications for α and β, the prior distribution for γ ($prior_\gamma$) was assumed to be either

1. diffuse so that $\gamma_{vj} \sim Beta(1,1)$, or
2. informative so that $\gamma_{vj} \sim Beta(5,17)$ with the center location being at 0.23.

With each model specification, the Gibbs sampling procedure illustrated in Sect. 2 was then implemented to fit the 3PNO multi-unidimensional model to the simulated data. Convergence was monitored using the R statistic (Gelman and Rubin 1992) as well as diagnostic plots.

For each simulated scenario, ten replications were conducted, and the accuracy of parameter estimates was evaluated using the root mean square error (*RMSE*) and bias, which were averaged over items to provide summary indices. Tables 1–3 summarize the results for each item parameter in the 3PNO multi-unidimensional model when the intertrait correlation was specified to be 0.2, 0.5, and 0.7, respectively. From these tables, we can observe that:

- When α_{vj} or β_{vj} assumed uniform priors or proper noninformative priors with a large variance, $\sigma^2 = 10^{10}$, the Markov chains did not reach convergence with a run length of 30,000 iterations for sample sizes less than 5,000. It is observed that even with $n = 5{,}000$, some of the Markov chains failed to converge within the specified number of iterations. One may improve the convergence by increasing the chain length or sample size.
- Increased sample sizes (n) consistently resulted in smaller average *RMSE* and bias for estimating α_{vj}, β_{vj}, and γ_{vj}. Hence, they play an important role in improving the accuracy of the posterior estimates with reduced bias.
- For either α, β or γ, it is generally the case that with a more informative prior (that is, if the prior density had a smaller variance), the error and bias in estimating these item parameters reduced. This implies that correct information needs to be obtained regarding the item parameters in order for them to be estimated accurately.
- It is also worth noting that when the prior distribution for γ_{vj} was informative $Beta(5,17)$, the error and bias in estimating α_{vj} and β_{vj} were smaller than those with a diffuse prior $Beta(1,1)$ for γ_{vj}. Hence, when appropriate information is available, setting a smaller prior variance for one set of parameters reduces the error and bias in estimating the other set of item parameters in the model.

Moreover, the intertrait correlation was estimated accurately for each of the simulated scenarios. Based on these results, we can conclude that the Gibbs sampler for the 3PNO multi-unidimensional model requires proper informative priors to be specified for the slope and intercept parameters to ensure convergence. Unlike what we observed for the 3PNO unidimensional model (see, e.g., Sheng 2010), it is suggested that priors for pseudo-chance-level parameters be specified to be informative. It should be noted that when there is a strong intertrait correlation,

Table 1 Average *RMSE* (bias) of estimating item parameters in the 3PNO multi-unidimensional model for tests with the intertrait correlation specified to be 0.2 ($k_1 = 9, k_2 = 9$)

		$n = 1,000$			$n = 2,000$			$n = 5,000$		
$prior_\gamma$	$prior_{\alpha\beta}$	α	β	γ	α	β	γ	α	β	γ
1	1	n.c.	n.c.	n.c.	n.c.	n.c.	n.c.	0.30 (0.16)	0.52 (0.24)	0.16 (0.08)
	2	n.c.	n.c.	n.c.	n.c.	n.c.	n.c.	0.33 (0.16)	0.58 (0.28)	0.16 (0.08)
	3	0.55 (0.37)	0.70 (0.41)	0.21 (0.12)	0.47 (0.26)	0.60 (0.26)	0.19 (0.11)	0.23 (0.11)	0.37 (0.18)	0.15 (0.07)
	4	0.23 (0.10)	0.42 (0.21)	0.19 (0.10)	0.24 (0.10)	0.41 (0.15)	0.19 (0.09)	0.15 (0.06)	0.32 (0.14)	0.17 (0.08)
2	1	n.c.	n.c.	n.c.	n.c.	n.c.	n.c.	0.23 (0.12)	0.26 (0.12)	0.08 (0.05)
	2	n.c.	n.c.	n.c.	n.c.	n.c.	n.c.	0.34 (0.16)	0.38 (0.17)	0.08 (0.05)
	3	0.43 (0.28)	0.48 (0.26)	0.09 (0.07)	0.34 (0.19)	0.34 (0.13)	0.08 (0.06)	0.19 (0.10)	0.22 (0.12)	0.07 (0.05)
	4	0.20 (0.09)	0.23 (0.13)	0.09 (0.06)	0.21 (0.08)	0.21 (0.07)	0.08 (0.05)	0.12 (0.05)	0.14 (0.07)	0.07 (0.04)

Note: n.c. = the Markov chain did not reach convergence with a run length of 30,000 iterations

Table 2 Average *RMSE* (bias) of estimating item parameters in the 3PNO multi-unidimensional model for tests with the intertrait correlation specified to be 0.5 ($k_1 = 9, k_2 = 9$)

		$n = 1{,}000$			$n = 2{,}000$			$n = 5{,}000$		
$prior_\gamma$	$prior_{\alpha\beta}$	α	β	γ	α	β	γ	α	β	γ
1	1	n.c.	n.c.	n.c.	n.c.	n.c.	n.c.	0.30 (0.14)	0.58 (0.23)	0.15 (0.07)
	2	n.c.	n.c.	n.c.	n.c.	n.c.	n.c.	0.43 (0.20)	0.74 (0.28)	0.15 (0.07)
	3	0.46 (0.31)	0.69 (0.38)	0.21 (0.12)	0.37 (0.20)	0.54 (0.26)	0.18 (0.09)	0.25 (0.10)	0.31 (0.12)	0.14 (0.07)
	4	0.25 (0.10)	0.41 (0.19)	0.20 (0.10)	0.21 (0.08)	0.38 (0.16)	0.19 (0.09)	0.18 (0.05)	0.30 (0.10)	0.16 (0.07)
2	1	n.c.	n.c.	n.c.	n.c.	n.c.	n.c.	0.24 (0.11)	0.43 (0.15)	0.07 (0.04)
	2	n.c.	n.c.	n.c.	n.c.	n.c.	n.c.	0.27 (0.13)	0.36 (0.13)	0.08 (0.05)
	3	0.38 (0.24)	0.44 (0.23)	0.09 (0.06)	0.33 (0.18)	0.36 (0.16)	0.08 (0.05)	0.19 (0.09)	0.25 (0.09)	0.07 (0.04)
	4	0.20 (0.08)	0.21 (0.11)	0.08 (0.05)	0.19 (0.08)	0.21 (0.09)	0.08 (0.05)	0.16 (0.05)	0.15 (0.04)	0.07 (0.04)

Note: n.c. = the Markov chain did not reach convergence with a run length of 30,000 iterations

Table 3 Average *RMSE* (bias) of estimating item parameters in the 3PNO multi-unidimensional model for tests with the intertrait correlation specified to be 0.7 ($k_1 = 9, k_2 = 9$)

		$n = 1,000$			$n = 2,000$			$n = 5,000$		
$prior_\gamma$	$prior_{\alpha\beta}$	α	β	γ	α	β	γ	α	β	γ
1	1	n.c.	n.c.	n.c.	n.c.	n.c.	n.c.	0.35 (0.17)	0.83 (0.40)	0.18 (0.10)
	2	n.c.	n.c.	n.c.	n.c.	n.c.	n.c.	0.32 (0.18)	0.76 (0.39)	0.18 (0.10)
	3	0.53 (0.35)	0.80 (0.47)	0.23 (0.15)	0.36 (0.20)	0.57 (0.30)	0.19 (0.11)	0.21 (0.11)	0.46 (0.23)	0.16 (0.09)
	4	0.26 (0.13)	0.48 (0.24)	0.21 (0.13)	0.20 (0.08)	0.38 (0.16)	0.19 (0.10)	0.15 (0.07)	0.38 (0.18)	0.17 (0.09)
2	1	n.c.	n.c.	n.c.	n.c.	n.c.	n.c.	0.23 (0.12)	0.54 (0.24)	0.08 (0.05)
	2	n.c.	n.c.	n.c.	n.c.	n.c.	n.c.	0.25 (0.13)	0.62 (0.27)	0.08 (0.05)
	3	0.35 (0.22)	0.47 (0.28)	0.09 (0.07)	0.25 (0.14)	0.44 (0.21)	0.08 (0.06)	0.18 (0.09)	0.40 (0.18)	0.08 (0.05)
	4	0.21 (0.09)	0.25 (0.13)	0.09 (0.06)	0.17 (0.06)	0.20 (0.09)	0.08 (0.05)	0.12 (0.05)	0.21 (0.09)	0.08 (0.04)

Note: n.c. = the Markov chain did not reach convergence with a run length of 30,000 iterations

i.e., $\rho > 0.7$, the use of a more informative prior distribution for α_{vj}, e.g., $\alpha_{vj} \sim N_{(0,\infty)}(0,1)$, requires their actual values to have a smaller upper bound. For example, α_{vj} need to be bounded between 0 and 1.5, instead of between 0 and 2, when $\rho = 1$ and $n = 2{,}000$ for the informative prior to be adopted. This is due to the reason that allowing for a nonzero lower asymptote leads to larger posterior estimates of α in the 3PNO model (see, e.g., Loken and Rulison 2010), and that higher intertrait correlations result in more overestimation. Hence, when the estimated values are farther away from the prior mean of 0.798, problems arise if we try to constrain α_{vj} to be close to it.

4 Simulation Study 2

In order to further evaluate the performance of the 3PNO multi-unidimensional model and compare it with two existing IRT models, a second simulation study was carried out where item responses for 20 items and 5,000 individuals were generated according to each of the following models:

1. the 3PNO unidimensional model;
2. the 2PNO multi-unidimensional model where $k_1 = k_2 = 10$ and $\rho = 0.5$;
3. the 3PNO multi-unidimensional model where $k_1 = k_2 = 10$ and $\rho = 0.5$.

Gibbs sampling was implemented to each simulated data set to fit these three models, where 10,000 iterations were obtained with the first half as burn-in. In particular, based on the results of simulation study 1, informative priors were used for the item parameters so that $\alpha \sim N_{(0,\infty)}(0,1)$, $\beta \sim N(0,1)$, and/or $\gamma \sim Beta(5,17)$.

For each simulated scenario, ten replications were conducted. Each implementation of the Gibbs sampler gave rise to Gelman–Rubin R statistics close to 1, indicating that the Markov chain converged to its stationary distribution within 10,000 iterations. The accuracy of parameter estimates was evaluated using average *RMSE* and bias. In addition, model performance was evaluated using the Bayesian deviance information criterion (*DIC*; Spiegelhalter et al. 2002). Their results in each simulated condition were averaged over the ten replications and are summarized in Tables 4–6, which display the average *RMSE* and bias in estimating α, β, γ, and ρ. In addition, the averaged estimates for the posterior expectation of the deviance ($\bar{D}$), the deviance of the posterior expectation ($D(\bar{\vartheta})$) values, the effective number of parameters (p_D), and the Bayesian *DIC* are also shown in these tables. Small deviance values indicate a better-fitting model. Generally more complicated models tend to provide better fit. Hence, penalizing for number of parameters makes *DIC* a more reasonable measure to use.

A close examination of the tables indicates that:

- When data conformed to the 3PNO unidimensional model (see Table 4), the 3PNO uni- and multi-unidimensional models performed similarly in involving smaller error and bias in estimating α, β, and γ, with a slight advantage to

Table 4 Parameter recovery and model-data fit using each of the three IRT models under the situation where simulated data conformed to a 3PNO unidimensional model ($n = 5,000$, $k = 20$)

	Model		
	3PNO uni	2PNO multi-uni	3PNO multi-uni
RMSE (bias)			
α	0.091 (0.034)	0.248 (−0.165)	0.089 (0.035)
β	0.187 (0.0750)	0.411 (−0.300)	0.194 (0.080)
γ	–	–	0.075 (0.044)
ρ	–	0.017 (−0.017)	0.005 (−0.005)
Deviance estimates			
$\bar{D}$	94,907.82	95,123.25	94,876.75
$D(\vartheta)$	90,929.33	91,164.94	90,863.81
p_D	3,978.49	3,958.31	4,012.94
DIC	98,886.31	99,081.56	98,889.70

Table 5 Parameter recovery and model-data fit using each of the three IRT models under the situation where simulated data conformed to a 2PNO multi-unidimensional model ($n = 5,000$, $k_1 = 10$, $k_2 = 10$, $\rho = 0.5$)

	Model		
	3PNO uni	2PNO multi-uni	3PNO multi-uni
RMSE (bias)			
α	0.476 (0.025)	0.057 (0.001)	0.144 (0.112)
β	0.520 (0.335)	0.039 (−0.002)	0.204 (0.153)
γ	0.189 (0.145)	–	0.133 (0.102)
ρ	–	0.008 (−0.002)	0.008 (0.003)
Deviance estimates			
$\bar{D}$	83,952.60	75,344.13	75,623.15
$D(\vartheta)$	79,886.26	68,133.49	68,282.23
p_D	4,066.34	7,210.64	7,340.92
DIC	88,018.93	82,554.77	82,964.07

the multi-unidimensional model. They also resulted in smaller *DIC* values and hence were preferred than the 2PNO multi-unidimensional model. The two three-parameter models had almost identical deviance results. This agrees with what we noted earlier that the 3PNO unidimensional model is a special case of the 3PNO multi-unidimensional model.

- When data conformed to the 2PNO multi-unidimensional model, the correct model resulted in much smaller error and bias in estimating α and β (see Table 5), and was suggested by *DIC* to be better than the two 3PNO models. On the other hand, the 3PNO unidimensional model was clearly the worst among the three models as far as parameter recovery and model-data fit are concerned. One may note that although the 2PNO multi-unidimensional model is said to be a special case of the 3PNO multi-unidimensional model when $\gamma = 0$, the latter tended to overestimate γ (i.e., estimated them to be nonzero) and had

Table 6 Parameter recovery and model-data fit using each of the three IRT models under the situation where simulated data conformed to a 3PNO multi-unidimensional model ($n = 5{,}000$, $k_1 = 10$, $k_2 = 10$, $\rho = 0.5$)

	Model		
	3PNO uni	2PNO multi-uni	3PNO multi-uni
RMSE (bias)			
α	0.505 (0.015)	0.383 (−0.269)	0.126 (0.055)
β	0.573 (0.277)	0.437 (−0.314)	0.147 (0.055)
γ	0.156 (0.076)	–	0.069 (0.038)
ρ	–	0.021 (0.007)	0.015 (0.004)
Deviance estimates			
$\bar{D}$	92,558.82	86,952.78	86,058.33
$D(\vartheta)$	88,649.73	80,305.46	79,047.50
p_D	3,909.09	6,647.32	7,010.83
DIC	96,467.91	93,600.09	93,069.16

slightly larger error and bias in estimating α and β. However, note that in the simulation results from Sect. 3, the average *RMSE* and bias in estimating item parameters for the 3PNO multi-unidimensional model when it was true (Table 2) were not much smaller. Hence, the relatively larger error and bias in estimating item parameters using the 3PNO multi-unidimensional model for data with a zero lower asymptote might be due to the complexity of the model and the estimation procedure.

- In situations where the 3PNO multi-unidimensional model was true with a moderate intertrait correlation (see Table 6), the correct model resulted in much smaller estimation error and bias, and had the smallest *DIC* value, which suggests that it fit the data the best even after penalizing for a large number of effective parameters. The latent structure agreed with multi-unidimensionality. Hence, the 2PNO multi-unidimensional model resulted in relatively less error in estimating item parameters and had a better model fit than the 3PNO unidimensional model.
- It is noted that when data were unidimensional, the two multi-unidimensional models involved a fairly small effective number of parameters (p_D), which was close to that for the unidimensional model (see Table 4). However, when data were multi-unidimensional, both 2PNO and 3PNO multi-unidimensional models had a substantially larger p_D than the unidimensional model (see Tables 5 and 6).
- When data conformed to the model with a nonzero lower asymptote (γ), the 2PNO multi-unidimensional model tended to underestimate both α and β (see Tables 4 and 6).
- It is further noted that no matter whether data assumed a zero or nonzero lower asymptote, both the 2PNO and 3PNO multi-unidimensional models estimated ρ fairly well, with a slight advantage to the correct model (see Tables 4–6).

In general, the 3PNO multi-unidimensional model is more general and flexible than the 3PNO unidimensional model and has advantages over it in large-sample situations. On the other hand, when it is clear that the test data do not assume a nonzero lower asymptote parameter or do not involve pseudo-chance, it is suggested that the 2PNO multi-unidimensional model be adopted for ease of implementing the Gibbs sampling procedure.

5 An Example with *CBASE* Data

As an illustration, the Gibbs sampler for the 3PNO multi-unidimensional model was implemented to a subset of *College Basic Academic Subjects Examination* (*CBASE*; Osterlind 1997) English data and its model-data fit was evaluated by comparing it with a 2PNO multi-unidimensional model and a 3PNO unidimensional model.

The overall *CBASE* exam contains an overall 41 multiple-choice items on English, 25 of which are on reading/literature and the remaining 16 are on writing. The data used in this study were from college students who took the LP form of *CBASE* in years 2001 and 2002. After removing those who attempted the exam multiple times and removing missing responses, a sample of 1,200 examinees was randomly selected. Gibbs sampling with each of the three models described in Sect. 4 was fit to the data and compared with one another in describing the data.

Each Gibbs sampler was implemented with a chain length of 10,000 iterations and a burn-in stage of 5,000 iterations. The Gelman–Rubin R statistics were used to assess convergence and they were found to be around or close to 1, suggesting that stationarity had been reached within the simulated Markov chains for the models. The Bayesian deviance estimates were subsequently obtained for each model and the results are summarized in Table 7. Among the three models considered, the 3PNO multi-unidimensional model had relatively smaller *DIC* and expected posterior deviance ($\bar{D}$) values. Hence, it provided a better description of the data. The latent structure of the data was suggested to agree with multi-unidimensionality, as the unidimensional model provided a worse description of the data than the 2PNO multi-unidimensional model. In addition, the p_D values for the two multi-unidimensional models were much larger than that for the unidimensional model. Given these results, it is reasonable to believe that the actual lower asymptote parameters for the *CBASE* English data are nonzero and the latent structure can be multi-unidimensional with a fairly strong intertrait correlation $\hat{\rho} = .826$.

Table 7 Bayesian deviance estimates for the three IRT models with the *CBASE* data ($n = 1,200$, $k_1 = 16$, $k_2 = 25$, $\text{chainlength} = 10,000$, $\text{burn} - \text{in} = 5,000$)

Model	$\bar{D}$	$D(\vartheta)$	p_D	*DIC*
3PNO uni	53,840.81	52,744.78	1,096.03	54,936.83
2PNO multi-uni	53,501.48	52,095.27	1,406.21	54,907.69
3PNO multi-uni	53,333.62	51,866.18	1,467.44	54,801.06

6 Discussion

In summary, fully Bayesian estimation for the three-parameter multi-unidimensional IRT model can be developed generalizing the approach for the two-parameter model by Lee (1995). Exploring different prior specifications, this study shows that the procedure requires a fairly informative prior for each set of the item parameters. When compared with the conventional three-parameter unidimensional or the two-parameter multi-unidimensional model, simulation results indicate that the more complex three-parameter multi-unidimensional model consistently provides a good if not better model description to the data that assume either a perfect intertrait correlation or a zero pseudo-chance level. It is noted that the three-parameter multi-unidimensional model, allowing for a nonzero lower asymptote, is more complicated than the two-parameter model. It requires informative priors or a much larger sample size for the Markov chains to work properly.

One has to also note that the advantages of the multi-unidimensional model over the unidimensional model demonstrated by the simulations of this study relied on the fact that the latent structure was correctly specified. For situations where such information is not readily available, a misspecified latent structure for the multi-unidimensional model could result in an insufficient description of the data. To avoid this, one can choose to use the simpler unidimensional model if the amount of dimensionality is suggested to be negligible. After all, unidimensional models have been predominant in educational research given the fact that many IRT applications are only possible with such models. Alternatively, if a test is believed to involve multiple distinct latent traits, which is more common in actual testing situations, the more general multidimensional IRT model (Reckase 2009) should be used to explore the dimensionality structure. The difference between the general multidimensional model and the multi-unidimensional model is analogous to the distinction made between exploratory and confirmatory factor analysis (Sheng 2012). As such, one can use the former to identify the latent structure when it is not available and use the latter to confirm this structure.

Given that previous research on Gibbs sampler for 3PNO unidimensional models found that the estimation accuracy of item parameters should improve with larger sample sizes, but not necessarily with larger test lengths (Sheng 2010), this study used fixed number of items in the simulation study. Certainly, additional studies are needed to empirically demonstrate the effect of test length on estimating 3PNO multi-unidimensional model parameters. In addition, this study only looked at nonhierarchical models where item hyperparameters take specific values. It will also be interesting to consider hierarchical Bayesian models where second-order priors are assumed for item hyperparameters. Given findings from Sheng (2013) on 3PNO unidimensional models, it is believed that hierarchical modeling provides advantages in modeling the complex 3PNO multi-unidimensional model. Further, only conjugate prior densities for item parameters were investigated in this paper. Future studies may adopt non-conjugate priors.

References

Adams, R. J., Wilson, M., & Wang, W. C. (1997). The multidimensional random coefficients multinomial logit model. *Applied Psychological Measurement*, *21*(1), 1–23.

Albert, J. H. (1992). Bayesian estimation of normal ogive item response curves using Gibbs sampling. *Journal of Educational Statistics*, *17*(3), 251–269.

Casella, G., & George, E. I. (1992). Explaining the Gibbs sampler. *The American Statistician*, *46*(3), 167–174.

Gelman, A., & Rubin, D. B. (1992). Inference from iterative simulation using multiple sequences (with discussion). *Statistical Science*, *7*(4), 457–511.

Geman, S., & Geman, D. (1984). Stochastic relaxation, Gibbs distributions, and the Bayesian restoration of images. *IEEE Transactions on Pattern Analysis and Machine Intelligence*, *6*(6), 721–741.

Lee, H. (1995). *Markov chain Monte Carlo methods for estimating multidimensional ability in item response analysis*. Unpublished Dissertation, Missouri, MO.

Loken, E., & Rulison, K. L. (2010). Estimation of a four-parameter item response theory model. *British Journal of Mathematical and Statistical Psychology*, *63*(3), 509–525.

McDonald, R. P. (1999). *Test theory: A unified approach*. Mahwah: Lawrence Erlbaum.

Osterlind, S. (1997). *A national review of scholastic achievement in general education: How are we doing and why should we care?* ASHE-ERIC Higher Education Report 25, No. 8. Washington, DC: The George Washington University Graduate School of Education and Human Development.

Reckase, M. D. (2009). *Multidimensional item response theory*. New York: Springer.

Sahu, S. K. (2002). Bayesian estimation and model choice in item response models. *Journal of Statistical Computation and Simulation*, *72*(3), 217–232.

Sheng, Y. (2008). Markov chain Monte Carlo estimation of normal ogive IRT models in MATLAB. *Journal of Statistical Software*, *25*(8), 1–15.

Sheng, Y. (2008). A MATLAB package for Markov chain Monte Carlo with a multi-unidimensional IRT model. *Journal of Statistical Software*, *28*(10), 1–19.

Sheng, Y. (2010). A sensitivity analysis of Gibbs sampling for 3PNO IRT models: Effects of prior specifications on parameter estimates. *Behaviormetrika*, *37*(2), 87–110.

Sheng, Y. (2013). An empirical investigation of Bayesian hierarchical modeling with unidimensional IRT models. *Behaviormetrika*, *40*(1), 19–40.

Sheng, Y., & Wikle, C. K. (2007). Comparing multi-unidimensional and unidimensional IRT models. *Educational & Psychological Measurement*, *67*(6), 899–919.

Sheng, Y., & Headrick, T. C. (2012). A Gibbs sampler for the multidimensional item response model. *ISRN Applied Mathematics, 2012*(269385), 1–14.

Spiegelhalter, D., Best, N., Carlin, B., & van der Linde, A. (2002). Bayesian measures of model complexity and fit (with discussion). *Journal of the Royal Statistical Society, Series B, 64*(4), 583–640.

The Effect of Response Model Misspecification and Uncertainty on the Psychometric Properties of Estimates

Kristian E. Markon and Michael Chmielewski

The effect of model uncertainty and model misspecification on test score properties has been a prominent issue in assessment for decades, manifesting implicitly or explicitly in a number of different domains. For example, measurement invariance (i.e., differential item or test functioning) is often of interest because of the possibility that test models otherwise might be misspecified for particular individuals or groups. Similar issues regarding predictive invariance also often arise from concerns about the effects of response models that might be misspecified (Borsboom et al. 2008; Millsap 1997, 2007). Impression management continues to be an area of focus because of concerns about misspecified assumptions during test scoring or trait estimation (Ziegler et al. 2012).

The prominence of these issues has led to substantial advances in methods for detecting and preventing possible model misspecification (e.g., Meijer 2003; Meredith 1993; Millsap and Everson 1993). Less well understood, however, are the effects of misspecified models on the psychometric properties of tests, such as test error and reliability (Wainer and Thissen 1987). For example, it is possible to test whether a model might be inappropriate for a certain person or subpopulation, but how does inappropriate use of that model affect overall test score accuracy and precision?

Understanding how model misspecification impacts the psychometric properties of tests is critically important for quantifying the impact of misspecification, but also because misspecification is likely endemic to the assessment process. From a pragmatic perspective, for instance, a certain proportion of misspecification cases will likely always go undetected simply due to unavoidable random errors of inference.

K.E. Markon (✉)
Department of Psychology, University of Iowa, Iowa City, IA 52242, USA
e-mail: kristian-markon@uiowa.edu

M. Chmielewski
Department of Psychology, Southern Methodist University, Dallas, TX, USA

R.E. Millsap et al. (eds.), *New Developments in Quantitative Psychology*, Springer Proceedings in Mathematics & Statistics 66, DOI 10.1007/978-1-4614-9348-8_7,

From a more theoretical perspective, individual variation and heterogeneity in response processes may be typical, implying that any purely nomothetic assessment approach will necessarily entail some model misspecification effects at the level of individuals, who may each be responding idiosyncratically (Borsboom et al. 2003; Molenaar 2004; von Eye 2004).

In this paper, we review the literature on model misspecification, to clarify how use of incorrect models impacts the actual and assumed accuracy and precision of trait estimates. First, we review the broader statistical literature on misspecification and its effects on estimation, and explore how misspecification affects the accuracy of estimates under common response models. We then explore the effects of misspecification on the precision of estimates. Interestingly, using analytic and simulation results, we show that although misspecification often decreases the accuracy of estimates, somewhat counterintuitively, it actually may also increase accuracy under certain circumstances. Moreover, depending on the form of misspecification, reliability can actually be increased under misspecification, in a way that provides a misleading characterization of test precision. We conclude with recommendations for applied use of tests when model uncertainty is a prominent concern.

1 Response Models and Their Misspecification: Overview

Throughout this paper, it is assumed that a probabilistic model of test response, at either the item or score level, is being used implicitly or explicitly. That is, the model can be written in some general form of $P(\boldsymbol{X}|\theta,\gamma)$, where the probability of some response $\boldsymbol{X}$ is modeled in terms of one or more person parameters (e.g., latent traits) θ and item parameters γ. In this paper, it is also generally assumed that the item parameters are assumed to be known (note that the assumed item parameters can be correct or incorrect), and the interest is in obtaining an estimate of respondents' standing on a single latent trait, $\widehat{\theta}$, using maximum likelihood (ML) unless otherwise stated (Bayesian estimation is briefly discussed at the end of the paper). Although these assumptions are admittedly somewhat simplistic, they are nevertheless arguably realistic and applicable to a wide variety of situations, simplify discussion, and likely generalize well to more complex scenarios.

Many familiar response models, including a variety of item response theory (IRT) and classical test theory (CTT) models, can be derived from a more general framework, that of generalized linear latent variable modeling (e.g., Mellenbergh 1994a; Moustaki and Knott 2000; Skrondal and Rabe-Hesketh 2004). In this framework, a model for the responses to a measure j by a person i can be written as

$$g\left(\tau_{ij}\right) = a_j\theta_i + b_j, \tag{1}$$

where g is a link function relating the latent trait to an expected value of the response variable and τ_{ij} is the expected value of the response variable given a value of the latent trait (i.e., $E(\boldsymbol{x}_{ij}|\theta_i)$). The link function g, which derives from generalized linear modeling, depends on the assumed distribution of the response variable and choices regarding the specific model of interest (e.g., normal versus logistic). It can be thought of as a function that transforms the scale of the latent variable (e.g., continuous) into the assumed scale and distribution of the response variable (e.g., an ordinal polytomous variable or a count variable). The parameter a reflects the discrimination or loading of the item and the parameter b is an intercept term reflecting the difficulty or severity of the item. For example, using a normal link function with variance ψ^2 equal to the residual variance, one obtains a family of continuous response models that include traditional (e.g., parallel, tau-equivalent) models as special cases; using a logit link one obtains the familiar two-parameter item response model.

The central question in this paper is: what happens if the form of the response model in Eq. (1) is different from the actual model governing an individual's responses to items? For example, what happens if the item parameters that are used to estimate trait scores [e.g., a and b in Eq. (1)] are different from the actual item parameters describing the process used to generate responses? What are the effects on trait estimate accuracy and reliability if measurement invariance does not hold across ethnic groups, but the response model describing a majority subpopulation is incorrectly applied to estimate scores in a minority subpopulation? Similarly, how is the accuracy of trait estimates affected if individual differences in impression management are ignored—or conversely, if impression management is assumed incorrectly?

Various authors have explored the effect of item parameter estimation errors on trait estimation (e.g., Thissen and Wainer 1990; Tsutakawa and Johnson 1990; Yang et al. 2012; Zhang et al. 2011). This can be considered a form of model misspecification due to stochastic sampling variation during the item parameter estimation process. Although important and relevant to the current discussion, here we focus on a different phenomenon: structural model misspecification, where misspecification is not due to stochastic sampling variation, and would occur even if the population item parameters were known (i.e., the misspecification will not disappear as the sample used to estimate item parameters becomes infinitely large).

2 Estimation Under Misspecification: Accuracy, Bias, and Variance

2.1 Estimates

Various authors have illustrated that, under misspecification, ML estimates—in this case, ML trait estimates—approach the value that minimizes the relative entropy (i.e., Kullback–Leibler distance) between the misspecified likelihood and the true likelihood (e.g., Akaike 1973; Gustafson 2001; White 1982). Specifically, under misspecification, ML estimates will tend toward (i.e., have expected values of) the value of $\widehat{\theta}$ that minimizes

$$\sum P\left(X \mid \theta^{*}, \gamma^{*}\right) \ln \left[\frac{P\left(X \mid \theta^{*}, \gamma^{*}\right)}{P\left(X \mid \widehat{\theta}, \gamma\right)}\right], \tag{2}$$

where θ^* is the true trait value and γ^* are the true item parameters, and the sum is taken over all possible response vectors. The relative entropy will be zero when the misspecified model produces likelihoods that are exactly the same as the true model likelihoods, and will increase as the misspecified likelihoods and true likelihoods diverge. Misspecification will produce trait estimates that come closest, on average across response patterns, to reproducing the probability of the data under the true model, minimizing the relative entropy in Eq. (2).

Note that the value being minimized in Eq. (2) by $\widehat{\theta}$ under the misspecified model is still defined even when direct comparisons between the parameters of the true model and the assumed model are not meaningful—e.g., in the case that responses do not actually involve trait or person parameters at all, or where true person parameters are on one scale of measurement (e.g., nominal) and the estimated parameters are on another (e.g., interval). In this case, $P(\boldsymbol{X}|\theta^*, \gamma^*)$ is arguably more accurately thought of in terms of $P(\boldsymbol{X}|M^*)$, where M^* is the true model, with misspecification still producing trait estimates that come closest, on average across response patterns, to reproducing the likelihood under the true model.

2.2 *Estimation Error, Bias, and Variance*

Assuming that the true model and the assumed model both have directly comparable trait parameters, how accurate are they? How close they are to the true values? Although the minimized value in Eq. (2) could be used to indirectly answer this question—with values closer to zero indicating accurate estimates and smaller effects of misspecification, and larger values indicating less accurate estimates and larger effects of misspecification—this would still not address how similar the estimated trait value is to the true trait value.

2.2.1 Mean Square Error

A more direct index of the accuracy of estimates, often used in statistical theory and research, is the mean square error (MSE):

$$MSE = E\left[\left(\widehat{\theta} - \theta^{*}\right)^{2}\right] \tag{3}$$

which is the expected—i.e., average—squared difference between the estimated trait value and true trait value. The MSE has the benefit of ignoring the direction of estimation errors; it also weights estimation errors more the greater they are.

Although the MSE under model misspecification can be derived for specific types of models, obtaining a general formula for the MSE under misspecification is challenging. Xu et al. (2004) present general lower bounds for the MSE under misspecification, relating the MSE with regard to a parameter to the log-likelihood ratio with regard to that parameter. They show that in general the MSE over a range of a parameter is lower bounded by the integrated error probability under the log-likelihood ratio test, using the misspecified model.

2.2.2 Bias–Variance Decomposition

Importantly, the MSE can be reexpressed as the sum of two components: the squared estimation bias and the estimation variance. That is,

$$MSE = \beta^2 + \sigma^2, \tag{4}$$

where β is the bias and σ^2 is the variance of the estimates:

$$\beta = E\left[\left(\widehat{\theta} - \theta^*\right)\right] \tag{5}$$

and

$$\sigma^2 = E\left[\left(\widehat{\theta} - E\left[\widehat{\theta}\right]\right)^2\right], \tag{6}$$

where $E[\widehat{\theta}]$ is the expected or average trait estimate [i.e., the estimate minimizing Eq. (2)]. The bias is therefore the average difference between the estimated and true trait value, and the variance is the variance of the trait estimates around their average (which is not necessarily the same as the true value). It is important to emphasize that the term bias here specifically refers to the extent to which trait estimates differ on average from their true values. This is related to, but different from, the use of the term "bias" in some of the applied and psychometric literature, where it is often used to refer to misspecification or misestimation of measurement models more broadly.

The bias–variance decomposition of the MSE significantly underscores that the accuracy of an estimate depends on both bias and variance, and that there may be compromises between the two in selecting a model. A model that increases bias may nevertheless produce more accurate estimates if the increased bias is sufficiently offset by decreased variance. Conversely, a model that decreases bias may produce less accurate estimates if it increases the variance of those estimates too much. This phenomenon is well documented in the broader statistical literature: more flexible models with fewer constraints, for example, are likely to produce less biased estimates but are also more susceptible to sampling variability; conversely, less flexible models are less susceptible to sampling variability but are more susceptible to bias (e.g., Forster 2000; Hero et al. 1996).

Similar phenomena may occur in trait estimation. For example, in some cases it may be that estimating ancillary person parameters (e.g., reflecting response style or impression management) together with trait level may introduce more estimation uncertainty than the amount of bias it reduces, decreasing the accuracy of trait estimates overall. Even among response models with only one parameter—the trait parameter—it may be the case that some response models introduce greater uncertainty into estimates, even as they decrease bias, by virtue of their structural features.

It is important to emphasize that these bias–variance compromises apply when comparing a misspecified model to the correct model just as they apply to comparisons between two misspecified models. In other words, a misspecified model may actually produce more accurate estimates than the correct model, by virtue of reducing uncertainty at the cost of increased bias. This phenomena has been observed in other areas of statistics (Lowerre 1974; Rao 1971; Todros and Tabrikian 2011), suggesting that use of an incorrect test response model may sometimes have little effect on test scores, and may actually improve the accuracy of the scores in some cases.

2.3 Example: Continuous Response Models

As an example, consider a continuous response model, obtained from Eq. (1) by using a normal link function with variance ψ^2 equal to the residual variance. As noted earlier, many traditional test models (e.g., parallel or tau-equivalent measures models) can be obtained as special cases from this model under certain constraints. As illustrated by Mellenbergh (1994b), for a single trait, ML trait estimates under this model are given by

$$\widehat{\theta}_i = \frac{\sum a_j \left(x_{ij} - b_j\right) / \psi_j^2}{\sum a_j^2 / \psi_j^2}. \tag{7}$$

This is equivalent to Bartlett's factor score estimator (Bartlett 1937) for a single trait. Moreover, as noted by Bartholomew and Knott (1999), this estimate is unbiased when the model is correctly specified.

Following Mellenbergh (1994b, page 231), and substituting $a_j^* \theta_i^* + b_j^* + e_{ij}^*$ for x_{ij} in Eq. (7), one obtains the following expression for the expected value of the trait estimate under misspecification, conditional on the true trait value:

$$E\left[\widehat{\theta} \mid \theta^*, \gamma\right] = \frac{\sum a_j \left[a_j^* \theta_i^* + \left(b_j^* - b_j\right)\right] / \psi_j^2}{\sum a_j^2 / \psi_j^2}. \tag{8}$$

Here, as elsewhere, the asterisks indicate the true parameters and the values without asterisks indicate the assumed parameters (e.g., a is the assumed loading and a^* is the true loading). Equation (8) can be used to estimate the expected bias at a given level of the trait, as $\beta(\theta) = E\left[\widehat{\theta} \mid \theta^*, \gamma\right] - \theta^*$. Expanding this gives the following value for the bias conditional on the true trait value:

$$\beta\left(\widehat{\theta} \mid \theta^*, \gamma\right) = \frac{\sum\left[a_j\left[a_j^*\theta_i^* + \left(b_j^* - b_j\right)\right] - a_j^2\theta_i^*\right]/\psi_j^2}{\sum a_j^2/\psi_j^2}. \tag{9}$$

Similarly, assuming uncorrelated error variances, the variance of the trait estimate under misspecification is given by

$$\sigma^2\left(\widehat{\theta} \mid \theta^*, \gamma\right) = \frac{\sum \frac{a_j^2}{\psi_j^2}\frac{\psi^{*2}_j}{\psi_j^2}}{\left[\sum \frac{a_j^2}{\psi_j^2}\right]^2}, \tag{10}$$

where again, ψ^{*2} is the true error variance and ψ^2 is the assumed error variance. The derivation of the variance under misspecification is explained in greater detail in the Appendix.

Note that if the true and assumed error variance are equal (i.e., there is no misspecification), then the variance becomes

$$\sigma^2\left(\widehat{\theta} \mid \theta^*, \gamma^*\right) = \frac{1}{\sum \frac{a_j^2}{\psi_j^2}} = \frac{1}{I}, \tag{11}$$

where I is the nominal test information (Mellenbergh 1994b), which will be constant.

Equations (9) and (10) reveal various characteristics of how continuous response model trait estimates behave under misspecification. Bias, for example, depends on the relative magnitudes of true versus assumed loadings and intercepts, but not the true error variances. Variance, in contrast, does not depend on the true loading, but does depend on the relative magnitudes of the true and assumed error variances. Similarly, bias depends on the true trait value, but variance is independent of it. Both bias and variance are affected by the assumed loadings and assumed error variances.

In order to illustrate the effects of misspecification on estimation accuracy, and verify the accuracy of Eqs. (8)–(10), a series of simulations were conducted. Values of the parameters were taken from measurement invariance analyses of the Spanish and English Neuropsychological Assessment Scales (SENAS; Mungas et al. 2011), a cognitive battery developed for use in multiethnic and multilingual applications. The SENAS provides an excellent example of how misspecification might impact accuracy of test score estimates, as its psychometric properties in differently responding groups of individuals are well documented.

Table 1 Bias, variance, and MSE under misspecification: continuous response model

	$\theta*=0$			$\theta*=1$			$\theta*=2$		
Model	σ^2	β	MSE	σ^2	β	MSE	σ^2	β	MSE
Model A, correctly specified	0.114	0.001	0.114	0.115	−0.001	0.115	0.114	−0.001	0.114
	0.114	0.000	0.114	0.114	0.000	0.114	0.114	0.000	0.114
Model A, misspecified	0.096	0.038	0.097	0.096	−0.056	0.099	0.096	−0.150	0.119
	0.096	0.038	0.097	0.096	−0.056	0.099	0.096	−0.149	0.118
Model B, correctly specified	0.087	0.000	0.087	0.088	0.000	0.088	0.088	−0.001	0.088
	0.088	0.000	0.088	0.088	0.000	0.088	0.088	0.000	0.088
Model B, misspecified	0.107	−0.041	0.109	0.108	0.057	0.111	0.108	0.154	0.131
	0.108	−0.041	0.110	0.108	0.057	0.111	0.108	0.155	0.132

Note: Values in table are variance, bias, and MSE at true trait values of 0, 1, and 2, for different correctly and incorrectly specified models. For each model specification condition, the top number is the value obtained in simulations; the bottom number is the predicted value based in Eqs. (8)–(10). Within each model specification condition, the predicted variance did not depend on trait value but is repeated across trait values to compare with simulation results, which did vary very slightly

Two models were used in the simulations, each of which was based on the Semantic/Language scales of the SENAS, which assess verbal reasoning or language ability. Model A corresponded to the SENAS parameter estimates among White individuals (loadings of 0.76, 0.74, 0.49, 0.42, 0.73; intercepts of 0.64, 0.63, 0.67, −0.03, 0.47; and residual variances of 0.20, 0.31, 0.22, 0.83, 0.19); Model B corresponded to the SENAS parameter estimates among English-speaking Hispanic individuals (loadings of 0.81, 0.82, 0.59, 0.54, 0.78; intercepts of 0.64, 0.63, 0.51, −0.03, 0.47; and residual variances of 0.20, 0.24, 0.22, 0.58, 0.19). Four sets of simulations conducted: one in which Model A was the true, data-generating model, and was correctly specified; another simulation in which Model A was the true model, but Model B was incorrectly specified as the data-generating model; a simulation in which Model B was the true model and was correctly specified; and a simulation in which Model B was the true model but Model A was incorrectly specified as the data-generating model. 1,00,000 response vectors were simulated for each condition, for trait values of 0, 1, and 2, and trait estimates were calculated using Eq. (7).

Table 1 presents the results of these simulations. Throughout the conditions, the simulated bias, variance, and MSE were nearly identical to predictions using Eqs. (8)–(10). Consistent with predictions, whereas the variance is constant across trait level, the bias changes with trait level. The results in Table 1 also illustrate that, under correct model specification, trait estimates are unbiased and MSE is constant across trait level. Under misspecification, the trait estimates exhibit varying degrees of bias, and the MSE changes across trait level.

Figure 1 also illustrates these trends, showing predicted MSE as a function of true trait level across the different conditions. Importantly, as is evident in the figure, the misspecified model does not in fact always produce the greatest estimation error. When Model B is used as the true model, error is in fact always greater for the

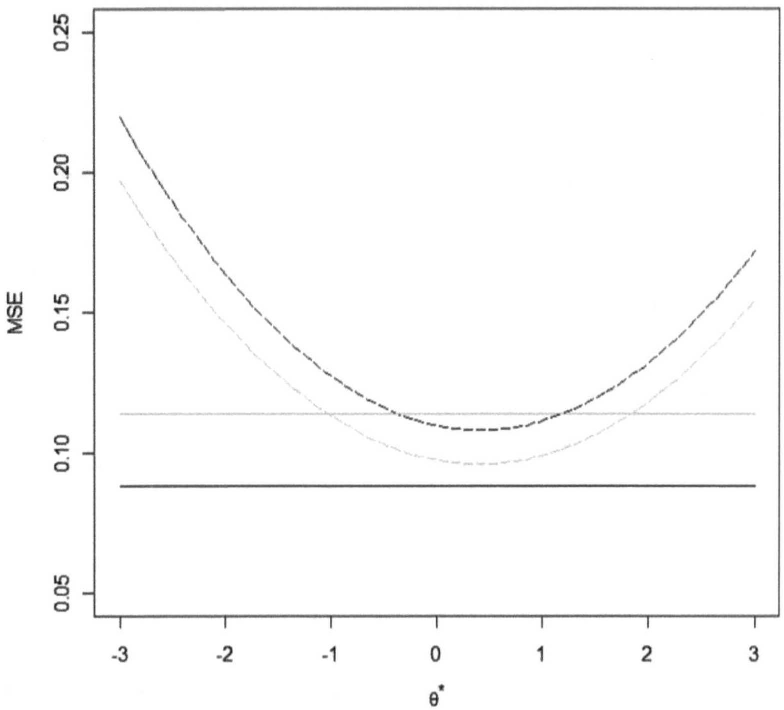

Fig. 1 Mean square error (MSE) as a function of true trait level, population model, and assumed model. MSE for population Model A is illustrated by the *gray lines*; MSE for population Model B is illustrated by the *black lines*. MSE for correctly specified models is illustrated by *solid lines*, MSE for misspecified models by *dashed lines*

misspecified model. However, when Model A is used as the true model, error is only sometimes greater for the misspecified model: for extreme values of the trait, the true model produces lower error, but for moderate values of the trait, the misspecified model actually produces less estimation error.

Figure 1 demonstrates that the effect of misspecification on estimation accuracy is complex, depending on the true model, the form of misspecification, and the distribution of true trait values in the population. For a standard normal population responding under Model A, for example, the misspecified model would actually result in slightly lower MSE overall than the correct model (simulations indicate an MSE of 0.106 for the misspecified model versus 0.114 for the correct model).

One important implication of these results is that ignoring measurement noninvariance does not always result in an overall increase in estimation error, and may actually decrease estimation error depending on the circumstances. Similar phenomena involving small or negligible effects of noninvariance or model misspecification have been observed empirically in various studies (e.g., Hendrawan et al. 2005; Reise et al. 2001; Roznowski and Reith 1999) but is illustrated here analytically and through simulations. The precise form of the bias, variance, and corresponding MSE provided by Eqs. (8)–(10) will help quantify the effect of measurement variance on estimation accuracy.

In this particular example, with the SENAS, failure to recognize measurement variance would likely result in decreased estimation accuracy. As Model B corresponds to test parameters among minorities, the most likely form of misspecification—incorrectly assuming that European American test parameters apply to other groups—would increase error. However, with other tests and other measurement invariance scenarios, other conclusions might be more appropriate.

2.4 Example: Discrete Response Models

In the case of discrete observed variables (e.g., with IRT models), the relationship between trait level, bias, variance, and MSE becomes more complex. For instance, with typical IRT models, the variance as well as the bias would be expected to change with trait level (consider the typical information function of IRT, which reflects this variance, and generally changes with trait level). Also, even with correct model specification, IRT estimates may be biased, in a form that depends on the true trait value (Lord 1983).

Both of these factors lead to potentially complex effects of misspecification on trait estimation. For example, if correctly specified models do in fact produce biased estimates, it is conceivable that a misspecified model might produce bias of a form that counteracts the bias of the correctly specified model—a sort of antibias—reducing estimation error overall. Similarly, a misspecified model might reduce overall estimation error in a trait range by decreasing variance in that range, even if it increases bias somewhat.

Impression management effects provide a useful context for exploring some of these issues. Although the effects of impression management on responding can be demonstrated well in experimental settings (e.g., Baer and Miller 2002), it has been difficult to demonstrate validity of impression management indices in observational settings (McGrath et al. 2010). This has led to apparent paradox and associated controversy, whereby putatively obvious, even known, effects of impression management on response processes are sometimes asserted to have no effect on test validity (Ziegler et al. 2012).

The current discussion provides one additional possible explanation for this phenomenon: if use of the correct impression management response model leads to sufficient uncertainty in trait estimation—i.e., sufficiently increases the variability of trait estimates—it may be inconsequential or even desirable to ignore the impression management and adopt an incorrect, biased model for the purposes of trait estimation. This phenomenon would hold even if it is known with certainty that the individual has used impression management during the response process.

2.4.1 The Asymptote-Shift Model of Impression Management

Consider, for example, models of impression management relying on a shift in the asymptotic response from extreme trait values. Under this scenario, in response to a binary response item (e.g., true–false), extreme individuals who are faking always have a finite probability of responding to an item in a direction that they might otherwise not respond. For example, on a measure of Big Five agreeableness, a very aggressive individual faking might always have a nonzero probability of responding "true" to the item "I would never harm someone." The three-parameter logistic (3PL) IRT model is often used in this scenario to model impression management, with the lower asymptote parameter reflecting effects of impression management. Similar four-parameter models have also been proposed, with both lower and upper asymptotic parameters (Loken and Rulison 2010; Waller and Reise 2009).

Simulations were conducted to investigate the effects of model misspecification in this scenario (e.g., using the correct impression management model or ignoring it). In this simulation, 4,000 responses were generated for each of 13 trait values, equally spaced from -3 to 3. In all cases, respondents were assumed to be responding using impression management to a 23-dichotomous-item test, under a process described by a 3PL IRT model, with the lower asymptote reflecting impression management. Item parameters were taken from Waller and Reise (2009); as those authors were studying the four-parameter model, population values of lower asymptotes for the simulations were obtained by taking one minus the estimated upper asymptotes from their results (many of their estimated lower asymptotes were near zero; note that which asymptote is upper or lower depends on a relatively arbitrary keying of the items).

To model the effects of item parameter estimation, every 100 simulee's trait values were estimated using item parameters estimated on a different 2,500-person calibration sample. In other words, 2,500 simulated responses were generated and used to estimate item parameters; these item parameters were used to estimate trait values from a different set of 100 randomly generated responses; this process was repeated 40 times for the 4,000 trait values to be estimated for each of the 13 trait values. Each 2,500-person calibration sample was assumed to come from a known population—i.e., item parameters from the 1PL and 2PL models were estimated on a zero-lower-asymptote population, and the 3PL item parameters were estimated on a nonzero-lower-asymptote population (to simulate the effects of experimentally modeling response processes). Ultimately, trait estimates were obtained for each of the 4,000 simulees using each of four models: the population 3PL model, the sample-estimated 3PL model, the sample-estimated two-parameter logistic (2PL) model (ignoring impression management), and the sample-estimated one-parameter logistic (1PL) model (again, ignoring impression management).

Figure 2 illustrates the results of these simulations. The top figure plots the bias of the estimates as a function of trait level; the middle figure plots the variance as a function of trait level, and the bottom figure plots overall MSE as a function of trait level. As is evident in the figure, in general, bias, variance, and overall MSE was smallest for moderate to large trait values, and larger for smaller trait values.

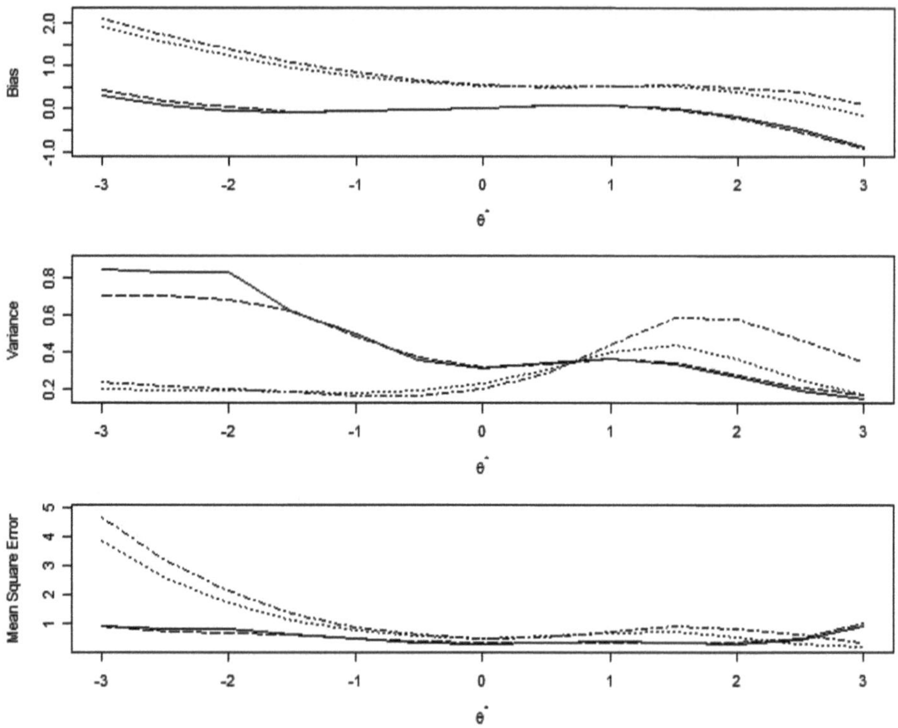

Fig. 2 Bias, variance, and MSE of trait estimates as a function of true trait level, for a population of individuals responding using impression management modeled by a three-parameter logistic (3PL) model, as described in the text. *Solid line* reflects trait estimates obtained using population 3PL item parameters; *dashed line*, trait estimates obtained using sample-estimated 3PL item parameters; *dashed* and *dotted line*, sample-estimated 2PL item parameters, and *dotted line*, sample-estimated 1PL item parameters

Also, in general, bias, variance, and MSE from the misspecified trait estimates were similar, as were those from the correctly specified estimates.

Consistent with what might be expected, trait estimates were more biased overall when using the incorrect 1PL and 2PL models for trait estimation, especially for smaller trait values. This is consistent with the idea that ignoring impression management would lead to increased bias in trait estimates. However, use of the correct impression management model also increases variance of the trait estimates relative to the incorrect models, especially at extreme trait levels. This increased variance offsets the decreased bias, leading to a scenario where for much of the range of the trait, the accuracy of trait estimates is extremely similar regardless of whether the correct or incorrect model is used. The incorrect model does produce less accurate estimates overall, especially for low levels of the trait. However, for moderate to high levels of the trait, the decrement in accuracy is slight.

2.4.2 The Intercept-Shift Model of Impression Management

Another possible account of impression management is the intercept-shift model. In this model, individuals utilizing impression management shift their thresholds for endorsing an item in a manner consistent with their impression management. For example, individuals engaging in positive impression management might raise their thresholds for endorsing socially undesirable items; individuals engaging in negative impression management might lower their thresholds for endorsing socially undesirable items. Multiple-group modeling in quasi-experimental designs suggests that this sort of intercept-shift model can account for at least some positive impression management (Ferrando and Anguiano-Carrasco 2009).

Simulations were again conducted in order to investigate the effects of model misspecification in this scenario (e.g., using the correct impression management model or ignoring it). Simulation conditions were the same as in the simulation study just described. In this study, however, impression management was modeled by a shift in intercept parameters relative to the normal response condition; the 2PL model was used in all conditions. Population parameters were based on the SNAP-2 (Clark et al. 1993) Negative Temperament scale, a 28-dichotomous-item measure of the tendency to experience negative emotions. Two-PL parameters of the SNAP-2 Negative Temperament scale in a general community sample (Simms et al. 2007) were used for the population normal response parameters. Impression management parameters were calculated using experimental estimates of the effect of impression management on the SNAP Negative Temperament scale (Simms and Clark 2001); each item's threshold was assumed to shift by an amount (in d units) equal to the corresponding observed shift in the Negative Temperament scale under impression management (i.e., each item's thresholds were assumed to shift by $1.56d$ in the negative impression management condition and $1.15d$ in the positive impression management condition).

Figure 3 illustrates the results of the simulations of positive impression management. Consistent with expectations, using the incorrect model resulted in downwardly biased estimates at higher (i.e., more pathological) levels of the trait—i.e., positive impression management resulted in estimates that were too low for high-trait individuals when the incorrect model was used. For low-trait individuals, the bias was actually reversed, such that low-trait individuals' estimates were somewhat too large. However, throughout the range of the trait, the variance of estimates was lower under the misspecified models compared to the true model, especially at lower trait levels. Overall MSE was generally greater when using the incorrect model, although this was primarily true of the upper range of the trait; for low-trait individuals the decrement in overall MSE was much less, and for moderately low trait values the misspecified model actually produced slightly more accurate estimates.

Figure 4 illustrates the results of simulating negative impression management. Again, consistent with expectations, using the incorrect model resulted in upwardly biased estimates throughout the range of the trait—i.e., negative impression management resulted in estimates that were generally too high (i.e., pathological) when

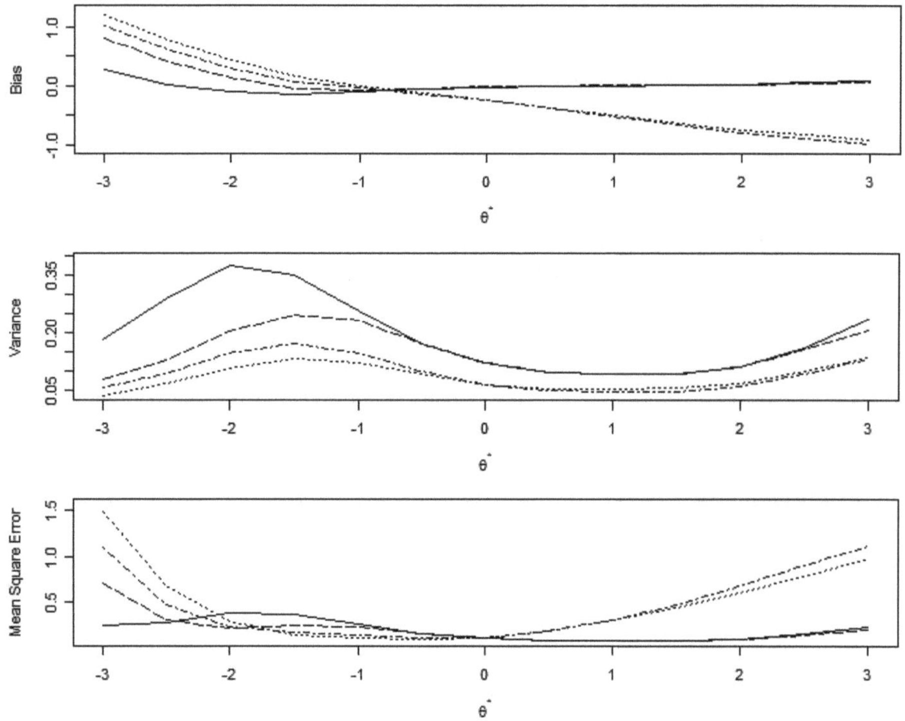

Fig. 3 Bias, variance, and MSE of trait estimates as a function of true trait level, for a population of individuals responding using positive impression management modeled by a two-parameter logistic (2PL) model, as described in the text. *Solid line* reflects trait estimates obtained using population item parameters; *dashed line*, trait estimates obtained using sample-estimated impression management item parameters; *dashed* and *dotted line*, sample-estimated 2PL normal response item parameters, and *dotted line*, sample-estimated 1PL normal response item parameters

the incorrect model was used. However, in contrast to the other two forms of impression management being simulated, the variance in estimates was generally similar across different models, although slightly greater for the incorrect models at lower trait levels, and slightly greater for the correct models at higher trait levels. Also, in contrast to the other forms of impression management, overall error was almost uniformly larger for the misspecified model, except for individuals at very high levels of the trait.

These three simulations are generally consistent with the findings for the continuous response model. Overall, misspecification does generally decrease the accuracy of estimates, at least for the cases examined here. However, these overall trends obscure the fact that, under particular circumstances, misspecification might not decrease estimation accuracy significantly, and might actually slightly improve estimates.

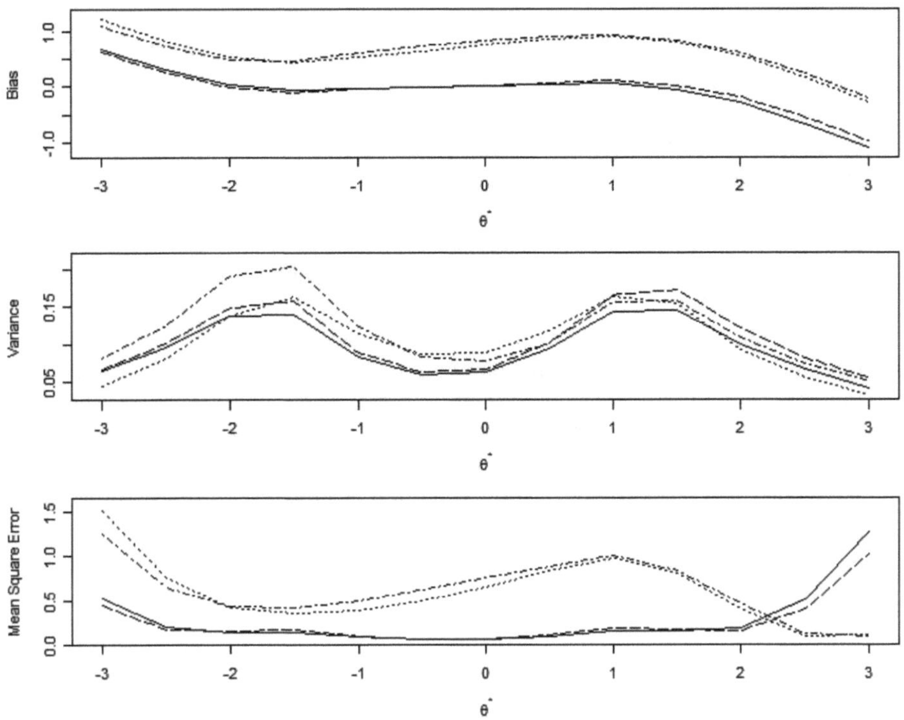

Fig. 4 Bias, variance, and MSE of trait estimates as a function of true trait level, for a population of individuals responding using negative impression management modeled by a two-parameter logistic (2PL) model, as described in the text. *Solid line* reflects trait estimates obtained using population item parameters; *dashed line*, trait estimates obtained using sample-estimated impression management item parameters; *dashed* and *dotted line*, sample-estimated 2PL normal response item parameters, and *dotted line*, sample-estimated 1PL normal response item parameters

For example, negative impression management of the form illustrated in Fig. 4 suggests that misspecification would result in decreased estimation accuracy in many scenarios. However, for settings where very high trait levels are encountered (e.g., in settings with high levels of psychopathology, such as hospital settings), ignoring the impression management might actually produce more accurate estimates. Moreover, for the other two forms of impression management being modeled, in samples having relatively low to moderate levels of the trait, ignoring the impression management might result in only a slight decrement in accuracy (in the case of the asymptote-shift form of impression management), or might actually improve accuracy slightly (in the case of the intercept-shift form of positive impression management).

Note that focusing entirely on the bias in responses (e.g., illustrated in the top of Figs. 2, 3, and 4), as is often the case in the literature, would give a misleading idea of how model misspecification affects estimation accuracy. In all three cases, the bias was generally larger under the misspecified model (albeit in different directions; Fig. 3). However, the variance was affected differently in the different scenarios, at different levels of the trait, producing more nuanced effects on actual estimation accuracy.

These phenomena may help explain some findings in the impression management literature, where effects of impression management on response can clearly be demonstrated, but use of this information to estimate trait values appears to have little impact on the validity of trait estimates (McGrath et al. 2010; Ziegler et al. 2012). It is possible that in certain cases, the form of impression management introduces so much uncertainty into trait estimation, that even if respondents were known with certainty to use impression management, overall trait estimation error would be relatively unaffected by making use of that information.

Considered together, these three simulations illustrate that use of a correct IRT model does not always improve estimation error, and may actually worsen it for certain individuals in certain circumstances. Even when use of a misspecified model increases bias, if it decreases the variance of the estimates sufficiently, it may decrease estimation error overall. Although in most cases, use of an incorrect response model will increase estimation error, in other cases—depending on the response process, test, and true value of the trait—using an incorrect model may have little effect on overall estimation error, or might in fact decrease it.

3 The Effects of Misspecification on Estimates of Precision

3.1 *Reliability*

Mellenbergh (1996) noted that the reliability of a test can be expressed in terms of the variance of the true trait values, the variance of the expected values of the estimates, and the expected variance of the estimates:

$$\rho = \frac{var(\theta^*)}{var\left[E\left[\widehat{\theta} \mid \theta^*, \gamma\right]\right] + E\left[\sigma^2\left(\widehat{\theta} \mid \theta^*, \gamma\right)\right]}. \tag{12}$$

In Eq. (12), ρ is the reliability and E again indicates the expectation (i.e., average). Reliability is the ratio of true trait variance to total trait estimate variance, where the total variance is the sum of the variance of the expected values of the estimates and the expected variance of the estimates conditional on the true trait values.

The reliability under misspecification can be obtained from Eq. (12) by noting that the expected value of the estimates conditional on trait value [the expectation in the first term in the denominator of Eq. (12)] is given by $\theta * + \beta$, where β is the bias [Eq. (5)]. Reinserting this gives reliability under misspecification:

$$\rho = \frac{var(\theta^*)}{var(\theta^*) + var\left(\beta \mid \theta^*, \gamma\right) + 2cov\left(\theta^*, \beta \mid \theta^*, \gamma\right) + E\left[\sigma^2\left(\widehat{\theta} \mid \theta^*, \gamma\right)\right]}. \tag{13}$$

Multiple consequences implied by Eq. (13) are worth noting. First, the reliability under misspecification depends on the variance of the bias across levels of the true trait value, not the absolute value of the bias. Most importantly, even if a test model is biased, if that bias is constant across different levels of the trait, it will not change reliability relative to a model that is completely unbiased. More accurately, even if an incorrectly specified model produces biased estimates relative to a correctly specified model, that bias will not affect reliability if the variance in bias across the population or sample of interest is the same as the variance in bias under the correctly specified model.

Initially, results such as those presented in Table 1 and Figs. 1, 2, 3, and 4 might seem to suggest that constant bias across the trait might be an unreasonable assumption. However, note that the variance involving bias in Eq. (13) applies to the trait distribution in the sample or population of interest, not the entire range of the trait. Moreover, even if the bias varies across the entire trait, if it varies similarly under misspecified and correct models, the reliability will be affected similarly. If the bias under a misspecified model is relatively constant within the population of interest—or does not vary more than the correctly specified model—it will not decrease reliability relative to a correctly specified model. In Fig. 2, for example, the bias under both the correct and misspecified model is relatively constant for trait values from 0 to 1; in a sample from that range, the reliability would be less affected by bias than a sample from elsewhere in the range of the trait where the bias varies more greatly.

A second notable consequence of Eq. (13) is that direction as well as magnitude of covariation between bias and trait level can substantially influence the observed variance in estimates, and therefore, the reliability. In particular, if the bias and latent trait negatively covary, the observed variance will decrease and the reliability will increase. In fact, if the covariance between the bias and trait is sufficiently negative, it might offset the other terms in Eq. (13) and produce a reliability greater than one. Similarly, if the bias and latent trait positively covary, the observed variance will increase and the reliability will decrease. In this way, the shape as well as variance of the bias also will affect reliability.

A final consequence implied by Eq. (13) is that the reliability under misspecification does depend on the absolute magnitude of the variance of the estimates. A decrease in variance under misspecification—as is illustrated in Figs. 2 and 3—will actually contribute to an increase in reliability.

In order to illustrate these phenomena, reliabilities were calculated under the three impression management scenarios illustrated in Figs. 1, 2, 3, and 4. In each case, the population of interest was assumed to have a trait distribution that was standard normal, and was assumed to be responding using one of the impression management scenarios illustrated in Figs. 1, 2, 3, and 4. Reliability was calculated for scores estimated using the correct population model as well for scores estimated an incorrect model, as described earlier and illustrated in the figures. Reliabilities were calculated in two ways: using Eq. (13), as well as directly using simulations. These new simulations were identical to those described earlier, except that 1,000 responses were generated from a standard normal population; the reliability was

Table 2 Reliabilities of estimates obtained using correct and incorrect models

	Analytic reliability estimates		Simulation reliability estimates	
Population model	Correct model	Incorrect model	Correct model	Incorrect model
Continuous, Model A	0.898	1.089	0.900	1.095
Continuous, Model B	0.919	0.762	0.890	0.738
Asymptote shift	0.713	1.082	0.757	1.058
Intercept shift: PIM	0.815	1.579	0.810	1.664
Intercept shift: NIM	0.782	0.978	0.857	1.099

Note: Analytic reliability estimates were obtained using Eq. (13) with values obtained from simulations whose results are illustrated in Figs. 2, 3, and 4. Reliabilities greater than one are discussed in the text. Simulation reliability estimates were calculated directly as the ratio of latent trait variance to observed estimate variance, using methods described in the text. PIM refers to positive impression management, NIM to negative impression management

calculated directly as the ratio of the latent trait variance to the observed estimate variance. For the continuous response models, the bias and variance functions were calculated directly using Eqs. (9) and (10). For the discrete response models, values used in Eq. (13) were derived from the previous simulations (e.g., Eq. (13) was calculated using the bias functions illustrated in Figs. 2, and 3).

Table 2 presents these reliabilities, for scores estimated using correct and incorrect models, for each of the impression management scenarios. The analytic estimates using Eq. (13) and the directly calculated reliabilities are similar, supporting the accuracy of Eq. (13).

Note that the reliabilities greater than one in Table 2 are not in error. The cases where this occurs involve scenarios in which an incorrect model is used and the bias is negatively related to the trait (compare with Table 1 and Figs. 2, 3, and 4). The negative covariance between the bias and the trait [Eq. (13)] decreases the observed variable variance to the point where the observed variance in estimates is actually less than the true trait variance, producing a reliability greater than one. For example, in the scenario where the normal-response 2PL model is incorrectly applied to a group of individuals responding under an asymptote-shift impression management model, the covariance between the bias and the trait in a standard normal population is approximately -0.201 and the variance in bias is 0.06, producing a variance in expected scores equal to 0.658; as the expected variance is 0.266, this produces an observed variable variance of approximately 0.924, and a reliability equal to 1.082. Note that in the one case where the bias of the incorrect model positively covaries with the trait ($\text{cov}(\theta^*, \beta) = 0.098$), in the case of continuous response population Model B, the reliabilities are less than one.

A related point important to emphasize about Table 2 is that the greater reliabilities under the incorrect models are not overestimates of the reliability—reliability is a property of a score or estimate, which will depend on the particular estimation model being used in addition to the test and sample. Although these examples illustrate that the reliability can provide a misleading sense of test precision when models are misspecified, it should be emphasized that the reliabilities under many of the incorrect models illustrated in the table are actually greater than the reliabilities under the correct models. That is, the ratio of the true trait variance to observed score variance will be greater when using an incorrect model in many settings.

3.2 *Information and Confidence Intervals*

Given that model misspecification can substantially impact the variance of estimates, it is important to determine how it impacts item or test information functions as summaries of measurement precision. A related, more general question is how misspecification affects indices of estimation precision, such as confidence intervals. Regardless of how the accuracy and precision of estimates are actually affected by misspecification, if that effect is represented well in indices of overall accuracy and precision, uncertainty due to misspecification can be quantified and used to make decisions based on the trait estimates. If, on the other hand, indices of overall accuracy and precision do not represent effects of misspecification well, it becomes difficult to know how to quantify uncertainty due to model misspecification and use it to make decisions.

3.2.1 Robust Information

A variety of authors (e.g., Freedman 2006; Huber 1967; Kent 1982; Vuong 1989; White 1982) have discussed estimates of information under misspecification. In the current setting, the information associated with an estimate of a single latent trait value from a very long test is given by

$$I_r\left(\widehat{\theta}\right) = \frac{H^2}{J} = \frac{\left[\sum lnP''\left(X_j\middle|\widehat{\theta}\right)\right]^2}{\sum\left[lnP'\left(X_j\middle|\widehat{\theta}\right)\right]^2}. \tag{14}$$

In Eq. (14), H is the sum of second derivatives of the log-likelihood across items, at the maximum likelihood estimate, and J is the sum of squared first derivatives of the log-likelihood at the same estimate (note that the derivatives are empirically observed values, not expected values under the model). The robust variance of the estimate at the maximum likelihood estimate is then given by $V_r = 1/I_r\left(\widehat{\theta}\right)$.

The robust information, I_r, is well known in the literature and holds asymptotically even when the model is misspecified. As many authors have noted, however, the robust information performs more poorly in scenarios involving small numbers of observations (e.g., in terms of confidence interval coverage or hypothesis tests), such as those scenarios typically encountered in psychological measurement. The robustness properties of I_r are asymptotic, for very large numbers of observations; in a psychological measurement scenario, this would correspond to very long tests that are rarely encountered in practice (e.g., tests that are 100s of items long). For this reason, it is unclear whether the robust information would be any more useful in typical psychological measurement scenarios than the assumed information under the misspecified model.

3.2.2 Simulations

Simulations were conducted in order to explore the accuracy of confidence intervals based on the robust information. Conditions were the same as in the previous simulations of impression management (i.e., the asymptote and intercept-shift models). Confidence intervals were created for each simulated trait estimate using two different estimators of information: the assumed model information and the robust information [Eq. (14)]. In all conditions, a nominal coverage of 0.95 was assumed, corresponding to an overall nominal 0.05 Type I error rate.

Results of these simulations are presented in Table 3. In interpreting the values in the tables, it is important to remember that sampling variation in item parameter estimates was included in simulations and therefore affected coverage.

Examining the results in Table 3, three broad trends become apparent. First, as would be predicted, intervals were generally, although not always, closer to nominal values for correctly specified models compared to incorrectly specified models. Second, intervals conditional on trait level varied substantially with trait level in terms of how close they were to nominal values. Finally, use of the assumed information generally, but again not always, produced confidence intervals that were closer to their nominal values than use of the robust information. However, actual coverage levels using robust information were not necessarily further from their nominal levels under misspecification, and differences between the different estimators were not large.

Overall, our results echo the conclusions of Freedman (2006), who argued that the possible benefits to be accrued from using robust information are likely small when weighed against the much larger effects of misspecification. In our results, use of the information under the assumed but possibly incorrect model performed approximately as well as the robust information, suggesting little difference between the two in practical use, especially given that the effects of misspecification could be large.

4 Important Areas of Inquiry

4.1 Model Averaged Estimates

Given the effects of misspecification demonstrated thus far, how might one obtain trait estimates and estimates of precision when there is uncertainty about the appropriate model? In general, two approaches have been developed: the model

Table 3 Actual confidence interval coverage using assumed and robust information

Model		True θ													
		−3.0	−2.5	−2.0	−1.5	−1.0	−0.5	0	0.5	1.0	1.5	2.0	2.5	3	Mean
NIM															
Incorrect	I	1.000	1.000	0.991	0.880	0.854	0.874	0.866	0.881	0.913	0.995	1.000	1.000	1.000	0.943
	I_r	1.000	1.000	0.994	0.904	0.922	0.951	0.942	0.925	0.918	0.992	1.000	1.000	1.000	0.965
Correct	I	1.000	1.000	0.997	0.907	0.886	0.895	0.883	0.886	0.916	0.995	1.000	1.000	1.000	0.951
	I_r	1.000	0.999	0.989	0.888	0.881	0.893	0.875	0.879	0.899	0.985	1.000	1.000	1.000	0.945
PIM															
Incorrect	I	1.000	1.000	1.000	0.990	0.944	0.938	0.941	0.939	0.943	0.941	0.943	0.930	0.939	0.957
	I_r	1.000	1.000	0.998	0.956	0.903	0.897	0.895	0.889	0.897	0.895	0.907	0.895	0.895	0.925
Correct	I	1.000	1.000	0.997	0.960	0.910	0.889	0.893	0.884	0.884	0.887	0.888	0.883	0.899	0.921
	I_r	0.999	0.995	0.981	0.883	0.873	0.851	0.861	0.861	0.858	0.860	0.856	0.847	0.835	0.889
ASIM															
Incorrect	I	0.867	0.860	0.873	0.871	0.870	0.880	0.884	0.899	0.898	0.882	1.000	1.000	1.000	0.906
	I_r	0.930	0.914	0.911	0.903	0.884	0.887	0.882	0.890	0.871	0.877	0.983	1.000	1.000	0.918
Correct	I	0.967	0.939	0.932	0.907	0.888	0.881	0.865	0.878	0.913	0.987	0.999	1.000	1.000	0.935
	I_r	0.925	0.897	0.887	0.856	0.850	0.855	0.853	0.875	0.886	0.954	0.990	1.000	1.000	0.910

Note: Values are median actual coverage (for a nominal 0.95 confidence interval) as a function of true latent trait value, assumed model (correct or incorrect), population model (asymptote-shift model or negative or positive impression management under intercept-shift model; ASIM, NIM, and PIM, respectively), and variance estimation method (using information under assumed model, I, or robust information assuming a normal sampling distribution, I_r)

selection approach and the model averaging approach (Buckland et al. 1997; Claeskens and Hjort 2008; Draper 1995). The model selection approach is relatively standard in the psychometric and assessment literature: in this approach to model uncertainty, one attempts to identify the optimal model for a given respondent, based on model selection statistics or appropriateness indices, and use that optimal model to estimate or make other inferences about trait level (a common variant of the model selection approach is to identify individuals for whom a desired model is inappropriate or less optimal, and not make inferences about their trait level).

The model averaging approach, in contrast, is a relatively novel approach to handling model uncertainty in assessment settings. In this approach, multiple trait estimates are obtained for each respondent, using the different models under consideration, and are averaged, weighting each estimate by the optimality of the corresponding models. Specifically, the model averaged estimate, $\tilde{\theta}$, is given by

$$\tilde{\theta} = \sum w_m \widehat{\theta}_m, \tag{15}$$

where w_m is some index of the relative optimality of model m for the respondent (e.g., a value of a person-fit or model selection statistic) and $\widehat{\theta}_m$ is the estimate obtained with model m. Usually the weights w_m are scaled so that they sum to one.

Model averaging offers a number of potential benefits over a model selection approach to handling modeling uncertainty in trait estimation. First and perhaps most importantly, research suggests that model averaging reliably improves the accuracy of estimates under conditions of model uncertainty (Burnham and Anderson 2004). This can be explained intuitively by noting that in a model selection approach, there will be errors of model selection, which will increase the variability of estimates. By weighting estimates under different models in a way that is inversely proportional to the risk of error, and then averaging, the variability of estimates due to selection error is decreased. This can also be seen by noting that a model selection approach is equivalent to a model averaging approach where unit weights are used in the latter (i.e., w_m is 1 for the best fitting model and 0 for all other models). Although this might be appropriate in certain settings, such weights will overstate the certainty of model selection in many cases, underestimating the effect of model selection errors on estimation variance (Leeb and Pötscher 2005).

Another advantage to model averaging is that it allows one to incorporate model uncertainty into indices of trait estimate uncertainty (e.g., in quantifying measurement information or calculating confidence intervals). Just as sampling variation contributes one source of uncertainty about trait level, model uncertainty contributes another. Rather than conceptualizing model misspecification as a problem requiring identification of misfitting response profiles, treating them as misfitting or not, one can instead assume that model uncertainty is part of the trait estimation process, and incorporate it into indices of estimation error.

Initial simulation results, not reported here, are consistent with previous research in suggesting that, in cases of model uncertainty, incorporating that uncertainty into estimates and associated confidence intervals through the use of model averaging produces more accurate estimates than if one used model selection to identify a best model to use for estimation. Model averaging accounts for errors in the model selection process by weighing different models by their likelihood of being optimal, thereby "hedging" estimates against different models. Further research is needed to verify these results and understand how different model averaging approaches perform.

4.2 *Bayesian Estimation*

Throughout this paper, we have assumed that trait estimates are obtained through maximum likelihood inference. One important question is how the conclusions drawn here might generalize to trait estimates obtained through Bayesian inference, which is increasingly being used in a number of assessment settings.

Some of the phenomena illustrated here are likely to generalize in a straightforward way to the Bayesian case. Bunke and Milhaud (1998), for example, demonstrated that under very general conditions, under misspecification, Bayesian estimates will converge to the same expected value as the maximum likelihood estimate [Eq. (2)], and will have a variance similar in form to the inverse of the robust information [Eq. (14); the exact form depends on the specific type of Bayesian estimator]. These results apply asymptotically, however, for very large tests, and it is unclear how they would generalize to finite samples of observations, with smaller tests. Bayesian inference itself can be seen as a form of estimation in which a potential bias is induced (through the prior; e.g., Bickel and Blackwell 1967) in order to reduce variance, raising further questions about the small-sample bias, variance, and error of Bayesian estimates under model misspecification.

Model averaged estimates, similarly, are formulated naturally within a Bayesian paradigm. In the case of Bayesian estimation, model averaged estimates are obtained by integrating the likelihood over the posterior distribution of the model, which itself can be decomposed into priors involving the model and its parameters and another likelihood (Draper 1995; Hoeting et al. 1999; Walker et al. 2001). How to integrate model uncertainty into Bayesian trait estimation, especially in applications such as computerized adaptive testing, is an important area for future inquiry. Questions about choices of priors, the form of Bayesian estimation, and how to integrate uncertainty into Bayesian adaptive testing design all require additional investigation.

4.3 *Random Model Misspecification and Multiparameter Models*

Random model misspecification is another critical area for future inquiry. The scenarios examined here reflected fixed forms of model misspecification, where the form of misspecification was the same for all individuals. Although this simplifies exploration of phenomena, it is likely unrealistic in many settings, where the degree of misspecification will likely vary randomly across individuals (due to, e.g., group or idiographic factors). Relatedly, many models will include multiple parameters, including parameters representing possible sources of misspecification—impression management or response style parameters, for example.

Various authors have explored the effects of model uncertainty in these settings. Claeskens and Hjort (2008; also Hjort and Claeskens 2003), for example, focus on the multiparameter setting, as do Liang et al. (2011). Results similar to those discussed here are obtained in the multiparameter case, but generally incorporate the effects of estimating one nuisance parameter on the parameter of interest (e.g., the effects of estimating an impression management parameter on estimation of a trait parameter).

5 Summary and Recommendations for Applied Assessment Settings

Model misspecification and uncertainty is an important issue arising in a number of measurement and assessment settings. Here, we have attempted to clarify the role of model misspecification in psychological measurement by addressing the effect of misspecification and uncertainty on the psychometric properties of estimates. Although model misspecification will often negatively impact estimates, its effects can be unintuitive and complex, helping to explain certain findings in the literature. We conclude by offering recommendations for applied assessment settings.

5.1 Consider Total Error, Including Variance as Well as Bias Effects, of Misspecified Models

It is our sense that the applied literature on misspecification has focused much more extensively on bias effects than variance effects, which can be misleading given that overall error is a function of both. There are various examples of this focus on bias in the literature (Meade 2010; Nye and Drasgow 2011). One explanation for this focus might be a seemingly reasonable but incorrect assumption that the form of misspecification will directly parallel its effects on estimation accuracy and precision. For example, it is tempting to assume that misspecification limited to a location shift (e.g., a shift in intercepts or thresholds) will result solely in a shift in expected values of estimates (i.e., bias). Although this might be true under certain circumstances (e.g., for continuous normal responses), the current results indicate that this will often not be the case (e.g., Fig. 3).

This is not to suggest bias effects can or should be ignored—intuitively, and as evidenced by the results presented here, bias can exert powerful effects on overall estimation error. Also, in certain settings where the effects of location shifts are amplified, bias effects might predominate. For example, in classification or selection settings, even if overall estimation error is similar using correct and incorrect models, if it is increased in the range of the classification or selection threshold, bias effects might exert strong effects (cf. Kalohn and Spray 1999).

As demonstrated here, variance effects of misspecification can substantially influence the overall error of estimates, either increasing or decreasing error. For this reason, we recommend that test users remain mindful of variance as well as bias effects of misspecification in test scoring, trait estimation, and interpretation.

5.2 *Explicitly Determine Misspecification Effects in a Given Setting*

Relatedly, we recommend that effects of misspecification on estimation accuracy and precision be explicitly determined when issues related to model uncertainty are important. In the case of continuous responses, equations presented here [Eqs. (3)–(10)] can be used to quantify the effects of misspecification on MSE; in the case of discrete responses, simulations could be used. If MSE is an undesirable index of estimation accuracy for a particular application, other indices (e.g., median absolute difference) could also be used (Heskes 1998; James 2003). Explicitly delineating misspecification effects is important because they can be unintuitive or complex, depending on the form of misspecification, the probability (e.g., base rate) of misspecification, and true trait level. Characterizing the most likely effects of misspecification can help prevent errors in interpretation and apparent paradoxes regarding misspecification.

One important possible example is provided by recent literature on the validity of impression management indices (McGrath et al. 2010). It is often assumed in that literature that indices of impression management should moderate the validity of trait estimates, such that estimates associated with greater values of such indices should be less valid. However, one important implication of the results obtained here [e.g., Eq. (13)] is that this assumption can be false: indices of model misspecification (e.g., validity scales) may not moderate criterion-related validity of test scores, even if model misspecification exists and negatively affects accuracy and precision.

For instance, consider an estimate of the bias, $\widehat{\beta}$, obtained through a validity scale or other index. As this estimate becomes more accurate, if one conditions on it, the variance in bias and the covariance between the bias and the trait will, by definition, go to zero. Examining Eq. (13), it becomes apparent that this will actually remove the component of the observed score variance due to bias, leaving only the true variance and expected error variance in trait estimates at each level of the estimated bias. If these two components of variance do not change across different levels of bias, $\widehat{\beta}$ will not moderate the validity of the estimates. In fact, if variance decreases with misspecification (e.g., as in Fig. 3), $\widehat{\beta}$ might moderate validity in the opposite direction, such that conditioning on $\widehat{\beta}$ becomes associated with more valid estimates. In fact, in this case, one would predict more accurate estimates of bias (e.g., more valid validity scales) to increase conditional validity even more. Similarly, in the case that error variance does not change across levels of bias, any moderation effect would decrease with more accurate estimates of bias.

The purpose of this example is not to weigh on the utility of impression management indices: many other issues regarding their validity and utility have been discussed (McGrath et al. 2010; Ziegler et al. 2012). However, the example does illustrate that misspecification effects can be unintuitive, and illustrate the importance of explicitly delineating these effects when model uncertainty is a concern.

Acknowledgment We would like to thank Katherine Jonas for her helpful comments on drafts of this manuscript.

Appendix

Throughout the appendix, to simplify notation, the trait estimate conditional on the true trait value and model parameters, $\left(\widehat{\theta} \mid \theta^*, \gamma\right)$, will be written as $\widehat{\theta}$. As noted in the text, the variance of the trait estimate can then be written as

$$\sigma^2 = E\left[\left(\widehat{\theta} - E\left[\widehat{\theta}\right]\right)^2\right] = E\left[\widehat{\theta}^2\right] - E\left[\widehat{\theta}\right]^2. \tag{16}$$

Let

$$f = \frac{\sum a_j\left[a_j^*\theta_i^* + \left(b_j^* - b_j\right)\right]/\psi_j^2}{\sum a_j^2/\psi_j^2} \quad \text{and} \quad g = \frac{\sum\left[a_j e_{ij}^*\right]/\psi_j^2}{\sum a_j^2/\psi_j^2}. \tag{17}$$

Then, following Mellenbergh (1994b), page 231, and substituting $a_j^*\theta_i^* + b_j^* + e_{ij}^*$ for x_{ij} in Eq. (7), one has $\widehat{\theta} = f + g$, and $E\left[\widehat{\theta}\right] = E[f+g] = E[f] + E[g]$. However, assuming that the mean true error e_{ij}^* is zero, the second term, E[g], equals zero, so $E\left[\widehat{\theta}\right] = E[f] = f$ [Eq. (8)]. Substituting back into Eq. (16), one has

$$\sigma^2 = E\left[(f+g)^2\right] - f^2 = E\left[f^2 + 2fg + g^2\right] - f^2 = E\left[f^2\right] + E[2fg] + E\left[g^2\right] - f^2. \tag{18}$$

However, if the expected true error e_{ij}^* is zero, the second term on the rightmost side is zero, and the first and last terms cancel, leaving E[g^2]:

$$\sigma^2 = E\left[g^2\right] = E\left[\frac{\left[\sum\left[a_j e_{ij}^*\right]/\psi_j^2\right]^2}{\left[\sum a_j^2/\psi_j^2\right]^2}\right]. \tag{19}$$

The denominator in the expectation can be treated as a constant. The numerator in the expectation expands to

$$\left[\sum\left[a_j e_{ij}^*\right]/\psi_j^2\right]^2 = \frac{a_1^2}{\left(\psi_1^2\right)^2}e_{i1}^{*\,2} + \frac{a_j^2}{\left(\psi_j^2\right)^2}e_{ij}^{*\,2} + \frac{a_1}{\psi_1^2}\frac{a_j}{\psi_j^2}e_{i1}^* e_{ij}^* + \cdots. \tag{20}$$

However, with uncorrelated errors, all the multiplicative terms [represented by the last term in Eq. (20)] equal zero in expectation. This gives

$$\begin{aligned} E\left[\left[\sum\left[a_j e_{ij}^*\right]/\psi_j^2\right]^2\right] &= E\left[\frac{a_1^2}{\left(\psi_1^2\right)^2}e_{i1}^{*\,2}\right] + E\left[\frac{a_j^2}{\left(\psi_j^2\right)^2}e_{ij}^{*\,2}\right] + \ldots \\ &= \frac{a_1^2}{\left(\psi_1^2\right)^2}E\left[e_{i1}^{*\,2}\right] + \frac{a_j^2}{\left(\psi_j^2\right)^2}E\left[e_{ij}^{*\,2}\right] + \cdots. \end{aligned} \tag{21}$$

Note, though, that $\psi{*}_j^2 = E[(e_{ij}^* - E[e_{ij}^*])^2] = E[e_{ij}^{*2}] - E[e_{ij}^*]^2$. Assuming the mean of the errors is zero, this implies $\psi{*}_j^2 = E[e_{ij}^{*2}]$. Substituting this back into Eq. (21), and combining with Eq. (19), this gives

$$\sigma^2 = \frac{\sum \frac{a_j^2}{\psi_j^2}\frac{\psi{*}_j^2}{\psi_j^2}}{\left[\sum \frac{a_j^2}{\psi_j^2}\right]^2}.$$

References

Akaike, H. (1973). Information theory and an extension of the likelihood principle. In B. N. Petrov & F. Csaki (Eds.), *Proceedings of the second international symposium of information theory* (pp. 267–281). Budapest: Akademiai Kiado.

Baer, R. A., & Miller, J. (2002). Underreporting of psychopathology on the MMPI-2: A meta-analytic review. *Psychological Assessment, 14*, 16–26.

Bartholomew, D. J., & Knott, M. (1999). *Latent variable models and factor analysis*. London: Arnold.

Bartlett, M. S. (1937). The statistical conception of mental factors. *British Journal of Psychology, 3*, 77–85.

Bickel, P., & Blackwell, D. (1967). A note on Bayes estimates. *Annals of Mathematical Statistics, 38*, 1907–1911.

Borsboom, D., Mellenbergh, G. J., & van Heerden, J. (2003). The theoretical status of latent variables. *Psychological Review, 110*, 203–219. doi:10.1037/0033-295X.110.2.203.

Borsboom, D., Romeijn, J., & Wicherts, J. M. (2008). Measurement invariance versus selection invariance: Is fair selection possible? *Psychological Methods, 13*, 75–98. doi:10.1037/1082-989X.13.2.75.

Buckland, S. T., Burnham, K. P., & Augustin, N. H. (1997). Model selection: An integral part of inference. *Biometrics, 53*, 603–618.

Bunke, O., & Milhaud, X. (1998). Asymptotic behavior of Bayes estimates under possibly incorrect models. *Annals of Statistics, 26*, 617–644.

Burnham, K. P., & Anderson, D. R. (2004). Multimodel inference: Understanding AIC and BIC in model selection. *Sociological Methods & Research, 33*, 261–304. doi:10.1177/0049124104268644.

Claeskens, G., & Hjort, N. L. (2008). *Model selection and model averaging*. Cambridge: Cambridge University Press.

Clark, L. A. (1993). *Schedule for nonadaptive and adaptive personality (SNAP). Manual for administration, scoring, and interpretation*. Minneapolis: University of Minnesota Press.

Clark, L. A., Simms, L. J., Wu, K. D., & Casillas, A. (1993). *Schedule for Nonadaptive and Adaptive Personality—Second edition* (*SNAP-2*). Minneapolis: University of Minnesota Press.

Draper, D. (1995). Assessment and propagation of model uncertainty. *Journal of the Royal Statistical Society: Series B (Statistical Methodology), 57*, 45–97.

Ferrando, P. J., & Anguiano-Carrasco, C. (2009). Assessing the impact of faking on binary personality measures: An IRT-based multiple-group factor analytic procedure. *Multivariate Behavioral Research, 44*, 497–524.

Forster, M. R. (2000). Key concepts in model selection: Performance and generalizability. *Journal of Mathematical Psychology, 44*, 205–231. doi:10.1006/jmps.1999.1284.

Freedman, D. A. (2006). On the so-called "Huber sandwich estimator" and "robust standard errors". *The American Statistician, 60*, 299–302.

Gustafson, P. (2001). On measuring sensitivity to parametric model misspecification. *Journal of the Royal Statistical Society, Series B: Statistical Methodology, 63*, 81–94.

Hendrawan, I., Glas, C. A. W., & Meijer, R. R. (2005). The effect of person misfit on classification decisions. *Applied Psychological Measurement, 29*, 26–44. doi:10.1177/0146621604270902.

Hero, A. O., Fessler, J. A., & Usman, M. (1996). Exploring estimator bias-variance tradeoffs using the uniform CR bound. *IEEE Transactions on Signal Processing, 44*, 2026–2041.

Heskes, T. (1998). Bias/variance decompositions for likelihood-based estimators. *Neural Computation, 10*, 1425–1433. doi:10.1162/089976698300017232.

Hjort, N., & Claeskens, G. (2003). Frequentist model average estimators. *Journal of the American Statistical Association, 98*, 879–899.

Hoeting, J. A., Madigan, D., Raftery, A. E., & Volinsky, C. T. (1999). Bayesian model averaging: A tutorial. *Statistical Science, 14*, 382–417.

Huber, P. J. (1967). The behavior of maximum likelihood estimates under nonstandard conditions. In L. M. Le Cam & J. Neyman (Eds.), *Proceedings of the fifth Berkeley symposium on mathematical statistics and probability* (Statistics, Vol. 1, pp. 221–233). Berkeley: University of California Press.

James, G. M. (2003). Variance and bias for general loss functions. *Machine Learning, 51*, 115–135.

Kalohn, J. C., & Spray, J. A. (1999). The effect of model misspecification on classification decisions made using a computerized test. *Journal of Educational Measurement, 36*, 47–59.

Kent, J. T. (1982). Robust properties of likelihood ratio tests. *Biometrika, 69*, 19–27.

Leeb, H., & Pötscher, B. M. (2005). Model selection and inference: Facts and fiction. *Econometric Theory, 21*, 21–59. doi:10.1017/S0266466605050036.

Liang, H., Zou, G., Wan, A. T. K., & Zhang, X. (2011). Optimal weight choice for frequentist model average estimators. *Journal of the American Statistical Association, 106*, 1053–1066.

Loken, E., & Rulison, K. L. (2010). Estimation of a four-parameter item response theory model. *British Journal of Mathematical and Statistical Psychology, 63*, 509–525. doi:10.1348/000711009X474502.
Lord, F. M. (1983). Unbiased estimators of ability parameters, of their variance, and of their parallel-forms reliability. *Psychometrika, 48*, 233–245.
Lowerre, J. M. (1974). On the mean square error of parameter estimates for some biased estimators. *Technometrics, 16*, 461–464.
McGrath, R. E., Mitchell, M., Kim, B. H., & Hough, L. (2010). Evidence for response bias as a source of error variance in applied assessment. *Psychological Bulletin, 136*, 450–470. doi:10.1037/a0019216.
Meade, A. W. (2010). A taxonomy of effect size measures for the differential functioning of items and scales. *Journal of Applied Psychology, 95*, 728–743. doi:10.1037/a0018966.
Meijer, R. R. (2003). Diagnosing item score patterns on a test using item response theory-based person-fit statistics. *Psychological Methods, 8*, 72–87. doi:10.1037/1082-989X.8.1.72.
Mellenbergh, G. J. (1994a). Generalized linear item response theory. *Psychological Bulletin, 115*, 300–307.
Mellenbergh, G. J. (1994b). A unidimensional latent trait model for continuous item responses. *Multivariate Behavioral Research, 29*, 223–236.
Mellenbergh, G. J. (1996). Measurement precision in test score and item response models. *Psychological Methods, 1*, 293–299.
Meredith, W. (1993). Measurement invariance, factor analysis and factorial invariance. *Psychometrika, 58*, 525–543.
Millsap, R. E. (1997). Invariance in measurement and prediction: Their relationship in the single-factor case. *Psychological Methods, 2*, 248–260.
Millsap, R. E. (2007). Invariance in measurement and prediction revisited. *Psychometrika, 72*, 461–473.
Millsap, R. E., & Everson, H. T. (1993). Methodology review: Statistical approaches for assessing measurement bias. *Applied Psychological Measurement, 17*, 297–334.
Molenaar, P. C. M. (2004). A manifesto on psychology as idiographic science: Bringing the person back into scientific psychology, this time forever. *Measurement: Interdisciplinary Research & Perspective, 2*, 201–218. doi:10.1207/s15366359mea0204_1.
Moustaki, I., & Knott, M. (2000). Generalized latent trait models. *Psychometrika, 65*, 391–411.
Mungas, D., Widaman, K. F., & Reed, B. R. (2011). Measurement invariance of neuropsychological tests in diverse older persons. *Neuropsychology, 25*, 260–269.
Nye, C. D., & Drasgow, F. (2011). Effect size indices for analyses of measurement equivalence: Understanding the practical importance of differences between groups. *Journal of Applied Psychology, 96*, 966–980. doi:10.1037/a0022955.
Rao, P. (1971). Some notes on misspecification in multiple regressions. *The American Statistician, 25*, 37–39.
Reise, S. P., Smith, L., & Furr, R. M. (2001). Invariance on the NEO PI-R neuroticism scale. *Multivariate Behavioral Research, 36*, 83–110. doi:10.1207/S15327906MBR3601_04.
Roznowski, M., & Reith, J. (1999). Examining the measurement quality of tests containing differentially functioning items: Do biased items result in poor measurement? *Educational and Psychological Measurement, 59*, 248–269.
Simms, L. J., & Clark, L. A. (2001). Detection of deception on the schedule for nonadaptive and adaptive personality: Validation of the validity scales. *Assessment, 8*, 251–266. doi:10.1177/107319110100800302.
Simms, L. J., Turkheimer, E., & Clark, L. A. (2007). *Novel approaches to the structure of personality disorder*. Symposium presented at the 21st annual meeting of the society for research in psychopathology, Iowa City.
Skrondal, A., & Rabe-Hesketh, S. (2004). *Generalized latent variable modeling: Multilevel, longitudinal, and structural equation models*. Boca Raton: Chapman & Hall/CRC.
Thissen, D., & Wainer, H. (1990). Confidence envelopes for item response theory. *Journal of Educational Statistics, 15*, 113–128.

Todros, K., & Tabrikian, J. (2011). Uniformly best biased estimators in non-Bayesian parameter estimation. *IEEE Transactions on Information Theory, 57*, 7635–7647. doi:10.1109/TIT.2011.2159958.

Tsutakawa, R. K., & Johnson, J. C. (1990). The effect of uncertainty of item parameter estimation on ability estimates. *Psychometrika, 55*, 371–390.

von Eye, A. (2004). The treasures of Pandora's box. *Measurement: Interdisciplinary Research and Perspectives, 2*, 244–247.

Vuong, Q. H. (1989). Likelihood ratio tests for model selection and non-nested hypotheses. *Econometrica, 57*, 307–333.

Wainer, H., & Thissen, D. (1987). Estimating ability with the wrong model. *Journal of Educational Statistics, 12*, 339–368.

Walker, S. G., Gutierrez-Pena, E., & Muliere, P. (2001). A decision theoretic approach to model averaging. *Journal of the Royal Statistical Society. Series D (The Statistician), 50*, 31–39.

Waller, N. G., & Reise, S. P. (2009). Measuring psychopathology with non-standard IRT models: Fitting the four parameter model to the MMPI. In S. Embretson & J. S. Roberts (Eds.), *New directions in psychological measurement with model-based approaches* (pp. 147–173). Washington, DC: American Psychological Association.

White, H. (1982). Maximum likelihood estimation of misspecified models. *Econometrica, 50*, 1–25.

Xu, W., Baggeroer, A. B., & Bell, K. L. (2004). A bound on mean-square estimation error with background parameter mismatch. *IEEE Transactions on Information Theory, 50*, 621–632. doi:10.1109/TIT.2004.825023.

Yang, J. S., Hansen, M., & Cai, L. (2012). Characterizing sources of uncertainty in item response theory scale scores. *Educational and Psychological Measurement, 72*(2), 264–290.

Zhang, J., Xie, M., Song, X., & Lu, T. (2011). Investigating the impact of uncertainty about item parameters on ability estimation. *Psychometrika, 76*, 97–118.

Ziegler, M., MacCann, C., & Roberts, R. D. (Eds.). (2012). *New perspectives on faking in personality assessment*. New York: Oxford University Press.

A State Space Approach to Modeling IRT and Population Parameters from a Long Series of Test Administrations

Richard G. Wanjohi, Peter W. van Rijn, and Alina A. von Davier

1 Introduction

In certain standardized educational assessments, there are many administrations of test forms of the same assessment over a specific period. The issue of equating these test forms from long series of test administrations is complicated, because the statistical properties of the items and the student populations can be volatile. Populations of test takers are always changing over time. For example, testing companies can target new groups or countries as to expand their business, where the ability level of these new groups can be quite different from the current group of test takers. In addition, external influences can have serious effects. For instance, if, at a certain point in time, a test is accredited for some sort of certification by a government, this can have a major and direct influence on the population of test takers. In addition, test preparation can become more and more popular, which can lead to increased scores. Most of the techniques and methodologies for equating are, however, assuming stable statistical properties for items, student population, or both. In addition, most equating techniques are concerned with relatively few forms to be equated (in the simplest case, there are two). The framework that we use for equating long series of test administrations is based on item response theory (IRT). The first step, then, is to estimate the parameters of an appropriate IRT model. If the test forms contain common items, then concurrent calibration procedures can be used to

R.G. Wanjohi (✉)
University of Arkansas, Fayetteville, AR, USA
e-mail: rwanjohi@uark.edu

P.W. van Rijn
ETS Global, Princeton, NJ, USA
e-mail: pvanrijn@ets.org

A.A. von Davier
Educational Testing Service, Princeton, NJ, USA
e-mail: avondavier@ets.org

R.E. Millsap et al. (eds.), *New Developments in Quantitative Psychology*, Springer Proceedings in Mathematics & Statistics 66, DOI 10.1007/978-1-4614-9348-8_8,

estimate the IRT model parameters. If the number of administrations becomes large, the model parameters might have drifted gradually over time or broken from their initial distribution. This may occur for any number of reasons, including changes in institutional arrangements, economics, or policy, or, more seriously, breaches of security and mistakes in test development. Drift in the model parameters is an important aspect to consider in equating long series of test forms, because, if it is ignored, it can seriously impact the scores of the test takers. Therefore, there is a need to develop methodology to detect such drift, so that it can be addressed quickly.

Commonly used quality control techniques in the field of educational testing have mainly focused on the detection of changes or drift in item parameters in the context of computerized adaptive testing (Veerkamp and Glas 2000; Glas 2000). These techniques include straightforward and effective visual inspection charts like the Shewhart control and cumulative sum (CUSUM) charts (Glas 1998). The use of such techniques in the context of equating large numbers of test forms can be limited. In particular, the standard CUSUM charts that have been used in educational measurement do not work well if the variables of interest exhibit correlation over time, even at low levels (VanBrackle and Reynolds 1997). Time series techniques are more suited to deal with such correlations and, therefore, will be used in the present paper.

In recent years, researchers have considered monitoring the distributions of various variables over a long series of test administrations (Li et al. 2011). Some of these variables are means and variances of the scaled and raw scores, means and variances of IRT parameters, IRT linking parameters, automated and human scoring data, and background variables (Keller and Keller 2011; Brinkhuis and Maris 2009). Li et al. (2011) monitored the distribution of the mean scaled scores using autoregressive integrated moving average (ARIMA) models. However, they assumed that the distribution of test takers' ability is stationary over time. There is a need to develop fast, flexible, and effective procedures to monitor the variables of interest over time and capture any unusual patterns in these large data streams in real time. For example, in the context of monitoring scale scores, Lee and von Davier (in press) discuss quality control charts and time series techniques, and von Davier (2012) provides an overview including data mining techniques.

We will demonstrate the use of state space modeling techniques to model IRT characteristics in the context of equating long series of test forms. In our approach, the item parameters from the 2-parameter logistic model (2PLM) are combined with population parameters from a Gaussian distribution (van Rijn et al. 2010). In this paper, we will focus on sudden breaks (change points or jumps), trends, seasonal effects, and outliers in the population means in this model, but the methodology can be applied to other parameters in the model as well (e.g., the item parameters or the population variance). In our case, however, the estimated population means from each administration serve as input for the state space model.

The outline of the present paper is as follows. First, the 2PLM and state space model for the population means are discussed. Next, models for breaks, trends, seasonal effects, and outliers in the population means are introduced. Then, we illustrate our approach through three different examples with simulated data. The paper ends with a discussion.

2 IRT and State Space Models

IRT models and their estimation are described in Lord and Novick (1968), van der Linden and Hambleton (1997), and Rao and Sinharay (2007). In the 2PLM, the probability of a correct answer to dichotomous item j is modeled as follows (Birnbaum 1968)

$$P(x_j = 1|\theta) = \frac{1}{1+\exp(-a_j(\theta - b_j))} \tag{1}$$

where a_j is an item discrimination parameter, b_j is an item difficulty parameter, and θ is the unobserved ability level. We assume that ability θ is normally distributed with mean μ and variance σ^2. In addition, we assume that there exists a series of T test administrations where a different population mean is assumed for each administration and that both item and population parameters can be calibrated concurrently through a linking design by means of marginal maximum likelihood estimation (see Li et al. 2011). In this paper, we will focus on the population means, and we denote the series of estimated populations $\hat{\mu}_t$ by y_t for $t = 1,\ldots,T$, so that we can retain straightforward notation for the state space model. However, whenever an item is used in multiple administrations, its parameters can be inspected for drift by the state space methods discussed next.

State space models provide an effective basis for practical time series analysis and forecasting. They are used in a wide range of fields including statistics, econometrics, genetics, and engineering (Lindquist and Picci 1981; West and Harrison 1997; Durbin and Koopman 2001). A state space model involves two processes: the observation process and the unobserved state process. The state-space approach to time series modeling focuses attention on the state vector process of a system, because the state vector contains all relevant information required to describe the system under investigation.

In our case, the observation process is the univariate series of estimated population means y_t, $t = 1,\ldots,T$ which are related to an unobserved state vector α_t of dimension p through an observation equation. Although we assume that we obtain this mean from the estimation of a general linear mixed model, this is not strictly necessary to specify a time series model. That is, simple estimated means from the scaled scores derived from equating techniques other than concurrent calibration can also serve as input. The dynamics of the state vector are captured in the state equation, and the state vector can contain different elements depending on the dynamic model that is used. Both equations can be given by

$$y_t = f(\alpha_t, v_t, \psi), \quad \text{(observationequation)} \tag{2}$$

$$\alpha_t = g(\alpha_{t-1}, w_t, \phi), \quad \text{(stateequation)} \tag{3}$$

where f and g are known functions, v_t and w_t are independent error sequences, and ψ and ϕ are vectors of unknown parameters in the model.

2.1 Linear State Space Models

Linear Gaussian state space models are also referred to as dynamic linear models (DLMs). In a DLM, the functions f and g are linear functions, and the distributions of the error sequences are assumed to be Gaussian. For our case, a DLM can be specified as follows

$$y_t = F_t\alpha_t + v_t, \quad v_t \sim N(0, V_t), \tag{4}$$

$$\alpha_t = G_t\alpha_{t-1} + w_t, \quad w_t \sim N(0, W_t). \tag{5}$$

where F_t and G_t are known design and transition matrices of order $1 \times p$ and $p \times p$, respectively, and v_t and w_t are two independent sequences of independent Gaussian random vectors with mean zero and known variance matrices V_t and W_t, respectively.

2.2 Particular Cases of the Linear State Space Model

We will make use of the three instances of the linear state space model to accommodate breaks, trends, and seasonality in the series of population means: the random walk plus noise model, the linear trend model, and

(i) The random walk model plus noise model, or *local level model*, can be denoted as

$$\begin{aligned} \mu_t &= \alpha_t + v_t, \quad v_t \sim N(0, V_t), \\ \alpha_t &= \alpha_{t-1} + w_t, \quad w_t \sim N(0, W_t), \end{aligned} \tag{6}$$

where $p = 1$ and $F = G = 1$. This model is appropriate for population means showing no clear trend and seasonal variations.

(ii) In the *local linear trend model*, the dimension of the state vector and associated error is two:

$$\begin{aligned} \mu_t &= \begin{bmatrix} 1 \\ 0 \end{bmatrix} \alpha_t + v_t \quad v_t \sim N(0, V_t), \\ \alpha_t &= \begin{bmatrix} 1 & 1 \\ 0 & 1 \end{bmatrix} \alpha_{t-1} + w_t, \quad w_t \sim N(0, W_t). \end{aligned} \tag{7}$$

These two cases, (i) and (ii) above, are polynomial DLMs with order one and two, respectively, where the order is the dimension of the state vector. Polynomial DLMs are commonly used for describing the trend of a time series.

(iii) *Seasonal model with linear trend*: If there is a seasonal pattern in the series of population means, then this can also be modeled in the DLM framework.

We first write the model for a series with S seasons as a structural time series model as follows (Harvey 1989)

$$\mu_t = \beta_{1t} + \beta_{2t} + \gamma_t + \varepsilon_t, \tag{8}$$

where β_{1t} and β_{2t} comprise a local linear trend model as specified above, ε_t is a white noise sequence, and the seasonal component γ_t is given by

$$\gamma_t = \sum_{j=1}^{S/2} \gamma_{jt}, \tag{9}$$

where each γ_{jt} follows

$$\begin{bmatrix} \gamma_{jt} \\ \gamma_{jt}^* \end{bmatrix} = \begin{bmatrix} \cos\lambda_j & \sin\lambda_j \\ -\sin\lambda_j & \cos\lambda_j \end{bmatrix} \begin{bmatrix} \gamma_{j,t-1} \\ \gamma_{j,t-1}^* \end{bmatrix} + \begin{bmatrix} \varepsilon_{jt} \\ \varepsilon_{jt}^* \end{bmatrix}, \tag{10}$$

where $\lambda_j = 2\pi j/S$ is the frequency in radians. For example, a model with quarterly observations, a trend, and a yearly cycle reduces to the following state space model:

$$\mu_t = \begin{bmatrix} 1 \\ 1 \\ 1 \\ 1 \\ 1 \\ 1 \end{bmatrix} \alpha_t + v_t \quad v_t \sim N(0, V_t),$$

$$\alpha_t = \begin{bmatrix} 1 & 1 & 0 & 0 & 0 & 0 \\ 0 & 1 & 0 & 0 & 0 & 0 \\ 0 & 0 & 0 & 1 & 0 & 0 \\ 0 & 0 & -1 & 0 & 0 & 0 \\ 0 & 0 & 0 & 0 & -1 & 0 \\ 0 & 0 & 0 & 0 & 0 & -1 \end{bmatrix} \alpha_{t-1} + w_t, \quad w_t \sim N(0, W_t), \tag{11}$$

where

$$\alpha_t = \begin{bmatrix} \beta_{1t} \\ \beta_{2t} \\ \gamma_{1t} \\ \gamma_{1t}^* \\ \gamma_{2t} \\ \gamma_{2t}^* \end{bmatrix}, \quad w_t = \begin{bmatrix} w_{1t} \\ w_{2t} \\ \varepsilon_{1t} \\ \varepsilon_{1t}^* \\ \varepsilon_{2t} \\ \varepsilon_{2t}^* \end{bmatrix} \tag{12}$$

When the seasonality (or periodicity) varies over time, an autoregressive process of order two with complex roots can be used. In a similar context, Lee and Haberman (2012) used harmonic regression to investigate the stability of mean scale scores.

We note that the assumption of equidistant estimated population means is only tenable when the test administrations are regular (e.g., weekly). Methods exist to allow for irregularly spaced test administrations (e.g., weekly, but not in winter and summer holidays). For strong irregularities, the model can be specified in continuous time, but the state space representation then accommodates the observations in discrete time (Harvey 1989; Oud and Singer 2008).

In this paper, we do not take into account the estimation error of the population mean. We find this reasonable because the sample sizes for the applications we have in mind are quite large (1,000+). In addition, Lee and Haberman (2012) make use of scale scores of a series of administrations from which the mean is computed and do not take into account the estimation error of the scale scores. In addition, note that estimating the variance from scale scores is susceptible to underdispersion, i.e., the variance is underestimated.

The estimation and prediction of the state vector is achieved by computing the conditional density $p(\alpha_k, \xi | y_{1:t})$, where ξ is a vector of all unknown parameters in the model. When $k = t$, we deal with what is referred to as the *filtering* problem, where we estimate α_t as data arrive. This is the case in many applications, including test administrations, where data is collected sequentially over time. When $k < t$, we have the *smoothing* problem, where the researcher has all the data and wants to study retrospectively the state process underlying the observed data. When $k > t$, we have the *prediction* problem, where the researcher is interested in forecasting future states.

Effective algorithms exist to filter, smooth, and predict the unobserved states and predict future observations. These algorithms include the Kalman filter (Kalman 1960) and the Forward Filtering Backward Sampling (FFBS) algorithm (Frühwirth-Schnatter 1994).

2.3 Detecting Outliers and Breaks

To account for observations and states that are unusual, Petris et al. (2009) replaced the Gaussian distributions of v_t and w_t with Student's t-distribution. Then, the error sequences in the DLM can be regarded as a mixture of normals, conditional on the scale parameters, and a vector of latent random variables (Petris et al. 2009; Shephard 1994). This class of conditionally linear Gaussian state space models offers a general and convenient framework for parameter learning, state filtering and detection of observational outliers, structural breaks, or scale drift (Petris et al. 2009).

Here, we follow Petris et al. (2009) and, therefore, assume that v_t follows a t-distribution with $\eta_{y,t}$ degrees of freedom and common scale parameter λ_y

$$\lambda_y^{1/2} v_t | \lambda_y, \eta_{y,t} \sim t(\eta_{y,t}). \tag{13}$$

Introducing the latent variable $\omega_{y,t}$, we can equivalently write

$$v_t | \lambda_y, \omega_{yt} \sim N(0, (\lambda_y \omega_{yt})^{-1}). \tag{14}$$

Following a similar argument, the conditional distribution of w_t can be expressed as

$$w_{t,i} | \lambda_{\alpha i}, \omega_{\alpha ti} \sim N(0, (\lambda_{\alpha i} \omega_{\alpha ti})^{-1}), \quad i = 1, 2, \ldots, p. \tag{15}$$

From (8) and (9) above, V_t and W_t in (4) can now be expressed as

$$V_t = (\lambda_y \omega_{y,t})^{-1}, \tag{16}$$

$$W_t = diagonal(\lambda_{\alpha i} \omega_{\alpha ti})^{-1}, \quad \text{for} i = 1, 2, \ldots, p, \tag{17}$$

and (4) now becomes:

$$y_t = F_t \alpha_t + v_t, \quad v_t \sim N(0, (\lambda_y \omega_{yt})^{-1}) \tag{18}$$

$$\alpha_t = G_t \alpha_{t-1} + w_t, \quad w_{ti} \sim N(0, (\lambda_{\alpha i} \omega_{\alpha ti})^{-1}). \tag{19}$$

The variable ω can be interpreted as the degree of non-normality of v and w. Small values of ω will produce large values of v and w. This can be observed by taking, as baseline, $v_t \sim N(0, \lambda_y^{-1})$ corresponding to $\omega_y = 1$. Values of ω_y less than 1 make larger absolute values of v_t more likely (Petris et al. 2009). Ideally, if there are no outliers or break points in the series, the values of the ω's are expected to be equal to 1. Specifically, from (16), a small value of ω_y corresponds to large variance V_t making a large v_t accounted for, easily, by the model. A small value of ω_y will therefore signal an outlier in the series. Similarly, from (17), a small value of $\omega_{\alpha i,t}$ corresponds to large variance $W_{t,i}$ ($W_{t,i}$ is the ith diagonal element of W_t). A small value of $\omega_{\alpha i,t}$ flags a break or jump in the ith component of the state vector.

Our goal is to estimate the unknown states $\alpha_{0:T}$ and parameters ξ given the data $y_{1:T}$. This inference is expressed through the joint posterior density

$$p(\alpha_{0:T}, \xi | y_{1:T}) \propto p(\alpha_{0:T} | \xi, y_{1:T}) p(\xi | y_{1:T}). \tag{20}$$

In practice, computing the density Eq. (20) is analytically intractable (Gilks et al. 1996), so we resort to Monte Carlo methods and, in particular, Markov Chain Monte Carlo (MCMC). The most commonly used approach is to implement a Gibbs sampler to draw from the joint posterior distribution of the states and the parameters given the data. As mentioned earlier, ξ is the vector of all unknown parameters, but, in this study, we are particularly interested in the ω's. A Gibbs sampler to draw from this posterior distribution can easily be implemented. For each $\xi^{(j)}$ in the MCMC sample of size N, we can draw $\alpha_{0:T}^{(j)}$ from $p(\alpha_{0:T}|\xi = \xi^{(j)}, y_{1:T})$ using the FFBS algorithm. The parameters are, in turn, drawn from their full conditional distributions given the states and observations, that is draw $\xi^{(j)}$ from $p(\xi|y_{1:T}, \alpha_{0:T} = \alpha_{0:T}^{(j)})$. This process is repeated for $j = 1, 2, \ldots, N$. The full conditional distributions for the parameters are easy to derive. For example, the full conditional distribution of ω_y for $t = 1, 2, \ldots, T$ is given by

$$\begin{aligned} p(\omega_y|\ldots) &\propto p(y_{1:T}|\alpha_{1:T}, \omega_y, \lambda_y) \cdot p(\omega_y|\eta_y) \\ &\propto \prod_{t=1}^{T} \omega_y^{\frac{1}{2}} \cdot \exp\left\{-\frac{\lambda_y \omega_{y,t}}{2}(y_t - F_t\alpha_t)^2\right\} \cdot \omega_y^{\frac{\eta}{2}-1} \cdot \exp\left\{-\omega_y \frac{\eta}{2}\right\} \\ &\propto \omega^{\frac{T+\eta_y}{2}-1} \cdot \exp\left\{-\omega_y\left[\frac{1}{2}\lambda_y \sum_{t=1}^{T}(y_t - F_t\alpha_t)^2\right]\right\} \end{aligned} \tag{21}$$

and, therefore,

$$\omega_y|\ldots \sim \text{Gamma}\left(\frac{T+\eta_y}{2}, \frac{\eta_y + \lambda_y \sum_{t=1}^{T}(y_t - F_t X_t)^2}{2}\right). \tag{22}$$

The entire sampler is available in Petris (2010).

3 Simulation Design

We simulated data with 20 common items in 100 test administrations, each test being administered to 100 test takers. A series of simulations was performed in which the time series of test takers' ability means contained seasonal effects, trends, and/or sudden breaks. In particular, test takers' ability means were simulated to cater for three different possible instances (a) when the ability means are assumed to be the same across different forms (b) when there is some linear growth in the ability means over time, and (c) when the ability means exhibit some seasonality over time. The results for each of the three cases are presented in the next section.

Difficulty parameters for each item were drawn from a standard normal distribution, while the discrimination parameters were drawn from a standard log-normal distribution. The simulated ability means together with the item parameters were then used to generate item responses under the two parameter logistic model, Eq. (1).

From the generated data, the item parameters and population means were estimated using the marginal maximum likelihood (MML) estimation method (van der Linden and Hambleton 1997). The design in this study is a *complete* data design where all the test takers took the same test with all common items (Kolen and Brennan 2004). The complete data design was employed to keep things straightforward and the concurrent calibration procedure effective. From this procedure, we obtained a set of estimated item parameters and, for each test administration, an estimated population mean and variance. The estimated means were then used as the observed data in the time series analysis. The MCMC methods were used to compute the joint posterior estimates of the states and the unknown parameters given the observed data, up to time t.

4 Results

4.1 Local Level Model

As explained earlier, this model is appropriate for series that do not exhibit any trend or seasonality. The test takers' mean abilities were drawn from a local level model (4). The assumption here is that the mean abilities of the different groups of test takers are the same across different administrations, apart from random fluctuations. We created intentionally a change point at test administration 73 ($t = 73$). The simulated and the estimated ability means are displayed in Fig. 1. We can clearly see that the two series overlap, an indication that the estimation method is quite accurate.

To compute the posterior estimates of the states and the parameters in this state space model, an MCMC algorithm using a random walk plus noise model was run.

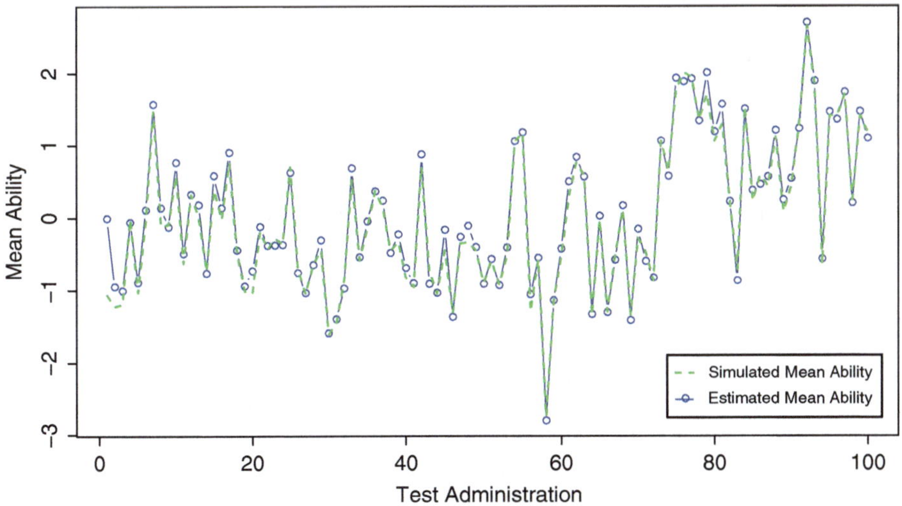

Fig. 1 Simulated and estimated mean abilities for local level model

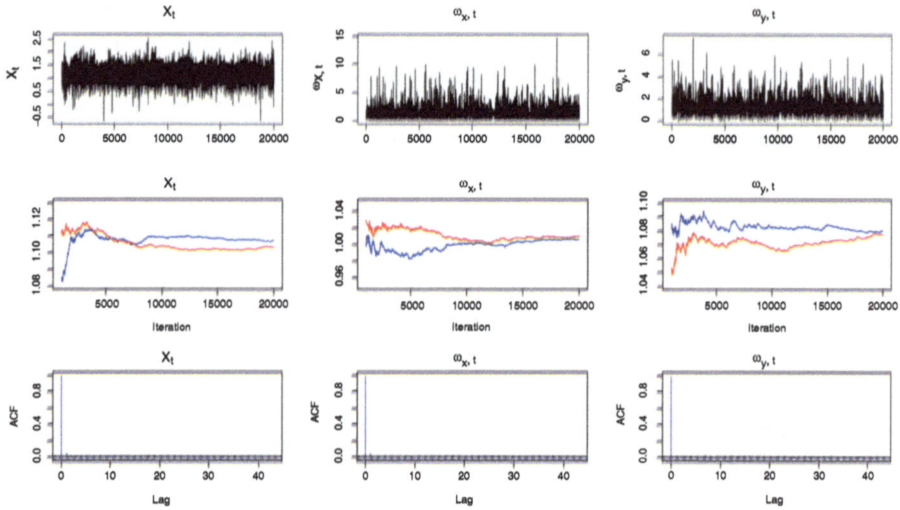

Fig. 2 MCMC diagnostic plots for local level model

The MCMC samples were set at 20,500, and the first 500 were removed as burn-in before the analysis. The MCMC diagnostic plots are displayed in Fig. 2.

From these MCMC diagnostic plots, it is very clear that the trace plots and the ergodic means —the running sample means—are very stable. The autocorrelation function (ACF) decays very fast. We can conclude that the convergence has been achieved and, therefore, go ahead and use the output from MCMC for analysis.

From Fig. 3, we can see that the unobserved states, X_t, which, in this model, correspond to the test takers' expected mean ability, are the same across the different test administrations. The change point at administration 73 is well captured in the plot. It is also clear that there are many observations that lie outside the 95 % probability interval of the test takers' expected mean ability. Observation at administration 58 is, however, very far from the rest.

We can see from Fig. 4, the left panel, that the major break or change point at administration $t = 73$ is captured. In the right panel, we can see that there are several outliers, and the furthest one at administration $t = 58$ has been captured.

4.2 Local Linear Trend Model

The test takers' ability means were drawn from a local linear trend model. The assumption here is that the mean ability of the different populations changes linearly through time. As discussed earlier, the state in this model is two-dimensional —the intercept and the slope or growth rate. The simulated test takers' mean abilities and the estimated ones, again, were highly correlated. Figure 5 shows the two plots for this model.

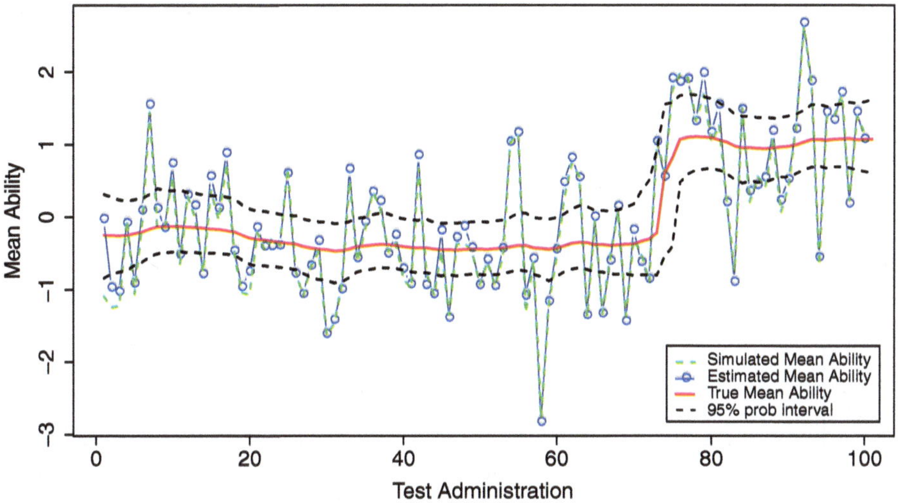

Fig. 3 MCMC output for local level model

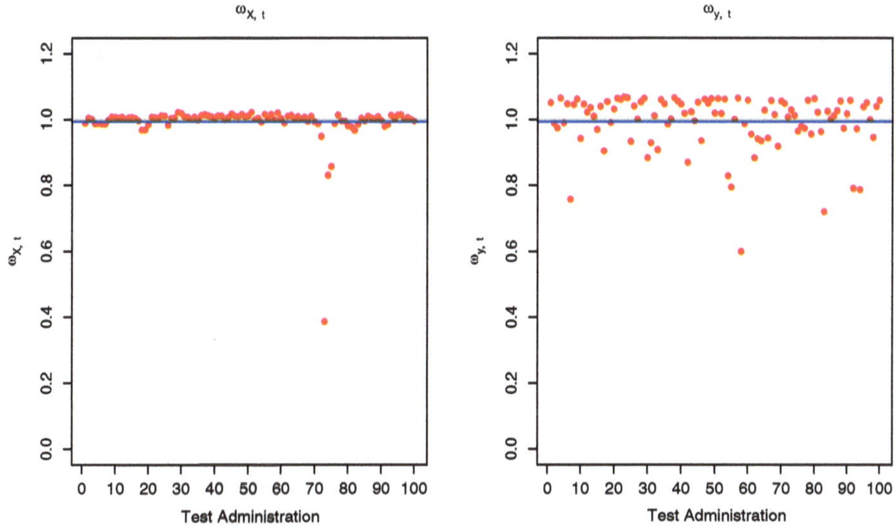

Fig. 4 Posterior estimates for ω in local level model (left = $\omega_{x,t}$, right = $\omega_{y,t}$)

To compute the posterior estimates of the states and the parameters in this model, an MCMC algorithm using the linear trend model was run. The MCMC samples were set at 20,500, and the first 500 were removed as burn-in before the analysis. Figure 6 shows the MCMC diagnostic plots.

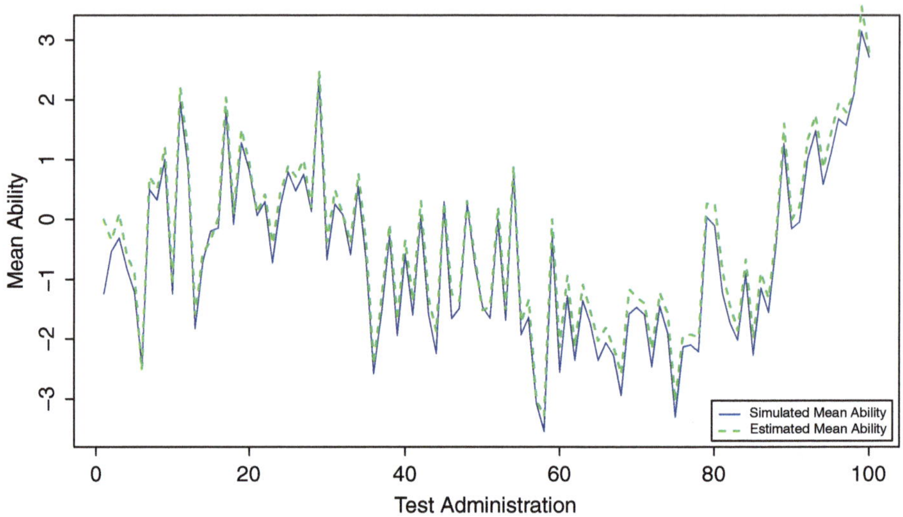

Fig. 5 Simulated and estimated mean abilities for local linear trend model

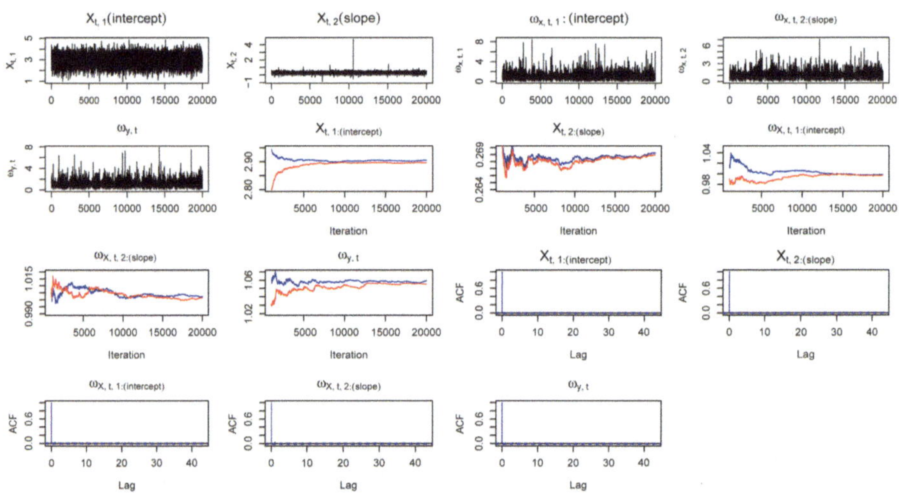

Fig. 6 MCMC diagnostic plots for linear trend model

From these plots, we can conclude that the convergence has been achieved. The ergodic means —the running sample means—are very stable, especially at the end of the iterations. The ACF decays very fast. Next, we use the output from MCMC for analysis.

Figure 7 shows the plots of the test takers' simulated, estimated, and true mean abilities and 95 % confidence interval for the expected mean. There are also several, but mild, observational outliers.

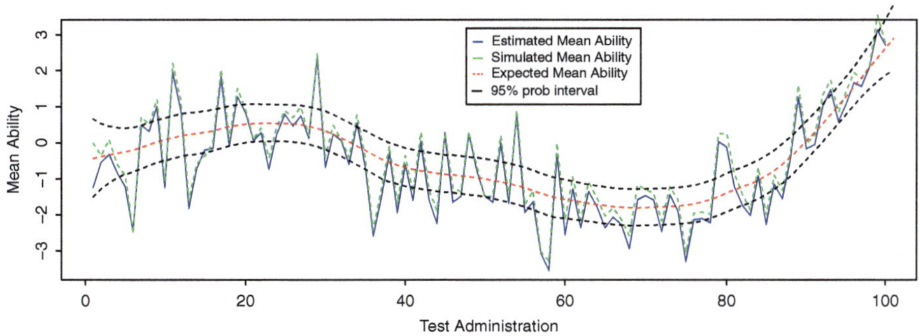

Fig. 7 MCMC output for local linear trend model

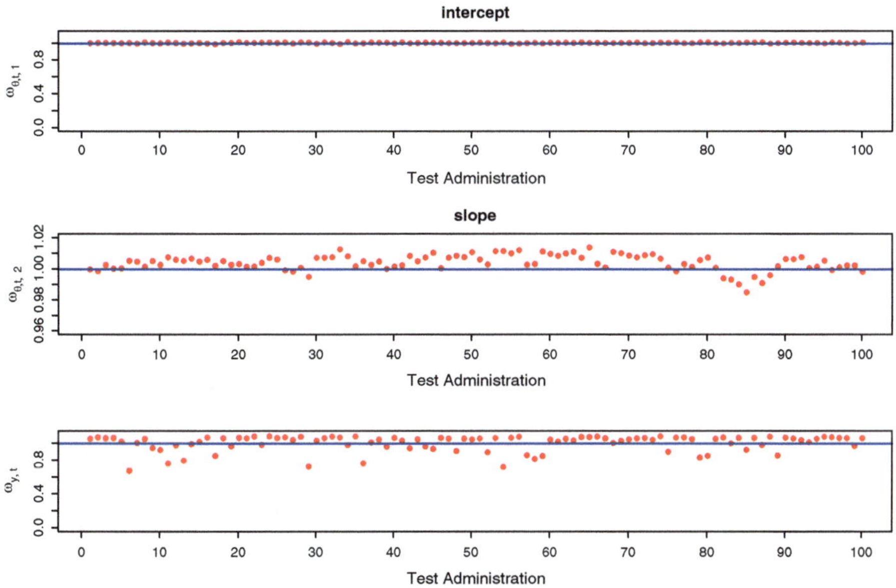

Fig. 8 Posterior estimates of ω for local linear trend model

From Fig. 8, we can see that there are several outliers, but they are relatively mild. The intercept component of the state vector is very stable. In the slope component, the major break at $t = 85$ has captured. The results from these plots are consistent with the plot of the expected mean abilities.

4.3 Seasonal Model with Linear Trend

This model has three-dimensional state space: the intercept, slope, and the seasonal component. The assumption here is that the mean abilities of test takers vary from one test administration to another, and the tests are administered at different seasons

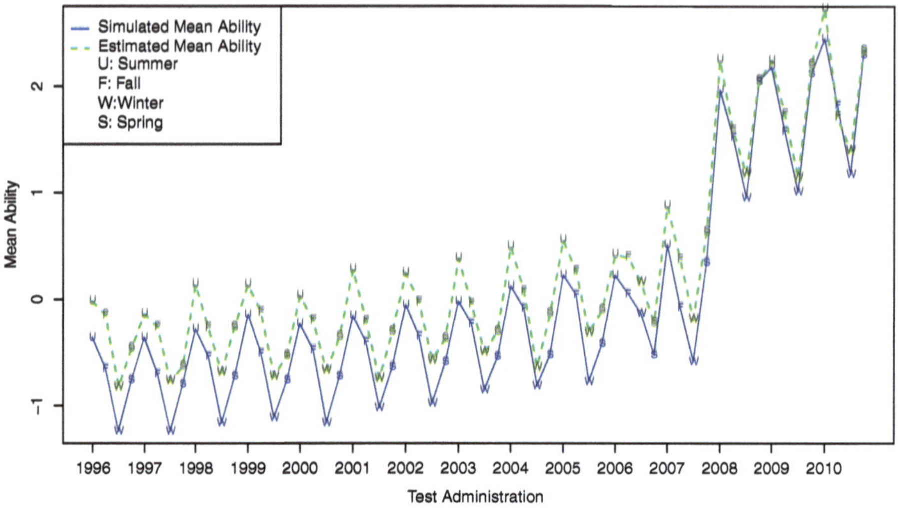

Fig. 9 Simulated and estimated mean abilities for seasonal model with linear trend

within a year. For a start, we assume one test form is given per season in any given year. We also consider four seasons in each year: Spring (S), Summer (U), Fall (F), and Winter (W). Multiple tests per season can also be modeled. The mean ability is simulated using linear trend plus seasonal component model. For illustration, we simulated from year 1996 to 2010, and we intentionally created a change point in spring of year 2008. The plots of simulated and estimated mean abilities are shown in Fig. 9.

To compute the posterior estimates of the states and the parameters in this model, an MCMC algorithm was run. The MCMC samples were set at 20,500, and the first 500 were removed as burn-in before the analysis. MCMC diagnostics plots are displayed in Fig. 10.

From these MCMC diagnostic plots, we can conclude that the convergence has been achieved. We can now go ahead and use the output from MCMC for analysis.

From Fig. 11, it is apparent that the linear trend is stable. This is also confirmed by the posterior estimates of ω for the slope component of the state. That is $\omega_{x,t,2}$ in Fig. 12. The major change point in Summer 2008 is well captured in the posterior estimates of ω for intercept component of the state, $\omega_{x,t,1}$ in Fig. 12. It is clear from Fig. 11 that we do not have any observational outliers; this is confirmed by very stable estimates of $\omega_{y,t}$ in Fig. 12.

The seasonal instability in Winter of 2006 and Fall and Winter of 2007 apparent in plots of simulated and estimated mean abilities is well captured by the posterior estimates of ω for seasonal component, $\omega_{x,t,3}$.

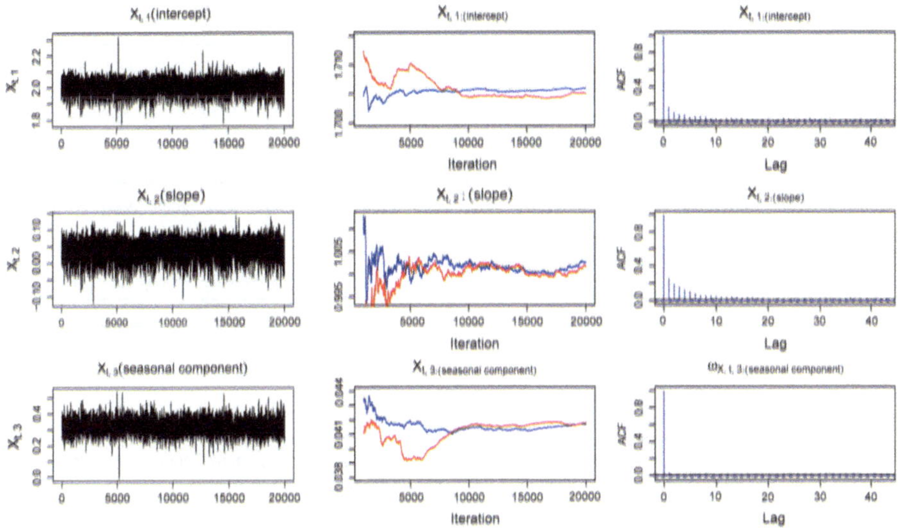

Fig. 10 MCMC diagnostic plots for seasonal model with linear trend

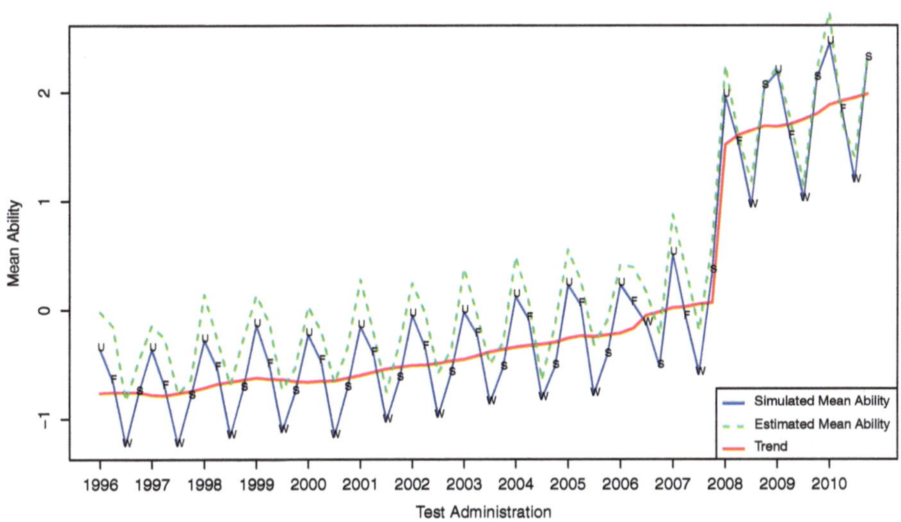

Fig. 11 Simulated and estimated mean abilities, and the trend for seasonal model with linear trend

5 Discussion and Future Directions

This paper investigates the use of DLM in an IRT framework. This approach allows us to detect, effectively and in real time, any outliers and structural breaks or change point(s) in population parameters in different test administrations over time. In

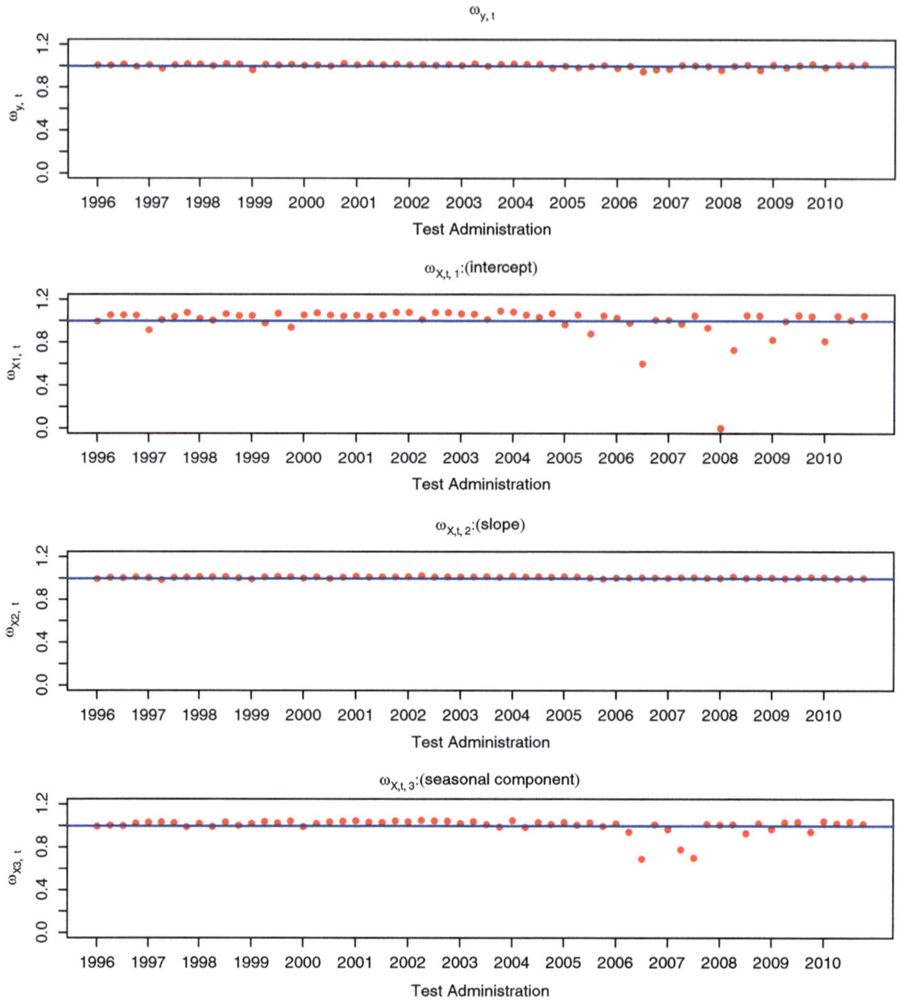

Fig. 12 Posterior estimate of ω for seasonal model with linear trend

principle, the methodology is capable of dealing with changes in both item and population parameters over time. The approach then is analogous to detection of differential item functioning (DIF) where one has to distinguish between actual differences in ability between groups (known as impact) and actual differences in item performance conditional on ability (known as DIF). It would, however, be the case that in studying changes in item parameters over time, this is performed on an item-by-item basis. Due to effectiveness of this approach on simulated data, its application to real data sets with complete or incomplete design is encouraged. Positive results are expected. The approach may also be extended to other different variables that are to be monitored over a long chain of administrations. Since the posterior estimate based on time t cannot be used to evaluate posterior based on time $(t+1)$, every time a new observation is made, a totally new Markov chain has to be simulated. This makes inference using MCMC limited, especially if the observations are made rapidly (in minutes or hours). We are currently in the process of designing a fast algorithm to detect the outliers and the breaks using sets of weighted particles —an approach commonly referred to as sequential Monte Carlo (Liu and West 2001; Pitt and Shephard 1999; Storvik 2002).

Acknowledgments The authors would like to thank Frank Rijmen and Lili Yao for helpful comments on an earlier draft of the manuscript. In addition, we are obliged to Kim Fryer for editorial assistance

References

Birnbaum, A. (1968). Some latent trait models and their use in inferring an examinee's ability. In F. Lord & M. Novick (Eds.), *Statistical theories of mental test scores* (pp. 397–472). Reading, MA: Addison-Wesley.

Brinkhuis, M., & Maris, G. (2009). *Dynamic parameter estimation in student monitoring systems* (Technical Report No. 2009–1). Arnhem: Cito.

Durbin, J., & Koopman, S. (2001). *Time series analysis by state space methods.* Oxford: Oxford University Press.

Frühwirth-Schnatter, S. (1994). Data augmentation and dynamic linear models. *Journal of Time Series Analysis, 15*, 183–202.

Gilks, W., Richardson, S., & Spiegelhalter, D. (1996). *Markov chain Monte Carlo in practice.* Boca Raton, FL: Chapman & Hall.

Glas, C. (1998). Detection of differential item functioning using Lagrange multiplier tests. *Statistica Sinica, 8*, 647–667.

Glas, C. (2000). Item calibration and parameter drift. In W. van der Linden & C. Glas (Eds.), *Computer adaptive testing: Theory and practice* (pp. 183–200). Boston, MA: Kluwer.

Harvey, A. (1989). *Forecasting, structural time series models and the Kalman filter.* Cambridge: Cambridge University Press.

Kalman, R. (1960). A new approach to linear filtering and prediction problems. *Journal of Basic Engineering, 82*, 35–45.

Keller, L., & Keller, R. (2011). The long-term sustainability of different item response theory scaling methods. *Educational and Psychological Measurement, 71*, 362–379.

Kolen, M., & Brennan, R. (2004). *Test equating, scaling, and linking: Methods and practices.* New York: Springer.

Lee, Y.-H., & Haberman, S. (2012). Harmonic regression and scale stability. In *IMPS.* Lincoln, NE.

Lee, Y.-H., & von Davier, A. (in press). Monitoring scale scores over time via quality control charts, model-based approaches, and time series techniques. *Psychometrika.*

Li, D., Li, S., & von Davier, A. (2011). Applying time series analysis to detect scale drift. In A. von Davier (Ed.), *Statistical models for test equating, scaling, and linking* (pp. 327–346). New York: Springer.

Lindquist, A., & Picci, G. (1981). State space models for Gaussian stochastic processes. In M. Hazewinkel & J. Willems (Eds.), *Stochastic systems: The mathematics of filtering and identification and applications* (pp. 169–204). Dordrecht: Reidel.

Liu, J., & West, M. (2001). Combined parameter and state estimation in simulation-based filtering. In A. Doucet, N. de Freitas, & N. Gordon (Eds.), *Sequential Monte Carlo methods in practice* (pp. 197–223). New York: Springer.

Lord, F., & Novick, M. (1968). *Statistical theories of mental test scores*. Reading, MA: Addison-Wesley.

Oud, J., & Singer, H. (2008). Continuous time modeling of panel data: SEM versus filter techniques. *Statistica Neerlandica, 62*, 4–28.

Petris, G. (2010). An R package for dynamic linear models. *Journal of Statistical Software, 36*, 1–16.

Petris, G., Petrone, S., & Campagnoli, P. (2009). *Dynamic linear models*. New York: Springer.

Pitt, M., & Shephard, N. (1999). Filtering via simulation: Auxiliary particle filters. *Journal of the American Statistical Association, 94*, 590–599.

Rao, C., & Sinharay, S. (Eds.). (2007). *Handbook of statistics, volume 26: Psychometrics*. Amsterdam: Elsevier.

Shephard, N. (1994). Partial non-Gaussian state space. *Biometrika, 81*, 115–131.

Storvik, G. (2002). Particle filters for state-space models with the presence of unknown static parameters. *IEEE Transactions on Signal Processing, 50*, 281–289.

VanBrackle, L., & Reynolds, M. (1997). EWMA and CUSUM control charts in the presence of correlation. *Communications in Statistics: Simulation and Computation, 26*, 979–1008.

van der Linden, W., & Hambleton, R. (Eds.). (1997). *Handbook of modern item response theory*. New York: Springer.

van Rijn, P., Dolan, C., & Molenaar, P. (2010). State space methods for item response modeling of multi-subject time series. In P. Molenaar & K. Newell (Eds.), *Individual pathways of change: Statistical models for analyzing learning and development* (pp. 125–151). Washington, DC: American Psychological Association.

Veerkamp, W., & Glas, C. (2000). Detection of known items in adaptive testing with a statistical quality control method. *Journal of Educational and Behavioral Statistics, 25*, 373–389.

von Davier, A. (2012). *The use of quality control and data mining techniques for monitoring scaled scores: An overview* (Technical Report No. RR-12-20). Princeton, NJ: Educational Testing Service

West, M., & Harrison, J. (1997). *Bayesian forecasting and dynamic models*. New York: Springer.

Detection of Unusual Test Administrations Using a Linear Mixed Effects Model

Yi-Hsuan Lee, Minzhao Liu, and Alina A. von Davier

1 Introduction

Nowadays, many educational standardized assessments have an (almost) continuous administration mode. With an increase in the number of administrations of test forms there is also an increase in the complexity of the quality assurance procedures needed to maintain the stability of the reported scores. Traditional methods for quality control (QC; Allalouf 2007) are not sufficient for detecting unusual scores in a rapid flow of administrations. This study investigates data from several consecutive administrations that follow a specific equating design (or braiding plan) and proposes a linear mixed effects model for the detection of abnormal results.

Monitoring and maintaining the quality and stability of the scale scores of a standardized assessment are perhaps the most important goals of the psychometricians' work. Global tests are taken all over the world by examinees from different language groups and different countries. Being responsible for the reported scores to millions of examinees implies that many layers of quality control are cautiously and seriously employed, since any mistake or unusual result might affect examinees' lives. For testing programs that provide a large number of administrations each year, the challenge of maintaining comparability of test scores is influenced by the potential rapid accumulation of errors and by the lack of time between administrations to apply the usual techniques for detecting and addressing scale drift or anomalous results. Many traditional techniques available to psychometricians for understanding and monitoring the equating results (Allalouf 2007) have been developed for tests

Y.-H. Lee (✉) • A.A. von Davier
Educational Testing Service, Princeton, NJ 08541, USA
e-mail: YLee@ets.org; avondavier@ets.org

M. Liu
University of Florida, Gainesville, FL, USA
e-mail: liuminzhao@ufl.edu

R.E. Millsap et al. (eds.), *New Developments in Quantitative Psychology*, 133
Springer Proceedings in Mathematics & Statistics 66, DOI 10.1007/978-1-4614-9348-8_9,

with only a small number of administrations per year, and therefore, while very valuable and necessary, they are not sufficient for a complex and rapid flow of scale scores (Lee and von Davier 2013; von Davier 2012). To assess the significance of the variability of scale scores over time, a different type of techniques is needed. In this paper, we investigate the usefulness of linear mixed effects models for detecting the effects of background variables, the administration, and the equating design (or braiding plan) on the variability of scale scores over time. This approach is illustrated with real data from 15 administrations of a global English assessment. In this study we fit a linear mixed effects regression model to test data to predict scores of certain subgroups and to help detect unusual results.

In recent years, research has been conducted on identifying promising statistical tools that can be used as QC procedures on assessment data over time. Lee and von Davier (2013) proposed the inspection of the QC charts, such as the Shewhart and CUSUM, to detect trends and the application of the change point models to detect abrupt changes in the flow of scores over time. Li et al. (2011) investigated the use of time series to model test scores data over time. Lee and Haberman (2013) proposed the use of harmonic regression to account for the seasonality observed in test scores over time. The study of Luo et al. (2011) had similar objectives as the current study, but used data from a test with a very different equating design (or braiding plan) than ours. They focused on mean score vectors and examined the effects of three background variables (i.e., testing country, native language, and reason of taking the test) on the mean scores. This method may lose some information about the data because the raw, individual data were aggregated by subgroups. Meanwhile, it had limitations in the selection of the independent variables in order to ensure decent sample sizes for each subgroup. Therefore, instead of working with mean scores, in this study we propose a linear mixed effects model with individual scores as responses to describe the data.

The rest of the paper proceeds as follows. The data set and the model will be described in Sect. 2. In Sect. 3, results from model selection will be presented, and interpretations and inferences will be made. The prediction method will be used to detect unusual score patterns in test administrations for a certain target population and it will be described in Sect. 4. In the last section, we discuss the limitations of the study and propose future research.

2 Methods

2.1 Data and Design

The data came from 15 administrations of an international English test. They included examinees' scaled scores and their responses to a background questionnaire. A random sample of 18,000 examinees was drawn from each of the

Fig. 1 Equating design involved in the 15 administrations (*each triangle* and *circle* stands for one administration. Three of them were given in country A, and the other two were given in country B)

administrations. The 15 administrations can be classified into three groups of five administrations each based on the equating design: within each group, the five administrations were linked in a certain way; three of them were assigned to country A and the other two were assigned to country B. The three groups were randomly selected from a large pool of administrations. Figure 1 demonstrates the equating design and data structure.

We looked at the Listening and Reading sections of the test. Each examinee received a score for each section on a scale from 5 to 495 points. In this study, Reading and Listening scores were modeled separately. The scores for each section were treated as a continuous variable.

The background questionnaire contained 14 questions. Basically, they could be divided into two parts: demographical information and learning experience, including level of education, major, working status, job, years of learning English, times of taking this test, daily study time, etc. After a preliminary exploratory investigation, several variables were selected as potential predictors. Table 1 shows the complete list of variables of interest as well as their properties and basic description. They are predictors (i.e., independent variables) considered in the model selection. The properties of these predictors are discussed in the following subsections.

Table 1 List of predictors and their properties

Term	Label	Property	Levels	Type	Description
Group	"group"	Random	3	Nominal	Group of administrations
Administration	"admin"	Random	15	Nominal	Administration
Gender	"gender"	Fixed	2	Binary	Examinee's gender
Country	"cntry"	Fixed	2	Binary	Examinee's country
Repeater	"repeater"	Fixed	2	Binary	Whether test previously taken
Education	"edu"	Fixed	3	Nominal	Level of education
Status	"status"	Fixed	3	Nominal	Employment status
Major	"major"	Fixed	7	Nominal	Examinee's major
Job	"job"	Fixed	3	Nominal	Industry of jobs
Years	"years"	Fixed		Integer	Years of study
Time	"time"	Fixed		Integer	Daily study time
English country	"engctry"	Fixed		Integer	Years abroad

Table 2 Frequency table for the "education" variable

Education	Frequency	Proportion
Missing value	8,957	0.03
Primary school	304	0.00
Junior high school	919	0.00
High school	13,507	0.05
Vocational/technical high school	1,804	0.01
Vocational/technical school after high school	5,515	0.02
Community/junior college	14,967	0.06
Undergraduate college or university	191,368	0.71
Graduate or professional school	31,676	0.12
Language institution	983	0.00

2.2 *Data Manipulation*

Based on the property of those independent variables, different data manipulations are needed for the predictors for fixed effects. Here are three major modifications.

1. Grouping: There are many possible response categories for variables such as "education," "job," and "status," so grouping some of the categories appears reasonable and necessary because the sample size might be too small in some categories. From Tables 2 and 3, it is easy to find that undergraduate students and graduate students are the major categories for "education," and full-time students and full-time employees are the majority for "status." By categorizing the two major levels and combining all the others into a separate level "others" for either variable, we might have a more meaningful and accurate model. For the "job" variable, there were 32 response categories, and we grouped the categories into three levels (manufacturing, service, and others).

Table 3 Frequency table for the "status" variable

Status	Frequency	Proportion
Missing value	7,838	0.03
Employed full-time (including self-employed)	89,034	0.33
Employed part-time and/or study part-time	13,428	0.05
Not employed	22,885	0.08
Full-time student	136,815	0.51

Table 4 Assigned scores for the ordinal variables

Question	Scores	Question	Scores
Years		Time	
(A) Less than or equal to 4	1	(A) None	1
(B) 4–6	2	(B) 1–10 %	2
(C) 6–10	3	(C) 11–20 %	3
(D) More than 10	4	(D) 21–50 %	4
		(E) 51–100 %	5
English country			
(A) No	1		
(B) Less than 6 months	2		
(C) 6–12 months	3		
(D) 12–24 months	4		
(E) 24 months more	5		

2. Assigning scores: Response categories of the variables "years" (how many years examinees have learned English), "time" (how often they use English in daily life), and "English country" (how long they stayed in English-speaking countries) have intrinsic ordering, so we treat them as ordinal variables and assign scores to the response categories. The most naïve method is to assign 1–n scores. Any other assignments would have a very similar Pearson correlation and similar inference from the model. Table 4 shows the assigned values for each response category of a question. Handling them in this manner also makes the approach more efficient (Agresti 1996, pp. 36–38).
3. Missing data: There were no missing data in the random predictors "group" and "administration" and the fixed predictor "country" because their values are determined when the examinees register for the test. When all the other fixed predictors ("repeater," "gender," "years," "time," "English country," "education," "status," "major," and "job") were considered, the number of missing observations is 36,565 out of 270,000 total number of observations (about 14 %). The simplest method for analyzing data with missing observations is to delete cases and obtain a data set that is complete, which is also the default method for many statistical packages. This method was used in our study under the assumption that the missingness of those predictors was irrelevant to test-takers' scores; i.e., missing covariates were missing completely at random (MCAR). If the MCAR assumption is reasonable, valid inferences can still be made based on the complete responses, even though we did not make full use of the

available data and might lack some accuracy in estimating the variance of the regression coefficients (Daniels and Hogan 2008, p. 92). Alternatively, one may impute the missing observations, but this approach often requires the missing at random (MAR) assumption and some distributional assumptions. As noted in Gelman and Hill (2007, Chap. 25), it is impossible to prove that data are missing (completely) at random because they are unobserved. For missing categorical predictors, one may avoid the assumption of MCAR or MAR by creating an extra category for the variable indicating missing. We did not consider this method because the proportion of missing values per variable of interest was very small (the maximum was about 7 %).

2.3 Univariate Linear Mixed Effects Model

We propose a linear mixed effects model to analyze the examinees' scores collected from the equating design shown in Fig. 1. Due to the equating design, the test scores possibly have two levels of variance components: (a) examinees taking the same administration are likely to have scores that are more correlated than those taking different administrations due to seasonality and (b) it is also possible that scores in a particular group of administrations are more correlated than those in different groups because of equating. Recall that the groups of administrations are a random sample from a large pool of groups of administrations, rather than pre-decided groups of administrations of interest. Therefore, we differentiate the two sources of variations by assigning "group" and "administration" as two independent categorical random effects and estimating the variance component attributable to either random effect. By nature of the equating design, each administration only appeared in one group (i.e., a nested design). Other background variables mentioned in Table 1 are taken as fixed independent variables when examining their contribution to individual scores.

Let Y_{ijk} be the random variable that represents the score of examinee k in administration j and group i, where $1 \leq k \leq 18{,}000$, $1 \leq j \leq 5$, and $1 \leq i \leq 3$, and let $\mathbf{X}_{ijk}$ be a vector of fixed predictors for this examinee. Following the convention in mixed models analysis and variance components estimation (e.g., Searle et al. 2006; Snijders and Bosker 2012), the proposed linear mixed effects model is defined as follows:

$$
\begin{aligned}
Y_{ijk} &= \mu_0 + G_i + A_{ij} + X'_{ijk}\beta + \epsilon_{ijk},\\
G_i &\sim N\left(0, \sigma_g^2\right),\\
A_{ij} &\sim N\left(0, \sigma_a^2\right),\\
\epsilon_{ijk} &\sim N\left(0, \sigma^2\right),
\end{aligned}
$$

where μ_0 is the grand mean, G_i is a random categorical variable indicating group i, A_{ij} is a random categorical variable indicating administration j in group i (i.e., A_{ij} is a factor nested within G_i), β is a coefficient vector for the predictors $\mathbf{X}_{ijk}$, and ϵ_{ijk} is the individual (random) error. The property that the random variables G_i, A_{ij}, and ϵ_{ijk} are independent of each other follows from the model specification (see, e.g., Snijders and Bosker 2012). The normality assumption about the individual error can be checked through residual diagnostics.

We first show how the random effect terms affect the expectation of an examinee' score:

(a) The expected score for an examinee in administration j of group i equals

$$E\left(Y_{ijk}\middle|G_i,A_{ij}\right)=\mu_0+X'_{ijk}\beta+G_i+A_{ij};$$

(b) the expected score for an examinee in group i equals and

$$E\left(Y_{ijk}\middle|G_i\right)=\mu_0+X'_{ijk}\beta+G_i;$$

(c) the expected score for any examinee equals

$$E\left(Y_{ijk}\right)=\mu_0+X'_{ijk}\beta.$$

Note that the constraints $E(G_i)=0$ and $E(A_{ij})=0$ not only involve no loss of generality in (a)–(c) but also make the estimation of μ_0 identifiable.

Next, we show how the random effect terms explain the variance of an examinee's score and the covariance between two individuals' scores: First,

$$\text{Var}\left(Y_{ijk}\right)=\sigma_g^2+\sigma_a^2+\sigma^2,$$

where σ_g^2, σ_a^2, and σ^2 are variance components of Var(Y_{ijk}). Second, consider two examinees' scores, Y_{ij1} and $Y_{i'j'2}$. It is clear that (a)

$$\text{Cov}\left(Y_{ij1},Y_{i'j'2}\right)=\sigma_g^2+\sigma_a^2$$

if $i=i'$ and $j=j'$ (i.e., they took the same administration and hence in the same group), (b)

$$\text{Cov}\left(Y_{ij1},Y_{i'j'2}\right)=\sigma_g^2$$

if $i=i'$ and $j\neq j'$ (i.e., different administrations in the same group), and (c)

$$\text{Cov}\left(Y_{ij1},Y_{i'j'2}\right)=0$$

if $i \neq i'$ (i.e., different groups, and hence different administrations). Clearly, this model describes our hypothesis that the scores of examinees from the same administration may have stronger correlation than those from the same group but different administrations. Whether this hypothesis is supported by the data is the main question to answer. Note that the current study addresses the issue of repeaters by including a fixed predictor that indicates whether an examinee repeated or not. This variable came from the background questionnaire. An alternative way to handle this issue is to model the correlation between scores of the same examinee (even if the scores came from administrations in different groups), which requires unique identification for each examinee across administrations in order to identify when a person retakes the test. The alternative method cannot be considered here because the information is not available in our data set. Although it is not impossible that some of the randomly selected examinees took more than one of the 15 administrations, the portion of such examinees is expected to be quite small. Thus, our model assumption about the correlation between scores should not limit our findings to a great extent.

Various models that include different numbers of predictors are considered, and a set of predictors that best explain the section scores is determined by the model/variable selection procedure described in the next subsection. All computation was done with R (R Development Core Team 2011) package "lme4" (Bates and Maechler 2010) and can also be done in SAS®.

2.4 Model Selection and Variable Selection

The model selection procedure begins with the selection of random effects terms. Suitable fixed predictors are then chosen from the ten available fixed predictors in Table 1 based on the forward selection procedure (Draper and Smith 1998, p. 336). We select predictors based on their contribution to the explanatory power of the model. In this case, a predictor will be retained in the model only when it leads to significant reduction in the estimated standard deviation of individual error (or root mean squared error). For purposes of illustration, a decrement of 0.5 % or more in the estimated standard deviation of error is considered significant in this paper. This criterion is chosen to facilitate the model selection procedure, and adopting the value 0.5 % roughly separates the models with useful predictors and those without in our study. This value may not be adequate for all applications. One should try different models to see the contribution of individual predictors in explaining the variability in test scores before setting up a fixed criterion to automate the model selection procedure.

3 Results

3.1 Variable Selection

Tables 5 and 6 show the log-likelihood (LogLik) value for each model and the percent reduction in the estimated standard deviation of individual error when extra random effect terms, group and/or administration (admin), were added to the null model. We can see from these tables that the "group" random effect is negligible in terms of reduction in $\hat{\sigma}$ or increase in log-likelihood values. For either section score, the administration random term was retained in the model because the variance reduction is greater than 0.5 %. Thus, we continued the variable selection based on the model with the "administration" random effect.

Tables 7 and 8 present the steps of forward selection for Reading and Listening, respectively. Recall that a fixed predictor is retained if its entry results in more than 0.5 % of reduction in $\hat{\sigma}$ from the previous step. Table 7 shows that predictors "English country," "years," "education," "repeater," and "major" were selected as main effects in the model by the forward selection procedure for Reading scores. For Listening score, Table 8 shows that the main effects are "English country," "years," "repeater," and "major." Note that we only consider a linear relationship between the section scores and the ordinal predictors ("years," "time," and "English country") because there is an evident linear trend between the scores and each of the predictors (see Fig. 2).

Results for the selection of interactions are presented in Tables 9 and 10, where "main" refers to the main effects terms in Tables 7 and 8. Tables 9 and 10 show that none of the interactions reduced $\hat{\sigma}$ significantly, so they were not chosen in the final model for either section scores.

To summarize, we obtained the final model with "education," "major," "repeater," "English country," and "years" as fixed predictors for Reading scores.

Table 5 Random effects terms selection for Reading scores

Model	Term	LogLik	$\hat{\sigma}$	Reduction (%)
Null model	Intercept	–1,612,582	94.97	
Model 1	Intercept + group	–1,612,459	94.93	0.05
Model 2	Intercept + group + admin	–1,610,178	94.12	0.90
Model 3	Intercept + admin	–1,610,178	94.12	0.90

Table 6 Random effects terms selection for Listening scores

Model	Term	LogLik	$\hat{\sigma}$	Reduction (%)
Null model	Intercept	–1,585,039	85.76	
Model 1	Intercept + group	–1,584,935	85.73	0.04
Model 2	Intercept + group + admin	–1,582,115	84.82	1.09
Model 3	Intercept + admin	–1,582,115	84.82	1.09

Table 7 Fixed effects terms selection for Reading score

Model	Term	LogLik	$\widehat{\sigma}$	Reduction (%)
Model 1	Intercept + admin	–1,391,315	93.79	
Model 2	Intercept + admin + engctry	–1,380,639	89.6	4.47
Model 3	Model 2 + years	–1,371,977	86.33	3.65
Model 4	Model 3 + edu	–1,367,952	84.86	1.7
Model 5	Model 4 + repeater	–1,364,375	83.57	1.52
Model 6	Model 5 + major	–1,361,969	82.71	1.03

Reduction was obtained by $(\widehat{\sigma}_0 - \widehat{\sigma}_1)/\widehat{\sigma}_0$, where $\widehat{\sigma}_0$ is the estimated standard deviation of individual error for Model 1, and $\widehat{\sigma}_1$ is that for a selected model

Table 8 Fixed effects terms selection for Listening score

Model	Term	LogLik	$\widehat{\sigma}$	Reduction (%)
Model 1	Intercept + admin	–1,367,021	84.52	
Model 2	Intercept + admin + engctry	–1,342,935	76.23	9.81
Model 3	Model 2 + years	–1,336,312	74.1	2.79
Model 4	Model 3 + repeater	–1,331,601	72.62	2
Model 5	Model 4 + major	–1,328,007	71.51	1.53

Reduction was obtained by $(\widehat{\sigma}_0 - \widehat{\sigma}_1)/\widehat{\sigma}_0$, where $\widehat{\sigma}_0$ is the estimated standard deviation of individual error for Model 1, and $\widehat{\sigma}_1$ is that for a selected model

Table 9 Selection of interaction terms for Reading score

Model	Term	LogLik	$\widehat{\sigma}$	Reduction (%)
Model 0	Intercept + admin + main	–1,361,969	82.71	
Model 1	Model 0 + engctry: years	–1,361,965	82.7089	0.001
Model 2	Model 0 + engctry: repeater	–1,361,755	82.6346	0.090
Model 3	Model 0 + engctry: major	–1,361,944	82.7014	0.081
Model 4	Model 0 + engctry: edu	–1,361,946	82.7024	0.001
Model 5	Model 0 + years: repeater	–1,361,969	82.7104	0.010
Model 6	Model 0 + years: major	–1,361,835	82.6631	0.057
Model 7	Model 0 + years: edu	–1,361,958	82.7066	0.053
Model 8	Model 0 + repeater: major	–1,361,906	82.6882	0.022
Model 9	Model 0 + repeater: edu	–1,361,917	82.6922	0.005
Model 10	Model 0 + major: edu	–1,361,704	82.6164	0.092

For Listening scores, the final model includes the following fixed predictors: "years," "English country," "repeater," and "major." Both models include the "administration" random predictor.

As in regression analysis, standard residual diagnostics can help to check model assumptions and assess model fit. As an example, we used individual residuals to check the normality assumption for individual errors. Figure 3 shows the QQ-plots based on the final models. From the figures, we can see the residuals were approximately normally distributed. Further checking could be executed through stratified residual plots over groups or administrations. Estimates of the random

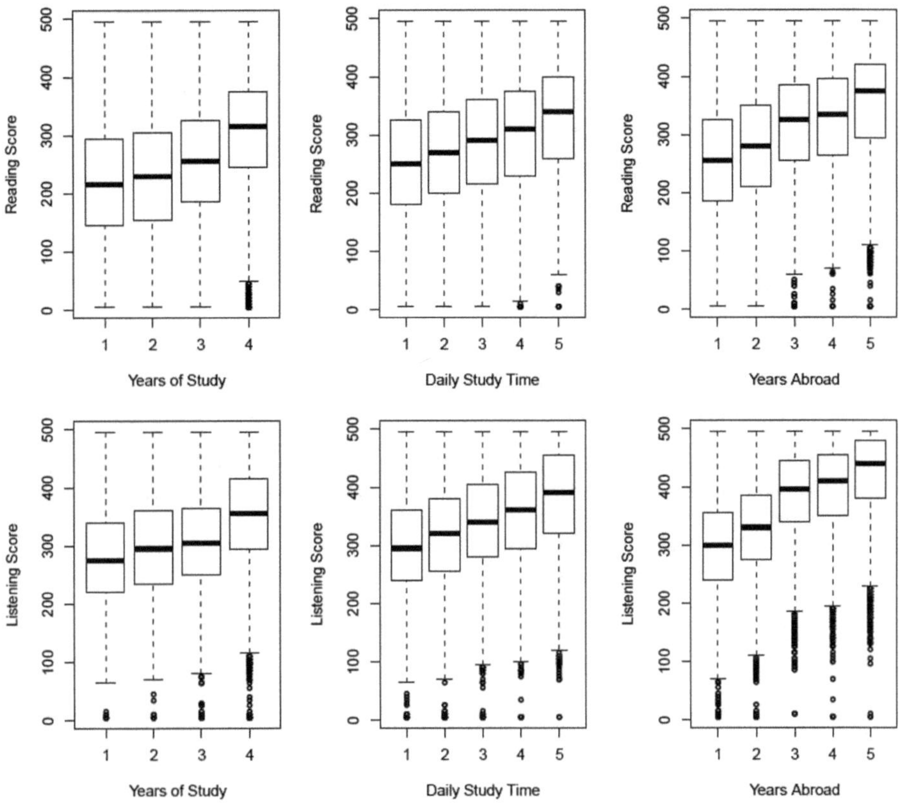

Fig. 2 Box plot of scores versus the three ordinal predictors (*years of study*, *daily study time*, and *years abroad*)

Table 10 Selection of interaction terms for Listening score

Model	Term	LogLik	$\hat{\sigma}$	Reduction (%)
Model 0	Intercept + admin + main	–1,328,007	71.51	
Model 1	Model 0 + engctry: years	–1,327,971	71.4990	0.015
Model 2	Model 0 + engctry: repeater	–1,327,716	71.4210	0.109
Model 3	Model 0 + engctry: major	–1,327,946	71.4914	0.099
Model 4	Model 0 + years: repeater	–1,328,002	71.5087	0.024
Model 5	Model 0 + years: major	–1,327,945	71.4912	0.025
Model 6	Model 0 + repeater: major	–1,327,973	71.4999	0.012

effect terms can be plotted to test the normality assumption about the random effects. The reader can refer to Draper and Smith (1998, Chaps. 2, 7 and 8) for an in-depth discussion about general model-fit assessment.

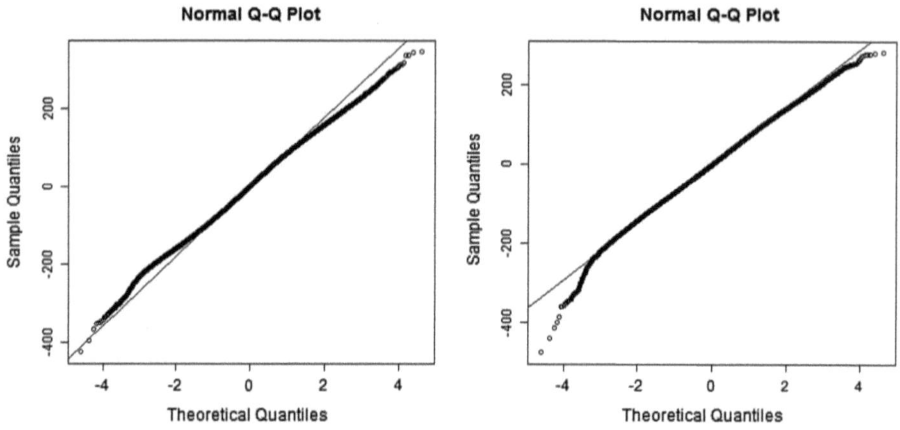

Fig. 3 Residual QQ-plots for Reading (*left*) and for Listening (*right*). Quantiles of the sample distribution and quantiles of standard normal distribution are plotted against each other. If the points in the QQ-plots approximately lie on the line $y = x$, then the sample (i.e., residual) distribution can be regarded as following the standard normal distribution approximately

3.2 *Inference and Interpretation of the Final Models*

Based on the final models, we found the "group" random effect was not significant. In other words, scores of examinees from the same group and different administrations were not significantly correlated. This indicates that the equating plan did not introduce a noticeable level of dependency to the scores examined here. As we expected, the "administration" random effect appeared to be significant, showing that scores of examinees from the same administration are significantly correlated. The intraclass correlation estimate based on the Reading final model was $\widehat{\sigma}_a^2 / \left(\widehat{\sigma}_a^2 + \widehat{\sigma}^2\right) = 0.02$, meaning that only 2 % of the variance in the Reading scores was between administrations. The estimated intraclass correlation was 0.03 for Listening scores.

Tables 11 and 12 show the estimated fixed effects for the Reading and Listening final models, respectively. All of the estimated fixed effects are significantly nonzero. Because the estimated coefficient for "English country" is positive, examinees who spent more time in English-speaking countries had higher scores than those who did not. Meanwhile, the longer the examinees studied English, the better the scores were. Also, examinees who had a college or higher degree tended to score higher. Another important finding is that repeaters scored higher than the first-timers. In terms of Reading score, examinees obtained approximately 22.83 more points when they spent 6 more months in English-speaking countries; while for Listening score, the increment was 30.12 points. Meanwhile, the examinees scored about 20.67 more points on Reading and 17.49 more points on Listening when they spent 3 more years studying English. For the predictor "education," undergraduate students were the baseline. For Reading score (Table 11), undergraduate students

Table 11 Fixed effects in the final model for Reading

Predictor	Interpretation	Estimate	Standard error
(Intercept)		152.31	3.09
Engctry		22.83	0.17
Years		20.67	0.21
Edu2	Graduate student	22.61	0.55
Edu3	Others	−38.47	0.55
Repeater1	Repeated examinee	37.14	0.43
Major2	Social study/law	5.84	0.58
Major3	Business	−2.36	0.55
Major4	Sciences	−17.32	0.64
Major5	Health	−6.61	0.95
Major6	Engineering/architecture	−27.63	0.51
Major7	Others/none	−19.50	0.84

Note: Reference categories of the categorical predictors are undergraduate students (Edu1), examinees taking the test for the first time (Repeater0), and examinees majoring in liberal arts (Major1)

Table 12 Fixed effects in the final model for Listening

Predictor	Interpretation	Estimate	Standard error
(Intercept)		202.01	3.50
Engctry		30.12	0.14
Years		17.49	0.18
Repeater1	Repeated examinee	37.35	0.37
Major2	Social study/law	−3.38	0.49
Major3	Business	−11.52	0.48
Major4	Sciences	−23.41	0.54
Major5	Health	−17.24	0.82
Major6	Engineering/architecture	−32.78	0.43
Major7	Others/none	−24.59	0.70

Note: Reference categories of the categorical predictors are examinees taking the test for the first time (Repeater0) and examinees majoring in liberal arts (Major1)

tended to score 38.47 more points than examinees who had a lower degree than bachelors (Edu3); while for graduate students (Edu2), their advantage was 22.61 points higher on the mean Reading score as compared to undergraduate students. For the predictor "major," students with a major of liberal arts were the baseline. Among the seven categories for "major," only the students who majored in social studies/law scored higher on average than the baseline.

4 Prediction

One important application of the linear mixed effects model is to construct a prediction interval for the mean score of a new administration based on the final model built on historical data that include necessary predictors to explain the test scores. By way of illustration, consider a 95 % prediction interval. One can be 95 % sure that the future mean score of an administration should fall within the 95 % prediction interval. If not, there might be something unusual with the administration so that the whole operational procedures should be checked for quality control purposes.

Following the notation in the previous sections, denote Y_{jk} as individual k's score (Reading or Listening) in administration j, and denote p as the number of predictors included in the final model built on historical data or a training set. Let $\mathbf{X}_{jk}$ be a p-dimensional vector of the predictors included in the final model for the section score, and let β be the p-dimensional coefficient vector. To simplify the formulas in this section, we further define a $(p+1)$-dimensional vector $\boldsymbol{W}_{jk} = [1, \boldsymbol{X}'_{jk}]'$ and a $(p+1)$-dimensional coefficient vector $\beta_1 = [\mu_0, \beta']'$ that includes the intercept of the model, and the final model can be rewritten as

$$\begin{aligned}
Y_{jk} &= W'_{jk}\,\beta_1 + A_j + \epsilon_{jk}, \\
A_j &\sim i.i.d.N\left(0, \sigma_a^2\right), \\
\epsilon_{jk} &\sim i.i.d.N\left(0, \sigma^2\right), \\
A_j &\perp \epsilon_{jk}.
\end{aligned}$$

The $\perp$ sign means two random variables are independent of each other. Let n be the number of examinees in administration j, and let $\mu_{jk} = \boldsymbol{W}'_{jk}\,\beta_1$. Then the expected mean score of administration j, $\overline{Y}_j$, conditioning on A_j, is equal to

$$E\left(\overline{Y}_{j.}\,\middle|A_j\right) = E\left(\frac{1}{n}\sum_{k=1}^{n} Y_{jk}\middle|A_j\right) = \frac{1}{n}\sum_{k=1}^{n}\mu_{jk} + A_j + E\left(\frac{1}{n}\sum_{k=1}^{n}\epsilon_{jk}\right)$$

where the last term equals zero.

However, if we are interested in predicting the mean score of a new administration, we need to find the marginal distribution of $\overline{Y}_j$ by integrating out A_j. Based on the properties of conditional expectation and the variance decomposition formula (e.g., Casella and Berger 2002, Chap. 4.4), one can find that

$$\overline{Y}_{j.} \sim N\left(\frac{1}{n}\sum_{k=1}^{n}\mu_{jk}, \frac{1}{n}\,\sigma^2 + \sigma_a^2\right).$$

From the final model built on historical data or a training set, we have the estimates for β_1, σ^2, and σ_a^2. Let

$$\mu_{j\cdot} = \frac{1}{n}\sum_{k=1}^{n}\mu_{jk} = \frac{1}{n}\sum_{k=1}^{n}W'_{jk}\,\beta_1 = \frac{1}{n}\,1'W'_j\beta_1, \tag{1}$$

where $\boldsymbol{W}_j = [\boldsymbol{W}_{j1}, \ldots, \boldsymbol{W}_{jn}]$ is a $(p+1)\times n$ matrix and $\mathbf{1} = [1, \ldots, 1]'$ is an n-dimensional vector. Therefore,

$$\overline{Y}_{j.} - \widehat{\mu}_{j.} \sim N\left(0, \mathrm{Var}\left(\overline{Y}_{j.} - \widehat{\mu}_{j.}\right)\right),$$

where $\widehat{\mu}_{j.} = \left(\mathbf{1}'W'_j\widehat{\beta}_1\right)/n$ is the prediction of the new value $\overline{Y}_{j.}$ with its predictors $\boldsymbol{W}_j$, and

$$\mathrm{Var}\left(\overline{Y}_{j.} - \widehat{\mu}_{j.}\right) = \left(\frac{1}{n}\,\sigma^2 + \sigma_a^2\right) + \frac{1}{n^2}\left(\mathbf{1}'W'_j\mathrm{Var}\left(\widehat{\beta}_1\right)W_j\mathbf{1}\right). \tag{2}$$

Thus, the 95 % approximate prediction interval for $\overline{Y}_j$, the mean score of the new administration of interest, is

$$\left(\widehat{\mu}_{j\cdot} \pm z_{2.5\,\%}\sqrt{\widehat{\mathrm{Var}}\left(\overline{Y}_{j\cdot} - \widehat{\mu}_{j\cdot}\right)}\right), \tag{3}$$

where $z_{2.5\,\%} = 1.96$, and the σ, σ_a, and $\mathrm{Var}\left(\widehat{\beta}_1\right)$ in Eq. (2) are replaced by their estimates, $\widehat{\sigma}^2, \widehat{\sigma}_a^2$ and $\widehat{\mathrm{Var}}\left(\widehat{\beta}_1\right)$, respectively. The approximation is more accurate with more administrations. Note that, for quality control purposes, the 95 % prediction interval may lead to too many false positives. One solution is to construct the prediction interval with a type I error $\alpha\% < 5\,\%$ by using $z_{(\alpha/2)\,\%}$ rather than $z_{2.5\,\%}$ in Eq. (3). In the quality control literature, $z_{(\alpha/2)\,\%} = 3$ is a common choice when the issue of multiple comparisons is involved.

An empirical example. To demonstrate the above formulas for detecting unusual test administrations, we used data from the earlier 14 administrations as the training set to build the linear mixed effects models for Reading and Listening. Following the procedure described in Sect. 2, the same final models resulted for the 14 administrations (of course, the estimated fixed effects and variance components had different values than those reported in Sect. 3). Based on the final models, we then constructed the 95 % approximate prediction intervals for the Reading mean score and the Listening mean score of the last administration. For Listening, the observed mean score was 348.81, and the 95 % approximate prediction interval from Eq. (3) was (335.78, 385.75). For Reading, the observed mean score was 292.61, and the 95 % approximate prediction interval from Eq. (3) was (290.68, 336.96). The observed mean scores of the last administration fall with the prediction intervals.

5 Conclusion

In this study we proposed a new way of conducting QC of test scores data over time for a specific operational setting. We proposed a linear mixed effects model to identify an unusual test administration in a flow of administrations by using a prediction interval for the mean scaled score of an administration. We applied this method to a set of operational data from a global English assessment.

In order to apply the linear mixed effects model we assumed that individual residuals were normally distributed. The "group" random effect turned out to be not significant, while examinees from the same "administration" still shared a small but significant random effect, which means the examinees' scores were slightly correlated due to seasonality. Approximate prediction intervals could be constructed from the model and can be used to detect unusual administrations for certain subgroups. In some sense, "country" and "administration" effects were confounded because of the equating design.

This procedure can be improved upon by increasing the number of administrations and the equating groups of administrations, thereby increasing the precision of the results. Then, the proposed prediction interval can be updated and computed at each administration for a detection of unusual results on-the-fly, if the time allotted for reporting scores permits extra analyses; otherwise, the interval can be updated after each administration in order to predict the next administration's results.

In the future, one might consider investigating a nonlinear link in the linear mixed effects model. In addition, further research may consider accounting for seasonality.

Acknowledgments The list of authors is alphabetical to reflect the equal contribution of each of them. The work presented here was conducted during the summer internship of Minzhao Liu with the Educational Testing Service in 2011. The authors thank Shelby Haberman, Andries van der Ark, Charlie Lewis, Frank Rijmen, and Yue Jia for their comments on earlier versions of the paper, and thank Kim Fryer for editorial help. Any opinions expressed in this paper are those of the authors and not necessarily of the Educational Testing Service or the University of Florida.

References

Agresti, A. (1996). *An introduction to categorical data analysis*. New York: Wiley.

Allalouf, A. (2007). An NCME instructional module on quality control procedures in the scoring, equating, and reporting of test scores. *Educational Measurement: Issues and Practice, 26*(1), 36–46.

Bates, D., & Maechler, M. (2010). *lme4: Linear mixed-effects models using S4 classes*. R package version 0.999375-34.

Casella, G., & Berger, R. L. (2002). *Statistical inference* (2nd ed.). Pacific Grove, CA: Duxbury Press.

Daniels, M. J., & Hogan, J. W. (2008). *Missing data in longitudinal studies: Strategies for Bayesian modeling and sensitivity analysis*. Boca Raton, FL: Chapman & Hall/CRC.

Draper, N. R., & Smith, H. (1998). *Applied regression analysis* (3rd ed.). New York: Wiley.

Gelman, A., & Hill, J. (2007). *Data analysis using regression and multilevel/hierarchical models*. Cambridge, UK: Cambridge University Press.

Lee, Y.-H., & Haberman, S. J. (2013). Harmonic regression and scale stability. *Psychometrika, 78*(4), 815–829. doi:10.1007/s11336-013-9337-1.

Lee, Y.-H., & von Davier, A. A. (2013). Monitoring scale scores over time via quality control charts, model-based approaches, and time series techniques. *Psychometrika, 78*(3), 557–575. doi:10.1007/s11336-013-9317-5.

Li, D., Li, S., & von Davier, A. A. (2011). Applying time-series analysis to detect scale drift. In A. A. von Davier (Ed.), *Statistical models for test equating, scaling, and linking* (pp. 327–346). New York: Springer.

Luo, L., Lee, Y.-H., & von Davier, A. A. (2011, April). *Pattern detection for scaled score means of subgroups across multiple test administrations*. Paper presented at the annual meeting of the American Educational Research Association, New Orleans, LA.

R Development Core Team. (2011). *R: A language and environment for statistical computing*. Vienna, Austria: R Foundation for Statistical Computing. ISBN 3-900051-07-0.

Searle, S. R., Casella, G., & McCulloch, C. E. (2006). *Variance components*. New York: Wiley-Interscience.

Snijders, T. A. B., & Bosker, R. J. (2012). *Multilevel analysis: An introduction to basic and advanced multilevel modeling* (2nd ed.). London, UK: Sage.

Von Davier, A. A. (2012). *The use of quality control and data mining techniques for monitoring scaled scores: An overview* (ETS Research Rep. No. RR-12-20). Princeton, NJ: ETS.

Heterogeneous Populations and Multistage Test Design

Minh Q. Duong and Alina A. von Davier

1 Introduction

In this paper we discuss the considerations involved in designing a test so that the difficulty of the test matches the distribution of the target population of test takers. The underlying idea is that an assessment brings together a set of items with a set of test takers and, if the attributes of these two sets are suitably matched, then measurement is improved and the validity of the assessment is better supported.

This applied research was motivated by operational experience: a linear achievement test of English skills was repurposed as a placement test. The assessment was initially designed for a population of highly educated professionals and then was administered, in several instances, to a less educated, more heterogeneous group of test takers. This change in the demographics led to poor measurement and biased equating results for some subgroups of test takers. These consequences were in violation of the fairness standards to which we adhere in the field of psychometrics.

In this paper we will discuss how the data were problematic in this testing situation, propose a change in the test design, and describe a simulation study that we conducted to investigate the potential performances of two multistage test (MST) designs. The remainder of this paper is structured as follows: first, the target population and test designs are briefly discussed. Next, an example using our data is presented, and the bias that occurred is discussed. We will conclude with a description of our simulation study, including the methods, results, and conclusions.

M.Q. Duong (✉)
Pacific Metrics, 1 Lower Ragsdale Drive, Building 1, Suite 150, Monterey, CA 93940, USA
e-mail: mduong@pacificmetrics.com

A.A. von Davier
Research and Development, Educational Testing Service, Rosedale Road, T-198, Princeton, NJ 08541, USA
e-mail: avondavier@ets.org

R.E. Millsap et al. (eds.), *New Developments in Quantitative Psychology*, Springer Proceedings in Mathematics & Statistics 66, DOI 10.1007/978-1-4614-9348-8_10,

2 Target Population

The target population for an assessment should be from a population of test takers for whom the test results should be valid. To ensure a good match between items and people, tests are designed for a target population. The items, tests, and equating results are expected to be (relatively) invariant with respect to the subgroups that comprise the target population (see Dorans and Holland 2000). These subgroups may be defined by language, gender, race, and so forth (Van de Vijver and Leung 1997). This requirement tends to hold for most traditional, well-constructed standardized assessments for which the target population is clearly defined (see Dorans and Holland 2000; von Davier and Wilson 2008). When subgroups of test takers have different ability levels in the skill measured by the test, then the test results might be dependent on which group being examined. In addition, the population of test takers might change over time and differ from the population initially targeted. In this case, the accuracy of the scores may decrease and the equating function may become dependent on subgroups of test takers with different skill levels. In addition, differing subgroup sample sizes across administrations may impact measurement (Qian et al. 2012). Together, these conditions could undermine the fairness of the assessment.

The following discussion addresses the issue of test design for these types of shifts in the testing population and how to choose a test design that matches the characteristics of the skill distribution of the target population.

3 Test Design

For many years, linear tests have been the most popular way to measure test takers' skills in educational assessments. In a linear test, all test takers are administered the same items, regardless of whether the items are too easy or too difficult for them (Rudner 1998). When properly developed, the construction of a linear test is easy and economical; moreover, the test could have a good reliability and relatively little measurement error.

A computer adaptive test (CAT) is a computer-based test that uses an algorithm to administer test items that match the test taker's estimated skill level, based on his/her pattern of responses as the test proceeds. With the right item pool, a CAT can be much more efficient than traditional linear tests, by shortening the test (Hambleton and Swaminathan 1985; Lord 1971, 1980; Wainer et al. 1992).

A multistage (adaptive) test is very similar to a CAT, but rather than selecting individual items, groups of items (modules) are selected, and the test is constructed in stages. In an MST, all test takers are administered an initial set of items at the first stage, and, based on the test taker's performance, the test taker is then routed to one of the several different modules in the second stage that are based on the test taker's estimated skill level. This routing process may continue to subsequent stages, depending on the test. For tests that are intended to measure a wide range of proficiency, MSTs are more effective than linear tests (Kim and Plake 1993; Lord 1971, 1980) and offer more control on the test development, in particular at module level, than a CAT does. An overview of the various designs, particularly of the MST design, is given in Hendrickson (2007) and Yan et al. (in press).

If the distribution of test takers' measured skill is clearly unimodal, then a linear test for measurement and placement purposes may be the appropriate design. If the distribution is bimodal or exhibits a very large variance, then a CAT or MST should be considered in an effort to increase the precision of measurement in the full range of skill levels without increasing the test length.

CATs and MSTs can be used with any type of population distributions, as long as other measurement requirements are met: (a) a very large item pool is available; (b) the calibration samples are large; and (c) a sophisticated algorithm for item selection is available to optimize the item selection based on multiple constraints, such as the difficulty and discrimination of items, content coverage, item exposure, and so forth.

4 Real Data Example

We illustrate how to match a skill (or ability) distribution with a test design using our data from an English linear achievement test that was administered to a polarized population of test takers for placement purposes—to those who speak some English, as well as those who speak little or no English. The test is long and very reliable, and it includes some very easy items that are appropriate for the low ability group. However, there is a concern that the measurement might not be as precise for these lower and middle levels of ability as would be appropriate. In addition, it has been found that test takers with very low English skill levels tend to perform less predictably on the anchor items of the test and guess more often on all test items, in general, thus endangering the quality of equating. The ability distribution for this heterogeneous group of test takers is plotted in Fig. 1. For these data, we propose reconsidering the test design.

The dataset was obtained from an administration of a 200-item English skills test to a group of test takers. The test consists of two parts, each part being constituted of 100 items measuring listening and reading skills, respectively. For illustration purpose in this study each part will be considered as a different form of the same test. For simplicity, we will call them Test Form X and Test Form Y, respectively. A total of 6,852 test takers were assigned to two different groups, P and Q, based on their reported educational background. Group P consists of 2,808 test takers (41 %) whose educational level was less than a bachelor's degree. Group Q is comprised of 4,044 test takers (59 %) whose educational level was equivalent to a bachelor's degree or higher. Descriptive statistics of the scores on the two forms for the two groups are presented in Table 1. An examination of Fig. 1 reveals that the score distributions for overall population, and particularly for the scores on Test Form Y, are bimodal.

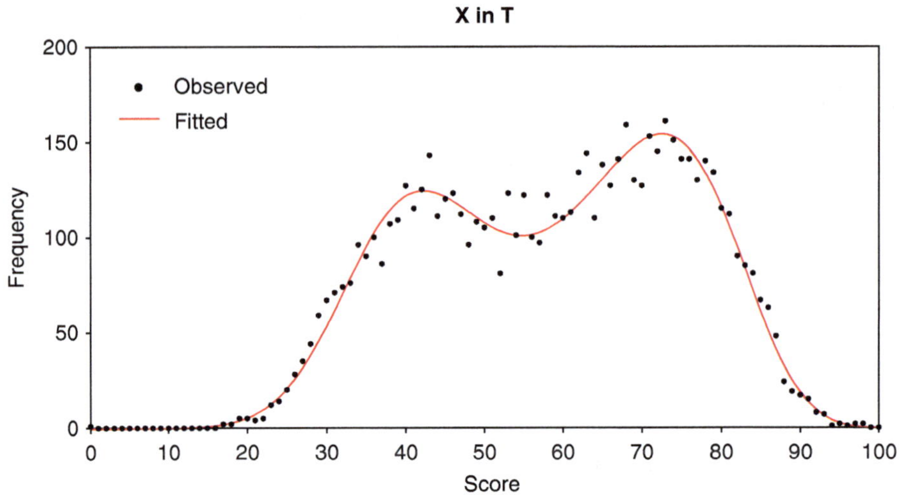

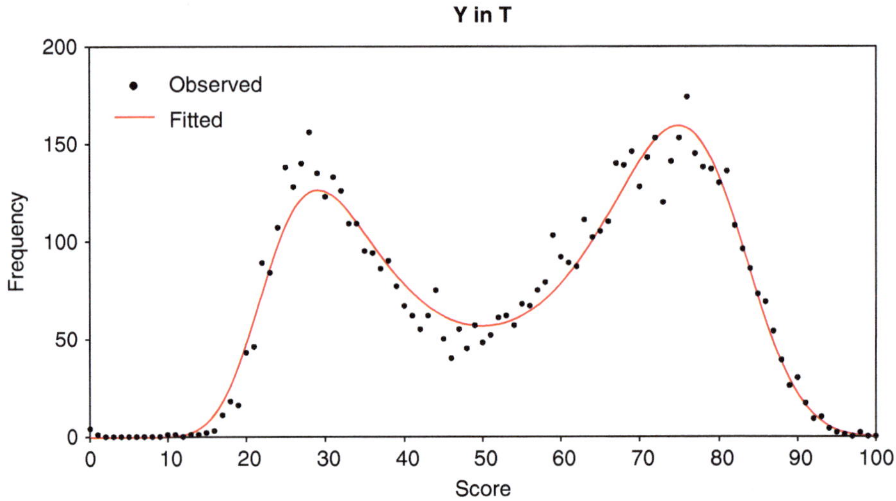

Fig. 1 Real data: distributions of X, Y in T

Table 1 Real Data: score descriptive statistics

		Form *X* score		Form *Y* score	
Group	Sample size	Mean	Std. Dev.	Mean	Std. Dev.
P	2,808	43.84	11.60	35.67	12.82
Q	4,044	68.89	11.41	69.25	12.97
T (total)	6,852	58.62	16.85	55.49	20.96

5 Procedures

Duong and von Davier (2012) analyzed these data and investigated the appropriate linking methods for them. Because the two forms measure different constructs, the process of mapping their scores is considered a *linking* rather than an *equating*. This distinction is not important here, as we only use the linking data for illustration purposes. In a real testing situation, one should never attempt to equate two tests that measure different constructs. The only purpose of linking the score distributions from these two sections of the test in this paper is to illustrate what would happen if one links two bimodal distributions and what subgroups of test takers might be impacted. In this particular case, this link is informative because the two distributions are very similar, as shown in Fig. 1.

Duong and von Davier (2012) linked Test Form X to Test Form Y using both the operational observed-score (kernel) equating (OSE) method (von Davier et al. 2004) and a two-parameter logistic (2PL) observed-score multigroup item response theory (IRT) method (Kolen and Brennan 2004) with multiple group calibration for each section. The data from the two sections, reading and listening, were calibrated separately. The factor structure in the data was preliminary analyzed for each of the two sections in order to ensure that the two modes in the distributions do not reflect different factors. One factor model underlines each of the two sets of data. The fit of the IRT model was acceptable. There is no evidence that the items function differently in the two groups of the mixture for either reading or listening. There seems to be sufficient evidence that the two groups in the sample differed mainly in their English ability and that there is no other factor that impacts the test results that leads to the bimodal distribution.

During the presmoothing step, the log-linear model that preserves the first five univariate moments and the first bivariate moment was chosen from among other (nested) models using several statistical indices available in the LOGLIN/KE Software (ETS 2011) for each of the datasets. In this example, three ways of using the data were considered during equating: (a) use both subgroups with weights that were proportional to group sample sizes; (b) use data only from P, that is, use weights $w_P = 1$ and $w_Q = 0$, denoted as *KE.P*; or (c) use data only from Q, that is, use weights $w_P = 0$ and $w_Q = 1$, denoted as *KE.Q*.

Figure 2 shows the equating differences when using the high-ability group ($w_P = 0$ and $w_Q = 1$) versus using the full distribution. It appears that, for scores greater than 67, using all the data or using only the most able group produced similar results.

If the test is used as a licensure or placement test with one or more cut scores at or below the score interval [55, 58] (where 55 and 58 are the means of the two tests for the overall group), then choosing only the higher ability group for equating might impact the results for those who score close to the cut score(s). Hence, if the test is used for placement purposes, then the placement of test takers in learning groups might not be accurate for all cut-score points and, therefore, the opportunities for efficient learning, as well as those for career advancement, might be in jeopardy.

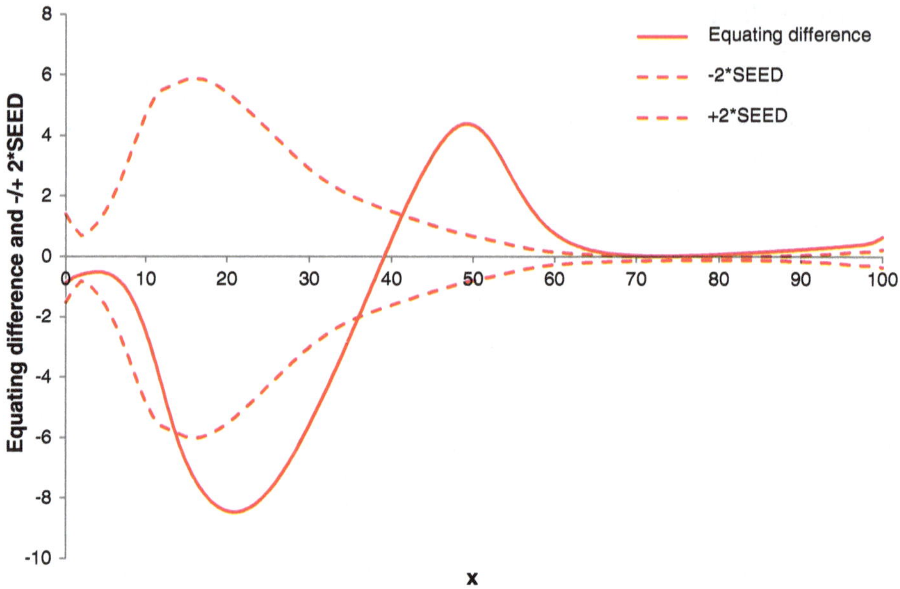

Fig. 2 Real data: difference between equating functions from high-ability group and all

A dilemma exists as to what to do with these issues. There are several options: (a) continue to use one linear test and pool the two ability groups (this might lower accuracy and lead to group dependent equating); (b) continue to use one linear test and remove one of the ability groups for equating, applying the equating results to the entire population (this might lead to scores that are not fair to all of the test takers as it was shown in Duong and von Davier 2012); (c) change the item difficulties to match the low ability group (which may cause the test to lose comparability with previous test forms, and the score scale may not have the same meaning); or (d) change the test design and use either an adaptive test, a CAT (which may be difficult for the users of this test to implement and use), or a multistage adaptive test. These options, together with the traditional operational practice, were discussed in detail by Duong and von Davier (2012).

In this paper we considered two research ideas: (a) choose an MST targeted to the bimodal population and (b) investigate two MST designs, both with two stages (see Figs. 3 and 4) where we use either one routing module and two second-stage modules or one routing module and three second-stage modules. These test designs will be presumably applied to each of the two sections separately. We will now describe these research studies using simulated data.

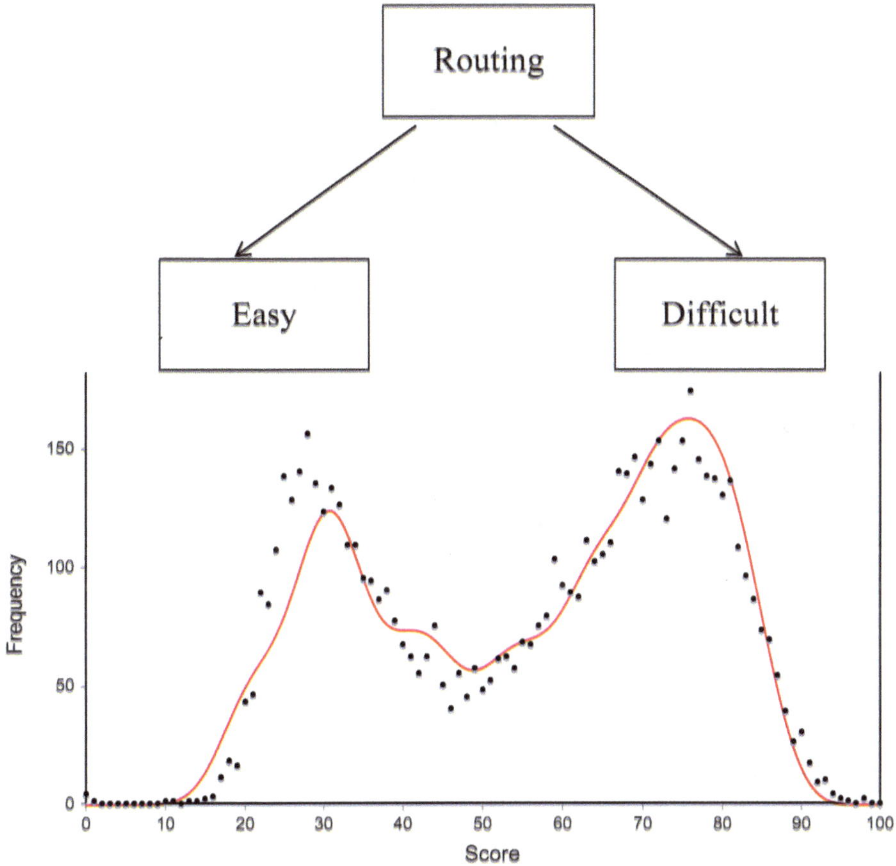

Fig. 3 A proposed MST design (with two modules on second stage) for a bimodal distribution

6 Simulation Study

6.1 Method

6.1.1 Design

In this study, two MST designs were employed, both consisting of two stages. Design *A* had two second-stage modules: easy and difficult. Design *B* had three modules in the second stage: easy, moderate, and difficult. The module structure was similar in the two designs. The routing module consisted of 40 items with a wide range of difficulty (*b* parameters). All second-stage modules consisted of 20 items with narrow ranges of difficulty. In terms of item parameters, all modules were similar except for the *b* parameters, which varied across modules to create various difficulty levels, as mentioned above.

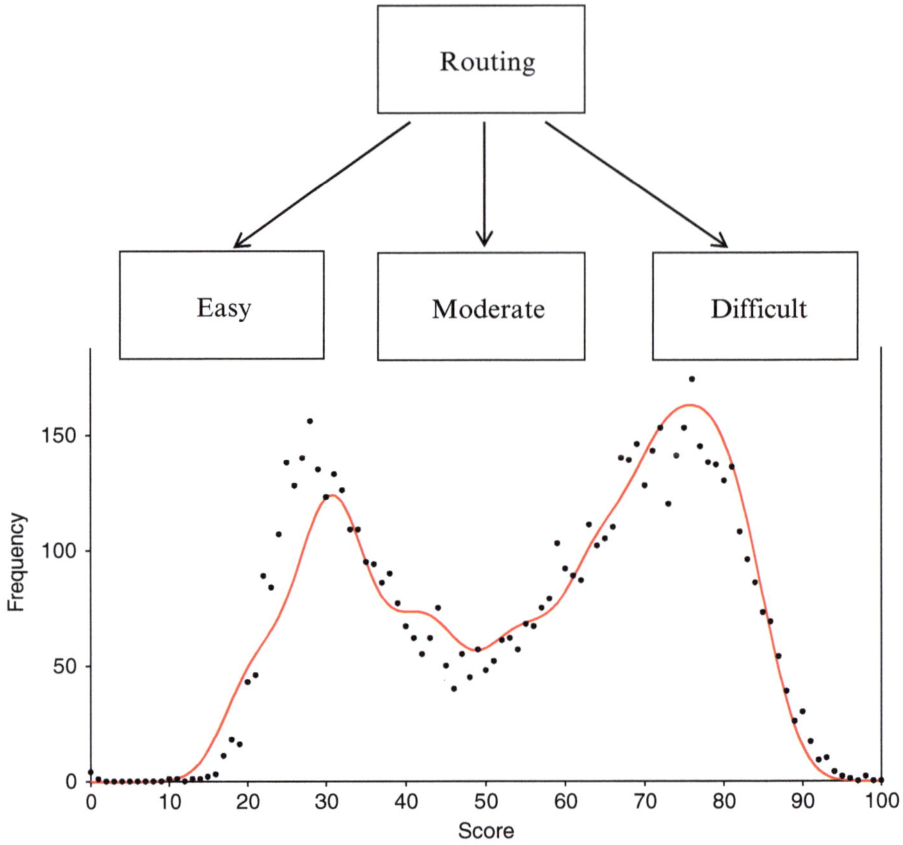

Fig. 4 A proposed MST design (with three modules on second stage) for a bimodal distribution

Data were simulated to closely match the real data in terms of the ability distribution, and the two simulated MST designs were analyzed. The data were simulated using a 3PL model because the first mode of the bimodal distribution is close to the guessing point, and, therefore, we assumed that perhaps many of the test takers from this new group guessed their answers. We also wanted to have a different model for the simulation of the data from the model used for the calibration so that some level of misspecification would be introduced, as is the case with test takers.

The item parameters for each module were simulated independently. The *a* parameters were simulated from a log-normal distribution *LN* ($\mu = -0.15, \sigma = 0.3$). In this paper, σ denotes the standard deviation. The *c* (guessing) parameters were simulated from a beta distribution Beta ($\alpha = 7, \beta = 34$), which has a mean of 0.17 and standard deviation of 0.058. The *b* parameters were simulated from a normal distribution *N* (μ, σ) with different values of μ and σ. For the routing modules, $\mu = 1.5$ and $\sigma = 1.6$. For all second-stage modules, σ was set at 1 and μ at –0.5

Table 2 Generating item parameter statistics

Module (number of items)	Item parameter	Design *A* (two modules on second stage)		Design *B* (three modules on second stage)	
		Mean	Std. Dev.	Mean	Std. Dev.
Routing (40)	*a*	0.873	0.256	0.879	0.278
	b	1.535	1.626	1.528	1.614
	c	0.134	0.046	0.134	0.044
Easy (20)	*a*	0.882	0.299	0.878	0.271
	b	−0.505	0.927	−0.556	0.908
	c	0.128	0.045	0.153	0.051
Moderate (20)	*a*	NA		0.911	0.265
	b			1.577	0.908
	c			0.131	0.058
Difficult (20)	*a*	0.886	0.285	0.875	0.300
	b	2.503	0.933	2.482	0.934
	c	0.134	0.045	0.131	0.041

Table 3 Population structure

Condition	Population *P*	*Q*	Total
1	22,500	7,500	30,000
2	15,000	15,000	30,000
3	7,500	22,500	30,000

for the easy module, 1.5 for the moderate module, and 2.5 for the difficult module. The summary statistics for the simulated item parameters are presented in Table 2. Those parameters were used as generating parameters to simulate data.

The test taker population was simulated as a bimodal population consisting of two distinct groups *P* and *Q*. *P* had a normal distribution $N\ (\mu = 0,\ \sigma = 1)$ while *Q* had a normal distribution with a larger mean $N\ (\mu = 3,\ \sigma = 1)$. The ability levels of the two groups were set far apart (i.e., the mean difference equaled three standard deviations) to produce a clear bimodal distribution, as in the real data. Table 3 shows the three sample structures that were investigated. These structures represent balanced and imbalanced sample sizes. The sample sizes were set large enough to exclude possible sample size effects on the calibration.

6.1.2 Data Simulation and Calibration

In an MST administration, test takers are administered the routing module and a specific second-stage module depending on their score on the routing module. To mimic that data structure, the data simulation included two steps. In the first step, test takers' responses to all modules were simulated using generated item parameters with the 3PL model. In the second step, responses to the routing module and one second-stage module were kept, resulting in the MST-like data. The second-stage module for which the test taker's responses were kept depended on his or her score on the routing module. In Design A, if the score on the routing module was less than or equal to 20, the response on the easy module was kept. Otherwise, the response on the difficult model was retained. In Design B (which had three modules in the second stage), if a score on the routing module was less than or equal to 13, the response on the easy module was kept. If the score was greater than or equal to 27, then the response on the difficult module was retained. Otherwise, the response on the moderate module was kept.

Simulated data were calibrated using the computer program BILOG-MG (Zimowski et al. 1996), using the multigroup procedure in order to reflect the bimodal nature of the data. Group P was set as a reference group, which, by the program's default, is assumed to have a standard normal distribution. Default priors were used for all item parameters.[1] Besides item parameter estimates, the expected a posteriori (EAP) of theta was also obtained for classifying test takers. Although the data were simulated using the 3PL model, both the 2PL and 3PL models were used in calibration. The 2PL model was used to determine if the model misfit had any impact on the results.

For each condition (i.e., sample structure presented in Table 3), 100 replications were conducted. Each replication included the following steps: (a) data simulation, (b) calibration, and (c) computation of evaluation statistics (which are presented in the next section). Across all replications, the generating item parameters remained unchanged.

6.1.3 Evaluation Statistics

Several evaluation statistics were used in this study. To evaluate item parameter recovery, bias and root mean square error (RMSE) between the estimated and true parameters were used. Standard errors were also used to evaluate the item parameter estimation.

To assess how well test takers were classified, two classification statistics were used, based on the true (simulated) theta and the estimated EAP. For simplicity, only dichotomous classifications were employed such that test takers falling below the cut score (on a theta or EAP scale) were classified as "nonmasters" and those meeting or exceeding the cut score were classified as "masters." The percentage of test takers who were classified at the same level on both true theta and EAP scales was used as the classification accuracy statistic. The other classification index was the kappa statistic, which indicates the magnitude of agreement between two classification procedures based on true theta and EAP values accounting for

---

[1] $\log(a) \sim N(\mu = 0, \sigma = 0.5)$
$b \sim N(\mu = 0, \sigma = 2)$
c is set to have a Beta distribution with the mean equal to 0.2 for the 3PL model or a mean of 0.001 for the 2PL model.

Table 4 Classification based on true theta and EAP

		EAP classification		
		Nonmaster	Master	Total
True theta classification	Nonmaster	a	b	t_0
	Master	c	d	t_1
	Total	e_0	e_1	N

agreement by chance. Several theta cut scores were used between −2 and 5 with a 0.5 increment to investigate how well test takers were classified at various cut scores, to cover a wide range of scores.

The kappa was computed using

$$\text{kappa} = \frac{p_0 - p_e}{1 - p_e} \tag{1}$$

where p_e and p_0 are expected and observed agreement calculated from

$$p_e = \frac{t_1}{N}\frac{e_1}{N} + \frac{t_0}{N}\frac{e_0}{N} \tag{2}$$

$$p_0 = \frac{a+d}{N} \tag{3}$$

All terms in (1)–(3) are presented in Table 4.

In addition, relative (IRT) information was used for all modules as a way to evaluate module quality. All evaluation statistics were computed for each replication and averaged across all replications.

6.2 Results

6.2.1 Score Distribution

The target population investigated in this study was bimodal, consisting of two distinct groups. Figure 5 presents score distributions for the routing module for one of the replications (used as an example for illustrative purpose) in all conditions (i.e., sample structure presented in Table 3) within each design. The simulated score distributions were obviously bimodal, especially in condition 2, where the population was equally represented by both Groups P and Q. It should be noted that the other distributions were skewed, due to an imbalanced population structure, but were also somewhat bimodal. In Fig. 5, A1 denotes Design A, Condition 1, A2 denotes Design A, Condition 2, and so on.

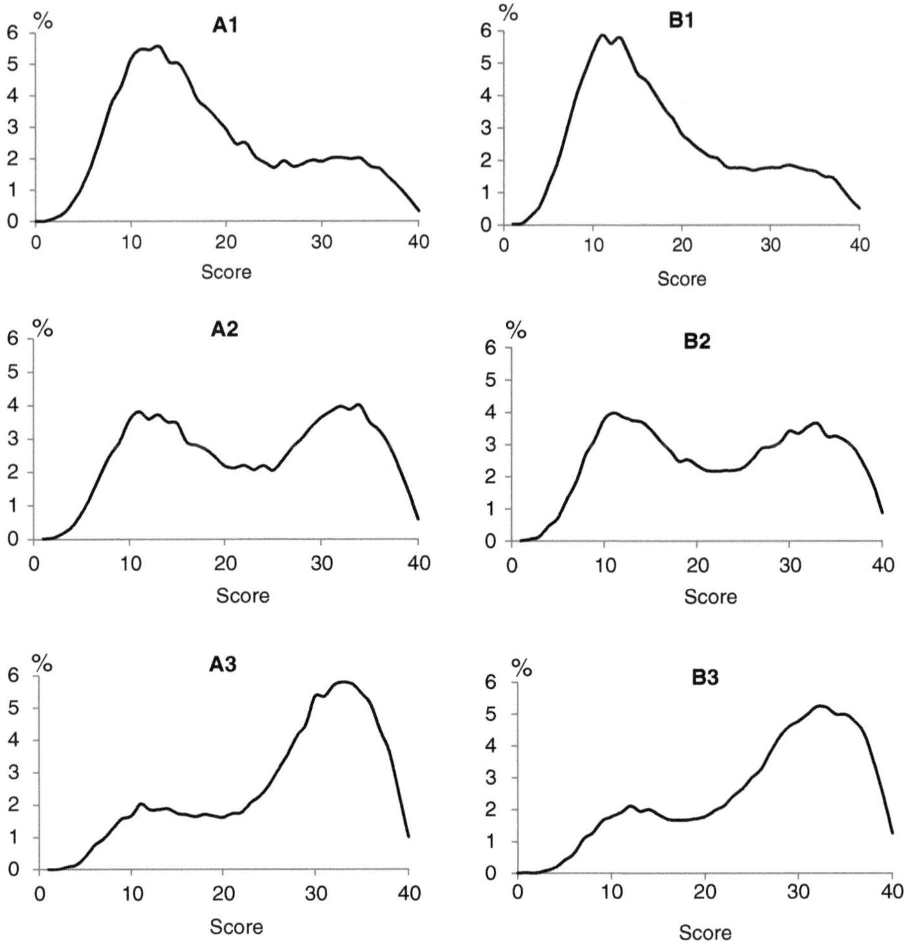

Fig. 5 Routing module score distribution (of one replication)

6.2.2 Calibration Results

All calibration runs converged with less than 30 cycles on the default criterion (0.01). The number of Gauss–Newton iterations following E-M cycle was set at two (default) for 3PL model and at three for 2PL model.

6.2.3 Bias, RMSE, and Standard Error

The results for bias, RMSE, and standard error are presented in Table 5 for all conditions described in Table 3 in both designs for both 2PL and 3PL calibration models.

Table 5 Bias, RMSE, and standard error

Design (number of items)	Condition	Item parameter	Bias 2PL	Bias 3PL	RMSE 2PL	RMSE 3PL	Standard error 2PL	Standard error 3PL
A (80)	1	*a*	−0.380	−0.044	0.465	0.059	0.010	0.031
		b	0.266	0.074	1.127	0.132	0.043	0.054
		c		0.002		0.023		0.020
	2	*a*	−0.374	−0.059	0.448	0.072	0.010	0.028
		b	0.166	0.085	0.937	0.152	0.036	0.055
		c		0.000		0.025		0.021
	3	*a*	−0.364	−0.077	0.431	0.099	0.012	0.029
		b	0.110	0.114	0.806	0.192	0.036	0.063
		c		0.003		0.034		0.025
B (100)	1	*a*	−0.400	−0.064	0.475	0.093	0.014	0.047
		b	0.229	0.085	0.970	0.165	0.067	0.077
		c		−0.002		0.029		0.028
	2	*a*	−0.403	−0.085	0.466	0.112	0.014	0.044
		b	0.157	0.094	0.842	0.183	0.057	0.079
		c		−0.004		0.032		0.030
	3	*a*	−0.402	−0.114	0.458	0.142	0.017	0.045
		b	0.122	0.110	0.785	0.233	0.058	0.088
		c		−0.008		0.036		0.033

Bias. In the 3PL model, Design *A* produced slightly less bias than Design *B*, especially for the *a* and *c* parameters. Biases increased, especially for the *a* and *b* parameters, when the number of high-ability test takers increased (i.e., moving from condition 1 to condition 2 and to condition 3).

Under the 2PL model, where the model misfit might have had an impact, Design *A* produced slightly less bias than Design *B* for the *a* parameter, but not for the *b* parameter. Unlike the 3PL model, bias decreased, especially for the *b* parameter, when the number of high-ability test takers increased.

It is obvious from Table 4 that using a 3PL model for calibration produced much better results than using a 2PL model. This observation was not unexpected, since the data were simulated using a 3PL model.

RMSE. Under the 3PL model, Design *A* produced a slightly smaller RMSE than Design *B* for all item parameters. As with bias, the RMSE increased when the number of high-ability test takers increased.

When the 2PL model was used for calibration, there was no clear advantage for either design. While Design *A* produced better results for the *a* parameter, Design *B* worked better in reducing the RMSE for the *b* parameter. It was not clear if the group structure had any impact on RMSE for both *a* and *b* parameters, although having more high-ability test takers had a slightly better advantage (e.g., a smaller RMSE moving from condition 1 to condition 2 and to condition 3). As with bias, the same pattern can be observed that using a 3PL model produced much better results compared to a 2PL model.

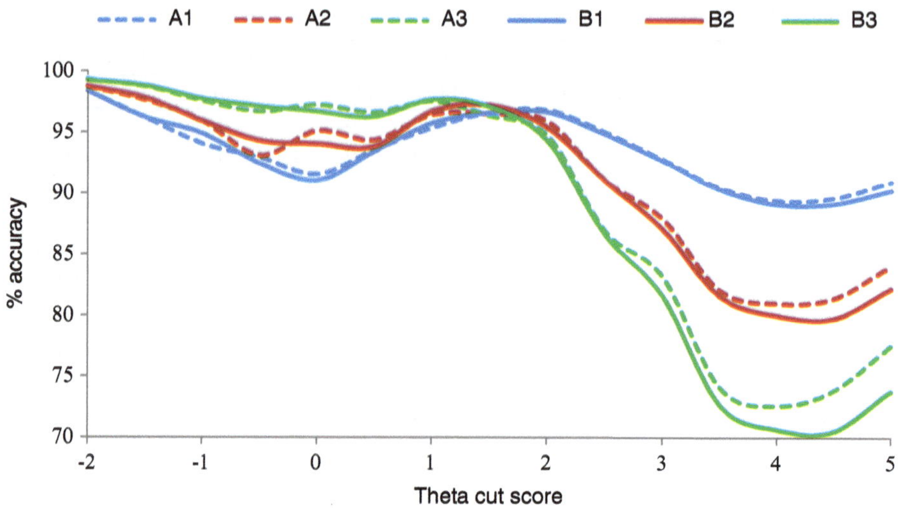

Fig. 6 2PL model classification accuracy

Standard error. If a 3PL model was used for calibration, Design *A* produced a smaller standard error than Design *B* for all of the item parameters. For the *b* and *c* parameters, having more high-ability test takers led to larger standard errors. It was not obvious whether the group structure had any impact on the standard error for the *a* parameter.

When a 2PL model was used to calibrate the data, Design *A* also produced a smaller estimation error. There was no clear impact of group structure on standard errors.

6.2.4 Classification Accuracy

The classification accuracy results for the 2PL and 3PL models are presented in Figs. 6 and 7, respectively.

It is obvious from Figs. 6 and 7 that the accuracy was low if the theta cut score was set to values where the majority of test takers were. When the majority of test takers were far from the theta cut score, the classification accuracy was high. For example, in condition 1 when the population was dominated by Group *P* (see Table 3), whose mean theta was 0, the classification accuracy was lowest when theta cut score was 0, and it was higher when the theta cut score was not near 0. That pattern is reasonable because classification accuracy tends to have more error if there are many test takers near the borderline, because this is where misclassification often occurs.

If a 2PL model was used to calibrate the data, the classification accuracy was lowered significantly with higher theta cut scores. That is because guessing, which

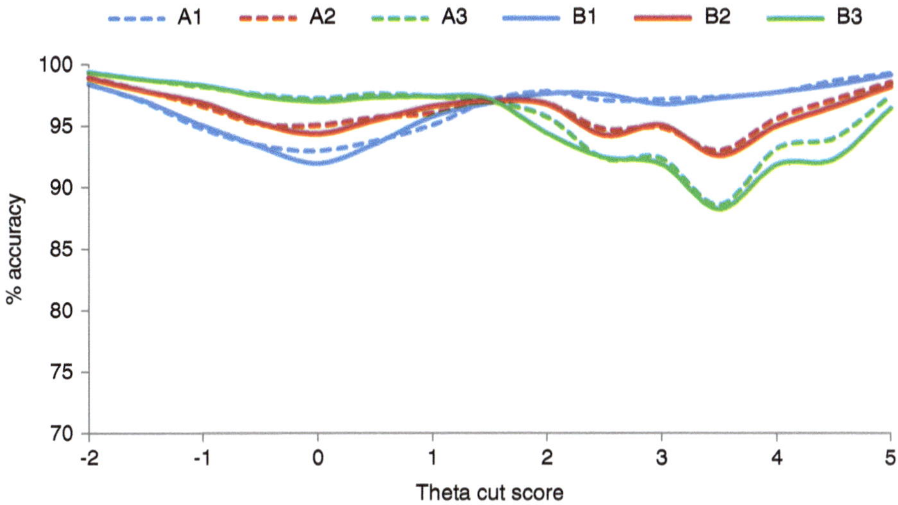

Fig. 7 3PL model classification accuracy

was integrated in the 3PL during data simulation, was not accounted for with the 2PL model. When the theta cut score was set high, more students whose true ability was not high enough were misclassified as "masters" because their scores were inflated by guessing.

There were no significant differences between Design *A* and Design *B* regardless of group structure. As can be seen in Figs. 6 and 7, in each condition of the group structure presented in Table 3, the curves representing both designs are close together, although the curve in Design *A* is slightly higher, that is, indicating a better accuracy classification.

6.2.5 Kappa Statistic

The results for the kappa statistic for the 2PL and 3PL models are presented in Figs. 8 and 9, respectively.

In Fig. 8, all of the curves approach zero at the ends. That means that when a 2PL model was used to calibrate the data, the kappa statistic decreased significantly when the theta cuts cores were set too low or too high. The same pattern is observed in Fig. 9, which represents the results when a 3PL model was used. However, compared to the kappa produced by the 2PL model, the kappa for the 3PL model was much higher and did not decrease as much at the ends. The kappa values are quite good, being higher than 0.6 for most of the score range. In both Figs. 8 and 9, the curves stay close together, indicating that there was no significant difference between Design *A* and Design *B* or among the different group structures.

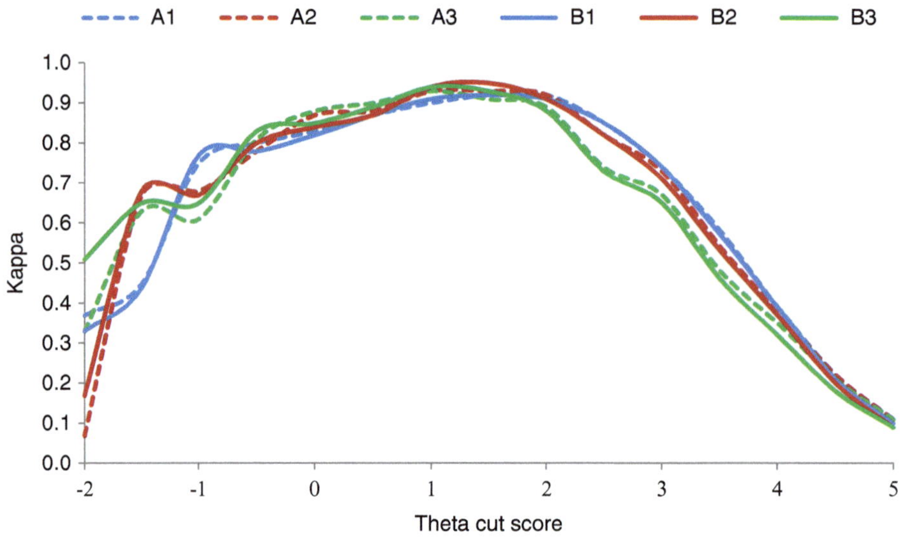

Fig. 8 2PL model kappa

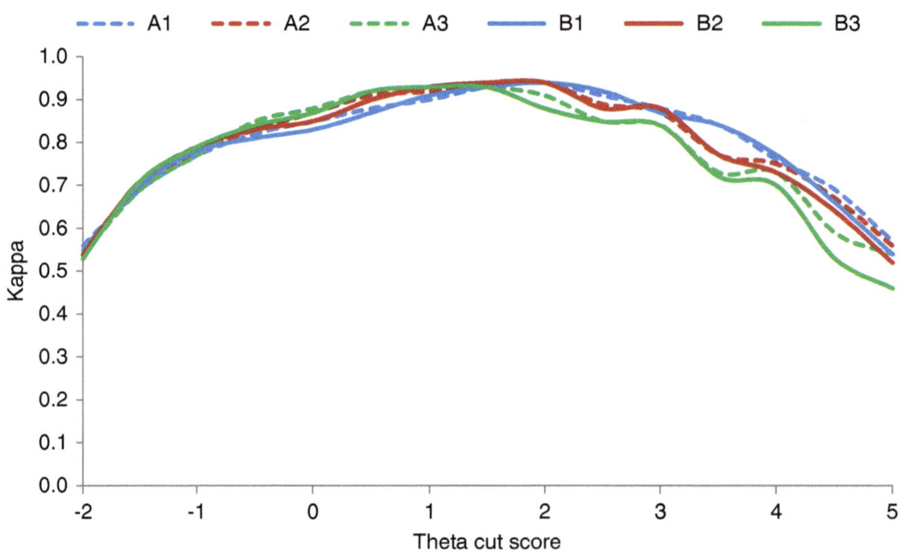

Fig. 9 3PL model kappa

6.2.6 Information

IRT-based relative information was computed for each module in all conditions for both designs. The relative information equals the average item information in each module. The average item information was used in comparing modules because the

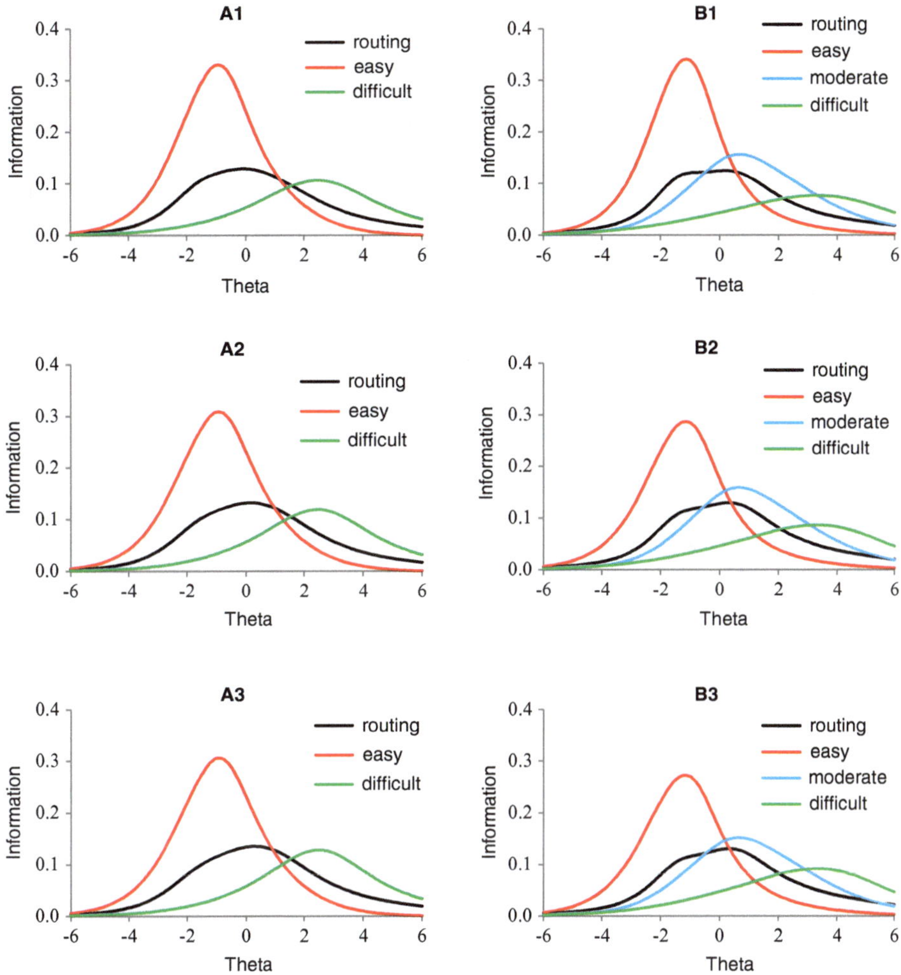

Fig. 10 2PL model information function

modules had different numbers of items. The information is presented in Figs. 10 and 11 for Design *A* and Design *B*, respectively.

It is clear from those figures that each relative information curve covers a specific area where its module was supposed to differentiate the test takers. The routing curves cover a wider range because it was supposed to differentiate test takers during the first stage, when students are not pre-classified. Except for the easy modules, using a 3PL model resulted in higher relative information. No significant differences were evident between the designs or conditions.

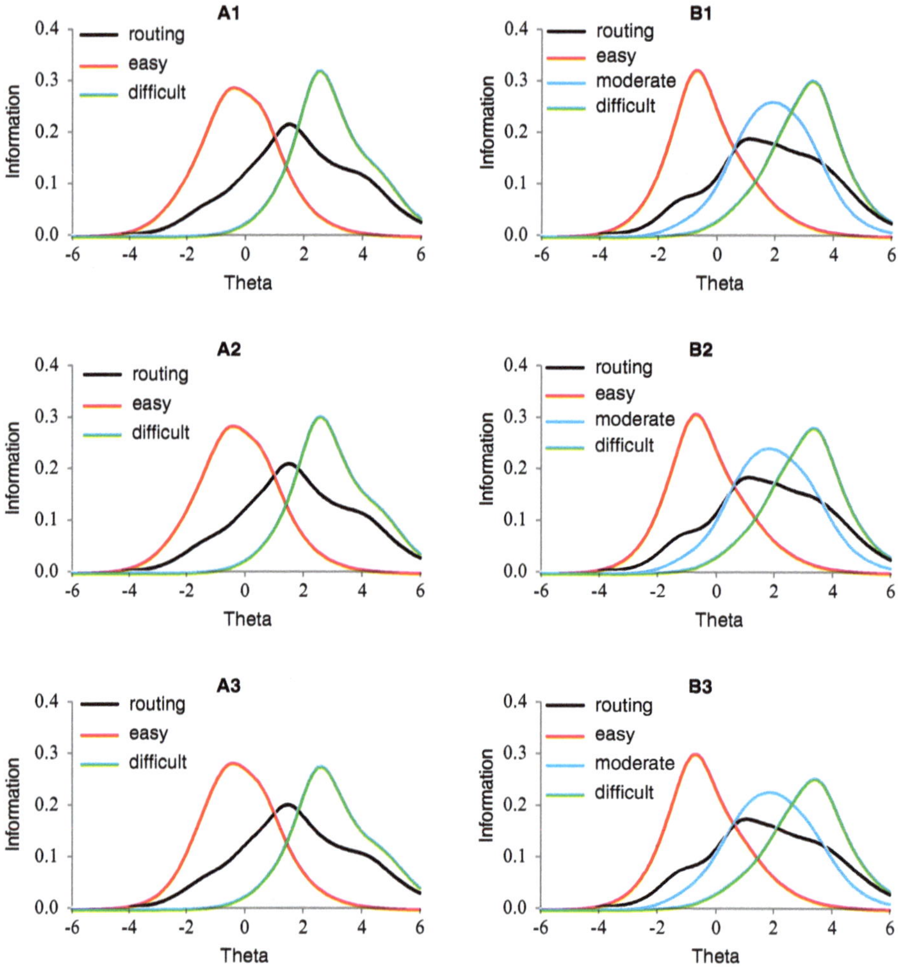

Fig. 11 3PL model information function

7 Conclusions

In this paper we investigated some of the considerations necessary for an assessment to transition from a linear test design to an MST, when there are shifts in the test taker population, leading to a bimodal distribution of test taker ability. Data were simulated to closely match the real data in terms of the ability distribution, and the two simulated MST designs were analyzed. The data were simulated using a 3PL model because the first mode of the ability distribution from the real data is close to the guessing point, and, therefore, we assumed that perhaps many of the test takers from this group would guess their answers. We also wanted to use a different model for the simulation of the data than from the model used for the calibration so that some level of misspecification would be introduced, as is the case in a real application.

As expected, the results indicate that using the 2PL model to calibrate the data is not as good as using the 3PL model. When the estimation errors are large, then the classification accuracy is lower, and the information is lower. If the hypothesis that the test takers with low ability tend to guess more holds, then a 3PL model might be more appropriate for this type of data.

No significant differences were found between using the two modules (Design *A*) and using the three modules (Design *B*) in the second stage, in terms of measurement and classification. This finding means that it may not be necessary to use three modules in the second stage if the population is bimodal and the test will not be equated. If the test continues to be post-equated, then perhaps adding a module in the middle might prove to be useful and might lead to less bias in the equating results of real data for test takers with scores in the middle of the distribution, as displayed in Fig. 2.

The population structure affects the classification accuracy, depending on the cut score. It is reasonable to assume that accuracy tends to be higher in the middle of the bimodal distribution and lower when the cut score is set to a location where the majority of test takers are located.

The investigations conducted here would definitely support the use of an MST to improve measurement and classification accuracy. The next step in this research project is to actually build the MST with the items from the item pools of the aforementioned English assessment. We will then investigate the different calibration and equatings and compare the pre-equating methods as they are known in the realm of MST to post-equating methods. The challenge presented in this particular situation is that the linear test will continue to be used in the other applications for which it was initially constructed, and, therefore, a request might be made to post-equate the test scores for this specific use of the test.

The data example considered in this paper is extreme, but real. In other testing situations the differences between different ability subgroups might not be as dramatic, and therefore, different operational decisions might be considered.

Acknowledgments The authors thank Shelby Haberman, Frederic Robin, and Duanli Yan for their comments on the manuscript. The authors also thank Kim Fryer for editorial help. The opinions expressed in this paper are those of the authors and not necessarily those of Pacific Metrics or Educational Testing Service.

References

Dorans, N. J., & Holland, P. W. (2000). Population invariance and equitability of tests: Basic theory and the linear case. *Journal of Educational Measurement, 37*(4), 281–306.

Duong, M. Q., & von Davier, A. A. (2012). Observed-score equating with a heterogeneous target population. *International Journal of Testing, 12*(3), 224–251. Retrieved from http://dx.doi.org/10.1080/15305058.2011.620725

ETS. (2011). *LOGLIN/KE software Version 2 [Computer software]*. Princeton, NJ: ETS.
Hambleton, R. K., & Swaminathan, H. (1985). *Item response theory, principles and applications*. Boston, MA: Kluwer Nijhoff.
Hendrickson, A. (2007). An NCME instructional module on multi-stage testing. *Educational Measurement: Issues and Practice, 26*, 44–52.
Kim, H., & Plake, B. S. (1993, April). *Monte Carlo simulation comparison of two-stage testing and computerized adaptive testing*. Paper presented at the annual meeting of the National Council on Measurement in Education, Atlanta, GA.
Kolen, M. J., & Brennan, R. J. (2004). *Test equating, scaling and linking* (2nd ed.). New York, NY: Springer.
Lord, F. M. (1971). A theoretical study of two-stage testing. *Psychometrika, 36*, 227–242.
Lord, F. M. (1980). *Applications of item response theory to practical testing problems*. Hillsdale, NJ: Lawrence Erlbaum Associates.
Qian, J., von Davier, A. A., & Jiang, Y. (2014). Achieving a Stable Scale for an Assessment with Multiple Forms: Weighting Test Samples in IRT Linking (this volume).
Rudner, L. (1998). *An on-line interactive computer adaptive testing tutorial*. Retrieved from http://edres.org/scripts/cat
Van de Vijver, F., & Leung, K. (1997). *Methods and data analysis for cross-cultural research*. Thousand Oaks, CA: Sage.
von Davier, A. A., Holland, P. W., & Thayer, D. T. (2004). *The kernel method of test equating*. New York, NY: Springer.
von Davier, A. A., & Wilson, C. (2008). Investigating the population sensitivity assumption of item response theory true-score equating across two subgroups of examinees and two test formats. *Applied Psychological Measurement, 32*(1), 11–26.
Wainer, H., Kaplan, B., & Lewis, C. (1992). A comparison of the performance of simulated hierarchical and linear testlets. *Journal of Educational Measurement, 29*, 243–251.
Yan, D., von Davier, A. A., Lewis, C. (Eds; 2014). *Computerized Multistage Testing: Theory and Applications*. London: Chapman & Hall.
Zimowski, M. F., Muraki, E., Mislevy, R. J., & Bock, R. D. (1996). *BILOG-MG: Multiple-group IRT analysis and test maintenance for binary items [Computer software and manual]*. Chicago: Scientific Software International.

Achieving a Stable Scale for an Assessment with Multiple Forms: Weighting Test Samples in IRT Linking

Jiahe Qian, Alina A. von Davier, and Yanming Jiang

1 Introduction

In quality control of an assessment with multiple forms, one way to ensure a stable scale for the reported scores is to achieve a stable linking process over time. For an assessment with multiple test forms, measurement precision and invariance in linking and equating are always a concern to test investigators (Holland 2007; Holland and Dorans 2006; Kolen and Brennan 2004; von Davier and Wilson 2008). In this paper, we use the term linking to describe a transformation of IRT parameters from two or more test forms to establish a common IRT scale (a linear transformation of the IRT parameters from the two test forms). Although the same specifications are used to construct forms for multiple test administrations, equating and linking procedures can still be unstable because of sample heterogeneity. There are two main sources of variation: general variability and seasonality. The general variability is largely due to the heterogeneity across the test taker samples over time, while seasonality is caused by some identifiable seasonal conditions and sources, such as curriculum schedule and college application deadlines (Guo et al. 2008; Li et al. 2011). The goal of this study is to obtain an improved sampling design to stabilize the estimates of the measurement model parameters, of the item response theory (IRT) linking parameters, and of the means and variances of the equated scores across numerous administrations (Qian et al. 2011). Specifically, statistical weighting techniques are applied to yield a weighted sample distribution that is consistent with the distribution of the target population of the test. In this way, the

J. Qian (✉)
Research and Development, ETS, MS 02-T, Rosedale Road, T-198, Princeton, NJ 08541, USA
e-mail: jqian@ets.org

A.A. von Davier • Y. Jiang
ETS, Princeton, NJ 08541, USA
e-mail: avondavier@ets.org; yxjiang@ets.org

R.E. Millsap et al. (eds.), *New Developments in Quantitative Psychology*, 171
Springer Proceedings in Mathematics & Statistics 66, DOI 10.1007/978-1-4614-9348-8_11,

disparity of the distributions of linking samples across administrations is reduced. The design in this study aligns the proportions of the examinee groups of interest in the sample to those of the target population. The objective of the study is to achieve a stable scale for an assessment with multiple forms and to explore an effective paradigm to evaluate the procedure. The future research is to explore a formal optimal sampling design for linking based on weighted samples and equating of multiple test forms over many administrations (Berger 1991, 1997; Berger and van der Linden 1992; Buyske 2005; Lord and Wingersky 1985; Stocking 1990; van der Linden and Luecht 1998).

The basis of achieving a stable linking is the consistency between a weighted distribution of a sample (for certain demographic variables) and the distribution of the test's target population. This idea is analogous to the idea of "sampling exchangeability," an assumption in the Draper–Lindley–de Finetti (DLD) measurement validity framework (Zumbo 2007). For linking based on weighted samples, whenever a target population is available, we can always adjust the marginal distributions in a sample and make them to be consistent with those in the target population. In addition, achieving a stable linking by applying weighted samples is essential for quality control. For example, in analyzing a test with multiple forms, the measurement invariance found in one administration sample may not be a valid presumption for another one. Or when a linking has to use partial data that are sometimes gathered with selection bias, a decision based on such results could differ from those based on the whole data set. So the linking function yielded from a partial data set or a specific sample could also be biased, and the quality of reporting could be compromised by the sample characteristics and heterogeneity. In order to perform IRT linking based on weighted samples, we first define the target population and the equating samples, and then apply weighting techniques to obtain an improved sampling design for invariant Stocking and Lord (1983) test characteristic curve (TCC) linking across testing seasons. The linking based on weighted samples process will result in more stable equating results.

The previous studies on population invariance in equating are focused on improving measurement precision and scale invariance across examinee subgroups within an administration sample (Kolen and Brennan 2004). The root mean square difference (RMSD) is often used to quantify group invariance in random group equating (Holland and Dorans 2006; Yang and Gao 2008; Yi et al. 2008). Based on RMSD using half a point as the criterion (Holland and Dorans 2006), Moses (2011) found that measurement invariance, including scaling invariance and regression invariance, was most likely when there were similarities in the tests being linked and in the examinee groups taking the tests but were not guaranteed to be invariant when the tests and/or groups are dissimilar. However, Huggins (2011) did identify tests that failed to possess either the measurement invariance or population invariance properties. As pointed out by Kolen (2004), most of these studies are sample relevant because linkings and equatings are data dependent. Some papers in the equating literature studied matching the equating sample to a target population (Duong and von Davier 2012; von Davier et al. 2004). As shown in this paper, our approach of weighting has similarities to the methods described in the equating literature.

For example, poststratification, one of the methods that we used here, has also been employed in observed-score equating for nonequivalent groups with anchor test (NEAT) design (Braun and Holland 1982; Livingston 2004), and in chain and poststratification equating (Sinharay et al. 2011). Although some studies have used poststratification to align the proportions of demographic groups to those in the reference sample in linking (Livingston 2007), no study has been based on total linking errors, and none has demonstrated that weighting effectively reduces the linking errors due to sample variability.

As mentioned previously, the focus of this study is the stability and accuracy of linking over time and is conceptually similar to that of optimal sampling design research. In this paper, the main research question is how to select the samples so that the estimates of the model parameters are stable or with less variability over many test forms and administrations. We aim to reduce the mean squared error (MSE) of the parameters and estimates of interest.

In Sect. 2 of this paper, we introduce the methodology of the study, including study design, weighting techniques, and the statistical tools employed for the evaluation of the proposed design. In Sect. 3 we document the empirical results of weighting examinee samples in IRT linking. The final section offers a summary and conclusions.

2 Methodology

In this section, we introduce the study design and the statistical tools applied in the analysis which include the linking procedure of Stocking and Lord (1983) based on test characteristic curves (S-L TCC), IRT true-score equating, the weighting techniques applied (including poststratification and raking), and complete grouped jackknife variance estimation.

2.1 Data Resources

In this study, we employed eight data sets from a large-scale international language assessment, four from the reading section and four from the listening section; these assessments were administered across different testing seasons. Table 1 shows the summary of the eight data sets and their subsamples used in the study.

For the reading test design, all of the examinees had responses to 42 operational items from two blocks having 14 and 28 items, respectively. The IRT linking was accomplished using both internal and external anchors. The anchor items were used to link the scale of a new test form to the scale of the reference forms. For the listening test design, all of the examinees had responses to 34 operational items that were evenly distributed in two blocks. Similar to the reading design, the linking in listening was accomplished using both internal and external anchors. In each data

Table 1 Basic statistics of the samples and their subsamples

Data set	Sample size	Nonlinking cases	Subsample size (40 %)	Nonlinking cases
Listening 1	10,433	32	4,173	14
Listening 2	8,760	293	3,504	121
Listening 3	9,566	311	3,826	132
Listening 4	10,293	0	4,117	0
Reading 1	10,313	32	4,125	17
Reading 2	8,628	288	3,451	118
Reading 3	9,454	307	3,782	120
Reading 4	10,120	0	4,048	0

set, there were some demographic variables available for analysis, such as gender, age, test location, reason and length of time of study. Some of them are correlated with general variability and seasonality across administration samples.

2.2 Study Design

As stated above, the procedure proposed in this paper is intended to yield a weighted sample distribution that is consistent with the distribution of the target population. If we have the baseline scale score of the target population, we can judge whether the weighted or unweighted results from the same administration sample have smaller linking errors and higher precision in estimation. Because we are unable to conduct an assessment on the whole target population, we are unable to make a judgment directly. Thus the evaluation becomes challenging due to a lack of a baseline for comparison.

To counter this issue, we selected a subsample from each of the eight original administration samples. The subsample was treated as a relative "sample" and the original administration sample was treated as a relative "pseudo target population." In making comparisons, the results, i.e., transformation parameters, etc., from the pseudo target population were treated as the baseline. Therefore, the two sets of subsample results (weighted and unweighted) can be compared with the results yielded from the original administration sample. If the results from the weighted subsample are closer to the results yielded by the original administration sample than those from the unweighted subsample, then the linking based on weighted samples process is better. RMSE was used as the evaluation criterion. In this study, we selected one subsample from each original administration sample and created one set of base weights for each subsample. By employing poststratification and trimming, we eventually yielded eight sets of weights for analysis for each set of the base weights. For details of poststratification and trimming, see the descriptions below.

In selecting subsamples from the original eight data sets, the sampling rate in selecting examinees is 40 %. In this study, the symbol $\mathfrak{R}$ refers to an original data set (i.e., the pseudo target population) and R refers to the sample selected from $\mathfrak{R}$ with a rate of 40 %.

2.3 Linking in an IRT Framework

In this study we used IRT true-score equating with separate calibrations to match the procedures used in operational practice. The equating process consisted of three steps: IRT calibration, item parameter transformation through S-L TCC linking, and IRT true-score equating. The two-parameter logistic (2PL) regression IRT model and/or the generalized partial credit model (GPCM) were chosen for item calibration (Allen et al. 2001; Lord 1980) using the PARSCALE software package (Muraki and Bock 2002). The same calibration procedure was carried out for each data set and for each weighting method.

In conducting the IRT calibration with weighted samples, weights are used to estimate a sample distribution including prior and posterior distributions in the calibration procedure. Each examinee in a weighted distribution is counted by the magnitude of its weight instead of one as in a size-based distribution. Correspondingly, weights are also used to calculate the values of means and standard deviations of different distributions. The definition of a weighted mean is given in Sect. 2.3. The results of IRT calibration with weighted samples usually differ from those with unweighted samples.

The results yielded by the calibration with weighted samples are the input to the linking step. Based on common items, the S-L TCC method transforms the item parameter and ability estimates of the new form to the scale of the reference forms or existing item pool through a linear transformation. The common items on the reference form are usually assembled from an item pool already on the base scale (Haberman 2009). The S-L TCC method obtains the linear transformation by minimizing the squared difference between the two TCCs for common items between the new and reference forms. See Stocking and Lord (1983) for the details of this method.

Let A and B, slope and intercept, be the solution of the linear transformation for the S-L TCC linking method. The expected values of A and B are 1 and 0 (Stocking and Lord 1983). Let $\widehat{\theta}_N$ and $\widehat{\theta}_N^*$ represent the ability scores for the same examinee on the new and reference forms, respectively. For item t, let $\widehat{a}_{Nt}$ and $\widehat{b}_{Nt}$ be the item parameter estimates of the 2PL IRT models on the new form, and let $\widehat{a}_{Nt}^*$ and $\widehat{b}_{Nt}^*$ be the item parameter estimates on the scale of the reference form. Then the score transformation between two forms is

$$\widehat{\theta}_N^* = A\widehat{\theta}_N + B, \tag{1}$$

and item parameters can be transformed by

$$\widehat{b}_{Nt}^* = A\widehat{b}_{Nt} + B, \tag{2}$$

and

$$\widehat{a}_{Nt}^* = \widehat{a}_{Nt}/A. \tag{3}$$

The step after S-L TCC linking is IRT true-score equating (i.e., obtaining the equated scores based on the conversion table). In this study we used IceDog software (Robin et al. 2006) to conduct IRT true-score equating. See Kolen and Brennan (2004) for a detailed description of the procedure.

2.4 *Weighting Techniques for Calibration Samples*

The objective of creating weights in this study was to make the weighted distribution of a subsample (representing a calibration and equating sample) consistent with the distribution of the original data (representing the reference population). The weighting process consisted of three steps: computing base weights for cases (examinees) that have participated in the assessment, conducting poststratification or raking, and performing weight trimming (Cochran 1977; Deming and Stephan 1940; Potter 1990).

Creation of base weights. Let N_g be the sample size of test center g in the total sample and n_g be the sample size of test center g in a subsample. We chose the variable test center because it reflected the mechanism of data collection. Other demographic variables may also be used, such as region, country, and native language. Although native language can serve the same function in creating base weights as test center, it usually contains more missing values than test center. Let $r_g = n_g/N_g$ be the ratio of sample sizes for test center g. Then the base weight for any examinee i in test center g in the subsample equals

$$w_{i,g} = r_g^{-1}. \tag{4}$$

For example, in applying weights in estimation, let x_i be the variable of interest and w_i be the weight for case i for a sample of size n. The Hurwitz–Thompson estimator of total statistic is $\sum_{i=1}^{n} w_i x_i$ (Cochran, 1977). Then, a weighted mean of x can be defined by $\overline{x} = \sum_{i=1}^{n} w_i x_i / \sum_{i=1}^{n} w_i$. Although $\overline{x}$ is biased, this bias vanishes with increasing n on the order of $O(1/n)$ (Cochran, 1977).

Poststratification and raking. The characteristics of a target population can be described by some demographic variables, such as gender, age, ethnicity, location, and experiences of study (Allen et al. 2001). After base weights were created, some demographic variables could show considerable gaps between a weighted subsample distribution and its corresponding original sample distribution. Such gaps were revealed in corresponding cells that were cross-classified by variables. These gaps were due to the inconsistency between the subsamples and its original sample, and such inconsistency was mainly caused by sample variability and/or by some undue factors such as holidays or storms that could led to nonparticipation. Raking and poststratification can be used to correct for these known gaps. Consequently, the linking based on the weighted sample will have improved precision such as reduced mean squared error. Based on data analysis, we first select several demographic variables (usually 3–5) that highlight the feature of a target population; then we conduct a poststratification or raking process.

Poststratification matches the weighted sample cell counts to the population cell counts by applying a proportional adjustment to the weights in each cell across the contingency table (Cochran 1977; Kish 1965). Sometimes though, the sample can be spread too thinly across the cells in the table, thus poststratification would produce extreme weights in cells with few cases and cause large design effects of weighting (Kish 1965). To avoid such flaws, raking is used to control marginal distributions for the variables of interest.

A raking procedure iteratively adjusts the case weights in the sample to make the weighted marginal distributions of the sample agree with the marginal distributions of the population on specified demographic variables (Deming 1943). The algorithm used in raking is called the Deming–Stephan algorithm (Haberman 1979). Again, this is conceptually similar to estimating the weights assigned to examinees or the parameters of a specified distribution of characteristics in an optimal sampling design, as described in Berger (1997, pp. 73–75).

In this study, the Deming–Stephan raking procedure is based on some or all of the following four demographic variables to adjust the base weights in Eq. (4): gender, age, time of language study, and reason for language study. As listed in the Appendix, a total of eight sets of weights were formed by different raking schemes.

Trimming weights. To reduce the design effects of weighting, the weight adjustment process usually includes a weight trimming step. The trimming process truncates extreme weights caused by unequal probability sampling or by raking and poststratification adjustment. It reduces variation caused by extremely large weights but introduces some bias in estimates. The process usually employs the criterion of minimum MSE (Potter 1990). To investigate the effects of different trimming criteria, though not optimal, we implemented ten criteria for the subsamples, which are given in the Appendix.

2.5 Evaluation Criterion and Complete Grouped Jackknifing

In this study, we used the RMSE of linking parameters and equated scores as the criterion to measure the stability of the whole complex linking procedure and to evaluate the effects of different weighting approaches. Bias estimation was used to evaluate the effects of reducing selection bias in the comparison of weighted and unweighted samples. The bias estimate measures the error due to selection bias and RMSE measures the overall variability due to both sampling and selection bias. In general, RMSE is preferred to standard error or bias in evaluating the effects of linking (van der Linden 2010). In computing the RMSE, the original samples from the eight administrations played the role of pseudo target populations, and the transformation parameters yielded from the original samples were treated as the true values. A subsample was then randomly selected from each original sample. Thus, it is viable to compare the RMSEs of the parameter estimates from the weighted subsamples against those from the unweighted subsamples. If the RMSEs of the linking parameter estimates for a weighted data set are smaller than those for its unweighted counterpart, we can conclude that the weighted sample is closer to its (pseudo) target population than the unweighted sample.

Recently, the jackknifing method was used to investigate the two types of errors involved in S-L TCC linking: errors due to the variability of examinee samples and errors due to the selection of anchor items. Compared with examinee selection, anchor item selection usually has comparatively small effects on linking and such effects are usually controllable by test developers (Haberman et al. 2009).

Complete grouped jackknifing. A complete grouped jackknife repeated replication (CGJRR; Haberman et al. 2009; Miller 1964; Qian 2005; Wolter 1985) method is used to estimate the standard errors of the whole linking procedure, including IRT calibration, item parameter scaling, and IRT linking. In the CGJRR we ran, the examinees in the sample were randomly aggregated into J (=120 in this study) groups of similar sizes. The jth jackknife replicate sample $R_{(j)}$ was formed by deleting the jth group from the whole sample, and therefore, 120 jackknife replicate samples were formed in total.

For the whole sample and each jackknife replicate sample, we conducted the same IRT calibration, scaling, and the equating procedure. Then we estimated the jackknifed standard errors of the parameters of interest. Let $\widehat{\theta}_{R,R}$ be the parameter estimated with weights from the subsample R. The first R in the subscript indicates the data set is being used in calibration; the second R indicates the data set used in linking. Let $\widehat{\theta}_{R_{(j)},R_{(j)}}$ be the weighted estimate from the jth jackknife replicate sample, and the replicate sample $R_{(j)}$ is used in both calibration and linking. The complete jackknifed variance of $\widehat{\theta}$ is estimated by

$$v_{[R_J,R_J]}\left(\widehat{\theta}\right) = \frac{J-1}{J}\sum\nolimits_{j=1}^{j}\left(\widehat{\theta}_{R(j),R(j)} - \widehat{\theta}_{\cdot,\cdot}\right)^2, \tag{5}$$

where $\widehat{\theta}_{\cdot,\cdot}$ is the mean of all $\widehat{\theta}_{R_{(j)},R_{(j)}}$ (Haberman et al. 2009). The MSE estimate is

$$MSE_{[R_J,R_J]}\left(\widehat{\theta}\right) = v_{[R_J,R_J]}\left(\widehat{\theta}\right) + \left(\widehat{\theta}_{R,R} - \widehat{\theta}_{\mathfrak{R},\mathfrak{R}}\right)^2. \tag{6}$$

The second term $\left(\widehat{\theta}_{R,R} - \widehat{\theta}_{\mathfrak{R},\mathfrak{R}}\right)^2$ in the equation is the estimate of squared bias and $\widehat{\theta}_{\mathfrak{R},\mathfrak{R}}$ is estimated from the original sample $\mathfrak{R}$ in both calibration and linking.

3 Results

3.1 The Sample Effects on S-L TCC Linking

To show the sample effects on S-L TCC linking, in Table 2 we present estimates of the bias and RMSE of the S-L TCC transformation parameters A and B in Eqs. (1)–(3) for the unweighted subsamples. The RMSEs of the linking parameters for subsamples measure the differences in the linking function between a whole sample and its subsamples. Given that the theoretical value of B equals zero, the RMSEs of B are sizable and these errors are nonnegligible. Similar results hold for other statistics such as converted mean scores. This evidence of the sample variation effects signals a need to reduce the variability in linking. The goal is to obtain a set of weights with RMSEs (for A and B or scale scores) that are smaller than those from the unweighted data, as shown in Table 2.

3.2 Sampling Baseline Characteristics of the Weighted A and B Estimates

One basic interest in evaluating weighting effects is to examine the characteristics of transformation coefficients A and B of S-L TCC linking. Because the expected values of A and B are 1 and 0, respectively (Stocking and Lord 1983), we examine which estimates of A and B, weighted or unweighted, deviate further from their expected values. Table 3 presents a summary of such comparisons. The analysis used the subsamples of eight data sets, and base weights were created from the variable of test center size (i.e., each base weight was the inverse of the sample ratio of test center sizes). The base weights of each subsample were further raked by some or all of the four variables listed in the Appendix.

Table 2 Bias and RMSE of the estimated A and B for subsamples (unweighted)

			A		*B*	
Data set	Whole sample size	Subsample size	Bias	RMSE	Bias	RMSE
Listening 1	10,433	4,125	−0.0018	0.0168	0.0196	0.0268
Listening 2	8,760	3,451	0.0101	0.0254	0.0178	0.0304
Listening 3	9,566	3,782	0.0104	0.0262	0.0129	0.0287
Listening 4	10,293	4,048	−0.0033	0.0219	−0.0014	0.0235
Reading 1	10,313	4,173	0.0145	0.0214	0.0335	0.0383
Reading 2	8,628	3,504	−0.0224	0.0293	−0.0156	0.0250
Reading 3	9,454	3,826	−0.0143	0.0274	−0.0217	0.0339
Reading 4	10,120	4,117	−0.0020	0.0198	0.0123	0.0262

Table 3 Baseline characteristics of weighted A and B estimates

	No. of the weighted *B* estimates closer to 0 than the unweighted ($N=32$)	No. of the weighted *A* estimates closer to 1 than the unweighted ($N=32$)
Listening	24 (75.0 %)	25 (78.1 %)
Reading	22 (68.8 %)	13 (40.6 %)

For the *B* transformation parameter, 75 % of weighted *B* estimates (24 out of 32) for listening were closer to 0 than their corresponding unweighted *B* estimates, and 68.8 % of the weighted *B* estimates (22 out of 32) for reading were closer to 0 than their unweighted counterparts. See Table 3. These results thus favor the weighted estimates, and this statement can be confirmed by a binomial test. Assume that the weighted estimates are no better than the unweighted counterparts. For listening in 24 out of 32 of weighted estimates, the *p*-value is 0.001 for a one-side binomial significance test, and the assumption is rejected at the 0.01 level. Similarly, for reading in 22 out of 32 weighted estimates, the assumption can be rejected at the 0.01 level with a *p*-value of 0.01. Correspondingly, binomial significance tests can be used to confirm the conclusions drawn from other tables.

For the *A* transformation parameter, 78.1 % of weighted *A* estimates for listening were closer to 1 than corresponding unweighted ones. However, the weighted *A* estimates from the reading test did not show the same characteristics. We analyzed different *A* parameter estimates from the reading data and found that when the unweighted estimates from a subsample were closer to 1 than the estimates from the original sample, the weighted estimates from the subsample could actually be closer to the estimates from the original sample than 1.

3.3 *Comparison of the Bias and RMSE of the Weighted A and B Estimates*

To evaluate weighting effects, we also compared the biases and RMSEs of *A* and *B* for the weighted and the unweighted subsamples; Table 4 contains the results of the comparisons. The base weights were created based on test center sizes with raking. For each listening or reading subsample, all eight sets of weights, trimmed by default scheme (i.e., the maximum weight size was set at 2), were used in the analysis. The detailed raking and trimming schedules are listed in the Appendix.

All the biases and RMSEs of the *B* parameter estimates obtained from weighted samples were smaller than those estimated from unweighted samples. More than 75 % of the weighted *A* estimates also had smaller biases and RMSEs than those of the unweighted estimates. These results thus favor the weighted estimates. At the 0.01 significance level for the one-side binomial test, all of the results favor weighted estimates. These results show that compared with the estimates from the

Table 4 Comparison of the Bias and RMSE of the weighted A and B estimates with those of the unweighted estimates

	No. of the bias of weighted *B* smaller than the unweighted ($N = 32$)	No. of the RMSE of weighted *B* smaller than the unweighted ($N = 32$)	No. of the bias of weighted *A* smaller than the unweighted ($N = 32$)	No. of the RMSE of weighted *A* smaller than the unweighted ($N = 32$)
Listening	32 (100.00 %)	32 (100.00 %)	24 (75.00 %)	32 (100.00 %)
Reading	32 (100.00 %)	32 (100.00 %)	28 (87.50 %)	28 (87.50 %)

unweighted samples, those from the weighted samples have smaller biases and overall variabilities. This verifies that the linking weighting procedure functions well for a sample that deviates greatly from its population when its sampling rate is small and selection bias is strong.

4 Discussion

In this study, we applied weighting techniques to samples of test takers in conducting IRT linking to achieve a stable scale for an assessment with multiple forms. In the method proposed here, the weighted distributions of different samples would be consistent, as if all of them were probability sample selected from the target population. In this way, the linking quality is controlled by a sampling design for numerous administrations over time.

The results obtained based on the proposed paradigm showed the effectiveness of weighting the samples in IRT linking procedures. Although this study is focused on reducing the variability across multiple samples, the evaluation procedure and weighting techniques can also be employed to analyze the precision of item calibration through item selection in test assembly. Thus, we think, this procedure may also be used for constructing a better test design.

Application has always been a focus of this study. The proposed weighting strategy can be employed in two scenarios. In the first scenario, one applies the weighting strategy in an assessment such as GRE® or TOEFL® with multiple forms and variability and seasonality among multiple test samples. In the second scenario, one applies the same strategy in analyzing partial data. A typical example is analyzing the data from state assessments where the available data for making initial equating decisions may be only about 20 % of the final data. Instead of using randomization, the initial data are often a convenient sample gathered from the school districts that complete testing early. So applying weighting techniques could help psychometricians avoid biased results based on the initial equating analysis. Note that if the initial sample of a state assessment is a random sample, the problem might not exist. In general, the weighting procedure can be used to correct the differences between a sample and its population, such as under- or over-representation of certain subgroups for a given administration. Moreover, applying weighting techniques, including creating weights and raking, is not very complex, although evaluating weighting efficiency as done in this study is computationally intensive.

In application, the process to create weights should follow the steps in Section 2.3: computing base weights, conducting poststratification or raking, and performing weight trimming. In poststratification and raking, we should, based on statistical analysis of data, choose several demographic variables, such as gender, age, ethnicity, location, and experiences of study, that are correlated with the estimates of interest in the target population.

As future research, we may consider a different strategy, such as imposing selection bias in samples by deliberately oversampling certain demographic groups to evaluate the effects of optimized weighting on reducing selection bias (Berger et al. 2000). In the future, we may conduct a comparison of the method that we proposed here to the formal optimal sampling design described by Berger (1997). The difficulty in following Berger's approach consists of formally modeling the three aspects of the situation: the background information, the IRT model parameters for each administration, and the IRT linking parameter for each pair of administrations, and all these for multiple test forms/administrations. One might focus first on linking only two test forms/administrations, in a simple way, say using a mean–mean IRT linking. The formal expression of the IRT linking expressed as a restriction function on the parameter space, as given in von Davier and von Davier (2011), could be useful for writing the constraints formally. Then as in von Davier and von Davier and using the definition of an optimal sampling design (Berger 1991, 1997), a sampling design is locally optimal if a specific optimality criterion (which is usually a function of the information matrix) is achieved. Writing the linking parameters as constraints as in von Davier and von Davier might aid with writing the constraints formally in linear programming for estimating the weights that lead to a sample for which the linking parameters are estimated most efficiently.

Acknowledgments The authors thank Jim Carlson, Shelby Haberman, Kentaro Yamamoto, Frank Rijmen, Xueli Xu, Tim Moses, and Matthias von Davier for their suggestions and comments. The authors also thank Shuhong Li and Jill Carey for their assistance in assembling data and Kim Fryer for editorial help. Any opinions expressed in this paper are those of the authors and not necessarily those of Educational Testing Service.

Appendix: Weights, Raking Variables, and Number of Trimming Criteria Applied in Analyses

Weight	Variable used for base weight	Variables used for raking[a]	Criteria used for trimming[b]	Note
W0A	Test center	V1, V2, V3, V4	10	Results reported
W0B	Test center	V1, V2, V3	10	Results reported
W0C	Test center	V1, V2	10	Results reported
W0YY	Test center	V1, V3	10	Results reported
W0ZZ	Test center	V2, V3	10	Results reported
W0X	Test center	V1	10	Results reported
W0Y	Test center	V2	10	Results reported
W0Z	Test center	V3	10	Results reported

[a]Symbols of the variables used in raking: V1 = gender, V2 = age, V3 = time of language study, V4 = reason for language study
[b]In trimming, the total of the weights was normalized to the size of each subsample. The default trimming criterion was set at 2. For the base weights based on test center, the criteria used for trimming ranged from 1.5 to 2.4 with an even interval of 0.1. The base weights based on native language only used the default trimming criterion

References

Allen, N., Donoghue, J., & Schoeps, T. (2001). *The NAEP 1998 technical report* (NCES 2001-509). Washington, DC: National Center for Education Statistics.

Berger, M. P. F. (1991). On the efficiency of IRT models when applied to different sampling designs. *Applied Psychological Measurement, 15*, 293–306.

Berger, M. P. F. (1997). Optimal designs for latent variable models: A review. In J. Rost & R. Langeheine (Eds.), *Application of latent trait and latent class models in the social sciences* (pp. 71–79). Muenster, Germany: Waxmann.

Berger, M. P. F., King, C. Y. J., & Wong, W. K. (2000). Minimax D-optimal designs for item response theory models. *Psychometrika, 65*, 377–390.

Berger, M. P. F., & van der Linden, W. J. (1992). Optimality of sampling designs in item response theory models. In M. Wilson (Ed.), *Objective measurement: theory into practice* (Vol. 1, pp. 274–288). Norwood, NJ: Ablex.

Braun, H. I., & Holland, P. W. (1982). Observed-score test equating: A mathematical analysis of some ETS equating procedures. In P. W. Holland & D. B. Rubin (Eds.), *Test equating* (pp. 9–49). New York, NY: Academic Press.

Buyske, S. (2005). Optimal design in educational testing. In M. P. F. Berger & W. K. Wong (Eds.), *Applied optimal designs* (pp. 1–19). New York, NY: Wiley.

Cochran, W. G. (1977). *Sampling techniques* (3rd ed.). New York, NY: Wiley.

Deming, W. E. (1943). *Statistical adjustment of data*. New York, NY: Wiley.

Deming, W. E., & Stephan, F. F. (1940). On a least squares adjustment of a sampled frequency table when the expected marginal tables are known. *Annals of Mathematical Statistics, 11*, 427–444.

Duong, M., & von Davier, A. A. (2012). Observed-score equating with a heterogeneous target population. *International Journal of Testing, 12*, 224–251.

Guo, H., Liu, J., Haberman, S., & Dorans, N. (2008, March). *Trend analysis in seasonal time series models*. Paper presented at the meeting of the National Council on Measurement in Education, New York, NY

Haberman, S. J. (1979). *Analysis of qualitative data* (Vol. 2). New York, NY: Academic Press.

Haberman, S. J. (2009). *Linking parameter estimates derived from an item response model through separate calibrations* (Research Report 09-40). Princeton, NJ: Educational Testing Service.

Haberman, S. J., Lee, Y., & Qian, J. (2009). *Jackknifing techniques for evaluation of equating accuracy* (Research Report 09-39). Princeton, NJ: Educational Testing Service.

Holland, P. W. (2007). A framework and history for score linking. In N. J. Dorans, M. Pommerich, & P. W. Holland (Eds.), *Linking and aligning scores and scales* (pp. 5–30). New York, NY: Springer.

Holland, P. W., & Dorans, N. J. (2006). Linking and equating. In R. L. Brennan (Ed.), *Educational measurement* (4th ed., pp. 187–220). Westport, CT: Greenwood.

Huggins, A. C. (2011, April). *Equating invariance across curriculum groups on a statewide fifth-grade science exam*. Paper presented at the meeting of the American Educational Research Association, New Orleans, LA

Kish, L. (1965). *Survey sampling*. New York, NY: Wiley.

Kolen, M. J. (2004). Population invariance in equating and linking: Concept and history. *Journal of Educational Measurement, 41*, 3–14.

Kolen, M. J., & Brennan, R. L. (2004). *Test equating, scaling, and linking: Methods and practices* (2nd ed.). New York, NY: Springer.

Li, D., Li, S., & von Davier, A. A. (2011). Applying time-series analysis to detect scale drift. In A. A. von Davier (Ed.), *Statistical models for test equating, scaling, and linking* (pp. 381–398). New York, NY: Springer.

Livingston, S. A. (2004). *Equating test scores (without IRT)*. Princeton, NJ: Educational Testing Service.

Livingston, S. A. (2007). *Demographically adjusted groups for equating test scores* (Unpublished manuscript). Princeton, NJ: Educational Testing Service.

Lord, F. M. (1980). *Applications of item response theory to practical testing problems*. Hillsdale, NJ: Erlbaum.

Lord, M. F., & Wingersky, M. S. (1985). Sampling variances and covariances of parameter estimates in item response theory. In D. J. Weiss (Ed.), *Proceedings of the 1982 IRT/CAT Conference* (pp 69–88). Minneapolis: University of Minnesota, Department of Psychology, CAT Laboratory

Miller, R. G. (1964). A trustworthy jackknife. *Annals of Mathematical Statistics, 53*, 1594–1605.

Moses, T. (2011). *Evaluating empirical relationships among prediction, measurement, and scaling invariance* (Research Report 11-06). Princeton, NJ: Educational Testing Service.

Muraki, E., & Bock, R. D. (2002). *PARSCALE (Version 4.1). [Computer software]*. Lincolnwood, IL: Scientific Software International.

Potter, F. J. (1990). A study of procedures to identify and trim extreme sampling weights. *Proceedings of the section on survey research methods* (pp. 225–230). Alexandria, VA: American Statistical Association

Qian, J. (2005, April). *Measuring the cumulative linking errors of NAEP trend assessments*. Paper presented at the meeting of the National Council on Measurement in Education, Montreal, Canada

Qian, J., von Davier, A., & Jiang, Y. (2011, April). *Effects of weighting examinee samples in TBLT IRT linking: Weighting test samples in IRT linking and equating*. Paper presented at the meeting of the National Council on Measurement in Education, New Orleans, LA.

Robin, F., Holland, P., & Hemat, L. (2006). *ICEDOG. [Computer software]*. Princeton, NJ: Educational Testing Service.

Sinharay, S., Holland, P. W., & von Davier, A. A. (2011). Evaluating the missing data assumptions of the chain and poststratification equating methods. In A. A. von Davier (Ed.), *Statistical models for test equating, scaling, and linking* (pp. 381–398). New York, NY: Springer.

Stocking, M. L. (1990). Specifying optimum examinees for item parameter estimation in item response theory. *Psychometrika, 55*, 461–475.
Stocking, M. L., & Lord, F. M. (1983). Developing a common metric in item response theory. *Applied Psychological Measurement, 7*, 201–210.
van der Linden, W. J. (2010). On bias in linear observed-score equating. *Measurement, 8*, 21–26.
van der Linden, W. J., & Luecht, R. M. (1998). Observed-score equating as a test assembly problem. *Psychometrika, 63*, 401–418.
von Davier, A. A., Holland, P. W., & Thayer, D. T. (2004). The chain and post-stratification methods for observed-score equating and their relationship to population invariance. *Journal of Educational Measurement, 41*, 15–32.
von Davier, M., & von Davier, A. A. (2011). A general model for IRT scale linking and scale transformation. In A. A. von Davier (Ed.), *Statistical models for test equating, scaling, and linking* (pp. 225–242). New York, NY: Springer.
von Davier, A. A., & Wilson, C. (2008). Investigating the population sensitivity assumption of item response theory true-score equating across two subgroups of examinees and two test formats. *Applied Psychological Measurement, 32*, 11–26.
Wolter, K. (1985). *Introduction to variance estimation*. New York, NY: Springer.
Yang, W.-L., & Gao, R. (2008). Invariance of score linkings across gender groups for forms of a testlet-based college-level examination program examination. *Applied Psychological Measurement, 32*, 45–61.
Yi, Q., Harris, D. J., & Gao, X. (2008). Invariance of equating functions across different subgroups of examinees taking a science achievement test. *Applied Psychological Measurement, 32*, 62–80.
Zumbo, B. D. (2007). Validity: foundational issues and statistical methodology. In C. R. Rao & S. Sinharay (Eds.), *Handbook of statistics* (Psychometrics, Vol. 26, pp. 45–79). Amsterdam, The Netherlands: Elsevier Science BV.

A Monte Carlo Approach for Nested Model Comparisons in Structural Equation Modeling

Sunthud Pornprasertmanit, Wei Wu, and Todd D. Little

1 Introduction

Model selection is an important issue in structural equation modeling (SEM). Model selection occurs when researchers have two or more competing research hypotheses (or models) and would like to know which provides a better explanation to the population behind the data. When the competing models are nested in a sense that one model can be created by fixing or relaxing some parameters in the other model, model selection can be done using likelihood ratio test (LRT, also termed chi-square difference test). The model that has more parameters is called the parent model and the model with fewer parameters is called the nested model. The LRT compares the chi-square test statistic (an absolute model fit index) of the two models. A significant LRT indicates that the nested model provides a poorer model fit than the parent model, leading to rejection of the nested model.

A major disadvantage of the LRT is its sensitivity to large sample size. As a result, even a trivial difference in fit between the parent and nested models could lead to rejection of the nested model. For example, suppose the parent model is a two-factor confirmatory factor analysis model (CFA) on six indicators with a correlation of 0.95 between the two factors. The nested model is a one-factor CFA on the same six indicators. The factor correlation is so high in the parent model that it is reasonable to deem the one-factor model (nested model) as good as the two-factor model (parent model). Unfortunately, the LRT would reject the nested model with a large enough sample size.

S. Pornprasertmanit (✉) • W. Wu
Department of Psychology and Center for Research Methods and Data Analysis, University of Kansas, Lawrence, KS 66045, USA
e-mail: psunthud@ku.edu; wwei@ku.edu; yhat@ku.edu

T.D. Little
Professor, Educational Psychology and Leadership Director, Institute for Measurement, Methodology, Analysis and Policy College of Education, Texas Tech University

R.E. Millsap et al. (eds.), *New Developments in Quantitative Psychology*, Springer Proceedings in Mathematics & Statistics 66, DOI 10.1007/978-1-4614-9348-8_12,

To solve the problem, many researchers have used difference in fit indices other than chi-square test statistic for nested model comparisons. For example, Cheung and Rensvold (2002) used a change in comparative fit index (CFI), gamma hat, or McDonald's noncentrality index to compare nested models with different levels of measurement invariance across groups. They suggested a cutoff of 0.01 for the change in CFI in keeping control of the Type I error rate. A later study by Meade et al. (2008) argued that a cutoff of 0.002 for the change in CFI would be more appropriate because the cutoff led to higher power to reject models without measurement invariance. Although cutoffs have been suggested for the multiple-group measurement invariance test, there are infinite types of nested model comparison (e.g., longitudinal measurement invariance test or a comparison between full and partial mediation models). It is unlikely that either of the cutoffs is suitable for all of them. In addition, the LRT and change in CFI are used to test the hypothesis that a nested model is equal to the parent model in model fit. In practice, a null hypothesis that the nested model approximates the parent model in model fit would be more realistic and meaningful.

We argue that a desirable method for nested model comparisons should have the following characteristics. First, the method is applicable to all nested model comparisons. Second, it should not be sensitive to sample size (Hu and Bentler 1999). Third, it should retain a nested model if it is only trivially different from the parent model and reject a nested model if it deviates substantially from the parent model. Taking the three criteria into consideration, we propose a Monte Carlo approach for nested model comparisons. This approach is an extension of the Monte Carlo approach for model fit evaluation developed by Millsap (2012). We argue that the Monte Carlo approach can satisfy all of the three criteria outlined above. The goal of the article is to demonstrate and evaluate the performance of the Monte Carlo approach.

The rest of the article is organized as follows. We start with a brief introduction of the Monte Carlo approach for model fit evaluation. We then illustrate how to extend this approach to nested model comparisons followed by a discussion of ways to account for a trivial difference between the nested models in the Monte Carlo approach. A simulation study is conducted to evaluate the approach. We conclude this paper by discussing the implications and limitations of the study and providing suggestions for applied researchers.

2 Monte Carlo Approach for Model Fit Evaluation

The basic idea of the Monte Carlo approach to model fit evaluation is to create an empirical sampling distribution of a fit index given the null hypothesis that the hypothesized model is approximately correct (Millsap 2007, 2010, 2012; Millsap and Lee 2008). A cutoff criterion for the fit index can be then derived from the sampling distribution and used for testing approximate fit.

To implement the approach, a target model is first fit to the original data and fit indices (e.g., RMSEA) are recorded. Second, an alternative model is created by adding trivial model errors to the target model such that the target model remains a good approximation of the alternative model (below, we describe how a trivial error can be added). A large number of simulated data sets (with the same sample size as the original data) are then generated from the alternative model. Third, the target model is fit to each of the simulated data sets. Target fit indices are saved from each of the resulting analyses of fitting simulated data sets. The fit indices are used to form sampling distributions. Because the target model is fit to the data generated from the alternative model and the target model is slightly different from the alternative model, the sampling distribution reflects the sampling variability of a fit index assuming that the target model is only an approximation of the population. Finally, after the sampling distribution of a fit index is established, the cutoff of the fit index is derived as the critical value based on an a priori alpha level (usually $\alpha = 0.05$) in the sampling distribution. The fit index from the original data is then compared to this cutoff to decide whether the target model should be rejected. Using RMSEA as an example, the cutoff criterion is the 95th percentile (one-tailed test) in the simulated sampling distribution of RMSEA. If the original RMSEA is larger than the cutoff, then the target model would not be considered a good approximation (it would be rejected in favor of the severely misspecified alternative). In other words, given the null hypothesis is true that the target model approximates the population, it is very unlikely to obtain such a large RMSEA in the sample, indicating that the sample is probably not from the population defined by the null hypothesis. Note that a plug-in p value can also be calculated to facilitate the decision. The p value is estimated as the proportion of the fit indices from simulated data that suggest worse fit than the observed fit index. The alternative model is rejected if the plugin p-value is smaller than or equal to the a priori alpha level ($p \leq \alpha$) or vice versa.

3 Monte Carlo Approach for Nested Model Comparison

Now we describe how to extend the procedure to nested model comparisons. Similar to the Monte Carlo approach to model fit evaluation, the purpose here is to derive a sampling distribution. However, because nested model comparisons use differences in fit indices, we derive the sampling distribution for the difference in a given fit index. After the sampling distribution is established, the cutoff criterion for the difference can be established correspondingly. To facilitate test of a more realistic hypothesis regarding the difference in model fit between nested models, the sampling distribution should be created based on the null hypothesis that the nested model fits the data approximately as well as the parent model. In other words, the difference between the nested and parent models or the parameter constraints in the nested model should be trivial.

This approach involves the following steps:

First, both nested and parent models are fit to the original data and the difference in a fit index is recorded.

Second, an alternative nested model is created by adding trivial misspecification to the nested model such that the target nested model is a good approximation of the alternative nested model. For example, small amounts of noise can be added to the constrained parameters in the nested model. Using a multiple-group measurement invariance test as an illustration, suppose that the parent model is a weak measurement invariance model (factor loadings are equal but intercepts are different across groups) and the nested model is a strong measurement invariance model (both factor loadings and intercepts are equal across groups). A good candidate for the alternative nested model is a model with trivial group difference in the intercepts.

Third, a large number of simulated data sets with the same sample size as the original data are generated from the alternative nested model. Both nested and parent models are then fit to each of the simulated data sets and the difference in a fit index (e.g., CFI) is recorded. The differences in the fit index from the simulated datasets form the sampling distribution of the difference. In this case, the parent model fits the simulated data well (because it is an over-specified model) and the target nested model fits the simulated data approximately well. The sampling distribution derived in this way would be consistent with the null hypothesis that the nested model fits approximately as well as the parent model.

Finally, the cutoff criterion for the difference in the fit index is the critical value based on a priori alpha level (usually 0.05) in the simulated sampling distribution. If the difference from the original sample exceeds the cutoff, the nested model is rejected. Again, a plug-in p value can be calculated as the proportion of the differences from the simulated data exceeds the observed difference to facilitate the decision.

4 Imposing Trivial Misspecifications in a Nested Model

As can be seen above, creating an alternative nested model by adding trivial misspecifications to the nested model is a key step in the Monte Carlo approach. In terms of specifying a misspecification, both the type and severity of the misspecification need to be considered. A misspecification can be considered as trivial if it is not of central interest to researchers and its magnitude is small. In this article, we focus on the case where the nested model underspecifies the population model. We define the severity of a model misspecification using the magnitude of the misspecified parameter or added noise following Millsap (2010) and Saris et al. (2009).

There are three possible methods to add a trivial misspecification. Millsap (2010, 2012) proposed using an exemplar of maximally acceptable misspecifications (e.g., a misspecified cross loading of size 0.3). We refer to this method as the *fixed method*. This method can be directly applied in nested model comparisons. An exemplar of maximally acceptable misspecifications can be added in a nested model (e.g., measurement intercept of 0.2 in standardized scale in the example above). The major disadvantage of this approach is that it only considers one form and one size of trivial misspecification out of a large number of possible misspecifications. As a consequence, the result might be sensitive to the selected misspecification. To take into account more variety of forms and sizes of potential misspecifications, Pornprasertmanit et al. (2012) proposed two new ways to introduce the trivial misspecification into the model: random and maximal methods.

The *random method* treats model misspecifications as random and assumes that they have a distribution (e.g., all measurement intercepts have uniform distribution from −0.2 to 0.2 in a standardized scale). In each replication, a set of values for the trivial misspecified parameters is drawn from the distribution based on which data set is generated. In other words, the set of values for the trivial misspecifications would be different for each replication. By doing this, multiple exemplars of possible misspecified models are taken into account.

The *maximal method* also accommodates the fact that there could be a range of trivial misspecifications. However, instead of randomly assigning values to misspecifications, the maximal method selects a combination of values that results in maximum misfit and uses it to generate data. Suppose any measurement intercepts fall in between −0.2 and 0.2 in a standardized scale are deemed as trivial, the maximal method will go through all possible combinations of the measurement intercepts within the range and pick the one that results in a maximum misfit. Note that the amount of misfit can be defined by a fit index such as LR, RMSEA (Browne and Cudeck 1992), or SRMR (Bentler 1995). This combination of values for the measurement intercepts are then used for data generation in each replication.

5 Simulation Study

Having described the Monte Carlo approach to nested model comparison, we now conduct a simulation study to evaluate this approach in comparison with the traditional LRT and change in CFI approach with a cutoff of 0.002.

In the simulation study, the data generation model is a longitudinal CFA model with three time points. At each time point, there was one latent factor indicated by three observed variables (see Fig. 1). The analysis model examines the measurement invariance of the single factor construct across time. The population values of the parameters in the data generation model are specified as follows. All factor loadings are equal to 1. Factor variances of each time point are 1, 1.2, and 1.4, respectively. The factor correlations between adjacent time points are 0.7 and the factor correlation between Times 1 and 3 is 0.49. All factor means and measurement intercepts are fixed at 0. The error variances are 0.4. The error correlation matrix follows a second-order autoregressive structure where the first-order autocorrelations are 0.2 and the second-order autocorrelations are 0.04.

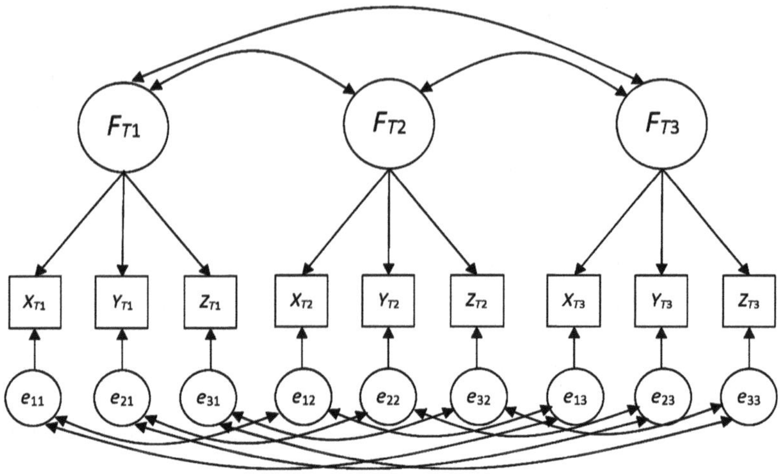

Fig. 1 The longitudinal CFA model

The parent model is a configural factorial invariance model in which the factor loadings are all freely estimated except that the loading of the marker variable is fixed to 1 at each time point. Note that the marker-variable method is only appropriate when the marker variable is known a priori to be invariant across time (which we assume here). The nested model is a weak factorial invariance model in which the factor loadings are constrained to be equal across time. Following the procedure outlined above, an alternative model is created by adding trivial misspecifications to the nested model. In this case, the trivial misspecifications are imposed by allowing the factor loadings of Y and Z at the third time point to be different from those at the previous time points.

Three factors are manipulated in this study. The first factor is the severity of the misspecifications in the nested model which has three levels: none, trivial, and severe. In the *none* condition, all factor loadings in the data generation model are 1. In this case, the nested model fits the data perfectly. In the *trivial* condition, the factor loadings of Y and Z at the third time point are 0.9 while all of the other factor loadings are set at 1. In this case, the nested model approximates the data generation model, assuming that a difference of 0.1 in factor loadings is trivial. In the *severe* condition, the factor loadings of Y and Z at the third time point are 0.4 while all of the other factor loadings are set at 1. Now the two factor loadings are different from those at the first and second time points by 0.6 points. We assume that this difference is large enough to falsify the weak factorial invariance assumption. In other words, the nested model would fit the data worse than the parent model. Note that for all of the conditions, the parent model (configural invariance model) fits the data perfectly.

The second factor is sample size which has four levels: 125, 250, 500, and 1,000. We consider both small and large sample sizes to examine whether the Monte Carlo approach is sensitive to sample size.

The third factor is the way to impose trivial misspecifications to create the alternative nested model in the Monte Carlo approach. This factor varied at four levels: none, fixed, random, and maximal methods. For the "none" misspecification, the simulated data in the Monte Carlo approach are created based on the nested model (weak factorial invariance model). For fixed misspecification, the simulated data are created based on the alternative nested model with the factor loadings of Y and Z at the last time point subtracted by 0.1s. With random misspecification, the factor loadings of Y and Z at all time points are subtracted by a random draw from a uniform distribution ranged from -0.1 to 0.1. For maximal misspecification, the factor loadings of Y and Z at all time points are subtracted by a value within the range between -0.1 to 0.1 such that the population RMSEA would be maximized comparing to the fitted parameters. Figure 2 shows examples of the simulated sampling distribution for the different methods of imposing trivial misspecification.

One thousand replications are generated for each condition. The rejection rate of the nested model is used to evaluate the performance of all methods. If the population misspecification is none or trivial, the nested model should be preferred and the rejection rate should be close to or less than 0.05. If the population misspecification is severe, the parent model should be preferred and the rejection rate should approach 1. We used the *simsem* package (Pornprasertmanit et al. 2012) in (R Core Development Team 2012) to conduct the simulation. The *simsem* package calls the *lavaan* package (Rosseel 2012) in R for SEM.

6 Results

Figure 3 shows the rejection rates for each condition. For the chi-square difference test, when there was no misspecification in the nested model, the rejection rate was 0.05, which is the nominal level of Type I error. When the misspecifications in the nested model were severe, the rejection rate was 1. When the misspecifications were trivial, the rejection rate increased as sample size increased (see Fig. 3a). For the change in CFI with the cutoff of 0.002, the rejection rates were all close to 0 indicating low power to detect severe misspecifications (see Fig. 3b). Note that the cutoff of 0.01 for the change in CFI (Cheung and Rensvold 2002) would lead to even lower rejection rates.

In comparison, when trivial misspecifications are not taken into account in the Monte Carlo approach, the Monte Carlo approach for the change in chi-square test statistic was essentially identical to the chi-square difference test (see Fig. 3c). However, with the trivial misspecifications taken into account, the Monte Carlo approach is superior to the chi-square difference test by correctly retaining the nested model with zero or trivial misspecifications while maintaining a sufficient power to reject the nested model with severe misspecification. The different methods

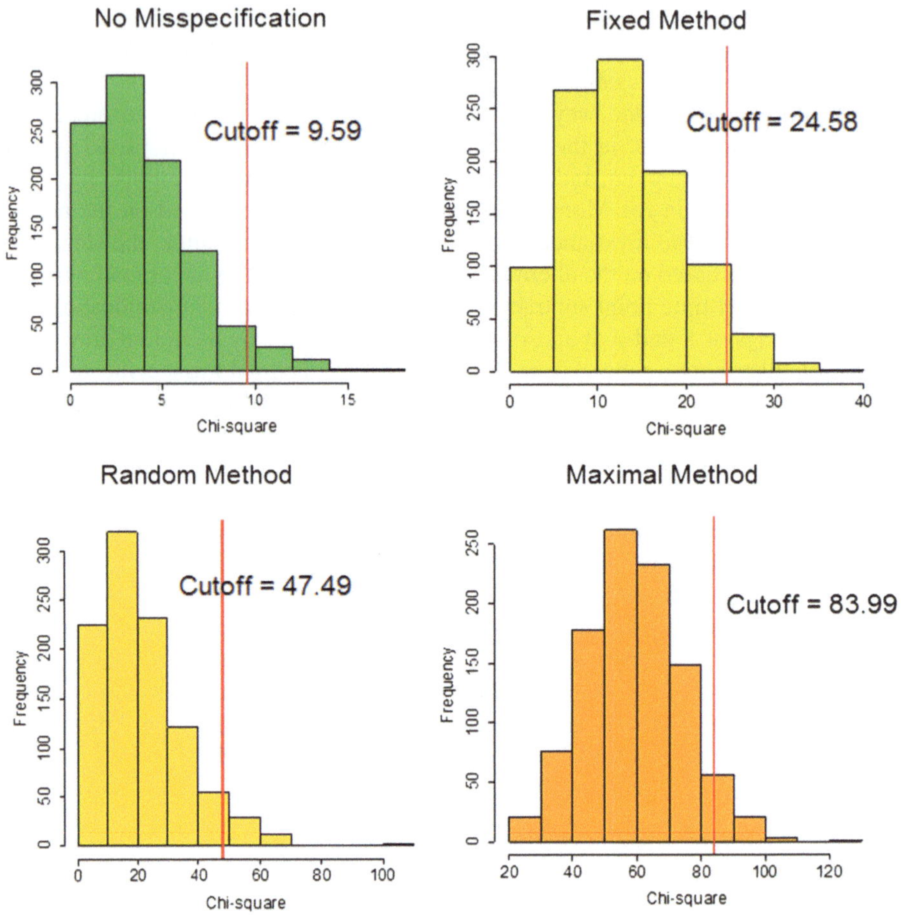

Fig. 2 The simulated sampling distribution of the difference in chi-square values between nested models for the different methods of imposing trivial misspecification

to impose trivial misspecifications resulted in similar results under all of the conditions with only one exception. When the sample size was small ($N = 125$), the random and maximal methods tended to have lower power than the fixed method to reject the nested model with severe misfit (see Fig. 3d–f). The power from both methods, however, was still greater than 0.8 which is generally deemed as a sufficient power. Note that we only presented the simulation results for the change in chi-square test statistic. The same result pattern was found for the Monte Carlo approach for the change in RMSEA, CFI, TLI, or SRMR

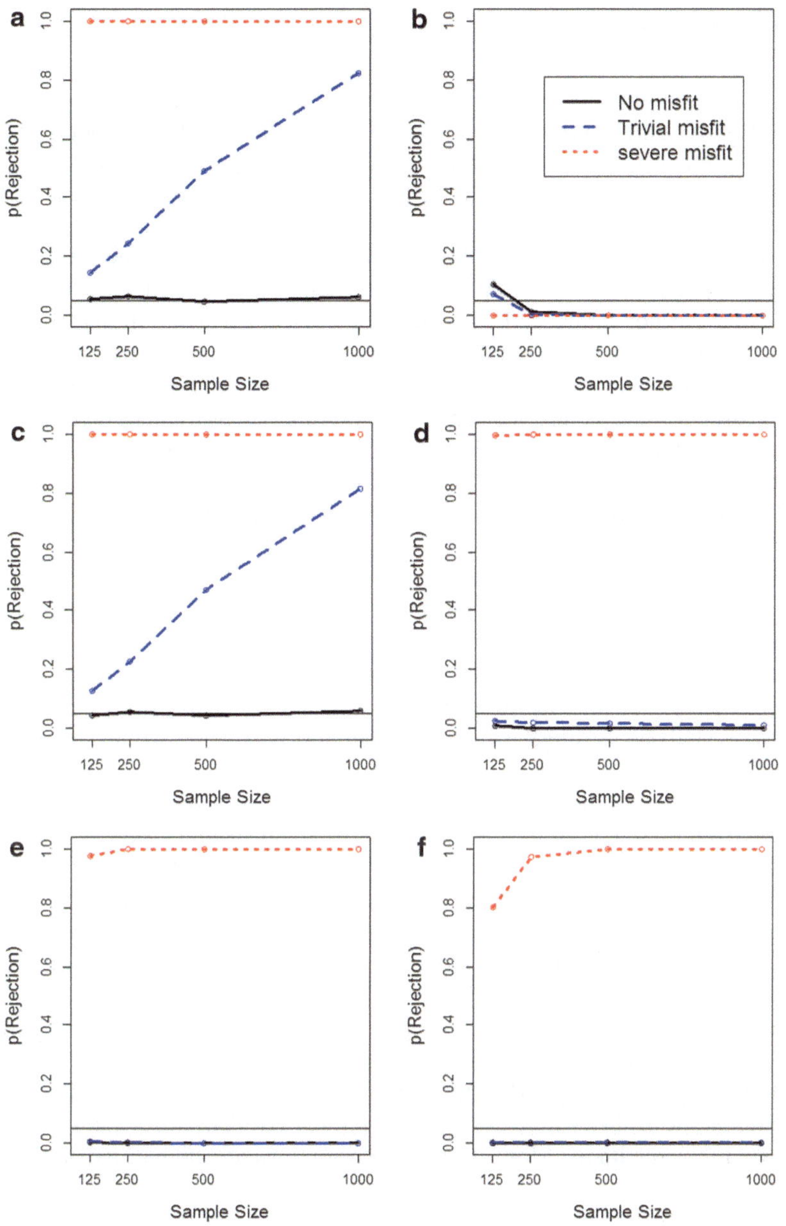

Fig. 3 The rejection rates of each condition. MC = Monte Carlo approach. (**a**) Chi-square difference test, (**b**) change in CFI, (**c**) MC: no misfit, (**d**) MC: fixed method with true misfit, (**e**) MC: Random method with uniform misfit, (**f**) MC: maximal method

7 Discussion

The current study examined the performance of a Monte Carlo approach to nested model comparison in the context of a longitudinal measurement invariance test. Different ways to incorporate trivial misspecifications in the Monte Carlo approach were also examined. The results suggest that the Monte Carlo approach is superior to the chi-square difference test by correctly rejecting the nested model with severe misspecifications without overrejecting the nested model with trivial misspecifications. In general, the rejection rates associated with the Monte Carlo approach were not influenced by sample size except that the nested model with trivial misspecification had small difference in rejection rates across sample sizes in the maximal method. The suggested cutoffs (either 0.002 or 0.01) for the change in CFI turned out to be too lenient for longitudinal measurement invariance tests, indicating that the cutoffs developed under one type of model might not work for another. The Monte Carlo approach proposed in the article then provides an excellent solution for researchers to develop the cutoffs appropriate for their target models.

The Monte Carlo method requires researchers to define trivial misspecification(s). The trivial misspecification(s) should be defined carefully based on theoretical consideration, experience, or past research. In practice, researchers may try out different trivial misspecifications to see how the result is sensitive to the different trivial misspecifications. This would be analogous to conducting a sensitivity analysis. Stronger evidence to support a decision would be obtained if the different trivial misspecifications lead to the same conclusion. Although this practice might be subjective, we believe that it is still better than applying the suggested cutoffs blindly as they might lead to misleading statistical inference regarding model selection. Note that although the different methods to impose trivial misspecifications led to similar results in the current simulation study, their performance might differ when the modeling context changes. More studies need to be conducted to fully understand the advantages and disadvantages of the different methods.

For all methods examined in this paper, the *simsem* package (Pornprasertmanit et al. 2013) provides an automated script for evaluating model fit and model selection using the Monte Carlo approach (see http://simsem.org/). The package also implements the Bollen–Stine bootstrap approach (Bollen and Stine 1992), which can be combined with the Monte Carlo approach to handle nonnormal data (Millsap 2012).

Acknowledgments Partial support for this project was provided by grant NSF 1053160 (Wei Wu & Todd D. Little, co-PIs) and by the Center for Research Methods and Data Analysis at the University of Kansas (when Todd D. Little was director). Todd D. Little is now director of the Institute for Measurement, Methodology, Analysis, and Policy at Texas Tech University. Any opinions, findings, and conclusions or recommendations expressed in this material are those of the authors and do not necessarily reflect the views of the funding agencies.

References

Bentler, P. M. (1995). *EQS structural equations program manual.* Encino, CA: Multivariate Software.

Bollen, K. A., & Stine, R. A. (1992). Bootstrapping goodness-of-fit measures in structural equation models. *Sociological Methods & Research, 21*, 205–229.

Browne, M. W., & Cudeck, R. (1992). Alternative ways of assessing model fit. *Sociological Methods & Research, 21*, 230–258.

Cheung, G. W., & Rensvold, R. B. (2002). Evaluating goodness-of-fit indexes for testing measurement invariance. *Structural Equation Modeling, 9*, 233–255.

Hu, L.-T., & Bentler, P. M. (1999). Cutoff criteria for fit indexes in covariance structure analysis: Conventional criteria versus new alternatives. *Structural Equation Modeling, 6*, 1–55.

Meade, A. W., Johnson, E. C., & Braddy, P. W. (2008). Power and sensitivity of alternative fit indices in tests of measurement invariance. *Journal of Applied Psychology, 93*, 568–592.

Millsap, R. E. (2007). Structural equation modeling made difficult. *Personality and Individual Differences, 2*, 875–881.

Millsap, R. E. (September, 2010). *A simulation paradigm for evaluating "approximate fit" in latent variable modeling.* Paper presented at the conference "Current topics in the Theory and Application of Latent Variable Models: A Conference Honoring the Scientific Contributions of Michael W. Browne", Ohio State University, Columbus, OH.

Millsap, R. E. (2012). A simulation paradigm for evaluating model fit. In M. C. Edwards & R. C. MacCallum (Eds.), *Current issues in the theory and application of latent variable models* (pp. 165–182). New York: Routledge.

Millsap, R. E. & Lee, S. (September, 2008). *Approximate fit in SEM without a priori cutpoints.* Paper presented at the Annual Meeting of Society of Multivariate Experimental Psychology, McGill University, Montreal, QC, Canada.

Pornprasertmanit, S., Miller, P. J., & Schoemann, A. M. (2013). *simsem: simulated structural equation modeling version 0.5-0* [Computer Software]. Available at the Comprehensive R Archive Network.

Pornprasertmanit, S., Wu, W., & Little, T. D. (May, 2012). *Monte Carlo approach to model fit evaluation in structural equation modeling: How to specify trivial misspecification.* Poster presented at the American Psychological Society Annual Convention, Chicago, IL.

Rosseel, Y. (2012). lavaan: An R package for structural equation modeling. *Journal of Statistical Software, 48*, 1–36.

R Development Core Team (2012). R: A language and environment for statistical computing [Computer software manual]. Retrieved from http://www.R-project.org/

Saris, W. E., Satorra, A., & van der Veld, W. M. (2009). Testing structural equation models or detection of misspecifications? *Structural Equation Modeling, 16*, 561–582.

Positive Trait Item Response Models

Joseph F. Lucke

1 Introduction

Measurement models from item response theory (IRT) (Embretson and Reise 2000) have been recently and increasingly applied to measures of addictive disorders such as alcohol use disorder (Keyes et al. 2011; Wu et al. 2009, and references therein), nicotine use disorder (Liu et al. 2012, and references therein), illicit drug use disorders (Saha et al. 2012; Wu et al. 2009, and references therein), and gambling behavior disorder (Sharp et al. 2012, and references therein). All of the above-cited studies have been concerned with the psychometric properties of various measures of addictive disorders, usually the Diagnostic and Statistical Manual of Mental Disorders (DSM-IV, American Psychiatric Association 1994). The research has primarily investigated whether a given disorder can be adequately represented as a unidimensional continuum rather than the traditional categories of *use*, *dependence*, *abuse*, and *addiction* (Orford 2001). *Standard* IRT models, including the above-referenced models, posit the *real trait assumption* that the latent trait follows a density, usually but not necessarily the standard normal density, whose support[1] is the entire real line. Intuitively, the assumption claims the range of a trait θ with positive probability density is $-\infty < \theta < \infty$. This assumption is appropriate for the traits of ability, achievement, or attitude for which everyone can be assigned a score, positive or negative, relative to an anchor at zero, representing the average level of the trait. However, the assumption of real traits creates several problems for addictions research.

[1]The topological closure of the union of all open sets of positive measure.

J.F. Lucke
Research Institute on Addictions, State University of New York at Buffalo, Buffalo, NY, USA
e-mail: jlucke@ria.buffalo.edu

R.E. Millsap et al. (eds.), *New Developments in Quantitative Psychology*, Springer Proceedings in Mathematics & Statistics 66, DOI 10.1007/978-1-4614-9348-8_13,

The first is that the assumption entrains trait scores that are not interpretable as a level of disorder. While it makes sense to assert that a person has a below-average ability in music or a right-of-center attitude towards gun control, it makes little or no sense to assert that a person has a below- or above-average level of addictive disorder. The more meaningful assertion is that person has a certain level of disorder, always relative to the level of *no disorder*.

The second problem arises from assigning the proper score to *no disorder*. A person with no disorder must be distinguished from one at risk for the disorder but endorses no items. The former is identified independently of the diagnostic test (e.g., one who never drinks alcohol cannot have an alcohol use disorder), whereas only a person at risk for the disorder is given the diagnostic test. The anchor for the scale should therefore be *no disorder*, and as there is no trait level less than that of *no disorder*, the anchor should be located at the infimum of the density's support. A person with a potential for the disorder but endorses no items should have a trait score bounded away from the infimum. Under the assumption of real trait, the trait representing no disorder must be located at $-\infty$ with probability zero, effectively excluding such persons from measurement. This problem could be remedied by allowing positive probability at $-\infty$, but the remedy would create a scale such that *no disorder* would be infinitely distant from any disorder.

The third and most important problem is that *the assumption violates current theories regarding the etiology of addictions*. Theories of addictive disorders, from neuropharmacology to social psychology, hold that "[an addictive disorder] can be usefully viewed as a behavioral manifestation of a chronic condition of the motivational system in which a reward-seeking behavior has become out of control" (West 2006, p. 174). The excessive behavior exhibited by the disorder is presumed to be caused by the motivational system's being subjected to ampliative effects that are inadequately regulated by impaired constraints such that the current level of the disorder is proportional to cumulative previous effects (Orford 2001). Conceptualizing the state of a motivational process as a latent trait and modeling the partially constrained, ampliative effects as infinitesimal multiplicative processes, Gibrat's "law of proportional effects" implies that the trait should follow a nonnegatively supported, right-skewed density that is asymptotically lognormal (Johnson et al. 1994, Chap. 14).

One of the advantages of IRT models is that they can be formulated to more realistically represent the underlying psychological processes that may explain an individual's response to items. Here I introduce a class of IRT models that attempts to account for a person's response to items on a diagnostic test by representing the latent trait according to our understanding of addictive disorders. The proposed positive trait item response model (PTIRM) posits that the trait for an addictive disorder follows a mixed density comprising a point-supported probability at zero representing the absence of disorder and the lognormal density representing the presence of disorder. The functions linking the trait to the response are formulated as multiplicative, rather than additive, models. IRT models with positive traits are not new. The original Rasch model posited fixed positive traits (Rasch 1966). Recently, van der Maas et al. (2011) proposed a *positive ability model* derived from cognitive information processing principles, but did not directly estimate the positive trait.

2 Positive Trait Item Response Models

Random variables are underlined (Hemelrijk 1966). Let $\underline{y}_{i1},\ldots,\underline{y}_{iK}$ be observable Bernoulli random variables denoting K items on a diagnostic test such that $\underline{y}_{ik}=1$ if a person i endorses the item and $\underline{y}_{ik}=0$ if not. Let $\underline{\theta}_i$, $i=1,\ldots,I$, be nonnegative latent random variables denoting i-th person's level of addictive disorder such that $\underline{\theta}_i=0$ if i has no disorder and $\underline{\theta}_i>0$ otherwise. Let F be an absolutely continuous distribution function with positive support, and let χ_A denote the indicator function for a set A. The PTIRM posits that the probability (Pr) that person i endorses item k is[2]

$$\pi_k(\theta_i)=\Pr\left(\underline{y}_k=1\,|\,\underline{\theta}_i=\theta_i,\beta_k,\alpha_k\right)=\chi_{]0:\infty[}(\theta_i)\,F\left(\frac{\theta_i^{\alpha_k}}{\beta_k}\right). \tag{1}$$

The parameter $\beta_k>0$ is the (multiplicative) intercept for the k-th item denoting the probability of endorsement β_k^{-1} for $\theta=1$. The parameter $\alpha_k>0$ is the (multiplicative) slope or *discriminability* of the k-th item with respect to severity, with larger α_k denoting finer discriminability. The derived parameter $\delta_k=\beta_k^{\alpha_k^{-1}}$ is the *severity* of the disorder as revealed by item k, and setting $\theta=\delta_k$ gives the probability $F(1)$ of endorsement. If the sample contains a person i with no disorder, then $\theta_i=0$, so that $\chi_{]0:\infty[}(0)=0$, and from Eq. (1), $\pi_k(0)=0$. In this case, the parameters β_k, α_k, and δ_k have no meaning.

Three specific PTIRMs are readily available. First is the *log-logistic*:

$$\pi_k^{\mathrm{LL}}(\theta_i)=\chi_{]0:\infty[}(\theta_i)\,\frac{\theta_i^{\alpha_k}}{\beta_k+\theta_i^{\alpha_k}}. \tag{2}$$

Second is the *lognormal* (Johnson et al. 1994, Chap. 14):

$$\pi_k^{\mathrm{LN}}(\theta_i)=\chi_{]0:\infty[}(\theta_i)\,\Phi\left[\log\left(\frac{\theta_i^{\alpha_k}}{\beta_k}\right)\right]. \tag{3}$$

[2]To conform with the more common parameterization, the item parameters α and β in original presentation have been reversed to β and α, and the person parameter z has been replaced with θ.

And third is the *Weibull* (Johnson et al. 1994, Chap. 21):

$$\pi_k^{\mathrm{W}}(\theta_i) = \chi_{]0:\infty[}(\theta_i)\left[1 - \exp\left(-\frac{\theta_i^{\alpha_k}}{\beta_k}\right)\right]. \tag{4}$$

As previously mentioned, the log-logistic with $\theta > 0$ and $\alpha_k = 1$ is a version of Rasch's original item response model (Rasch 1966). The log-normal with $\theta > 0$ is a statistical version of a psychophysical stimulus–response function (Thomas 1983). The Weibull model with $\theta > 0$, although used in other fields, is, I believe, new as a psychometric model. For $\theta > 0$, these three models can also be expressed as a log-linear extension of generalized linear item response models (Mellenbergh 1994), namely as $h[\pi(\theta)] = \alpha\log(\theta) - \log(\beta)$, where h is the logit, probit, or complementary log–log link function.

The item characteristic curves (ICC's) are given by Eqs. (2)–(4) for all nonnegative θ. The point $\theta = 0$ supplies no additional information, so from here on out we assume θ is positive. The trait quantile $\pi_k^{-1}(p)$ for a given endorsement probability p to item k is

$$\pi_k^{-1}(p) = \left[\beta_k F^{-1}(p)\right]^{\frac{1}{\alpha_k}}.$$

Dropping the item subscript k, log-logistic quantile function is

$$\pi_{\mathrm{LL}}^{-1}(p) = \left[\beta\frac{p}{1-p}\right]^{\frac{1}{\alpha}}; \tag{5}$$

the lognormal quantile function is

$$\pi_{\mathrm{LN}}^{-1}(p) = \left\{\beta\exp\left[\Phi^{-1}(p)\right]\right\}^{\frac{1}{\alpha}}; \tag{6}$$

and the Weibull quantile function is

$$\pi_{\mathrm{W}}^{-1}(p) = \left[-\beta\log(1-p)\right]^{\frac{1}{\alpha}}. \tag{7}$$

For the log-logistic and lognormal PTIRMs, the median trait quantile for a specific item occurs at the item's severity, that is,

$$\pi_k^{-1}(.5) = \beta_k^{\frac{1}{\alpha_k}} = \delta_k \quad \text{and} \quad \pi_k(\delta_k) = .5$$

The equality between the median trait quantile and severity does not hold for the Weibull PTIRM. In this case

$$\pi_k^{-1}(.5) = [\log(2)\beta_k]^{\frac{1}{\alpha_k}} \quad \text{but} \quad \pi_k(\delta_k) = 1 - e^{-1} \approx .63.$$

One could restore the equality by additionally scaling the severity for the Weibull model as $[\log(2)\beta_k]^{\frac{1}{\alpha_k}}$, but that not pursued here.

The item (Fisher) information function provides an index of item precision as a function of the latent trait. For a given item k and dropping subscripts, the item information function for the general model (1) is

$$I(\theta) = E\left[\left(\frac{d\log\left\{\left[F\left(\frac{\theta^\alpha}{\beta}\right)\right]^y\left[1-F\left(\frac{\theta^\alpha}{\beta}\right)\right]^{1-y}\right\}}{d\theta}\right)^2\right]$$

$$= \frac{\left[\frac{\alpha\theta^{\alpha-1}}{\beta}f\left(\frac{\theta^\alpha}{\beta}\right)\right]^2}{F\left(\frac{\theta^\alpha}{\beta}\right)\left[1-F\left(\frac{\theta^\alpha}{\beta}\right)\right]}.$$

The log-logistic item information function is

$$I^{\mathrm{LL}}(\theta) = \frac{\beta\alpha^2\theta^{\alpha-2}}{(\beta+\theta^\alpha)^2} = \left(\frac{\alpha}{\theta}\right)^2\pi(\theta)\left[1-\pi(\theta)\right]. \tag{8}$$

The log-normal item information function is

$$I^{\mathrm{LN}}(\theta) = \frac{\left\{\frac{\alpha}{\theta}\phi\left[\log\left(\frac{\theta^\alpha}{\beta}\right)\right]\right\}^2}{\Phi\left[\log\left(\frac{\theta^\alpha}{\beta}\right)\right]\left\{1-\Phi\left[\log\left(\frac{\theta^\alpha}{\beta}\right)\right]\right\}} = \frac{\left\{\frac{\alpha}{\theta}\phi\left[\log\left(\frac{\theta^\alpha}{\beta}\right)\right]\right\}^2}{\pi(\theta)\left[1-\pi(\theta)\right]}, \tag{9}$$

where ϕ is the standard normal density function. The Weibull item information function is

$$I^{\mathrm{W}}(\theta) = \left[\frac{\alpha\theta^{\alpha-1}}{\beta}\right]^2\frac{\exp\left(-\frac{\theta^\alpha}{\beta}\right)}{1-\exp\left(-\frac{\theta^\alpha}{\beta}\right)} = \left[\frac{\alpha\theta^{\alpha-1}}{\beta}\right]^2\frac{1-\pi(\theta)}{\pi(\theta)}. \tag{10}$$

3 Inference

Bayesian inference was used to obtain parameter estimates. Let $[y_{ik}]$ be the $I \times K$ matrix of observed binary outcomes denoting the i-th person's response to item k. Under the standard IRT assumptions of independence among subjects and local independence among items along with no missing data and prior independence among parameters, the joint posterior density (pr) of the model parameters given the observed responses is

$$\text{pr}\left(\underline{\beta}_1,\ldots,\underline{\beta}_K,\underline{\alpha}_1,\ldots,\underline{\alpha}_K,\underline{\theta}_1,\ldots,\underline{\theta}_I \,|\, y_{11},\ldots,y_{1K},\ldots,y_{I1},\ldots,y_{IK}\right)$$
$$\propto \prod_{i=1}^{I}\text{pr}(\underline{\theta}_i)\prod_{k=1}^{K}\pi_k(\theta_i)^{y_{ik}}\left[1-\pi_k(\theta_i)\right]^{1-y_{ik}}\text{pr}(\underline{\beta}_k)\,\text{pr}(\underline{\alpha}_k).$$

Markov chain Monte Carlo (MCMC) methods were used to obtain the $2K+I$ marginal parameter distributions (Fox 2010, Chap. 4). The parameters were given mutually independent, low information prior densities, namely $\underline{\beta}_k \sim \text{gamma}(.1,.1)$ and $\underline{\alpha}_k \sim \text{gamma}(.1,.1)$, so that $\Pr(0<\underline{\beta}_k<6)=.95$ and $\Pr(0<\underline{\alpha}_k<6)=.95$ for all k. Following the reasoning given in Sect. 1 on page 199 the prior density for the trait was $\underline{\theta}_i \sim \text{lognormal}(0,1)$ for all i. The analyses were conducted in R (R Development Core Team 2012) under Rstudio (RStudio, Inc 2012) using JAGS (Plummer 2011) and the R2jags package (Su and Yajima 2012) for the MCMC analyses and the lattice package (Sarkar 2008) for graphics.

4 Data Set

The data sources were two public-use files from the Clinical Trials Network for the methadone and non-methadone maintenance trials for abstinence-based contingency management (Peirce et al. 2006; Petry et al. 2005) which had previously been analyzed using a standard IRT model (Wu et al. 2009). The data comprised 854 subjects responding to the seven alcohol dependency items of the DSM-IV (American Psychiatric Association 1994) at baseline, prior to any intervention. Of the 854 subjects, 167 (19.6 %) reported they had never used alcohol in the past nor were currently using alcohol. These subjects were given a trait score of $\theta=0$. The remaining 687 were assumed to be potentially addicted to alcohol and assumed to have a trait score $\theta>0$. The DSM-IV items were

1. *toler*—increasing tolerance of alcohol,
2. *wdraw*—experience withdrawal symptoms,
3. *amount*—using larger amounts,
4. *unable*—unable to control use,
5. *time*—large amount of time spent in acquiring alcohol,
6. *giveup*—giving up important activities, and
7. *contin*—continued use despite accompanying problems.

Two MCMC simulations were run to obtain the marginal densities of the 2×7 item $+\,687$ person parameters. The first comprised three chains with a burn-in of 1,000 replications followed by estimation based on 1,000 replications. The Brooks–Gelman–Rubin (BGR) potential scale reduction statistic was less than 1.1 for all parameters (Gelman et al. 2004). The final 1,000 samples from each of the three chains became the estimated marginal densities for the analysis.

5 Results

Figure 1 presents the ICC's for the three models according to Eqs. (2)–(4). The curves, constrained to the positive real line, are not symmetric around any trait score. Although the curves showed, as would be expected, slightly different forms, the ordering of the curves along the latent trait axis (Alcohol Disorder Score) was the same for all three models. Visual inspection revealed that six of the seven characteristic curves showed roughly the same item severity (δ_k) and discriminability (α_k) with the exception being the item *wdraw*, which had the greatest severity the least discriminability.

Table 1 on page 207 presents for each item the posterior means of the intercept, discrimination, and severity parameters along with their respective standard errors. The mean severity across items within each model induced the same rank ordering among models, so the items are ranked by increasing mean severity. For each item, the log-logistic tended to generate the smallest severity estimates, the lognormal the next largest, the Weibull the largest. As there is no intrinsic scale, only the ordering of the items is meaningful. The deviance information criterion (DIC), a Bayesian measure similar to the Akaike information criterion (Spiegelhalter et al. 2002), indicated that all three models had similar goodness of fit, with the lognormal model showing the best fit and the Weibull the worst.

The item *unable* indicated the least severity and *wdraw* indicated the greatest for all three models. Also, as previously mentioned, all of the items except *wdraw* showed similar estimates of severity. The mean discriminabilities of the items were not consistent across the three models. The item *wdraw* showed the least discriminability for the log-logistic and lognormal models, whereas *unable* showed the least for the Weibull. For item analysis, the relative severity of the items appears independent of the model, but the relative discriminability depends on the model.

Figure 2 on page 208 presents the item information curves for the three models according to (8)–(10). The item information curves are not consistent across models. The log-logistic model shows greatest precision for *unable*, followed by the precisions for *contin* and *giveup*. In contrast, the log-normal model shows greatest precision for *giveup* followed by *unable* and next *contin*. In further contrast, the Weibull model shows greatest precision for *giveup* followed by *contin* then by *time* and *amount*. However, all models show the least precision for *wdraw*.

Figure 3 on page 209 presents the total item information curves, the sum of all seven item information curves, for each model. The log-logistic and lognormal models showed similar curves, but with the lognormal peak being slightly lower and skewed further to the right. The Weibull curve was considerably lower and more right-skewed than the other two.

Apart from item analysis, the goal of a PTIRM is to provide person scores. Figure 4 on page 210 presents the posterior person score densities, obtained from the MCMC analysis, for eight selected item response patterns under the log-logistic model. The thin line appearing the same in each panel displays the prior standard log-normal density for the person score. The thick line presents the posterior density of the score for that pattern. The upper left panel presents the posterior score density

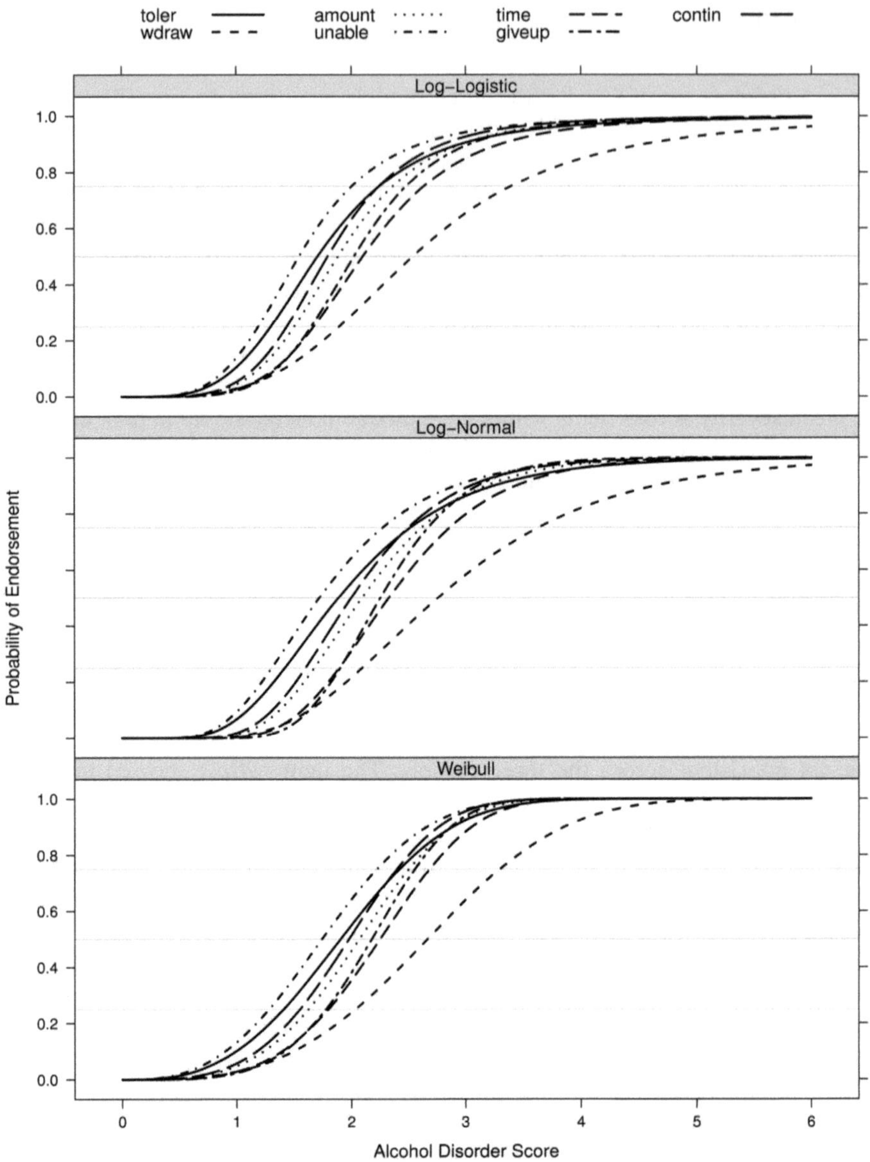

Fig. 1 Item characteristic curves of the seven dependence items of the DSM-IV for the log-logistic, log-normal, and Weibull PTIRMs

Table 1 Posterior means and (standard errors) of each item's intercept (β), discrimination (α), and severity (δ) parameters for the log-logistic, log-normal, and Weibull PTIRMs

	Log-logistic						Log-normal						Weibull					
Item	β		α		δ		β		α		δ		β		α		δ	
unable	6.3	(1.6)	4.2	(0.5)	1.5	(0.1)	3.7	(0.7)	2.4	(0.3)	1.7	(0.1)	7.0	(1.5)	2.8	(0.3)	2.0	(0.1)
toler	8.6	(2.2)	4.0	(0.4)	1.7	(0.1)	4.5	(0.7)	2.4	(0.3)	1.9	(0.1)	9.3	(2.3)	2.9	(0.3)	2.2	(0.1)
contin	18.1	(6.2)	5.0	(0.5)	1.8	(0.1)	8.1	(2.3)	3.0	(0.4)	2.0	(0.1)	16.8	(4.7)	3.6	(0.4)	2.2	(0.1)
amount	21.8	(7.6)	4.9	(0.6)	1.9	(0.1)	9.5	(2.7)	3.0	(0.4)	2.1	(0.1)	20.3	(6.1)	3.6	(0.4)	2.3	(0.1)
giveup	46.1	(15.6)	5.4	(0.6)	2.0	(0.1)	25.2	(9.6)	4.0	(0.5)	2.2	(0.1)	42.1	(12.6)	4.3	(0.4)	2.4	(0.1)
time	36.8	(12.3)	4.9	(0.5)	2.1	(0.1)	15.8	(6.1)	3.3	(0.4)	2.3	(0.1)	34.9	(10.7)	3.9	(0.4)	2.5	(0.2)
wdraw	33.5	(10.6)	3.8	(0.4)	2.5	(0.2)	12.0	(3.4)	2.4	(0.3)	2.7	(0.2)	34.8	(10.0)	3.3	(0.3)	3.0	(0.2)
DIC	2,325						2,245						2,347					

The items are ordered by increasing severity. The last row presents each model's goodness of fit by the DIC

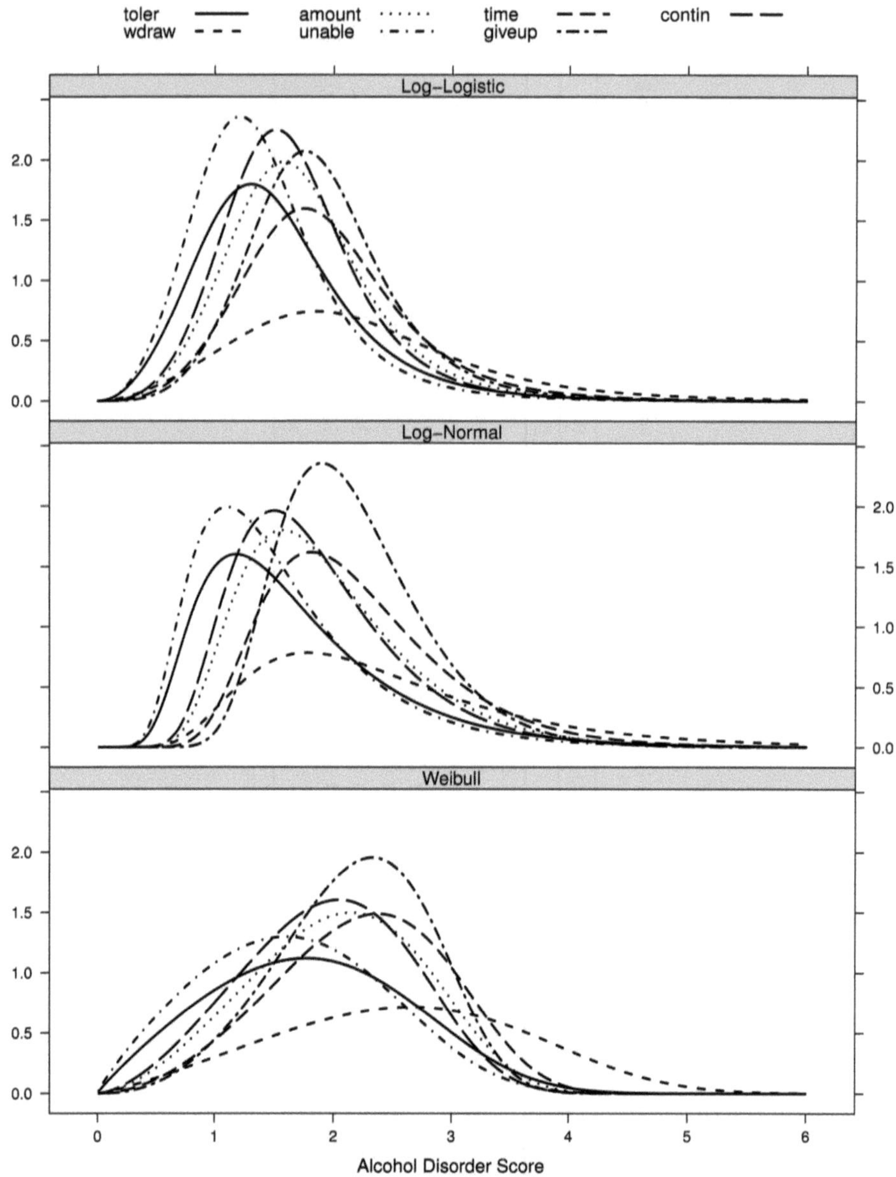

Fig. 2 Item information curves for the seven dependence items of the DSM-IV for the log-logistic, lognormal, and Weibull PTIRMs

for a person endorsing none (0000000) of the seven items and the lower right panel presents that for one endorsing all (1111111) of the items. The upper right panel presents the posterior density for a person endorsing only the seventh item *contin* (0000001) and the lower left panel presents that for one endorsing all but the second

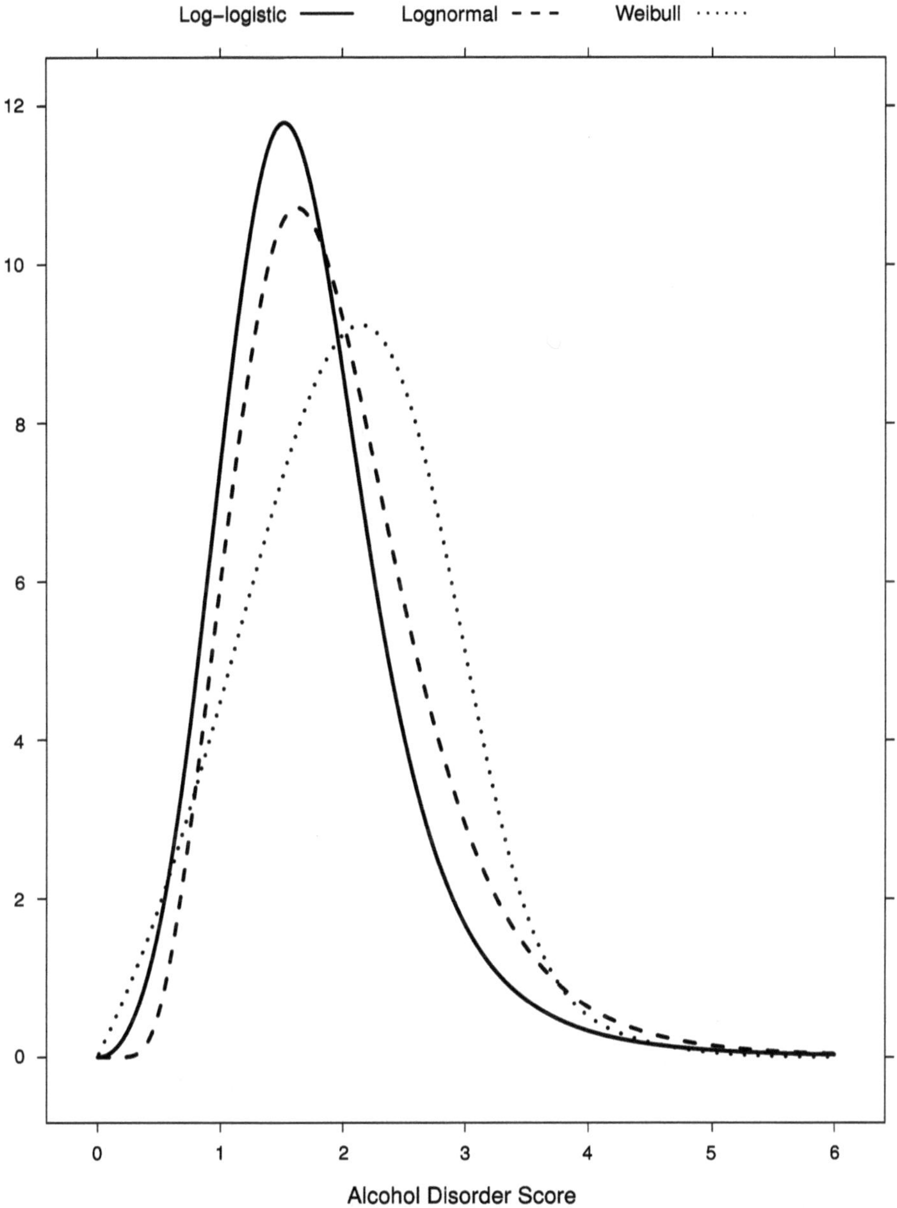

Fig. 3 Total item information curves for the seven dependence items of the DSM-IV for the log-logistic, lognormal, and Weibull PTIRMs

item *wdraw* (1011111). The remaining panels have similar interpretations. Also given are the mean score and its standard error for each response pattern. The upper six panels have posterior densities with standard errors smaller than the prior, but

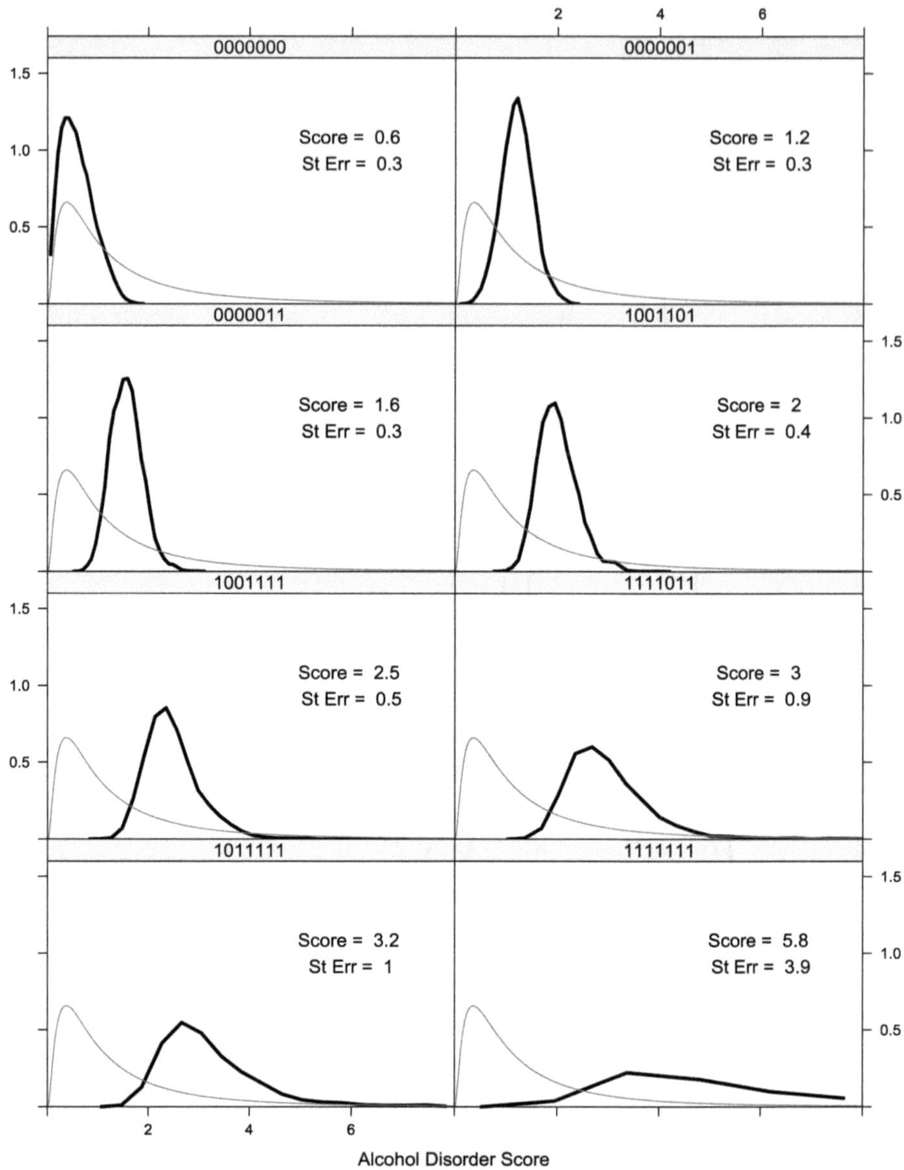

Fig. 4 Posterior distribution of trait scores for eight selected response patterns with posterior means and standard errors from the log-logistic PTIRM

the lowest right panel has a density with large standard error, possibly associated that score's being the extreme along with the poor discriminability of the second item *wdraw*.

6 Discussion

The purpose here was to introduce a class of item response models that more realistically represent traits such as addictive disorders. This new class of models was proposed on theoretical rather than empirical grounds. Theories of addictive disorders emphasize the increasingly ampliative effects worsening the disorder over a baseline of no disorder. This theoretical premise is not consistent with the standard IRT assumption that the trait can lie anywhere along the real line. The PTIRM introduced here assumes the trait representing an addictive disorder to be positive with the baseline of no disorder fixed at zero. Three PTIRM models were introduced—the log-logistic, the lognormal, and the Weibull—as special cases of a general PTIRM. Subsidiary derivations yield the trait quantile functions and item information functions.

These models were applied to a data set measuring alcohol use disorder. Bayesian inference via MCMC methods provided a satisfactory method for obtaining posterior distributions for item parameters and the person trait. Different PTIRMs yielded differently shaped ICC's that nonetheless retained the same ordering of items across models. The item severity parameters were ranked in the same order across all three models, but the discriminability parameters were not similarly ranked. Likewise, different PTIRMS yielded different item information curves, with some items showing greater precision under one model but other items showing greater precision under another. Also presented were the densities of a selected subset of person scores.

PTIRMs are a multiplicative transformation of standard IRT models. For purely item analyses, the ranking of items in terms of severity scores from a PTIRM should correspond to the ranking of severity from the corresponding IRT model. Indeed, analyzing these data with standard IRT models yielded the same ordering of items with respect to severity which was, in turn, the same order as in the original analyses (Wu et al. 2009). One can also estimate the moments of the trait scores for PTIRM from the moments of trait scores from a standard IRT model that assumes a standard normal trait density. An occasional question is whether the PTIRM fits the data better than a standard IRT model. Although I consider the empirical question of fit secondary to the theoretical properties of the PTIRM, I note that the logistic IRT with a standard normal density for the trait applied to these data yields a DIC of 2,341, which is only slightly worse than the DIC of 2,325 of the corresponding log-logistic PTIRM.

PTIRMs provide a viable alternative to the standard IRT models for phenomena such as addiction disorders.

References

American Psychiatric Association (1994). *Diagnostic and statistical manual of mental disorders* (4th ed.). Washington, DC: American Psychiatric Association.

Embretson, S. E., & Reise, S. P. (2000). *Item response theory for psychologists*. Mawah, NJ: Lawrence Erlbaum Associates.

Fox, J. P. (2010). *Bayesian item response modeling: Theory and applications*. New York, NY: Springer.

Gelman, A., Carlin, J. B., Stern, H. S., & Rubin, D. B. (2004). *Bayesian data analysis* (2nd ed.). London: Chapman & Hall.

Hemelrijk, J. (1966). Underlining random variables. *Statistica Neerlandica, 20*(1), 1–7.

Johnson, N. L., Kotz, S., & Balakrishnan, N. (1994). *Continuous univariate distributions* (Vol. 1), (2nd ed.). New York, NY: Wiley.

Keyes, K. M., Krueger, R. F., Grant, B. F., & Hasin, D. S. (2011). Alcohol craving and the dimensionality of alcohol disorders. *Psychological Medicine, 41*(03), 629–640. doi:10.1017/S003329171000053X. http://dx.doi.org/10.1017/S003329171000053X, http://journals.cambridge.org/article_S003329171000053X

Liu, L. C., Hedeker, D., & Mermelstein, R. J. (2012). Modeling nicotine dependence: An application of a longitudinal IRT model for the analysis of Adolescent Nicotine Dependence Syndrome Scale. *Nicotine & Tobacco Research*. doi:10.1093/ntr/nts125. http://ntr.oxfordjournals.org/content/early/2012/05/13/ntr.nts125.abstract, http://ntr.oxfordjournals.org/content/early/2012/05/13/ntr.nts125.full.pdf+html

Mellenbergh, G. J. (1994). Generalized linear item response theory. *Psychological Bulletin, 115*(2), 300–307.

Orford, J. (2001). Addiction as excessive appetite. *Addiction, 96*(1), 15–31. http://search.ebscohost.com/login.aspx?direct=true&db=a9h&AN=3991026&site=ehost-live&scope=site

Peirce, J. M., Petry, N. M., Stitzer, M. L., Blaine, J., Kellogg, S., Satterfield, F., et al. (2006). Effects of lower-cost incentives on stimulant abstinence in methadone maintenance treatment: A National Drug Abuse Treatment Clinical Trials Network study. *Archives of General Psychiatry, 63*(2), 201–208. doi:10.1001/archpsyc.63.2.201. http://archpsyc.ama-assn.org/cgi/content/abstract/63/2/201, http://archpsyc.ama-assn.org/cgi/reprint/63/2/201.pdf

Petry, N. M., Peirce, J. M., Stitzer, M. L., Blaine, J., Roll, J. M., Cohen, A., et al. (2005). Effect of prize-based incentives on outcomes in stimulant abusers in outpatient psychosocial treatment programs: A National Drug Abuse Treatment Clinical Trials Network study. *Archives of General Psychiatry, 62*(10), 1148–1156. doi:10.1001/archpsyc.62.10.1148. http://archpsyc.ama-assn.org/cgi/content/abstract/62/10/1148, http://archpsyc.ama-assn.org/cgi/reprint/62/10/1148.pdf

Plummer, M. (2011). JAGS version 3.1.0 user manual. http://sourceforge.net/projects/mcmc-jags/files/Manuals/3.x/jags_user_manual.pdf/download

R Development Core Team (2012). *R: A language and environment for statistical computing*. Vienna: R Foundation for Statistical Computing. http://www.R-project.org/, ISBN: 3-900051-07-0.

Rasch, G. (1966). An individualistic approach to item analysis. In P. F. Lazarsfeld, & N. W. Henry (Eds.), *Readings in mathematical social science* (pp. 89–108). Chicago, IL: Chicago Science Research Associates.

RStudio, Inc. (2012). Rstudio. http://www.rstudio.org/

Saha, T. D., Compton, W. M., Chou, S. P., Smith, S., Ruan, W. J., Huang, B., et al. (2012). Analyses related to the development of DSM-5 criteria for substance use related disorders: 1. toward amphetamine, cocaine and prescription drug use disorder continua using item response theory. *Drug and Alcohol Dependence, 122*(1–2), 38–46. doi:10.1016/j.drugalcdep.2011.09.004. http://www.sciencedirect.com/science/article/pii/S0376871611003917

Sarkar, D. (2008). *Lattice: Multivariate data visualization with R*. New York, NY: Springer.

Sharp, C., Steinberg, L., Yaroslavsky, I., Hofmeyr, A., Dellis, A., Ross, D., et al. (2012). An item response theory analysis of the Problem Gambling Severity Index. *Assessment, 19*(2), 167–175. doi:10.1177/1073191111418296. http://asm.sagepub.com/content/19/2/167.abstract, http://asm.sagepub.com/content/19/2/167.full.pdf+html

Spiegelhalter, D. J., Best, N. G., Carlin, B. P., & van der Linde, A. (2002). Bayesian measures of model complexity and fit. *Journal of the Royal Statistical Society: Series B (Statistical*

Methodology), 64(4), 583–639. http://www.blackwell-synergy.com/doi/abs/10.1111/1467-9868.00353, http://www.blackwell-synergy.com/doi/pdf/10.1111/1467-9868.00353

Su, Y. S., & Yajima, M. (2012). R2jags: A Package for running JAGS from R. http://cran.r-project.org/web/packages/R2jags/R2jags.pdf

Thomas, H. (1983). Parameter estimation in simple psychophysical models. *Psychological Bulletin, 93*(2), 396–403.

van der Maas, H. L. J., Molenaar, D., Maris, G., Kievit, R. A., & Borsboom, D. (2011). Cognitive psychology meets psychometric theory: On the relation between process models for decision making and latent variable models for individual differences. *Psychological Review, 118*(2), 339–356. http://search.ebscohost.com/login.aspx?direct=true&db=pdh&AN=rev-118-2-339&site=ehost-live&scope=site

West, R. (2006). *Theory of addiction*. Oxford: Blackwell. http://66.199.228.237/boundary/addiction/Theoryofaddictionfirsthalf.pdf

Wu, L. T., Pan, J. J., Blazer, D. G., Tai, B., Stitzer, M. L., et al. (2009). An item response theory modeling of alcohol and marijuana dependences: A National Drug Abuse Treatment Clinical Trials Network study. *Journal of Studies on Alcohol and Drugs, 70*(3), 414–425.

A Comparison of Algorithms for Dimensionality Analysis

Sedat Sen, Allan S. Cohen, and Seock-Ho Kim

1 Introduction

Item response theory (IRT) models have been widely used for various educational and psychological testing purposes such as detecting differential item functioning (DIF), test construction, ability estimation, equating, and computer adaptive testing. The main assumption underlying these models is that local independence holds with respect to the latent ability being modeled (Lord and Novick 1968). It is important, therefore, to show that the unidimensionality assumption holds before any unidimensional IRT modeling is applied. Otherwise, violations of the unidimensionality assumption may have a considerable and negative effect on parameter estimation (Ackerman 1989; Reckase 1979). Ackerman (1992) also showed that the presence of multidimensionality may also cause DIF. Correct identification of the internal test structure also helps to examine how well the test measures the underlying structure. Tate (2003) noted that strict dimensionality and essential dimensionality are two types of dimensionality in the traditional IRT context. The former refers to the minimum number of examinee latent abilities required to estimate a monotone and locally independent model (McDonald 1981; Stout 1990) while the latter refers to a test with a single dominant factor and one or more minor factors (Stout 1987, 1990).

Because of the centrality of the unidimensionality assumption to many applications of IRT, the dimensionality assessment problem has been the focus of considerable study. Excellent reviews are provided by Hattie (1984) and Tate (2003). Dimensionality assessment is more problematic for categorical variables than continuous variables. When the variables are continuous, traditional factor analysis techniques can be used to identify factors that may be used to explain the observed data. Data in social science are often categorical in nature (e.g., dichotomous

S. Sen (✉) • A.S. Cohen • S.-H. Kim
University of Georgia, Athens, GA 30602, USA
e-mail: sedatsen@uga.edu; acohen@uga.edu; shkim@uga.edu

R.E. Millsap et al. (eds.), *New Developments in Quantitative Psychology*, Springer Proceedings in Mathematics & Statistics 66, DOI 10.1007/978-1-4614-9348-8_14,

and polytomous item responses). These types of data normally fail to meet the distributional requirements of the traditional linear factor analysis. As a result, factor analysis may not be directly applicable to categorical variables because spurious factors (called difficulty factors) may emerge when using Pearson product-moment correlations (Ackerman et al. 2003; McLeod et al. 2001). As a result, the number of dimensions may be overestimated (Bock et al. 1988). In order to deal with this situation, tetrachoric correlations can be used instead of Pearson correlations to deal with dichotomous nature of item scores (Hulin et al. 1983; Knol and Berger 1991; Parry and McArdle 1991). However, it should be noted that tetrachoric matrices for item-level data may not always be positive definite, as required for modern factor analysis techniques. Another problem with this method is the estimation of tetrachoric correlations which can be difficult to implement when correlations are very close to unity (Thissen and Wainer 2001).

A number of different methods have been proposed to assess test dimensionality for item-level, beginning with work by Christoffersson (1975) and Muthén (1977). Some relatively new methods based on item factor analysis (IFA) have also been proposed. There are a wide range of IFA models within structural equation modeling (SEM) and IRT including full-information maximum-likelihood (FIML) estimation (Bock et al. 1988), the algorithm in the software package LISCOMP (Muthén 1978), nonlinear factor analysis (McDonald 1982), and factor analysis of the tetrachoric correlations between all item pairs (Knol and Berger 1991). The FIML estimation method is based on analyzing the entire item response pattern while the other three use bivariate information. These parametric approaches also differ in the estimation algorithms used. There are several methods available for IFA model parameter estimations. Among these are FIML, unweighted least squares (ULS), weighted least squares (WLS), and its modified extensions such as modified WLSM and WLSMV. In addition to these parametric approaches, there are also some nonparametric approaches for dimensionality assessment such as the algorithm in the computer software DIMTEST (Nandakumar and Stout 1993) and in the software DETECT (Kim 1994; Zhang and Stout 1999a,b). These techniques are designed to test essential dimensionality of a set of test items.

More recently, a number of studies of dimensionality have focused on comparison of different methods (e.g., Nandakumar 1994; Nandakumar and Yu 1996; Tate 2003), the effect of applying unidimensional IRT to multidimensional items (e.g., Ackerman 1989), and the effect of guessing parameter (Tate 2003; Stone and Yeh 2006). Although it has been more than three decades since Lord's (1980) call for a statistical significance test for assessing dimensionality of a test, there is still no general test for dichotomous items. Hattie (1984) noted that most indices were inappropriate for dimensionality assessment for the case of dichotomous variables.

Even though substantial work has been done on techniques used for dimensionality checking, there has been a lack of study on the effectiveness of different software packages implementing these techniques. The purposes of this study were to (1) compare two popular software packages, Mplus and TESTFACT, with respect to their effectiveness for checking dimensionality in multiple-choice tests and (2) compare different criteria used in these programs. We also included SAS in our empirical analyses to examine what would happen if Pearson correlations instead of tetrachoric correlations were used. In addition to use of Pearson correlations, we also analyzed the empirical data set with SAS to provide a tetrachoric correlation for completeness. Guessing parameters and the size of correlations between dimensions were manipulated to explore possible interaction between these effects. Three indices based on the proportion of variance, RMSR reduction, and a chi-square difference test were used to examine dimensionality. The research included two parts, a simulation study using a Monte Carlo approach and an application with data from a large midwestern university mathematics placement testing program.

1.1 Software

There are a number of computer programs used for both parametric and nonparametric approaches. Because the focus of this study is on parametric approaches, software packages designed for nonparametric approaches (e.g., DIMTEST) are not discussed in detail. IFA-based procedures for applications with dichotomously scored items can be implemented in software programs, including Mplus (Muthén and Muthén 2010), NOHARM (Fraser and McDonald 1988), and TESTFACT (Wilson et al. 2003). Although the goal of these three programs is the same, the methods employed by each are different. They differ in sample statistics, estimation methods, and how guessing is handled (Stone and Yeh 2006).

1.1.1 Mplus

Mplus can handle categorical, continuous, and ordinal types of data. The software permits users to perform both exploratory factor analysis (EFA) and confirmatory factor analysis (CFA) to estimate unidimensional or multidimensional models. Estimation of dichotomous data is done using tetrachoric correlations via the following methods: ULS, WLS, WLSM, and WLSMV. Mplus also provides several fit indices including chi-square test statistics, root mean square residuals (RMSR), root mean square error of approximation (RMSEA), and comparative fit index (CFI). In addition, both orthogonal (varimax) and oblique (promax) rotations of the initial solution are available. There is no option for handling the guessing parameter in the three-parameter model. The Mplus manual also indicates that the relationship between the extracted factors and the observed indicators is provided using probit regression of items on factors.

1.1.2 TESTFACT

TESTFACT was designed to perform nonlinear, exploratory full-information IFA on dichotomous items. This software uses marginal maximum likelihood (MML) estimation in combination with an expectation-maximization (EM) algorithm. The estimates are obtained in TESTFACT using all of the information in the item responses rather than use of an item covariance or correlation matrix as is implemented in Mplus, and TESTFACT can handle the guessing parameter for factor analyses. TESTFACT prompts the user to specify the number of factors and the guessing parameters, if guessing is assumed in the model. The guessing parameter can be input by either assuming a single value or providing estimated guessing parameters for each item from another software package such as BILOG or MULTILOG. TESTFACT calculates chi-square statistics which can be used for model comparison. However, TESTFACT requires nonzero frequencies for each item pattern in order to calculate this value. Problematic correlations due to extreme proportions are replaced with admissible values using Thurstone's centroid method (Tate 2003). A smoothing option is also available if the correlation matrix is nonpositive definite. Although TESTFACT can produce the output of a residual matrix, there is no residual-based fit index. RMSR value can be calculated from residual matrix. As with Mplus, varimax and promax rotations of the initial solution can be obtained in TESTFACT.

1.1.3 SAS

SAS provides a way of doing common-factor and component analysis using the proc factor statement. It offers a range of methods in EFA to select the number of factors, extraction and rotation methods. These analyses can be done using either raw data or correlation/covariance matrix. SAS is often used for continuous variables with Pearson correlation coefficients. Although it is not very practical, one can conduct factor analysis for dichotomous type data by providing a tetrachoric correlation matrix. The extraction methods available in SAS include principal component analysis, principal factor analysis, iterated principal factor analysis, ULS factor analysis, maximum likelihood (canonical) factor analysis, alpha factor analysis, image component analysis, and Harris component analysis. Proc factor produces the residual correlation matrix and the partial correlation matrix. EQUAMAX, ORTHOMAX, QUARTIMAX, PARSIMAX, and VARIMAX; and two oblique rotation methods, PROCRUSTES and PROMAX, can be obtained with proc factor statement. In order to help in determining the number of components or factors, the scree plot, percentage of variance, and Kaiser's rule can be obtained from output.

2 Method

Dimensionality assessment results for the simulated data are given first, followed by results for the real data. Only the results of applying Mplus and TESTFACT are presented in the simulation study. Additional results from SAS are reported for the real data study. As mentioned earlier, number of dimensions, correlation, and guessing parameter were manipulated. Results from uncorrelated factors and those from correlated ($r = 0.3$) factors are presented for both Mplus and TESTFACT in results section. Values in the each cell represent the correct number of identifications out of ten replications. First rows of two tables are the same since only the uncorrelated condition is possible for unidimensional data. EFA was carried out using WLSM for all Mplus analyses. Similarly, exploratory analyses in TESTFACT were conducted using FIML for one to five factors. Hereafter, we refer Mplus as it is applied with WLSM and TESTFACT as it is applied with FIML in simulated data analyses. Maximum likelihood extraction method was used for SAS analyses in empirical data set.

2.1 Simulated Data

Examinees' responses to ten different 60-item tests were simulated based on the dichotomous, multidimensional logistic IRT model. Each of the ten tests was replicated ten times. One-, two-, and three-dimensional data sets were simulated for each replication. Two guessing conditions were simulated in which the guessing parameter was set at 0 and 0.25. There is a certain amount of correlation among factors in most educational tests. To simulate this, a correlation of 0.3 was used in addition to correlations of 0 between factors. Data were generated for 2,000 respondents for each test using WINGEN 3.0 (Han 2006) software. Following the conditions in (Yeh 2007), distribution of latent traits was normal with mean of zero and standard deviation of 0.1 for unidimensional data. While mean of latent traits remained the same for each dimension, different values for standard deviations were used to obtain the desired correlation ($r = 0.3$) between dimensions. Because this was the only way to obtain correlated dimensions in WINGEN. Item parameter distributions were $N(1,\ 0.36)$ and $N(0,\ 1.43)$ for discrimination and difficulty parameters, respectively. Ten data conditions were simulated by changing correlation, guessing, and the number of dimensions.

2.2 Real Data

The data used in this study were from a test designed to measure calculator proficiency in pre-calculus mathematics. A total of 765 students took a special, experimental form of this 28-item test. Each item had five choices. Students were allowed to use a calculator on the first 14 items, but were not allowed to do so on the second 14 items. Only the second 14 items, which allowed no calculator use, were analyzed for this study. The test was originally constructed as a unidimensional instrument.

The multidimensional item response theory (MIRT) model for dichotomously scored items with a guessing parameter (Bock et al. 1988) was used to analyze the data. The probability of a correct response to item j can be given as

$$P(U_j = 1|\theta) = g_j + (1 - g_j)\Phi[z_j(\theta)] = g_j + (1 - g_j)\frac{1}{\sqrt{2\pi}}\int_{-\infty}^{z_j(\theta)} \exp(-t^2/2)dt, \tag{1}$$

where

$$\Phi[z_j(\theta)] = \Phi\left(c_j + \sum_{k=1}^{K} a_{jk}\theta_k\right) = \Phi\left(\frac{\delta_j + \sum_{k=1}^{K} \alpha_{jk}\theta_k}{\sigma_j}\right), \tag{2}$$

g_j is the guessing parameter, c_j is the intercept or easiness parameter, a_{jk}s are the slopes, θ_ks are latent variables equivalent to the vector θ, δ_j is the standard difficulty or negative threshold (i.e., $-\gamma_j$), α_{jk}s are items regression coefficients or factor loadings to the respective dimensions from 1 to K (i.e., λ_{jk}), and $\sigma_j = \sqrt{1 - \sum_{k=1}^{K} \alpha_{jk}^2}$. If we let $d_j = \sqrt{1 + \sum_{k=1}^{K} a_{jk}^2}$, then $\alpha_{jk} = a_{jk}/d_j$ and $\delta_j = c_j/d_j$ (cf. McLeod et al. 2001, p. 199).

TESTFACT was used to obtain the a_{jk}s and c_j for each item under MMLE. The g_j parameters are not estimated with other parameters in TESTFACT and must be specified by the user. BILOG-MG (Zimowski et al. 2002; see also Mislevy and Bock 1990) was used to obtain the lower asymptote estimates using all default options with an exception of the option for items with five choices.

2.3 Decision Criteria

Several methods for determining the number of factors have been proposed. Eigenvalues, fit indices, and proportions of variance are typically used to examine the factor structure of a set of items. Scree plots involve plotting the eigenvalues for all possible numbers of factors and looking for the elbow in the plot (i.e., the point at which the eigenvalues tend to stop decreasing). The number of factors is taken as one fewer than the solution corresponding to the elbow. This approach is criticized as being very subjective because the location of the elbow is not always very clear. Kaiser (1960) proposed a heuristic rule called the eigenvalue-greater than-one (K1) rule in which each eigenvalue greater than one is taken to indicate a component, and his rule was applied by some to common-factor analysis (Mulaik 2009, p. 186). The proportion of variance is an index for the substantive importance of factors. This procedure is fairly straightforward and suggests keeping the number of factors needed to account for a specified percentage of the variance (e.g., 80% or 90%).

In addition to using eigenvalues, there are several residuals and fit indices that can be used for dimensionality assessment such as chi-square fit statistics, RMSEA, and RMSR. These statistics indicate the differences between observed values and estimated values. Smaller values are taken to indicate better fit. A cutoff value of 0.05 or less for the RMSR and RMSEA statistic has been suggested as a guide indicating an acceptable number of factors (Browne and Cudeck 1993). Hu and Bentler (1999) offer different cutoff values for these indices, specifically RMSR < 0.08 and RMSEA < 0.06. The chi-square test evaluates whether the observed data correspond to the expected data. The chi-square statistic is dependent on sample size, but RMSEA is not. Thus, for larger samples, it may be more appropriate to use RMSR and RMSEA to assess the model fit. In addition to using cutoff values, the model fit decision can be made based on the percentage of reduction of the

RMSR (Tate 2003). Tate (2003) suggests that factors be added to the model until the percent of RMSR reduction is less than 10%.

Dimensionality decisions in this study were based on the following three criteria: percentage of the RMSR reduction, chi-square difference test, and proportion of variance. As mentioned earlier, the assessment of test dimensionality in TESTFACT can be done using a test of the change of the chi-square fit statistic due to adding a factor to the model. In Mplus, RMSR reduction approach was used. However, proportion of variance criterion was used for all of the software packages.

3 Results

3.1 Simulated Data Results

3.1.1 One-Dimensional Tests

One-dimensional data with two guessing situations were analyzed in Mplus and TESTFACT programs. The fit statistics of the bifactor model were compared with those for the 1-factor model. As can be seen in the first rows of the two tables, TESTFACT and Mplus did not correctly identify the unidimensional structure when no guessing was simulated. When guessing was simulated, however, TESTFACT performed better than Mplus as expected (Table 1).

3.1.2 Two-Dimensional Tests

Within each test form, the correlations between factors were fixed at either 0 or 0.30. Mplus provided no correct identification when no guessing was simulated regardless of the simulated correlation. TESTFACT correctly identified 80% and 50% in the no-guessing simulation, however, for uncorrelated and correlated cases, respectively. As in the one-dimensional case, TESTFACT did better than Mplus, when guessing was simulated for two-dimensional data. Mplus correctly identified four cases when two-dimensional uncorrelated data were simulated with a guessing effect.

Table 1 Number of correct identification for TESTFACT and Mplus for 1- to 3-factor models ($r = 0$)

	$c = 0$		$c = 0.25$	
# of dimensions	TESTFACT	Mplus	TESTFACT	Mplus
1	0/10	0/10	10/10	6/10
2	8/10	4/10	5/10	4/10
3	4/10	2/10	10/10	10/10

Table 2 Number of correct identifications for TESTFACT and Mplus for 1- to 3-factor models ($r = 0.3$)

	$c = 0$		$c = 0.25$	
# of dimensions	TESTFACT	Mplus	TESTFACT	Mplus
1	0/10	0/10	10/10	6/10
2	5/10	0/10	8/10	0/10
3	9/10	1/10	7/10	0/10

3.1.3 Three-Dimensional Tests

The results from applying the 3-factor models indicated that TESTFACT performed better than Mplus in each of the four conditions. Correct identification rates range for TESTFACT ranged from 40% to 100%. Similar rates for Mplus were low in each of the three conditions except for the case for which guessing with zero correlation was simulated (Table 1).

3.2 *Real Data Results*

3.2.1 Full-Information Item Factor Analysis with TESTFACT

Summary indices for TESTFACT, Mplus, and SAS are presented in Table 3 for 1- to 4-factor solutions. The TESTFACT/BILOG rows show indices for the MIRT model with the g_j estimates from BILOG-MG since TESTFACT cannot estimate the lower asymptote. The TESTFACT/C rows show the results from the same MIRT model but the g_j were assumed to have a fixed value of 0.20 (because all items had five choices). The g_j parameters in this case are not separately estimated. The TESTFACT rows contain MIRT models without the g_j term.

The difference between the chi-squared goodness of fit values from the 1-factor solution to 2-factor solution was not significant for all the three cases with TESTFACT. (The critical value at the 0.05 level is $\chi^2(13) = 19.19$.) The respective critical values at the 0.05 nominal level are $\chi^2(12) = 21.20$ and $\chi^2(11) = 8.52$ for the 2-factor to 3-factor solution and for the 3-factor to the 4-factor solution. Although the 2-factor solution to the 3-factor solution shows a significant reduction in the goodness of fit values, the 1-factor solution seems to be a reasonable choice for the data.

The cumulative proportions of the variance accounted for appear to increase as the number of factors increases. The 1-factor solution for TESTFACT/C yielded a higher proportion of variance accounted for than was observed for a higher number of factors. Table 3 contains the summary of items with high Promax loadings (i.e., α_{jk} or $\lambda_{jk} > 0.30$). Although all TESTFACT methods yielded proper extraction results for the 4-factor solution for the TESTFACT/BILOG, TESTFACT/C, and TESTFACT cases, the Promax rotation failed to yielded reasonable loading results

Table 3 Numbers of items with high promax loadings and correlations between factors

	One factor	Two factors		Three factors			Four factors			
	I	I	II	I	II	III	I	II	III	IV
Mplus/WLSMV	14	6	6	6	3	4	Heywood case			
Mplus/WLS	14	6	7	Heywood case due to over-factoring						
Mplus/ULS	14	8	5	4	3	4	8	1	3	1
TESTFACT/BILOG	14	10	1	6	2	3	Not available			
TESTFACT/C	14	10	1	6	2	3	Not available			
TESTFACT	14	9	1	6	1	3	Not available			
SAS	13	8	7	7	5	6	4	6	4	4
SAS/Tetrachoric	14	9	7	7	3	6	7	4	4	3
Correlation between factors										
Mplus/WLSMV										
II		0.71		0.58						
III				0.70	0.53					
IV							Heywood case			
Mplus/WLS										
II		0.68								
III				Heywood case due to over-factoring						
IV										
Mplus/ULS										
II		0.64		0.57			0.48			
III				0.68	0.52		0.75	0.51		
IV							0.39	0.34	0.32	
TESTFACT/BILOG										
II		0.65		0.66						
III				0.73	0.59					
IV							Not available			
TESTFACT/C										
II		0.65		0.67						
III				0.73	0.59					
IV							Not available			
TESTFACT										
II		0.64		0.68						
III				0.75	0.61					
IV							Not available			
SAS										
II		0.31		0.25			0.25			
III				0.27	0.17		0.28	0.11		
IV							0.16	0.07	0.17	
SAS/Tetrachoric										
II		0.43		0.42			0.38			
III				0.36	0.33		0.20	0.31		
IV							0.22	0.33	0.30	

Table 4 TESTFACT/BILOG loadings for 1- to 4-factor solutions

	One factor	Two factors		Three factors			Four factors
Item	I	I	II	I	II	III	I II III IV
1	0.50	0.55	−0.09	0.56	−0.09	−0.04	Not available
2	0.44	0.21	0.29	0.27	0.31	−0.07	
3	0.45	0.48	−0.04	−0.03	−0.12	0.59	
4	0.34	−0.22	0.60	−0.18	0.62	−0.05	
5	0.49	0.35	0.19	−0.02	0.16	0.41	
6	0.49	0.49	0.01	0.29	−0.02	0.26	
7	0.47	0.27	0.25	0.19	0.25	0.09	
8	0.44	0.47	−0.04	0.54	−0.03	−0.07	
9	0.48	0.25	0.29	0.16	0.28	0.12	
10	0.47	0.54	−0.09	0.50	−0.10	0.06	
11	0.42	0.41	0.01	0.37	0.00	0.07	
12	0.49	0.43	0.09	0.03	0.04	0.39	
13	0.50	0.32	0.23	0.34	0.24	−0.05	
14	0.50	0.52	−0.03	0.49	−0.04	0.04	
Correlation between factors							
Factor							
II		0.65		0.66			
III				0.73	0.59		
IV							Not available

and, therefore, are reported as "Not available." For the 2-factor solution, one item consistently loaded on the second factor while other items mainly loaded on the first factor. High correlations were obtained between pairs of the factors under the 2- and 3-factor solutions.

Tables 4–6 contain the loadings for the 1-factor, 2-factor, and 3-factor solutions for TESTFACT/BILOG, TESTFACT/C, and TESTFACT, respectively. In Table 4, the 2-factor solution yielded only one item, Item 4, on the second factor. This item asks for the complete factoring of $12ax^2 - 9ax - 3a$. The same item as well as Item 2 yielded relatively high loadings on the second factor. Items 3, 5, and 12 had high loadings on the third factor for the 3-factor solution. Also for the 3-factor solution, the number of items loading on the first factor decreased from ten on the 2-factor solution to six on the 3-factor solution. Similar patterns of loadings were observed for the TESTFACT/C and TESTFACT solutions.

3.2.2 Factor Analysis with Mplus

Summary results are presented in Table 3 for results from Mplus for each of the three different estimation methods. For the EFA, WLSMV (i.e., weighted least squares parameter estimates using a diagonal weight matrix with standard errors and mean- and variance-adjusted chi-square test statistics that use a full weight matrix) is the default estimation in Mplus (Muthén and Muthén 2010, pp. 531–532). Two other

Table 5 TESTFACT/C loadings for 1- to 4-factor solutions

	One factor	Two factors		Three factors			Four factors
Item	I	I	II	I	II	III	I II III IV
1	0.50	0.56	−0.11	0.56	−0.19	−0.05	Not available
2	0.44	0.21	0.29	0.27	0.30	−0.08	
3	0.44	0.46	−0.03	−0.05	−0.12	0.59	
4	0.34	−0.23	0.61	−0.18	0.63	−0.06	
5	0.49	0.34	0.20	0.00	0.16	0.38	
6	0.49	0.48	0.01	0.29	−0.02	0.25	
7	0.47	0.27	0.26	0.18	0.27	0.09	
8	0.44	0.47	−0.04	0.53	−0.02	−0.07	
9	0.49	0.25	0.30	0.16	0.29	0.11	
10	0.49	0.55	−0.09	0.52	−0.10	0.05	
11	0.42	0.42	0.01	0.37	0.00	0.07	
12	0.47	0.41	0.09	0.03	0.04	0.35	
13	0.50	0.32	0.23	0.33	0.25	−0.04	
14	0.49	0.50	−0.04	0.47	−0.04	0.03	
Correlation between factors							
Factor							
II		0.66		0.67			
III				0.73	0.59		
IV							Not available

Table 6 TESTFACT loadings for 1- to 4-factor solutions

	One factor	Two factors		Three factors			Four factors
Item	I	I	II	I	II	III	I II III IV
1	0.50	0.56	−0.10	0.57	−0.07	−0.03	Not available
2	0.42	0.27	0.21	0.31	0.26	−0.09	
3	0.41	0.43	−0.03	−0.06	−0.12	0.58	
4	0.31	−0.19	0.60	−0.19	0.63	−0.04	
5	0.47	0.35	0.16	0.00	0.15	0.37	
6	0.46	0.47	−0.00	0.27	−0.03	0.26	
7	0.41	0.28	0.18	0.19	0.19	0.08	
8	0.41	0.48	−0.09	0.57	−0.09	−0.08	
9	0.46	0.30	0.22	0.17	0.25	0.12	
10	0.45	0.53	−0.11	0.51	−0.12	0.04	
11	0.40	0.42	−0.02	0.39	−0.01	0.03	
12	0.50	0.45	0.07	0.03	0.04	0.45	
13	0.40	0.28	0.16	0.28	0.19	−0.01	
14	0.43	0.45	−0.03	0.37	−0.03	0.10	
Correlation between factors							
Factor							
II		0.64		0.68			
III				0.75	0.61		
IV							Not available

estimation methods used in this study were WLS and ULS. The proportions of variance accounted for by the respective factors were based on the varimax rotated loadings instead of the initial extraction. The total variance accounted for is reported as sum (see Table 7).

In terms of the model selection using the various indices from Mplus-type computer programs, Hu and Bentler (1999) recommend a model with a value of RMSR less than 0.08 for selection of a model. That recommendation, however, was not based on analysis of binary variables. The values of RMSR's from the Mplus runs using Hu and Bentler's RMSR < 0.08 suggested 1-factor solution provided reasonably good fit under all estimation methods. Stone and Yeh (2006) suggested a model with a value of RMSR less than 0.05 could be chosen in conjunction with factor analysis for a set of dichotomously scored items. Using the Stone and Yeh suggestion, then WLSMV and ULS estimation methods yielded a 2-factor solution rather than a 1-factor solution.

Hu and Bentler (1999) suggested a value of an RMSEA less than 0.06 as indicating good fit. Using this criterion, WLSMV and WLS both would suggest a 1-factor solution. Stone and Yeh (2006) recommended an RMSEA of less than 0.05. Using this criterion, a 1-factor solution would be recommended. In addition to RMSR and RMSEA, Stone and Yeh also suggested a chi-square divided by its degrees of freedom of less than 1.4 as an indicator of reasonable fit. Using this latter criterion, the 1-factor solution would be selected based on WLSMV and WLS estimates. Tate (2003) recommended a 10% reduction. Using this criterion, WLSMV would have yielded a 3-factor solution, WLS a 2-factor solution; and ULS a 4-factor solution.

As can be seen in Table 3, Heywood cases resulted for both WLSMV and WLS estimation, possibly due to over-factoring. The patterns of factor loadings were different from those with TESTFACT although high correlations were obtained between pairs of the available Promax factors. Tables 8–10 contain the factor loadings for 1- to 4-factor solutions for the three estimation methods using Mplus. The 2-factor solution presented in Table 8 shows six items as loading on the first factor (Items 1, 6, 8, 10, 11, and 14) and six items on the second factor (Items 2, 3, 4, 5, 9, and 12). For the 3-factor solution, six items (Items 1, 6, 8, 10, 11, and 14) loaded on the first factor, three items (Items 2, 4, and 9) on the second factor, and four items (Items 3, 5, 6, and 12) on the third factor. Similar patterns were observed for WLS and ULS.

3.2.3 Factor Analysis with SAS

Two different sets of SAS results are reported based on Phi coefficients (Table 11) and Tetrachoric correlations (Table 12). Adding factors increased the cumulative proportions of variance (see Table 7). Using the 20 % criterion suggested in Reckase (1979), results for both coefficients yielded a 1-factor solution.

The 2-factor solution shown in Table 11 indicated nine items loaded on the first factor (Items 1, 3, 4, 6, 8, 10, 11, 12, and 14), and seven items on the second factor

Table 7 Indices for item factor analyses

	One factor	Two factors		Three factors			Four factors			
	I	I	II	I	II	III	I	II	III	IV
Mplus/WLSMV										
$\chi^2(df)\ p$	73.7(65) 0.22	55.7(55) 0.45		40.4(46) 0.70			Heywood case			
RMSEA	0.013	0.004		0.000			Heywood case			
RMSR	0.0540	0.0462		0.0377			Heywood case			
Mplus/WLS										
$\chi^2(df)\ p$	97.7(77) 0.06	67.1(64) 0.37		Heywood case due to over-factoring						
RMSEA	0.019	0.008		Heywood case due to over-factoring						
RMSR	0.0649	0.0570		Heywood case due to over-factoring						
Mplus/ULS										
RMSR	0.0538	0.0457		0.0371			0.0318			
TESTFACT/BILOG										
$\chi^2(df)$	1533.46(736)	1512.80(723)		1488.25(711)			1478.97(700)			
$\Delta\chi^2(df)$		20.66(13)		24.55(12)			9.28(11)			
TESTFACT/C										
$\chi^2(df)$	1540.08(736)	1519.16(723)		1493.91(711)			1485.50(700)			
$\Delta\chi^2(df)$		20.92(13)		25.25(12)			8.41(11)			
TESTFACT										
$\chi^2(df)$	1538.78(736)	1519.59(723)		1498.39(711)			1489.87(700)			
$\Delta\chi^2(df)$		19.19(13)		21.20(12)			8.52(11)			
Proportion of variances accounted for by factors										
Mplus/WLSMV										
Proportion	0.27	0.16	0.14	0.14	0.09	0.11	Heywood case			
Sum	0.27	0.30		0.34			Heywood case			
Mplus/WLS										
Proportion	0.30	0.17	0.16	Heywood case due to over-factoring						
Sum	0.30	0.33		Heywood case due to over-factoring						
Mplus/ULS										
Proportion	0.27	0.18	0.12	0.14	0.09	0.11	0.15	0.06	0.11	0.07
Sum	0.27	0.30		0.34			0.39			
TESTFACT/BILOG										
Proportion	0.22	0.21	0.02	0.19	0.02	0.02	0.17	0.02	0.02	0.01
Cumulative	0.22	0.21	0.23	0.19	0.21	0.23	0.17	0.19	0.21	0.22
TESTFACT/C										
Proportion	0.30	0.20	0.02	0.18	0.02	0.02	0.17	0.02	0.02	0.01
Cumulative	0.30	0.20	0.22	0.18	0.20	0.22	0.17	0.19	0.21	0.22
TESTFACT										
Proportion	0.17	0.18	0.02	0.17	0.02	0.02	0.17	0.02	0.02	0.01
Cumulative	0.17	0.18	0.20	0.17	0.19	0.21	0.17	0.19	0.21	0.22
SAS										
Proportion	0.21	0.21	0.08	0.21	0.08	0.07	0.21	0.08	0.07	0.07
Cumulative	0.21	0.21	0.29	0.21	0.29	0.36	0.21	0.29	0.36	0.44
SAS/Tetrachoric										
Proportion	0.32	0.32	0.08	0.32	0.08	0.07	0.32	0.08	0.07	0.07
Cumulative	0.32	0.32	0.40	0.32	0.40	0.47	0.32	0.40	0.47	0.54

Table 8 Mplus/WLSMV factor loadings for models with 1- to 4-factors

	One factor	Two factors		Three factors			Four factors			
Item	I	I	II	I	II	III	I	II	III	IV
1	0.67	0.73	0.01	0.81	0.03	−0.11	Heywood case			
2	0.48	0.21	0.31	0.27	0.39	−0.07				
3	0.45	0.08	0.41	0.01	−0.08	0.57				
4	0.33	−0.13	0.48	−0.17	0.65	0.01				
5	0.57	−0.01	0.63	−0.00	0.23	0.45				
6	0.57	0.34	0.27	0.33	−0.01	0.30				
7	0.46	0.20	0.29	0.20	0.25	0.10				
8	0.48	0.61	−0.08	0.58	−0.06	−0.01				
9	0.57	0.14	0.47	0.17	0.40	0.12				
10	0.53	0.55	0.03	0.55	−0.07	0.09				
11	0.47	0.41	0.11	0.42	0.07	0.04				
12	0.68	0.07	0.68	−0.05	0.12	0.76				
13	0.44	0.26	0.22	0.26	0.24	0.02				
14	0.48	0.37	0.15	0.34	0.02	0.17				
Correlation between factors										
Factor										
II		0.71		0.58						
III				0.70	0.53					
IV							Heywood case			

(Items 2, 4, 5, 7, 9, 12, and 13). For the 3-factor solution, seven items loaded on the first factor (Items 1, 2, 4, 8, 10, 11, and 14), five items on the second factor (Items 2, 3, 5, 6, and 12), and six items (Items 2, 4, 5, 7, 9, and 13) on the third factor. For the 4-factor solution, four items loaded on the first factor (Items 3, 5, 6, and 12), six items loaded on the second factor (Items 1, 2, 4, 8, 10, and 11), four items loaded on the third factor (Items 4, 7, 13, and 14), and four items (Items 2, 4, 5, and 9) on the fourth factor. Results in Table 12 yielded complex patterns similar to those in Table 11. The lower part of Tables 11 and 12 contains the correlations between promax factors for SAS and SAS/Tetrachoric, respectively.

4 Discussion

The primary purpose of this study was to compare two popular software packages, Mplus and TESTFACT, on their capabilities for checking dimensionality in multiple-choice tests. Consistent with previous research (Stone and Yeh 2006; Tate 2003), analyses of the guessing condition indicated that TESTFACT was more accurate at detecting the simulated number of dimensions than Mplus. Both TESTFACT and Mplus, however, failed to detect unidimensionality, when no guessing was simulated. TESTFACT detected unidimensionality, when guessing was simulated, but Mplus overestimated the number of factors, because it has no

Table 9 Mplus WLS factor loadings for models with 1- to 4-factors

	One factor	Two factors		Three factors			Four factors			
Item	I	I	II	I	II	III	I	II	III	IV
1	0.68	0.72	0.05	Heywood case due to over-factoring						
2	0.53	0.27	0.28							
3	0.49	0.17	0.37							
4	0.36	−0.17	0.54							
5	0.61	0.07	0.57							
6	0.60	0.46	0.19							
7	0.50	0.09	0.44							
8	0.50	0.67	−0.10							
9	0.61	0.05	0.60							
10	0.54	0.55	0.04							
11	0.52	0.34	0.24							
12	0.72	0.10	0.68							
13	0.44	0.13	0.36							
14	0.50	0.35	0.21							
Correlation between factors										
Factor										
II		0.68								
III				Heywood case due to over-factoring						
IV										

option for handling guessing. With respect to the estimated number of dimensions, TESTFACT generally was more accurate than Mplus for both guessing and no guessing conditions. Mplus with WLSM using RMSR criteria tended to over estimate the number of dimensions when guessing was simulated. Similarly, Mplus performed less well when factors were correlated. TESTFACT performed similarly with correlated and uncorrelated factors.

In the real data analysis example, both TESTFACT and Mplus yielded similar results. Although the true underlying factor structure of the data was unknown, the mathematics test itself was designed to be unidimensional. According to results for both algorithms, a 1-factor solution appeared to be a reasonable choice for the data. In addition, results for SAS were consistent with those for TESTFACT and Mplus. The results for TESTFACT were consistent with previous research by Stone and Yeh (2006) and Tate (2003).

A second purpose of this study was to compare different indices used for detection of dimensionality for dichotomous items. The main finding was that the proportion of variance was not a good indication of dimensionality. The RMSR reduction in Mplus, recommended by Tate (2003), also did not appear to work well, whereas the chi-square test was successful in most conditions. The RMSR reduction criterion of 10% (Tate 2003) was more sensitive, overestimating the simulated dimensionality under most conditions. RMSR reduction yielded a 3-factor solution for the real data. The RMSR criterion of < 0.08 proposed by Hu and Bentler (1999)

Table 10 Mplus/ULS factor loadings for the models of one factor, two factors, three factors, and four factors

	One factor	Two factors		Three factors			Four factors			
Item	I	I	II	I	II	III	I	II	III	IV
1	0.67	0.71	−0.01	0.83	0.00	−0.08	0.87	−0.11	−0.16	0.11
2	0.48	0.19	0.35	0.29	0.44	−0.14	0.12	0.03	0.03	0.69
3	0.44	0.32	0.15	−0.04	−0.07	0.61	0.10	−0.05	0.49	−0.11
4	0.33	−0.23	0.66	−0.20	0.61	0.06	−0.14	0.91	−0.08	0.03
5	0.57	0.22	0.42	−0.00	0.29	0.41	0.04	0.07	0.17	0.14
6	0.56	0.48	0.12	0.26	−0.02	0.39	0.46	0.05	0.19	−0.14
7	0.46	0.22	0.29	0.14	0.23	0.18	0.31	0.20	0.08	−0.07
8	0.48	0.57	−0.06	0.52	−0.03	0.04	0.57	−0.05	−0.05	0.03
9	0.57	0.19	0.47	0.19	0.44	0.08	0.22	0.13	0.19	0.22
10	0.53	0.60	−0.04	0.49	−0.05	0.15	0.57	−0.07	0.03	0.01
11	0.48	0.44	0.08	0.42	0.09	0.03	0.42	−0.05	0.14	0.14
12	0.67	0.37	0.37	−0.05	0.17	0.69	−0.10	−0.07	0.93	0.05
13	0.44	0.25	0.24	0.23	0.22	0.07	0.38	0.18	−0.01	−0.04
14	0.48	0.43	0.08	0.28	0.03	0.22	0.38	0.01	0.14	−0.04
Correlation between factors										
Factor										
II		0.64		0.57			0.48			
III				0.68	0.52		0.75	0.51		
IV							0.39	0.34	0.32	

seemed to work well, given the conditions simulated, but the criterion of < 0.05 recommended by Stone and Yeh (2006) suggested a 2-factor solution. Results for RMSEA using the criteria from both Yeh and Stone and Tate yielded a 1-factor solution. Overall results provided no clear-cut answer to the practical question of which method should be used in all circumstances. Results from the chi-square test in TESTFACT were similar to previous research by Stone and Yeh and by Tate whereas results for the RMSR reduction index with Mplus were not consistent with these studies.

Although Mplus is easy to use and provides more fit indices, one suggestion is that using the chi-square test in TESTFACT might be more useful based on the higher number of correct identifications. Additionally, it would seem wise at this point to use a combination of these indices rather than relying on a single one. Substantive theory also should be considered as a meaningful explanation is more important than simply fitting a statistical model (Cudeck 2000). Finally, factor loadings should also be examined when determining the number of factors.

Table 11 SAS/Phi factor loadings for 1- to 4-factor solutions

	One factor	Two factors		Three factors			Four factors			
Item	I	I	II	I	II	III	I	II	III	IV
1	0.52	0.53	0.07	0.59	0.06	0.06	0.12	0.57	−0.07	0.22
2	0.36	0.03	0.46	0.34	−0.32	0.50	−0.16	0.34	−0.16	0.70
3	0.40	0.42	0.04	−0.09	0.73	−0.05	0.78	−0.09	−0.09	−0.11
4	0.30	−0.30	0.79	−0.30	0.03	0.78	−0.01	−0.35	0.43	0.53
5	0.51	0.24	0.41	0.01	0.39	0.35	0.51	0.00	−0.08	0.36
6	0.50	0.50	0.09	0.17	0.52	0.02	0.54	0.16	0.03	−0.01
7	0.44	0.21	0.35	0.10	0.23	0.31	0.11	0.04	0.47	0.11
8	0.44	0.56	−0.08	0.65	0.01	−0.08	−0.09	0.60	0.25	−0.05
9	0.52	0.15	0.53	0.12	0.14	0.51	0.21	0.10	0.08	0.50
10	0.49	0.58	−0.03	0.47	0.25	−0.06	0.21	0.44	0.14	−0.04
11	0.43	0.42	0.08	0.54	−0.04	0.08	−0.02	0.51	0.04	0.20
12	0.61	0.44	0.30	0.11	0.54	0.23	0.53	0.08	0.18	0.13
13	0.41	0.21	0.32	0.19	0.12	0.30	−0.11	0.11	0.71	0.02
14	0.44	0.46	0.04	0.33	0.27	0.01	0.07	0.27	0.52	−0.18
Correlation between factors										
Factor										
II		0.31		0.25			0.25			
III				0.27	0.17		0.28	0.11		
IV							0.16	0.07	0.17	

Table 12 SAS/Tetrachoric factor loadings for the 1- to 4-factor solutions

	One factor	Two factors		Three factors			Four factors			
Item	I	I	II	I	II	III	I	II	III	IV
1	0.70	0.68	0.11	0.66	0.12	0.08	0.61	0.13	0.26	−0.01
2	0.53	0.13	0.53	0.37	−0.21	0.55	0.30	−0.18	0.80	−0.10
3	0.49	0.50	0.04	−0.10	0.86	−0.11	−0.07	0.87	−0.11	−0.07
4	0.37	−0.33	0.89	−0.28	0.02	0.86	−0.36	−0.02	0.46	0.60
5	0.61	0.29	0.45	0.00	0.49	0.35	−0.02	0.51	0.44	−0.06
6	0.61	0.59	0.09	0.20	0.60	−0.02	0.19	0.59	−0.03	0.08
7	0.51	0.24	0.39	0.15	0.20	0.34	0.09	0.15	0.05	0.50
8	0.53	0.65	−0.08	0.76	0.07	−0.07	0.70	−0.09	0.00	0.16
9	0.62	0.18	0.59	0.14	−0.16	0.54	0.08	0.17	0.58	0.09
10	0.58	0.68	−0.05	0.57	0.23	−0.09	0.54	0.22	0.06	−0.02
11	0.53	0.50	0.10	0.60	−0.05	0.10	0.54	−0.04	0.28	−0.02
12	0.70	0.50	0.32	0.14	0.59	0.21	0.11	0.58	0.17	0.12
13	0.50	0.24	0.36	0.32	−0.02	0.36	0.23	−0.11	−0.08	0.76
14	0.53	0.54	0.04	0.47	0.18	0.01	0.41	0.13	−0.18	0.40
Correlation between factors										
Factor										
II		0.43		0.42			0.38			
III				0.36	0.33		0.20	0.31		
IV							0.22	0.33	0.30	

References

Ackerman, T. A. (1989). Unidimensional IRT calibration of compensatory and noncompensatory multidimensional items. *Applied Psychological Measurement, 13*, 113–127.

Ackerman, T. A. (1992). A didactic explanation of item bias, item impact, and item validity from a multidimensional perspective. *Journal of Educational Measurement, 29*, 67–91.

Ackerman, T. A., Gierl, M. J., & Walker, C. M. (2003). Using multidimensional item response theory to evaluate educational and psychological tests. *Educational Measurement: Issues and Practice, 22*(3), 37–51.

Bock, R. D., Gibbons, R., & Muraki, E. (1988). Full-Information item factor analysis. *Applied Psychological Measurement, 12*, 261–280.

Browne, M. W., & Cudeck, R. (1993). Alternative ways of assessing model fit. In K. A. Bollen & J. S. Long (Eds.), *Testing structural equation models* (pp. 136–162). Newbury Park, CA: Sage.

Christoffersson, A. (1975). Factor analysis of dichotomized variables. *Psychometrika, 40*, 5–32.

Cudeck, R. (2000). Exploratory factor analysis. In H. E. A. Tinsley & S. D. Brown (Eds.), *Handbook of applied multivariate statistics and mathematical modeling* (pp. 265–296). San Diego, CA: Academic.

Fraser, C., & McDonald, R. P. (1988). NOHARM: Least squares item factor analysis. *Multivariate Behavioral Research, 23*, 267–269.

Han, K. T. (2006). WinGen: Windows software that generates IRT parameters and item responses. *Applied Psychological Measurement, 31*, 457–459.

Hattie, J. (1984). An empirical study of various indices for determining unidimensionality. *Multivariate Behavioral Research, 19*, 49–78.

Hu, L.-T., & Bentler, P. M. (1999). Cutoff criteria for fit indexes in covariance structure analysis: Conventional criteria versus new alternatives. *Structural Equation Modeling, 6*, 1–55.

Hulin, C. L., Drasgow, F., & Parsons, L. K. (1983). *Item response theory*. Homewood, IL: Dow-Jones-Irwin.

Kaiser, H. F. (1960). The application of electronic computers to factor analysis. *Educational and Psychological Measurement, 20*, 141–151.

Kim, H. R. (1994). *New techniques for the dimensionality assessment of standardized test data* (Unpublished doctoral dissertation). University of Illinois, Urbana–Champaign.

Knol, D. L., & Berger, M. P. F. (1991). Empirical comparison between factor analysis and multidimensional item response models. *Multivariate Behavioral Research, 26*, 457–477.

Lord, F. M. (1980). *Application of item response theory to practical testing problems*. Hillsdale, NJ: Lawrence Erlbaum.

Lord, F. M., & Novick, M. R. (1968). *Statistical theories of mentaltest scores*. Reading, MA: Addison-Wesley.

McDonald, R. P. (1981). The dimensionality of tests and items. *British Journal of Mathematical and Statistical Psychology, 34*, 100–117.

McDonald, R. P. (1982). Linear versus nonlinear models in item response theory. *Applied Psychological Measurement, 6*, 379–396.

McLeod, L. D., Swygert, K. A., & Thissen, D. (2001). Factor analysis for items scored in two categories. In D. Thissen & H. Wainer (Eds.), *Test scoring* (pp. 189–216). Mahwah, NJ: Erlbaum.

Mislevy, R. J., & Bock, R. D. (1990). *BILOG-MG 3: Item analysis and test scoring with binary logistic models* [Computer software]. Chicago, IL: Scientific Software International.

Mulaik, S. A. (2009). *The foundations of factor analysis*. New York: CRC.

Muthén, B. (1977). *Statistical methodology for structural equation models involving latent variables with dichotomous indicators* (Unpublished doctoral dissertation). Department of Statistics, University of Uppsala, Uppsala.

Muthén, B. (1978). Contributions to factor analysis of dichotomous variables. *Psychometrika, 43*, 551–560.

Muthén, L. K., & Muthén, B. O. (2010). *Mplus user's guide*. Los Angeles, CA: Author.

Nandakumar, R. (1994). Assessing the dimensionality of a set of item responses: Comparison of different approaches. *Journal of Educational Measurement, 31*, 17–35.

Nandakumar, R., & Stout, W. (1993). Refinements of Stout's procedure for assessing latent trait unidimensionality. *Journal of Educational Statistics, 18*, 41–68.

Nandakumar, R., & Yu, F. (1996). Empirical validation of DIMTEST on nonnormal ability distributions. *Journal of Educational Measurement, 33*, 355–368.

Parry, C. D., & McArdle, J. J. (1991). An applied comparison of methods for least-squares factor analysis of dichotomous variables. *Applied Psychological Measurement, 15*, 35–46.

Reckase, M. D. (1979). Unifactor latent trait models applied to multifactor tests: Results and implications. *Journal of Educational Statistics, 4*, 207–230.

Stone, C. A., & Yeh, C.-C. (2006). Assessing the dimensionality and factor structure of multiple-choice exams: An empirical comparison of methods using the multistate bar examination. *Educational and Psychological Measurement, 66*, 193–214.

Stout, W. (1987). A nonparametric approach for assessing latent trait unidimensionality. *Psychometrika, 52*, 589–617.

Stout, W. (1990). A new item response theory modeling approach with applications to unidimensionality assessment and ability estimation. *Psychometrika, 55*, 293–325.

Tate, R. (2003). A comparison of selected empirical methods for assessing the structure of responses to test items. *Applied Psychological Measurement, 27*, 159–203.

Thissen, D., & Wainer, H. (2001). *Test scoring*. Mahwah, NJ: Lawrence Erlbaum Associates.

Wilson, D. T., Wood, R., & Gibbons, R. (2003). *TESTFACT: Test scoring, item statistics, and item factor analysis* [Computer program]. Chicago, IL: Scientific Software International.

Yeh, C.-C. (2007). The effect of guessing on assessing dimensionality in multiple-choice tests: A Monte Carlo study with application. Unpublished dissertation. University of Pittsburg.

Zhang, J., & Stout, W. (1999a). Conditional covariance structure of generalized compensatory multidimensional items. *Psychometrika, 64*, 129–152.

Zhang, J., & Stout, W. (1999b). The theoretical DETECT index of dimensionality and its application to approximate simple structure. *Psychometrika, 64*, 213–249.

Zimowski, M. F., Muraki, E., Mislevy, R. J., & Bock, R. D. (2002). *BILOG-MG for windows* [Computer software]. Lincolnwood, IL: Scientific Software International.

Evaluating CTT- and IRT-Based Single-Administration Estimates of Classification Consistency and Accuracy

Nina Deng and Ronald K. Hambleton

1 Introduction

In many testing contexts, it is necessary to classify the examinees into mutually exclusive performance categories based on a set of performance standards (e.g., the pass–fail decisions on the credentialing exams and the advanced, proficient, basic, and failing classifications on the achievement tests). The classification often provides an appropriate and convenient way to report and interpret the candidates' test performance. For tests designed for such purposes, the classical approach to reliability estimate may not be particularly useful. It has been agreed that the consistency and accuracy of such classifications, rather than the test scores, are of more concern. *The Standards for Educational and Psychological Testing* (AERA et al. 1999, p. 35) calls that "when a test or combination of measures is used to make categorical decisions, estimates should be provided of the percentage of examinees who would be classified in the same way on two applications of the procedure."

A couple of methods have been proposed to determine the consistency and accuracy of the proficiency classifications (Hambleton and Novick 1973; Swaminathan et al. 1974) and substantial amounts of research on these and other methods have continued. Of special interest are the methods that are capable of providing single-administration decision consistency and accuracy (DC/DA) estimates given that the parallel administrations of assessments are rarely possible in practice. Among the limited comparative studies, the Livingston and Lewis (1995) method

N. Deng (✉)
Department of Quantitative Health Sciences, University of Massachusetts Medical School, Worcester, MA 01655, USA
e-mail: nina.deng@umassmed.edu

R.K. Hambleton
Center for Educational Assessment, University of Massachusetts Amherst, Amherst, MA 01003, USA
e-mail: rkh@educ.umass.edu

R.E. Millsap et al. (eds.), *New Developments in Quantitative Psychology*, Springer Proceedings in Mathematics & Statistics 66, DOI 10.1007/978-1-4614-9348-8_15,

was found to outperform several other classical test theory (CTT) model-based methods (Wan et al. 2007). Furthermore, the item response theory (IRT) model-based methods were found, generally, having a better fit than the beta-binomial model-based methods to the real data (Lee et al. 2002). Additionally, the IRT-based DC/DA estimates were found to be slightly higher than the beta-binomial model-based DC/DA estimates in several studies (Lee et al. 2002; Li 2006; Lee 2010), as well as with our own experiences with these methods (Deng 2011). Nevertheless, it is not clear which method provides more accurate estimates. Given the discrepancies found between the CTT- and IRT-based DC/DA estimates, and the fact that the IRT-based methods are comparatively new, further comparative studies of these methods seem highly desirable.

A series of simulation studies were conducted in this paper to investigate: (1) how accurate these CTT- and IRT-based DC/DA methods are. The accuracy could potentially be assessed given that the "true" scores are possibly known in the simulation; (2) how robust these DC/DA methods are to various less-standard testing conditions. The most widely used CTT model-based Livingston and Lewis method (denoted as "LL") and the newly developed IRT model-based Lee (2010) method were compared and investigated under a variety of simulated conditions by varying the test length, shape of true score distribution, and degree of local item dependence (LID).

2 Decision Consistency and Accuracy Methods

The DC/DA indices were proposed for the purpose of describing the reliability and validity of the proficiency classifications. The DC index refers to the percentage of candidates who are classified into the same proficiency category across two independent administrations (or parallel forms) of the same test. The DA index refers to the percentage of candidates who are classified into the same proficiency category as that classified based on their "true" or criterion scores. Specifically, the DC/DA indices can be expressed in Eq. (1)

$$P = \sum_{j=1}^{J} p_{jj} \tag{1}$$

where J is the number of proficiency categories. When p_{jj} stands for the proportion of examinees consistently classified into the jth proficiency category across the two independent administrations, the summed percentage P stands for the DC index. If one administration is replaced with the examinee's "true" score or another criterion score, the summed percentage P stands for the DA index. Kappa (Cohen 1960) is an alternate way of calculating the DC index by correcting for the chance agreement. It is defined as

$$k = \frac{P - p_c}{1 - p_c} \tag{2}$$

where p_c is the agreement percentage expected by chance and is computed as

$$p_c = \sum_{j=1}^{J} p_{j.}p_{.j} \tag{3}$$

where $p_{j.}$ and $p_{.j}$ are the marginal proportions of the jth proficiency category in the two independent administrations, respectively.

The notion of DC/DA indices is appealing and the calculation is straightforward. However, the requirement of two administrations is not attractive. Therefore, the single-administration based methods were introduced to overcome the two-administration restriction (Huynh 1976; Subkoviak 1976). The single-administration based methods call for an underlying measurement model to estimate the true and the observed score distributions of a parallel form (or a re-administration) of the test without actually administering it. Based on the underlying measurement model, the available DC/DA methods can generally be divided into two categories: the CTT model-based method and the IRT model-based method. The former assumes a binomial or an extension (Huynh 1976; Subkoviak 1976; Hanson and Brennan 1990; Livingston and Lewis 1995; Lee et al. 2009) and the latter assumes a family of IRT models (Huynh 1990; Wang et al. 2000; Rudner 2001, 2005; Bourque et al. 2004; Li 2006; Lee 2010).

The Livingston and Lewis (1995) method, denoted as "LL" in this study, is the first and so far the most widely used binomial model-based method for handling tests with a mixture of polytomously and dichotomously scored items. By creating a concept of "effective test length," denoted as n, the LL method converts the original test into a new scale of n discrete, dichotomously scored, and locally independent items necessary to produce the total scores having the same precision (i.e., reliability) as the observed scores being actually used in the real test to classify the candidates. The formula to solve n suggested by the authors is shown in Eq. (4)

$$n = \frac{(\mu_x - X_{\min})(X_{\max} - \mu_x) - r\sigma_x^2}{\sigma_x^2 (1 - r)} \tag{4}$$

where $X_{\min}$ is the lowest possible score, $X_{\max}$ is the highest possible score, μ_x is the mean score, σ_x^2 is the test score variance, and r is the classical reliability estimate of the test. It can be implied from the formula that three types of inputs are required to calculate n: (1) the observed test score distribution (mean and variance), (2) the possible maximum and minimum test scores, and (3) the reliability estimate of the test. The Cronbach's coefficient alpha (Cronbach 1951) is the most commonly used reliability estimate and was used by the authors in the LL method. Lastly, the cut-off scores are needed for computing the DC/DA indices.

Adopting a different approach, Lee (2010) proposed to compute the DC/DA indices based on the conditional observed score distribution derived from IRT models. Specifically, provided with IRT models, the probability of a vector of item responses (U_1, U_2, $\ldots U_n$) given the true score θ can be expressed as

$$P\left(U_1,U_2,\ldots,U_n\middle|\theta\right)=\prod_{i=1}^{n}P\left(U_i\middle|\theta\right) \tag{5}$$

where $P(U_i|\ \theta)$ is the probability of endorsing the response U_i for item i conditional on the latent ability θ, as defined in the IRT models. The conditional probability is summed up for all possible vectors of item responses which have a sum equal to the test score X, which in turn, becomes the conditional probability of having an observed summed score X, denoted as $P(X|\theta)$. The summed conditional probability is then integrated across the true score distribution to obtain the observed score distribution. There are generally two approaches to providing the true score distribution: (1) the estimated quadrature points and weights provided in the IRT calibration outputs are used to approximate the true score distribution. It was called the D-method by the author since a distributional assumption for the true scores was made and (2) the classification indices are calculated for each candidate and then averaged over the population. It was called the P-method. The author found that the two approaches produced very similar results. To implement the Lee method, the item parameter estimates from the chosen IRT model(s), and the true score distribution are needed for computing the observed score distribution. And again the cut-off scores are needed for computing the DC/DA indices. The software BB-CLASS (Brennan 2004) and IRT-CLASS (Lee and Kolen 2008) were used to implement the LL and Lee methods, respectively.

3 Simulation Studies

3.1 Data

The data were generated using the item parameter estimates from an item pool in a US statewide standardized achievement test (an English Language Arts test at the grade 10 level). The pool had 84 dichotomously scored multiple-choice items and 12 polytomously scored open-response items (scored 0–4 per item). The three-parameter logistic (3PL) IRT model (Birnbaum 1968) and the two-parameter graded response model (GRM) (Samejima 1969), which were used to calibrate the operational test, were used to generate the unidimensional data for the dichotomous and polytomous items, respectively. The 3PL and GRM Testlet Response Theory (TRT) models (Wainer et al. 2000) were used to generate the data with various degrees of LID to study their effects on the DC/DA indices estimates. Adopted from the operational test, three cut-off scores on the theta scale (−1.75, −0.81, and 0.58) were used to classify the candidates into four proficiency categories. The percentages of candidates in the four proficiency categories observed from the operational test were 4, 17, 51, and 28 %, respectively, which were the same as the percentages found in a normal distribution using the three cut-off scores.

3.2 Study 1: Test Length

The DC/DA methods were found sensitive to the test length in the previous studies (Wan et al. 2007; Li 2006). Therefore, four different test lengths were studied: 10/1, 20/2, 40/4, and 80/8 (the numbers before the slashes denote the total number of items in the test and the numbers after denote the number of polytomously scored items in the test). These lengths are in the range typically found with the educational and psychological tests and subscales. And their Cronbach's alpha estimates were 0.73, 0.85, 0.92 and 0.96, respectively, which are in the range of reliability estimates found acceptable in practice. The proportion of polytomous items in each test was fixed to eliminate the possible effects of the proportion of polytomous items on the DC/DA indices. For each test length condition, the designated numbers of items were randomly drawn from the item pool described above.

3.3 Study 2: Ability Distribution

Different from the test length, there is less known about how robust the DC/DA methods are to the different shapes of score distributions. All of the research to date has been carried out with normal score distributions. Therefore, five different score distributions were investigated: one normal distribution (mean of 0 and standard deviation of 1) and four skewed beta distributions. Specifically, the four beta distributions were $B(\alpha=2, \beta=4)$, $B(\alpha=2, \beta=3)$, $B(\alpha=3, \beta=2)$, and $B(\alpha=4, \beta=2)$, representing positively skewed, slightly positively skewed, slightly negatively skewed, and negatively skewed distributions, respectively. The means of scores were ± 1 for the negatively/positively skewed distributions and ± 0.6 for the slightly negatively/positively skewed distributions. The standard deviations of scores were all around 1.0. A graphic illustration of the five distributions is displayed in Fig. 1. The skewed distributions may be less atypical with educational tests but are more common with psychological and social behavior tests. (The ability scores were later linearly transformed back onto a scale of mean of 0 and standard deviation of 1 so that they were on the same scale as the IRT score estimates. More details were provided in the section of Evaluation Criterion).

3.4 Study 3: Local Item Dependence

Although both the underlying CTT- and IRT-based measurement models assume that the items are conditionally independent given the candidates' true scores, it is not unusual in practice to have items interrelated with each other due to reasons other than the measured latent trait, such as a common format, stimuli, or sub-domain. The consequence of having interrelated items is called LID. It is of interest to study the

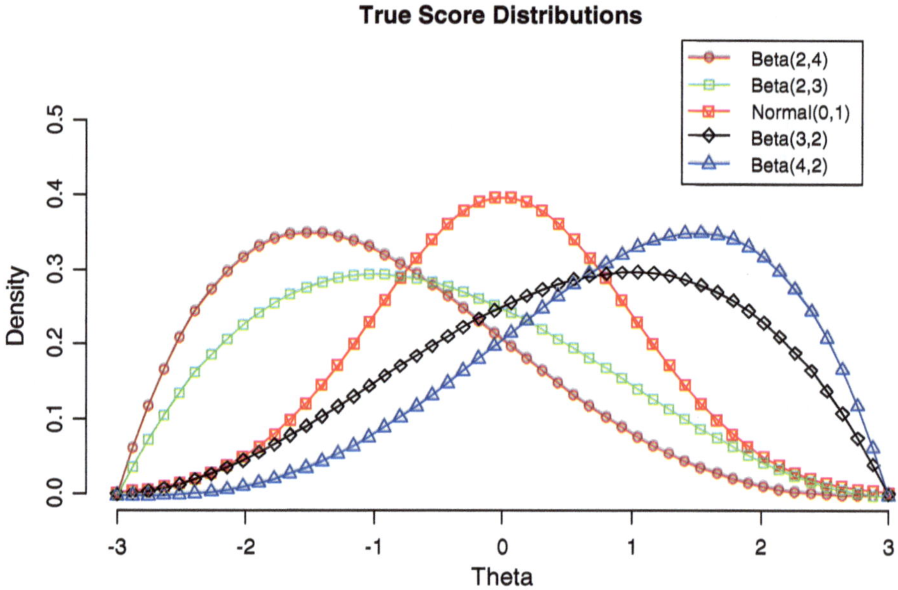

Fig. 1 Five simulated true score distributions

impacts of LID when it comes to the DC/DA indices. The TRT model was used to simulate the data with four degrees of LID by varying the variance of testlet effect parameters to 0, 0.2, 0.5, and 1, where 0 means no LID and 1 indicates a high level of LID among the items within the testlets. It was not clear what values might be typically seen in practice, thus a wide range of values were chosen for the study. The 3PL and GRM TRT models were used to generate the data which had two testlet effects associated with the item format, one associated with the multiple-choice questions and the other associated with the open-response questions. The principal component analysis (PCA) was used to double check the test dimensionality.

3.5 Evaluation Criteria

A main advantage of simulation studies is that the truth is known and can be used as a criterion for evaluating the results of interest. To calculate the "true" DA index, the classification based on the simulated data was compared with that based on the "true" scores, and the percentage of candidates consistently classified across the two classifications was computed as the "true" DA index. It deserves a special note for the LID study in which the general factor was regarded as the "true" score, while the testlet factors were regarded as the method effects and thus were not taken into account in computing the "true" score. To calculate the "true" DC index, a second data set was simulated using the "true" scores and "true" item parameters, which was considered a parallel form of the first simulated data set, and the percentage of candidates who were consistently classified across the two classifications based on the two parallel forms was computed as the "true" DC index. The "true" Kappa index was computed accordingly based on the classification contingency table.

Biases of the DC/DA indices estimates were calculated to reflect both the systematic error (by the sign of the statistic) and the random error (by the absolute value of the statistic). The statistic of bias is given by

$$BIAS\left(\widehat{P}\right) = \widehat{P} - P \tag{6}$$

where P is the "true" DA/DC/Kappa index and $\widehat{P}$ is the DA/DC/Kappa estimate. Since sample size was eliminated as a factor in this study, rather than calculating $\widehat{P}$ across a number of replications and taking the average, a large sample size of 50,000 examinees was used to essentially eliminate the sampling error as a concern in the interpretation of the results. For the IRT-based Lee method, all the 50,000 examinees were used to obtain the item parameter estimates, which were in turn read as the input for the Lee method.

A special note on the "true" DA index for the conditions of skewed ability distributions should be mentioned. Because the software PARSCALE (Version 4.1) (Muraki and Bock 2003), which was used in this study for IRT calibration, arbitrarily rescales the ability estimates to a scale of mean of 0 and standard deviation (SD) of 1 to eliminate the indeterminacy problem, therefore, the "true" scores in the skewed ability distributions were rescaled to mean of 0 and SD of 1 to put them on the same scale as the IRT score estimates for computing the "true" DA index. The cut-off theta scores were rescaled accordingly too. This problem is resolved in practice by the test score equating process.

4 Results

4.1 Test Length

The "true" DC/DA/Kappa indices with different test lengths are plotted in Fig. 2. As we expected, a longer test resulted in greater "true" DC/DA/Kappa indices due to a greater degree of score reliability. The biases of DC/DA/Kappa estimates of the LL and Lee methods are plotted in Fig. 3. It shows that the biases were reasonably small across different test lengths. That said, the biases for both methods decreased as the test length increased. Comparatively speaking, the Lee method had smaller biases and was more robust to the short tests. On the contrary, the LL method had much larger biases of the DC and Kappa estimates with the short tests, e.g., the LL method had biases of −0.04 and −0.06 for the DC and Kappa estimates with 10 items, versus both biases of −0.01 with 80 items.

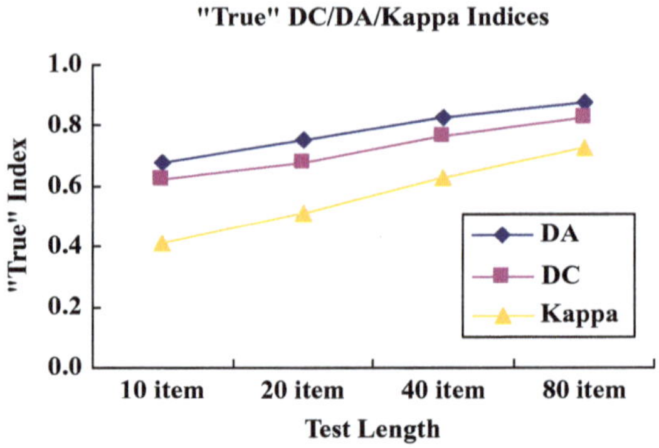

Fig. 2 "True" DC/DA/Kappa indices by test length

4.2 Ability Distribution

The "true" DC/DA/Kappa indices with different ability distributions when the test had 40 items are displayed in Fig. 4. The labels of "++", "+", "0", "−", "− −" on the x-axis stand for the positively skewed, slightly positively skewed, normal, slightly negatively skewed, and negatively skewed distributions, respectively. Interestingly, it is found that the "true" DC/DA/Kappa indices with the negatively skewed distributions were higher than those with the normal and positively skewed distributions. This is suspected due to the effects of the location of cut-off scores relative to the ability distribution. Since the cut-off scores (−1.75, −0.81, 0.58) were more on the lower end of the ability scale, there were more candidates in the positively skewed distributions around the cut-off scores, which in turn had a greater chance of misclassification and lower DC/DA indices. The biases of the DC/DA/Kappa estimates with different ability distributions are illustrated in Fig. 5. Two findings are clear—(1) the biases in the estimates are generally small and (2) the LL method had consistently larger biases than the Lee method, especially with the negatively skewed distributions.

Combining the previous results, it seemed reasonable to assume that the LL method was more sensitive to both short tests and skewed distributions. Some further efforts were attempted to investigate the potential negative effects of a joint condition of short test length and skewed ability distribution on the DC/DA estimates. Figure 6 displays the biases with different ability distributions when the test had ten items. It was found that the LL method had generally larger biases with those non-normal distributions in a short test. Specifically, the LL method over-estimated the DA index in the positively skewed distributions and under-estimated in the negatively skewed distributions. Furthermore, the LL method consistently under-estimated the DC/Kappa indices across all distributions, having especially large biases with negatively skewed distributions. In contrast with the LL method, the Lee method performed relatively consistently and had reasonably small biases across the different ability distributions. Additionally, the findings that the LL method performed very differently across the five ability distributions suggested

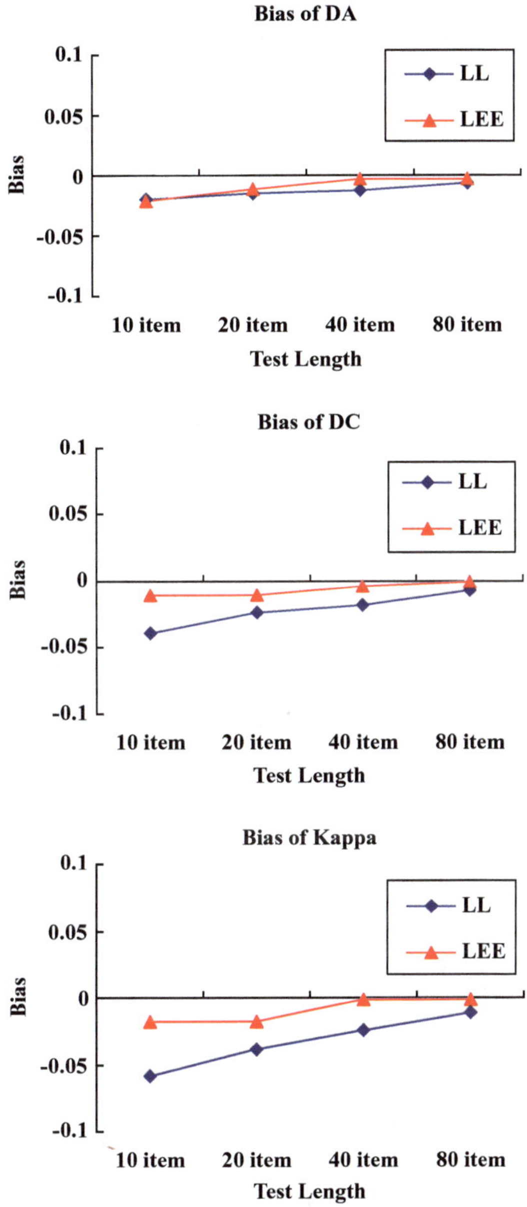

Fig. 3 Bias of DC/DA/Kappa estimates by test length

a negative interaction between ability distribution and cut-off score location on the LL method for the short tests. In fact, using another set of cut-off scores (−0.414, 0.384, and 1.430), the differences of bias of the LL method across the different distributions diminished but still were larger than the Lee method (plots not shown).

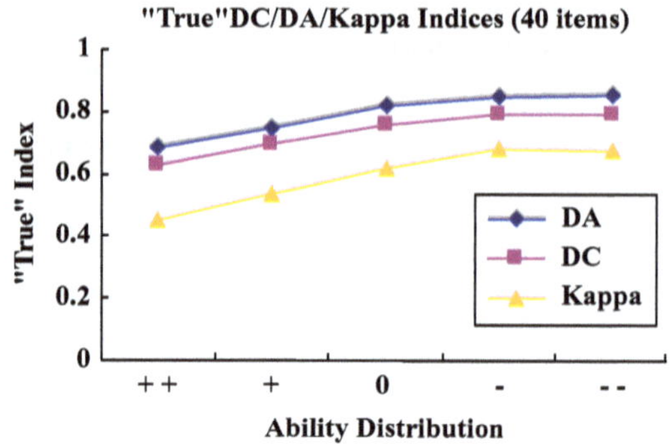

Fig. 4 "True" DC/DA/Kappa indices by ability distribution (40 items)

4.3 Local Item Dependence

The PCA was conducted as a validity check of the test dimensionality with various degrees of LID. The first five eigenvalues are summarized in Table 1 (in the order of increasing LID levels). It shows that along with an increasingly high level of LID, the tests presented from strong unidimensionality to moderate multidimensionality (with an emerging stronger second factor). Table 1 also suggests that the ratio of the first factor to the second factor was much more sensitive to the LID than the proportion of total variance explained by the first factor.

Figure 7 displays the "true" DA/DC/Kappa indices at various levels of LID. It was found that the "true" DA index decreased noticeably when the test had a higher level of LID. By contrast, the "true" DC and Kappa indices stayed more or less stable across the various levels of LID. When it comes to the bias of the estimates (Fig. 8), both methods excessively over-estimated the DA index when the test had a moderate or high level of LID (e.g., bias close to 0.2 for a high level of LID). Yet, the biases of the DC and Kappa indices were much smaller and less consequential. Comparatively speaking, the Lee method was more sensitive to the LID and had larger biases of the DC/Kappa indices when the test had a high level of LID (e.g., when the variance of testlet parameters was equal to 1).

5 Conclusions

A series of comprehensive simulation studies were conducted to compare a widely used CTT-based method and a newly developed IRT-based method (the LL and Lee methods) for computing the single-administration decision consistency and accuracy (DC/DA) estimates under various standard and nonstandard testing conditions. Both methods had reasonably small biases when the conditions were standard, that is, when the tests were reasonably long, the ability scores were normally distributed, and the data were unidimensional without the LID. In the less-typical or nonstandard situations, in general, we found that the Lee method provided more

Fig. 5 Bias of DC/DA/Kappa estimates by ability distribution (40 items)

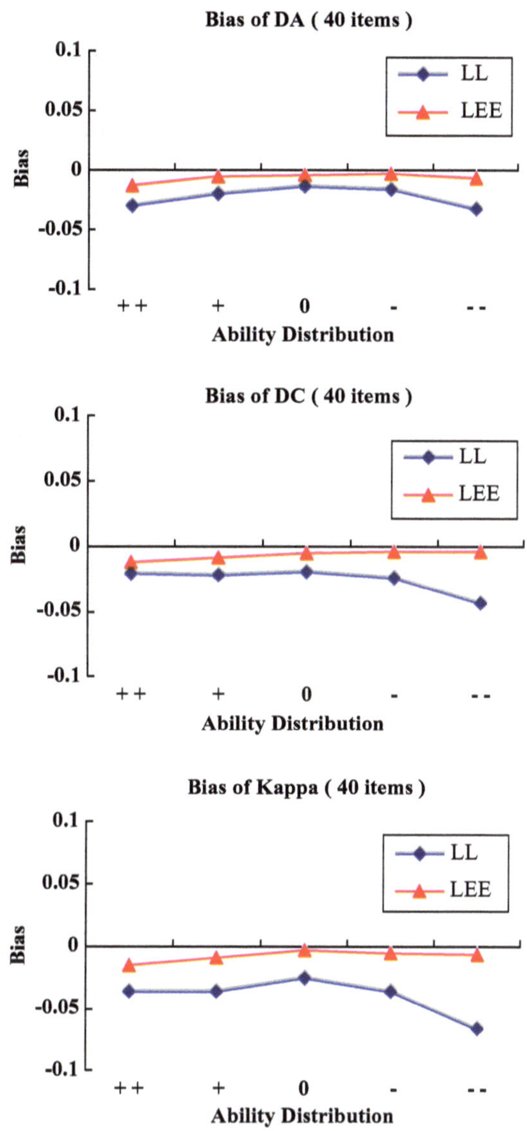

accurate estimates than the LL method. One exception was the condition of LID, where the underlying assumption of IRT was violated, and here, the LL method outperformed the Lee method when the test had a high level of LID. In addition, there was a negative interaction between the ability distribution and cut-off score location with the LL method for the short tests, and this finding was not observed with the Lee method.

The simulation results also confirmed a sometimes reported finding in the literature on the discrepancies between the CTT- and IRT-based single-administration

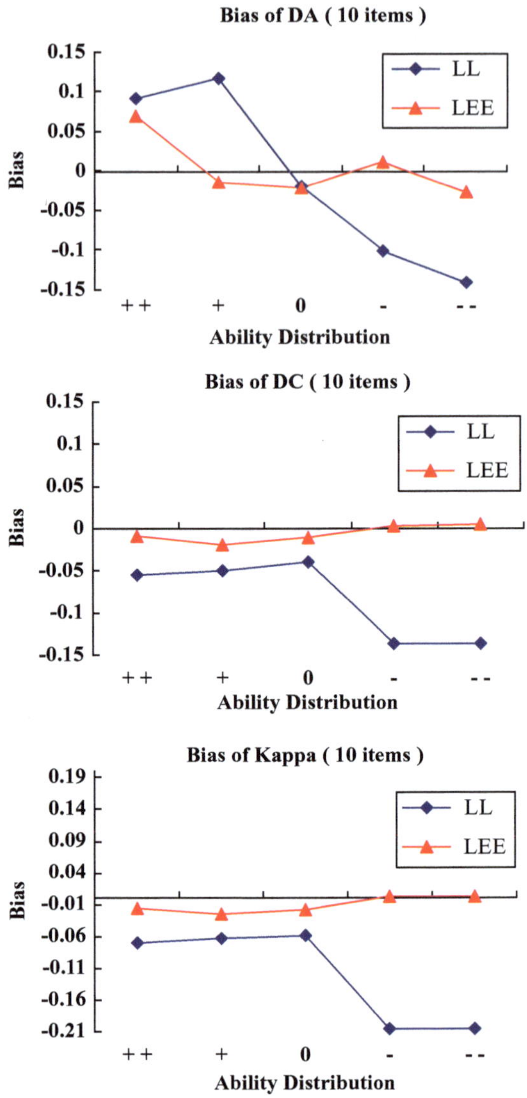

Fig. 6 Bias of DC/DA/Kappa estimates by ability distribution (10 items)

Table 1 Eigenvalues of tests with different levels of local item dependence (40 items)

LID level	First five eigenvalues 1	2	3	4	5	Variance (%) explained by first eigenvalue	Ratio of first to second eigenvalues
0	15.2	0.89	0.85	0.79	0.79	38.1	17.2
0.2	15.7	1.07	0.87	0.82	0.78	39.3	14.7
0.5	16.5	1.74	0.85	0.79	0.73	41.3	9.5
1	17.7	2.39	0.82	0.75	0.68	44.3	7.4

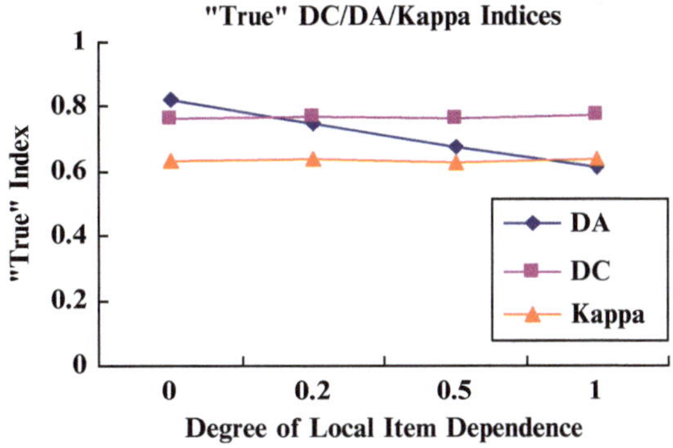

Fig. 7 "True" DC/DA/Kappa indices by level of local item dependence (40 items)

DC/DA estimates. Specifically, the LL method consistently under-estimated the decision consistency indices across the simulated conditions, while the Lee method reduced the under-estimation in many conditions by providing somewhat higher values of the estimates. This is an important finding because it suggests that the often reported DC/DA findings using the LL method for the tests are probably underestimates of the true DC/DA results. Recall too, that many tests today are using IRT models in the test development and analyses.

This study has important implications for both methods in practice. First, for the LL method, it suggested that it provided poor estimates with both short tests and skewed ability distributions. In addition, the results suggest the under-estimation of the LL method for the decision consistency indices. Given that there are a couple of reliability estimates available (e.g., Cronbach's alpha, stratified alpha, test–retest reliability, parallel-form reliability, etc.), the practitioners may want to evaluate and pick the most suitable available reliability estimate before applying the LL method. For the Lee method, it is important that the assumptions of IRT models, namely, the unidimensionality and local item independence, be met to ensure the accurate DC/DA estimates. The IRT model fit is also assumed with the Lee method and therefore should always be checked. Finally, the IRT parameter estimates need to be precise since they are used in computing the observed score distributions. When the assumption of local item independence was violated as illustrated in this paper, interestingly, it was found that the DA estimates were much more negatively affected than the DC and Kappa estimates. One possible explanation could be that the problems with the LID were consistent with the two parallel forms, which made the effects on the decision consistency indices much less consequential. Nevertheless, the testlet factors can vary from form to form, and from testlet to testlet in the real world, and the content- or paragraph-related testlet factors could have more negative effects on the DC estimates than the format-related testlet factors as simulated in this study, and thus deserve further research. The effects of multidimensionality, although related with the LID but having a more complex factor structure, provide the possibility of future investigation too. Lastly, there are fewer works investigating the effects on the DA estimate than on the DC estimate and more such studies would be desirable.

Fig. 8 Bias of DC/DA/Kappa estimates by level of local item dependence (40 items)

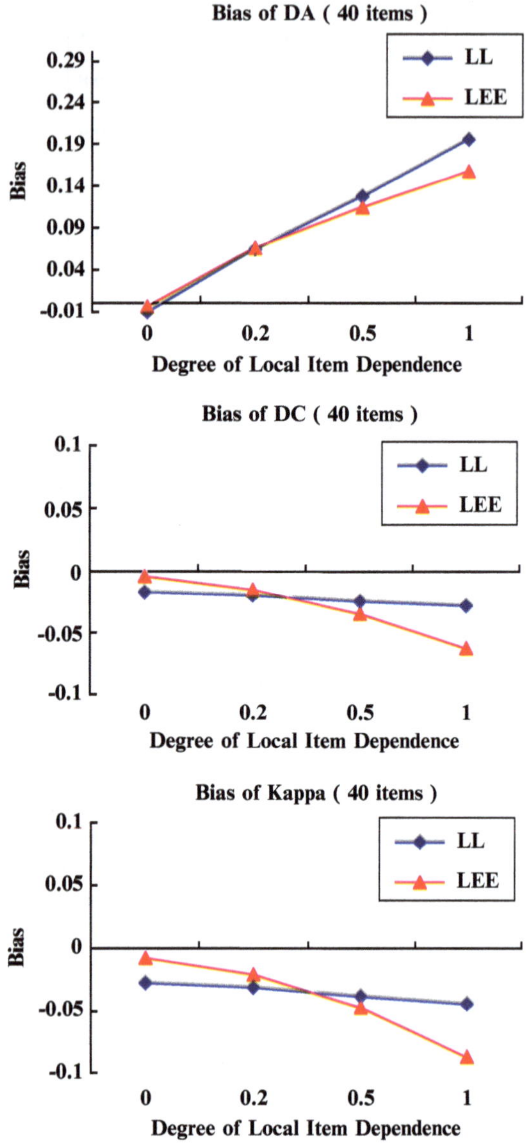

One criticism of the study could be that the data were simulated within the IRT framework. This could result in a bias in favor of the Lee Method. Nevertheless, the IRT models often show more than adequate fit with many tests in use and these models are widely used in test development, equating, and the study of differential item functioning. More studies using the Lee method with IRT models that fail to fit the data well would be worth carrying out. Another possible limitation is associated with the assumption of the random parallel forms made for the CTT-based method, which would in turn have lager error variances than the strict parallel forms (namely, the parallel forms have exactly the same items) assumed for the IRT-based methods. Future simulation studies using a large item pool to randomly generate the parallel forms may facilitate a more in-depth understanding of the discrepancies between the two approaches. Lastly, the comparison with other existing DC/DA methods, e.g., the IRT-based Rudner (2005) method, is of interest and should be included in the future studies.

Acknowledgment The authors are grateful for the valuable comments from the editor Daniel Bolt, which strengthened the study considerably.

References

American Educational Research Association, American Psychological Association, & National Council on Measurement in Education. (1999). *Standards for educational and psychological testing*. Washington, DC: Author.

Birnbaum, A. (1968). Some latent trait models and their use in inferring an examinee's ability. In F. M. Lord & M. R. Novick, *Statistical theories of mental test scores* (pp. 397–472). Reading, MA: Addison-Wesley.

Bourque, M. L., Goodman, D., Hambleton, R. K., & Han, N. (2004). *Reliability estimates for the ABTE tests in elementary education, professional teaching knowledge, secondary mathematics and English/language arts* (Final report). Leesburg, VA: Mid-Atlantic Psychometric Services.

Brennan, R. L. (2004). *BB-CLASS: A computer program that uses the beta-binomial model for classification consistency and accuracy* (Version 1.0, CASMA Research Report No. 9). Iowa City, IA: University of Iowa, Center for Advanced Studies in Measurement and Assessment. Available at http://www.education.uiowa.edu/casma

Cohen, J. (1960). A coefficient of agreement for nominal scales. *Educational and Psychological Measurement, 20*, 37–46.

Cronbach, L. J. (1951). Coefficient alpha and the internal structure of tests. *Psychometrika, 16*, 297–334.

Deng, N. (2011). *Evaluating IRT- and CTT-based methods of estimating classification consistency and accuracy indices from single administrations* (Unpublished doctoral dissertation). Amherst, MA: University of Massachusetts.

Hambleton, R. K., & Novick, M. (1973). Toward an integration of theory and method for criterion-referenced tests. *Journal of Educational Measurement, 10*(3), 159–170.

Hanson, B. A., & Brennan, R. L. (1990). An investigation of classification consistency indexes estimated under alternative strong true score models. *Journal of Educational Measurement, 27*, 345–359.

Huynh, H. (1976). On the reliability of decisions in domain-referenced testing. *Journal of Educational Measurement, 13*, 253–264.

Huynh, H. (1990). Computation and statistical inference for decision consistency indexes based on the Rasch model. *Journal of Educational Statistics, 15*, 353–368.

Lee, W. (2010). Classification consistency and accuracy for complex assessments using item response theory. *Journal of Educational Measurement, 47*(1), 1–17.

Lee, W., Brennan, R. L., & Wan, L. (2009). Classification consistency and accuracy for complex assessments under the compound multinomial model. *Applied Psychological Measurement, 33*, 374–390.

Lee, W., Hanson, B. A., & Brennan, R. L. (2002). Estimating consistency and accuracy indices for multiple classifications. *Applied Psychological Measurement, 26*, 412–432.

Lee, W., & Kolen, M. J. (2008). *IRT-CLASS: A computer program for item response theory classification consistency and accuracy (Version 2.0)*. Iowa City, IA: University of Iowa, Center for Advanced Studies in Measurement and Assessment. Available at http://www.education.uiowa.edu/casma

Li, S. (2006). *Evaluating the consistency and accuracy of proficiency classifications using item response theory* (Unpublished dissertation). Amherst, MA: University of Massachusetts.

Livingston, S. A., & Lewis, C. (1995). Estimating the consistency and accuracy of classifications based on test scores. *Journal of Educational Measurement, 32*, 179–197.

Muraki, E., & Bock, R. D. (2003). *PARSCALE 4: IRT item analysis and test scoring for rating-scale data [Computer program]*. Chicago, IL: Scientific Software International, Inc.

Rudner, L. M. (2001). Computing the expected proportions of misclassified examinees. *Practical Assessment Research & Evaluation, 7*(14). Available online: http://pareonline.net/getvn.asp?v=7&n=14

Rudner, L. M. (2005). Expected classification accuracy. *Practical Assessment Research & Evaluation, 10*(13). Available online: http://pareonline.net/getvn.asp?v=10&n=13

Samejima, F. (1969). Estimation of latent ability using a response pattern of graded scores. *Psychometrika* (Monograph Supplement, 17).

Subkoviak, M. J. (1976). Estimating reliability from a single administration of a criterion-referenced test. *Journal of Educational Measurement, 13*, 265–276.

Swaminathan, H., Hambleton, R. K., & Algina, J. (1974). Reliability of criterion referenced tests: A decision-theoretic formulation. *Journal of Educational Measurement, 11*, 263–267.

Wainer, H., Bradlow, E. T., & Du, Z. (2000). Testlet response theory: An analog for the 3PL model useful in testlet-based adaptive testing. In W. J. van der Linden & C. A. W. Glas (Eds.), *Computerized adaptive testing: Theory and practice* (pp. 245–269). Amsterdam: Kluwer Academic Publishers.

Wan, L., Brennan, R. L., & Lee, W. (2007). *Estimating classification consistency for complex assessments* (CASMA Research Report No. 22). Iowa City, IA: University of Iowa, Center for Advanced Studies in Measurement and Assessment. Available at http://www.education.uiowa.edu/casma

Wang, T., Kolen, M. J., & Harris, D. J. (2000). Psychometric properties of scale scores and performance levels for performance assessments using polytomous IRT. *Journal of Educational Measurement, 37*, 141–162.

Modeling Situational Judgment Items with Multiple Distractor Dimensions

Anne Thissen-Roe

Multiple choice situational judgment items (SJI) are often used in employee selection assessment. Such SJIs pair an item stem describing a realistic on-the-job problem scenario with response options describing specific problem-solving actions. In addition to information about problem-solving skills and job-related procedural knowledge, SJIs may contribute information about personality traits, as in Motowidlo et al.'s (2006) implicit trait policy (ITP) model. Schmitt and Chan (2006) advised that SJIs be modeled so as to obtain information about multiple distinct personality antecedents of work behaviors, independent of contextual behavior effectiveness. Both development and scoring processes for SJIs stand to benefit from the application of item response theory (IRT), and specifically from the use of a diagnostic item response model capable of distinguishing the effects of multiple latent traits on response option selection, which may vary across distractors. The multidimensional nominal response model (MNRM; Bolt and Johnson 2009) fits intrinsically multidimensional items, e.g., where response sets or skill component information are present (Bolt and Newton 2010, 2011). Appropriately constrained, the MNRM can model differential personality antecedents to SJI response options as continuous latent variables, as well as in-context problem solving. The present study demonstrates an application of the MNRM to employee selection SJIs.

1 Situational Judgment Items in Employee Selection Assessment

When considering candidates for employment, a hiring organization may be interested in predicting their performance on a job. Making that prediction is

A. Thissen-Roe (✉)
777 Mariners Island Blvd, Suite 200, San Mateo, CA 94404, USA
e-mail: athissenroe@comiratesting.com

R.E. Millsap et al. (eds.), *New Developments in Quantitative Psychology*,
Springer Proceedings in Mathematics & Statistics 66, DOI 10.1007/978-1-4614-9348-8_16,

not always as simple as administering an intelligence test; it may be as complex and multidimensional as the evaluation metrics, and the behavioral antecedents, of job performance itself. In service of such a prediction, assessments taken during the application and hiring process can provide information about candidates' knowledge, skills, and abilities as well as their preferences, inclinations, beliefs, and behavior patterns.

Situational judgment tests are often used in employee selection assessment. SJI pose realistic on-the-job problem scenarios and offer specific problem-solving responses. They can be developed to assess problem solving, job-related procedural knowledge, work styles, work preferences, and/or personality expression. Relative to general measures of ability and personality, they provide a distinct measurement of contextual reasoning, potentially capturing interactions between person and role (Gessner and Klimoski 2006; Swander 2001; Motowidlo and Beier 2009). An additional benefit of SJIs in an employee selection context is that they are capable of functioning as a realistic job preview. After taking a situational judgment test tailored to the job to which they are applying, candidates' expectations of the job align better with the hiring organization's. A candidate who fits the role well might be motivated to apply, while one likely to be quickly dissatisfied is encouraged to self-select out of the application process. Such self-selection is beneficial in cases where the candidates, if hired, would quit too quickly for the organization to recoup hiring and training costs.

An example of a multiple choice SJI is as follows:

> On one of your breaks some of your co-workers start gossiping about an apparent romance taking place between a supervisor and another employee. Which of the following would you most likely do?
>
> A. Tell your co-workers that they should not be gossiping.
> B. Join the conversation so that you can change the topic to something more appropriate.
> C. Tell your supervisor about the conversation.
> D. Listen to the conversation, but don't say anything.

This item was administered to candidates for entry-level, customer-facing hourly retail jobs. It functions as a realistic job preview, in that it presents a situation an hourly retail employee may encounter that isn't covered in the recruitment job description, a situation that is uncomfortable to some degree.

Not all SJIs are alike. Some SJIs, such as this one, tap "other duties as required": dealing with rude customers, frustrating co-workers, unglamorous tasks, inter-task conflict, and encroachment of work on personal time. Despite such duties being captured only in the catch-all portion of a job description, the SJIs are designed to measure the same attributes, such as diligence and social skills, that help with primary task performance. They are not intended to make demands on the candidate's fluid reasoning or creativity. By contrast, SJIs used for specialized professions, such as military or medical jobs, sometimes look for good intuitions about unfamiliar situations, or practical solutions to novel problems (McDaniel et al. 2001; Gessner and Klimoski 2006).

The development of SJI content and scoring methods tend to be pragmatic and practically rooted. The purpose of this article is to advance the psychometric science of SJIs through application of a flexible item response model. To that end, the following sections briefly review the state of measurement theory and existing scoring methods for SJIs; then, the MNRM (Bolt and Johnson 2009) is presented as an alternative. Finally, as a demonstration, the model is applied to real job candidate responses to a situational judgment test, and compared with the fit of a simpler alternative model.

2 Measurement Theory for Situational Judgment Items

Over the years, some theoretical understanding has developed of the psychology of SJI responses. Some of this understanding is general, while some is specific to one presentation or response format. This article concerns itself with SJIs formatted as multiple choice items, having K response options.

Responses to K-option multiple choice items have $K - 1$ degrees of freedom, and can distinguish respondents on up to $K - 1$ dimensions (Cronbach 1946). Although Cronbach's early conception of secondary measurement dimensions within multiple choice items involved nuisance dimensions such as response sets, there is no reason items cannot be written to simultaneously address multiple constructs.

The first axis of differentiation within an SJI is usually considered to be *effectiveness*. One of the responses is, or several of the responses are, more effective work behavior than the others. However, Schmitt and Chan (2006) recommend coding responses for personality antecedents, independent of effectiveness. If personality traits are not strongly related to effectiveness, they constitute secondary measurement dimensions, about which the remaining axes of differentiation in each SJI may provide information. In a related approach, Stemler and Sternberg (2006) wrote seven-response SJIs in which each response endorsed one of seven categorically differentiated interpersonal strategies, which were more or less effective in the context of the situation given, but could also be preferred or avoided across items independent of context. In both of these cases, SJIs are meaningfully multidimensional at the item level.

Motowidlo et al. (2006) presented an ITP model, in which SJI responses reflect personality expression in an interactionist sense. An ITP is defined as an implicit belief about the contextual effectiveness of trait expression. ITPs moderate the effect of the latent trait on behavior choices. Although the traits in question are personality traits, the policies are implicit cognition and contingent on the situation, and can be a form of procedural job knowledge. By their situational context and cognitive framing, SJIs measure ITPs directly and traits indirectly, via dispositional fit (Motowidlo and Beier 2009) and, presumably, familiarity with the results of personality-consonant actions. Again, multiple traits and policy moderators may affect responses to a single item, leading to differentiation on multiple axes.

Based on these descriptions, it appears that a model of SJI responses should permit intrinsic multidimensionality within each item. It is illuminating, further, to consider the distinction between these joint effectiveness-approach models of SJIs and cognitive diagnostic models of skill items. Cognitive diagnostic models such as DINA (Junker and Sijtsma 2001) also call for a primary latent trait that permits problem-solving effectiveness, along with a set of individual component skills that may be present or absent. However, no underlying theory of SJI response requires a personality trait, an ITP, or even a preference for or against an interpersonal strategy to be explicitly two-valued. Most of them are better conceptualized as continua.

Returning to our example SJI, its four responses can be divided along two axes of general behavioral expression, each of which has an unknown degree of relationship to effectiveness overall and within the given context. One axis reflects an orientation toward active (versus passive) responses. Another axis is a relative prioritization of either the needs of the team or the rules of the organization—an ITP axis, reflecting a choice between two possible trait expressions. One response reflects each combination of the two ends of the two axes:

> On one of your breaks some of your co-workers start gossiping about an apparent romance taking place between a supervisor and another employee. Which of the following would you most likely do?
>
> A. Tell your co-workers that they should not be gossiping. (Active, rule priority)
> B. Join the conversation so that you can change the topic to something more appropriate. (Active, team priority)
> C. Tell your supervisor about the conversation. (Passive, rule priority)
> D. Listen to the conversation, but don't say anything. (Passive, team priority)

3 Scoring Situational Judgment Items

To date, SJIs have been scored with a variety of methods, from the ad hoc to the theory driven. There are dichotomous and polytomous variations on the assignment of credit for the selection of effective or ineffective responses. The simplest, dichotomous version involves assignment of one point for the best response and no points to any other; partial-credit variations include assigning each response points equal to its mean effectiveness rating or according to a regression model derived empirically from validation data. In both of these cases, simple accumulation of test scores over items is implied (Weekley et al. 2006; Zu and Kyllonen 2012).

Realistic SJIs are not written in a vacuum. Commonly, the situations are obtained through a *critical incidents* methodology, in which anecdotes of real job situations, capable of provoking good or bad job performance, are distilled into an appropriate length and level of specificity (Weekley et al. 2006). Given that practical, largely atheoretical origin for the stem and sometimes response text, the issue of key provenance merits some attention. Rationally derived keys may be obtained through incumbent consensus; based on the ratings of "subject matter experts" including supervisors, trainers, customers, and outside stakeholders; or based on psychologist review according to a theory of job performance (Weekley et al. 2006; McDaniel et al. 2009; Motowidlo and Beier 2009). Empirical models, in addition to regression derived from concurrent or predictive validation, may include models of group membership and nonmembership. Finally, hybrid keys combine elements of rational and empirical keying, use multiple sources to generate the keys, or use multiple sources to eliminate inconsistently keyed items.

An alternative to accumulative scoring algorithms is latent trait estimation according to IRT. The use of IRT to score SJIs is relatively novel. Zu and Kyllonen (2012) tested five item response models in comparison to non-IRT methods on two skill-focused situational judgment tests, and found the nominal response model (NRM) to produce more reliable and valid scores than the alternatives, particularly in cases of ambiguous or multiply keyed responses, the same type of cases that led to recommendations for partial credit summed-score methods.

Both of the assessments studied by Zu and Kyllonen (2012) were unidimensional, written to assess single latent traits: the ability to manage emotions, and teamwork. By contrast, Mangos et al. (2012) studied SJIs written to assess both ability and work style traits simultaneously, and considered one- and three-dimensional IRT models. Most of the models addressed only the multidimensionality of the test, allowing for differences in measurement between items; Mangos et al. suggested the MNRM as an effective alternative for modeling intrinsic multidimensionality in SJIs. Except for issues of dimensionality, Mangos et al. generally corroborated Zu and Kyllonen's findings.

The use of IRT models to score SJIs, in general, reduces but does not eliminate the problem of initial keying. An imprecise key according to expected trait-response relationships is sufficient to orient an IRT model for calibration, but the initial key still determines which of two or more ultimate models emerge from the calibration process. (The minimum is two models: every IRT model has a trivial counterpart where the latent trait's high and low anchors are exchanged.)

4 The Multidimensional Nominal Response Model

The MNRM (Bolt and Johnson 2009) can be written as:

$$T(i,k) = \frac{e^{z_{ik}}}{\sum_h e^{z_{ih}}}$$

where

$$z_{ik} = \sum_j a_{ij} * s_{ijk} * \theta_j + c_{ik}$$

for item i, dimension j, and category k. $T(i,k)$ traces the probability of a response in category k as a function of the j-dimensional latent variable θ. The parameter c_{ik} is an intercept parameter for each response category, while discrimination for each dimension j is decomposed into a slope a_{ij} and a set of scoring functions s_{ijk}. This decomposition is consistent with Thissen et al. (2010, p. 59) and (prior to the imposition of cross-item equality constraints) Johnson and Bolt (2010, p. 99). The scoring functions for each dimension can be thought of as giving the order of response categories; spacing is determined by s_{ijk} jointly with a_{ij}.

A more constrained multidimensional form of the NRM (Thissen et al. 2010) is usually used, for example, in the estimation software IRTPRO (Cai et al. 2011). In this version,

$$z_{ik} = \sum\nolimits_j a_{ij} * s_{ik} * \theta_j + c_{ik}$$

for item i, dimension j, and category k; a single vector s_{ik} applies across all dimensions. While an NRM item may measure in a multidimensional space *relative to other items*, it has only one dimension of *intrinsic* measurement.

The constraint imposed by the NRM upon the general form of the MNRM, and conversely, the advantage offered by MNRM, is particularly salient in the case of SJIs. Multiple scoring functions s_{ijk} allow the MNRM to fit intrinsically multidimensional items, e.g., where response sets or skill component information are present (Bolt and Newton 2010, 2011). SJIs have the potential to be intrinsically multidimensional as well. A K-response SJI can differentiate applicants on up to $K-1$ dimensions, with the responses in a different order on each. Recall that in our recurring example, two responses were coded active and two passive; two were coded for rule priority and two were coded for team priority. The effectiveness judgments of subject matter experts produced a third response ordering, corresponding exactly to neither work style dimension. Appropriately constrained, the MNRM can model differential personality antecedents to SJI response options as continuous latent variables, as well as in-context problem solving.

While the intrinsic unidimensionality constraint may be excessive, some identification constraints are needed to fit the MNRM to I items, J dimensions, and K categories. It is sufficient, as an alternative to the identification practices used by Bolt and Johnson (2009), to constrain J of the discrimination parameters a_{ij}, leaving $J(I-1)$ free; to constrain one intercept parameter c_{ik} per item, leaving $K-1$ free; and to constrain two scoring function parameters s_{ijk} per item per dimension, leaving $K-2$ free. For example, one may use structural zeroes: $c_{i0}=0$ for all i, intended lowest $s_{ijk}=0$ and intended highest $s_{ijk}=K-1$ for all ij. (The remaining s_{ijk} are expected to fall between 0 and $K-1$ but can vary outside that range if the expected order is not supported by the data.) Further constraint may, of course, be needed for *practical* identification; that is, to obtain convergence of item parameter estimates given a real dataset.

The practice of constraining two scoring function values in a particular direction, and also constraining discrimination parameters a_{ij} to be greater than zero, has consequences for the factor rotation. As with the intrinsic unidimensionality constraint, a positive discrimination parameter constraint is theoretically significant, potentially useful and potentially too constricting for the data.

Here, in Table 1, initial parameters are presented for our example SJI under NRM and MNRM. In this example, the three dimensions measured, in order, are expected

Table 1 Initial parameters for calibration of an example item, under NRM and MNRM

	NRM	MNRM			
	$a_{i0}=1, a_{i1}=1, a_{i2}=1$		$j=0$ $a_{i0}=1$	$j=1$ $a_{i1}=1$	$j=2$ $a_{i2}=1$
(A) $k=0$	$c_{i0}=0$*; $s_{i0}=2$	$c_{i0}=0$*	$s_{i00}=2$	$s_{i10}=3$*	$s_{i20}=1$
(B) $k=1$	$c_{i1}=0$; $s_{i1}=3$*	$c_{i0}=0$	$s_{i01}=3$*	$s_{i11}=2$	$s_{i21}=2$
(C) $k=2$	$c_{i2}=0$; $s_{i2}=1$	$c_{i0}=0$	$s_{i02}=1$	$s_{i12}=1$	$s_{i22}=0$*
(D) $k=3$	$c_{i3}=0$; $s_{i3}=0$*	$c_{i0}=0$	$s_{i03}=0$*	$s_{i13}=0$*	$s_{i23}=3$*

Subscript i indexes the current item. Starred values are fixed; others are starting values for calibration

to be effectiveness or problem solving, active (versus passive) response orientation (initiative), and team (versus rule) priority. Judged effectiveness was used to set the scoring function order for NRM and the first dimension of MNRM; if appropriately scaled, average SME ratings could be used directly, as could trait level estimates, but the value of conferred precision in scoring function values is unknown.

On one of your breaks some of your co-workers start gossiping about an apparent romance taking place between a supervisor and another employee. Which of the following would you most likely do?

A. Tell your co-workers that they should not be gossiping. (Active, rule priority)
B. Join the conversation so that you can change the topic to something more appropriate. (Active, team priority)
C. Tell your supervisor about the conversation. (Passive, rule priority)
D. Listen to the conversation, but don't say anything. (Passive, team priority)

5 Empirical Study

SJI response data were collected from four million individuals' job applications to 22 organizations in the United States over a 3-year period. Job candidates took one of several forms of a screening assessment as a part of the initial application process, following minimal screening. The screening assessment in question is designed to predict customer service performance in hourly jobs in industries such as retail, by way of measuring work styles and preferences. It is a multiple-section assessment that includes SJIs as well as other item formats.

Responses were collected from each job candidate to some, but not all, of a set of 20 SJIs. Candidates were presented a minimum of 4 and a maximum of 15 SJIs, on average 7.3. The number of SJIs presented to any particular job candidate was limited out of respect for the candidate's effort in completing the application, but candidates were not permitted to skip items presented. Missing responses are considered to be missing at random, because the presence or absence of response data was under the control of the assessment's creator, not the job candidate.

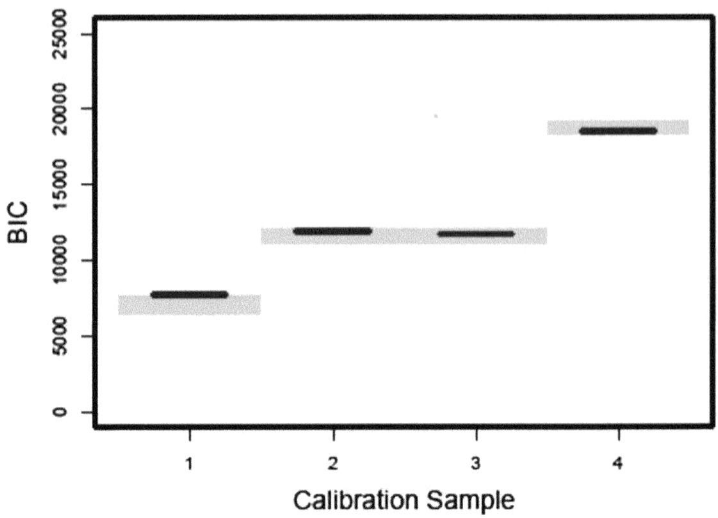

Fig. 1 Difference in BIC between MNRM and NRM for each sample, with cross-fit range

Some individuals applied to more than one job; subsequent repeat applications after the first, from the same individual, were discarded in order to satisfy the assumption of local independence between response patterns. The remaining response data was divided into four replication samples of approximately one million response patterns each, based on the remainder of a unique database key attached to the application after division by four.

The NRM and MNRM were separately calibrated against each of the four samples, using the same starting parameters, and the Bayesian Information Criterion (BIC) was calculated for model comparison. In addition, the obtained MNRM parameters from each sample were cross-validated against the other three samples; the BIC was calculated for each set of parameters on the three samples *not* used to obtain them. These cross-fit values give a sense of the degree of overfit or capitalization on chance due to the larger number of free parameters in MNRM, separately from variable success in calibration when using different samples.

In all cases, MNRM fit the data better than NRM. Figure 1 shows the difference in BIC between MNRM and NRM for each sample; black lines represent the difference in fit for models calibrated on the same sample, whereas the gray represents the range of differences resulting from cross-validation. (In order to account for small variations in sample size, differences were always calculated between fit statistics for the same sample, no matter on which sample the parameter calibration was done.)

It is readily apparent from Fig. 1 that the obtained improvement of MNRM on NRM varies considerably by calibration sample; differences in BIC for models calibrated and fit on the same sample range from 7,721 to 18,516. (With 50 additional free parameters, a significant χ^2, at $\alpha = 0.05$, is at least 71.4.) The narrow

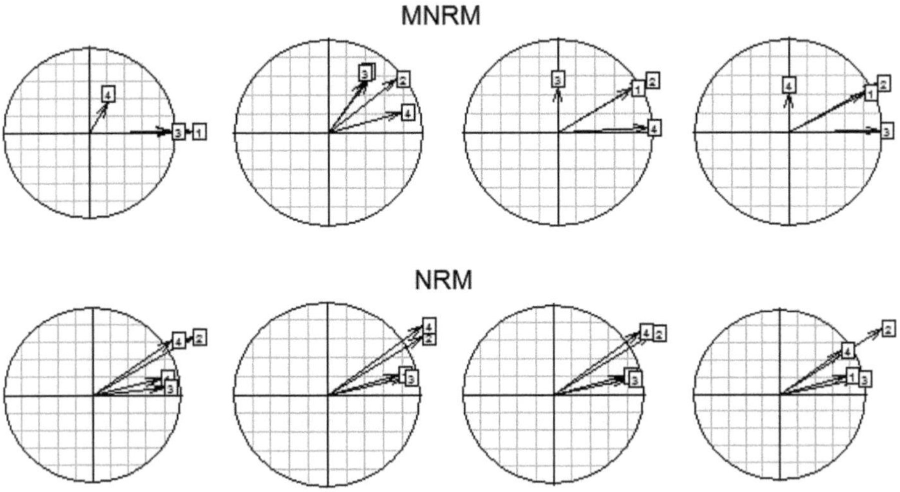

Fig. 2 Rotational indeterminacy in practice. Obtained factor loading configurations differed more between calibration samples under MNRM than under NRM

cross-fit ranges suggest that model overfit, or capitalization on chance, is not a large determinant in the obtained improvement; the mean advantage in BIC conferred by MNRM calibration and fit evaluation on the same sample was 380. Instead, calibration on certain data samples resulted in universally better or worse parameter vectors. This pattern could result from local minima in the loglikelihood surface for the model in parameter space, but it might also simply indicate large nearly flat regions in the same surface, over which minimization algorithms do not readily traverse. Either way, the loglikelihood surface is not well suited to minimization. Further evidence toward rotational near-indeterminacy, as suggested by Bolt and Johnson (2009), is provided by comparison of the configurations of loadings of four representative items across two dimensions, as shown in Fig. 2. NRM generated much more consistent patterns of loadings between calibration samples than did MNRM.

The problem of rotational indeterminacy can, at least some of the time, be ameliorated through the use of anchor items which can be constrained to load on particular dimensions, or in general modeled with fewer free parameters. In this case, six additional items were drawn from the assessment's paired preference section, and modeled with the two-parameter logistic model (2PL; Birnbaum 1968). As shown in Fig. 3, the improvement of MNRM over NRM was much more consistent when anchor items were used, although the anchor items themselves were modeled identically in both conditions. Differences in BIC for models calibrated and fit on the same sample, with anchors, ranged from 17,621 to 22,000, less than half the range of the models fit without anchors.

Figure 4 shows that, while less dramatic, the problem of rotational indeterminacy has not been eliminated. In the third replication sample, but not the first, second or fourth, one plotted item loads only on the second dimension (vertical axis).

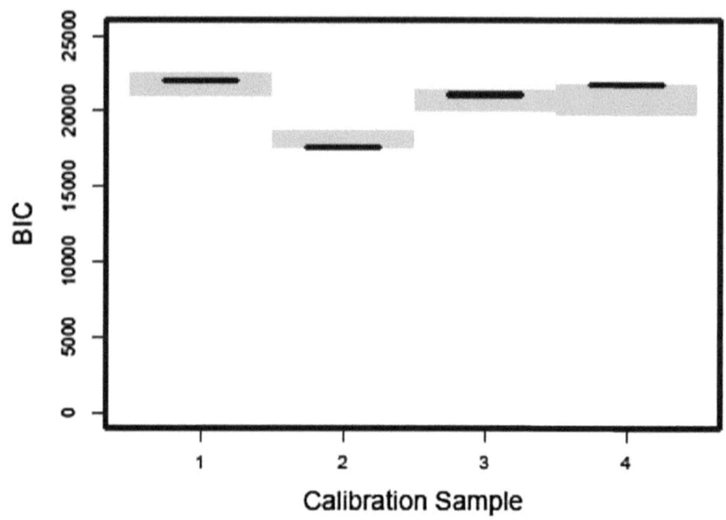

Fig. 3 Difference in BIC between MNRM and NRM for each sample when anchor items were used, with cross-fit range

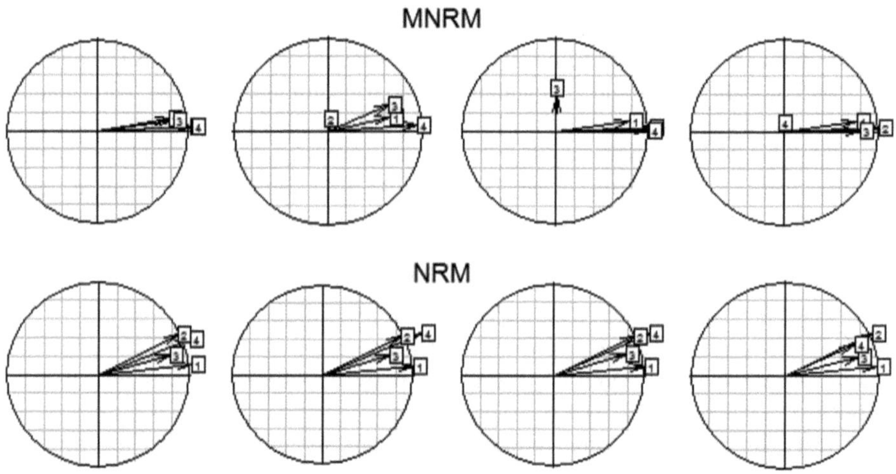

Fig. 4 Less configural variation was observed between MNRM factor loadings derived under different calibration samples when six anchor items were used

Furthermore, under both the NRM and MNRM, two of the anchor items "stole theta" on the second dimension; that is, a relatively high correlation between those two items manifested not as local dependence, but as high loadings on that trait while all other items' loadings were suppressed. This might be a case where more or better-chosen anchors could do a better job of stabilizing the models. In short, anchor items are a practical amelioration strategy, not a panacea.

Returning once again to our example item, Fig. 5 compares the trace lines under NRM and MNRM. Under NRM, the item loads mostly on the third dimension; its trace lines correspond closely to MNRM's third dimension, but left–right reversed. The difference is a side effect of the choice of initial high and low categories for each dimension on MNRM; the third dimension category anchor orders were sufficiently opposed to the first dimension category anchor orders (used for all three dimensions under NRM) that the two models fit that dimension with high and low ends reversed.

In addition, the other two dimensions of MNRM picked up a lower-discrimination pattern. The first two dimensions in this case correspond closely, although they are distinct from the third dimension, team priority. This is visible in the first two trace lines in the second panel of Fig. 5.

Another way of visualizing the two patterns is to look at the latent trait regions where each item response is dominant, jointly on two axes of differentiation. In Fig. 6, dominant response regions are plotted on a composite of dimensions 1 and 2 (horizontal) against team priority (vertical). It is immediately apparent that the four item responses do not fall in a line, as NRM enforces.

NRM's intrinsic single dimension of measurement is generally aligned with the vertical axis. In the two-dimensional display of Fig. 6, it is apparent that the vertical axis, team priority, differentiates three response options that don't involve getting one's teammates in trouble from one response option that does—and the option to be a "supervisor proxy" ends up in the middle. Contrary to expectations, initiative or action orientation appears to be primarily relevant in distinguishing between the two high team priority options.

6 Discussion

At least in the case of the screening assessment studied, the intrinsic multidimensionality of the MNRM allows better fit to SJI response data, compared to the NRM, even when extrinsic (between-items) multidimensionality is permitted in both cases. It further appears from the preceding empirical study that the "exploratory-like" flexibility of the MNRM, and even NRM, allows some data-driven rotation of the latent measurement axes.

Starting parameters for the study were based on the expectation of problem solving (overall effectiveness), action orientation (initiative), and team priority factors. The measures actually obtained were better labeled as customer priority (attentiveness), initiative, and team priority. Customer priority can be described as a willingness to drop routine tasks in order to attend a customer, and does not appear to be a general problem-solving measure. Several items do not load on the first factor; if that latent trait were problem solving, they should.

All of the obtained measures can be characterized as work styles contrasts, not ability components. Is situational performance in retail jobs then more a matter of ITP than ability? Such a finding would be consistent with Motowidlo and Beier's (2009) findings that novice-derived SJI keys contained only ITP information,

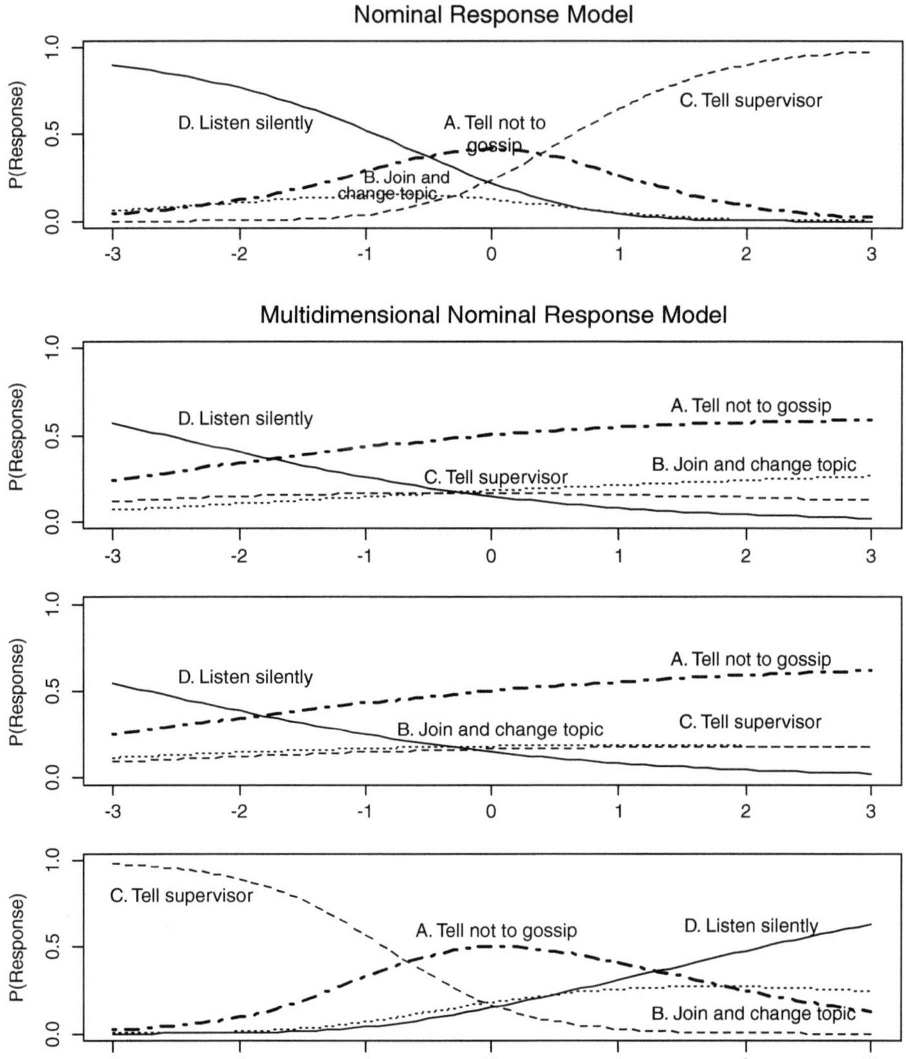

Fig. 5 Trace lines for an example item under NRM (*top panel*) and MNRM (*bottom panel*). Under NRM, the horizontal axis is aligned to the item's intrinsic single dimension of measurement; under MNRM, three orthogonal axes are shown for the three modeled dimensions, in each case with the other two thetas held constant at zero

whereas experienced employees produced keys with additional performance-relevant information; Motowidlo and Beier labeled that information job-relevant knowledge. However, as a practical matter, the selection of critical incidents to translate into SJIs acts as a filter on the types of performance and performance determinants represented by a set of SJIs. The present study is by no means

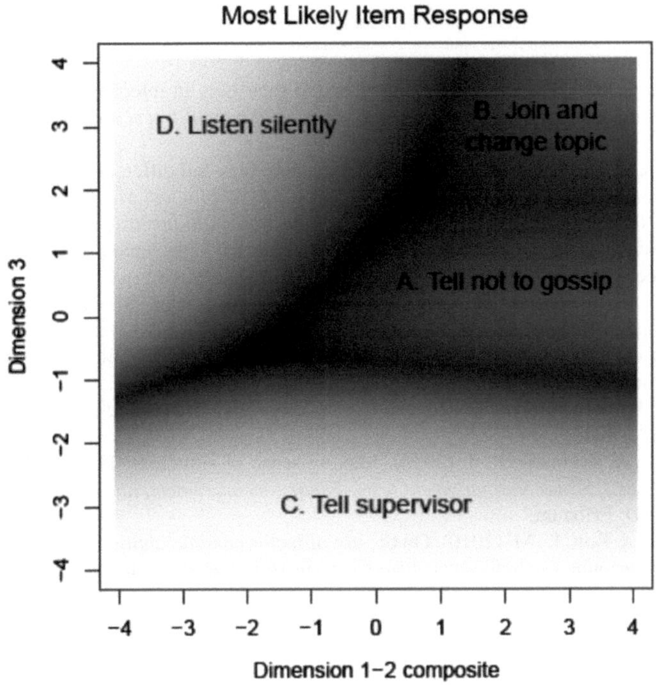

Fig. 6 Dominant response regions for an example item under MNRM. The horizontal axis is a composite of two constructs, customer priority and initiative; the vertical axis is team (as opposed to rule) priority

sufficiently broad or deep to determine conclusively whether and under what conditions problem-solving ability remains relevant to situational performance in retail jobs. It merely suggests the question.

7 Conclusions

The MNRM can be used to model multiple constructs antecedent to situational judgment item responses; for example, $K-1$ work styles contrasts within a K-response SJI, which jointly predict an overall assessment of job performance. However, due to the complexity of the MNRM, when modeling SJIs with it, it is a good idea to constrain the model according to theory, anchor it to constructs with non-SJIs, or both.

Acknowledgments The author thanks Phil Mangos, Ryan Robinson, and John Morrison for insight into SJIs in general and the particular SJIs in the empirical study; Dave Thissen for a number of helpful comments on parameter estimation; and Marc Schluper for assistance with the empirical study data.

References

Birnbaum, A. (1968). Some latent trait models and their uses in inferring an examinee's ability. In F. M. Lord & M. R. Novick, *Statistical theories of mental test scores* (Part 5, pp. 397–479). Reading, MA: Addison-Wesley

Bolt, D. M., & Johnson, T. R. (2009). Addressing score bias and differential item functioning due to individual differences in response style. *Applied Psychological Measurement, 33*, 335–352.

Bolt, D., & Newton, J. (2010, May 3). *Application of a multidimensional partial credit model allowing within-item slope heterogeneity*. Paper presented at the annual meeting of the National Conference on Measurement in Education (NCME), Denver, CO.

Bolt, D. M., & Newton, J. R. (2011). Multiscale measurement of extreme response style. *Educational and Psychological Measurement, 71*, 814–833.

Cai, L., Thissen, D., & du Toit, S. H. C. (2011). *IRTPRO for Windows [Computer software]*. Lincolnwood, IL: Scientific Software International.

Cronbach, L. J. (1946). Response sets and test validity. *Educational and Psychological Measurement, 6*, 475–494.

Gessner, T. L., & Klimoski, R. J. (2006). Making sense of situations. In J. A. Weekley & R. E. Ployhart (Eds.), *Situational judgment tests: Theory, measurement, and application* (pp. 13–38). Mahwah, NJ: Erlbaum.

Johnson, T. R., & Bolt, D. M. (2010). On the use of factor-analytic multinomial logit item response models to account for individual differences in response style. *Journal of Educational and Behavioral Statistics, 35*, 92–114.

Junker, B. W., & Sijtsma, K. (2001). Cognitive assessment models with few assumptions, and connections with nonparametric item response theory. *Applied Psychological Measurement, 25*, 258–272.

Mangos, P., Thissen-Roe, A., & Robinson, R. (2012, April 27). *Recovering ability and non-ability components underlying situational judgment*. Paper presented at the annual meeting of the Society for Industrial-Organizational Psychology (SIOP), San Diego, CA.

McDaniel, M. A., Morgeson, F. P., Finnegan, F. B., Campion, M. A., & Braverman, E. P. (2001). Use of situational judgment tests to predict job performance: A clarification of the literature. *Journal of Applied Psychology, 86*, 730–740.

McDaniel, M. A., Psotka, J., & Legree, P. J. (2009, April). *Toward an understanding of situational judgment item validity*. Paper presented at the annual meeting of the Society for Industrial-Organizational Psychology (SIOP), New Orleans, LA.

Motowidlo, S. J., & Beier, M. E. (2009, April). *Differentiating specific job knowledge from implicit trait policies in procedural knowledge measured by a situational judgment test*. Paper presented at the annual meeting of the Society for Industrial-Organizational Psychology (SIOP), New Orleans, LA.

Motowidlo, S. J., Hooper, A. C., & Jackson, H. L. (2006). A theoretical basis for situational judgment tests. In J. A. Weekley & R. E. Ployhart (Eds.), *Situational judgment tests: Theory, measurement, and application* (pp. 57–82). Mahwah, NJ: Erlbaum.

Schmitt, N., & Chan, D. (2006). Situational judgment tests: Method or construct? In J. A. Weekley & R. E. Ployhart (Eds.), *Situational judgment tests: Theory, measurement, and application* (pp. 135–156). Mahwah, NJ: Erlbaum.

Stemler, S. E., & Sternberg, R. J. (2006). Using situational judgment tests to measure practical intelligence. In J. A. Weekley & R. E. Ployhart (Eds.), *Situational judgment tests: Theory, measurement, and application* (pp. 107–131). Mahwah, NJ: Erlbaum.

Swander, C. J. (2001). *Video-based situational judgment test characteristics: Multidimensionality at the item level and impact of situational variables* (Doctoral dissertation). Virginia Polytechnic Institute. http://scholar.lib.vt.edu/theses/available/etd-05152001-125408/unrestricted/etd.pdf

Thissen, D., Cai, L., & Bock, R. D. (2010). The nominal categories item response model. In M. L. Nering & R. Ostini (Eds.), *Handbook of polytomous item response theory models: Development and applications* (pp. 43–75). New York, NY: Taylor & Francis.

Weekley, J. A., Ployhart, R. E., & Holtz, B. C. (2006). On the development of situational judgment tests: issues in item development, scaling and scoring. In J. A. Weekley & R. E. Ployhart (Eds.), *Situational judgment tests: Theory, measurement, and application* (pp. 157–182). Mahwah, NJ: Erlbaum.

Zu, J., & Kyllonen, P. (2012, April). *Scoring situational judgment tests with item response models*. Paper presented at the annual meeting of the National Conference on Measurement in Education (NCME).

Theory Development as a Precursor for Test Validity

Klaas Sijtsma

The two classical main themes in psychological measurement are reliability and validity. The other topics psychological measurement addresses are directly or indirectly concerned with investigating aspects of reliability and validity or contribute directly to making measurements more reliable and more valid. For example, equating of different scales assumes that the scales measure the same attribute, thus producing a common scale that is a valid representation of the attribute. Adaptive testing aims at selecting the items for the measured individual from the item bank that produce the most reliable measurement of the individual using the smallest number of items. Differential item functioning research identifies items that measure different attributes in different populations in addition to the dominant attribute, hence suggesting removing the items that threaten test validity. Person-fit analysis identifies respondents whose responses were driven by the intended attribute (e.g., intelligence) but also by attributes the test was not constructed to measure (e.g., test anxiety) or that even replaced the intended attribute (e.g., guessing, cheating), and person-fit analysis suggests studying such aberrant respondents or removing their data from the dataset. Componential item response models and cognitive diagnosis models hypothesize theories explaining how respondents produce item scores, thus providing a more solid basis for understanding what the test measures and thus improving its validity.

Reliability is a more technical subject and a narrower concept than validity; hence, it is a less problematic concept even though the estimation of

This chapter was based on a paper presented in the Invited Symposium "Metaphors and Measurement: An Invited Symposium on Validity", at the International Meeting of the Psychometric Society 2012, July 9–12, 2012, in Lincoln, NE, USA.

K. Sijtsma (✉)
Department of Methodology and Statistics, Tilburg School of Social and Behavioral Sciences, Tilburg University, P.O. Box 90153, 5000 LE Tilburg, The Netherlands
e-mail: k.sijtsma@tilburguniversity.edu

R.E. Millsap et al. (eds.), *New Developments in Quantitative Psychology*, Springer Proceedings in Mathematics & Statistics 66, DOI 10.1007/978-1-4614-9348-8_17,

reliability (group-level characteristic) and measurement precision (individual-level characteristic) is not devoid of discussion (Mellenbergh 1996). The broader and less technical, hence more problematic validity concept has been debated since it originated in the 1920s (Sireci 2009; for a discussion of the validity concept, see Zumbo 2007) and has proven to be more intangible than reliability. The ongoing debate about validity's main issue still is the same as it was then: What is valid, the test or the test score? If the focus is on the test the question is what the test measures, and if the focus is on the test score the question is for which purposes the test score can be used. Present-day validity conceptions predominantly focus on the practical usefulness of the test score and the question of what the test measures is largely suppressed. This contribution discusses the necessity to do research aimed at establishing what the test measures and touches upon the surprisingly modest role psychometrics plays in the validation of measurement.

1 Brief History

In the 1920s, the psychological attribute was considered the causal agent of responses persons provide to items and a test was considered a measurement instrument of such a causal agent. The novel technique known as factor analysis that had been introduced recently (Spearman 1904) played a crucial role, and psychologists saw factors not so much as summaries of variance but more as representing entities with an ontological status. The view on validity strongly influenced the early ideas of Cronbach and Meehl (1955). Their nomological network describes the relationships of the test score with other variables and represents the attributes' theory. Soon attention shifted from what (i.e., a "construct") the test measures to studying relationships in the nomological network from which the meaning of the test score could be derived, and with this shift the view of an attribute as a causal agent disappeared and was replaced by studying relationships with other variables. The meaning of measurement was derived from these relationships, thus weakening the role of theory as a guiding principle in the development of tests and questionnaires.

In the 1920s already another viewpoint emerged, which was that a test can be valid for many different purposes. This view was inspired by the use of tests for selecting military personnel in WWI and in personnel selection in civil society. The idea developed that a test is valid to the degree to which it relates to a criterion. For example, a criterion may operationalize an applicant's suitability for a particular job and for each job one may define a different criterion. As there are many different criteria, a test can have many different validities. For each criterion, the test's validity was expressed in the product–moment correlation, which like factor analysis at the time was still quite new (Pearson 1896). Soon the need emerged to distinguish different types of criteria and consequently different types of validity, such as convergent, divergent, incremental, differential, concurrent, and synthetic validity. Finally, Messick (1989, p. 13) proposed that "Validity is an integrated evaluative judgment of the degree to which empirical evidence and theoretical rationales support the *adequacy* and *appropriateness* of *inferences* and *actions* based on test scores and other modes of assessment." Thus, validity became both an encompassing but also a fuzzier concept that referred to the degree to which available sources support a particular interpretation or a particular use of the test score. As a result, what the test measures moved to the background and validity focused on technology, emphasizing that a test fulfilling its practical purpose is a good test and that in principle one does not need to know what the test measures.

The technological approach to validity is a practical approach that avoids difficult questions for which one would need an elaborate founding theory of the attribute of interest, as if such a theory does not matter. The approach reminds one of a consumer who simply wants an apparatus to work and is uninterested in the mechanics responsible for its successful performance. But test constructors are not consumers and it is difficult to imagine that test constructors do not purposefully construct tests as measures of a particular attribute. The idea that one would assemble a set of items only because they seem to have predictive power for one or two criteria, at the same ignoring what the items measure in common, seems preposterous. It is as if scientific curiosity no longer is of interest. The *Standards for Educational and Psychological Testing* (AERA et al. 1999, p. 9) indeed shows that the question what a test measures does not seem to play a role in modern views on validity.

2 Modern Resistance

Recently, several authors have expressed their concern about the technological approach to validity. Michell (1999) posited that psychological measurement must be based on a theory about the attribute but also noticed that very few measurement instruments are based on this point of departure. The basic problem in psychological measurement is the absence in most cases of well-founded and well-tested theories about attributes. If theories are available, the problem usually is that there are too many competing theories for the same attribute, and that there are no crucial experiments that allow a decision that favors one theory with respect to the others. Intelligence is an excellent example for which several theories exist next to one another so that different tests for intelligence can be based on different theories, such as Spearman's 2-factor theory, Thurstone's 7-factor theory, and Guilford's three-dimensional 120-factor theory, whereas other tests are based on binary distinctions between verbal and performal intelligence and crystallized and fluid intelligence. The richness of the field in fact signifies its weakness as different intelligence conceptions continue to exist next to one another. However, for many personality traits such as leadership and social intelligence the situation is much grimmer, as propositions, hypotheses, and guesses replace theories and are often expressed by inaccurate associations between the test score and other variables.

The general complaint is that many tests and questionnaires are based on vague "theories" that are not well founded and well tested. As a result, test construction often entails the selection of a set of items that define what the test measures instead of a theory that guides the operationalization of the attribute into a set of items. The psychometric analysis of the collected data and the analysis of the correlations of test score and a limited number of other variables then serve as the basis for establishing validity. The researcher relying on psychometrics to find out what his test measures thus interprets the structure that factor analysis or item response theory reveals and in hindsight accepts this interpretation as the explanation of how the respondent answered the items. The Achilles heel of this approach is that in hindsight one is always able to interpret structures found in data. On the contrary, the availability of a theory prior to data collection enables one to formulate hypothesis that can be tested using the data. The dominant approach using items to define what the test measures rather than theory about the attribute is known as operationism. Following operationism, the attribute coincides with the operations used to measure it.

Cronbach and Meehl (1955) proposed investigating a test score's validity through the relations a test score entertains with the other variables in the test's nomological network. Borsboom et al. (2009) noticed that in psychology nomological networks do not exist; hence, they cannot be investigated. Thus, it is unclear which variables would have to be investigated to ascertain test-score validity and how a selection of variables can give rise to a correct inference of what the test measures. Indeed, in much practical validity research the test score is correlated with one or two other similar test scores, which is supposed to give evidence of convergent validity, while correlations with a limited number of other, dissimilar variables should provide evidence of discriminant validity. These two pieces of information together are important aspects of a methodology for the investigation of the nomological network known as the multi-method multi-trait approach (Campbell and Fiske 1959).

Can a few correlations be a sound basis for the inference of what the test measures? The abundance of theories for some attributes and the absence of theories for other attributes necessitate the reliance on the nomological network or whatever is available (see Cronbach's 1988, weak program), and much test construction work reports correlations with variables that are available and replace convergent and discriminant validity. Borsboom et al. (2009) argue that the development of attribute theories is necessary to know what a test measures, and for this purpose one has to investigate what persons do when they respond to items: Which cognitive processes are activated? Which affective processes are activated? Psychometrics can lend a helping hand by means of cognitive processing models (e.g., De Boeck and Wilson 2004) and cognitive diagnostic models (Rupp et al. 2010). A relatively simple example of a cognitive processing model is the linear logistic test model (Fischer 1995), which explains item locations from contributions of different operations that students have to perform when they attempt to solve a cognitive problem. Psychometric models contribute to theory development in the intelligence domain, for example, investigating solution strategies in Raven's Progressive Matrices test (Verguts and De Boeck 2002) and competing theories for transitive reasoning (Bouwmeester et al. 2007), and in the emotion domain for investigating the process structure of guilt (Smits and De Boeck 2003).

3 Cycle of Measurement

Sijtsma (2012) extensively discussed how either the presence or the absence of a well-developed theory affects the construction of a test. Figure 1 shows a cycle the development of a test goes through. I assume that one starts the test construction by selecting the theory for the attribute for which one intends to construct a measurement instrument. In rare cases a well-developed theory is available, such as for proportional reasoning and transitive reasoning; in other cases the researcher has to choose one from multiple, possibly well-developed theories, as with intelligence; and in many cases theory takes the appearance of notions, abstractions, and traditions, intuitions and educated guesses, that define hypotheses at best but no well-developed theory supported by sound empirical research and replicated on several research occasions. The dashed box "Attribute Theory" in Fig. 1 represents this initial state of theory development, and the solid box "Attribute Theory" represents the other two, better-developed states.

Theories define attributes at a high abstraction level, but attributes only become "tangible" in behavior. Hence, the theoretical attribute structures need to be translated into observable behaviors that are typical of the attribute. This process is known as operationalization (Fig. 1); that is, the specification of the operations needed to measure the attribute. The typical behaviors are provoked by well-chosen items that require respondents to provide solutions or give answers that are informative of the attribute. This only works well with a strong, well-developed attribute theory but not with a weak, immature attribute theory when subjectivity guides the operationalization. For example, with weak theory one has little more "theory" available than general statements referring to weak relations, such as "depressive people are inclined to sleep shorter and worry more." Even though this may be true, people sleeping shorter and worrying more often are not depressive. Hence, these are behaviors that are not typical of depression and a better-developed depression theory would provide more guidance for operationalization and test construction.

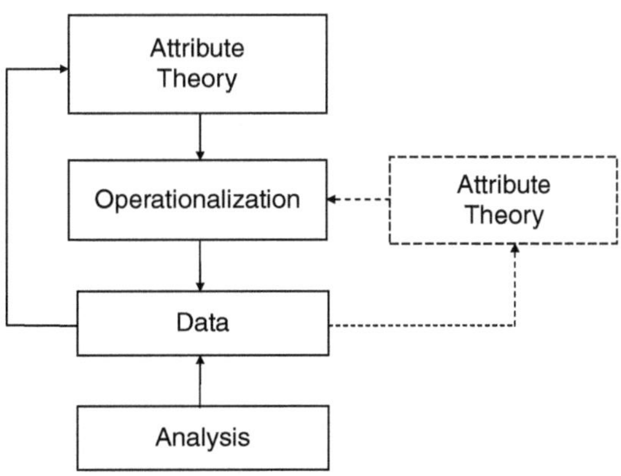

Fig. 1 Cycle of test construction

	Does not apply				Applies
Items: I sometimes feel gloomy	☐	☐	☐	☐	☐
I wish I were cheerful more often	☐	☐	☐	☐	☐
Now and then I have pessimistic thoughts	☐	☐	☐	☐	☐
I am not always as gay as I should be	☐	☐	☐	☐	☐

Fig. 2 Imaginary four-item questionnaire for measuring melancholy

After a set of items has been defined irrespective of the status of the underlying theory, next a preliminary test is constructed, administered to a representative sample from the population of interest producing qualitative responses, and the responses are transformed into numbers or item scores constituting the data (Fig. 1). The transformation follows the general principle that a higher score reflects a higher level of the attribute. This is a hypothesis, which may be proven wrong by data analysis, for example, using item response theory models. The psychometric analysis (Fig. 1) of the data produces results that are informative about the structure of the data and the quality of the test, but which may also be fed back to the theory of the attribute. The feedback loops in Fig. 1 show that outcomes of psychometric analysis have more repercussions for better-developed theories than for immature theories. It is important to notice that without a theory that guides the operationalization data analysis can only provide information about the *data*, not about the *non-existing theory*.

A generally accepted idea among test constructors seems to be that in the absence of a well-developed attribute theory the analysis of the collected data helps to develop the attribute theory. This way theory is inferred from data. Why do people believe that data can provide such information? I contend that they are misguided by the structure data always display (unless a computer generated random data), and which is revealed by clever statistical modeling. Statistical modeling always comes up with "something" but why would that "something" be informative about a theory? All that was revealed is the structure of the data. I use an example to clarify my point. The example is made up for didactical purposes, and not based on a real questionnaire that was used to collect real data.

The example concerns the measurement of the inclination to having feelings of melancholy. Figure 2 shows four items that each are hypothesized to represent different aspects of melancholy. My prediction is that a principal components analysis or a confirmatory factor analysis of data collected in a sample of respondents supports a 1-factor model. I have not done this experiment and may be wrong but the point I want to make is that a researcher may readily infer the existence of a causal attribute from the 1-factor solution, and that this is what happens in the absence of a theory for melancholy that guides the construction of the items. The 1-factor structure simply suggests that an underlying trait caused the responses to the items. This practice led Kagan (2005) to conclude that self-descriptions rely too much on "the semantic structures activated when participants answer questionnaires." Thus, respondents reflect on the situation in which they find themselves answering questions and tend to come up with a consistent picture. But is this trait measurement? Or is this a linguistic phenomenon? Or something else? Without theory one cannot know this.

This discussion serves to emphasize the importance of having a theory available when one constructs a measurement instrument. In the absence of theory, all efforts should be invested in the development of such a theory. Only if test construction is based on theory guidance can tests be decided to be valid.

4 Conclusion

My advice to researchers is to use whatever theory about the attribute in question that is available to design a first draft of the test. However, the best they could do is to actively contribute to the development of the theory, provided a theory is absent or in its infancy. Then, researchers may use psychometric cognitive processing models to study the psychological processes that subjects employ to solve or answer the items and to use the results of the statistical data analysis to amend the test and the theory that stood at the basis of the test construction. The flexibility of modern cognitive processing models including variations on item response theory models, latent class models, and factor models suggests that one has much leeway to describe such processes well and make huge contributions to better measurement. The end result is a test that measures the intended attribute. Finally, after the test has been constructed it should be investigated how well it can be used to predict a particular criterion, such as an applicant's suitability for a particular job or the classification of persons for treatment. The degree to which the test produces valid positives and valid negatives qualifies the test for the particular purpose but does not say anything about what the test measures; this was established in the previous stage of test construction.

The discussion about validity has become too complex. There are basically two problems that have to be tackled. First, one has to establish whether a test is a valid measurement instrument for the intended attribute. Second, one has to establish whether the test can be used effectively for a particular practical usage. Both aspects of validity are essential; constructing a test to measure an attribute without intending to ever use it in practice is a useless enterprise, and using a test in practice without having established what it measures is bad science.

References

American Educational Research Association, American Psychological Association, & National Council on Measurement in Education (1999). *Standards for educational and psychological testing*. Washington, DC: American Educational Research Association.

Borsboom, D., Cramer, A. O. J., Kievit, R. A., Zand Scholten, A., & Franić, S. (2009). The end of construct validity. In R. W. Lissitz (Ed.), *The concept of validity. Revisions, new directions, and applications* (pp. 135–170). Charlotte, NC: Information Age Publishing, Inc.

Bouwmeester, S., Vermunt, J. K., & Sijtsma, K. (2007). Development and individual differences in transitive reasoning: A fuzzy trace theory approach. *Developmental Review, 27*, 41–74.

Campbell, D. T., & Fiske, D. W. (1959). Convergent and discriminant validation by the multitrait-multimethod matrix. *Psychological Bulletin, 56*, 81–105.

Cronbach, L. J. (1988). Five perspectives on the validity argument. In H. Wainer & H. I. Braun (Eds.), *Test validity* (pp. 3–17). Hillsdale, NJ: Lawrence Erlbaum.

Cronbach, L. J., & Meehl, P. E. (1955). Construct validity in psychological tests. *Psychological Bulletin, 52*, 281–302.

De Boeck, P., & Wilson, M. (2004). *Explanatory item response models: A generalized linear and nonlinear approach*. New York: Springer.

Fischer, G. H. (1995). The linear logistic test model. In G. H. Fischer & I. W. Molenaar (Eds.), *Rasch models. Foundations, recent developments, and applications* (pp. 131–156). New York: Springer.

Kagan, J. (2005). A time for specificity. *Journal of Personality Assessment, 85*, 125–127.

Mellenbergh, G. J. (1996). Measurement precision in test score and item response models. *Psychological Methods, 1*, 293–299.

Messick, S. (1989). Validity. In R. L. Linn (Ed.), *Educational measurement* (3rd ed., pp. 13–103). Washington, DC: American Council on Education and National Council on Measurement in Education.

Michell, J. (1999). *Measurement in psychology. A critical history of a methodological concept.* Cambridge: Cambridge University Press.

Pearson, K. (1896). Mathematical contributions to the theory of evolution. III regression, heredity and panmixia. *Philosophical Transactions of the Royal Society A, 187*, 253–318.

Rupp, A. A., Templin, J., & Henson, R. A. (2010). *Diagnostic measurement: Theory, methods, and applications*. New York: Guilford Press.

Sijtsma, K. (2012). Psychological measurement between physics and statistics. *Theory & Psychology, 22*, 786–809.

Sireci, S. G. (2009). Packing and unpacking sources of validity evidence. In R. W. Lissitz (Ed.), *The concept of validity. Revisions, new directions, and applications* (pp. 19–37). Charlotte, NC: Information Age Publishing, Inc.

Smits, D. J. M., & De Boeck, P. (2003). A componential IRT model for guilt. *Multivariate Behavioral Research, 38*, 161–188.

Spearman, C. (1904). 'General intelligence', objectively determined and measured. *American Journal of Psychology, 15*, 201–293.

Verguts, T., & De Boeck, P. (2002). The induction of solution rules in Raven's progressive matrices test. *European Journal of Cognitive Psychology, 14*, 521–547.

Zumbo, B. D. (2007). Validity: Foundational issues and statistical methodology. In C. R. Rao & S. Sinharay (Eds.), *Handbook of statistics* (Psychometrics, Vol. 26, pp. 45–79). Amsterdam: Elsevier.

Bayesian Methods and Model Selection for Latent Growth Curve Models with Missing Data

Zhenqiu (Laura) Lu, Zhiyong Zhang, and Allan Cohen

1 Introduction

There has been widespread interest in the analysis of change in social and behavioral sciences (e.g., Singer and Willett 2003). Growth modeling, in particular, is becoming increasingly important in these areas. Among the most popular growth models, *latent growth curve models* (LGCMs) are statistical models designed to study individuals' latent growth trajectories by analyzing the variables of interest on the same individuals repeatedly through time (e.g., Bollen and Curran 2006). With an increase in complexity of LGCMs, comes an increase in difficulties estimating such models. First, missing data are almost inevitable with longitudinal data (e.g., Jelicic et al. 2009). Second, using conventional likelihood procedures may be challenging when estimating model parameters in complex models with complicated data structures. And third, even with effective estimation methods, model selection in such complex situations becomes difficult.

1.1 Missing Data

As LCGMs involve data collection on the same participants through multiple waves of surveys, tests, or questionnaires, missing data are almost inevitable. This is because some students may miss a test because of absence or fatigue or research

Z. Lu (✉) • A. Cohen
University of Georgia, Athens, GA 30602, USA
e-mail: zlu@uga.edu; acohen@uga.edu

Z. Zhang
University of Notre Dame, Notre Dame, IN 46556, USA
e-mail: zhangzhiyong@nd.edu

R.E. Millsap et al. (eds.), *New Developments in Quantitative Psychology*, Springer Proceedings in Mathematics & Statistics 66, DOI 10.1007/978-1-4614-9348-8_18,

participants may drop out of a study (e.g., Schafer 1997). Missing data can be investigated from their mechanisms, that is, by examining why missing data occur. Little and Rubin (2002) distinguished two mechanisms for missing data, *ignorable* and *non-ignorable*. For ignorable missingness, estimates are usually asymptotically consistent when the missingness is ignored (Little and Rubin 2002). This is because parameters that govern the missing process either are distinct from the parameters that govern the model outcomes or depend on the observed parameters in the fitted model. The non-ignorable missingness is also referred to as *missing not at random (MNAR)*, in which the missing data probability depends on unobserved outcomes or on some unobserved latent variables in the model.

With the appearance of missing data comes the challenge in estimating growth model parameters. Although there is a large literature addressing the problems of missing data in applied and quantitative psychology (e.g., Yuan and Lu 2008; Roth 1994), particularly in longitudinal studies (e.g., Jelicic et al. 2009), the majority of the literature is on ignorable missingness. This is mainly because (1) analysis models or techniques for non-ignorable missing data are traditionally difficult to implement and not yet well suited for widespread use (e.g., Baraldi and Enders 2010); and (2) missingness mechanisms are not testable (Little and Rubin 2002). At the same time, however, the analysis of non-ignorable missingness is a crucial and a serious concern in applied research areas, in which participants may be dropping out for reasons closely related to the response being measured (e.g., Enders 2011). Not attending to the non-ignorable missingness may result in severely biased statistical estimates, standard errors, and associated confidence intervals (e.g., Schafer 1997), and thus poses substantial risk of leading researchers to incorrect conclusions. Accordingly, this paper focuses on non-ignorable missingness and investigates its influences on model estimation for different types of missingness.

In a recent study of latent growth models, Lu et al. (2011) investigated non-ignorable missingness. However, the missingness in that study was only allowed to depend on latent class membership. In practice, the non-ignorable missingness in latent growth models can depend on many other latent variables such as individual starting level and growth rate. Furthermore, Lu et al. (2011) did not discuss how to identify the missingness mechanisms.

1.2 Bayesian Approach

In this study, a full Bayesian approach is used for parameter estimation. Previously, maximum likelihood methods were adopted for most of the studies, and statistical inferences were carried out using conventional likelihood procedures (e.g., Yuan and Lu 2008). Recently, Bayesian methods have been proposed as an alternative approach (e.g., Muthén and Asparouhov 2012) to estimate complex models. The advantages of Bayesian methods include their intuitive interpretations of statistical results, their flexibility in incorporating prior information about how data behave in similar contexts and findings from experimental research, their capacity for dealing with small sample sizes (such as occur with special populations), and their expandability in the analysis of complex statistical models with complicated data structure (e.g., Lee 2007).

In a Bayesian approach, when the joint distribution is complex or unknown but the conditional distribution of each variable is available for each set of variables, Gibbs sampling algorithm (Geman and Geman 1984) can be adopted. The Gibbs sampling generates Markov chains which can be shown to be ergodic (Geman and Geman 1984), and thus the sequence of samples after convergence can be viewed from the joint probability distribution of all parameters. It is also shown that each variable from the Markov chain converges to the marginal distribution of that variable (Robert and Casella 2004).

1.3 Model Selection Criteria

Model selection criteria can be used to compare models to identify the best-fit model. Akaike (1974) proposed the Akaike's information criterion (AIC). AIC offers a relative measure of the information lost. For Bayesian models, the Bayes factor is used for hypothesis testing. But the Bayes factor is usually difficult or even impossible to calculate, especially for models that involve many random effects, large numbers of unknowns parameters, or improper priors. To approximate the Bayes factor, Schwarz (1978) developed the Bayesian information criterion (BIC) or Schwarz criterion. To obtain more precise criteria, Bozdogan (1987) proposed the consistent Akaike Information Criterion (CAIC) and Sclove (1987) proposed the sample-size adjusted Bayesian information criterion (ssBIC) which is based on the Rissanen Information Criteria (RIC, Rissanen 1978) for auto-regressions. The deviance information criterion (DIC) (Spiegelhalter et al. 2002) is a recently developed criterion designed for complex hierarchical models. It is based on the posterior distribution of the log-likelihood, following the original suggestion of Dempster (1974) for model choice in the Bayesian framework, and it is particularly useful in Bayesian model selection problems where the posterior distributions of the models have been obtained by Markov chain Monte Carlo (MCMC) simulation. DIC is usually regarded as a Bayesian version or generalization of the AIC and BIC. For all these criteria, the model with a smaller value is better supported by data.

In a Bayesian context, currently there are no well-defined model selection criteria for latent growth models with missing data (e.g., Celeux et al. 2006). The problem is mainly due to random effects and missing data. For random effects models, the likelihood function can be an observed-data likelihood, a complete-data likelihood, or a conditional likelihood. Briefly speaking, an observed-data likelihood does not explicitly include latent variables, such as random-effects; a complete-data likelihood includes all auxiliary variables in the model; and a conditional likelihood is the joint likelihood function of the observed outcomes and the missingness indicator conditional on the random-effects, and thus the likelihood only includes random-effects, with no fixed-effects involved (e.g., Celeux et al. 2006). Also, the missing data part can be either included in or excluded from the log-likelihood functions.

1.4 Goals and Structure

The goals of the paper are to propose latent growth models with non-ignorable missingness, to estimate the models via a Bayesian approach, and to evaluate the performance of model selection criteria.

The rest of the paper consists of six sections. Section 2 describes the proposed growth models. Three non-ignorable missingness selection models are presented and formulated. Section 3 presents a full Bayesian method to estimate the latent growth models through data augmentation and Gibbs sampling algorithms. Section 4 proposes model selection criteria in a Bayesian context for growth models with missing data. Section 5 conducts simulation studies. Estimates from models with different non-ignorable missingness and different sample sizes are summarized, analyzed, and compared. Conclusions based on the simulation studies are drawn. Section 6 discusses the implications and future directions of this study. In addition, the Appendices present some technical details.

2 Latent Growth Models

The LGCMs can be expressed by a regression equation with latent variables being regressors. Specifically, for a longitudinal study with N subjects and T measurement time points, let $\mathbf{y}_i = (y_{i1}, y_{i2}, \ldots, y_{iT})'$ be a $T \times 1$ random vector, where y_{it} stands for the outcome or observation of individual i on occasion t ($i = 1,2,\ldots,N$; $t = 1,2,\ldots,T$), and let η_i be a $q \times 1$ random vector containing q continuous latent variables. A LGCM for the outcome $\mathbf{y}_i$ related to the latent η_i can be written as

$$\mathbf{y}_i = \Lambda \eta_i + \mathbf{e}_i \tag{1}$$

$$\eta_i = \beta + \xi_i, \tag{2}$$

where Λ is a $T \times q$ matrix consisting of factor loadings, $\mathbf{e}_i$ is a $T \times 1$ vector of residuals or measurement errors that are assumed to follow a T-dimensional multivariate normal distribution, i.e., $\mathbf{e}_i \sim MN_T(\mathbf{0}, \Theta)$, and ξ_i is a $q \times 1$ vector that is assumed to follow a q-dimensional multivariate distribution, i.e., $\xi_i \sim MN_q(\mathbf{0}, \Psi)$. In LGCMs, β is a vector of *fixed effects* and ξ_i is a vector of *random effects* (e.g., Fitzmaurice et al. 2004). The vector β, η_i, and the matrix Λ determine the growth trajectory of the model.

2.1 Selection Models for Non-ignorable Missingness

To address the non-ignorable missingness, there are two general approaches, *pattern-mixture models* (Little and Rubin 1987) and *selection models* (Glynn et al. 1986). In both cases, the statistical analysis requires joint modeling of dependent variable and missing data processes. In this research, selection models are used, mainly because (1) substantively selection models seem more natural for considering the behavior of the response variable in the full target population of interests, rather than in the sub-populations defined by missing data patterns (e.g., Fitzmaurice et al. 2008), and (2) the selection models formulation leads directly to the joint distribution of both dependent variables and the missingness (e.g., Fitzmaurice et al. 2008):

$$p(\mathbf{y}_i,\mathbf{m}_i|\nu,\phi,\mathbf{x}_i) = p(\mathbf{y}_i|\nu,\mathbf{x}_i)\,p(\mathbf{m}_i|\mathbf{y}_i,\nu,\phi,\mathbf{x}_i)$$

where $\mathbf{x}_i$ is a vector of covariates for individual i, $\mathbf{y}_i$ is a vector of individual i's outcome scores, $\theta = (\nu,\phi)$ are all parameters in the model, in which ν are parameters for the growth model and ϕ are parameters for the missingness, and $\mathbf{m}_i$ is a vector $\mathbf{m}_i = (m_{i1}, m_{i2}, \ldots, m_{iT})'$ that indicates the missingness status for $\mathbf{y}_i$. Specifically, if y_i is missing at time point t, then $m_{it} = 1$. Otherwise, $m_{it} = 0$.

Let $\tau_{it} = p(m_{it} = 1)$ be the probability that y_{it} is missing, then m_{it} follows a Bernoulli distribution of τ_{it}, and the density function of m_{it} is

$$p(m_{it}) = \tau_{it}^{m_{it}}(1-\tau_{it})^{1-m_{it}}. \tag{3}$$

For different non-ignorable missingness patterns, the expressions of τ_{it} are different. In Lu et al. (2011), τ_{it} is a function of latent class membership and thus the missingness is *latent class dependent (LCD)*. However, the non-ignorable missingness mechanism could be much more complex in reality. For example, the missingness may be related to the latent intercept, the latent slope of growth, or the potential outcome variables. In these cases, the missing data probabilities depend on latent variables, and thus missingness is non-ignorable. We propose three basic non-ignorable missingness models in detail as follows.

(1) Latent Intercept-Dependent (LID) Missingness: This pattern assumes that the missingness depends on individual's latent intercept, or initial level, I_i, and some observed covariates $\mathbf{x}_i$. The rate of missingness τ_{Iit} is expressed as a probit link function of I_i and $\mathbf{x}_i$

$$\tau_{Iit} = \Phi(\gamma_{0t} + I_i\gamma_{It} + \mathbf{x}_i'\gamma_{xt}) = \Phi(\omega_{Ii}'\gamma_{It}), \tag{4}$$

where $\mathbf{x}_i$ is an r-dimensional vector, $\omega_{Ii} = (1, I_i, \mathbf{x}_i')'$ and $\gamma_{It} = (\gamma_{0t}, \gamma_{It}, \gamma_{xt}')'$. Note that if the vector $\gamma_{It} = 0$, then the missingness is ignorable. A path diagram of the LGCM with an LID missingness is illustrated in Fig. 1.

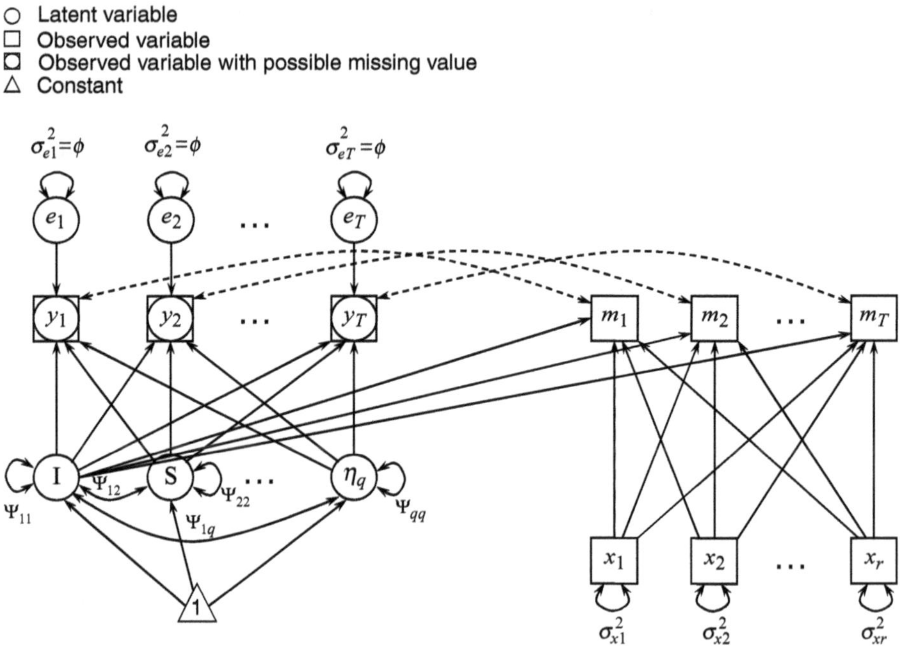

Fig. 1 Path diagram of a latent growth model with latent intercept-dependent missingness (LID), where the rate of missingness $p(m_t)$ depends on covariates x_rs and individual's latent intercept, or initial level, I

(2) Latent Slope-Dependent (LSD) Missingness: This pattern assumes the missingness depends on the latent slope of individuals, S_i. The missing data rate τ_{it} is expressed as a probit link function of S_i and covariates $\mathbf{x}_i$,

$$\tau_{Sit} = \Phi(\gamma_{0t} + S_i\gamma_{St} + \mathbf{x}_i'\gamma_{xt}) = \Phi(\omega_{Si}'\,\gamma_{St}), \tag{5}$$

with $\omega_{Si} = (1, S_i, \mathbf{x}_i')'$ and $\gamma_{St} = (\gamma_{0t}, \gamma_{St}, \gamma_{xt}')'$. Its path diagram is drawn in Fig. 2.

(3) Latent Outcome-Dependent (LOD) Missingness: This pattern assumes that the missing data rates depend on the potential outcomes that may be missing. With covariates $\mathbf{x}_i$, we express τ_{it} as a probit link function as follows.

$$\tau_{yit} = \Phi(\gamma_{0t} + y_{it}\gamma_{yt} + \mathbf{x}_i'\gamma_{xt}) = \Phi(\omega_{yit}'\,\gamma_{yt}), \tag{6}$$

with $\omega_{yit} = (1, y_{it}, \mathbf{x}_i')'$ and $\gamma_{yt} = (\gamma_{0t}, \gamma_{yt}, \gamma_{xt}')'$. The path diagram illustrating the LGCMs with LOD missingness is illustrated in Fig. 3.

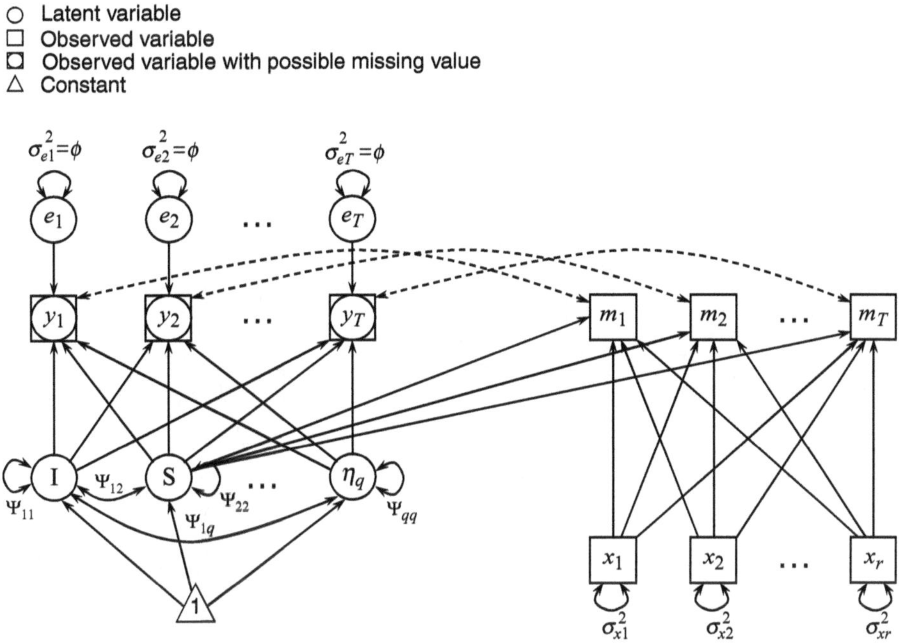

Fig. 2 Path diagram of a latent growth model with latent slope-dependent missing data where $p(m_t)$ depends on covariates x_rs and the latent slope S

3 Bayesian Estimation

In this research, a full Bayesian estimation approach is used to estimate growth models. The algorithm is described as follows. First, model-related latent variables are added via the data augmentation method (Tanner and Wong 1987). By including auxiliary variables, the likelihood function for each model is obtained. Second, proper priors are adopted. Third, with the likelihood function and the priors, based on the Bayes' Theorem, the posterior distribution of the unknown parameters is readily available. We obtain conditional posterior distributions instead of the joint posteriors because the integrations of marginal posterior distributions of the parameters are usually hard to obtain explicitly for high-dimensional data. Fourth, with conditional posterior distributions, Markov chains are generated for the unknown model parameters by implementing a Gibbs sampling algorithm (Geman and Geman 1984). Finally, the statistical inferences are conducted based on converged Markov chains.

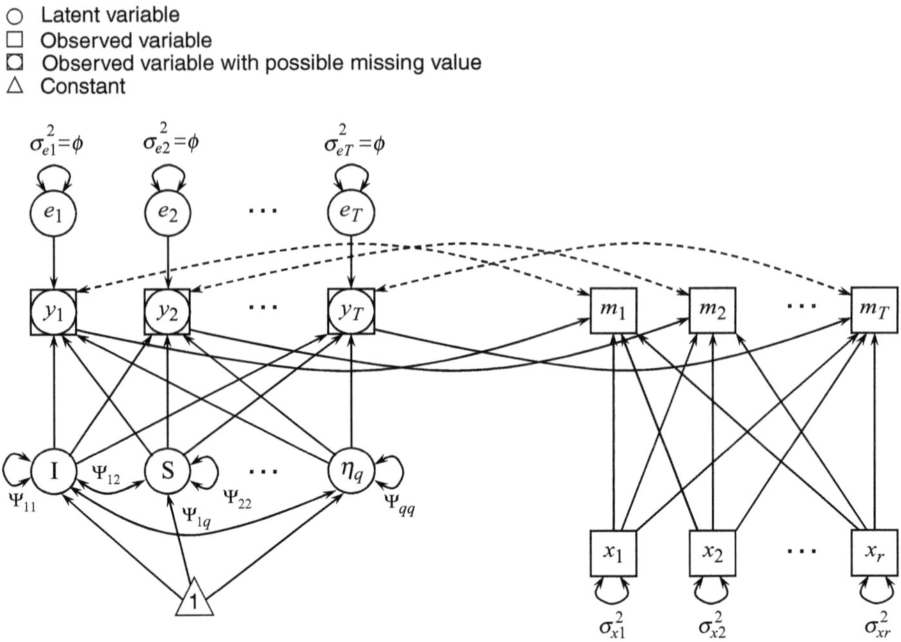

Fig. 3 Path diagram of a latent growth model with potential outcome-dependent missing data where $p(m_t)$ depends on covariates x_rs and the outcome y

3.1 Data Augmentation and Likelihood Functions

In order to construct the likelihood function explicitly, we use the data augmentation algorithm (Tanner and Wong 1987). The observed outcomes $\mathbf{y}_i^{obs}$ can be augmented with the missing values $\mathbf{y}_i^{mis}$ such that $\mathbf{y}_i = (\mathbf{y}_i^{obs}, \mathbf{y}_i^{mis})'$ for individual i. Also, the missing data indicator variable $\mathbf{m}_i$ is added to models. Then the joint likelihood function of the selection model for the ith individual can be expressed as

$$L_i(\eta_i, \mathbf{y}_i, \mathbf{m}_i) = [p(\eta_i)\, p(\mathbf{y}_i|\eta_i)]\; p(\mathbf{m}_i|\mathbf{y}_i, \eta_i, \mathbf{x}_i).$$

For the whole sample, the likelihood function is specifically expressed as

$$\begin{aligned} L(\mathbf{y},\eta,\mathbf{m}) \propto \prod_{i=1}^{N} \Bigg\{ & |\Psi|^{-1/2} \exp\left[-\frac{1}{2}(\eta_i-\beta)'\Psi^{-1}(\eta_i-\beta)\right] \\ & \times |\phi|^{-T/2} \exp\left[-\frac{1}{2\phi}(\mathbf{y}_i-\Lambda\eta_i)'(\mathbf{y}_i-\Lambda\eta_i)\right] \\ & \times \prod_{t=1}^{T}\left[\tau_{it}^{m_{it}}(1-\tau_{it})^{1-m_{it}}\right] \Bigg\}, \end{aligned} \tag{7}$$

where τ_{it} is defined by Eq. (4) for the LID missingness, (5) for the LSD missingness, and (6) for the LOD missingness.

3.2 Priors, Posteriors, and Gibbs Sampling

We assume that all posterior distributions exist in this study. Commonly used proper priors (e.g., Lee 2007) are adopted. Specifically, (1) an inverse Gamma distribution prior is used for $\phi \sim IG(v_0/2, s_0/2)$ where v_0 and s_0 are given hyper-parameters. The density function of an inverse Gamma distribution is $p(\phi) \propto \phi^{-(v_0/2)-1}\exp(-s_0/(2\phi))$. (2) An inverse Wishart distribution prior is used for Ψ. With hyper-parameters m_0 and $\mathbf{V}_0$, $\Psi \sim IW(m_0, \mathbf{V}_0)$, where m_0 is a scalar and $\mathbf{V}_0$ is a $q \times q$ matrix. Its density function is $p(\Psi) \propto |\Psi|^{-(m_0+q+1)/2}\exp[-\mathrm{tr}(\mathbf{V}_0\Psi^{-1})/2]$. (3) For β a multivariate normal prior is used, and $\beta \sim MN_q(\beta_0, \Sigma_0)$ where the hyper-parameter β_0 is a q-dimensional vector and Σ_0 is a $q \times q$ matrix. (4) The prior for γ_t $(t = 1, 2, \ldots, T)$ is chosen to be a multivariate normal distribution $\gamma_t \sim MN_{(2+r)}(\gamma_{t0}, \mathbf{D}_{t0})$, where γ_{t0} is a $(2+r)$-dimensional vector, $\mathbf{D}_{t0}$ is a $(2+r) \times (2+r)$ matrix, and both are pre-determined hyper-parameters.

After constructing the likelihood function and assigning the priors, the joint posterior distribution for unknown parameters is readily available. Considering the high-dimensional integration for marginal distributions of parameters, the conditional distribution for each parameter is obtained instead. The derived conditional posteriors are provided by the equations for parameters in the Appendix. In addition, the conditional posteriors for the latent variable η_i and the augmented missing data $\mathbf{y}_i^{mis}$ $(i = 1, 2, \ldots, N)$ are also provided by their corresponding equations in the Appendix.

After obtaining conditional posteriors, the Markov chain for each model parameter is generated by implementing a Gibbs sampling algorithm (Geman and Geman 1984). Specifically, suppose $\theta = (\theta_1, \theta_2, \ldots, \theta_M)$ is a vector of model parameters, latent variables, and missing values. We start with a set of initial values for θs. At the sth iteration, $\theta^{(s)}$ is generated. To obtain $\theta^{(s+1)}$, each $\theta^{(s+1)}$ is generated from its corresponding posterior distribution, derived in the Appendix, with renewed parameters.

3.3 Statistical Inference

After passing convergence tests, the generated Markov chains can be viewed as from the joint and marginal distributions of all parameters. The statistical inference can then be conducted based on the generated Markov chains.

For different loss functions of θ, the point estimates are different. For example, if a square loss function, $LF = (\theta - \hat{\theta})^2$, is used, then the posterior mean is the estimate of θ; but if an absolute loss function, $LF = |\theta - \hat{\theta}|$, is used, then its estimate is the posterior median. There are other function forms, such as 0–1 loss function, but in this research we take the square loss function.

Let $\theta = (\theta_1, \theta_2, \ldots, \theta_p)'$ denote a vector of all the unknown parameters in the model. Then the converged Markov chains can be recorded as $\theta^{(s)}, s = 1, 2, \ldots, S$, and each parameter estimate $\widehat{\theta}_j$ $(j = 1, 2, \ldots, p)$ can be calculated as $\widehat{\theta}_j = \Sigma_{s=1}^{S} \theta_j^{(s)}/S$ with standard error (SE) $s.e.(\widehat{\theta}_j) = \sqrt{\Sigma_{s=1}^{S}(\theta_j^{(s)} - \widehat{\theta}_j)^2/(S-1)}$. To get the credible (confidence) intervals, both percentile intervals and the highest posterior density intervals (HPD, Box and Tiao 1973) of the Markov chains can be used. Percentile intervals are obtained by sorting $\theta_j^{(s)}$. HPD intervals may also be referred to as minimum length confidence intervals for a Bayesian posterior distribution, and for symmetric distributions HPD intervals obtain equal tail area probabilities.

4 Model Selection Criteria

Model selection criteria play an important role in comparing competing models. In this section, Bayesian model selection criteria are proposed for latent growth models with missing data.

The general mathematical forms of selection criteria are closely related to each other. Almost all of them try to find a balance between the accuracy and the complexity of a model. First, the accuracy of a model can be measured by deviance, which is defined as $D(\theta) = -2log(p(\mathbf{y}|\theta)) + C$ for some constant C. In a Bayesian context, the most popular way to calculate the deviance is to plug the expectation of θ. So we have $D(\hat{\theta}) = -2log(p(\mathbf{y}|E_{\theta|\mathbf{y}}[\theta])) + C$, which can be estimated by $D(\hat{\theta}) \approx -2log(p(\mathbf{y}|\hat{\theta})) + C$. For latent growth models with missing data, $D(\hat{\theta})$ can be calculated as

$$D(\hat{\theta}) = -2\sum_{i=1}^{N}\sum_{t=1}^{T}\left[(1-m_{it})l_{it}(y|\hat{\theta}) + l_{it}(m|\hat{\theta})\right] \tag{8}$$

in which m_{it} is the missing data indicator for individual i at occasion t, $\hat{\theta}$ is the posterior mean of parameter estimates across S converged Markov iterations, and $l_{it}^{(s)}(y)$ and $l_{it}^{(s)}(m)$ are the conditional likelihood functions of y_{it} and m_{it}, respectively, for individual i at occasion t. When y_{it} is missing, $m_{it} = 1$, the likelihood of y_{it} is excluded. When y_{it} are normally distributed, the log-likelihood function is

$$l_{it}(y_N) = -\frac{1}{2}log(2\pi|\phi|) - \frac{(y_{it} - I_i - tS_i)^2}{2\phi}$$

Table 1 Model selection criteria

Criterion(Index) =	Deviance +	Penalty
Dhat.AIC	$D(\hat{\theta})$	2 p
Dhat.BIC	$D(\hat{\theta})$	log(N) p
Dhat.CAIC	$D(\hat{\theta})$	(log(N)+1) p
Dhat.ssBIC	$D(\hat{\theta})$	log((N+2)/24) p
DIC	$D(\hat{\theta})$	$2(\overline{D(\theta)} - D(\hat{\theta}))$
rough DIC	$\overline{D(\theta)}$	var($D(\theta)$)/2

where I_i and S_i are obtained from the random effect model. For the missing data indicator m_{it}, the log-likelihood function is

$$l_{it}(m) = m_{it} log(\tau_{it}) + (1 - m_{it}) log(1 - \tau_{it}),$$

where τ_{it} varies for different missingness models.

The second part of a criterion is the complexity of a model, which is also called a penalty term. For AIC, the penalty is $2p$, where p is the number of model parameters. As the penalty of AIC is sometimes considered to be too lenient in that it selects saturated models in large samples (e.g., Janssen and De Boeck 1999), BIC uses $log(N)p$ as the penalty, where N is the sample size. CAIC is another improved version of AIC. Compared with BIC, CAIC adds an extra p in penalty, which makes CAIC favor smaller models slightly more than BIC. Also, ssBIC improves BIC. The penalty in ssBIC is $log((N+2)/24)\,p$. For DIC, the penalty takes the difference between $E_{\theta|y}[D]$ and $D(E_{\theta|y}[\theta])$, where $E_{\theta|y}[D] = E_{\theta|\mathbf{y}}[-2log(p(\mathbf{y}|\theta))] + C$ is a Monte Carlo estimation of the expectation deviance and can be estimated as the posterior mean across the converged Markov chain,

$$\overline{D(\theta)} = -\frac{2}{S}\sum_{s=1}^{S}\sum_{i=1}^{N}\sum_{1=t}^{T}\left[(1 - m_{it}) l_{it}^{(s)}(y) + l_{it}^{(s)}(m)\right]. \tag{9}$$

In DIC, $pD = E_{\theta|y}[D] - D(E_{\theta|y}[\theta])$ is a measure of the effective model parameters or the complexity of the model, and it is approximated by $pD = \overline{D(\theta)} - D(\hat{\theta})$. In practice, rough DIC (RDIC, sometimes called DICV in some literature, e.g., Oldmeadow and Keith 2011) is an approximation of formal DIC (e.g., Sturtz et al. 2005). It takes $\overline{D(\theta)}$ as its deviance and $pV = Var(D(\theta))/2$ as its penalty.

In summary, the model selection criteria for latent growth models with missing data in this study are listed in Table 1.

5 Simulation Studies

In this section, simulation studies are conducted to evaluate the performance of the proposed latent growth models and the model selection criteria in a Bayesian context.

5.1 Simulation Design and Implementation

In the simulation we focus on linear LGCMs to simplify the presentation. Higher order LGCMs can be easily expanded by adding quadratic or higher order terms.

First, four waves of complete LGCM data $\mathbf{y}_i$ are generated based on Eqs. (1) and (2). The random effects consist of the intercept I_i and the slope S_i, with $Var(I_i) = 1$, $Var(S_i) = 4$, and $Cov(I_i, S_i) = 0$. The fix-effects are (I,S) $= (1,3)$. The measurement errors are assumed to follow a normal distribution with mean 0 and standard deviation 1. In the simulation we also assume there is one covariate X generated from a normal distribution, $X \sim N(1, sd = 0.2)$. Missing data are created based on different pre-designed missingness rates. We assume the true missingness is LSD (also noted as the XS missingness in this study because the missingness depends on the latent individual slope S and covariate X). With LSD, the bigger the slope is, the more the missing data. For the sake of simplicity in the simulation, the missingness rate is set the same for every occasion. Specifically, we set the missingness probit coefficients as $\gamma_0 = (-1,-1,-1,-1)$, $\gamma_x = (-1.5,-1.5,-1.5,-1.5)$, and $\gamma_S = (0.5,0.5,0.5,0.5)$. With the setting, missingness rates are generated based on Eq. (5). If a participant has a latent growth slope 3, with a covariate value 1, his or her missingness rate at each wave is $\tau \approx 16\%$; and if the slope is 5, with the same covariate value, the missing rate increases to $\tau \approx 50\%$; but when the slope is 1, the missingness rate decreases to $\tau \approx 2.3\%$.

Next, we fit data with LGCMs with different missingness. Specifically, the model design with different missingness is shown in Table 2, where the symbol "✓" shows the related factors on which the missing data rates depend. For example, when both "X" and "I" are checked, the missingness depends on the individual's latent intercept "I" and the observed covariate "X." Four types of missingness are studied: LID (also noted as XI in Table 2), LSD (XS), LOD (XY), and ignorable (X). The shaded model, LSD (XS), is the true model we used for generating the simulation data. Five levels of sample size (N = 1,000, N = 500, N = 300, N = 200 and N = 100) are investigated, and for each sample size, 100 converged replications are analyzed and summarized.

The simulation studies are implemented by the following algorithm. (1) Set the counter $R = 0$. (2) Generate complete longitudinal growth data according to predefined model parameters. (3) Create missing data according to missing data mechanisms and missing data rates. (4) Generate Markov chains for model parameters through the Gibbs sampling procedure. (5) Test the convergence of

Table 2 Model design in the simulation study

LGCM: N = 1000, 500, 300, 200 and 100				
	Missingness			
Model	X[2]	I[3]	S[4]	Y[5]
Ignorable (X)	√			
LID (XI)	√	√		
LSD (XS)[1]	√		√	
LOD (XY)	√			√

[1] The shaded model is the true model.
[2] Observed covariates.
[3] Individual latent intercept. If checked, the missingness is non-ignorable.
[4] Individual latent slope. If checked, the missingness is non-ignorable.
[5] Individual potential outcome y. If checked, the missingness is non-ignorable.

generated Markov chains. (6) If the Markov chains pass the convergence test, set $R = R + 1$ and calculate and save the parameter estimates. Otherwise, set $R = R$ and discard the current replication of simulation. (7) Repeat the above process till $R = 100$ to obtain 100 replications of valid simulation.

In step 4, priors carrying little prior information are adopted (Zhang et al. 2007). Specifically, for φ_1, we set $\mu_{\varphi_1} = \mathbf{0}_2$ and $\Sigma_{\varphi_1} = 10^3\mathbf{I}_2$. For ϕ, we set $v_{0k} = s_{0k} = 0.002$. For β, it is assumed that $\beta_{k0} = \mathbf{0}_2$ and $\Sigma_{k0} = 10^3\mathbf{I}_2$. For Ψ, we define $m_{k0} = 2$ and $\mathbf{V}_{k0} = \mathbf{I}_2$. Finally, for γ_t, we let $\gamma_{t0} = \mathbf{0}_3$ and $\mathbf{D}_{t0} = 10^3\mathbf{I}_3$, where $\mathbf{0}_d$ and $\mathbf{I}_d$ denote a d-dimensional zero vector and a d-dimensional identity matrix, respectively. In step 5, the iteration number of burn-in period is set. The Geweke convergence criterion indicated that less than 10,000 iterations were adequate for all conditions in the study. Therefore, a conservative burn-in of 20,000 iterations was used for all iterations. And then the Markov chains with a length of 20,000 iterations are saved for convergence testing and data analysis. After step 7, twelve summary statistics are reported based on 100 sets of converged simulation replications. For the purpose of presentation, let θ_j represent the jth parameter, also the true value in the simulation. The twelve statistics are defined below. (1) The average estimate (est.$_j$) across 100 converged simulation replications of each parameter is obtained as est.$_j = \bar{\hat{\theta}}_j = \sum_{i=1}^{100} \hat{\theta}_{ij}/100$, where $\hat{\theta}_{ij}$ denotes the estimate of θ_j in the ith simulation replication. (2) The simple bias (BIAS.smp$_j$) of each parameter is calculated as BIAS.smp$_j = \bar{\hat{\theta}}_j - \theta_j$. (3) The relative bias (BIAS.rel$_j$) of each parameter is calculated using BIAS.rel$_j = (\bar{\hat{\theta}}_j - \theta_j)/\theta_j$ when $\theta_j \neq 0$ and BIAS.rel$_j = \bar{\hat{\theta}}_j - \theta_j$ when $\theta_j = 0$. (4) The empirical standard error (SE.emp$_j$) of each parameter is obtained as SE.emp$_j = \sqrt{\sum_{i=1}^{100}(\hat{\theta}_{ij} - \bar{\hat{\theta}}_j)^2/99}$. (5) The average standard error (SE.avg$_j$) is calculated by SE.avg$_j = \sum_{i=1}^{100} \hat{s}_{ij}/100$, where $\hat{s}_{ij}$ denotes the estimated standard error of $\hat{\theta}_{ij}$. (6) The average mean square error (MSE) of each parameter is obtained by $\text{MSE}_j = \Sigma_{i=1}^{100} \text{MSE}_{ij}/100$, where MSE_{ij} is the mean square error for the jth parameter in the ith simulation replication, $\text{MSE}_{ij} = (\text{Bias}_{ij})^2 + (\hat{s}_{ij})^2$. (7) The average lower and (8) upper limits of the 95% percentile confidence interval (CI.low_j and CI.upper_j) are, respectively, defined as $\text{CI.low}_j = \Sigma_{i=1}^{100} \hat{\theta}_{ij}^{l}/100$, and $\text{CI.upper}_j = \Sigma_{i=1}^{100} \hat{\theta}_{ij}^{u}/100$ where $\hat{\theta}_{ij}^{l}$ and $\hat{\theta}_{ij}^{u}$ denote the 95% lower and upper limits of CI for the jth parameter, respectively. (9) The coverage probability of the 95% percentile confidence interval (CI.cover_j) of each parameter is obtained using $\text{CI.cover}_j = [\#(\hat{\theta}_{ij}^{l} \leq \theta_j \leq \hat{\theta}_{ij}^{u})]/100$. (10) The average lower, (11) upper limits, and (12) the coverage probability of the 95% highest posterior density credible interval (HPD, Box and Tiao 1973) of each parameter are similarly defined by HPD.low_j, HPD.upper_j, and HPD.cover_j, respectively.

5.2 *Simulation Results*

In this section, we show simulation results for the estimates obtained from the true model and mis-specified models, and the performance of model selection criteria.

First, we investigate the estimates obtained from the true model. Tables 3 and 4 show the summarized estimates for different sample sizes (N = 1,000, N = 500, N = 300, N = 200, and N = 100). From both tables, except for the small sample size N = 100, one can see that (1) all the estimate biases are very small; (2) the difference between the empirical SEs and the average SEs is very small, which indicates the SEs are estimated accurately; (3) both percentile interval and HPD interval coverage probabilities are very close to the theoretical percentage 95%, which means the type I error for each parameter is close to the specified 5% so that we can use the estimated confidence intervals to conduct statistical inference; and (4) this true model has 100% convergence rate.

In order to conveniently compare estimates for different sample sizes, we further summarize Tables 3 and 4 by calculating five summary statistics across all parameters, which are shown in Table 5. The first statistic is the average absolute relative biases (|Bias.rel|) across all parameters, which is defined as $|\text{Bias.rel}| = \Sigma_{j=1}^{p} |\text{Bias.rel}_j|/p$, where p is the total number of parameters in a model. Second, we obtain the average absolute differences between the empirical SEs and the average Bayesian SEs (|SE.diff|) across all parameters by using $|\text{SE.diff}| = \Sigma_{j=1}^{p} |\text{SE.emp}_j - \text{SE.avg}_j|/p$. Third, we calculate the average percentile coverage probabilities (CI.cover) across all parameters by using $\text{CI.cover} = \Sigma_{j=1}^{p} \text{CI.cover}_j/p$. Fourth, we calculate the average HPD coverage probabilities (HPD.cover) across all parameters by using $\text{HPD.cover} = \Sigma_{j=1}^{p} \text{HPD.cover}_j/p$. Fifth, the convergence rate for the study is calculated.

Table 5 shows that, except for the case for N = 100, the true mode can recover model parameters very well, by checking (1) the small average absolute relative biases of estimates, |Bias.rel|, (2) the small average absolute differences between the empirical SEs and the average SEs, |SE.diff|, and (3) the almost 95%

Table 3 Summarized estimates of the true models with LSD (XS) missingness

					BIAS		SE			95% percentile CI			95% HPD interval		
		Parameter	True	est.[a]	smp.[b]	rel.[c]	emp.[d]	avg.[e]	MSE[f]	Lower	Upper	Cover	Lower	Upper	Cover
N = 1,000, Summarized based on 100 converged replications with a convergence rate of 100/100 = 100%.															
Growth curve		I	1	0.998	−0.002	−0.002	0.05	0.053	0.005	0.894	1.101	0.99	0.894	1.101	0.98
		S	3	3.003	0.003	0.001	0.079	0.077	0.012	2.853	3.155	0.97	2.853	3.154	0.96
		var(I)	1	1.011	0.011	0.011	0.105	0.102	0.022	0.82	1.22	0.94	0.814	1.213	0.94
		var(S)	4	3.99	−0.01	−0.003	0.232	0.232	0.107	3.56	4.468	0.94	3.545	4.449	0.93
		cov(IS)	0	0.001	0.001	0.001	0.119	0.112	0.026	−0.221	0.217	0.94	−0.218	0.218	0.94
		var(e)	1	1	0	0	0.043	0.042	0.004	0.92	1.086	0.92	0.918	1.084	0.93
Missingness parameters	Wave 1	γ_{01}	−1	−1.025	−0.025	0.025	0.184	0.174	0.065	−1.375	−0.694	0.93	−1.365	−0.69	0.94
		γ_{x1}	−1.5	−1.541	−0.041	0.027	0.138	0.123	0.036	−1.795	−1.314	0.92	−1.783	−1.307	0.93
		γ_{S1}	0.5	0.515	0.015	0.03	0.066	0.062	0.008	0.4	0.641	0.9	0.397	0.636	0.92
	Wave 2	γ_{02}	−1	−1.038	−0.038	0.038	0.191	0.171	0.067	−1.385	−0.714	0.96	−1.376	−0.711	0.97
		γ_{x2}	−1.5	−1.551	−0.051	0.034	0.129	0.119	0.034	−1.798	−1.33	0.95	−1.786	−1.323	0.94
		γ_{S2}	0.5	0.521	0.021	0.042	0.066	0.06	0.008	0.41	0.643	0.95	0.408	0.639	0.94
	Wave 3	γ_{03}	−1	−1.067	−0.067	0.067	0.186	0.172	0.069	−1.417	−0.741	0.94	−1.407	−0.737	0.94
		γ_{x3}	−1.5	−1.557	−0.057	0.038	0.117	0.116	0.03	−1.796	−1.341	0.97	−1.785	−1.334	0.97
		γ_{S3}	0.5	0.529	0.029	0.058	0.063	0.058	0.008	0.42	0.648	0.89	0.418	0.643	0.91
	Wave 4	γ_{04}	−1	−1.034	−0.034	0.034	0.18	0.173	0.063	−1.384	−0.709	0.94	−1.374	−0.704	0.93
		γ_{x4}	−1.5	−1.539	−0.039	0.026	0.122	0.114	0.029	−1.773	−1.325	0.95	−1.763	−1.319	0.94
		γ_{S4}	0.5	0.514	0.014	0.027	0.058	0.057	0.007	0.407	0.63	0.95	0.405	0.625	0.95

(continued)

Table 3 (continued)

N = 500, Summarized based on 100 converged replications with a convergence rate of 100/100 = 100%.

Growth curve		I	1	0.986	−0.014	−0.014	0.076	0.074	0.011	0.841	1.132	0.93	0.841	1.132	0.95
		S	3	3.001	0.001	0	0.097	0.109	0.021	2.789	3.216	0.97	2.788	3.213	0.97
		var(I)	1	0.976	−0.024	−0.024	0.146	0.144	0.042	0.712	1.274	0.97	0.7	1.26	0.97
		var(S)	4	4.001	0.001	0	0.388	0.329	0.258	3.403	4.691	0.9	3.373	4.652	0.9
		cov(IS)	0	−0.009	−0.009	−0.009	0.155	0.157	0.049	−0.324	0.294	0.96	−0.319	0.297	0.96
		var(e)	1	1.014	0.014	0.014	0.06	0.061	0.007	0.901	1.141	0.96	0.897	1.136	0.96
Missingness parameters	Wave 1	γ_{01}	−1	−1.082	−0.082	0.082	0.254	0.255	0.137	−1.609	−0.608	0.95	−1.587	−0.596	0.97
		γ_{x1}	−1.5	−1.606	−0.106	0.071	0.181	0.186	0.079	−2.002	−1.275	0.95	−1.975	−1.258	0.97
		γ_{S1}	0.5	0.54	0.04	0.081	0.083	0.092	0.017	0.375	0.735	0.95	0.368	0.722	0.94
	Wave 2	γ_{02}	−1	−1.096	−0.096	0.096	0.281	0.252	0.152	−1.61	−0.624	0.89	−1.591	−0.615	0.89
		γ_{x2}	−1.5	−1.615	−0.115	0.077	0.204	0.18	0.088	−1.996	−1.291	0.91	−1.971	−1.275	0.94
		γ_{S2}	0.5	0.546	0.046	0.092	0.104	0.088	0.021	0.385	0.73	0.87	0.379	0.719	0.88
	Wave 3	γ_{03}	−1	−1.068	−0.068	0.068	0.32	0.248	0.169	−1.572	−0.602	0.93	−1.555	−0.594	0.93
		γ_{x3}	−1.5	−1.613	−0.113	0.075	0.279	0.174	0.123	−1.978	−1.295	0.9	−1.958	−1.283	0.93
		γ_{S3}	0.5	0.536	0.036	0.072	0.116	0.084	0.022	0.381	0.71	0.92	0.378	0.702	0.91
	Wave 4	γ_{04}	−1	−1.123	−0.123	0.123	0.261	0.257	0.15	−1.652	−0.647	0.94	−1.628	−0.633	0.95
		γ_{x4}	−1.5	−1.579	−0.079	0.053	0.174	0.168	0.066	−1.933	−1.274	0.95	−1.913	−1.261	0.96
		γ_{S4}	0.5	0.543	0.043	0.086	0.089	0.085	0.017	0.388	0.719	0.92	0.382	0.71	0.92

N = 300, Summarized based on 100 converged replications with a convergence rate of 100/100 = 100%.

Growth curve		I	1	1.001	0.001	0.001	0.104	0.097	0.02	0.81	1.192	0.89	0.811	1.192	0.89
		S	3	2.984	−0.016	−0.005	0.149	0.14	0.042	2.712	3.262	0.93	2.71	3.259	0.93
		var(I)	1	1.014	0.014	0.014	0.183	0.19	0.07	0.673	1.418	0.96	0.654	1.392	0.96
		var(S)	4	3.975	−0.025	−0.006	0.416	0.425	0.354	3.22	4.886	0.96	3.174	4.82	0.96
		cov(IS)	0	0.054	0.054	0.054	0.212	0.205	0.09	−0.359	0.449	0.94	−0.351	0.454	0.93
		var(e)	1	1.011	0.011	0.011	0.073	0.08	0.012	0.867	1.179	0.96	0.86	1.17	0.96

Missingness parameters	Wave 1	γ_{01}	−1	−1.094	−0.094	0.094	0.341	0.345	0.249	−1.822	−0.468	0.97	−1.778	−0.441	0.97
		γ_{x1}	−1.5	−1.65	−0.15	0.1	0.265	0.253	0.162	−2.209	−1.217	0.92	−2.155	−1.185	0.94
		γ_{S1}	0.5	0.548	0.048	0.097	0.121	0.124	0.033	0.331	0.82	0.97	0.318	0.794	0.97
	Wave 2	γ_{02}	−1	−1.106	−0.106	0.106	0.452	0.34	0.341	−1.819	−0.486	0.93	−1.782	−0.467	0.93
		γ_{x2}	−1.5	−1.692	−0.192	0.128	0.345	0.253	0.23	−2.243	−1.254	0.89	−2.196	−1.227	0.90
		γ_{S2}	0.5	0.566	0.066	0.132	0.158	0.121	0.046	0.354	0.827	0.93	0.343	0.807	0.92
	Wave 3	γ_{03}	−1	−1.139	−0.139	0.139	0.397	0.335	0.293	−1.845	−0.527	0.91	−1.801	−0.503	0.92
		γ_{x3}	−1.5	−1.648	−0.148	0.099	0.305	0.236	0.175	−2.152	−1.233	0.86	−2.115	−1.21	0.92
		γ_{S3}	0.5	0.566	0.066	0.132	0.141	0.115	0.038	0.361	0.811	0.9	0.352	0.794	0.91
	Wave 4	γ_{04}	−1	−1.217	−0.217	0.217	0.411	0.356	0.347	−1.976	−0.576	0.9	−1.932	−0.552	0.90
		γ_{x4}	−1.5	−1.681	−0.181	0.121	0.263	0.241	0.163	−2.203	−1.257	0.9	−2.161	−1.231	0.92
		γ_{S4}	0.5	0.583	0.083	0.165	0.138	0.118	0.041	0.372	0.839	0.88	0.363	0.82	0.91

[a] The parameter estimate, defined by $\text{est.}_j = \bar{\hat{\theta}}_j = \sum_{i=1}^{100} \hat{\theta}_{ij}/100$

[b] The simple bias, defined by $\text{BIAS.smp}_j = \bar{\hat{\theta}}_j - \theta_j$

[c] The relative bias, defined by $\text{BIAS.rel}_j = (\bar{\hat{\theta}}_j - \theta_j)/\theta_j$ when $\theta_j \neq 0$ and $\text{BIAS.rel}_j = \bar{\hat{\theta}}_j - \theta_j$ when $\theta_j = 0$

[d] The empirical standard errors, defined by $\text{SE.emp}_j = \sqrt{\sum_{i=1}^{100}(\hat{\theta}_{ij} - \bar{\hat{\theta}}_j)^2/99}$

[e] The average standard errors, defined by $\text{SE.avg}_j = \sum_{i=1}^{100} \hat{s}_{ij}/100$

[f] The mean square error, defined by $\text{MSE}_j = \sum_{i=1}^{100} \text{MSE}_{ij}/100$, where $\text{MSE}_{ij} = (\text{Bias}_{ij})^2 + (\hat{s}_{ij})^2$

Table 4 Summarized estimates of the true models with LSD (XS) missingness (cont'd)

		Parameter	True	est.	BIAS smp.	BIAS rel.	SE emp.	SE avg.	MSE	95% percentile CI Lower	95% percentile CI Upper	95% percentile CI Cover	95% HPD interval Lower	95% HPD interval Upper	95% HPD interval Cover
N = 200, Summarized based on 100 converged replications with a convergence rate of 100/106 = 94.34%.															
Growth curve		I	1	1.011	0.011	0.011	0.099	0.119	0.024	0.779	1.244	0.98	0.779	1.243	0.98
		S	3	2.975	−0.025	−0.008	0.177	0.171	0.061	2.643	3.314	0.93	2.642	3.312	0.94
		var(I)	1	1.011	0.011	0.011	0.228	0.233	0.107	0.601	1.516	0.94	0.572	1.476	0.92
		var(S)	4	4	0	0	0.474	0.522	0.498	3.095	5.135	0.97	3.029	5.041	0.96
		cov(IS)	0	0.065	0.065	0.065	0.257	0.252	0.134	−0.447	0.549	0.92	−0.436	0.557	0.92
		var(e)	1	1.027	0.027	0.027	0.098	0.099	0.02	0.851	1.238	0.95	0.84	1.224	0.95
Missingness parameters	Wave 1	γ_{01}	−1	−1.3	−0.3	0.3	0.671	0.5	0.901	−2.399	−0.449	0.93	−2.306	−0.402	0.94
		γ_{x1}	−1.5	−1.874	−0.374	0.249	0.745	0.424	1.113	−2.868	−1.227	0.88	−2.735	−1.169	0.91
		γ_{S1}	0.5	0.647	0.147	0.293	0.323	0.197	0.202	0.334	1.1	0.91	0.311	1.045	0.92
	Wave 2	γ_{02}	−1	−1.278	−0.278	0.278	0.69	0.468	0.838	−2.303	−0.463	0.87	−2.227	−0.426	0.89
		γ_{x2}	−1.5	−1.779	−0.279	0.186	0.456	0.349	0.451	−2.578	−1.209	0.91	−2.487	−1.163	0.9
		γ_{S2}	0.5	0.627	0.127	0.254	0.244	0.171	0.117	0.343	1.014	0.9	0.324	0.976	0.91
	Wave 3	γ_{03}	−1	−1.191	−0.191	0.191	0.505	0.436	0.5	−2.133	−0.419	0.91	−2.05	−0.377	0.93
		γ_{x3}	−1.5	−1.721	−0.221	0.147	0.502	0.314	0.426	−2.428	−1.193	0.9	−2.348	−1.15	0.94
		γ_{S3}	0.5	0.586	0.086	0.172	0.183	0.152	0.068	0.326	0.926	0.91	0.309	0.889	0.95
	Wave 4	γ_{04}	−1	−1.27	−0.27	0.27	0.594	0.467	0.67	−2.304	−0.457	0.86	−2.209	−0.404	0.90
		γ_{x4}	−1.5	−1.808	−0.308	0.205	0.397	0.336	0.382	−2.56	−1.24	0.82	−2.48	−1.195	0.89
		γ_{S4}	0.5	0.618	0.118	0.236	0.204	0.16	0.085	0.345	0.98	0.88	0.325	0.942	0.89

N = 100, Summarized based on 100 converged replications with a convergence rate of 100/142 = 70.42%.																
Growth curve		I	1	1.031	0.031	0.031	0.167	0.168	0.057	0.701	1.359	0.96	0.701	1.359	0.97
		S	3	2.983	−0.017	−0.006	0.236	0.242	0.115	2.514	3.467	0.95	2.51	3.46	0.94
		var(I)	1	0.933	−0.067	−0.067	0.305	0.323	0.206	0.408	1.665	0.93	0.355	1.574	0.91
		var(S)	4	3.965	−0.035	−0.009	0.829	0.747	1.261	2.743	5.656	0.91	2.623	5.458	0.91
		cov(IS)	0	0.069	0.069	0.069	0.333	0.357	0.246	−0.666	0.748	0.93	−0.646	0.762	0.95
		var(e)	1	1.078	0.078	0.078	0.157	0.151	0.054	0.82	1.409	0.93	0.801	1.38	0.94
Missingness parameters	Wave 1	γ_{01}	−1	−3.257	−2.257	2.257	5.794	1.333	42.792	−6.264	−1.131	0.84	−5.922	−1.018	0.86
		γ_{x1}	−1.5	−4.314	−2.814	1.876	7.492	1.277	69.337	−7.171	−2.396	0.8	−6.739	−2.251	0.85
		γ_{S1}	0.5	1.626	1.126	2.252	2.881	0.55	10.353	0.788	2.857	0.8	0.746	2.698	0.84
	Wave 2	γ_{02}	−1	−3.011	−2.011	2.011	5.719	1.322	41.711	−6.062	−1.027	0.85	−5.696	−0.893	0.88
		γ_{x2}	−1.5	−3.772	−2.272	1.515	6.947	1.283	61.237	−6.811	−1.927	0.82	−6.385	−1.774	0.85
		γ_{S2}	0.5	1.436	0.936	1.871	2.57	0.549	8.564	0.653	2.71	0.81	0.586	2.527	0.86
	Wave 3	γ_{03}	−1	−2.877	−1.877	1.877	5.93	1.2	42.401	−5.493	−0.898	0.89	−5.233	−0.806	0.91
		γ_{x3}	−1.5	−3.86	−2.36	1.573	6.955	1.153	58.835	−6.508	−2.086	0.83	−6.125	−1.932	0.85
		γ_{S3}	0.5	1.388	0.888	1.776	2.567	0.467	7.977	0.641	2.428	0.85	0.596	2.289	0.89
	Wave 4	γ_{04}	−1	−2.831	−1.831	1.831	5.646	1.297	39.835	−5.902	−0.891	0.89	−5.522	−0.753	0.90
		γ_{x4}	−1.5	−3.386	−1.886	1.257	5.379	1.127	37.532	−6.048	−1.745	0.81	−5.622	−1.586	0.88
		γ_{S4}	0.5	1.222	0.722	1.444	1.944	0.457	4.854	0.552	2.312	0.84	0.491	2.152	0.88

Note: Abbreviations are as given in Table 3

Table 5 Summary and comparison of simulation results of the true model

		$\lvert$Bias.rel$\rvert$[a]	$\lvert$SE.diff$\rvert$[b]	MSE[c]	CI.cover[d]	HPD.cover[e]	CVG.rate[f] (%)
	1,000	0.025	0.007	0.033	0.942	0.942	100
	500	0.052	0.021	0.079	0.932	0.939	100
N	300	0.089	0.031	0.150	0.922	0.930	100
	200	0.160	0.090	0.366	0.909	0.924	94.34
	100	1.202	2.664	23.743	0.869	0.893	70.42

[a]The average absolute relative bias across all parameters, defined by $|\text{Bias.rel}| = \sum_{j=1}^{p} |\text{Bias.rel}_j|/p$. The smaller, the better

[b]The average absolute difference between the empirical SEs and the average Bayesian SEs across all parameters, defined by $|\text{SE.diff}| = \sum_{j=1}^{p} |\text{SE.emp}_j - \text{SE.avg}_j|/p$. The smaller, the better

[c]The Mean Square Errors (MSE) across all parameters, defined by $MSE = \sum_{j=1}^{p} [(\text{Bias}_j)^2 + (\hat{s}_j)^2]/p$. The smaller, the better

[d]The average percentile coverage probability across all parameters, defined by $\text{CI.cover} = \sum_{j=1}^{p} \text{CI.cover}_j/p$, with a theoretical value of 0.95

[e]The average highest posterior density (HPD) coverage probability across all parameters, defined by $\text{HPD.cover} = \sum_{j=1}^{p} \text{HPD.cover}_j/p$, with a theoretical value of 0.95

[f]The convergence rate

average percentile coverage probabilities, CI.cover, and the average HPD coverage probabilities, HPD.cover. With the increase of the sample size, both the point estimates and standard errors get more accurate.

Second, we compare the estimates obtained from the true model and different mis-specified models. In this study the true model is the LGCM with LSD (XS) missingness, and there are three mis-specified models, the LGCM with LID (XI) missingness, the LGCM with LOD (XY) missingness, and the LGCM with ignorable missingness (see Table 2 for simulation design). The estimates from the mis-specified models, such as LID (XI) missingness, LOD (XY) missingness, and ignorable missingness, are also summarized, but not included in this paper due to limit space.

To compare estimates from different models, we further summarize and visualize some statistics. Figure 4a compares the point estimates of intercept and slope for all models when N = 1,000. The true value of slope is 3 but the estimate is 2.711 when the missingness is ignored. Actually, for the model with ignorable missingness, the slope estimates are all less than 2.711 for all sample sizes in our study. Figure 4b focuses on the coverage of slope. When the missingness is ignored, it is as low as 4% for N = 1,000, and 21% for N = 500 (the coverage for N = 1,000 is lower because the SE for N = 1,000 is smaller than the SE for N = 500). As a result, conclusions based on the model with ignorable missingness will be severely misleading. Figure 4b also shows that the slope estimate from the model with the mis-specified missingness, LID (XI), has low coverage, with 76% for N = 1,000 and 87% for N = 500. So the conclusions based on this model may still be incorrect. Figure 4c compares the true model and the model with another type of mis-specified missingness, LOD (XY) for N = 1,000. For the wrong model, the coverage is 51%

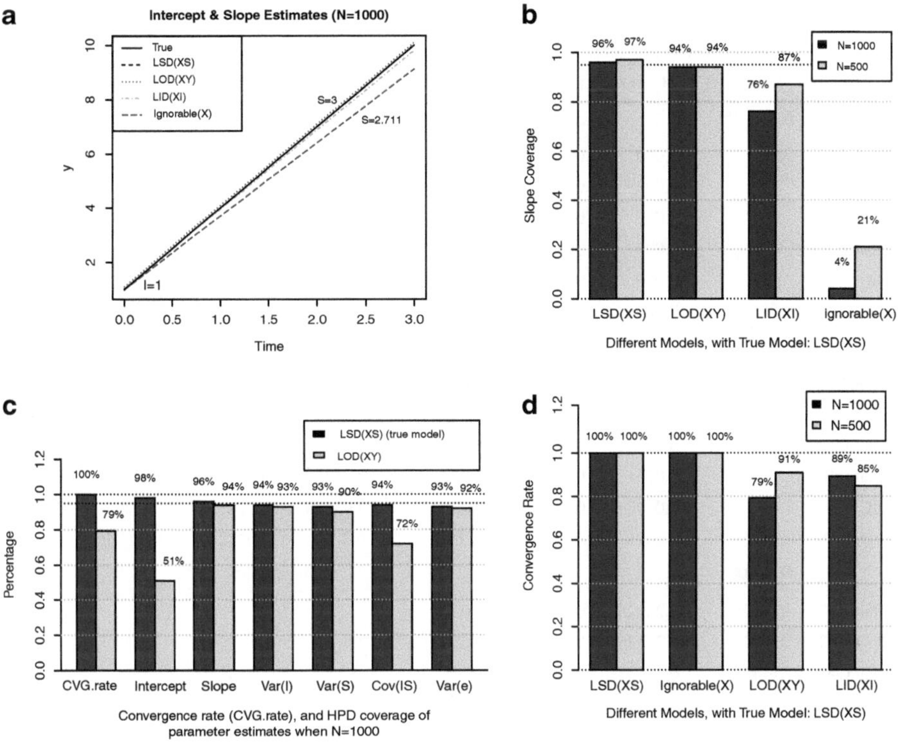

Fig. 4 Comparison of four models/missingness mechanisms. (**a**) Intercept and slope estimates for all models (True Int=1, True Slope=3), (**b**) Slope coverage for all models (Theoretical coverage=95%), (**c**) Parameter coverage for LSD(XS) and LOD (XY) (Theoretical value=95%), and (**d**) Convergence rates for all models (The closer to 100%, the better)

for intercept, and 72% for Cov(I,S). Finally, Fig. 4d compares the convergence rates for all models. One can see that the convergence rates of LOD (XY) and LID (XI) models are much lower than those of the true model LSD (XS) and the model with ignorable missingness. When the missingness is ignored, the number of parameters is smaller than that of non-ignorable models, and then convergence rate gets higher.

In summary, the estimates from mis-specified models may result in severely misleading conclusions, especially when the missingness is ignored. Also, the convergence rate of a mis-specified model is usually lower than that of the true model.

Third, regarding model selection, Table 6 lists the selection proportions across all replications. It shows that almost all the criteria, except for the rough DIC, can correctly identify the true model with high certainty.

Table 6 Model selection proportion

Criterion[1]	Non-ignorable missingness LSD (XS)[2]	LOD (XY)	LID (XI)	ignorable missingness	Non-ignorable missingness LSD (XS)	LOD (XY)	LID (XI)	ignorable missingness
	N = 1000				N = 500			
Dhat.AIC	1	0.000	0.000	0.000	1	0.000	0.000	0.000
Dhat.BIC	1	0.000	0.000	0.000	1	0.000	0.000	0.000
Dhat.CAIC	1	0.000	0.000	0.000	1	0.000	0.000	0.000
Dhat.ssBIC	1	0.000	0.000	0.000	1	0.000	0.000	0.000
DIC	1	0.000	0.000	0.000	1	0.000	0.000	0.000
Rough DIC	0.013	0.000	0.987	0.000	0.038	0.000	0.962	0.000
	N = 300				N = 200			
Dhat.AIC	0.95	0.05	0.000	0.000	0.9375	0.06875	0.000	0.000
Dhat.BIC	0.95	0.05	0.000	0.000	0.9375	0.06875	0.000	0.000
Dhat.CAIC	0.95	0.05	0.000	0.000	0.9375	0.06875	0.000	0.000
Dhat.ssBIC	0.95	0.05	0.000	0.000	0.9375	0.06875	0.000	0.000
DIC	1	0.000	0.000	0.000	0.98125	0.0125	0.00625	0.000
Rough DIC	0.1125	0.000	0.8875	0.000	0.2	0.03125	0.76875	0.000
	N = 100							
Dhat.AIC	0.7125	0.28125	0.00625	0.000				
Dhat.BIC	0.7125	0.28125	0.00625	0.000				
Dhat.CAIC	0.7125	0.28125	0.00625	0.000				
Dhat.ssBIC	70625	0.28125	0.00625	0.000				
DIC	0.70625	0.175	0.11875	0.000				
Rough DIC	0.1125	0.04375	0.84375	0.000				

[1] The definition of each criterion is given in Table 1.

[2] The shaded model is the true model.

[3] The shaded cell has the largest proportion. For each criterion, the sum of all proportions might be larger than 1 because models may have the same lowest index value.

5.3 Simulation Conclusions

Based on the simulation studies, we conclude as follows. (1) The proposed Bayesian method can accurately recover model parameters (both point estimates and standard errors). (2) The small difference between the empirical SE and the average SE indicates that the Bayesian method used in the study can estimate the standard errors accurately. (3) With the increase of the sample size, estimates get closer to their true values and standard errors become more accurate. (4) Ignoring the non-ignorable missingness can lead to severely incorrect conclusions. (5) Mis-specified missingness may also result in misleading conclusions. (6) Almost all the criteria, except for the rough DIC, can correctly identify the true model with high certainty. (7) The non-convergent model might be a sign of a wrong model.

6 Real Data Analysis

In this section, we illustrate the application of the Bayesian latent growth curve model with missing data through the analysis of mathematical ability growth data from the NLSY97 survey (Bureau of Labor Statistics, U.S. Department of Labor 1997). The data set available to us consisted of $N = 362$ youths who were administered the Peabody Individual Achievement Test (PIAT) Mathematics Assessment yearly from 1997, when they were 12 years old and in Grade 7, to 2000, when they were 15 years old and in Grade 10. Figure 5 plots the data, which shows the four measures of mathematical ability increased over time with a roughly linear trend.

Table 7 presents the summary statistics. The missing data rates range from 5.801% to 12.707%. Information on mothers' education (in years) was also included in the sample. In this analysis, we are interested to see how mathematical ability grew over the 4-year period, and if mothers' education influenced the missing data pattern.

First, for comparison purposes, we fit four models with different types of missingness, LSD, LID, LOD, and ignorable. For each model, the burn-in period for Gibbs sampling was generated long enough to make sure Markov chains for parameters converged. To test convergence, the history plot and Geweke test statistic

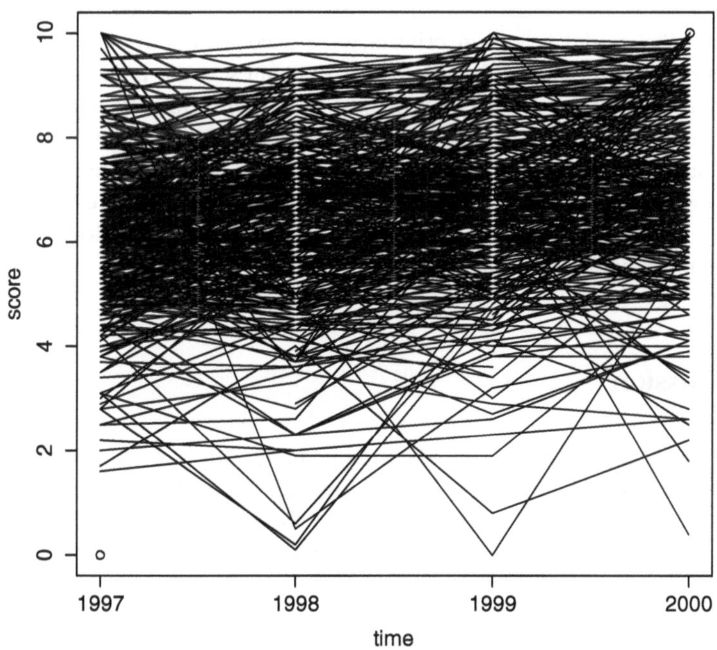

Fig. 5 Plot for the PIAT math data

Table 7 Summary statistics for the PIAT math data

	1997	1998	1999	2000
Mean	6.110	6.309	6.722	6.959
Standard deviation	1.560	1.698	1.679	1.770
Missing data (count)	22	21	39	46
Missing data rate (%)	6.077	5.801	10.773	12.707

for each unknown model parameter were examined. Except for the LID model, all the other three models converged. Table 8 shows the Geweke test statistics for all the model parameters are smaller than 1.96, which indicates the convergence of Markov chains (Geweke 1992). The next 90,000 iterations are then saved for data analysis. The results of the three models are provided in Table 8. In the table, the ratio of Monte Carlo error (MC error) and standard deviation (SD) for each parameter is around or smaller than 0.05, which indicates parameter estimates are accurate (Spiegelhalter et al. 2003). MC error is an important statistic providing a measure of the variability of each parameter estimate in the MCMC chain. The lower the MC error, the more precise the parameter estimate. Overall, we conclude that the results from the real data analysis can be used for further inference. A quick look at the results from the three models shows that the growth parameters do not differ much, even for the model with ignorable missingness. This is due to the low missing data rates for our data set. However, for missingness parameters, different missingness models have different results which, in turn, leads to different interpretations of the data.

Second, the model selection criteria were used to identify the best-fit model. Table 9 shows all the available indices. As one can see, the LSD model is favored by all the criteria. The results from the best-fit model, LSD, reveal that (1) none of γ_{xt}s, the coefficients for the covariate, are significant at the α level of 0.05, which implies that the missingness is not related to mothers' education level; however, (2) the missingness is significantly negatively correlated with the latent slope in 1999 and 2000, which implies that in these 2 years the youth with a low mathematical growth is more likely to miss a test.

7 Discussion

Latent growth curve models are becoming increasingly complex and with this comes an increase in concerns about estimating these models. In this study, we examined several growth models designed to address problems common to almost all longitudinal research, namely, that of missing data. Three new non-ignorable missingness mechanisms were considered: latent intercept missingness, latent slope missingness, and outcome-dependent missingness. A fully Bayesian approach was implemented using data augmentation and Gibbs sampling to estimate these models in the presence of the three types of non-ignorable missingness. Simulation results

Table 8 Estimates from different models in real data analysis

			Mean	S.D.[1]	MCs.e./S.D.[2]	Lower[2.5%]	Upper[97.5%]	Geweke t[3]
			Model with LSD (XS) missingness [4]					
Growth Curve	Parameters	Intercept	6.060 [5]	0.083	0.001	5.895	6.223	−0.718
		Slope	0.288	0.030	$7.3E-4$	0.230	0.348	0.170
		Var(I)	1.697	0.171	0.002	1.387	2.057	0.928
		Var(S)	0.078	0.020	$7.4E-4$	0.046	0.121	−1.280
		Cov(I,S)	−0.039	0.038	$8.7E-4$	−0.120	0.031	−0.199
		Var(e)	1.011	0.054	0.001	0.909	1.121	1.734
Missingness Parameters	1997	γ_{01}	−2.574	0.625	0.033	−3.847	−1.450	−1.448
		γ_{x1}	0.081	0.046	0.002	−0.004	0.175	1.512
		γ_{S1}	−0.089	0.840	0.030	−1.797	1.550	0.205
	1998	γ_{02}	−1.656	0.516	0.025	−2.681	−0.636	−0.162
		γ_{x2}	0.022	0.039	0.002	−0.054	0.103	0.313
		γ_{S2}	−0.926	0.796	0.025	−2.613	0.526	−0.989
	1999	γ_{03}	−1.710	0.695	0.039	−3.164	−0.407	1.387
		γ_{x3}	0.083	0.054	0.003	−0.020	0.195	−1.146
		γ_{S3}	−4.332	2.878	0.073	−12.457	−1.170	−1.201
	2000	γ_{04}	−0.875	0.482	0.025	−1.823	0.021	0.484
		γ_{x4}	0.009	0.037	0.002	−0.061	0.085	−0.230
		γ_{S4}	−1.838	0.920	0.032	−3.967	−0.319	−1.258
			Model with LOD (XY) missingness					
Growth Curve	Parameters	Intercept	6.002	0.084	$8.8E-4$	5.838	6.167	0.315
		Slope	0.333	0.032	$6.0E-4$	0.271	0.396	0.205
		Var(I)	1.738	0.187	0.002	1.396	2.128	0.035
		Var(S)	0.103	0.022	$3.2E-4$	0.064	0.150	0.437
		Cov(I,S)	−0.057	0.050	$6.6E-4$	−0.161	0.036	0.243
		Var(e)	0.972	0.053	$4.7E-4$	0.873	1.080	−1.124
Missingness Parameters	1997	γ_{01}	−0.986	0.760	0.041	−2.491	0.539	0.204
		γ_{x1}	0.102	0.052	0.003	0.005	0.211	−0.466
		γ_{Y1}	−0.345	0.117	0.006	−0.591	−0.133	0.201
	1998	γ_{02}	−1.794	0.681	0.036	-3.213	−0.543	−0.162
		γ_{x2}	0.026	0.040	0.002	−0.053	0.104	−0.593
		γ_{Y2}	−0.019	0.082	0.004	−0.178	0.145	0.902
	1999	γ_{03}	−1.258	0.586	0.031	−2.344	−0.034	−1.477
		γ_{x3}	0.050	0.038	0.001	−0.024	0.124	1.272
		γ_{Y3}	−0.092	0.069	0.003	−0.230	0.045	0.804
	2000	γ_{04}	−1.638	0.606	0.033	-2.740	−0.371	−0.142
		γ_{x4}	4.4E-4	0.032	0.002	−0.060	0.064	−0.464
		γ_{Y4}	0.067	0.070	0.004	−0.076	0.187	0.529
			Model with ignorable (X) missingness					
Growth Curve	Parameters	Intercept	6.051	0.082	$4.7E-4$	5.890	6.210	1.303
		Slope	0.311	0.030	$2.5E-4$	0.252	0.369	−1.376
		Var(I)	1.683	0.183	0.001	1.349	2.064	1.431
		Var(S)	0.100	0.021	$3.0E-4$	0.062	0.145	1.052
		Cov(I,S)	−0.043	0.049	$5.7E-4$	−0.144	0.049	−1.945
		Var(e)	0.966	0.052	$3.8E-4$	0.869	1.072	−1.446

(continued)

Table 8 (continued)

Missingness Parameters	1997	γ_{01}	−2.554	0.553	0.029	−3.640	−1.433	−0.254
		γ_{x1}	0.080	0.043	0.002	−0.007	0.163	0.305
	1998	γ_{02}	−1.906	0.541	0.028	−2.963	−0.869	−0.282
		γ_{x2}	0.026	0.043	0.002	−0.058	0.109	0.294
	1999	γ_{03}	−1.784	0.420	0.021	−2.598	−0.978	−0.394
		γ_{x3}	0.044	0.033	0.002	−0.021	0.109	0.389
	2000	γ_{04}	−1.189	0.381	0.019	−1.914	−0.463	−0.287
		γ_{x4}	0.004	0.031	0.002	−0.056	0.061	0.281

Note:
Standard deviation.
Ratio of MC error to standard deviation. A value around or less than 0.05 indicates that the corresponding estimate is accurate (Spiegelhalter et al. 2003).
Geweke test t value. An absolute value less than 1.96 indicates
The shaded model is selected to be the best-fit model by all criteria in this study.
The shaded parameter estimate is significant from zero.

Table 9 Model selection in real data analysis

	non-ignorable missingness			ignorable
Criterion	LOD (XY)	LSD (XS)	LID (XI)	missingness
Dhat.AIC	4125.000	4083.000	N/A	4151.000
Dhat.BIC	4195.050	4153.050	N/A	4205.483
Dhat.CAIC	4213.050	4171.050	N/A	4219.483
Dhat.ssBIC	4137.944	4095.944	N/A	4161.067
DIC	4959.000	4953.000	N/A	4979.000
rough DIC	5730.878	5714.752	N/A	5731.980

Note:
The definition of each criterion is given in Table 1.
The shaded cell has the smallest value.

showed that the Bayesian method was able to accurately recover parameters in all models considered.

Next, Bayesian model selection criteria were studied to identify the best-fit model in the context of the correct missing mechanisms. Almost all the criteria were able to correctly identify the true model with high certainty.

We also illustrated the application of the Bayesian latent growth curve model with missing data through the analysis of mathematical ability growth data from the NLSY97 survey. In this example, the focus was on seeing how mathematical ability grew over the 4-year period, and whether mothers' education influenced the missing data pattern. Using the model selection criteria introduced in this study, we were able to identify the best-fit of the models considered. The results obtained from the best-fit model showed that mathematical ability grew significantly, and the missing data mainly depended on student's latent rate of growth. Further, mothers' education did not significantly influence the missing data pattern.

The models proposed in this paper can be further developed in various ways. First, the missingness in the simulation was assumed to be independent across time points. If this assumption is violated, likelihood functions will be different. For example, if the missingness depends on the previous session, then autocorrelations might be involved, and the likelihood will be much more complicated. Furthermore, the missingness in practice can be a combination of different types of missingness, quite probably leading to development of increasingly more complex models. Second, additional model selection criteria could be considered, for example, Bayes factors and predictive posterior probabilities. Also, designing new criteria is an interesting topic for future work. It might be useful, for example, to consider observed-data or complete-data likelihood functions for random effects models for $p(\mathbf{y}|\boldsymbol{\theta})$. Third, the data considered in the study were assumed to be normally distributed. However, in reality data are seldom normally distributed, particularly in behavioral and educational sciences (e.g., Micceri 1989). When data have heavy tails, or are contaminated with outliers, robust models (e.g., Huber 1996) should be adopted to help reduce the sensitivity to small deviations from the assumption of normality. Fourth, latent population heterogeneity (e.g., McLachlan and Peel 2000) may exist in the collected longitudinal data. Growth mixture models (GMMs) can be considered to provide a flexible set of models for analyzing longitudinal data with latent or mixture distributions (e.g., Bartholomew and Knott 1999).

Appendix

The Derived Posteriors for LGCMs with Non-ignorable Missingness:

(1) Let $\eta = (\eta_1, \eta_2, \ldots, \eta_N)$, and the conditional posterior distribution for ϕ can be easily derived as an Inverse Gamma distribution,

$$\phi|\eta, \mathbf{y} \sim IG(a_1/2, b_1/2),$$

where $a_1 = v_0 + NT$, and $b_1 = s_0 + \Sigma_{i=1}^{N}(\mathbf{y}_i - \Lambda\eta_i)'(\mathbf{y}_i - \Lambda\eta_i)$.

(2) Notice that $tr(\mathbf{AB}) = tr(\mathbf{BA})$, so the conditional posterior distribution for Ψ is derived as an Inverse Wishart distribution,

$$\Psi|\beta, \eta \sim IW(m_1, \mathbf{V}_1),$$

where $m_1 = m_0 + N$, and $\mathbf{V}_1 = \mathbf{V}_0 + \Sigma_{i=1}^{N}(\eta_i - \beta)(\eta_i - \beta)'$.

(3) By expanding the terms inside the exponential part and combining similar terms, the conditional posterior distribution for β is derived as a multivariate normal distribution,

$$\beta|\Psi, \eta \sim MN(\beta_1, \Sigma_1),$$

where $\beta_1 = \left(N\Psi^{-1} + \Sigma_0^{-1}\right)^{-1}\left(\Psi^{-1}\Sigma_{i=1}^{N}\eta_i + \Sigma_0^{-1}\beta_0\right)$, and $\Sigma_1 = \left(N\Psi^{-1} + \Sigma_0^{-1}\right)^{-1}$.

(4) The conditional posterior for γ_t, $(t = 1, 2, \ldots, T)$, is a distribution of

$$p(\gamma_t|\omega,\mathbf{x},\mathbf{m}) \propto \exp\left[-\frac{1}{2}(\gamma_t-\gamma_{t0})'\mathbf{D}_{t0}^{-1}(\gamma_t-\gamma_{t0}) + \sum_{i=1}^{N}\left\{m_{it}\log\Phi(\omega_i'\gamma_t)+(1-m_{it})\log[1-\Phi(\omega_i'\gamma_t)]\right\}\right].$$

where $\Phi(\omega_i'\gamma_t)$ is defined by Eqs. (4), (5), or (6).

(5) By expanding the terms inside the exponential part and combining similar terms, the conditional posterior distribution for η_i, $i=1,2,\ldots,N$, is derived as a Multivariate Normal distribution,

$$\eta_i|\phi,\Psi,\beta,\mathbf{y}_i \sim MN(\mu_{\eta i},\Sigma_{\eta i}),$$

where $\mu_{\eta i} = \left(\frac{1}{\phi}\Lambda'\Lambda+\Psi^{-1}\right)^{-1}\left(\frac{1}{\phi}\Lambda'\mathbf{y}_i+\Psi^{-1}\beta\right)$, and $\Sigma_{\eta i} = \left(\frac{1}{\phi}\Lambda'\Lambda+\Psi^{-1}\right)^{-1}$.

(6) The conditional posterior distribution for the missing data $\mathbf{y}_i^{mis}$, $i=1,2,\ldots,N$, is a normal distribution,

$$\mathbf{y}_i^{mis}|\eta_i,\phi \sim MN\left[\Lambda\eta_i,\mathbf{I}_T\phi\right],$$

where $\mathbf{I}_T$ is a $T\times T$ identity matrix. The dimension and location of $\mathbf{y}_i^{mis}$ depend on the corresponding $\mathbf{m}_i$ value.

References

Akaike, H. (1974). A new look at the statistical model identification. *IEEE Transactions on Automatic Control, 1919*(6), 716–723.

Baraldi, A. N., & Enders, C. K. (2010). An introduction to modern missing data analyses. *Journal of School Psychology, 48*, 5–37.

Bartholomew, D. J., & Knott, M. (1999). *Latent variable models and factor analysis: Kendall's library of statistics* (2nd ed., Vol. 7). New York, NY: Edward Arnold.

Bollen, K., & Curran, P. (2006). *Latent curve models: A structural equation perspective*. Hoboken, NJ: Wiley.

Box, G. E. P., & Tiao, G. C. (1973). *Bayesian inference in statistical analysis*. Hoboken, NJ: Wiley.

Bozdogan, H. (1987). Model selection and Akaike's Information Criterion (AIC): The general theory and its analytical extensions. *Psychometrika, 52*, 345–370.

Bureau of Labor Statistics, U.S. Department of Labor. (1997). *National longitudinal survey of youth 1997 cohort, 1997–2003 (rounds 1–7)*. [computer file]. Produced by the National Opinion Research Center, the University of Chicago and distributed by the Center for Human Resource Research, The Ohio State University. Columbus, OH, 2005. Available from http://www.bls.gov/nls/nlsy97.htm

Celeux, G., Forbes, F., Robert, C., & Titterington, D. (2006). Deviance information criteria for missing data models. *Bayesian Analysis, 4*, 651–674.

Dempster, A. (1974). The direct use of likelihood for significance testing. In *Proceedings of Conference on Foundational Questions in Statistical Inference* (pp. 335–352). University of Aarhus: Aarhus.

Enders, C. K. (2011). Missing not at random models for latent growth curve analyses. *Psychological Methods, 16*, 1–16.

Fitzmaurice, G., Davidian, M., Verbeke, G., & Molenberghs, G. (Eds.). (2008). *Longitudinal data analysis*. Boca Raton, FL: Chapman & Hall.

Fitzmaurice, G. M., Laird, N. M., & Ware, J. H. (2004). *Applied longitudinal analysis*. Hoboken, NJ: Wiley.

Geman, S., & Geman, D. (1984). Stochastic relaxation, Gibbs distributions, and the Bayesian restoration of images. *IEEE Transactions on Pattern Analysis and Machine Intelligence, 6*, 721–741.

Geweke, J. (1992). Evaluating the accuracy of sampling-based approaches to calculating posterior moments. In J. M. Bernado, J. O. Berger, A. P. Dawid, & A. F. M. Smith (Eds.), *Bayesian Statistics 4* (pp. 169–193). Oxford, UK: Clarendon.

Glynn, R. J., Laird, N. M., & Rubin, D. B. (1986). Drawing inferences from self-selected samples. In H. Wainer (Ed.), (pp. 115–142). New York: Springer.

Huber, P. (1996). *Robust statisticalprocedures* (2nd ed.). Philadelphia: SIAM.

Janssen, R., & De Boeck, P. (1999). Confirmatory analyses of componential test structure using multidimensional item response theory. *Multivariate Behavioral Research, 34*, 245–268.

Jelicic, H., Phelps, E., & Lerner, R. M. (2009). Use of missing data methods in longitudinal studies: The persistence of bad practices in developmental psychology. *Developmental Psychology, 45*, 1195–1199.

Lee, S. Y. (2007). *Structural equation modeling: A Bayesian approach*. Chichester, UK: Wiley.

Little, R. J. A., & Rubin, D. B. (1987). *Statistical analysis with missing data*. New York, NY: Wiley.

Little, R. J. A., & Rubin, D. B. (2002). *Statistical analysis with missing data* (2nd ed.). New York: Wiley-Interscience.

Lu, Z., Zhang, Z., & Lubke, G. (2011). Bayesian inference for growth mixture models with latent-class-dependent missing data. *Multivariate Behavioral Research, 46*, 567–597.

McLachlan, G. J., & Peel, D. (2000). *Finite mixture models*. New York, NY: Wiley.

Micceri, T. (1989). The unicorn, the normal curve and the other improbable creatures. *Psychological Bulletin, 105*, 156–166.

Muthén, B., & Asparouhov, T. (2012). Bayesian SEM: A more flexible representation of substantive theory. *Psychological Methods, 17*(3), 313–335.

Oldmeadow, C., & Keith, J. M. (2011). Model selection in Bayesian segmentation of multiple DNA alignments. *Bioinformatics, 27*, 604–610.

Rissanen, J. (1978). Modeling by shortest data description. *Automatica, 14*, 465–471.

Robert, C. P., & Casella, G. (2004). *Monte Carlostatistical methods*. New York, NY: Springer.

Roth, P. L. (1994). Missing data: A conceptual review for applied psychologists. *Personnel Psychology, 47*, 537–560.

Schafer, J. L. (1997). *Analysisof incomplete multivariate data*. Boca Raton, FL: Chapman & Hall/CRC.

Schwarz, G. E. (1978). Estimating the dimension of a model. *Annals of Statistics, 6* (2), 461–464.

Sclove, L. S. (1987). Application of mode-selection criteria to some problems in multivariate analysis. *Psychometrics, 52*, 333–343.

Singer, J. D., & Willett, J. B. (2003). *Applied longitudinal data analysis: Modeling change and event occurrence*. New York, NY: Oxford University Press.

Spiegelhalter, D. J., Best, N. G., Carlin, B. P., & Van Der Linde, A. (2002). Bayesian measures of model complexity and fit. *Journal of the Royal Statistical Society: Series B (Statistical Methodology), 64*(4), 583–639.

Spiegelhalter, D. J., Thomas, A., Best, N., & Lunn, D. (2003). WinBUGS manual Version 1.4. (Cambridge CB2 2SR, UK: MRC Biostatistics Unit, Institute of Public Health, Robinson Way. http://www.mrc-bsu.cam.ac.uk/bugs)

Sturtz, S., Ligges, U., & Gelman, A. (2005). R2WinBUGS: A package for running WinBUGS from R. *Journal of Statistical Software, 12*, 1–16.

Tanner, M. A., & Wong, W. H. (1987). The calculation of posterior distributions by data augmentation. *Journal of the American Statistical Association, 82*, 528–540.

Yuan, K.- H., & Lu, Z. (2008). SEM with missing data and unknown population using two-stage ML: Theory and its application. *Multivariate Behavioral Research, 43*, 621–652.

Zhang, Z., Hamagami, F., Wang, L., Grimm, K. J., & Nesselroade, J. R. (2007). Bayesian analysis of longitudinal data using growth curve models. *International Journal of Behavioral Development, 31*(4), 374–383.

Notes on the Estimation of Item Response Theory Models

Xinming An and Yiu-Fai Yung

1 Introduction

Item response theory (IRT) was first proposed in the field of psychometrics for the purpose of educational testing and personality assessment. During the last 10 years, it has become increasingly popular in other fields, such as health behavior and health policy research. The most widely used estimation method for IRT models is the Gauss–Hermite quadrature-based EM algorithm proposed by Bock and Aitkin (1981). Because of its several appealing properties, it has become the gold standard and the most popular method used by all the major IRT packages, such as BILOG and TESTFACT. However, there are several issues associated with the G–H quadrature-based EM algorithms that have been overlooked. There are generally two issues associated with this algorithm: the first being the approximation accuracy of the G–H quadrature and the second being the computational properties of the EM algorithm. These issues will be explored in detail in Sects. 2 and 3 by using an example. In this example, binary responses are fitted by the uni-dimensional IRT model, which can be expressed by the following equations:

$$y_i = \Lambda \eta_i + \epsilon_i, \tag{1}$$

and

$$P(u_{ij} = 1) = P(y_{ij} > \alpha_j), \tag{2}$$

where u_{ij} is the observed binary response from subject i for item j, y_{ij} is a continuous latent response underlying u_{ij}, $\alpha = (\alpha_1, \ldots, \alpha_J)$ is a vector of difficulty (or threshold) parameters, Λ is a matrix of the slopes (or discrimination) parameters,

X. An (✉) • Y.-F. Yung
SAS Institute, Cary NC, USA
e-mail: Xinming.An@sas.com; Yiu-Fai.Yung@sas.com

R.E. Millsap et al. (eds.), *New Developments in Quantitative Psychology*, Springer Proceedings in Mathematics & Statistics 66, DOI 10.1007/978-1-4614-9348-8_19,

η_i and ϵ_i are the latent factor and unique factor for subject i. $\eta_i \sim N(0,I)$, $\epsilon_i \sim N_J(0,I)$ or $L_J(0,I)$. η_i and ϵ_i are independent.

Based on the above model specifications, we have

$$P_{ij} = P(u_{ij} = 1) = P(y_{ij} > \alpha_j) = \int_{\alpha_j - \lambda_j \eta_i}^{\infty} f(y;0,1)dy, \tag{3}$$

where $f(y;0,1)$ is the density function of the normal or logistic distribution with mean 0 and variance 1. To simplify the notation, let $Q_{ij} = 1 - P_{ij}$ and $v_{ij} = 1 - u_{ij}$.

Parameter estimates for this model are often obtained by maximizing the marginal likelihood, which can be expressed as

$$L(\theta|U) = \prod_{i=1}^{N} \int \prod_{j=1}^{J} P_{ij}^{u_{ij}} Q_{ij}^{v_{ij}} \phi(\eta)d\eta, \tag{4}$$

where θ is a set of all the model parameters and U represents responses from all subjects, and $\phi(\eta)$ is the density function of the prior distribution for latent factor η. The corresponding log likelihood is

$$\log L(\theta|U) = \prod_{i=1}^{N} \log \int L_i(\eta)d\eta = \prod_{i=1}^{N} \log \int \prod_{j=1}^{J} P_{ij}^{u_{ij}} Q_{ij}^{v_{ij}} \phi(\eta)d\eta. \tag{5}$$

Because the integrands, $L_i = \prod_{j=1}^{J} P_{ij}^{u_{ij}} Q_{ij}^{v_{ij}} \phi(\eta)$, involved in the above likelihood are not linear functions of η, integrations cannot be solved analytically. They are usually approximated by numeric integration, most often Gauss–Hermite quadrature.

2 Likelihood Approximation with Numeric Integration

For latent variable models with categorical responses, such as IRT, parameter estimates based on numerical integration, mostly Gauss–Hermite (G–H) quadrature, have been shown to be the most accurate and reliable (Schilling and Bock 2005). However there are two scenarios where G–H quadrature becomes inadequate (Rabe-Hesketh et al. 2002). The first scenario occurs when the number of latent variables is large, since the number of quadrature points grows exponentially as the number of latent variables increases. The second scenario involves the approximation accuracy of G–H quadrature under certain situations. It is commonly believed that 20 G–H quadrature points per dimension produces accurate approximation of the likelihood and as a result, reliable parameter estimates (Lesaffre and Spiessens 2001). However, several cases have been reported where a large number of quadrature points are required to obtain valid estimates (Lesaffre and Spiessens 2001; Rabe-Hesketh et al. 2002).

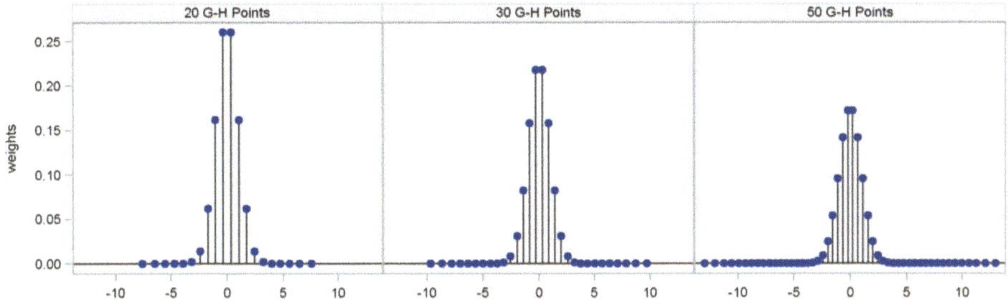

Fig. 1 Illustrations of three Gaussian–Hermite quadratures with 20 (*left*), 30 (*center*), 50 (*right*) quadrature points, respectively

While the issue associated with high dimensional quadrature is widely known, the approximation accuracy issue has only been reported for the generalized linear mixed model (GLMM) under certain cases. Its effects on IRT have not been investigated.

In general the G–H quadrature can be presented as follows:

$$\int_{-\infty}^{\infty} g(x)dx = \int_{-\infty}^{\infty} f(x)\phi(x)dx \approx \sum_{g=1}^{G} f(x_g)w_g, \tag{6}$$

where G is the number of quadrature points, x_g and w_g are the integration points and weights, which are uniquely determined by the integration domain and the weighting kernel $\phi(x)$. Traditional G–H quadrature often uses e^{-x^2} as the weighting kernel. In the field of statistics, the density of standard normal distribution is more widely used instead, because for the estimation of various statistical models, the Gaussian density is often a factor of the integrand. In the case when the Gaussian density is not a factor of the integrand, the integral is transformed into the form in 6 by dividing and multiplying the original integrand by the standard normal density. Graphical illustrations of G–H quadrature with the number of quadrature points ranging from 20 to 50 are included in Fig. 1. From Fig. 1 we can observe that (1) the positions and weights of the quadrature points are symmetric around zero, and (2) as the number of quadrature points increases, the quadrature points extend gradually to the two ends.

The G-point quadrature approximation is exact if $f(x)$ or $g(x)/\phi(x)$ is a polynomial of order $2G-1$ (Skrondal and Rabe-Hesketh 2004). However, as many studies note, $f(x)$ for various statistical models often has a sharp peak and cannot be well approximated by a low degree polynomial (Rabe-Hesketh et al. 2002). Furthermore, the peak may be far from zero so that substantial contributions to the integral are lost unless a large number of quadrature points are used. Three cases when the G–H quadrature will become inadequate are shown in Fig. 2. The locations of 30 G–H quadrature points are plotted along the x axis. The solid curve represents the case when $f(x)$ has a sharp peak. The dashed curve shows the

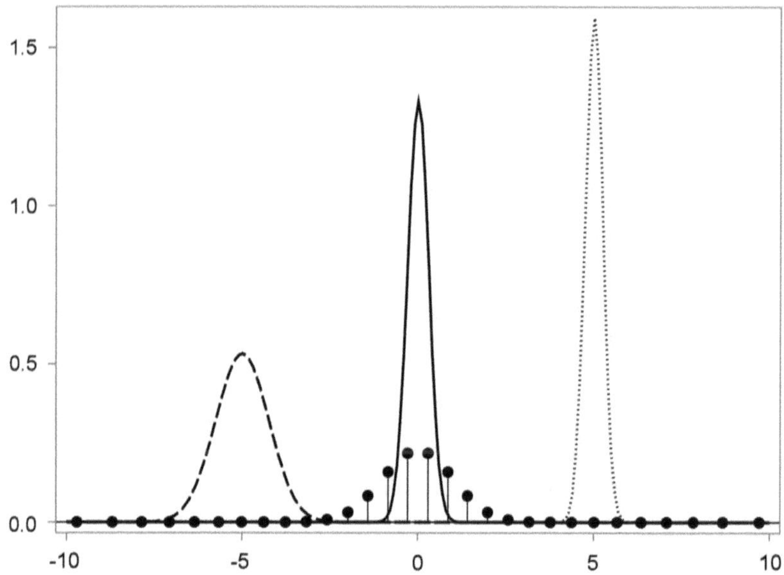

Fig. 2 Illustration of three situations when the Gaussian–Hermite quadrature becomes inadequate

case where the peak of the integrand is far from zero. The most troublesome case is illustrated by the dotted curve, in which $f(x)$ has a sharp peak and the peak is far from zero. Among these 30 quadrature points, only 6, 2, and 1 quadrature points make significant contributions to the approximation, respectively, for the three cases from left to right in Fig. 2.

G–H quadrature has been widely used along with optimization techniques, such as EM and Newton methods, to estimate various latent variable models with categorical responses. Several cases have been reported that a larger number of quadrature points are needed to get reliable estimates for generalized linear mixed models with categorical responses (Lesaffre and Spiessens 2001). These problems are often caused by the fact that the peak for some integrands involved in the model are far from zero and/or the integrands are very sharp around the peak. Although these problems have not been clearly recognized, they can also occur in latent variable models with categorical responses, such as IRT models.

Using the unidimensional IRT model presented in Sect. 1, we investigate how the integrand's peak location and sharpness are affected by the items and parameters of the IRT model. Equation (5) suggests that the integrand, $L_i(\eta) = \prod_{j=1}^{J} P_{ij}^{u_{ij}} Q_{ij}^{1-u_{ij}} \phi(\eta)$, can be considered as the unnormalized posterior distribution of latent variable η for a subject i with response $u_i = (u_{i1}, \ldots, u_{iJ})$. Let $\hat{\eta}_i$ and H_i denote the location of the peak and the corresponding Hessian of $-\log L_i(\eta)$, respectively. Then $\hat{\eta}_i$ can be used as estimates for the posterior mean and $\frac{1}{H_i}$ as an estimate of its variance.

Table 1 Number of Gaussian–Hermite quadrature points needed for the integrands with the sharpest peak, MaxH_i, or the peak furthest from zero, Max abs($\hat{\eta}_i$), in IRT models with different item sizes (J = 30, 100, 200). In column two, $\hat{\eta}_i$ and these values between the parentheses represent the locations where the Max Hessian, H_i, is obtained. In Column five, H_i and these values between the parentheses represent the Hessian corresponding to Max $\hat{\eta}_i$. Ave H_i and Ave $abs(\hat{\eta}_i)$ are the average of Hessian and average absolute value of peak locations across all the response patterns with different marginal means

J	MaxH_i ($\hat{\eta}_i$)	G–H	AveH_i	Max abs[$\hat{\eta}_i$](H_i)	G–H	Ave abs[$\hat{\eta}_i$]
30	20.10(0)	55	15.89	1.926(4.83)	15	0.72
100	64.65(0)	170	49.61	2.378(6.71)	15	0.77
200	128.30(0)	340	97.68	2.610(7.80)	20	0.78

The default setting includes 30 items and one latent factor. Factor loadings are set to be 1 and difficulty parameters are set to be 0. Under these settings, responses that have the same marginal mean will produce roughly the same integrand, since P_{ij} are the same for different items. Thus instead of keeping track of all the possible response patterns, we will only consider the J response patterns with different marginal means. In the following studies, the average absolute values of $\hat{\eta}_i$, Ave $abs(\hat{\eta}_i)$, and the maximum value of H_i, Max $\hat{\eta}_i$, across these J response patterns will be investigated under different settings. For the integrand with the maximum $\hat{\eta}_i$ or H_i, the number of quadrature points that is needed to approximate the integration with an error smaller than 0.01 will be reported.

It is known that as the number of items increases, the shape of the integrand becomes closer to a normal density function but sharper (the posterior variance becomes smaller), causing problems for the G–H quadrature (Schilling and Bock 2005). Results for item sizes of 30, 100, and 200 are summarized in Table 1, including the average and maximum $\hat{\eta}_i$ and H_i and the number of quadrature points needed to accurately approximate these integrands with the maximum $\hat{\eta}_i$ or H_i. These results suggest that item size has a significant impact on the posterior variance ($\frac{1}{H_i}$) which in turn strongly affects the number of quadrature points required. As the item size moves from 30 to 200, the maximum H_i increases from 20 to 128; and to obtain equal accuracy, the number of quadrature points moves from 55 to 340.

Next, we want to examine how factor loadings affect the maximum and average value of H_i and $\hat{\eta}_i$ and whether they will cause problems for the G–H quadrature. Table 2 summarizes the results for three cases where factor loadings are set to 0.5, 1, and 2 respectively. These results suggest that factor loadings have a great impact on the maximum and average values of H_i and in turn the G–H quadrature.

In this section, we investigate several different factors that will affect the G–H quadrature for IRT model. Results suggest that item size and the value of factor loadings have great impact on G–H quadrature. The same problem also applies to other latent variable models, such as structural equation modeling with categorical responses, when G–H quadrature is used for model estimation. Adaptive G–H quadrature (Liu and Pierce 1994) has been shown to solve this problem effectively (Lesaffre and Spiessens 2001) and has also been used to improve computational

Table 2 Number of Gaussian–Hermite quadrature points needed for the integrands with the sharpest peak (MaxH_i) or the peak furthest from zero (Max abs($\hat{\eta}_i$)) in IRT models with different factor loadings (λ). In Column Two, $\hat{\eta}_i$ and these values between the parentheses represent the locations where the Max Hessian, H_i, is obtained. In Column Five, H_i and these values between the parentheses represent the Hessian corresponding to Max $\hat{\eta}_i$. Ave H_i and Ave $abs(\hat{\eta}_i)$ are the average of Hessian and average absolute value of peak locations across all the response patterns with different marginal means

λ	MaxH_i ($\hat{\eta}_i$)	G–H	AveH_i	Max abs($\hat{\eta}_i$)(H_i)	G–H	Ave abs($\hat{\eta}_i$)
0.5	5.77(0)	15	4.95	2.680(3.03)	9	1.1611
1	20.10(0)	55	15.89	1.926(4.83)	15	0.7165
2	77.39(0)	210	59.11	1.221(7.02)	18	0.3885

efficiency for high dimensional latent variable models (Rabe-Hesketh et al. 2002; Schilling and Bock 2005). While several statistical packages, such as SAS PROC GLMMIX, have changed their default numeric integration method from G–H to adaptive G–H quadrature, there are a large number of packages for IRT that still use G–H as their default and many of them do not have adaptive G–H available. A suggestion from the findings in this paper to applied researchers is to make the adaptive G–H quadrature the default integration technique if it is available, otherwise increase the number of quadrature points until the change in parameter estimate becomes very small.

3 Likelihood Maximization with Numerical Algorithms

One of the most popular estimation methods for latent variable models with categorical responses is based on the marginal likelihood. Parameter estimates can be obtained by maximizing the marginal likelihood using numerical algorithms, such as EM and Newton type algorithms.

3.1 EM Algorithm

The EM algorithm starts from the complete data log likelihood that can be expressed as follows:

$$\begin{aligned} \log L(\theta|u,\eta) &= \sum_{i=1}^{N}\left[\left(\sum_{j=1}^{J} u_{ij}\log(P_{ij}) + (v_{ij})\log(Q_{ij})\right) + \log\phi(\eta_i)\right] \\ &\propto \sum_{j=1}^{J}\sum_{i=1}^{N}\left[u_{ij}\log(P_{ij}) + (v_{ij})\log(Q_{ij})\right], \end{aligned} \tag{7}$$

where $\phi(\eta_i)$ is the prior distribution for latent factor η_i.

In the E step, we calculate the expectation of the complete data log likelihood with respect to the conditional distribution of η, $f(\eta_i|u_i,\theta^{(t)})$,

$$f(\eta_i|u_i,\theta^{(t)}) = \frac{f(u_i|\eta,\theta^{(t)})\phi(\eta)}{\int f(u_i|\eta,\theta^{(t)})\phi(\eta)d\eta} = \frac{f(u_i|\eta,\theta^{(t)})\phi(\eta)}{f(u_i)}. \tag{8}$$

Let $Q(\theta|\theta^{(t)})$ denote the conditional expectation of the complete data log likelihood, and we have

$$Q(\theta|\theta^{(t)}) = \sum_{j=1}^{J}\sum_{i=1}^{N}\left[u_{ij}E\left[\log P_{ij}|u_i,\theta^{(t)}\right] + (v_{ij})E\left[\log(Q_{ij})|u_i,\theta^{(t)}\right]\right] = \sum_{j=1}^{J} Q_j. \tag{9}$$

Expectations involved in the above equation are often approximated by either numerical or Monte Carlo integration. Let $\tilde{Q}(\theta|\theta^{(t)})$ denote the approximated conditional expectation of the complete data log likelihood.

In the M step of the EM algorithm, parameters are updated by maximizing $\tilde{Q}(\theta|\theta^{(t)})$. To summarize, the EM algorithm consists of the following two steps:

E Step: Approximate $Q(\theta|\theta^{(t)})$ with either numerical or Monte Carlo integration;
M Step: Update parameter estimates by maximizing $\tilde{Q}(\theta|\theta^{(t)})$ with a one step Newton–Raphson algorithm.

Technical details about the EM algorithm are provided in Appendix 1. Interested readers can refer to (McLachlan and Krishan 2007) for general discussions about the EM algorithm.

3.2 *Newton Type Algorithms*

Compared with EM type algorithms which start from the complete data log likelihood, Newton type algorithms maximize the marginal log likelihood directly. Based on the model specified in Sect. 1, the marginal likelihood is

$$L(\theta|U) = \prod_{i=1}^{N}\int\prod_{j=1}^{J}(P_{ij})^{u_{ij}}(Q_{ij})^{v_{ij}}\phi(\eta)d\eta, \tag{10}$$

where $\phi(\eta)$ is the density function for latent factor η. The corresponding log likelihood is

$$\log L(\theta|U) = \sum_{i=1}^{N}\log L_i = \sum_{i=1}^{N}\log\int\prod_{j=1}^{J}(P_{ij})^{u_{ij}}(1-P_{ij})^{1-u_{ij}}g(\eta)d\eta. \tag{11}$$

Similar to EM type algorithms, integrations involved in the above equation are often approximated by either numerical or Monte Carlo integration.

Let $Log\tilde{L}(\theta|U)$ denote the approximated marginal log likelihood. Parameter estimates can be obtained by maximizing $Log\tilde{L}(\theta|U)$ with Newton type algorithms. Two of the most widely used estimation algorithms are Newton–Raphson and Fisher Scoring which rely on the gradient and Hessian of the log likelihood. However, for latent variable models with categorical responses, the Hessian matrix is often expensive to compute. As a result, several Quasi-Newton algorithms only requiring gradients have been proposed. In the field of IRT, Bock and Lieberman (1970) proposed replacing the Hessian with the following information matrix

$$I(\theta) = E\left[\frac{\partial Log\tilde{L}(\theta|U)}{\partial\theta}\left(\frac{\partial Log\tilde{L}(\theta|U)}{\partial\theta}\right)^T\right] = \sum_{h=1}^{2^J}\left[\frac{\partial \log\tilde{L}_i}{\partial\theta}\left(\frac{\partial \log\tilde{L}_i}{\partial\theta}\right)^T\right]. \quad (12)$$

To calculate the above expectation, we need to sum over not just the observed but all 2^J possible response patterns which will become very computationally intensive when the number of items is large. Fortunately, other Quasi-Newton algorithms that do not suffer from this computational difficulty have been proposed. However, they have not been used for IRT. Notable examples include the Broyden–Fletcher–Goldfarb–Shanno (BFGS) method, one of the most popular Quasi-Newton algorithms that approximate the Hessian matrix with the gradient. It is a general algorithm that does not rely on any statistical properties and its usage is far beyond statistics. The second method was proposed by Berndt et al. (1974), which replaces the expectation in (12) with summation runs over only the observed response patterns. The accuracy of this approximation depends on two statistical properties: that the model is correct and the sample size is relatively large. This algorithm has been used for the estimation of generalized linear mixed model (GLMM) and is shown to work well even with bad starting values (Skrondal and Rabe-Hesketh 2004). Technical details about the Quasi-Newton algorithm corresponding to the model used here are included in Appendix 2.

3.3 *Comparison of Computational Efficiency*

In this section, we will investigate the relative computational properties of the EM and the Quasi-Newton type algorithms. Since the EM and Quasi-Newton algorithms use different convergence criteria and computational efficiency of the algorithm can be greatly affected by the implementation, it is very hard to conduct a meaningful comparison with numerical examples. Thus, we will discuss some analytical results that will affect the performance of these algorithms. The purpose of this study is to illustrate the potential advantage of Quasi-Newton algorithms in the field of IRT.

As shown by (9), the Q function is a summation of J functions that involve independent parameters. As a result, maximizing the Q function is equivalent to maximizing J separate functions with two parameters each. In contrast, directly maximizing the marginal likelihood of (11) requires handling all $2J$ parameters

Table 3 Computation time measured in seconds for the calculation of different number of exponential functions and standard normal CDFs using SAS IML

Number of summations	EXP	CDF
2000	0.01	0.01
20000	0.09	0.12
400000	1.7	2.3

Table 4 Computation time measured in seconds for solving a system of linear equations with different number of parameters using SAS IML

	Number of parameters					
	2	10	100	500	1000	2000
Computation time	9e−05	1e−4	6e−4	0.04	0.29	2.2

simultaneously. This is the most important advantage for the EM algorithm. This advantage becomes more significant as the number of items increases. On the other hand, the advantage of the Quasi-Newton algorithms lies in the calculation of derivatives. To implement the Quasi-Newton algorithm, we only need to calculate the gradient that involves $2J$ elements. In contrast, the M step of the EM algorithm needs to calculate $3J$ elements of the Hessian matrix on top of the gradient. For a multidimensional IRT model with d latent factors, EM algorithms will need to do $2+\frac{d}{2}$ times more calculations than the Quasi-Newton algorithm. Thus as the number of latent factor, d, increases, this advantage for Quasi-Newton algorithm becomes more obvious.

Technical details provided in the appendices suggest that both algorithms involve similar calculations for each iteration which can be divided into two steps. The first step calculates the gradient and/or Hessian, which is accomplished by a nested loop that involve $N \times G$ summations in total. The key components for each summation are the calculations of exponential function (EXP) and/or the cumulative distribution function (CDF) of standard normal distribution. The total number of summations ranges from thousands to millions. Table 3 lists the computation time measured in seconds for the calculation of different number of exponential functions and standard normal CDFs.

Then in the second step, parameters are updated with the Newton type equation as follows

$$\theta_{t+1} = \theta_t - \frac{f'(\theta_t)}{f''(\theta_t)}, \tag{13}$$

which is equivalent to solving a system of linear equations. With current computational techniques and resources, solving a system of linear equations is easy and fast. In Table 4 we list the computation time measured in seconds for solving system of linear equations with different number of parameters.

While the actual computational time might be different if different programming tools other than SAS IML are used, we assume the relative computational time to be similar across languages. Comparing Tables 3 and 4, we can observe that computations for the first step often dominate the computation time for each iteration unless the number of parameters is very large, for example above 1000. Thus the advantages of the EM algorithm on the total computational time decrease with each iteration, and as a result, we can expect that the Quasi-Newton will be as fast as, if not faster than, the EM for each iteration.

EM algorithm's convergence rate is linear at most. In contrast, Quasi-Newton is super linear. As a result, it can be expected that the Quasi-Newton algorithm would use less iterations to reach the same convergence criteria as compared with EM. Furthermore, with the extension of IRT to multidimensional models, confirmatory analysis becomes increasingly useful and desirable. When parameter restrictions are applied across different items, the Q function in (9) cannot be decomposed into the summation of independent functions and consequently the above advantage for EM algorithm will be impaired.

In this section, we demonstrated that under most cases, Quasi-Newton algorithms for IRT model are computationally as efficient as EM algorithms and at the same time avoid problems typically associated with EM algorithms.

4 Discussion

In this paper, we explored several computational issues associated with the G–H quadrature-based EM algorithm for the estimation of IRT models. There are several other practical issues associated with EM type algorithms. First, standard errors are not readily available. While several attempts such as the SEM algorithm (Meng and Rubin 1991) have been made, the problem has not been well addressed. Second, the convergence rate of the EM algorithm is slow, especially when the fraction of missing information is large. Last, the convergence of EM type algorithms is often monitored by the biggest parameter change. This approach is much less reliable than the gradient-based convergence criteria used by Newton type algorithms, since small parameter changes can also be caused by a slow convergence rate instead of convergence. As a result, EM type algorithms might sometimes mistake slow sub-linear convergence as a sign of [NON?convergence] <- NOT SURE WHAT YOU MEAN!!! and produce incorrect maximum likelihood estimates (Bentler and Tanaka 1983). Our results suggest that the combination of adaptive G–H quadrature with Quasi-Newton algorithm can avoid most of these issues without sacrificing computational efficiency. We do not claim that this combination is the best for all different situations. EM algorithms, especially Monte Carlo EM, are usually easier to implement. That makes EM very popular among methodology researchers who need to implement estimation algorithms for newly developed modeling techniques, especially for well-controlled simulations under standard statistical conditions. However, these disadvantages make EM algorithm a poor candidate for commercial software that require higher standards of estimation accuracy and computational efficiency to deal with all kinds of anomalies encountered in practical applications.

Hybrid algorithms that start with EM and then switch to Newton type algorithms have also been proposed (McLachlan and Krishan 2007), but more explorations are needed to identify these situations for IRT.

Appendix 1: Technical Details for EM

The conditional distribution $f(\eta|u_i,\theta^{(t)})$ is

$$f(\eta|u_i,\theta^{(t)}) = \frac{f(u_i|\eta,\theta^{(t)})\phi(\eta)}{\int f(u_i|\eta,\theta^{(t)})\phi(\eta)d\eta} = \frac{f(u_i|\eta,\theta^{(t)})\phi(\eta)}{f(u_i)}. \quad (14)$$

Then these conditional expectations involved in the Q function can be expressed as follows:

$$E[\log P_{ij}|u_i,\theta^{(t)}] = \int \log P_{ij} f(\eta|u_i,\theta^{(t)})d\eta, \quad (15)$$

$$E[\log(1-P_{ij})|u_i,\theta^{(t)}] = \int \log(1-P_{ij}) f(\eta|u_i,\theta^{(t)})d\eta, \quad (16)$$

and

$$E[\log\phi(\eta)|u_i,\theta^{(t)}] = \int \log\phi(\eta) f(\eta|u_i,\theta^{(t)})d\eta. \quad (17)$$

Then we have

$$\begin{aligned} Q_{1j} &= \int \sum_{i=1}^{N} \left[u_{ij}\log P_{ij} f(\eta|u_i,\theta^{(t)}) + (1-u_{ij})\log(1-P_{ij}) f(\eta|u_i,\theta^{(t)})\right] d\eta \\ &= \int \left[\log P_{ij}\left[\sum_{i=1}^{N} u_{ij} f(\eta|u_i,\theta^{(t)})\right] + \log(1-P_{ij})\left[\sum_{i=1}^{N}(1-u_{ij}) f(\eta|u_i,\theta^{(t)})\right]\right] d\eta \\ &= \int \left[\log P_{ij} r_j(\theta^{(t)}) + \log(1-P_{ij})[n(\theta^{(t)}) - r_j(\theta^{(t)})]\right] \phi(\eta|\theta^{(t)}))d\eta, \end{aligned} \quad (18)$$

where $r_j(\theta^{(t)}) = \sum_{i=1}^{N} u_{ij}\frac{f(u_i|\eta,\theta^{(t)})}{f(u_i)}$, and $n(\theta^{(t)}) = \sum_{i=1}^{N} \frac{f(u_i|\eta,\theta^{(t)})}{f(u_i)}$.

Integrations in the equations above can be approximated as follows using G–H quadrature. Note that these quadrature points, x_g, and weights, w_g, correspond to $\phi(\eta|\theta^{(t)})$ which is the density function of $N(0,\Phi^{(t)})$.

$$\tilde{Q}_{1j} = \sum_{g=1}^{G} \left[\log P_{ij}(x_g) r_j(x_g,\theta^{(t)}) + \log(1-P_{ij}(x_g))(n(x_g,\theta^{(t)}) - r_j(x_g,\theta^{(t)}))\right] w_g. \quad (19)$$

We take the derivatives of Q_{1j} with respect to model parameters

$$\frac{\partial \tilde{Q}_{1j}}{\partial \alpha_j} = \sum_{g=1}^{G} \left[\frac{r_j(x_g,\theta^{(t)})}{P_{ij}(x_g)} - \frac{n(x_g,\theta^{(t)}) - r_j(x_g,\theta^{(t)})}{1-P_{ij}(x_g)}\right] \frac{\partial P_{ij}(x_g)}{\partial \alpha_j} w_g, \quad (20)$$

$$\frac{\partial \tilde{Q}_{1j}}{\partial \lambda_j} = \sum_{g=1}^{G} \left[\frac{r_j(x_g, \theta^{(t)})}{P_{ij}(x_g)} - \frac{n(x_g, \theta^{(t)}) - r_j(x_g, \theta^{(t)})}{1 - P_{ij}(x_g)} \right] \frac{\partial P_{ij}(x_g)}{\partial \lambda_j} w_g, \tag{21}$$

$$\frac{\partial^2 \tilde{Q}_{1j}}{\partial \alpha_j^2} = \sum_{g=1}^{G} \left[\left[\frac{-r_j}{P_{ij}^2} - \frac{n - r_j}{(1 - P_{ij})^2} \right] \left[\frac{\partial P_{ij}(x_g)}{\partial \alpha_j} \right]^2 + \left[\frac{r_j}{P_{ij}} - \frac{n - r_j}{1 - P_{ij}} \right] \frac{\partial^2 P_{ij}(x_g)}{\partial \alpha_j^2} \right] w_g, \tag{22}$$

$$\frac{\partial^2 \tilde{Q}_{1j}}{\partial \lambda_j^2} = \sum_{g=1}^{G} \left[\left[\frac{-r_j}{P_{ij}^2} - \frac{n - r_j}{(1 - P_{ij})^2} \right] \left[\frac{\partial P_{ij}(x_g)}{\partial \lambda_j} \right]^2 + \left[\frac{r_j}{P_{ij}} - \frac{n - r_j}{1 - P_{ij}} \right] \frac{\partial^2 P_{ij}(x_g)}{\partial \lambda_j^2} \right] w_g, \tag{23}$$

and

$$\frac{\partial^2 \tilde{Q}_{1j}}{\partial \alpha_j \partial \lambda_j} = \sum_{g=1}^{G^d} \left[\left[\frac{-r_j}{P_{ij}^2} - \frac{n - r_j}{(1 - P_{ij})^2} \right] \left[\frac{\partial P_{ij}(x_g)}{\partial \alpha_j} \frac{\partial P_{ij}(x_g)}{\partial \lambda_j} \right] + \left[\frac{r_j}{P_{ij}} - \frac{n - r_j}{1 - P_{ij}} \right] \frac{\partial^2 P_{ij}(x_g)}{\partial \alpha_j \partial \lambda_j} \right] w_g. \tag{24}$$

In the above equations, we have

$$\frac{\partial P_{ij}(x_g)}{\partial \alpha_j} = -\phi(\alpha_j - \lambda_j x_g) = -\frac{\partial Q_{ij}(x_g)}{\partial \alpha_j}, \tag{25}$$

$$\frac{\partial P_{ij}(x_g)}{\partial \lambda_j} = \phi(\alpha_j - \lambda_j x_g) x_g = -\frac{\partial Q_{ij}(x_g)}{\partial \lambda_j}, \tag{26}$$

$$\frac{\partial^2 P_{ij}(x_g)}{\partial \alpha_j^2} = -\frac{\partial \phi(\alpha_j - \lambda_j x_g)}{\partial \alpha_j} = \phi(\alpha_j - \lambda_j x_g)(\alpha_j - \lambda_j x_g) = -\frac{\partial^2 Q_{ij}(x_g)}{\partial \alpha_j^2}, \tag{27}$$

$$\frac{\partial^2 P_{ij}(x_g)}{\partial \alpha_j \partial \lambda_j} = -\frac{\partial \phi(\alpha_j - \lambda_j x_g)}{\partial \lambda_j} = -\phi(\alpha_j - \lambda_j x_g)(\alpha_j - \lambda_j x_g) x_g = -\frac{\partial^2 Q_{ij}(x_g)}{\partial \alpha_j \partial \lambda_j}, \tag{28}$$

and

$$\frac{\partial^2 P_{ij}(x_g)}{\partial \lambda_j^2} = \frac{\partial \phi(\alpha_j - \lambda_j x_g) x_g}{\partial \lambda_j} = \phi(\alpha_j - \lambda_j x_g)(\alpha_j - \lambda_j x_g) x_g^2 = -\frac{\partial^2 Q_{ij}(x_g)}{\partial \lambda_j^2}. \tag{29}$$

Appendix 2: Technical Details for the Quasi-Newton Algorithm

For our objective function, $Log\tilde{L}(\theta)$, the first derivative with respect to θ_j, the latent trait for the jth item, is

$$\frac{\partial \log \tilde{L}(\theta|U)}{\partial \theta_j} = \sum_{i=1}^{N} \left[(\tilde{L}_i)^{-1} \frac{\partial \tilde{L}_i}{\partial \theta_j} \right] = \sum_{i=1}^{N} \left[(\tilde{L}_i)^{-1} \sum_{g=1}^{G} \left[\frac{\partial f_i(x_g)}{\partial \theta_j} w_g \right] \right], \tag{30}$$

where

$$\tilde{L}_i = \sum_{g=1}^{G} \left[\prod_{j=1}^{J} (P_{ij}(x_g))^{u_{ij}} (Q_{ij}(x_g))^{1-u_{ij}} \right] w_g = \sum_{g=1}^{G} f_i(x_g) w_g, \tag{31}$$

$$\frac{\partial f_i(x_g)}{\partial \theta_j} = \frac{\partial [P_{ij}(x_g)^{u_{ij}} Q_{ij}(x_g)^{1-u_{ij}}]}{\partial \theta_j} \frac{f_i(x_g)}{P_{ij}(x_g)^{u_{ij}} Q_{ij}(x_g)^{1-u_{ij}}}. \tag{32}$$

For the probit link

$$\frac{\partial P_{ij}(x_g)}{\partial \alpha_j} = -\phi(\alpha_j - \lambda_j x_g) = -\frac{\partial Q_{ij}(x_g)}{\partial \alpha_j}, \tag{33}$$

$$\frac{\partial P_{ij}(x_g)}{\partial \lambda_j} = \phi(\alpha_j - \lambda_j x_g) x_g = -\frac{\partial Q_{ij}(x_g)}{\partial \lambda_j}. \tag{34}$$

References

Bentler, P. M., & Tanaka, J. S. (1983). Problems with EM algorithms for ML factor analysis. *Psychometrika, 48*(2), 247–251.

Berndt, E., Hall, B., Hall, R., & Hausman, J. (1974). Estimation and inference in nonlinear structural models. *Annals of Economic and Social Measurement, 3*, 653–666.

Bock, R. D., & Aitkin, M. (1981). Marginal maximum likelihood estimation of item parameters: Application of an EM algorithm. *Psychometrika, 46*(4), 443–459.

Bock, R. D., & Lieberman, M. (1970). Fitting a response model for n dichotomously scored items. *Psychometrika, 35*, 179–197.

Lesaffre, E., & Spiessens, B. (2001). On the effect of the number of quadrature points in a logistic random effects model: an example. *Journal of the Royal Statistical Society, Series C, 50*, 325–335.

Liu, Q., & Pierce, D. (1994). A note on Gauss–Hermite quadrature. *Biometrika, 81*(3), 624.

McLachlan, G., & Krishan, T. (2007). *The EM algorithm and extensions.* Hoboken, NJ: Wiley.

Meng, X. L., & Rubin, D. B. (1991). Using EM to obtain asymptotic variance-covariance matrices: the SEM algorithm. *Journal of the American Statistical Association, 86*(416), 899–909.

Rabe-Hesketh, S., Skrondal, A., & Pickles, A. (2002). Reliable estimation of generalized linear mixed models using adaptive quadrature. *The Stata Journal, 2*(1), 1–21.

Schilling, S., & Bock, R. D. (2005). High-dimensional maximum marginal likelihood item factor analysis by adaptive quadrature. *Psychometrika, 70*(3), 533–555.

Skrondal, A., & Rabe-Hesketh, S. (2004). *Generalized latent variable modeling: Multilevel, longitudinal, and structural equation models.* Boca Raton, FL: Chapman & Hall/CRC.

Some Comments on Representing Construct Levels in Psychometric Models

Ronli Diakow, David Torres Irribarra, and Mark Wilson

1 Introduction

There is increasing interest in the development of *diagnostic* assessments that can provide actionable information to teachers to help them plan and target instructional activities. In order to successfully implement a system of assessments that provides such diagnostic information, it is necessary to coordinate cognitive theories about learning, our observations of student performance, and the interpretation of the evidence gathered during those observations. These are the components of the *assessment triangle* (National Research Council 2001) presented in Fig. 1. The alignment of these three areas is usually challenging, but is a necessary step to adequately embed meaning into the assessments used throughout the educational system.

This paper is concerned with one aspect of this process: tracing the connection between the substantive theory that serves as a basis for an assessment and the mathematical models that are used to analyze and rate student responses. We are interested in exploring this connection in the context of hypothesized variables that (a) have multiple ordered levels, (b) have been assessed with polytomous items that are meant to capture the aforementioned ordered performance levels, and (c) are modeled as continuous rather than ordinal.

R. Diakow • D. Torres Irribarra (✉) • M. Wilson
Graduate School of Education, University of California, 1501 Tolman Hall,
Berkeley, CA 94720-1670, USA
e-mail: rdiakow@berkeley.edu; dti@berkeley.edu; markw@berkeley.edu

R.E. Millsap et al. (eds.), *New Developments in Quantitative Psychology*, Springer Proceedings in Mathematics & Statistics 66, DOI 10.1007/978-1-4614-9348-8_20,

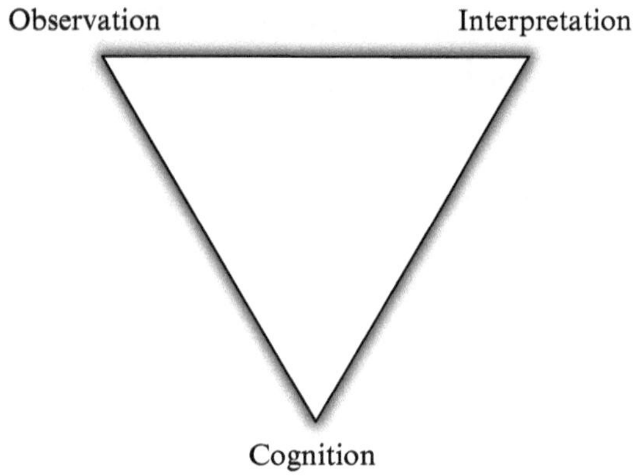

Fig. 1 The NRC assessment triangle

1.1 Setting Performance Standards

Points (a) and (c) characterize the common case where the original theory that motivates the assessments classifies students into an ordered set of performances (e.g., "below basic," "basic," "proficient," "advanced") but the assessment models rely on the assumption of a continuous latent variable (e.g., Rasch Model, 2PL, 3PL). Traditionally when these conditions arise in the context of a criterion referenced assessment (Glass 1978), stakeholders will use standard setting methods (see Cizek and Sternberg 2001) to provide cut-points in order to link the individual ability estimates back to the original levels of proficiency that the assessment was meant to differentiate.

It is worth noting that the term "standard setting" does not refer to a single procedure, but to a myriad of techniques (Cizek et al. 2004), such as the *Bookmark Method* (Lewis et al. 1996), the *Angoff Methods* (Angoff 1971) and its variations, and more recent *Holistic Methods* named in that way because "they require participants to focus judgment on a sample or collection of examinee work greater than a single item or task at a time." (p. 42) (Cizek et al. 2004). Overall the practice of standard setting has been described by Cizek as "the proper following of a prescribed, rational system of rules or procedures resulting in the assignment of a number to differentiate between two or more states or degrees of performance" (p. 100) (Cizek 1993). A specific method of standard setting has been developed for the context where constructs have been designed based on identifying sequences of qualitatively different levels, such as the focus of this paper. The method is referred to as Construct Mapping (Wilson and Draney 2002) and is essentially a blend of the item-mapping concept behind the Bookmark method, and holistic methods. Recent examples are shown in work by Wilmot et al. (2011) and Schwartz et al. (2011).

1.2 Connecting Levels to Polytomous Tasks

The second point mentioned before, namely the use of polytomous items that are meant to capture the aforementioned ordered performance levels, is both more specific and less common than the other two. While many assessments are subject to a standard setting procedure, few of them have a strong connection between the theoretical levels of performance and the scoring procedures that would yield graded responses associated with specific performance levels.

We contend that the additional effort required for the development of items and scoring procedures with these characteristics can provide us with a good alternative to standard setting methods thanks to the alignment of the original theory, the assessment tasks, and the statistical model. In this paper we use an empirical dataset to illustrate how we can achieve traceability from the meaning based on substantive theory to the mathematical model used to estimate each student's location.

We address the overall question about how to connect the original theory (which contains levels) to the assessment model by answering three more specific questions:

1. How to delimit the boundaries between the levels (i.e., set cut-points)?
2. How to characterize the respondents whose estimates lie within a level?
3. How to evaluate if the estimated levels are consistent with the theoretical levels?

We answer the first question by illustrating a simple method for estimating interpretable level boundaries. We then introduce some graphical methods that can help practitioners address the second and third questions, namely, the interpretation of the performances associated with each level and the comparison to the levels originally predicted by the theory.

2 The Empirical Illustration

The empirical data for the illustration of the proposed methods comes from a larger multi-year project to assess adolescent literacy. The *Striving Readers* project focuses on a literacy intervention implemented by the San Diego Unified School District and funded by the Institute for Education Sciences called *Strategies for Literacy Independence across the Curriculum* (SLIC) (Institute for Education Sciences 2006; McDonald et al. 2009). Students are taught how authors use different text forms to present particular types of information and how the features convey information about the content of the text.

A team from the Berkeley Evaluation and Assessment Research (BEAR) Center developed a system of assessments that would be embedded in the curriculum and also would be used as part of the evaluation of SLIC. The assessment development and refinement followed the Bear Assessment System (BAS) (Wilson 2005). A full description of the development of the assessments can be found in the project technical report (Dray et al. 2011).

Overall, 16 different assessments were developed for the SLIC curriculum, spanning the four grades covered by the curriculum (7th through 10th) and four assessment times in each school year (September, December, March, and June). Each assessment asks students to respond to a different text, and the genre of the text varies across the assessments. The same item types (questions that are similarly worded and address the same topics, e.g. main idea or inference) are used across the 16 texts as appropriate. Both the genres of text and the item types are a direct reflection of the instructional strategy implemented in the SLIC curriculum. All items on the SLIC assessments are scored polytomously. Since each of the 16 assessments relies on a different text, there are technically no common items across the assessments. A calibration sample, obtained in New Zealand[1] in the summer of 2008, was used to link the assessments; students in grades 7–10 took the assessments in an overlapping design that allowed linking through common persons.

The construct, assessments, items, and scoring guides were developed and refined jointly by the curriculum developers, district personnel, and assessment team. All 16 assessments were designed to assess the same underlying construct (Fig. 2). The final construct had five levels, corresponding to increasingly sophisticated levels of reading comprehension. The literature suggests that the comprehension of written texts requires understanding the ways textual forms present particular types of information. The construct contains successive levels of identifying both how a text works and what the text means.

Each assessment consisted of an authentic text (i.e., a published text, not written by the test developers) and 10–12 open-ended questions. Figure 3 shows an example copied from the scoring guide for one of the 7th grade assessments; it displays a portion of the text and one question. The text for this assessment is a persuasive text (a magazine article on the benefits of exercise) and the second question asks students to anticipate the content of the article based on the text features. The figure also points out the relevant text features for the rater (these hints were not given to the students).

Each response was scored from 0 to 4 with the score categories corresponding to one of the construct levels. Figure 2 shows another part of the scoring guide for the example item. Note how the score categories on the far left side of Fig. 2 match the construct levels on the left side of the same figure. The tests were scored by the teachers, curriculum developers, and other district personnel.

The subset of data used in this article comes from the calibration sample collected in New Zealand in the summer of 2008. It consists of the responses of 202 7th graders with complete data for the 12 items of the 7th grade assessment using the persuasive text shown in the above example.

[1]The calibration required that the assessments be taken by students who had used the new curriculum but were not potentially part of the experimental study in San Diego; schools in New Zealand, where the curriculum was first designed, were used.

	Construct Description	Scoring Guide
4	**Synthesizing - Creating New Key Ideas** - new understanding based upon the text - new understanding based upon multiple texts - evaluating author's intent - literary and/ or rhetorical criticism	Response is **complete in relation to the information contained:** *Example* : This article is convincing you to get healthy by describing a program of exercise and eating right. It also encourages to do exercise and suggests that it is not hard.
3	**Cross-checking - Coordinating Key Ideas in the Text** - claim - argument - theme - identifying author's intent	Student responds with **multiple items from tactics-based sources and cross-checks or combines items of information:** *Example* : This article is about convincing us to stay fit and healthy.
2	**Discriminating - Key Ideas in the Text** - idea structure - supporting statement - plot - characterization	Student responds with **at least two items from tactics-based sources:** *Example* : Exercise is good for you. We should all exercise.
1	**Engaging - Ideas in the Text** - topic - main idea of a paragraph	Student responds with **one item of information from tactics-based source:** *Examples:* - A fitness plan - Exercise is good for you - Everyone should exercise - Changing your diet can enhance fitness results
0	**Disengaging - Ideas Not in the Text** - not challenging existing knowledge - no new ideas	Student gives an **incorrect response:** *Example* : It's about how you should exercise

Fig. 2 The *Striving Readers* construct map and the scoring guide for one item

3 The Analysis and the Levels

The *Striving Readers* example nicely illustrates a construct that has a well-defined set of ordered performance levels and a set of assessment tasks and scoring guides directly informed by those levels. However, it is in the final step, the measurement model used for analysis, that this connection is usually lost.

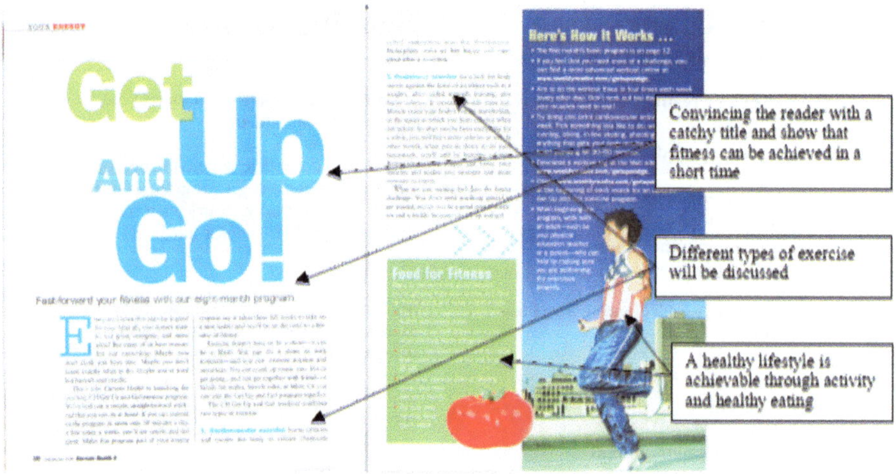

Fig. 3 A *Striving Readers* sample item

A standard approach would be, for instance, to use a model like Master's Partial Credit Model (PCM) (Masters 1982), where the logit of the probability of person p of answering item i at level j is:

$$logit[Pr(x_{pij} = 1 \mid \theta_p)] = \eta_{pij} = \theta_p - \delta_{ij} \tag{1}$$

In this model, the person proficiency is represented by θ_p, which indicates the person's location on the latent variable. Similarly, the difficulty associated with each category j in item i is represented by the δ_{ij} term.

This parameter represents the point on the latent variable when category j becomes more likely than category $j-1$. As we can see in Fig. 4, δ_{11} is located at the intersection of the category characteristic curve (CCC) for category 0 and category 1, and similarly, δ_{12} and δ_{13} are located at the intersection of the CCC's of the respective adjacent categories.

As represented in the left panel of Fig. 5, each δ_{ij} represents the interaction between the item and the category level, which means that the "levels" that are differentiated are effectively item specific and not common across the items. An alternative way to express the PCM, presented in the right panel in Fig. 5, illustrates this more clearly by decomposing the interaction term δ_{ij} into the main effect of the item $\delta_{i.}$ (represented by the black diamonds) and an interaction term τ_{ij} (represented by the dashed lines).

When the PCM is expressed in this way it is possible to see that there is no parameter associated with the level main effect, which effectively means that the original levels specified in the substantive theory are no longer directly represented as model parameters in this traditional parameterization of the PCM.

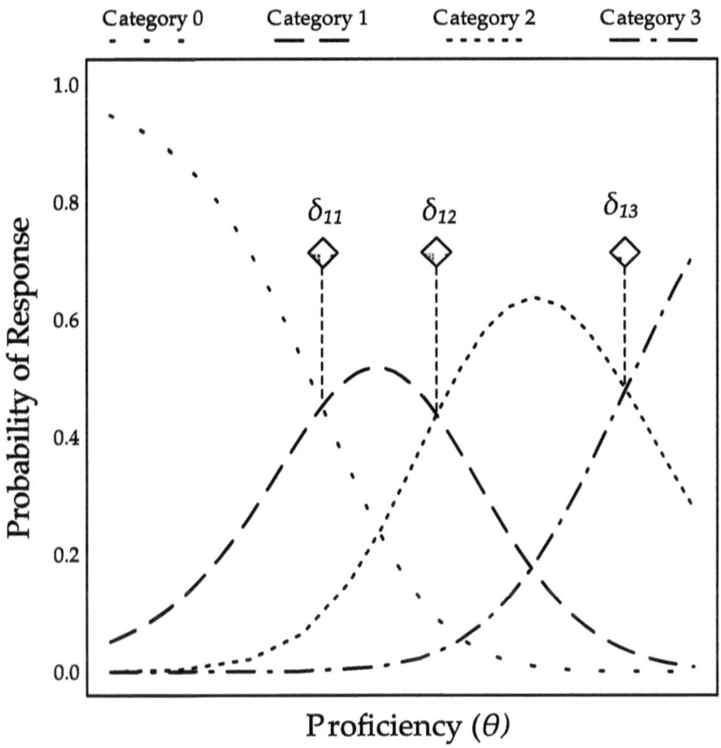

Fig. 4 Sample illustration of the locations of δ_{ij} parameters in a category characteristic curve plot

The PCM, like other polytomous logit models such as the graded response model (Samejima 1969) or continuation ratio models such as the sequential model (Tutz 1990), estimates these interaction terms. Because of this, they provide a better model fit than more restrictive models such as Andrich's Rating Scale Model (RSM) (Andrich 1978). Instead of including an interaction term, the RSM relies on the use of main effects for both items and levels; however, the parsimony of the RSM often proves too restrictive, and the PCM is then preferred for the better fit it provides. For instance, in the *Striving Readers* example, the PCM fit the data significantly better than the RSM ($\chi^2_{(22)} = 207.040, p < 0.001$).

It is possible to obtain the benefits of an overall level main effect (i.e., a $\delta_{.j}$ parameter) without resorting to the RSM by simply reparameterizing the PCM accordingly:

$$logit[Pr(x_{pij} = 1 \mid \theta_p)] = \eta_{pij} = \theta_p - (\delta_{.j} + \lambda_{ij}) \quad (2)$$

This simple reparameterization is graphically represented in Fig. 6. It includes an overall level parameter $\delta_{.j}$ (represented by the dashed horizontal lines) that directly estimates a location for each boundary between the levels. The λ_{ij}, estimated as deviations from the level effects, are constrained such that the sum of the λ_{ij} for a given level j is 0.

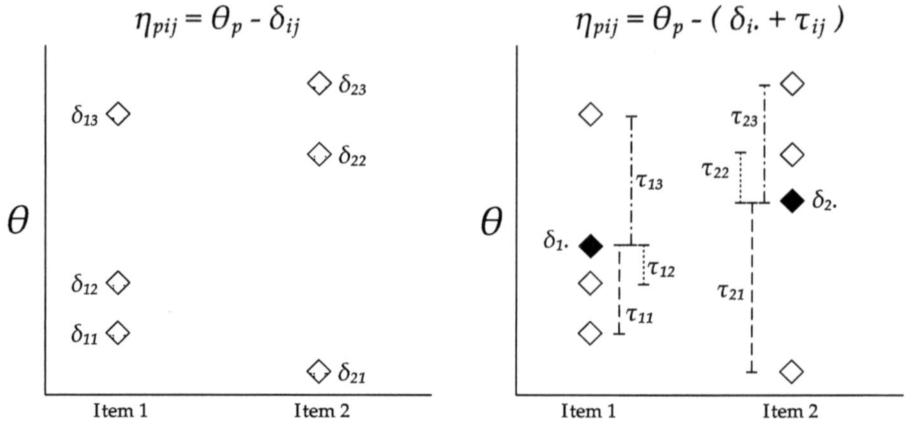

Fig. 5 Sample illustration comparing Master's parameterization of the PCM and a "rating scale" parameterization of the same model

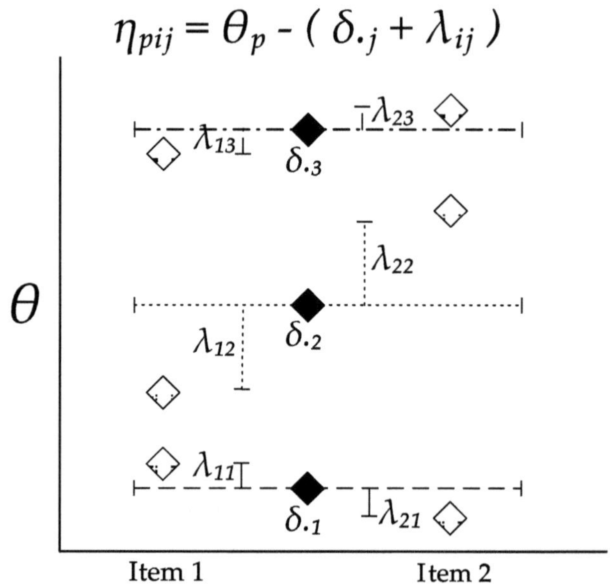

Fig. 6 Sample illustration illustrating the L-PCM reparametirization of the PCM including level main effects

Using this alternative parameterization (henceforth L-PCM for level-PCM), we can preserve the link to the original theory and examine how closely the interaction terms λ_{ij} follow the overall level parameters $\delta_{.j}$ by examining their dispersion as shown in Fig. 7. The item map in the figure organizes the λ_{ij} parameters around the overall level parameters, and the amount of observed variation in each level provides information about the quality of the overall levels as predictors of the item difficulty.

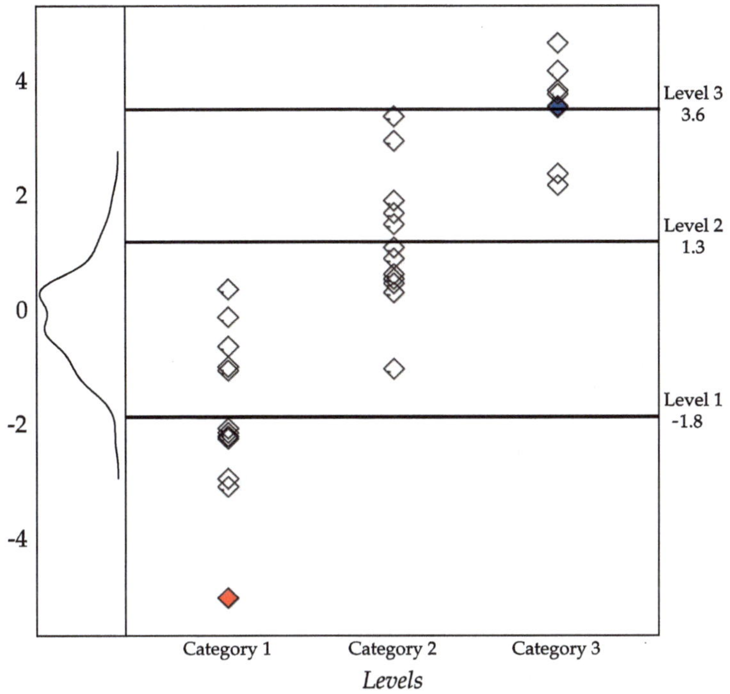

Fig. 7 Wright map organizing the λ_{ij} parameters as deviations of the $\delta_{.j}$ level parameters

In this example we can see that, although the dispersion of the λ_{ij} is considerable in all three levels, it is possible to appreciate a reasonable degree of separation between the three clusters of item by category parameters.

We have addressed the first of the questions raised in the introduction, namely how to estimate the boundaries (i.e., cut-points) between the levels. Based on these cut-points we can separate persons into the different levels of proficiency, fulfilling at least one of the goals that are usually pursued in standard setting exercises. However, it is one thing to determine cut-points, an another entirely different is to claim that those newly created levels in the latent variable correspond to the originally hypothesized performance levels.

4 Interpreting the Levels

Evaluating whether the estimated levels can be considered an accurate reflection of the theoretical levels is a critical issue that needs to be addressed in order to make tenable inferences about the respondents. We propose two complementary approaches to examine the "fit" of the estimated levels to the original hypothesis.

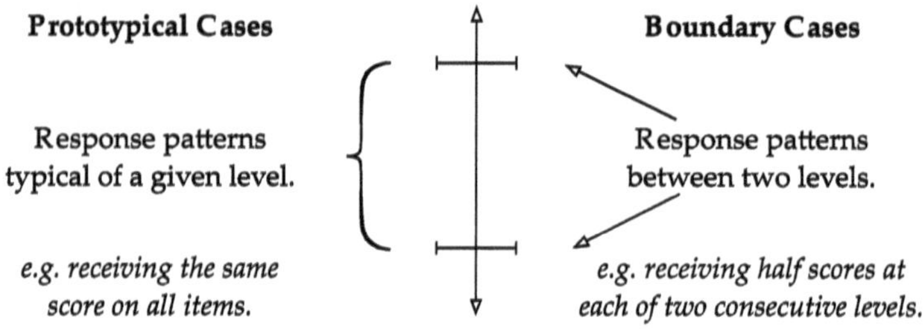

Fig. 8 Illustration of both kinds of ideal cases: prototypes and boundary cases

4.1 Identifying Ideal Cases

The first alternative for characterizing the proficiency levels estimated by the model is to consider them in relation to "ideal" cases, by which we mean response patterns that would canonically represent a performance level according to the original theory and task design.

We focus on two kinds of ideal cases, namely, prototypical and boundary cases (see Fig. 8):

1. *Prototypical cases:* refer to response patterns that would be considered exemplary of a given level, for instance, a respondent at level three that answers all the items at that level.
2. *Boundary cases:* refer to response patterns that would be prototypical for a respondent that is "in between" two levels. For example, a respondent that is transitioning from level one to level two may answer exactly half of the tasks at level one and half of the tasks at level two.

Using these ideal cases as a guide, we can produce a plot, an example of which is shown in Fig. 9, that "crosses" the average item scores of each one of these cases with the cut-points estimated directly by the model.

For example, the prototypical case of a respondent at level three, answering all the items at level three, would have an average item score of 3 and the boundary case of a respondent transitioning from level one to level two, answering exactly half of the tasks at level one and half of the tasks at level two, would have an average item score of 1.5. In this plot, the "prototypical" cases (shown by gray dashed vertical lines) should indicate the centroid of the level, while the "boundary" cases (shown by black solid vertical lines) should signal the cut-points between the levels. The horizontal black solid lines indicate the model estimates of the cut-points between the levels. Thus, the areas highlighted in gray indicate the regions where we expect our actual data to fall if the estimated levels match the hypothesized levels. We would compare the estimated person ability for each person[2] (given by solid

[2]Note that when fitting a partial credit model on complete data, each average item score is a sufficient statistic for ability estimate; the figure would be messier but interpreted the same way if incomplete data was used.

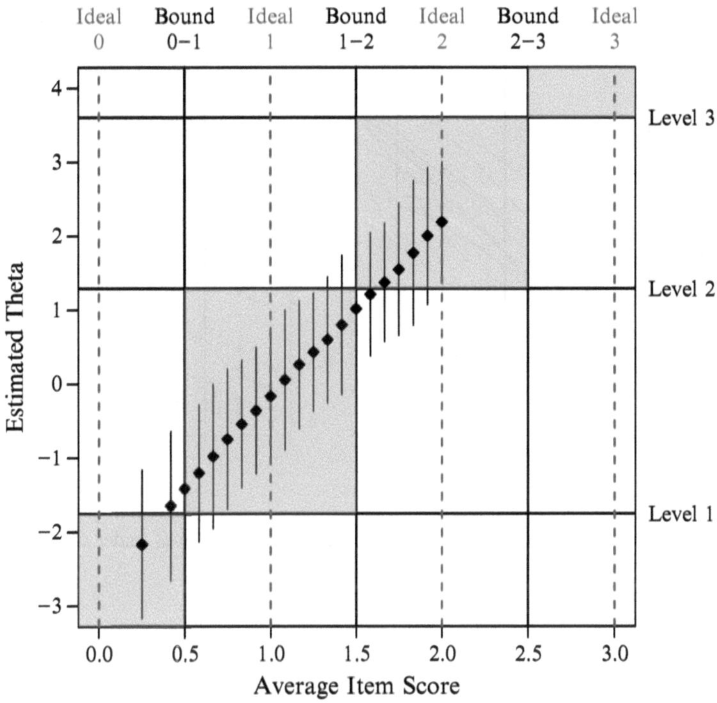

Fig. 9 Plotting proficiency estimates in relation to estimated cut-points and ideal cases

black points) and their standard errors (the vertical gray lines around each black point) to the gray regions to check.

Figure 9 shows the results for the *Striving Readers* example. The unusual linear relationship between average item score and estimated theta is due to the even coverage of the sample ability range by the item parameters. Most of the points fall within the gray regions, indicating good fit between the hypothesized and estimated levels for this dataset. Perhaps the level two cut-point is slightly overestimated and the level one cut-point is slightly underestimated, since the data falls slightly outside the highlighted zones at those boundaries. Overall, the estimated level cut-points by the model appear to match the hypothesized levels.

This plot shows the zones in which we would expect the respondents to be located if there is a good match between the levels demarcated by the estimated cut-points and the levels hypothesized by the construct and allows us to compare the estimated person locations to those zones. Information about both kinds of ideal cases (Fig. 8) is used to provide evidence regarding the match between the hypothesized and estimated levels.

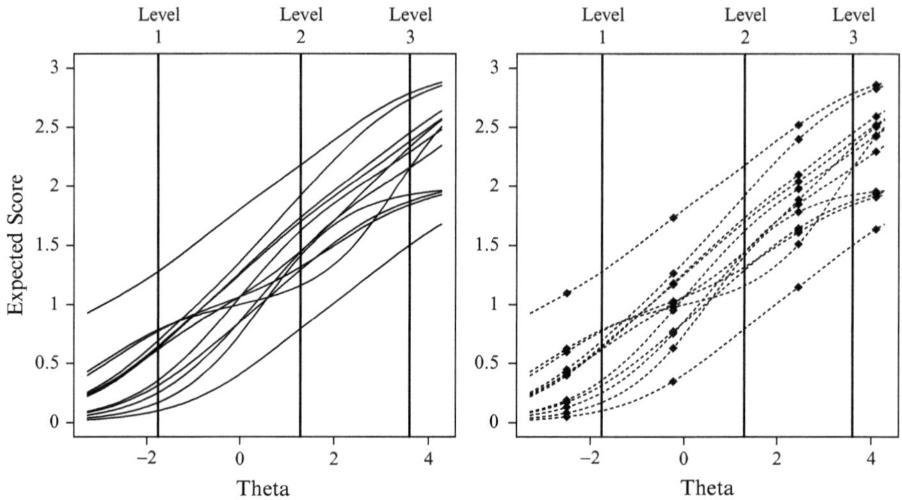

Fig. 10 Two approaches for calculating the expected responses: area under the curbe (*left*) and expected item score (*right*)

4.2 Examining Expected Score Ranges

The second alternative for characterizing the proficiency levels that are being demarcated by the model cut-points is to examine the expected responses for the items within the range of each level. The expected item score for each item i is a function of θ_p and can be calculated by:

$$\sum_j jPr(x_{pij} = 1 \mid \theta_p) \tag{3}$$

using the estimated values for the item parameters.

Figure 10 shows the expected item scores for the 12 *Striving Readers* items from the 7th grade persuasive assessment. In order to examine the expected scores for a given level, we could use the area under each curve within that level, for example by integrating each curve in the left-hand side of the figure over each of the four estimated levels. Alternatively, we could examine the expected score for one (or more) discrete values of theta, as in the right-hand side of the figure. The two methods will yield similar results unless the expected score curves are irregularly shaped, and the latter method has the advantage of simplicity in calculation, presentation, and interpretation.

If we look at the range of the expected item scores associated with level two (i.e., between the 1–2 and the 2–3 cut-points), we would anticipate that the expected scores on that range are (a) aggregated closely around the value associated with

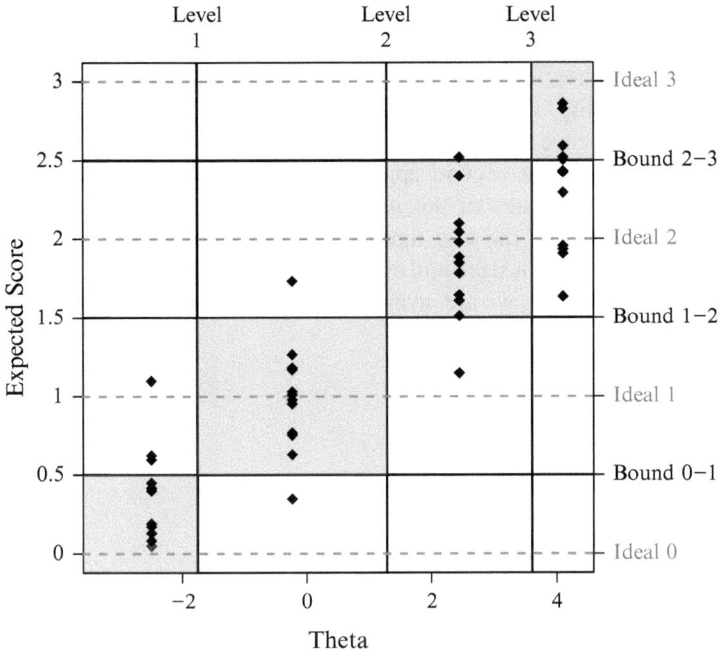

Fig. 11 Plotting proficiency estimates in relation to estimated expected scores

a prototypical case and (b) within the range established by the boundary cases. An example of the kind of graph to do this is presented in Fig. 11.

In this figure, the gray dashed vertical lines indicate the expected score for prototypical cases at each level and the solid black horizontal lines indicate the expected score for boundary cases between each successive pair of levels. The horizontal black solid lines indicate the model estimates of the cut-points between the levels. Thus, the areas highlighted in gray indicate the regions where we expect our actual data to fall if the estimated levels match the hypothesized levels. The black solid points give the expected item score for each item i at a given θ_p that is representative of the level.[3]

Figure 11 shows the results for the *Striving Readers* example. In general, the expected item scores are centered around the gray dashed lines within each level and fall within the gray regions, indicating good fit between the hypothesized and estimated levels. There is possibly one item that is too easy and one that is too difficult; these items could be removed from further analysis. Note that there is not much data regarding level three, so in this particular example, we would conclude

[3]The representation of standard errors in this figure is not straightforward considering that the standard errors in the logit scale would be presented as horizontal bars, which would not contribute to the inference in the plot.

that the hypothesized levels zero, one, and two are well recovered by the model but we would not make strong statements about the location of level three.

The two approaches, identifying ideal cases (as in Fig. 9) and examining expected score ranges (as in Fig. 11), provide complementary but distinct evidence. The first approach uses evidence from the person side of the model (the estimates of the person ability), while the second approach uses information from the item side of the model (the estimates of the item parameters). Since the person and item estimates are connected, the two figures will provide consistent evidence of the match between the hypothesized and estimated levels from alternative views of what the levels mean. However, we are investigating if one method is preferred in specific circumstances.

5 Discussion

5.1 Next Steps

Splitting a continuous variable into proficiency groups and then interpreting those groups, as is done in standard setting, is common practice. The methods to do so discussed in this paper could be extended by the use of located latent class models (Lindsay et al. 1991; Formann 1995), which directly model proficiency groups as in latent class analysis (Lazarsfeld and Henry 1968; Hagenaars and McCutcheon 2002), and a similar reparametrization to estimate a level main effect:

1. Located Latent Classes (LLC)

$$\eta_{pij} = \theta_{c(p)} - \delta_{ij}$$

2. Level Located Latent Classes (L-LLC)

$$\eta_{pij} = \theta_{c(p)} - (\delta_{.j} + \lambda_{ij})$$

These models could be used to directly estimate the centroids of each level, represented by the $\theta_{c(p)}$, concurrently with the level cut-points. This would provide an alternative to the use of prototypical score patterns to characterize each level.

A second area where the direct estimation of level cut-points could be useful is in the context of previous work on Structured Construct Models (SCM) (Wilson 2009; Diakow et al. 2011). In SCM, the relations between constructs are specified as conditional relations between specific levels of two different constructs. In other words, to reach level 4 of my "target" construct, the respondent is not only required to be at level 3 of that same construct, but also achieve a specific level, say level 3, of a "requirement" construct. So far, these models have relied exclusively on the use of latent class models to allocate the respondents into the different proficiency levels, but the estimation of the cut-points directly within the item response model opens the possibility of modeling these relations directly on a continuous latent variable.

5.2 Summary

In this paper we have presented a simple idea for improving the connection between the substantive theory used to create an assessment and the measurement model used to analyze it. Additionally, we have introduced two graphical representations that can help characterize the groups that have been established by the estimated cut-points by contrasting the observed performances of those groups to the performance levels originally hypothesized.

We believe that this kind of procedure can help practitioners make meaningful interpretations and provide more accurate diagnostic information to respondents in general. Furthermore, the procedure described in this paper can provide additional evidence to support, corroborate, or potentially raise questions about the results of traditional standard setting procedures.

It is important to note, however, that the methodological simplicity of this procedure requires a considerable amount of work in the definition of the construct, the creation of the assessment tasks, and the elaboration of the scoring guides. It is our hope that the possibility of generating this kind of analysis will encourage test developers to invest effort in those earlier stages in order to improve the quality and interpretation of their assessments.

References

Andrich, D. (1978). A rating formulation for ordered response categories. *Psychometrika, 43*(4), 561–573.

Angoff, W. H. (1971). Scales, norms, and equivalent scores. In R. L. Thorndike (Ed.), *Educational measurement* (pp. 508–600). Washington, DC: American Council on Education.

Cizek, G. J. (1993). Reconsidering standards and criteria. *Journal of Educational Measurement, 30*(2), 93–106.

Cizek, G. J., & Sternberg, R. J. (2001). *Setting performance standards: Concepts, methods, and perspectives.*. Mahwah, NJ: Lawrence Erlbaum.

Cizek, G. J., Bunch, M. B., & Koons, H. (2004). Setting performance standards: contemporary methods. *Educational Measurement: Issues and Practice, 23*(4), 31–50.

Diakow, R., Torres Irribarra, D., & Wilson, M. (2011). *Analyzing the complex structure of a learning progression: structured construct models.* Paper presented at the annual meeting of the national council of measurement in education, New Orleans, LA, April 2011.

Dray, A. J., Brown, N. J. S., Lee, Y., Diakow, R., & Wilson, M. (2011). *Striving readers BEAR assessment report.* Berkeley, CA: Berkeley Evaluation and Assessment Research Center.

Formann, A. K. (1995). Linear logistic latent class analysis and the Rasch model Rasch models: Foundations, recent developments, and applications. In G. H. Fischer & I. W. Molenaar (pp. 239–256). New York: Springer.

Glass, G. V. (1978). Standards and criteria. *Journal of Educational Measurement, 15*(4), 237–261.

Hagenaars, J. A., & McCutcheon, A. L. (2002). *Applied latent class analysis.*. New York: Cambridge University Press.

Institute for Education Sciences (2006). Striving Readers Program. Retrieved from http://www2.ed.gov/programs/strivingreaders/index.html. Cited December 10 2012.

Lazarsfeld, P. F., & Henry, N. W. (1968). *Latent structure analysis.* New York: Houghton, Mifflin.

Lewis, D. M., Mitzel, H. C., & Green, D. R. (1996, June). Standard setting: Abook- mark approach. In D. R. Green (Chair), *IRT-based standard setting procedures utilizing behavioral anchoring*. Symposium conducted at the Council of Chief State School Officers National Conference on Large-Scale Assessment, Phoenix, AZ.

Lindsay, B., Clogg, C. C., & Grego, J. (1991). Semiparametric estimation in the Rasch model and related exponential response models, including a simple latent class model for item analysis. *Journal of the American Statistical Association, 86*(413), 96–107.

Masters, G. N. (1982). A Rasch model for partial credit scoring. *Psychometrika, 47*(2), 149–174.

McDonald, T., Thornley, C., Staley, R., & Moore, D. W. (2009). The San Diego striving readers' project: building academic success for adolescent readers. *Journal of Adolescent & Adult Literacy, 52*(8), 720–722.

National Research Council (2001). *Knowing what students know: the science and design of educational assessment.* Washington, DC: National Academy Press.

Samejima, F. (1969). *Estimation of latent ability using a response pattern of graded scores* (Psychometrika Monograph Supplement, No. 17). Richmond, VA: Psychometric Society.

Schwartz, R., Ayers, E., & Wilson, M. (2011, July). *Mapping a learning progression using unidimensional and multidimensional item response models.* Paper presented at the International Meeting of the Psychometric Society, Hong Kong.

Tutz, G. (1990). Sequential item response models with an ordered response. *British Journal of Mathematical and Statistical Psychology, 43*(1), 39–55.

Wilmot, D.B., Schoenfeld, A., Wilson, M., Champney, D., & Zahner, W. (2011). Validating a learning progression in mathematical functions for college readiness. *Mathematical Thinking and Learning, 13*(4), 259–291.

Wilson, M., & Draney, K. (2002). A technique for setting standards and maintaining them over time. In S. Nishisato, Y. Baba, H. Bozdogan, & K. Kanefugi (Eds.), *Measurement and multivariate analysis* (Proceedings of the International Conference on Measurement and Multivariate Analysis, Banff, Canada, May 12–14, 2000), pp 325–332. Tokyo: Springer.

Wilson, M. (2005). *Constructing measures: An item response modeling approach.* New York: Routledge.

Wilson, M. (2009). Measuring progressions: Assessment structures underlying a learning progression. *Journal of Research in Science Teaching, 46*(6), 716–730.

The Comparison of Two Input Statistics for Heuristic Cognitive Diagnosis

Hans-Friedrich Köhn, Chia-Yi Chiu, and Michael J. Brusco

1 Introduction

In the past decade, cognitive diagnosis models (CDMs) of educational test performance, a special form of constrained latent class models, have received increasing attention among educational researchers as a new and promising paradigm of formative assessment. CDMs decompose ability in a domain into a set of specific binary skills called *attributes*. (Non-)mastery of attributes documents an examinee's strengths and weaknesses in the domain as a profile of mental aptitude. Distinct profiles define classes of intellectual proficiency. Methods for fitting CDMs to educational test data and assigning examinees to proficiency classes are typically based on maximum likelihood estimation (MLE) procedures such as Expectation Maximization (EM) and Markov Chain Monte Carlo (MCMC). These procedures often encounter difficulties in practice (e.g., the need for specialized, complex software that tends to be proprietary and difficult to use for educational practitioners; the sensitivity to the starting values of the iterative MLE procedures; no guarantee of optimal solutions; CPU time and convergence issues; the requirement of large samples that are often not available in small- or medium-sized testing programs). In response to these difficulties, a number of researchers (Ayers et al. 2008; Chiu 2008; Chiu and Douglas 2013; Chiu et al. 2009; Park and Lee 2011; Willse et al. 2007) have proposed nonparametric (i.e., model-free) classification techniques

H.-F. Köhn (✉)
University of Illinois at Urbana-Champaign, Champaign, IL 61820, USA
e-mail: hkoehn@cyrus.psych.uiuc.edu

C.-Y. Chiu
Rutgers, the State University of New Jersey, New Jersey, NJ 08901, USA
e-mail: chia-yi.chiu@gse.rutgers.edu

M.J. Brusco
Florida State University, Tallahassee, FL 32306, USA
e-mail: mbrusco@cob.fsu.edu

R.E. Millsap et al. (eds.), *New Developments in Quantitative Psychology*, Springer Proceedings in Mathematics & Statistics 66, DOI 10.1007/978-1-4614-9348-8_21,

(cluster analysis) as heuristic or approximate alternatives to MLE procedures for assigning examinees to proficiency classes. (A heuristic method solves a nontrivial optimization problem using clever computational approximations so that the obtained solution is very close to the desired optimal solution.) These classification techniques first aggregate each examinee's test item scores into a profile of attribute sum-scores, which then form the basis for clustering examinees into groups that serve as proxies for the proficiency classes in cognitive diagnosis. One difficulty of this approach is that aggregating distinct observed item scores of examinees, who belong to different proficiency classes, can result in their having identical attribute sum-score profiles and therefore risks misclassification of those examinees. This study demonstrates that clustering examinees into proficiency classes based on their item scores rather than on their attribute sum-score profiles results in a more accurate classification of examinees. First, a brief review of relevant definitions and technical key concepts concerning CDMs and classification techniques adapted to cognitive diagnosis is provided. The results of a simulation study are then presented. The discussion addresses two questions regarding the theoretical and empirical implications raised by the findings.

2 Definitions and Technical Concepts

2.1 Cognitive Diagnosis Models

Let Y_{ij} denote the observed response of examinee i, $i = 1, \dots, N$, to binary item j, $j = 1, \dots, J$. Consider N examinees who belong to K distinct latent classes of intellectual proficiency. The general (unconstrained) latent class model defines the conditional probability of examinee i in proficiency class $\mathscr{C}_k$, $k = 1, \dots, K$, answering correctly item j by the item response function, $P(Y_{ij} = 1 | i \in \mathscr{C}_k) = \pi_{jk}$, where π_{jk} is constant for item j across all members i in proficiency class $\mathscr{C}_k$. (For J items, the item response function is characterized by $J \times K$ parameters, π_{jk}.) The proficiency-class membership of the examinees is estimated from the observed item responses, Y_{ij}, using MLE; local independence is assumed for the observed item responses. No further restrictions are imposed on the relation between the latent variable—proficiency-class membership—and the observed item response. In contrast, CDMs constrain the relation between the latent variable and the observed item response so that the mastery of cognitive attributes characteristic for distinct latent proficiency classes is assumed to determine the observed response to an item.

Suppose that A latent binary attributes constitute a certain ability domain; there are then 2^A distinct attribute profiles composed of these A attributes representing K distinct latent proficiency classes. (An attribute profile for a proficiency class can consist of all zeroes, because it is possible for an examinee not to have mastered any attributes at all.) Let the A-dimensional vector, $\alpha_k = (\alpha_1, \dots, \alpha_A)'$, represent the binary attribute profile of proficiency class $\mathscr{C}_k$, where the ath entry indicates whether the respective attribute has been mastered. (For brevity, the attribute profile of examinee $i \in \mathscr{C}_k$, $\alpha_{i \in \mathscr{C}_k}$, will often be written $\alpha_i = (\alpha_{i1}, \ldots, \alpha_{iA})'$.) Consider a test of J items for assessing ability in that domain. Each individual item j is associated with a binary attribute profile that specifies or constrains the particular skills required for answering it correctly. Item-attribute profiles that consist entirely of zeroes, however, are inadmissible, because they correspond to items whose answers require no skills at all; hence, given A attributes, there are at most $2^A - 1$ distinct item-attribute profiles. The entire set of constraints specifying the associations between J items and A attributes constitutes the Q-matrix, $\mathbf{Q} = \{q_{ja}\}_{(J \times A)}$, $a = 1, \ldots, A$, where $q_{ja} = 1$ if a correct answer to the jth item requires mastery of the ath attribute, and 0 otherwise (Tatsuoka 1985); thus, the rows of $\mathbf{Q}$ represent the item-attribute profiles, $\mathbf{q}_j$.

2.2 *Model-Free Classification Adapted to Cognitive Diagnosis*

Let $\mathbf{Y}_i$ denote the J-dimensional item-score profile, $\mathbf{Y}_i = (Y_{i1}, \ldots, Y_{iJ})'$, of examinee i (for brevity, the examinee index is omitted when the context permits). For input to classification techniques, (Ayers et al. 2008; Willse et al. 2007), and (Chiu et al. 2009) aggregated each examinee's item-score profile, $\mathbf{Y}_i$, into an A-dimensional profile of attribute sum-scores, $\mathbf{W}_i$, defined as $\mathbf{W}_i = (W_{i1}, \ldots, W_{iA})' = \mathbf{Y}_i\mathbf{Q}$, where $W_{ia} = \sum_{j=1}^{J} Y_{ij} q_{ja}$. Because each cell entry of $\mathbf{Q} = \{q_{ja}\}$ represents the association between an item and an attribute, each element of $\mathbf{W}_i$ consists of the sum of the correct answers of examinee i to all items requiring mastery of the ath attribute. (Items that require mastery of more than one attribute for their solution contribute to multiple elements of $\mathbf{W}_i$.) Across examinees, the attribute sum-score profiles, $\mathbf{W}_i$, form the rows of a rectangular $N \times A$ matrix.

Many techniques exist for the model-free classification of a set of objects (such as the rows of a matrix). The principal objective shared by all of these techniques is to identify maximally homogeneous groups ("clusters") that are maximally separated. To adapt one popular technique, hierarchical agglomerative cluster analysis (HACA), to cognitive diagnosis requires transforming the $N \times A$ matrix of examinees' attribute sum-score profiles into an $N \times N$ symmetric matrix of inter-examinee Euclidean distances. Popular HACA algorithms include single-link, complete-link, and average-link clustering (Johnson 1967) and Ward's (Ward 1963) minimum-variance method. HACA algorithms all sequentially merge or agglomerate examinees (or groups of examinees) closest to each other at each step into an inverted tree-shaped hierarchy of nested classes that represents the relationship between examinees. The inter-examinee distances are updated after each merger to reflect the latest status of examinee/cluster cohesion as input for the next agglomeration step; the specific manner of re-calculating these distances distinguishes the link algorithms. (Ward's method uses a different strategy that does not rely upon inter-examinee distances but instead attempts to minimize the increase in total within-cluster variance after merging.)

The Asymptotic Classification Theory of Cognitive Diagnosis (ACTCD) (Chiu et al. 2009) provided a theoretical foundation for using HACA as a heuristic for assigning examinees to proficiency classes for educational data conforming to the conjunctive non-compensatory Deterministic Input Noisy Output "AND" Gate (DINA) model (Junker and Sijtsma 2001; Macready and Dayton 1977), which is perhaps the most popular of the many available CDMs. (A conjunctive non-compensatory model assumes that an examinee cannot make up for a lack of mastery of a specific attribute or attributes by mastery of another attribute or attributes.) The item response function of the DINA model for item j and examinee i is

$$P(Y_{ij}=1|\alpha_i,s_j,g_j)=(1-s_j)^{\eta_{ij}}g_j^{(1-\eta_{ij})} \tag{1}$$

where $s_j = P(Y_{ij}=0|\eta_{ij}=1)$ and $g_j = P(Y_{ij}=1|\eta_{ij}=0)$ are item parameters formalizing the probabilities of "slipping" (failing to answer item j correctly despite having the skills required to do so) and "guessing" (answering item j correctly despite lacking the skills required to do so), respectively. The conjunction parameter η_{ij} indicates whether examinee i has mastered all the attributes needed to answer correctly item j and is defined as $\eta_{ij}=\prod_{a=1}^{A}\alpha_{ia}^{q_{ja}}$ (thus, η_{ij} represents the ideal response when neither slipping nor guessing occurs; an examinee's entire vector of J ideal responses is written as η).

The ACTCD consists of three lemmas, each of which specifies a condition necessary for a consistency theorem to hold; this theorem states that the probability that complete-link HACA assigns examinees correctly to their true proficiency classes approaches 1 as the length of a test (i.e., the number of test items) increases, provided that each examinee's item-score profile, $\mathbf{Y}$, has been aggregated into an attribute sum-score profile, $\mathbf{W}$ (Consistency Theorem of Classification of the ACTCD; Chiu et al. 2009, pp. 645–647).

3 Proposition: Y as Input to Heuristic Classification

Lemma 2 of the ACTCD justifies using $\mathbf{W}$ as a statistic for α. Let $\mathbf{T}(\alpha)=E(\mathbf{W}|\alpha)$ be the conditional expectation of the attribute sum-score profile, $\mathbf{W}$, given attribute profile α, where the ath element of $\mathbf{T}(\alpha)$ is defined as $T_a(\alpha)=E(W_a|\alpha)=\sum_{j=1}^{J}E(Y_j|\alpha)q_{ja}$. (For the DINA model, the expected response, $E(Y_j|\alpha)$, equals $(1-s_j)^{\eta_j}g_j^{(1-\eta_j)}$.) Loosely speaking, $\mathbf{T}(\alpha)$ can be regarded as the center of the proficiency class characterized by α. Consider two attribute profiles, α and α^*. Lemma 2 of the ACTCD states that if the Q-matrix is complete (i.e., allows identification of all possible attribute profiles), then $\alpha\neq\alpha^*\Rightarrow\mathbf{T}(\alpha)\neq\mathbf{T}(\alpha^*)$ always holds (Chiu et al. 2009) (pp. 645–647). Thus, $\mathbf{W}$ guarantees distinct, well-separated centers of the different proficiency classes, which is a requirement for proving the Consistency Theorem. (At present, Lemma 2 has been proven only for item responses conforming to the DINA model.)

The ACTCD does not address the relative advantages of assigning examinees to proficiency classes based on their attribute sum-score profiles, **W**, or their item-score profiles, **Y**, but focuses on only **W** because of its direct conceptual relation to the underlying constrained latent class model. However, as indicated earlier, using attribute sum-score profiles, **W**, as input to heuristic classification techniques may encounter difficulties. Specifically, aggregating each examinee's item-score profile, **Y**, into an attribute sum-score profile, **W**, can result in the representation of distinct **Y**, where examinees possibly belong to different proficiency classes, by identical **W**, which may then lead to the misclassification of those examinees. Consider the following example. Suppose that $A = 2$ and $J = 5$, with the Q-matrix defined as

$$\mathbf{Q} = \begin{pmatrix} 1 & 0 \\ 1 & 0 \\ 0 & 1 \\ 0 & 1 \\ 1 & 1 \end{pmatrix}.$$

Let $\mathbf{Y} = (00011)$ and $\mathbf{Y}^* = (01110)$ denote the observed item-score profiles of two examinees who belong to distinct proficiency classes. However, aggregating **Y** and $\mathbf{Y}^*$ results in identical attribute sum-score profiles, $\mathbf{W} = \mathbf{W}^* = (12)$, which then leads to the assignment of the two examinees to the identical proficiency class. Thus, to avoid these potential ambiguities, it is proposed to use **Y** as input to heuristic classification for assigning examinees to proficiency classes (note that **Y** is linked to α through η; hence, **Y** can also be regarded as a statistic for α).

4 Simulation Study

A simulation study was conducted to compare the performance of item-score profiles, **Y**, with that of attribute sum-score profiles, **W**, when used as input to complete-link HACA for assigning examinees to proficiency classes.

4.1 Generation of Item Scores

Examinees' item scores conforming to the DINA model were simulated according to the method described in Chiu et al. (2009). The experimental design included three variables: (a) number of examinees, $N = 100, 500$; (b) number of attributes, $A = 3, 4$; and (c) number of items, $J = 20, 40, 80$. For the levels of variable A, $2^3 - 1 = 7$ and $2^4 - 1 = 15$ distinct binary item-attribute profiles were generated (profiles consisting of all zeroes being omitted) to form template Q-matrices of tests containing $J = 20$

items (Chiu et al. 2009) (Table 2, p. 650). These Q-matrix designs guaranteed that all attributes occurred with equal frequencies. The Q-matrices for tests containing 40 or 80 items were created by stacking the 20-item template Q-matrices.

An examinee's attribute profile was drawn either from a discrete uniform distribution (i.e., the attribute profile for each proficiency class, α_k, had the same probability, $1/K$, where $K = 2^A$) or from a more realistic and complex multivariate normal distribution ($\theta = (\theta_1, \ldots, \theta_A)' \sim N_A \ (\mathbf{0}, \Sigma)$, where $\mathbf{0}$ indicates the location vector and Σ, the covariance matrix, with values along the main diagonal equal to 1.00 and off-diagonal entries set to either 0.25 or 0.50), so that each binary attribute, α_a, was linked to a latent continuous ability dimension, θ_a. For each examinee, a vector θ_i was randomly sampled; if its component values exceeded a predetermined threshold, then the corresponding entry in the examinee's attribute profile, α_i, was set to 1:

$$\alpha_{ia} = \begin{cases} 1 \text{ if } \theta_{ia} \geq \Phi^{-1}\left(\frac{a}{A+1}\right) \\ 0 \text{ otherwise} \end{cases}$$

The simulated item responses, Y_{ij}, were sampled from a Bernoulli distribution with $\pi_{ij} = P(Y_{ij} = 1)$ defined by (1), the item response function of the DINA model. The slipping and guessing parameters, s_j and g_j, respectively, were drawn from the continuous uniform distribution $U(0, 0.15)$, allowing only minor deviations from the ideal item responses, or $U(0, 0.30)$, adding more noise. Completely crossing the three distributions for examinees' attribute profiles and the two distributions for the slipping and guessing parameters with the levels of the variables N, A, and J resulted in an experimental design with $3 \times 2 \times 2 \times 2 \times 3 = 72$ cells. Twenty-five paired ($\mathbf{Y}$ and $\mathbf{W}$) data sets were generated for each cell, for a total of 1,800 paired data sets.

4.2 Clustering Attribute Sum-Score Profiles and Item-Score Profiles

From examinees' observed attribute sum-score profiles, $\mathbf{W}$, and observed item-score profiles, $\mathbf{Y}$, the inter-examinee Euclidean distances were computed and collected into two $N \times N$ input proximity matrices. The examinees were grouped into $K = 2^A$ proficiency classes using the complete-link HACA algorithm (Johnson 1967) as implemented in the `hclust` routine in `R`.

For the simulated data sets, the true proficiency-class membership of each examinee is known and provides a standard for quantifying the results of the cluster analysis. However, because complete-link HACA does not label the clusters representing the proficiency classes with their respective attribute profiles, it is not possible to compute rates of correct classification. Instead, a measure of agreement between the true classification of the examinees and the classification assigned by complete-link HACA was computed using the Hubert–Arabie Adjusted Rand Index (ARI) (Hubert and Arabie 1985; Steinley 2004), which has bounds 0 and 1 indicating perfect disagreement and perfect agreement, respectively. A major advantage of the ARI over "true-false" classification-rate indices is that it incorporates a sophisticated adjustment for random correct classifications.

4.3 Results

Table 1 presents the results separately for each of the three distributions used to generate examinees' attribute profiles. For each combination of N, A, J, and the distribution of the slipping and guessing parameters, Table 1 reports the average (mean) ARI computed across the 25 simulated data sets when attribute sum-score profiles, **W**, and item-score profiles, **Y**, served as input to complete-link HACA. For comparison, the table column labeled "EM" reports the average ARI computed across 25 replications of examinee classification based on the DINA-model parameters produced by EM. Of course, because the simulated item responses conform perfectly to the DINA model, EM should outperform complete-link HACA.

Table 1 shows that, for all of the 72 cells of the experimental design, the performance of complete-link HACA in assigning examinees to their true proficiency classes is better when item-score profiles, **Y**, rather than attribute sum-score profiles, **W**, served as input. Table 1 also demonstrates that the assignment of the examinees to their true proficiency classes deteriorates when either the number of attributes or the level of error perturbation (as reflected by the slipping and guessing parameters) increases; the number of examinees does not seem to have an effect. Interestingly, for both levels of error perturbation, (a) a larger number of items led to more accurate classification regardless of whether attribute sum-score profiles, **W**, or item-score profiles, **Y**, served as input, and (b) the difference between the accuracy of examinee classification when **W** or **Y** served as input decreased as the number of items increased.

5 Discussion

The simulation study demonstrated that, for item responses conforming to the DINA model, assignment of test examinees to their true proficiency classes was more accurate when their item-score profiles, **Y**, rather than their attribute sum-score profiles, **W**, served as input to complete-link HACA. Two questions regarding the theoretical and empirical implications of these findings are briefly addressed here.

First, does the inferior performance of the attribute sum-score profiles contradict the Consistency Theorem of Classification of the ACTCD (Chiu et al. 2009), which states that the probability that complete-link HACA assigns examinees correctly to their true proficiency classes based on their attribute sum-score profiles approaches 1 as the length of a test (i.e., the number of items, J) approaches infinity? The results of the simulation study suggest the opposite. Recall that generally a larger number of items led to more accurate classification regardless of whether attribute sum-score profiles, **W**, or item-score profiles, **Y**, served as input and that the difference between the accuracy of examinee classification when **W** or **Y** served as input decreased as the number of items increased. Therefore, the empirical findings support rather than contradict the Consistency Theorem.

Table 1 Average ARIs for complete-link HACA of the simulated data sets using attribute sum-score profiles, **W**, and item-score profiles, **Y**, as input

Discrete uniform distribution of attribute profiles

			$s_j, g_j \sim U(0, 0.15)$			$s_j, g_j \sim U(0, 0.30)$		
N	A	J	EM	**W**	**Y**	EM	**W**	**Y**
100	3	20	0.936	0.676	0.766	0.815	0.467	0.560
100	3	40	0.945	0.893	0.974	0.953	0.688	0.810
100	3	80	0.990	0.988	0.998	0.991	0.809	0.871
100	4	20	0.818	0.470	0.657	0.626	0.251	0.354
100	4	40	0.952	0.756	0.874	0.782	0.399	0.534
100	4	80	0.993	0.862	0.972	0.986	0.713	0.824
500	3	20	0.965	0.603	0.807	0.879	0.476	0.593
500	3	40	0.995	0.874	0.964	0.958	0.620	0.789
500	3	80	1.000	0.988	0.992	0.995	0.828	0.950
500	4	20	0.886	0.427	0.657	0.619	0.222	0.298
500	4	40	0.970	0.651	0.841	0.884	0.420	0.576
500	4	80	0.991	0.897	0.986	0.979	0.581	0.801

MVN distribution of attribute profiles ($\rho = 0.25$)

			$s_j, g_j \sim U(0, 0.15)$			$s_j, g_j \sim U(0, 0.30)$		
N	A	J	EM	**W**	**Y**	EM	**W**	**Y**
100	3	20	0.954	0.688	0.858	0.803	0.495	0.579
100	3	40	0.985	0.877	0.940	0.954	0.746	0.863
100	3	80	0.987	0.979	0.995	0.986	0.816	0.892
100	4	20	0.857	0.547	0.723	0.722	0.322	0.448
100	4	40	0.950	0.674	0.835	0.884	0.390	0.509
100	4	80	0.989	0.827	0.917	0.954	0.596	0.699
500	3	20	0.976	0.697	0.895	0.828	0.433	0.525
500	3	40	0.998	0.810	0.973	0.992	0.737	0.925
500	3	80	1.000	0.972	0.999	0.999	0.818	0.943
500	4	20	0.914	0.486	0.714	0.796	0.311	0.461
500	4	40	0.984	0.679	0.922	0.929	0.469	0.637
500	4	80	0.990	0.816	0.987	0.979	0.604	0.833

MVN distribution of attribute profiles ($\rho = 0.50$)

			$s_j, g_j \sim U(0, 0.15)$			$s_j, g_j \sim U(0, 0.30)$		
N	A	J	EM	**W**	**Y**	EM	**W**	**Y**
100	3	20	0.886	0.655	0.725	0.847	0.389	0.556
100	3	40	0.985	0.813	0.924	0.960	0.605	0.721
100	3	80	0.996	0.984	0.991	0.988	0.856	0.874
100	4	20	0.865	0.499	0.664	0.687	0.275	0.356
100	4	40	0.937	0.609	0.797	0.864	0.338	0.471
100	4	80	0.971	0.723	0.869	0.936	0.552	0.689
500	3	20	0.965	0.652	0.878	0.886	0.527	0.643
500	3	40	0.996	0.831	0.969	0.975	0.678	0.841
500	3	80	1.000	0.994	0.999	0.999	0.834	0.968
500	4	20	0.892	0.476	0.682	0.696	0.250	0.399
500	4	40	0.989	0.644	0.919	0.939	0.468	0.705
500	4	80	1.000	0.830	0.967	0.995	0.592	0.863

Second, the results of the simulation study suggest that item-score profiles might be more sensitive than attribute sum-score profiles in preserving true proficiency-class membership. Hence, the Consistency Theorem of Classification might also apply when item-score profiles, **Y**, rather than attribute sum-score profiles, **W**, serve as input to complete-link HACA. At present, however, there is no definite explanation of this phenomenon, and the dilemma that the theoretically well-supported statistic, **W**, is outperformed empirically by the theoretically indeterminate statistic, **Y**, remains unresolved and awaits further study.

References

Ayers, E., Nugent, R., & Dean, N. (2008). Skill set profile clustering based on student capability vectors computed from online tutoring data. In R. S. J. de Baker, T. Barnes, & J. E. Beck (Eds.), *Educational data mining 2008: Proceedings of the 1st International Conference on Educational Data Mining* (pp. 210–217). Montréal, Québec, Canada: International Data Mining Society.

Chiu, C.-Y. (2008). *Cluster analysis for cognitive diagnosis: Theory and applications* (Doctoral dissertation). Available from ProQuest Dissertations and Theses database. (UMI No. 3337778)

Chiu, C.-Y., & Douglas, J. A. (2013). A nonparametric approach to cognitive diagnosis by proximity to ideal response patterns. *Journal of Classification*, *30*(2), 225–250.

Chiu, C.-Y., Douglas, J. A., & Li, X. (2009). Cluster analysis for cognitive diagnosis: Theory and applications. *Psychometrika*, *74*, 633–665.

Hubert, L., & Arabie, P. (1985). Comparing partitions. *Journal of Classification*, *2*, 193–218.

Johnson, S. C. (1967). Hierarchical clustering schemes. *Psychometrika*, *32*, 241–254.

Junker, B. W., & Sijtsma, K. (2001). Cognitive assessment models with few assumptions, and connections with nonparametric item response theory. *Applied Psychological Measurement*, *25*, 258–272.

Macready, G. B., & Dayton, C. M. (1977). The use of probabilistic models in the assessment of mastery. *Journal of Educational Statistics*, *2*, 99–120.

Park, Y. S., & Lee, Y.-S. (2011). Diagnostic cluster analysis of mathematics skills. *IERI Monograph Series: Issues and Methodologies in Large-Scale Assessments*, *4*, 75–107.

Steinley, D. (2004). Properties of the Hubert-Arabie adjusted rand index. *Psychological Methods*, *9*, 386–396.

Tatsuoka, K. K. (1985). A probabilistic model for diagnosing misconception by the pattern classification approach. *Journal of Educational Statistics*, *10*, 55–73.

Ward, J. H., Jr. (1963). Hierarchical grouping to optimize an objective function. *Journal of the American Statistical Association*, *58*, 236–244.

Willse, J., Henson, R., & Templin, J. (2007, April). *Using sum scores or IRT in place of cognitive diagnostic models: Can more familiar models do the job?* Paper presented at the Annual Meeting of the National Council on Measurement in Education, Chicago, IL.

Does Model Misspecification Lead to Spurious Latent Classes? An Evaluation of Model Comparison Indices

Ying-Fang Chen and Hong Jiao

1 Introduction

In recent decades, researchers have paid increasing attention to developing extended item response theory (IRT) models. These models were developed primarily because of the need to resolve the violation of the strong assumptions of IRT models, to more clearly reflect the nature of real-world testing scenarios, and to generate more accurate estimates of model parameters. One such extension is mixture IRT modeling (Kelderman and Macready 1990; Mislevy and Verhelst 1990; Rost 1990), which integrates an IRT or a Rasch model with latent class analysis (LCA) (Dayton 1999; McCutcheon 1987) to accommodate heterogeneity in examinee population.

In educational or psychological assessments, examinees/respondents may not be qualitatively homogeneous in terms of item response patterns. If examinees form a mixture of latent subgroups but a single latent population is assumed, the assumption of local independence in IRT models is violated. When such violations are not taken into account, the estimation of model parameters can be affected. For these reasons, the mixture modeling approach—which can identify the number of latent classes as well as describe multiple latent classes in the examinee population—has been progressively used in assessments (e.g., Cohen and Bolt 2005; De Ayala et al. 2002; Finch and Pierson 2011; Maij-de Meij et al. 2010; Mislevy and Verhelst 1990; Samuelsen 2005; Smith et al. 2012).

In the framework of mixture IRT modeling, the most frequently used mixture model is the mixture Rasch model (MRM) (Rost 1990). The MRM combines the Rasch measurement model (Rasch 1960) and LCA, allowing for multiple latent populations. For example, two examinees who have identical ability levels but belong

Y.-F. Chen (✉) • H. Jiao
Department of Human Development and Quantitative Methodology,
University of Maryland, College Park, MD 20742, USA
e-mail: pie@umd.edu; hjiao@umd.edu

R.E. Millsap et al. (eds.), *New Developments in Quantitative Psychology*, Springer Proceedings in Mathematics & Statistics 66, DOI 10.1007/978-1-4614-9348-8_22,

to qualitatively heterogeneous subgroups are allowed to perform differentially on items (i.e., different item difficulties). The unconditional probability of a response vector can be expressed as

$$\mathrm{P}\left(\mathrm{x}\middle|\theta\right) = \sum_{\mathrm{c}=1}^{\mathrm{C}} \pi_{\mathrm{c}} \mathrm{P}\left(\mathrm{x}\middle|\theta,\mathrm{c}\right), \tag{1}$$

and the conditional probability of success given the latent class membership and model parameters for a specific latent class in the MRM is

$$\mathrm{P}\left(\mathrm{x}=1\middle|\theta_{\mathrm{c}},\mathrm{c}\right) = \frac{\exp\left(\theta_{\mathrm{jc}}-\beta_{\mathrm{ic}}\right)}{1+\exp\left(\theta_{\mathrm{jc}}-\beta_{\mathrm{ic}}\right)}, \tag{2}$$

where $x = (x_1, \ldots, x_{\mathrm{I}})$ represents the response vector, π_{c} is the mixing proportion with a constraint $\sum \pi_c = 1$, β_{ic} is the difficulty for item i conditional on latent class c $(c = 1, \ldots, \mathrm{C})$, and θ_{jc} denotes the ability parameter for an examinee j in latent class c. For each latent class, the Rasch model is assumed. Both item and ability parameters are conditional on a discrete latent class. For scale identification, item difficulties within a class are usually constrained with $\sum_i^I \beta_{ic} = 0$ (Rost 1990). If a one-class solution is suggested for the data, the MRM is reduced into the Rasch model.

Given that the estimation of model parameters in mixture modeling depends on the identification of latent class membership, accurately extracting latent classes is important. If errors in latent class extraction occur, the estimation and interpretation of model parameters will be accordingly biased (e.g., Alexeev et al. 2011; Cho et al. 2012; Li et al. 2009). Alexeev et al. (2011) have recently demonstrated that model misspecification contributed to the creation of spurious latent classes in the MRM. The authors applied the MRM to the data generated as 2PLM. Their simulation results showed that at least two classes were extracted despite the fact that only one class was simulated. Their findings suggest that the extraction of latent classes did not result from examinee heterogeneity, but from model misspecification in the MRM.

Alexeev et al. (2011) provided valuable insights into potential nuisance sources that cause the formation of spurious latent classes. A major limitation in their simulation study, however, is that only varying item discrimination was considered as a single source of model misspecification (i.e., only 2PLM data were generated). Consequently, little is known as to whether their findings are generalizable to other testing conditions, such as model misspecification due to an addition of item guessing and/or slipping parameters that are not represented in the Rasch model.

In addition to item difficulty and discrimination, guessing and slipping parameters can also characterize items. A logistic IRT model that contains four item parameters (4PLM) (Barton and Lord 1981) is expressed as

$$P\left(x=1\middle|\alpha_i,\beta_i,\gamma_i,\lambda_i,\theta_j\right) = \gamma_i + \frac{\lambda_i-\gamma_i}{1+\exp(-\alpha_i(\theta_j-\beta_i))}, \tag{3}$$

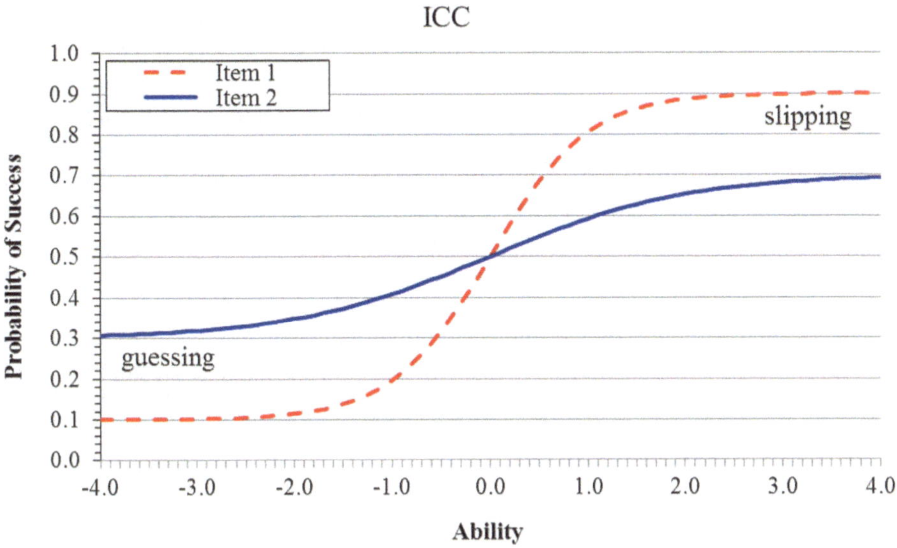

Fig. 1 Two 4PLM ICCs (item 1: $\alpha = 2.0$, $\gamma = 0.1$, $\lambda = 0.9$; item 2: $\alpha = 1.0$, $\gamma = 0.3$, $\lambda = 0.7$)

where α_i, β_i, γ_i, λ_i, and θ_i represent item discrimination, item difficulty, item guessing, item slipping, and ability parameter, respectively. In the plot of item characteristic curves (ICCs), item difficulty and discrimination represent the location and slope of an ICC, and the guessing parameter refers to the lower asymptote of an ICC and slipping is the upper asymptote of the ICC. Figure 1 illustrates two 4PLM ICCs, in which item 2 ($\alpha = 1.0$, $\gamma = 0.3$, $\lambda = 0.7$) exhibits stronger degrees of item guessing and slipping but weaker item discrimination than does item 1 ($\alpha = 2.0$, $\gamma = 0.1$, $\lambda = 0.9$). The probability of success in the 4PLM ranges from the lower asymptote to the upper asymptote across the ability continuum (Fig. 1). A guessing parameter is defined as the probability of a correct response by a very low-ability examinee. It can result from the use of a multiple choice format (e.g., the probability of success is 0.25 for a four-option item if a respondent guesses) and can be affected by flaws in an item (e.g., clues hidden in the item options or distractions are unattractive). A slipping item parameter is defined as the probability of an incorrect response to an item by a high-proficiency examinee. For some items, a high-ability examinee may unintentionally misread a question or overthink an easy item in a unique or creative manner. In a computer-based testing scenario, an item slipping effect may occur because of a special item response interface (Rulison and Loken 2009).

In the psychometric literature, the 3PLM with guessing is more prevalently used than IRT models with slipping. This predominance may be attributed to the fairly limited software available for estimating slipping parameters. Item slipping effects have been found to improve model-data fit and the accuracy of model parameter estimates in many empirical applications. For example, Barton and Lord

(1981) fitted the 4PLM and 3PLM to several large-scale assessment data sets and found that the former provided better model-data fit to the SAT verbal and math sections. In Loken and Rulison (2010), the 4PLM provided better fit (than did the 2PLM and 3PLM) to the delinquency data that were extracted from the large-scale *Monitoring the Future* (MTF) national survey (Johnston et al. 2006); in particular, the 4PLM yielded more information about moderate delinquency levels. Barton and Lord also demonstrated the adverse consequences of fitting the 3PLM and 2PLM to 4PLM data. Jiao et al. (2011) demonstrated how a 3PLM with slipping (i.e., 3PLM-λ) better fit a cognitive psychological test. Yen et al. (2012) indicated that in computerized adaptive testing scenarios, the 4PLM improved the ability estimates for a national sample data set that was drawn from the *English Ability Test* for college entrance in Taiwan. The above-mentioned studies suggest the practical need for and importance of including slipping effects to improve overall model-data fit and accuracy of parameter estimates.

The (mixture) Rasch model assumes no guessing or slipping effects. Therefore, model misspecification can also occur if one fits the (mixture) Rasch model to data with item guessing and/or slipping. To more comprehensively investigate the psychometric issue of the over-extraction of latent classes arising from model misspecification, the current study aims to examine whether the violation of assumptions regarding item discrimination, as well as guessing and slipping parameters, in the applications of the Rasch model causes the artificial extraction of latent classes. This research is expected to provide a more thorough discussion of the concerns about the over-extraction of latent classes. To sum up, this study intends to answer the following questions:

1. Which of the model-fit indices better selects the correct number of latent classes?
2. Does model misspecification cause the extraction of spurious latent classes in the MRM?
3. Do sample size and test length contribute to the extraction of spurious latent classes in the MRM?
4. How latent classes are extracted in real data applications?

2 Method

A simulation study was conducted to examine whether the extraction of spurious latent classes can be attributed to model misspecification. This research also explored the extraction of latent classes under real data scenarios. The succeeding section introduces the simulation design, real data sources, and data analysis methods used in this work.

Table 1 Simulation design

Manipulated factors	Levels
Item discrimination	1.0, 2.0
Item guessing	0.1, 0.3
Item slipping	0.7, 0.9
Test length	20, 40
Sample size	500, 1,000, 3,000

2.1 Simulation Study

This study was designed as a $3 \times 2 \times 2 \times 2 \times 2$ experimental design, in which sample size, test length, and magnitude of item discrimination, guessing, and slipping were manipulated. For each condition, 100 replications were simulated. Data were generated under a unidimensional IRT 4PLM [see Eq. (3)]. The data matrix comprises 500, 1,000, or 3,000 examinees' responses to 20 or 40 dichotomously scored items. Ability and item difficulty parameters were simulated from a standard normal distribution with a mean of 0 and a variance of 1.

Model misspecification in the Rasch model was manipulated using varying item discrimination and incorporating item guessing parameters (i.e., γ is greater than 0) and slipping parameters (i.e., λ is smaller than 1). Two levels of item discrimination, namely, 1.0 and 2.0, were used to represent low and high discrimination, respectively; these levels are identical to those adopted in previous studies (i.e., Emons et al. 2004; Li et al. 2009). Two levels of guessing (i.e., 0.1 and 0.3) and slipping effects (i.e., 0.7 and 0.9) were also manipulated as model misspecification factors. The extent of slipping was manipulated on the basis of slipping parameter estimates observed in previous empirical studies (i.e., $\lambda = 0.72$–0.89, Loken and Rulison 2010; $\lambda = 0.565$–0.998, Jiao et al. 2011). A discrimination of 2.0, a guessing level of 0.3, or a slipping level of 0.7 represents a strong violation of the Rasch model; that is, in the Rasch model, item discrimination is equal to 1, guessing is equal to 0, and slipping is equal to 1. The specifications used in the simulation study are summarized in Table 1.

Item response data were then analyzed with the MRM, which incorporates only difficulty parameters in the model [see Eqs. (1) and (2)]. The software *mdltm* developed by von Davier (2005) was used for estimation; it applies marginal maximum likelihood estimates with an expectation-maximization algorithm. Given that more than two extracted classes (e.g., two classes, three classes, and so on) indicate the presence of spurious latent classes (i.e., in the data generation, one latent class was simulated), this study reports the percentages of replications that suggest multiple-class solutions in the data. The outcome statistics for evaluating model-data fit are Akaike information criterion (AIC; Akaike 1974), Bayesian information criterion (BIC; Schwarz 1978), corrected Akaike information criterion (AICc; Burnham and Anderson 2002), and sample-size adjusted Bayesian information criterion (SABIC; Sclove 1987). These statistics are expressed as Eqs. (4)–(7). The

AIC and BIC measures were output from *mdltm*, and SABIC and AICc—which have penalties greater for a large number of parameters or small samples—were computed from Eqs. (6) and (7). The outcome statistics were computed across 100 replications:

$$\mathrm{AIC} = -2\mathrm{LL} + 2\mathrm{k}, \tag{4}$$

$$\mathrm{BIC} = -2\mathrm{LL} + \mathrm{k}\ln(\mathrm{N}), \tag{5}$$

$$\mathrm{AICc} = \mathrm{AIC} + \frac{2\mathrm{k}(\mathrm{k}+1)}{\mathrm{N}-\mathrm{k}-1}, \tag{6}$$

$$\mathrm{SABIC} = -2\mathrm{LL} + \mathrm{k}\ln\left(\frac{\mathrm{N}+2}{24}\right), \tag{7}$$

where LL = log-likelihood, k = number of parameters, and N = sample size.

2.2 *Empirical Examples*

Two real data sets were used. The first was extracted from a standardized large-scale assessment—the Progress in International Reading Literacy Study (PIRLS) 2006 (PIRLS 2006 Assessment 2007) conducted by the International Association for the Evaluation of Educational Achievement (Green et al. 2009; Mullis et al. 2007). PIRLS is designed to measure the reading comprehension abilities of fourth grade students. The extracted sample data set contains 1,398 examinees' responses to 21 items, in which the items were originally constructed under the 2PL or the 3PL model.

The second data set was extracted from the 2005 national MTF survey of 12th grade students (Johnston et al. 2006). The extracted data set contains 2,463 examinees' responses to 14 self-report questions of delinquency according to a 5-point Likert scale (i.e., students reported the frequency of delinquency acts; 1 = not at all to 5 = five or more times within the past year). The item responses were re-coded in binary format (i.e., 1 = at least once, 0 = never). Loken and Rulison (2010) demonstrated that the 4PLM satisfactorily fit this data set; the estimates of slipping parameters ranged from 0.72 to 0.89, which implicitly suggests that individuals at high levels of delinquency did not necessarily commit all delinquency acts. The data analysis procedure for the empirical examples is identical to that implemented in the above-mentioned simulation study.

3 Results

3.1 Simulation Study

Table 2 shows the average hit rates of latent class selection under each simulated condition, while Table 3 reveals the percentages of replications that extracted spurious latent classes in the MRM. The performance ranking of the model-fit indices followed the order BIC, SABIC, AICc, and AIC, with overage hit rates of 97.10 %, 86.30 %, 75.90 %, and 70.50 %, respectively (Table 2). Among the model-fit indices, BIC exhibited the best performance in selecting the correct number of latent classes, particularly under small- (i.e., sample size = 500) and moderate-sized (i.e., sample size = 1,000) samples (i.e., average hit rate = 100 %). BIC showed a relatively satisfactory and consistent performance across all simulated conditions (average hit rate = 91.25–100 %). By contrast, AIC produced the worst model selection, particularly when item discrimination was violated in the Rasch model (i.e., $\alpha = 2.0$) and when sample sizes increased (Table 3).

The inclusion of item guessing and slipping parameters did not contribute to the extraction of spurious latent classes in the MRM (Table 3). However, the model misspecification resulting from item discrimination was an influential factor for such extraction. At an item discrimination of 1 (i.e., as the constraint of item discrimination in the Rasch model), spurious latent classes were imperceptibly extracted even under item guessing and slipping effects.

Table 2 Average hit rates for latent class selection under simulated conditions (%)

	AIC	BIC	SABIC	AICc
Overall	70.50	97.10	86.30	75.90
Sample sizes				
500	94.63	100.00	100.00	100.00
1,000	65.25	100.00	96.19	74.19
3,000	51.63	91.25	62.56	53.63
Test lengths				
20	74.04	99.25	87.54	78.79
40	66.96	94.92	84.96	73.08
Item discrimination				
1.0	99.29	100.00	100.00	99.79
2.0	41.71	94.17	72.50	52.08
Item guessing				
0.1	64.83	94.71	80.83	71.46
0.3	76.17	99.46	91.67	80.42
Item slipping				
0.7	75.33	95.92	89.33	80.71
0.9	65.67	98.25	83.17	71.17

Table 3 Percentages of replications that extracted spurious classes in the mixture Rasch model (%)

				Fit indices											
				AIC			BIC			SABIC			AICc		
Sample sizes															
Item	α	γ	λ	500	1,000	3,000	500	1,000	3,000	500	1,000	3,000	500	1,000	3,000
20	1	0.1	0.7	0	0	0	0	0	0	0	0	0	0	0	0
20	1	0.1	0.9	0	0	0	0	0	0	0	0	0	0	0	0
20	1	0.3	0.7	0	0	0	0	0	0	0	0	0	0	0	0
20	1	0.3	0.9	0	0	0	0	0	0	0	0	0	0	0	0
40	1	0.1	0.7	0	0	16	0	0	0	0	0	0	0	0	5
40	1	0.1	0.9	0	0	0	0	0	0	0	0	0	0	0	0
40	1	0.3	0.7	0	0	0	0	0	0	0	0	0	0	0	0
40	1	0.3	0.9	0	0	1	0	0	0	0	0	0	0	0	0
20	2	0.1	0.7	0	**69**	**100**	0	0	1	0	0	**100**	0	22	**100**
20	2	0.1	0.9	3	**93**	**100**	0	0	14	0	0	**100**	0	**74**	**100**
20	2	0.3	0.7	0	0	**58**	0	0	0	0	0	0	0	0	44
20	2	0.3	0.9	6	**94**	**100**	0	0	3	0	0	**99**	0	**69**	**100**
40	2	0.1	0.7	49	**100**	**100**	0	0	**97**	0	**56**	**100**	0	**99**	**100**
40	2	0.1	0.9	15	**99**	**100**	0	0	15	0	4	**100**	0	**85**	**100**
40	2	0.3	0.7	0	1	**99**	0	0	0	0	0	0	0	0	**93**
40	2	0.3	0.9	13	**100**	**100**	0	0	10	0	1	**100**	0	**64**	**100**

When item discrimination varied from one as a kind of model misspecification in the Rasch model, the extraction of spurious latent classes increased; in particular, all the indices tended to extract spurious latent classes as sample sizes and test lengths increased. Overall, BIC was the least influenced by model misspecification resulting from item discrimination. For example, when $\alpha = 1$, all the model-fit indices produced perfect or nearly perfect hit rates (i.e., average hit rate = 99.29–100 %). When $\alpha = 2$, however, the average hit rate of BIC remained high (94.17 %), whereas those of the other indices visibly decreased (41.71 %, 52.08 %, and 72.50 % for AIC, AICc, and SABIC, respectively). Across all model misspecification conditions (i.e., $\alpha = 2.0$, $\gamma = 0.1$ or 0.3, $\lambda = 0.7$ or 0.9), BIC resulted in high hit rates that ranged from 94.17 to 99.46 % (Table 2).

3.2 *Empirical Examples*

Tables 4 and 5 show the results of the latent class selection for the PIRLS and the MTF data sets, respectively. In the empirical examples, the model-fit indices generated conflicting results, making the determination of the number of latent classes difficult. For both real data sets, BIC suggested a one-class solution, whereas SABIC recommended a two-class solution and AIC and AICc selected three-class solutions. Given that BIC effectively selected the correct number of latent classes, the one-class solution was adopted for both real data sets. AIC, SABIC, and AICc

Table 4 Latent class selection for the PIRLS

	AIC (rank)	BIC (rank)	AICc (rank)	SABIC (rank)
One-class solution	30,299 (4)	30,414 (1)	30,299 (4)	30,344 (2)
Two-class solution	30,225 (3)	30,461 (2)	30,228 (2)	30,318 (1)
Three-class solution	30,212 (1)	30,569 (4)	30,219 (1)	30,353 (3)
Four-class solution	30,216 (2)	30,694 (3)	30,229 (3)	30,404 (4)

Table 5 Latent class selection for the MTF

	AIC (rank)	BIC (rank)	AICc (rank)	SABIC (rank)
One-class solution	18,963 (3)	19,271 (1)	18,966 (4)	19,103 (3)
Two-class solution	18,666 (2)	19,288 (2)	18,676 (2)	18,948 (1)
Three-class solution	18,642 (1)	19,578 (3)	18,665 (1)	19,066 (2)
Four-class solution	18,666 (2)	19,915 (4)	18,707 (3)	19,232 (4)

tended to select a model that had many latent classes in both empirical examples, echoing the results of the simulation study.

4 Summary and Discussion

This research investigated whether model misspecification results in an extraction of spurious latent classes in the MRM and assessed the effectiveness of model-fit indices in latent class selection. BIC was the most promising model-fit index for selecting the correct number of latent classes, whereas AIC and AICc tended to select a model with spurious latent classes in the MRM. Our findings are consistent with those of previous studies, in which BIC performed effectively and AIC functioned poorly in latent class selection (i.e., Alexeev et al. 2011; Cho and Cohen 2010; Cho et al. 2012, Li et al. 2009; Preinerstorfer and Forman 2012). As stated earlier, model parameter estimation considerably depends on the identification of latent class membership; therefore, inaccurate estimates of the number of latent classes can cause severe biases in model parameter estimates. Given that no consensus regarding the best indicator of latent class numeration in mixture modeling has been reached (Nylund et al. 2007), researchers and practitioners should be particularly cautious in choosing model-fit measures. As indicated by the current and previous findings, BIC is favorable for latent class selection in data.

In Alexeev et al. (2011), BIC extracted spurious latent classes under large sample sizes, long test lengths, and a distribution of item discrimination parameters that corresponds to a violation of uniform item discrimination in the MRM. In the current work, however, BIC reduces concerns over the extraction of spurious latent class resulting from model misspecification. More specifically, BIC extracted spurious latent classes only when the constraint of item discrimination in the MRM was violated in few large-sample conditions. Sample size and test length were not the primary influential factors in the current study. AIC, SABIC, and AICc over-extracted latent classes under large item discrimination combined with large sample sizes—a finding that corresponds with that of Alexeev et al. (2011). The slight differences in findings between the current study and Alexeev et al. (2011) may be due to the different estimation programs used (Mplus was used in the latter). An interesting and new finding from the present research is that the model misspecification resulting from item guessing and slipping effects did not contribute to the extraction of spurious latent classes in the MRM.

Finally, the empirical examples show that the model-fit indices presented inconsistent results, also an observed occurrence in previous studies that used real data (e.g., Cho and Cohen 2010; Li et al. 2009; Willse 2011). Inconsistent latent class selection in real data can be a serious concern because the true number of latent classes in real data is usually unknown. In our real data application, both sets of real data, which contain items best modeled with guessing and/or slipping parameters, did not lend themselves to additional latent classes (i.e., possibly spurious latent classes), as indicated by the BIC values.

References

Akaike, H. (1974). A new look at the statistical model identification. *IEEE Transactions on Automatic Control*, *19*, 716–723.

Alexeev, N., Templin, J., & Cohen, A. (2011). Spurious latent classes in the mixture Rasch model. *Journal of Educational Measurement*, *48*, 313–332.

Barton, M. A., & Lord, F. M. (1981). *An upper asymptote for the three-parameter logistic item response model* (Report No. RR-81-20). Princeton, NJ: Educational Testing Service.

Burnham, K. P., & Anderson, D. R. (2002). *Model selection and multimodel inference: A practical information-theoretic approach* (2nd ed.). Berlin, Germany: Springer.

Cho, S.-J., & Cohen, A. S. (2010). A multilevel mixture IRT model with an application to DIF. *Journal of Educational and Behavioral Statistics*, *35*, 336–370.

Cho, Y., Jiao, H., & Macready, G. B. (2012). *Assessing the effects of different item parameter profiles in mixture Rasch models*. Paper presented at the meeting of the American Educational Research Association (AERA), Vancouver, Canada.

Cohen, A. S., & Bolt, D. M. (2005). A mixture model analysis of differential item functioning. *Journal of Educational Measurement*, *42*, 133–148.

Dayton, C. M. (1999). *Latent class scaling analysis*. Thousand Oaks, CA: Sage.

De Ayala, R. J., Kim, S.-H., Stapleton, L. M., & Dayton, C. M. (2002). Differential item functioning: A mixture distribution conceptualization. *International Journal of Testing*, *2*, 243–276.

Emons, W. H. M., Sijtsma, K., & Meijer, R. R. (2004). Testing hypotheses about the person-response function in person-fit analysis. *Multivariate Behavioral Research*, *39*, 1–35.

Finch, H., & Pierson, E. (2011). A mixture IRT analysis of risky youth behavior. *Frontiers in Psychology*, *2*, 98. doi:10.3389/fpsyg.2011.00098

Green, P. J., Herget, D., Rosen, J., & Provasnik, S. (2009). *User's guide for the Progress in International Reading Literacy Study* (*PIRLS*). Washington, DC: National Center for Education Statistics, Institute of Education Sciences.

Jiao, H., Macready, G., Zhu, J., & An, W. (2011). *A three parameter item response theory model with varying upper asymptote effects*. Paper presented at the meeting of the Psychometric Society, Hong Kong, China.

Johnston, L. D., Bachman, J. G., O'Malley, P. M., & Schulenberg, J. E. (2006). *Monitoring the future: A continuing study of American youth (12th-grade survey), 2005* [Computer file]. ICPSR04536-v3. Ann Arbor, MI: Inter-university Consortium for Political and Social Research [distributor], 2007-07-18. doi:10.3886/ICPSR04536.v3

Kelderman, H., & Macready, G. B. (1990). The use of loglinear models for assessing differential item functioning across manifest variables and latent examinee groups. *Journal of Educational Measurement*, *27*, 307–327.

Li, F., Cohen, A. S., Kim, S.-H., & Cho, S.-J. (2009). Model selection methods for mixture dichotomour IRT models. *Applied Psychological Measurement*, *33*, 353–373.

Loken, E., & Rulison, K. L. (2010). Estimation of a four-parameter item response theory model. *British Journal of Mathematical and Statistical Psychology*, *63*, 509–525.

Maij-de Meij, A. M., Kelderman, H., & van der Flier, H. (2010). Improvement in detection of differential item functioning using a mixture item response theory model. *Multivariate Behavioral Research*, *45*, 975–999.

McCutcheon, A. L. (1987). *Latent class analysis*. Beverly Hills, CA: Sage.

Mislevy, R. J., & Verhelst, N. (1990). Modeling item responses when different subjects employ different solution strategies. *Psychometrika*, *55*, 195–215.

Mullis, I. V. S., Martin, M. O., Kennedy, A. M., & Foy, P. (2007). *PIRLS 2006 International Report*. Boston, MA: TIMSS & PIRLS International Study Center, Lynch School of Education, Boston College.

Nylund, K. L., Asparouhov, T., & Muthen, B. (2007). Deciding on the number of classes in latent class analysis and growth mixture modeling: A Monte Carlo simulation study. *Structural Equation Modeling*, *14*, 535–569.

PIRLS 2006 Assessment. (2007). *International Association for the Evaluation of Educational Achievement (IEA)*. Boston, MA: TIMSS & PIRLS International Study Center, Lynch School of Education, Boston College.

Preinerstorfer, D., & Forman, A. K. (2012). Parameter recovery and model selection in mixed Rasch model. *British Journal of Mathematical and Statistical Psychology*, *65*, 252–262.

Rasch, G. (1960). *Probabilistic models for some intelligence and attainment tests*. Copenhagen, Denmark: Nielsen & Lydiche.

Rost, J. (1990). Rasch models in latent classes: An integration of two approaches to item analysis. *Applied Psychological Measurement*, *14*, 271–282.

Rulison, K. L., & Loken, E. (2009). I've fallen and I can't get up: Can high-ability students recover from early mistakes in CAT? *Applied Psychological Measurement*, *33*, 83–101.

Samuelsen, K. (2005). *Examining differential item from a latent class perspective* (Doctoral dissertation). Available from ProQuest Dissertations and Theses database. (UMI No. 3175148)

Schwarz, G. (1978). Estimating the dimension of a model. *Annals of Statistics*, *6*, 461–464.

Sclove, S. L. (1987). Application of model-selection criteria to some problems in multivariate analysis. *Psychometrika*, *52*, 333–43.

Smith, E. V., Jr., Ying, Y., & Brown, S. W. (2012). Using the mixed Rasch model to analyze data from the beliefs and attitudes about memory survey. *Journal of Applied Measurement, 13*, 23–40.

Von Davier, M. (2005). *Mdltm: Software for the general diagnostic model and for estimating mixture of multidimensional discrete latent traits models* [Computer software]. Princeton, NJ: Educational Testing Service.

Willse, J. T. (2011). Mixture Rasch models with joint maximum likelihood estimation. *Educational and Psychological Measurement*, *71*, 5–19.

Yen, Y.-C., Ho, R.-G., Laio, W.-W., Chen, L.-J., & Kuo, C.-C. (2012). An empirical evaluation of the slip correction in the four parameter logistic models with computerized adaptive testing. *Applied Psychological Measurement*, *36*, 75–87.

Modeling Differences in Test-Taking Motivation: Exploring the Usefulness of the Mixture Rasch Model and Person-Fit Statistics

Marie-Anne Mittelhaëuser, Anton A. Béguin, and Klaas Sijtsma

1 Modeling Differences in Test-Taking Motivation: Exploring the Usefulness of the Mixture Rasch Model and Person-Fit Statistics

Item response theory (IRT) models are useful in educational measurement for supporting the construction of measurement instruments, linking and equating of measurements, and evaluation of test bias (Scheerens et al. 2007). However, the IRT model must fit the data so as to be applicable to practical testing problems and yield correct proficiency level and item parameter estimates. Unfortunately, researchers often implicitly assume that scores on a test are valid indicators of a student's best effort (Wolf and Smith 1995) but Wainer (1993, p. 12) noted that: "If a test doesn't count for specific individuals, how can we be sure that they are trying as hard as they might if it mattered?". Over the years, evidence has accumulated that if item performance does not contribute to the test score or if no feedback is provided, students may not give their best effort and perform to their best ability (e.g., Wise and DeMars 2005; O'Neil et al. 1996; Kiplinger

M.-A. Mittelhaëuser (✉)
Department of Methodology and Statistics,
Tilburg School of Social and Behavioral Sciences, Tilburg University,
P.O. Box 90153, 5000 LE Tilburg, The Netherlands

Cito, Institute for Educational Measurement, 6801 MG Arnhem, The Netherlands
e-mail: Marie-Anne.Mittelhaeuser@cito.nl

A.A. Béguin
Cito, Institute for Educational Measurement, 6801 MG Arnhem, The Netherlands
e-mail: Anton.Beguin@cito.nl

K. Sijtsma
Department of Methodology and Statistics, Tilburg School of Social and Behavioral Sciences, Tilburg University, P.O. Box 90153, 5000 LE Tilburg, The Netherlands
e-mail: k.sijtsma@tilburguniversity.edu

R.E. Millsap et al. (eds.), *New Developments in Quantitative Psychology*, Springer Proceedings in Mathematics & Statistics 66, DOI 10.1007/978-1-4614-9348-8_23,

and Linn 1996). Under-performance is typical for tests administered in a low-stakes administration condition. Consequently, performance on items administered in a low-stakes condition may differ from performance on items administered in a high-stakes condition, resulting in unusual patterns of item scores or in relatively poor performance on the low-stakes items. Within an IRT framework, low-stakes performance threatens the correct estimation of the proficiency and item parameters. For example, Mittelhaëuser et al. (2011) found that using low-stakes common items to link two high-stakes tests yielded different conclusions about the ability distributions compared to using high-stakes common items.

This article explores the usefulness of two methods that may be helpful in removing bias in parameter estimation caused by the low-stakes administration condition of a test. The first method uses a mixture Rasch model that assumes that the data are a mixture of different datasets from two or more latent populations (Rost 1997; Von Davier and Yamamoto 2004), also called latent classes. If the mixture assumption is correct, a Rasch model does not hold for the entire population but different model parameters are valid for different subpopulations. Let X_i denote the score on item i and let k denote the number of items in the test. According to the mixture Rasch model, the probability of passing item i ($X_i = 1$) depends on a class-specific person parameter, θ_{jg}, which denotes the proficiency of student j if he/she belongs to latent class g. The conditional response probability is defined as:

$$P\left(X_i = 1 \middle| \theta_{jg}\right) = \frac{\exp(\theta_{jg} - \beta_{ig})}{1 + \exp(\theta_{jg} - \beta_{ig})} \tag{1}$$

where β_{ig} is a class-specific difficulty parameter. The probability of obtaining an item-score vector, $\mathbf{x} = \{x_1, x_2, \ldots, x_k\}$, given proficiency θ_{jg} equals

$$P\left(\boldsymbol{x}_j \middle| \theta_{jg}\right) = \prod_{i=1}^{k} \frac{\exp[x_i(\theta_{jg} - \beta_{ig})]}{1 + \exp(\theta_{jg} - \beta_{ig})} \tag{2}$$

Let π_g denote the proportion of the population that belongs to class g ($g = 1, \ldots, G$). The probability for an individual j to belong to class g, also known as the posterior probability, depends on the item-score vector x_j; that is,

$$p\left(g \middle| \boldsymbol{x}_j\right) = \frac{\pi_g p\left(\boldsymbol{x}_j \middle| g\right)}{\sum_{g=1}^{G} \pi_g p\left(\boldsymbol{x}_j \middle| g\right)} \tag{3}$$

Mixture IRT models can be used to identify classes resulting from different types of response behavior. Consequently, the mixture strategy can also be used to handle known sources of contamination in item parameter estimates. For example, Bolt et al. (2002) used a mixture Rasch model with ordinal constraints to help remove the effect of test speededness on item parameter estimates. We used other constraints facilitating identification of latent classes such that one of the latent classes represents "high-stakes response behavior" and the other latent class "low-stakes response behavior" (Béguin 2005; Béguin and Maan 2007). As the probability for each individual to belong to a latent class (i.e., posterior probability) can be estimated, it is possible to identify the item-score vectors the low-stakes administration condition of the test affect. The posterior probabilities represent the probabilities for a student to respond in either a "low-stakes manner" or a "high-stakes manner."

Alternatively, person-fit methods assign a value to each individual vector of item scores, and a statistical test is used to determine whether the underlying IRT model fits the item scores (Embretson and Reise 2000). Significant person-fit values identify item-score vectors for which the IRT model does not fit, and the researcher may decide to remove the aberrant item-score vectors from the dataset (Meijer and Sijtsma 1995). The remaining set of item-score vectors for which the IRT model fits are expected to produce correct parameter estimates. The l_z statistic is a well-known person-fit statistic (Drasgow et al. 1985). By estimating the l_z statistic on a low-stakes item-score vector given the ability parameter estimated on a high-stakes test, it may be possible to detect students driven by unmotivated response behavior.

The goal of this study was to explore whether indicators of non-typical response behavior, such as the posterior probabilities from a mixture IRT model and the l_z person-fit statistic can be used to model motivational differences between students. We investigated the relationship between student's self-reported motivation on the one hand and the posterior probabilities of the mixture Rasch model and the l_z statistic on the other hand.

2 Method

2.1 Participants and Design

Four different scales were used to collect data: the Eindtoets Basisonderwijs 2012 (End of Primary Education Test), the pre-test of the Eindtoets Basisonderwijs 2013, a scale measuring test-taking motivation (TTM), and a scale measuring social desirability. The order in which the different scales are discussed below corresponds to the order in which they were administered to the students.

Pre-test. Subsets of items intended for use in a high-stakes test are usually pre-tested on different samples of students to examine the statistical characteristics of the items before including them in a high-stakes test. To pre-test math items for the Eindtoets Basisonderwijs 2013, eighth-grade primary-school students ($N = 9{,}124$) were presented with a pre-test containing math items. Items most suitable for the population were selected for the Eindtoets Basisonderwijs 2013. Twenty-seven different pre-test versions also called test booklets were constructed, varying in test length from 30 to 60 items and including 585 multiple-choice items in total. The responses were coded 0 representing a wrong answer and 1 representing a right answer. The number of respondents per test booklet ranged from 7 to 516.

Table 1 Test-taking motivation items with mean scores and component loadings

Item		M	Loadings A1	A2	A3
1	I enjoy going to school	3.00	−0.121	0.061	**0.853**
2	I enjoy learning math	2.86	0.011	−0.107	**0.817**
3	I did my best on the math items	3.80	**0.705**	0.066	0.103
4	My teacher wants me to do my best on the math items	3.80	−0.034	**0.841**	0.001
5	My parents want me to do my best on the math items	3.83	0.009	**0.823**	0.055
6	I did a good job on the math items	3.21	**0.525**	−0.178	0.205
7	The kids in my class did their best on the math items	3.53	**0.409**	0.202	−0.061
8	I could have worked harder on the math items	2.88	**0.788**	−0.097	−0.115
9	I'm curious about how many math items I answered correctly	3.66	0.203	0.132	**0.422**

However, as a given pre-test item was administered in more than one pre-test booklet, the number of observations per item ranged from 332 to 1,424. The pre-test was used in most schools to practice for the high-stakes Eindtoets Basisonderwijs 2012, but the students were aware that they would not receive a score on the pre-test. Therefore, the pre-test is considered to be administered in a low-stakes administration condition.

Test-Taking Motivation. After the administration of the pre-test, a subsample of 1,512 students was administered a questionnaire containing nine items that measured TTM. The construction of the items was inspired by existing scales, such as the test-taking motivation questionnaire (Eklöf 2006), the student opinion scale (Thelk et al. 2009), and a subset of items from the self-report questionnaires of the Education Quality Accountability Office (Zerpa et al. 2011). Each item was answered on a four-point Likert-scale (1 = No, 2 = Not so much, 3 = Kind of, 4 = Yes). Table 1 shows English translations of the items.

Social Desirability. To check whether the tendency to answer in a socially desirable way influenced self-reported motivation, the students were administered six items stating desirable but uncommon behavior. The construction of the items was inspired by the children's social desirability scale (Baxter et al. 2004). Each item was answered as Not True (1) or True (2). Table 2 provides English translations of the items.

Eindtoets Basisonderwijs 2012. Each year in February, the Eindtoets Basisonderwijs is administered to students who are in the last year of Dutch primary education. The test results provide an independent advice to primary-school teachers, parents and secondary-schools about the most appropriate type of secondary education for a student. The test is administered in a high-stakes condition, and secrecy of the items is vital; hence, the test form is renewed each year. The Eindtoets

Table 2 Social desirability items with mean scores and standard deviations

Item		*M*	*SD*
1	I like all the kids in my class	1.49	0.50
2	I always tell the truth	1.35	0.48
3	I never fight	1.15	0.36
4	I always do what my teacher tells me to do	1.60	0.49
5	I always behave well	1.44	0.50
6	I never lie	1.27	0.45

Basisonderwijs 2012 contained 60 multiple-choice math items. The responses were coded 0 representing a wrong answer and 1 representing a right answer. In total, 144,708 students completed the math items of the Eindtoets Basisonderwijs 2012.

2.2 Analyses

All analyses were performed using SPSS version 20 unless stated otherwise.

Principal Components Analysis. A principal components analysis (PCA) was performed to investigate the internal structure of the TTM scale. After motivational components of the TTM scale were identified, the reliability estimate known as the greatest lower bound (GLB) was calculated for the total TTM scale using factor 8.1 (Lorenzo-Seva and Ferrando 2006).

Mixture Rasch Model. The data of the pre-test and the data of the Eindtoets Basisonderwijs 2012 were combined, providing 9,124 item-score vectors containing items administered in a low-stakes condition (pre-test items) and different items administered in a high-stakes condition (items from the Eindtoets Basisonderwijs 2012). A mixture Rasch model was estimated for this dataset using a dedicated version of the OPLM software (Verhelst et al. 1995; Béguin 2008). We anticipated that we would not find motivational differences in the high-stakes administration condition. Therefore, the item-score vectors of the Eindtoets Basisonderwijs 2012 were modeled as being exclusively part of the first latent class by setting $\pi_{g=0} = 0$ and $\pi_{g=1} = 1$ in Eq. (3). The item-score vectors of the pre-test could be in either the first or the second latent class. To identify the model, it was assumed that student's abilities did not differ across latent classes.

After estimating the mixture Rasch model for the 9,124 item-score vectors, the posterior probabilities of the 1,512 students who completed the TTM scale were related to their self-reported motivation. This was done by estimating the correlation coefficient and inspecting the mean posterior probability for each separate TTM sum score. Furthermore, the item difficulty parameters of both latent classes were plotted to inspect the differences between the latent classes.

Person-Fit. The l_z statistic (Drasgow et al. 1985; Meijer and Sijtsma 1995) is a person-fit statistic that assesses the likelihood of an item-score vector under a specific IRT model. The l_z statistic is given by

$$l_z = \frac{l - E(l)}{\sqrt{Var(l)}} \tag{4}$$

where l denotes the unstandardized likelihood of the item-score vector and $E(l)$ and $Var(l)$ denote the expected likelihood and the variance of the likelihood, respectively. These three quantities are given by:

$$l = \sum_{i=1}^{k} \{X_i \ln P_i(\theta) + (1 - X_i) \ln [1 - P_i(\theta)]\} \tag{5}$$

with

$$E(l) = \sum_{i=1}^{k} \{P_i(\theta) \ln [P_i(\theta)] + [1 - P_i(\theta)] \ln [1 - P_i(\theta)]\} \tag{6}$$

and

$$Var(l) = \sum_{i=1}^{k} P_i(\theta) [1 - P_i(\theta)] \left[\ln \frac{P_i(\theta)}{1 - P_i(\theta)} \right]^2. \tag{7}$$

The l_z statistic is assumed to be a standard normal deviate, with large negative values providing evidence of misfit.

For each student, the l_z statistic was calculated using the statistical program R (R Development Core Team 2010) by means of the following three steps:

1. Item parameters of the Rasch model were estimated for the Eindtoets Basisonderwijs 2012 and pre-test concurrently.
2. The item parameters estimated in step 1 were fixed and the proficiency parameters of the Rasch model were estimated for the Eindtoets Basisonderwijs 2012.
3. The l_z statistic was calculated for the pre-test items, given the item parameters and proficiency parameters estimated in steps 1 and 2, respectively.

The l_z statistic provided a likelihood measure of the low-stakes item-score pattern of the pre-test given the ability estimate based on the high-stakes item-score pattern of the Eindtoets Basisonderwijs 2012. High negative l_z values suggested motivational differences between the administration conditions.

After having estimated the l_z statistic for the 9,124 item-score vectors, the l_z statistics of the 1,512 students who completed the TTM scale were related to their self-reported motivation. This was done by estimating the correlation coefficient and analyzing the mean l_z statistic for each sum score on the TTM scale.

Social Desirability. We used the Kruskal–Wallis test to investigate the relationship between the score on the TTM scale and the social desirability (SD) scale so as to determine whether social desirability influenced the TTM scores.

3 Results

3.1 Principle Components Analysis

A PCA was performed on the nine items from the TTM scale. After 53 cases having missing values were deleted, the analysis was performed using data from 1,459 students. Prior to performing the PCA, the suitability of the data for PCA was assessed. Bartlett's test of sphericity (Bartlett 1954) reached statistical significance and the Kaiser–Meyer–Oklin (Kaiser 1974) value was 0.639, indicating that the data were suitable for PCA.

The PCA produced three components having eigenvalues exceeding 1 that explained 24.1, 16.4, and 12.7% of the variance, respectively. Analysis of the screeplot did not show a clear elbow. However, the loadings of the three-component solution revealed a simple structure. To aid the interpretation of the components, oblimin rotation was performed. The loadings are presented in Table 1, where the highest loadings per item are presented in boldface. The three-component solution explained a total of 53.2% of the variance. The first component can be interpreted as a "general TTM" component, the second component as an "external motivation" component, and the third component as measuring "general attitudes." The small number of items in each subscale renders the usefulness of the separate subscales that might be constructed based on these components limited. Therefore, we decided to use the sum score on the total TTM scale in all subsequent analyses.

The GLB was calculated for the total TTM scale and equaled 0.71. This value suggests a reliability that allows less important decisions about individuals (Evers et al. 2010).

3.2 Mixture Rasch Model

We computed the correlations between students' self-reported motivation and their posterior probabilities in a subsample of 1,453 students without incomplete data patterns. A significant but small positive relation between the variables was found, $r = 0.09, p = 0.001$.

We inspected the mean posterior probability for each sum score on the TTM scale. Figure 1 (upper panel) shows the results. Each of the sum scores of 16, 18, and 20 was produced by just one examinee, so that 95% confidence intervals for the mean posterior probabilities could not be determined. The student having the lowest score of 16 on the TTM scale had a very low posterior probability of belonging to the "motivated" class. However, the student having a sum score of 20 on the TTM scale had a very high posterior probability of belonging to the "motivated" class. The student having a TTM sum score of 16 indeed performed better on the high-stakes Eindtoets Basisonderwijs (95% of the items correctly answered) than on the low-stakes pre-test (41.67% of the items correctly answered). The student having a sum score of 20 performed better on the low-stakes pre-test (66.67% of the items correctly answered) than on the high-stakes Eindtoets Basisonderwijs (56.67% of the items correctly answered). The mean percentage of correctly answered items in the sample of 1,512 students on the Eindtoets Basisonderwijs was 72.56, and the mean percentage of correctly answered items on the pre-test was 64.96. It appears that the administration condition indeed influenced the student having a sum score of 16. Furthermore, the student having a sum score of 20 showed an average performance on the pre-test but scored below average on the Eindtoets Basisonderwijs.

As the number of observations on the lower sum scores on the TTM scale was very low (sum score 16: $n = 1$, 18: $n = 1$, 20: $n = 1$, 21: $n = 7$, 22: $n = 5$, 23: $n = 12$), we combined the observations for the low sum scores. Figure 1 (lower panel) shows the relationship between the mean posterior probability and the TTM sum score.

The mean posterior probability was low for the lower TTM sum scores and stabilized starting from sum score 27 onward at a mean posterior probability of 0.6. The 95% confidence interval for the mean posterior probability for sum score 36 was slightly wider than the confidence intervals for sum score 27 onward.

Figure 2 shows the item difficulty parameters of both latent classes. The difficulty parameters for most items were higher in the "unmotivated" class than in the "motivated" class, which was expected. However, for a few items the difficulty parameters were higher in the "motivated" class than in the "unmotivated" class.

3.3 Person-Fit

The correlation between students' self-reported motivation and their l_z statistics equaled $r = 0.15, p < 0.001$ ($N = 1{,}453$, incomplete cases removed). Figure 3 (upper panel) the mean l_z statistic for each TTM sum score. Due to the low frequency of one observation, sum scores 16, 18, and 20 are presented without a 95% confidence interval. The results for sum scores 16–23 were combined to facilitate the interpretation of the results. Figure 3 (lower panel) shows the results. The student having the lowest TTM sum score of 16 had a very low l_z statistic. Figure 3 (upper panel) shows that the mean l_z value stabilized starting from sum score of 25 onward at a mean l_z value just under 0. This result indicates that starting from sum score of 25 onward, the item-score patterns on the low-stakes pre-test were consistent with the proficiency parameters estimated for the high-stakes Eindtoets Basisonderwijs. The low-stakes administration condition of the pre-test did not (or very little at most) influence these item-score vectors. The 95% confidence interval for the mean l_z statistic for TTM sum score 36 was only little wider than that for sum score 25 onward.

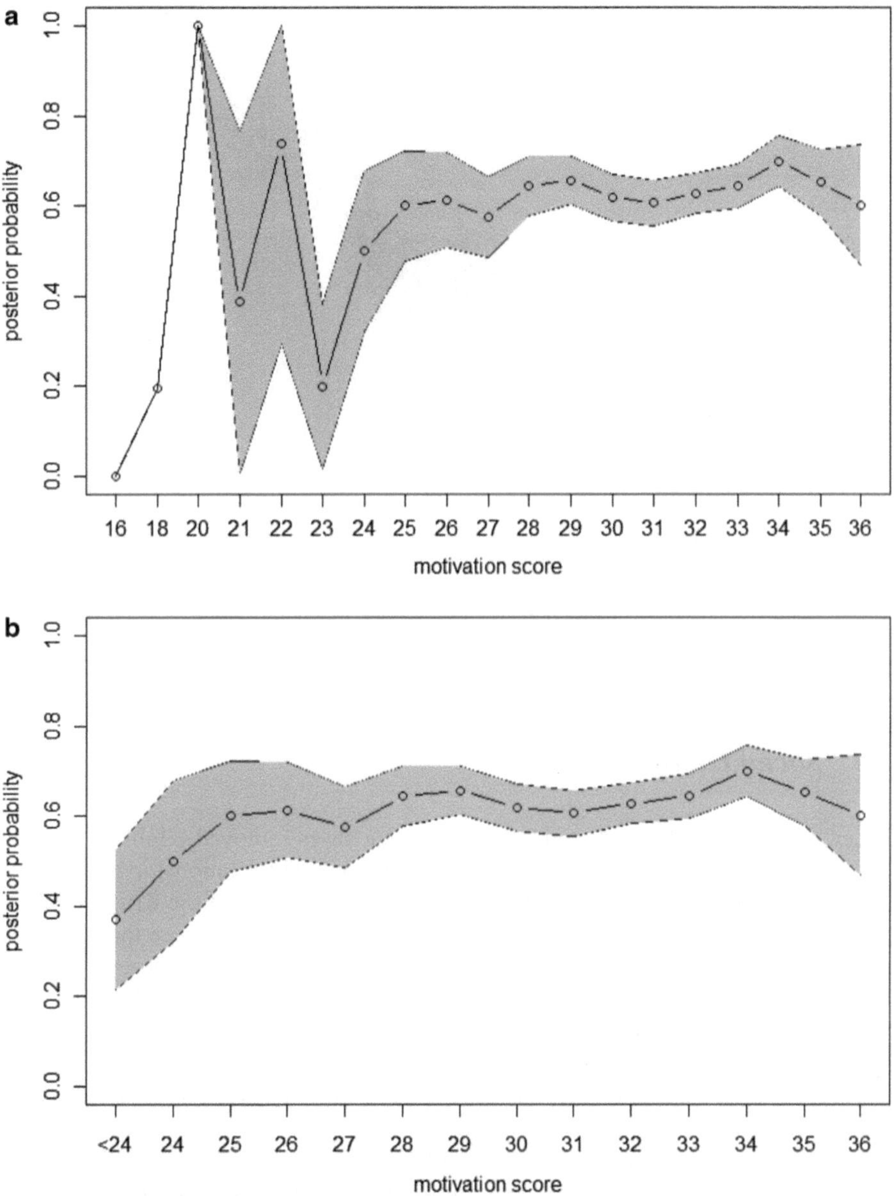

Fig. 1 (**a**) Mean posterior probability per motivation score, (**b**) mean posterior probability per motivation score with the lowest sum scores on the TTM scale combined. The *gray area* represents the 95% confidence interval for the mean posterior probability

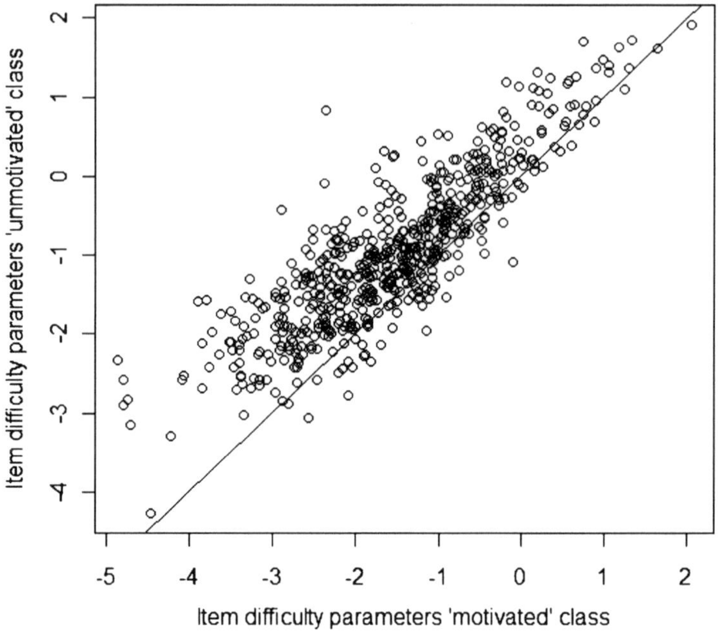

Fig. 2 Comparison of the item parameters estimated for the two latent classes

3.4 Social Desirability

Based on the data of 1,484 students (incomplete cases removed), Table 2 presents the SD items and their means and standard deviations. The relationship between the TTM score and the SD scale score was investigated by means of the Kruskal–Wallis test. The results revealed a statistically significant difference between the TTM sum score across the seven different SD scores (group 1, $n = 286$: sum score 6; group 2, $n = 259$: sum score 7; group 3, $n = 269$: sum score 8; group 4, $n = 231$: sum score 9; group 5, $n = 196$: sum score 10; group 6, $n = 131$: sum score 11; group 7, $n = 65$: sum score 12), $\chi^2(6, n = 1{,}437) = 92.08$, $p < 0.001$. The higher SD sum scores, 11 and 12, recorded a higher median sum score on the TTM scale ($Md = 32$) than the SD sum scores 7–10 ($Md = 31$) and the SD sum score equal to 6 ($Md = 30$). As the results showed a statistically significant difference between the TTM sum scores across the different SD scores, the analyses were rerun without the highest SD sum score, which was equal to 12. Removing these cases from the analyses did not change the results regarding the relationship of the TTM scale sum score and the posterior probabilities of the mixture Rasch model on the one hand and the l_z statistic on the other hand. Therefore, the results of the complete dataset were interpreted.

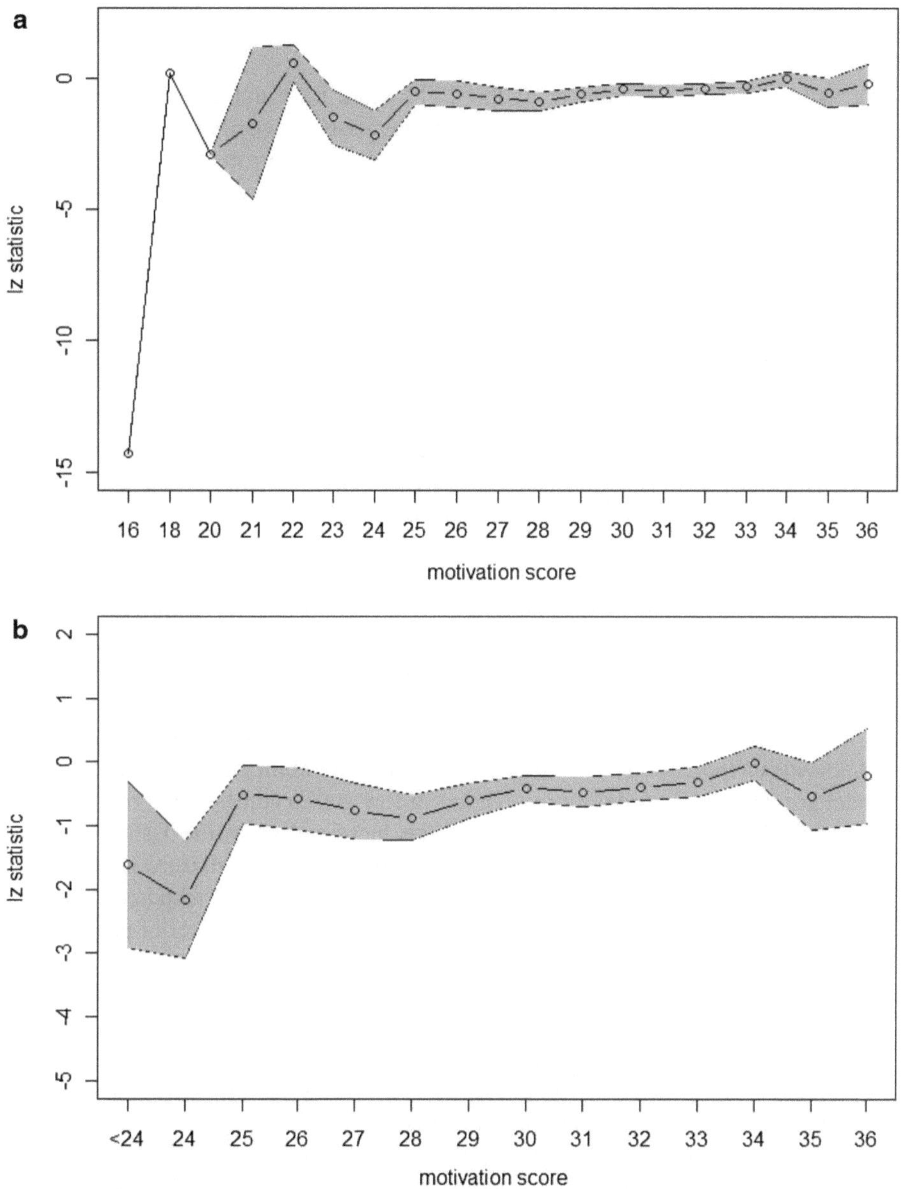

Fig. 3 (**a**) Mean l_z statistic per motivation score, (**b**) mean l_z statistic per motivation score with the lowest sum scores on the TTM scale combined. The *gray area* represents the 95% confidence interval for the mean l_z statistic

4 Discussion

The validity and the reliability of the TTM scale have not been investigated in earlier studies. Consequently, the question that arises is whether the TTM scale is appropriate as a measure of self-reported motivation. A more extensive investigation of the TTM scale is desirable. The reliability (GLB) was appropriate for the type of inference envisaged (Evers et al. 2010). The PCA revealed an internal structure approximately corresponding to results reported in existing literature on TTM (Eklöf 2006). For example, two of three motivational components that Eklöf found in the development of the TTM Questionnaire (TTM, general attitudes and performance expectancy) were also found for our TTM scale. The fact that we did not find a "performance expectancy" component might be due to the limited number of items in the TTM scale measuring performance expectancy. Furthermore, our TTM scale was administered to younger children who are probably affected more by "external motivation" than older children. The relationship between the TTM sum score and SD was as we expected. Higher SD scores were associated with higher TTM scores. Most likely, this result explains why the 95% confidence intervals found with the highest TTM sum score in Figs. 1 and 3 are slightly wider than the confidence intervals found with the sum scores just below the highest TTM sum score. This result was probably due to response tendencies or the influence of SD on the maximum TTM score. We conclude that the TTM sum score can be used in our research as a measure of self-reported motivation.

The relationship between the posterior probability and the TTM sum score did not provide an indication of whether the posterior probabilities of the mixture Rasch model are useful for modeling motivation in low-stakes administration conditions. Even though the mean posterior probabilities increased when the TTM sum score increased, it is not certain whether the two latent classes the mixture Rasch model estimated actually represent "low-stakes" and "high-stakes" response behavior. After all, the correlation between the TTM sum score and the posterior probabilities was low. Furthermore, the mean posterior probability stabilized at approximately 0.6. If the latent classes truly represented "low-stakes" and "high-stakes" response behavior, the mean posterior probability likely would increase more among the higher TTM sum scores. Possibly, the classes did not represent "low-stakes" and "high-stakes" response behavior, but instead reflected something else. Furthermore, the lower difficulty of items in the class representing "low-stakes" response behavior might indicate that assuming that the student's ability did not differ across latent classes was incorrect. An in-depth analysis of the interpretation of the latent classes is needed. For now, we conclude that the posterior probabilities of the mixture Rasch model have a limited usefulness in modeling motivational differences.

The l_z statistic seemed a more promising approach to model motivational differences. First, the correlation between the l_z statistic and the TTM sum score suggested a stronger relationship. Second, not only did the student having the lowest TTM sum score have the lowest l_z statistic, the mean l_z statistic stabilized just below 0 among the higher TTM sum scores, which was expected. Even though the l_z statistic seems more useful in modeling motivational differences, the results should be interpreted with caution. The parameter estimates on which the l_z statistic is based were estimated in a dataset including highly misfitting item-score vectors. Consequently, the data of a relatively small cluster of students showing extreme response behavior might have influenced the parameter estimates. Therefore it is advisable to only use the l_z statistic as a means for identifying the most extreme cases instead of whole classes displaying "low-stakes" response behavior. Without using an iterative procedure to update the parameter estimates and the l_z statistics, identification of a whole classes displaying "low-stakes" response behavior is likely to fail. For now, we conclude that the l_z statistic may be useful in modeling motivational differences, specifically in identifying students showing extreme differences in response behavior between low-stakes and high-stakes administration conditions.

References

Bartlett, M. S. (1954). A note on the multiplying factors for various chi square approximations. *Journal of the Royal Statistical Society, 16* (Series B), 296–298.

Baxter, S. D., Smith, A. F., Litaker, M. S., Baglio, M. L., Guinn, C. H., & Shaffer, N. M. (2004). Children's social desirability and dietary reports. *Journal of Nutrition Educational and Behaviour, 36*, 84–89.

Béguin, A. A. (2005). *Bayesian IRT equating with correction for unmotivated respondents on the anchor-test*. Paper presented at the International Meeting of the Psychometric Society, Tilburg, The Netherlands.

Béguin, A. A. (2008). *Application of mixed IRT models in IRT linking: Combining high-stakes tests with a low-stakes anchor.* Paper presented at the International Meeting of the Psychometric Society, Durham, NC.

Béguin, A. A., & Maan, A. (2007, April 10–12). *IRT linking of high-stakes tests with a low-stakes anchor*. Paper presented at the 2007 Annual National Council of Measurement in Education (NCME) Meeting, Chicago, IL.

Bolt, D. M., Cohen, A. S., & Wollack, J. A. (2002). Item parameter estimation under conditions of test speededness: Application of a mixture Rasch model with ordinal constraints. *Journal of Educational Measurement, 39*, 331–348.

Drasgow, F., Levine, M. V., & Williams, E. A. (1985). Appropriateness measurement with polychotomous item response models and standardized indices. *British Journal of Mathematical and Statistical Psychology, 38*, 67–86.

Eklöf, H. (2006). Development and validation of scores from an instrument measuring student test-taking motivation. *Educational and Psychological Measurement, 66*, 643–656.

Embretson, S. E., & Reise, S. P. (2000). *Item response theory for psychologists*. Mahwah, NJ: Lawrence Erlbaum.

Evers, A., Lucassen, W., Meijer, R., & Sijtsma, K. (2010). *COTAN Beoordelingssysteem voor de Kwaliteit van Tests (geheel herziene versie)* [COTAN rating system for test quality (completely revised edition)]. Amsterdam: NIP.

Kaiser, H. (1974). An index of factorial simplicity. *Psychometrika, 39*, 31–36.

Kiplinger, V. L., & Linn, R. L. (1996). Raising the stakes of test administration: The impact on student performance on the National Assessment of Educational Progress. *Educational Assessment, 3*, 111–133.

Lorenzo-Seva, U., & Ferrando, P. J. (2006). FACTOR: A computer program to fit the exploratory factor analysis model. *Behavioral Research Methods, Instruments and Computers, 38*, 88–91.
Meijer, R. R., & Sijtsma, K. (1995). Detection of aberrant item score patterns: A review and new developments. *Applied Measurement in Education, 8*, 261–272.
Mittelhaëuser, M., Béguin, A. A., & Sijtsma, K. (2011). *Comparing the effectiveness of different linking designs: The internal anchor versus the external anchor and pre-test data* (Report No. 11-01). Retrieved from Psychometric Research Centre website http://www.cito.nl/~/media/cito_nl/Files/Onderzoek%20en%20wetenschap/cito_mrd_report_2011_01.ashx
O'Neil, H. F., Sugrue, B., & Baker, E. L. (1996). Effects of motivational interventions on the National Assessment of Educational Progress mathematics performance. *Educational Assessment, 3*, 135–157.
R Development Core Team. (2010). *R: A language and environment for statistical computing [Computer software]*. Vienna: R Foundation for Statistical Computing.
Rost, J. (1997). Logistic mixture models. In W. Van der Linden & R. K. Hambleton (Eds.), *Handbook of modern item response theory* (pp. 449–463). New York: Springer.
Scheerens, J., Glas, C., & Thomas, S. M. (2007). *Educational evaluation, assessment, and monitoring*. New York, NY: Taylor & Francis.
Thelk, A., Sundre, D. L., Horst, J. S., & Finney, S. J. (2009). Motivation matters: Using the student opinion scale (SOS) to make valid inferences about student performance. *Journal of General Education, 58*, 129–151.
Verhelst, N. D., Glas, C. A. W., & Verstralen, H. H. F. M. (1995). *One-parameter logistic model (OPLM)*. Arnhem: Cito, National Institute for Educational Measurement.
Von Davier, M., & Yamamoto, K. (2004). Partially observed mixtures of IRT models: An extension of the generalized partial-credit model. *Applied Psychological Measurement, 28*, 389–406.
Wainer, H. (1993). Measurement problems. *Journal of Educational Measurement, 30*, 1–21.
Wise, S. L., & DeMars, C. E. (2005). Low examinee effort in low-stakes assessment: Problems and potential solutions. *Educational Assessment, 10*, 1–17.
Wolf, L. F., & Smith, J. K. (1995). The consequence of consequence: Motivation, anxiety and test performance. *Applied Measurement in Education, 8*, 227–242.
Zerpa, C., Hachey, K., van Barneveld, C., & Simon, M. (2011). Modeling student motivation and students' ability estimates from a large-scale assessment of mathematics. *SAGE open*. doi:10.1177/2158244011421803.

A Recursive Algorithm for IRT Weighted Observed Score Equating

Yuehmei Chien and Ching David Shin

1 Introduction

Item weighting has historically received much attention. Gulliksen (1950) said that as long as an overall score is to be formed from separate test scores, the weighting problem arises. Large-scale tests are usually composed of multiple test sections. One of the reasons for weighting is that for tests with multiple sections, administrators commonly incorporate weights to account for, or to correct for, perceived inequalities between test sections (Stucky 2009; Wainer and Thissen 1993).

Another reason for weighting tests with different item types is to weight in order to achieve equal contributions to the score for each of several test sections. For example, a ten-item multiple choice test section (ten points maximum) is coupled with a single essay question (five points maximum). To achieve equality a weight of 2 is attached to the essay question. No matter what the reasons that test scores are weighted, testing programs that report a single score based on multiple choice and performance components must face the issue of how to derive the component scores (Rudner 2001).

There are various ways to select weights of the test components. Early methods attempted to account for items with differing length, difficulty, or assumed validity. For example, Gulliksen (1950) provided formulae and rationales for basing weights on the reliabilities, the standard deviations of the test or subtest scores, or factor analysis results. McDonald (1968) proposed a "unified treatment of the weighting problem," classifying the approaches described by Gulliksen and others as special cases of a general approach. Wang and Stanley (1970) reviewed approaches to determining weights for tests, subtests, and items, and added a consideration of differential weighting of response options within item.

Y. Chien (✉) • C.D. Shin
Pearson, 2510 N Dodge St., Iowa City, IA, 52245 USA
e-mail: yuehmei.chien@pearson.com; david.shin@pearson.com

R.E. Millsap et al. (eds.), *New Developments in Quantitative Psychology*, Springer Proceedings in Mathematics & Statistics 66, DOI 10.1007/978-1-4614-9348-8_24,

As large-scale assessments increasingly use both constructed-response (CR) and multiple choice (MC) items, recent studies have focused on issues related to creating weighted composites from tests or subtests consisting of mixed formats of items. For example, Wainer and Thissen (1993) compared approaches to combine a test consisting of MC items with one consisting of CR items. Lukhele and Sireci (1995) discussed this problem in the context of the conversion of the writing skills section of the General Educational Development (GED) test from classical test theory analysis to an item response theory (IRT) analysis. Traditionally, the GED test had weights of 0.64 and 0.36 for the MC and CR sections, respectively, which were arbitrarily chosen to allow the essay section to adequately contribute without overly reducing the composite reliability. Ito and Sykes (2000) and Sykes et al. (2001) examined the effects on composite test scores of increasing the weights of extended response, CR, or MC items, as compared to the effects of adding an equivalent number of items of the relevant type. The standard error of the scores that included weighted components were higher across the latent trait scale, though the difference was greater in the lower and upper parts of the scale than in the middle. Sykes and Hou (2003) used a more direct approach to combine weighting with IRT. Sykes and Hou demonstrate that for tests composed of combined item types (CR and MC), weights may be applied prior to IRT estimation of scores. This weighting was accomplished by increasing the portion of the test characteristic curve (TCC) that was contributed by CR items and then using the modified TCC to create a weighted-summed-score to IRT-score conversion table. In the example considered by Sykes and Hou, all CR items were weighted by 2, with the MC items receiving unit weights. In the study of Schaeffer et al. (2002), the CR items were weighted so that MC and CR items contributed the same number of points to the total score.

Not only were various methods developed to weight test components to form a composite score, but also these methods were compared in some studies, and issues regarding the impact of these methods on reliability and validity were discussed. For example, Chang (2009) compared five weighting schemes: the equally weighted model, the reliability weighting model, the standard deviation weighting model, the error measurement weighting model, and the effective score point model. The comparison found that, overall, the SD and the error of measurement weighting models seemed to perform better in establishing the composites than the reliability or the effective score point model. Rudner (2001) expresses concern that the focus on the reliability of the composite score may cause researchers to lose sight of the effect of weighting on validity. For example, a MC subtest may have higher reliability, but a lower correlation with a criterion measure, than a CR subtest. In such a case, determining weights may involve a trade-off between the reliability of the composite and its validity. Ercikan et al. (1998), similarly, describe the value of CR items as increasing test validity. In their study, they compare scores and information from MC and CR items calibrated together and calibrated separately using IRT models, but they do not create a composite score from the results of the separate calibrations. Related to the issue of score validity, Wilson and Wang (1995) compared the contributions of MC and performance-based items to define the latent variable in IRT analyses and to test information, concluding that performance-based items contributed more information than MC items but that MC items did affect the definition of the latent variable.

Although a number of research studies have investigated the psychometric properties of weighted scale scores and approaches to computing standard error for such scores, fewer have addressed the method of equating of the weighted scores. If test scores are weighted to obtain desired properties, it is equally critical to equate the test forms properly so that the desired properties can be generalized across test sessions/forms.

2 IRT Observed Score Equating

Using IRT to equate different test forms is not uncommon since the IRT models are popular in many testing programs for test development, test assembling, and scoring. Two assumptions are made for using IRT to equate test forms: (1) data used need to fit the IRT model assumption and (2) precise item parameter estimates are necessary. When those assumptions hold, the test taker's ability estimate is independent of test forms. Then, when the test forms have been put on the same scale, the same ability estimate will be obtained regardless of which test form the test taker has taken. This is referred to as sample invariance property in IRT. Based on the sample invariance property in IRT, obviously, the first step to equate test forms is to place the item parameters of the test forms on the same scale. After all of the items' parameters are placed on the same scale for different test forms, the ability estimates of the test takers can be compared across different test forms; therefore, the test forms are equated. If the ability estimates on the θ scale are used for score reporting, the equating process is actually finished at this point. In practice, the number-correct scores, however, are more commonly used than the ability estimates for score reporting of fixed forms due to some issues associated with the ability estimates. If the ability estimates on the θ scale are *NOT* used for score reporting, a further step of equating process is a necessity—that is, to develop a relationship between the number-correct scores on test forms.

Two equating methods are commonly used when using IRT to equate test forms—IRT true score equating and IRT observed score equating. The concept of the IRT true score equating is to equate number-correct scores on two test forms through true scores, in which the true score of a given θ on one form is considered to be equivalent to the true score of that given θ on another form. Different from the IRT true score equating, the IRT observed score equating develops a relationship directly from the number-correct scores by producing estimated distributions of observed scores on both forms and then equating those forms through the conventional equipercentile methods, which identify scores on one form that have the same percentile ranks as scores on another form. (See Kolen and Brennan 2004, for details of these two methods.)

Table 1 An estimated distribution of observed scores for a test form with four items

x	$f(x)$	F(x)	P(x)
0	0.2	0.2	10
1	0.3	0.5	35
2	0.2	0.7	60
3	0.2	0.9	80
4	0.1	1.0	95

To equate test forms for weighted scores, the IRT true score equating can still be applied by simply changing the score unit from one to the weighted unit for each of the score categories. Currently, the computer program named WITSE (Chien and Shin 2008) can conduct the weighted IRT true score equating. No procedures, however, exist for conducting IRT weighted observed score equating. The main reason is that there is no algorithm that can be used to systematically obtain the estimated distributions of weighted scores and it is laborious to do it manually. In this paper, an extended algorithm based on the recursive formula described by Lord and Wingersky (1984) is proposed to solve this predicament. To introduce this extended algorithm, the recursive formula by Lord and Wingersky (1984) is described first. Then, the extended algorithm is introduced in the next section.

The essential component of the IRT observed score equating is to obtain the estimated distributions of observed scores for both forms being equated. To understand the estimated distribution of observed scores, a simple example for a specific population is presented in Table 1. In Table 1, x refers to test scores of one form, $f(x)$ is to the proportion of examinees gaining the score x, $F(x)$ is the cumulative proportion at or below score x, and $P(x)$ is the percentile rank of score x. Based on the assumption of local independence in IRT, $f(x)$ is calculated by multiplying each of the probabilities for the responses of score x. For example, the probability of earning score four for ability θ_i is $f(x=4|\theta_i)=p_1(\theta_i)p_2(\theta_i)p_3(\theta_i)p_4(\theta_i)$, where $p_j(\theta_i)$ is the probability to answer the j - th item correctly given θ_i. (To simplify the notation, $p_j(\theta_i)$ is labeled as p_{ij} thereafter.) To obtain the distribution of observed scores based on the ability distribution of test takers, the formula below is used to accumulate the probability across different theta points:

$$f(x) = \sum_i f\left(x \middle| \theta_i\right) \psi(\theta_i), \tag{1}$$

where $\psi(\theta)$ is the discrete ability distribution. Note that even though the ability θ is a continuous scale, in practice, the ability distribution is characterized by a discrete distribution on a finite number of equally spaced theta points. One can use the estimated posterior distribution of ability obtained from BILOG as the discrete ability distribution in Eq. (1) when the software is used for item calibration.

In a real situation, the test length is much longer than four items and, therefore, obtaining $f(x|\theta_i)$ for a given discrete ability distribution becomes laborious. Fortunately, Lord and Wingersky (1984) proposed a recursive formula presented in Eq. (2) to calculate $f(x|\theta_i)$ and it has become commonly used

$$f_r\left(x\middle|\theta_i\right) = f_{r-1}\left(x\middle|\theta_i\right)(1-p_{ir}), \qquad x=0$$
$$= f_{r-1}\left(x\middle|\theta_i\right)(1-p_{ir}) + f_{r-1}\left(x-1\middle|\theta_i\right)p_{ir}, \quad 0<x<r \qquad (2)$$
$$= f_{r-1}\left(x-1\middle|\theta_i\right)p_{ir}, \qquad x=r,$$

where $f_r(x|\theta_i)$ is the distribution of number-correct scores over the first r items for the ability θ_i for $r>1$. The initial step for $r=1$ is $f_1(0)=1-p_1$ for $x=0$ and $f_1(1)=p_1$ for $x=1$.

This recursive formula works when items are dichotomously scored and not weighted. As described previously, the items might be weighted for various purposes. Thus, how to obtain the estimated distribution of weighted score seems problematic because the total number of the weighted scores is possibly huge, depending on the variety of weights on items. However, in this paper, a solution that is based on the recursive formula (Lord and Wingersky 1984) is proposed and described in detail in the next section.

3 The Extended Recursive Algorithm

3.1 Algorithm

The extended recursive algorithm is proposed to obtain $f(z|\theta_i)$, where z is the weighted score based on the weights and test score x and $f(z|\theta_i)$ is the probability earning weighted score z for the test takers of ability θ_i. To further describe this algorithm, the following variables are first defined:

x_{rl}: score of category l on item r
p_{ijl}: probability earning a score l on item j given θ_i
z_r: weighted scores over the first r items
w_r: weight on item r

For the first item $r=1, f_1(z_1|\theta_i)=p_{i1l}$, where $z_1=w_1x_{1l}$. For example, if the first item has three categories scored 0, 1, and 2, respectively, and is weighted by 1.5, $f_1(z_1=0|\theta_i)=p_{i10}$, $f_1(z_1=1.5|\theta_i)=p_{i11}$, and $f_1(z_1=3|\theta_i)=p_{i12}$. The extended formula in Eq. (2) can be recursively used to generalize the procedure for the rest of items (i.e., $r>1$) following the steps below.

Step 1: Calculate $f_r(z_r|\theta_i)=f_r(z_{r-1}+w_rx_{rl}|\theta_i)$ for each of different scores x_{rl} and each of different z_{r-1}.
Step 2: Sort $f_r(z_r|\theta_i)$ by z_r.
Step 3: Sum up $f_r(z_r|\theta_i)$ and $f_r(z_r^{'}|\theta_i)$ from Step 2 if $z_r=z_r^{'}$.

Table 2 IRT weighted observed score distribution recursion formula example with three items for test takers of θ_i

r	x_{rl}	$z^r = z^{r-1} + w_i x_{rl}$	Calculate $f_r(z^r \mid \theta_i)$	Sort	Sum up
1	0	0	$f_1(z_1 = 0) = f_1(0) = p_{i10}$	$f_1(0)$	$f_1(0)$
	1	1.5	$f_1(z_1 = 1.5) = p_{i11}$	$f_1(1.5)$	$f_1(1.5)$
2	0	$0+0$	$f_2(z_2 = 0 + 1.5 \times 0) = f_2(0) = f_1(0)p_{i20}$	$f_2(0)$	$f_2(0)$
	1	$0+1.5\times 1$	$f_2(z_2 = 0 + 1.5 \times 1) = f_2(1.5) = f_1(0)p_{i21}$	$f_2(1.5)$	$f_2(1.5)$
	0	$1.5+0$	$f_2(z_2 = 1.5 + 1.5 \times 0) = f_2(1.5) = f_1(1.5)p_{i20}$	$f_2(1.5)$	
	1	$1.5+1.5\times 1$	$f_2(z_2 = 1.5 \times 1 + 1.5 \times 1) = f_2(3) = f_1(1.5)p_{i21}$	$f_2(3)$	$f_2(3)$
3	0	$0+0$	$f_3(z_3 = 0 + 2 \times 0) = f_3(0) = f_2(0)p_{i30}$	$f_3(0)$	$f_3(0)$
	1	$0+1.5\times 1$	$f_3(z_3 = 0 + 1.5 \times 1) = f_3(1.5) = f_3(0)p_{i31}$	$f_3(1.5)$	$f_3(1.5)$
	2	$0+1.5\times 2$	$f_3(z_3 = 0 + 1.5 \times 2) = f_3(3) = f_3(0)p_{i32}$	$f_3(1.5)$	
	0	$1.5+0$	$f_3(z_3 = 1.5 + 1.5 \times 0) = f_3(1.5) = f_3(1.5)p_{i30}$	$f_3(3)$	$f_3(3)$
	1	$1.5+1.5\times 1$	$f_3(z_3 = 1.5 + 1.5 \times 1) = f_3(3) = f_3(1.5)p_{i31}$	$f_3(3)$	
	2	$1.5+1.5\times 2$	$f_3(z_3 = 1.5 + 1.5 \times 2) = f_3(4.5) = f_3(1.5)p_{i32}$	$f_3(3)$	
	0	$3+0$	$f_3(z_3 = 3 + 1.5 \times 0) = f_3(3) = f_3(3)p_{i30}$	$f_3(4.5)$	$f_3(4.5)$
	1	$3+1.5$	$f_3(z_3 = 3 + 1.5 \times 1) = f_3(4.5) = f_3(3)p_{i31}$	$f_3(4.5)$	
	2	$3+1.5\times 2$	$f_3(z_3 = 3 + 1.5 \times 2) = f_3(6) = f_3(3)p_{i32}$	$f_3(6)$	$f_3(6)$

An example of using the extended recursive algorithm is presented in Table 2 for two dichotomous items and one 3-category polytomous item with the weight 1.5 for all three items.

The extended recursive algorithm is used to calculate the weighted observed score distribution for test takers of a given ability θ_i. To accumulate the weighted observed score distribution over ability distribution of test takers, Eq. (1) is used with x replaced by z to obtain $f(z)$. After $f(z)$ is available for each of the weighted scores, obtaining $F(z)$, the cumulative proportion at or below score z, and $P(z)$, the percentile rank of score z, is straightforward. After $f(z)$, $F(z)$, and $P(z)$ are obtained for both forms, the conventional equipercentile methods can be applied to equate the two forms.

3.2 *Equating Example*

To demonstrate the use of the extended recursive algorithm, the IRT weighted observed score equating was conducted using two real test forms administered in two consecutive years, which are referred to as Form X and Form Y. For illustration purposes, the IRT unweighted observed score equating, IRT true score equating for weighted scores, and IRT true score equating for unweighted scores were also conducted. Both test forms contain 70 items, including 65 dichotomous items and 5 polytomous items with 3, 3, 4, 4, and 4 score categories, respectively. The IRT weighted and unweighted observed score equating conducted were implemented using Equating Recipes (Brennan et al. 2009). Equating Recipes provides a set of open source functions to perform all types of equating discussed by Kolen and Brennan (2004). The weighted and unweighted IRT true score equating were conducted using WITSE (Chien and Shin 2008).

The purpose of the equating conducted is simply to demonstrate the extended recursive algorithm. Therefore, how to weigh the items was not seriously considered and weights were arbitrarily set to 1 for those 65 dichotomous items and to 0.5 for those 5 polytomous items. Tables 3, 4, 5, and 6 present the equating results for the two different equating methods—IRT observed score vs. IRT true score—and two different types of scores—weighted vs. unweighted.

The unweighted scores are from 0 to 81 and the weighted scores are from 0 to 73. The weighted scores listed in the tables contain only rounded integer scores. The form differences (Form Y equivalent minus Form X score) are plotted in Fig. 1. In the legend of Fig. 1, OB stands for IRT observed score equating, TRUE stands for IRT true score equating, WT stands for weighted scores, and UWT stands for unweighted scores. The relationship for the weighted score equating differs noticeably from the relationship for the unweighted score equating for both IRT equating methods. In this example, the two different IRT equating methods have slightly closer form differences on the weighted scores than on the unweighted scores. Also, the shapes of the form differences as shown in Fig. 1 are different between the weighted scores and unweighted scores for each of the IRT equating methods. This is an example of demonstrating the IRT weighted score equating using the extended recursive algorithm; therefore, further discussion about the results is not essential.

4 Summary

In this study, an extended recursive algorithm, which is used to construct the estimated score distribution in the process of the IRT weighted observed score equating, has been proposed and demonstrated using a real data set. As the use of different weighting schemes has increased to accommodate different purposes under different testing situations, the proposed extended recursive algorithm allows the practitioners and the researchers to equate test forms using the IRT weighted observed score equating. Therefore, further researches on the IRT weighted observed score equating is achievable and desirable.

Table 3 IRT unweighted observed score equating results

Form X score	Form Y equivalent	Form X weighted score	Form Y equivalent
0	−0.33	41	34.67
1	0.08	42	35.66
2	0.61	43	36.63
3	1.05	44	37.60
4	1.46	45	38.56
5	1.91	46	39.50
6	2.54	47	40.44
7	3.23	48	41.37
8	4.00	49	42.29
9	4.78	50	43.21
10	5.53	51	44.12
11	6.34	52	45.01
12	7.09	53	45.90
13	7.62	54	46.78
14	8.06	55	47.64
15	8.49	56	48.49
16	9.08	57	49.40
17	9.88	58	50.29
18	10.80	59	51.11
19	11.75	60	51.73
20	12.72	61	52.35
21	13.71	62	53.07
22	14.71	63	54.00
23	15.71	64	55.00
24	16.72	65	56.01
25	17.72	66	57.02
26	18.73	67	58.04
27	19.74	68	59.06
28	20.75	69	60.09
29	21.76	70	61.15
30	22.78	71	62.22
31	23.80	72	63.33
32	24.85	73	64.46
33	26.01	74	65.63
34	27.40	75	66.85
35	28.61	76	68.15
36	29.66	77	69.92
37	30.67	78	73.27
38	31.68	79	75.06
39	32.68	80	76.67
40	33.68	81	78.83

Table 4 IRT weighted observed score equating results

Form X score	Form Y equivalent	Form X weighted score	Form Y equivalent
0	−0.33	37	28.54
1	0.09	38	29.46
2	0.86	39	30.38
3	1.30	40	31.32
4	1.72	41	32.26
5	2.16	42	33.21
6	2.79	43	34.16
7	3.50	44	35.12
8	4.26	45	36.09
9	5.04	46	37.06
10	5.78	47	38.04
11	6.60	48	39.03
12	7.33	49	40.02
13	7.77	50	41.02
14	8.23	51	42.02
15	8.71	52	43.04
16	9.21	53	44.05
17	9.91	54	45.04
18	11.13	55	45.87
19	11.67	56	46.99
20	12.34	57	47.76
21	13.64	58	48.87
22	14.47	59	50.10
23	15.30	60	50.83
24	16.12	61	52.05
25	16.92	62	53.31
26	18.21	63	54.59
27	19.04	64	55.43
28	19.88	65	56.84
29	20.73	66	57.80
30	21.58	67	59.22
31	22.44	68	60.70
32	23.32	69	62.11
33	24.29	70	65.50
34	25.29	71	67.35
35	26.73	72	68.90
36	27.63	73	71.10

Table 5 Form Y equivalents of Form X scores using IRT true score equating

Form X score	θ Equivalent	Form Y equivalent	Form X score	θ Equivalent	Form Y equivalent
0	−99.00	0.00	41	−0.15	34.94
1	−3.56	0.39	42	−0.11	35.93
2	−3.10	0.82	43	−0.07	36.90
3	−2.82	1.29	44	−0.03	37.84
4	−2.61	1.80	45	0.00	38.76
5	−2.44	2.33	46	0.04	39.65
6	−2.30	2.88	47	0.08	40.52
7	−2.17	3.45	48	0.12	41.37
8	−2.06	4.05	49	0.15	42.19
9	−1.96	4.66	50	0.19	43.00
10	−1.86	5.29	51	0.22	43.80
11	−1.77	5.94	52	0.26	44.59
12	−1.69	6.61	53	0.29	45.38
13	−1.61	7.31	54	0.32	46.17
14	−1.54	8.02	55	0.35	46.97
15	−1.47	8.76	56	0.39	47.78
16	−1.40	9.53	57	0.42	48.61
17	−1.34	10.34	58	0.45	49.46
18	−1.28	11.18	59	0.49	50.33
19	−1.22	12.06	60	0.52	51.23
20	−1.16	12.97	61	0.55	52.15
21	−1.10	13.91	62	0.59	53.09
22	−1.05	14.89	63	0.63	54.05
23	−1.00	15.89	64	0.66	55.03
24	−0.94	16.90	65	0.70	56.02
25	−0.89	17.93	66	0.74	57.02
26	−0.84	18.97	67	0.78	58.04
27	−0.79	20.01	68	0.83	59.07
28	−0.74	21.07	69	0.87	60.13
29	−0.70	22.13	70	0.93	61.23
30	−0.65	23.19	71	0.98	62.38
31	−0.60	24.27	72	1.05	63.59
32	−0.56	25.36	73	1.13	64.89
33	−0.51	26.45	74	1.21	66.28
34	−0.46	27.54	75	1.31	67.77
35	−0.42	28.63	76	1.44	69.38
36	−0.37	29.71	77	1.58	71.12
37	−0.33	30.79	78	1.77	73.00
38	−0.28	31.85	79	2.03	75.08
39	−0.24	32.90	80	2.46	77.46
40	−0.19	33.93	81	99.00	81.00

Table 6 Form Y equivalents of Form X scores using IRT weighted true score equating

Form X weighted score	θ Equivalent	Form Y equivalent	Form X weighted score	θ Equivalent	Form Y equivalent
0	−99.00	0.00	37	−0.29	28.44
1	−3.56	0.39	38	−0.24	29.42
2	−3.10	0.82	39	−0.19	30.40
3	−2.82	1.30	40	−0.15	31.38
4	−2.61	1.80	41	−0.10	32.35
5	−2.44	2.33	42	−0.06	33.31
6	−2.30	2.88	43	−0.01	34.27
7	−2.17	3.46	44	0.03	35.21
8	−2.05	4.05	45	0.07	36.15
9	−1.95	4.66	46	0.11	37.07
10	−1.86	5.29	47	0.16	37.98
11	−1.77	5.94	48	0.20	38.89
12	−1.69	6.60	49	0.24	39.79
13	−1.61	7.27	50	0.29	40.69
14	−1.53	7.97	51	0.33	41.59
15	−1.46	8.68	52	0.37	42.51
16	−1.39	9.41	53	0.41	43.45
17	−1.33	10.17	54	0.46	44.41
18	−1.27	10.95	55	0.50	45.39
19	−1.21	11.75	56	0.55	46.41
20	−1.15	12.57	57	0.59	47.45
21	−1.09	13.42	58	0.64	48.51
22	−1.03	14.28	59	0.69	49.60
23	−0.98	15.16	60	0.75	50.70
24	−0.93	16.06	61	0.80	51.84
25	−0.87	16.96	62	0.86	53.00
26	−0.82	17.87	63	0.93	54.20
27	−0.77	18.79	64	1.00	55.47
28	−0.72	19.72	65	1.08	56.81
29	−0.67	20.66	66	1.17	58.23
30	−0.62	21.61	67	1.28	59.75
31	−0.58	22.57	68	1.41	61.38
32	−0.53	23.53	69	1.56	63.12
33	−0.48	24.51	70	1.75	65.00
34	−0.43	25.49	71	2.01	67.07
35	−0.38	26.47	72	2.44	69.45
36	−0.34	27.45	73	99.00	73.00

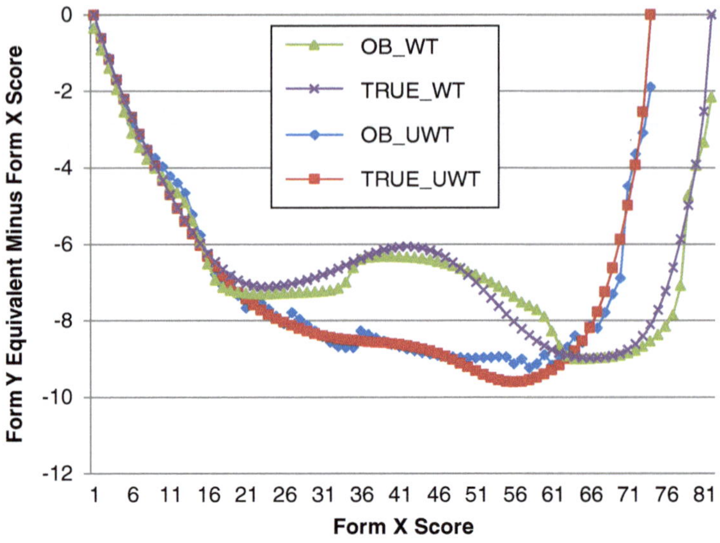

Fig. 1 Score difference between Form X and Form Y equivalent

References

Brennan, R. L., Wang, T., Kim, S., & Seol, J. (2009). *Equating recipes* (CASMA Monograph Number 1). Iowa City, IA: Center for Advanced Studies in Measurement and Assessment, the University of Iowa. Available from the web address: http://www.uiowa.edu/~casma

Chang, S. (2009). Choice of weighting scheme in forming the composite. *Bulletin of Educational Psychology, 40*(3), 489–510.

Chien, Y., & Shin, D. C. (2008). *WITSE: A program for weighted IRT true score equating, Version 1.0*. Iowa City, IA: Pearson.

Ercikan, K., Schwarz, R. D., Julian, M. W., Burket, G. R., Weber, M. M., & Link, V. (1998). Calibration and scoring of tests with multiple-choice and constructed-response item types. *Journal of Educational Measurement, 35*, 137–154.

Gulliksen, H. (1950). *Theory of mental tests*. New York: Wiley.

Ito, K., & Sykes, R. C. (2000, June). *An evaluation of "intentional" weighting of extended-response or constructed-response items in tests with mixed item types*. Paper presented at the annual national conference on large scale assessment, Snowbird, Utah.

Kolen, M. J., & Brennan, R. L. (2004). *Test equating, scaling, and linking*. New York, NY: Springer.

Lord, F. M. & Wingersky, M. S. (1984). Comparison of IRT true-score and equipercentile observed-score equatings. *Applied Psychological Measurement*, 8, 453–461.

Lukhele, R., & Sireci, G. (1995). *Using IRT to combine multiple-choice and free-response sections of a test onto a common scale using a priori weights*. Paper presented at the annual meeting of the National Council on Measurement in Education, San Francisco, CA.

McDonald, R. P. (1968). A unified treatment of the weighting problem. *Psychometrika, 33*, 351–381.

Rudner, L. M. (2001). Informed test component weighting. *Educational Measurement: Issues and Practice, 20*(1), 16–19.

Schaeffer, G. A., Henderson-Montero, D., & Julian, M. (2002). A comparison of three scoring methods for tests with selected-response and constructed-response items. *Educational Assessment, 8*(4), 317–340.

Stucky, B. D. (2009). *Item response theory for weighted summed scores* (Unpublished manuscript).

Sykes, R. C., & Hou, L. (2003). Weighting constructed-response items in IRT-based exams. *Applied Measurement in Education, 16*, 257–275.

Sykes, R. C., Truskosky, D., & White, H. (2001, April). *Determining the representation of constructed-response items in mixed-item format exams.* Paper presented at the annual meeting of the National Council on Measurement in Education, Seattle, WA.

Wainer, H., & Thissen, D. (1993). Combining multiple-choice and constructed response test scores: Toward a Marxist theory of test construction. *Applied Measurement in Education, 6*(2), 103–118.

Wang, M. D., & Stanley, J. C. (1970). Differential weighting: A review of methods and empirical studies. *Review of Educational Research, 40*, 663–705.

Wilson, M., & Wang, W. (1995). Complex composites: Issues that arise in combining different modes of assessment. *Applied Psychological Measurement, 19*, 51–71.

Bartlett Factor Scores: General Formulas and Applications to Structural Equation Models

Yiu-Fai Yung and Ke-Hai Yuan

This paper is based on a presentation by the first author at the International Meeting of Psychometric Society held in Lincoln, Nebraska, July 2012.

1 Bartlett Factor Scores and Its Applications to Structural Equation Modeling

Bartlett (1937) derives a formula for computing factor scores in the context of exploratory factor analysis. Yuan and Hayashi (2010) adapt Bartlett's method and provide extended formulas to compute factor scores in the LISREL-type structural equation model. The main purpose of the current paper is to continue the effort to provide more general formulas to compute factor scores in structural equation modeling. Related formulas that are useful for residual diagnostics, outlier and leverage point detection, and robust estimation are also derived.

To describe Bartlett's formula for computing factor scores, it would be useful to introduce the factor model and its notation. In a factor model, observed variables $\boldsymbol{y}$ are said to be "explained" by a set of factors $\boldsymbol{f}$, where $\boldsymbol{y}$ is a $p \times 1$ random vector of observed variables and $\boldsymbol{f}$ is an $m \times 1$ random vector of latent factors. Typically, the number of variables p should be much larger than the number of factors m.

Y.-F. Yung (✉)
SAS Institute Inc., 100 SAS Campus Drive, Cary, NC 27513-2414, USA
e-mail: Yiu-Fai.Yung@sas.com

K.-H. Yuan
University of Norte Dame, 123B Haggar Hall, Notre Dame, IN 46556-5636, USA
e-mail: kyuan@nd.edu

R.E. Millsap et al. (eds.), *New Developments in Quantitative Psychology*, Springer Proceedings in Mathematics & Statistics 66, DOI 10.1007/978-1-4614-9348-8_25,

The relationships between observed variables and latent factors are described by the following factor model equation:

$$\boldsymbol{y} = \nu + \Lambda \boldsymbol{f} + \boldsymbol{e} \tag{1}$$

where ν is a $p \times 1$ vector of intercepts, Λ is a $p \times m$ matrix of factor loadings, and $\boldsymbol{e}$ is a $p \times 1$ vector of errors. The latent factors $\boldsymbol{f}$ are centered at zero with a covariance matrix Φ (that is, $\mathscr{E}\boldsymbol{f} = \boldsymbol{0}$ and $\mathscr{E}\boldsymbol{ff}' = \Phi$). The errors $\boldsymbol{e}$ are centered at zero with a covariance matrix Θ (that is, $\mathscr{E}\boldsymbol{e} = \boldsymbol{0}$ and $\mathscr{E}\boldsymbol{ee}' = \Theta$). Usually, Θ is assumed to be a diagonal matrix, although it is not necessary to make such an assumption in the current context. Latent factors and errors are uncorrelated ($\mathscr{E}\boldsymbol{fe}' = \boldsymbol{0}$). Moreover, with the assumption of multivariate normality of factors and errors, this also means that latent factors and errors are independent.

Moving the intercept term ν in Eq. (1) to the left side of the equation shows the decomposition of the "true" and "error" components of the centered version of $\boldsymbol{y}$:

$$\boldsymbol{y} - \nu = \Lambda \boldsymbol{f} + \boldsymbol{e} \tag{2}$$

where $\Lambda\boldsymbol{f}$ and $\boldsymbol{e}$ are regarded as the "true" score and error components, respectively, of the mean-adjusted observed score $\boldsymbol{y}$.

Because factors are unobserved or theoretically unobservable, formulas have been derived to estimate the factors given the factor model and the observed variables $\boldsymbol{y}$. Bartlett (1937) proposes the following formula for estimating factor scores:

$$\widehat{\boldsymbol{f}} = \left(\Lambda'\Theta^{-1}\Lambda\right)^{-1}\Lambda'\Theta^{-1}(\boldsymbol{y} - \nu) \tag{3}$$

Due to its form, Eq. (3) is also referred to as the weighted least squares method for computing factor scores. Bartlett's method is not the only formula to compute factor scores. For example, the regression method has also been proposed (see, for example, Chap. 9 of Johnson and Wichern 2007). However, as discussed in Yuan and Hayashi (2010), Bartlett's formula has some nice geometric properties. Define a projection matrix $\boldsymbol{P}$ by the following equation:

$$\boldsymbol{P} = \Lambda\left(\Lambda'\Theta^{-1}\Lambda\right)^{-1}\Lambda'\Theta^{-1} \tag{4}$$

Then the true score component of $\boldsymbol{y} - \nu$ is estimated by:

$$\Lambda\widehat{\boldsymbol{f}} = \Lambda\left(\Lambda'\Theta^{-1}\Lambda\right)^{-1}\Lambda'\Theta^{-1}(\boldsymbol{y} - \nu) = \boldsymbol{P}(\boldsymbol{y} - \nu) \tag{5}$$

which is a projection of $(\boldsymbol{y} - \nu)$ onto the space spanned by the columns of Λ (or the true score space). In addition, the error or residual is estimated by:

$$\widehat{\boldsymbol{e}} = \boldsymbol{y} - \widehat{\boldsymbol{y}} = \boldsymbol{y} - \left(\nu + \Lambda\widehat{\boldsymbol{f}}\right) = (\boldsymbol{y} - \nu) - \Lambda\widehat{\boldsymbol{f}} = (\boldsymbol{I} - \boldsymbol{P})(\boldsymbol{y} - \nu) \tag{6}$$

Hence, Eqs. (5) and (6) show that Bartlett's formula results in an orthogonal decomposition of $(y - \nu)$ for estimating the true and error scores. This property is important. As $\widehat{e}$ is not correlated with $\widehat{f}$, residual analysis based on $\widehat{e}$ would not be confounded with the estimation of factor scores. Other desirable properties of Bartlett factor scores, as compared with the regression factor scores, are discussed in Yuan and Zhong (2008) and Yuan and Hayashi (2010).

To estimate factor scores in practical applications, the model parameters are replaced with their estimates (with the "hat" notation) from samples so that Eq. (3) becomes

$$\widehat{f} = \left(\widehat{\Lambda}'\widehat{\Theta}^{-1}\widehat{\Lambda}\right)^{-1}\widehat{\Lambda}'\widehat{\Theta}^{-1}(y - \widehat{\nu}) \tag{7}$$

Because the "population" form of Bartlett's formula in Eq. (3) essentially defines the computation, for simplicity the "sample" form in Eq. (7), which uses the "hat" notation, will not be presented in subsequent derivations. It is understood that in practical applications sample estimates must be obtained in place of the population parameters in the formulas.

Certainly, factor score estimation is useful in itself as a data reduction technique. Instead of dealing with a large number of observed variables, one can reduce the data to a much smaller number of factor scores when the factor model is appropriate. Moreover, factor score estimation facilitates the adaptation of traditional regression techniques to general structural equation modeling. Recall that the factor model in Eq. (1) has a similar form to the regression model. The critical difference is only that the predictors in Eq. (1) are latent variables. If these latent variables can be estimated reasonably well, then regression techniques such as outlier and leverage point detection can be applied to the factor model in very much the same way as they are applied to the regression model. Many other regression techniques might also be applicable to structural equation modeling once the factor scores are available. In this regard, using Bartlett factor scores is a good choice for the factor model. The harder problem is to make Bartlett factor scores also work in general structural equation modeling.

Recently, Yuan and Hayashi (2010) propose the use of Bartlett's method to estimate factor scores in LISREL-type structural equation models. They provide extended formulas for estimating factor scores in situation where endogenous latent variables might be present in the system. With the use of Bartlett factor scores, they also derive related formulas for outlier and leverage point detection, residual diagnostics, and robust estimation.

In summary, Bartlett's method of computing factor scores is very useful not only because it is a data reduction tool but also it would make some techniques in regression adaptable to structural equation modeling. However, the original Bartlett formula is limited as it can only deal with exogenous latent factors. Yuan and Hayashi (2010) provide extended formulas to deal with endogenous latent factors, but more general formulas are still needed. As shown in Table 1, there is another dimension that the original Bartlett formula and the extended formulas of Yuan

Table 1 Different sets of formulas for computing Bartlett factor scores

	No endogenous factors	Endogenous factors possible
No exogenous observed variables	Bartlett (1937)	Yuan and Hayashi (2010)
Exogenous observed variables possible	(NA)	Current extension

and Hayashi (2010) have not dealt with general structural equation modeling. This dimension is the presence of *exogenous* observed variables in structural equation models. Hence, the main goal of this paper is to derive more general formulas to fill this gap. The next section describes the general setting and derives the main formulas for computing Bartlett factor scores. Related results for outlier and leverage point detection and residual diagnosis are also derived. Next, the derived formulas are illustrated by using a simulated data set. Finally, the last section concludes the current findings and suggests further applications.

2 Estimating Bartlett Factor Scores in General Structural Equation Models

Figure 1a shows the path diagram of a structural equation model. Error terms are omitted for simplicity. Essentially, ξ_1 in the path diagram is a latent factor for the observed variables y_1, y_2, and y_3. If the observed variable x and its arrows pointing to the two y variables were omitted, the path diagram would have represented a typical confirmatory factor model. In that case, the Bartlett factor scores for ξ_1 can be computed directly by using Eq. (3). With the presence of the x variable, however, neither Eq. (3) nor the formulas in Yuan and Hayashi (2010) are applicable.

It is emphasized here that the model in Fig. 1a is not an unrealistic example created only for motivating the current problem with exogenous observed variables in structural equation models. In practical situations, response variables $\mathbf{y}$ might indeed covariate with some other variables in a factor model. The model shown in Fig. 1a represents a covariate variable x with response variables y_1 and y_2. It is desirable to estimate Bartlett factor scores with the covariate effects taken into account. Moreover, there are certainly many other practical analyses in which exogenous observed variables play important roles in the models, much like the predictors in regression analysis.

To circumvent the problem with exogenous observed variables, one might suggest a common "trick" that specifies dummy latent variables to represent exogenous observed variables perfectly. Figure 1b shows this idea for the current example. A dummy latent variable ξ_2 is created and its path to the x variable is fixed at 1. In addition, a fixed zero error variance is represented by a double-headed arrow attaching to the x variable. Statistically, the model in Fig. 1b is equivalent to that in Fig. 1a. Both models will have exactly the same model fit given the data. However, with regard to the estimation of Bartlett factor scores, the trick

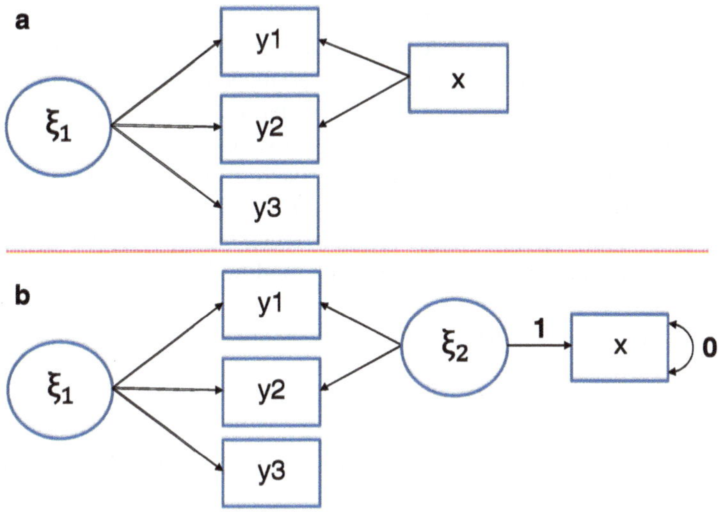

Fig. 1 A structural equation model with an exogenous observed variable

in Fig. 1b does not work as desired. If the model in Fig. 1b is specified in any SEM (structural equation modeling) software, ξ_2 will be treated literally as a latent factor (SEM software does not know whether a latent factor is a real or a dummy one). As a result, factor scores for ξ_1 and ξ_2 would be estimated simultaneously. However, because one of the error variance is fixed at zero, the matrix Θ will have a zero entry in its diagonal. Hence, Θ is not invertible in Eq. (3). Even if SEM software can distinguish between "dummy" and "real" latent variables, it is still scientifically better to have theoretically sound formulas to compute the factor scores in general situations. Relying on "tricks" to solve an important problem might make the software implementation unnecessarily complicated and difficult to maintain. It might not even work as desired. An approach that explicitly includes exogenous observed variables is needed, and will be described below.

With no loss of generality, the structural equation model of interest can be represented by the following model equation:

$$\begin{pmatrix} \boldsymbol{y} \\ \eta \end{pmatrix} = \begin{pmatrix} \nu_{\boldsymbol{y}} \\ \nu_\eta \end{pmatrix} + \mathbf{B} \begin{pmatrix} \boldsymbol{y} \\ \eta \end{pmatrix} + \Gamma \begin{pmatrix} \boldsymbol{x} \\ \xi \end{pmatrix} + \begin{pmatrix} \varepsilon \\ \zeta \end{pmatrix} \tag{8}$$

where $\begin{pmatrix} \boldsymbol{y} \\ \eta \end{pmatrix}$ is a random vector of endogenous manifest variables $\boldsymbol{y}$ and latent factors η, $\begin{pmatrix} \boldsymbol{x} \\ \xi \end{pmatrix}$ is a random vector of exogenous manifest variables $\boldsymbol{x}$ and latent factors ξ, $\begin{pmatrix} \varepsilon \\ \zeta \end{pmatrix}$ is a vector of error terms, which are independent of $\begin{pmatrix} \boldsymbol{x} \\ \xi \end{pmatrix}$, $\begin{pmatrix} \nu_{\boldsymbol{y}} \\ \nu_\eta \end{pmatrix}$

is a vector of intercepts for manifest variables $\boldsymbol{y}$ and latent factors η, respectively, $\mathbf{B}$ is a matrix of effects among the endogenous variables (with zero diagonal elements), and Γ is a matrix of effects of the exogenous variables on the endogenous variables.

Therefore, the current system covers the general situation where observed and latent variables could be either endogenous or exogenous. To derive the formulas for computing Bartlett factor scores, the approach of Yuan and Hayashi (2010) is adopted. Basically, the model in Eq. (8) would be "reduced" to a form that matches the factor model in Eq. (1). Then, Bartlett factor scores for general structural equation models are computed by Eq. (3), with modified definitions of the parameter matrices.

First, expand the $\boldsymbol{y}$ component in Eq. (8) to obtain the following:

$$\boldsymbol{y} = \boldsymbol{A}_{11}\nu_{\boldsymbol{y}} + \boldsymbol{A}_{12}\nu_{\eta} + \boldsymbol{G}_{11}\boldsymbol{x} + \boldsymbol{G}_{12}\xi + \boldsymbol{A}_{12}\zeta + \boldsymbol{A}_{11}\varepsilon \tag{9}$$

where $\boldsymbol{A}_{11}, \boldsymbol{A}_{12}$, $\boldsymbol{G}_{11}$, and $\boldsymbol{G}_{12}$ are sub-matrices defined by the following equalities:

$$\begin{pmatrix} \boldsymbol{A}_{11} & \boldsymbol{A}_{12} \\ \boldsymbol{A}_{21} & \boldsymbol{A}_{22} \end{pmatrix} \equiv \boldsymbol{A} = (\boldsymbol{I} - \mathbf{B})^{-1}$$
$$\begin{pmatrix} \boldsymbol{G}_{11} & \boldsymbol{G}_{12} \\ \boldsymbol{G}_{21} & \boldsymbol{G}_{22} \end{pmatrix} \equiv \boldsymbol{G} = (\boldsymbol{I} - \mathbf{B})^{-1}\,\Gamma$$

Invertibility of $(\boldsymbol{I} - \mathbf{B})$ is assumed, but this is a common assumption to all kinds of structural equation models. The essence of Eq. (9) is that it is identified with the following form of factor model:

$$\boldsymbol{y}^* = \nu + \Lambda \boldsymbol{f} + \boldsymbol{e} \tag{10}$$

Following Yuan and Hayashi (2010), two set of definitions of the variables and parameter matrices can be used in Eq. (10).

Definition 1 Treating ζ as factors. Let

$$\boldsymbol{y}^* = \boldsymbol{y} - \boldsymbol{G}_{11}\boldsymbol{x}, \quad \boldsymbol{f} = \begin{pmatrix} \xi \\ \zeta \end{pmatrix}, \quad \boldsymbol{e} = \boldsymbol{A}_{11}\varepsilon$$
$$\nu = \boldsymbol{A}_{11}\nu_{\boldsymbol{y}} + \boldsymbol{A}_{12}\nu_{\eta}, \quad \Lambda = \begin{pmatrix} \boldsymbol{G}_{12} & \boldsymbol{A}_{12} \end{pmatrix}$$

The reduced factor model in Eq. (10) removes the effects of $\boldsymbol{x}$ on $\boldsymbol{y}$ by using the transformed response $\boldsymbol{y}^*$, which is then functionally related to factors $\boldsymbol{f}$ in a way that it bears the same form as the factor model in Eq. (1). Hence, with these new definitions, Eq. (3) can be used for estimating the Bartlett factor scores in the current general structural equation model. That is, the Bartlett factor scores are computed by:

$$\widehat{\boldsymbol{f}} = (\Lambda'\,\Theta^{-1}\Lambda)^{-1}\Lambda'\Theta^{-1}(\boldsymbol{y}^* - \nu) = (\Lambda'\Theta^{-1}\Lambda)^{-1}\Lambda'\Theta^{-1}(\boldsymbol{y} - \boldsymbol{G}_{11}\boldsymbol{x} - \nu) \tag{11}$$

where

$$\Theta = \boldsymbol{A}_{11}\Theta_{\varepsilon}\boldsymbol{A}'_{11} \tag{12}$$

and $\Theta_{\varepsilon} \equiv \text{COV}(\varepsilon, \varepsilon')$ (Covariance matrix of ε), which is a parameter matrix in the general structural equation model defined in Eq. (8). Yuan and Hayashi (2010) argue that Definition 1 with $\boldsymbol{f} = \begin{pmatrix} \xi \\ \zeta \end{pmatrix}$ can be used when the model structures are theoretically sound. Otherwise, ζ should be treated as errors with the following alternative set of definitions for Eqs. (10)–(12):

Definition 2 Treating ζ as errors. Let

$$\boldsymbol{y}^* = \boldsymbol{y} - \boldsymbol{G}_{11}\boldsymbol{x}, \quad \boldsymbol{f} = \xi, \quad \boldsymbol{e} = \boldsymbol{A}_{12}\zeta + \boldsymbol{A}_{11}\varepsilon$$
$$\nu = \boldsymbol{A}_{11}\nu_{\boldsymbol{y}} + \boldsymbol{A}_{12}\nu_{\eta}, \quad \Lambda = \boldsymbol{G}_{12}$$

With Definition 2, the error covariance matrix Θ in Eqs. (11) and (12) for estimating Bartlett factor scores is now defined by:

$$\Theta = \boldsymbol{A}_{12}\Psi\boldsymbol{A}'_{12} + \boldsymbol{A}_{11}\Theta_{\varepsilon}\boldsymbol{A}'_{11} + \boldsymbol{A}_{12}\text{COV}\left(\zeta, \varepsilon'\right)\boldsymbol{A}'_{11} + \boldsymbol{A}_{11}\text{COV}\left(\varepsilon, \zeta'\right)\boldsymbol{A}'_{12} \tag{13}$$

where $\Theta_{\varepsilon} \equiv \text{COV}(\varepsilon, \varepsilon')$, $\Psi \equiv \text{COV}(\zeta, \zeta')$, and $\text{COV}(\zeta, \varepsilon') = (\text{COV}(\varepsilon, \zeta'))'$ are all parameter matrices in the general structural equation model defined in Eq. (8). In most practical applications, the errors ζ for endogenous latent factors and errors $\boldsymbol{e}$ for endogenous observed variables are not correlated. In this case, the last two terms of Eq. (13) vanish. However, if for any reason $\text{COV}(\zeta, \varepsilon')$ is non-null, the full form of Eq. (13) must be used.

In fact, when $\text{COV}(\zeta, \varepsilon')$ is non-null, only Definition 2 for the reduced factor model should be used. The reason is that Definition 1 treats ζ as factors. If $\text{COV}(\zeta, \varepsilon')$ is not null, factors in ζ would correlate with the corresponding error terms $\boldsymbol{e} = \boldsymbol{A}_{11}\varepsilon$ in Definition 1. This violates the assumption of the factor model in Eq. (1) and would render the use of Eq. (3) invalid for computing Bartlett factor scores.

3 Applications to Outlier and Leverage Point Detection and Residual Diagnostics

This section builds upon the preceding results to derive formulas that are needed to conduct outlier and leverage point detection and residual diagnosis. In regression analysis, residuals are well defined because the predicted values $\widehat{\boldsymbol{y}}$ can be computed easily by putting the model estimates and the observed values $\boldsymbol{y}$ into the regression equation. The residuals are simply defined by:

$$\widehat{\boldsymbol{e}} = \boldsymbol{y} - \widehat{\boldsymbol{y}} \tag{14}$$

Outlier detection and residual diagnosis are then based on the residuals defined in Eq. (14). In structural equation modeling, two additional issues need to be resolved before implementing similar types of regression techniques. First, residuals $\widehat{\boldsymbol{e}}$ in structural equation modeling are multi-dimensional. An overall measure of residuals is needed to facilitate the outlier detections and residual diagnosis. Second, the computation of the predicted values $\widehat{\boldsymbol{y}}$ is not as straightforward due to the presence of unobserved values in latent variables. To an extent, the derived results in the preceding section address the second issue quite satisfactorily. The first issue has been addressed by using the M-distance (Mahalanobis distance) measure of residuals (see Yuan and Hayashi 2010). Because the M-distance can be viewed as a kind of statistically standardized distance measure, the residual M-distance has the following familiar form:

$$d_r = \sqrt{\widehat{\boldsymbol{e}}' \Omega_{\widehat{\boldsymbol{e}}}^{-1} \widehat{\boldsymbol{e}}} \tag{15}$$

where $\widehat{\boldsymbol{e}}$ can be computed conveniently by Eq. (6) and $\Omega_{\widehat{\boldsymbol{e}}}$ is the covariance matrix of the error components in $\widehat{\boldsymbol{e}}$. With modified definitions for ν and Λ in Definition 1 or 2, and for Θ in Eq. (12) or (13), $\widehat{\boldsymbol{e}}$ can be obtained from the following formula:

$$\widehat{\boldsymbol{e}} = (\boldsymbol{I} - \Lambda P)\boldsymbol{y}^* = (\boldsymbol{I} - \Lambda P)\left(\boldsymbol{y} - \boldsymbol{G}_{11}\boldsymbol{x} - \nu\right) \tag{16}$$

and $\Omega_{\widehat{\boldsymbol{e}}}$ is given by the following formula:

$$\Omega_{\widehat{\boldsymbol{e}}} = (\boldsymbol{I} - \Lambda P)\Theta \tag{17}$$

However, $\Omega_{\widehat{\boldsymbol{e}}}$ might not have a full rank in general structural equation modeling. Its rank is reduced by the number of factors, m, in the reduced factor model—that is, m is the dimension of $\boldsymbol{f}$ in Definition 1 or 2. If m is not zero, the covariance matrix $\Omega_{\widehat{\boldsymbol{e}}}$ is rank deficient. Hence, $\Omega_{\widehat{\boldsymbol{e}}}$ is not invertible in Eq. (15). To deal with this issue, Yuan and Hayashi (2010) proposed a modified M-distance measure for the multivariate residuals based on extracting the orthogonal components of $\widehat{\boldsymbol{e}}$. The following formula is used instead of Eq. (15) to define the residual M-distance:

$$d_r = \sqrt{(\boldsymbol{L}\widehat{\boldsymbol{e}})'\left(\boldsymbol{L}\Omega_{\widehat{\boldsymbol{e}}}\boldsymbol{L}'\right)^{-1}(\boldsymbol{L}\widehat{\boldsymbol{e}})} \tag{18}$$

where $\boldsymbol{L}$ is a $(p-m) \times p$ matrix that extracts a set of $(p-m)$ orthogonal components of $\widehat{\boldsymbol{e}}$. Principal component techniques can be used to find such an $\boldsymbol{L}$ matrix.

Model outliers are determined by the magnitude of d_r, which is computed for each observation in the data set. By referring d_r to a χ-distribution (i.e., square-root of the χ^2-distribution), one can set the outlier detection criterion with the desired probability level of control, given that the model is reasonably accurate.

Because of the potential presence of exogenous observed variables in the general structural equation model, a related diagnostic measure—the leverage M-distance—also needs to be modified. Previous definition of the leverage M-distance involves only the Mahalanobis distance in the factor space, as shown in the following equation:

$$d_f = \sqrt{\hat{f}'\Omega_{\hat{f}}^{-1}\hat{f}} \tag{19}$$

where $\Omega_{\hat{f}}$ is the covariance matrix $\mathrm{COV}\left(\hat{f},\hat{f}'\right)$ of the estimated factor scores and is derived by Lawley and Maxwell (1971, p. 110) as:

$$\Omega_{\hat{f}} = \mathrm{COV}\,(f,f') + \left(\Lambda'\Theta^{-1}\Lambda\right)^{-1} \tag{20}$$

where $\mathrm{COV}(f,f) \equiv \Phi$ is the model parameter matrix for factor covariances.

With the inclusion of exogenous observed variables $\boldsymbol{x}$, Eq. (19) should be replaced with the following extended formula:

$$d_{x\hat{f}} = \sqrt{\left((x-\bar{x})'\;\left(\hat{f}-\kappa\right)'\right)\Omega_{x\hat{f}}^{-1}\begin{pmatrix} x-\bar{x} \\ \hat{f}-\kappa \end{pmatrix}} \tag{21}$$

where $\bar{\boldsymbol{x}}$ is the mean of the $\boldsymbol{x}$ variables, κ is the model parameter vector for factor means (which is fixed zero in factor model, but could be a free parameter vector in general structural equation models), and $\Omega_{x\hat{f}}$ is the covariance matrix of all $\boldsymbol{x}$ and $\hat{f}$ variables, which is given by:

$$\Omega_{x\hat{f}} = \begin{pmatrix} \Sigma_{xx} & \mathrm{COV}\,(x,f') \\ \mathrm{COV}\left(\hat{f},x'\right) & \mathrm{COV}\left(\hat{f},\hat{f}'\right) \end{pmatrix} \tag{22}$$

where Σ_{xx} is the covariance matrix of $\boldsymbol{x}$, $\mathrm{COV}\left(\hat{f},x'\right)$ is the covariance matrix between $\hat{f}$ and $\boldsymbol{x}$, and $\mathrm{COV}\left(\hat{f},\hat{f}'\right)$ is the same as $\Omega_{\hat{f}}$, as defined in Eq. (20). Because Σ_{xx} is a model matrix and can be estimated from samples, the only quantity that needs to be further defined in Eq. (22) is $\mathrm{COV}\left(\hat{f},x'\right)$. By using Eq. (11) for Bartlett factor scores, the covariance matrix between Bartlett factor scores $\hat{f}$ and $\boldsymbol{x}$ can be expressed as:

$$\begin{aligned} \mathrm{COV}\left(\hat{f},x'\right) &= \mathrm{COV}\left(\left(\Lambda'\Theta^{-1}\Lambda\right)^{-1}\Lambda'\Theta^{-1}\,(y-G_{11}x-\nu)\,,x'\right) \\ &= \left(\Lambda'\Theta^{-1}\Lambda\right)^{-1}\Lambda'\Theta^{-1}\left\{\mathrm{COV}(y,x')-\mathrm{COV}(G_{11}x,x')\right\} \\ &= \left(\Lambda'\Theta^{-1}\Lambda\right)^{-1}\Lambda'\Theta^{-1}\left(\Sigma_{yx'}-G_{11}\Sigma_{xx'}\right) \end{aligned} \tag{23}$$

However, using model Eqs. (9) and (10), it is easy to derive that:

$$\Sigma_{\boldsymbol{yx}'} = \boldsymbol{G}_{11}\Sigma_{\boldsymbol{xx}'} + \Lambda\,\mathrm{COV}\left(\boldsymbol{f},\boldsymbol{x}'\right) \tag{24}$$

By using Eq. (24), Eq. (23) simplifies to:

$$\mathrm{COV}\left(\widehat{\boldsymbol{f}},\boldsymbol{x}'\right) = \left(\Lambda'\Theta^{-1}\Lambda\right)^{-1}\Lambda'\Theta^{-1}\Lambda\,\mathrm{COV}\left(\boldsymbol{f},\boldsymbol{x}'\right) = \mathrm{COV}\left(\boldsymbol{f},\boldsymbol{x}'\right) \tag{25}$$

Because $\mathrm{COV}(\boldsymbol{f},\boldsymbol{x}')$ is a parameter matrix (that is, the covariance matrix for all exogenous non-error variables) in the general structural equation model, it can be estimated in practical situations. Using the results in Eqs. (20) and (25), $\Omega_{\boldsymbol{x}\widehat{\boldsymbol{f}}}$ in Eq. (22) is now given by the following formula that contains only population parameter matrices:

$$\Omega_{\boldsymbol{x}\widehat{\boldsymbol{f}}} = \begin{pmatrix} \Sigma_{\boldsymbol{xx}} & \mathrm{COV}\left(\boldsymbol{x},\boldsymbol{f}'\right) \\ \mathrm{COV}\left(\boldsymbol{f},\boldsymbol{x}'\right) & \mathrm{COV}\left(\boldsymbol{f},\boldsymbol{f}'\right) + \left(\Lambda'\Theta^{-1}\Lambda\right)^{-1} \end{pmatrix} \tag{26}$$

Hence, with the formula for $\Omega_{\boldsymbol{x}\widehat{\boldsymbol{f}}}$ in Eq. (26), the leverage M-distance computed with Eq. (21) is now well defined.

Equation (25) is worth of note because it shows another nice property of the Bartlett factor scores. That is, even though the true factor scores are *unknown* in the population, its covariances with any exogenous observed variables in the model are reflected truthfully by the covariances of the *computable* Bartlett factor scores and the exogenous observed variables.

Another nice property of Bartlett factor scores is that all the derived results in this paper will not be affected if nonzero factor means κ is assumed for factors. That is, even if Eq. (1) assumes nonzero factors for $\boldsymbol{f}$ (so that $\mathscr{E}\boldsymbol{f} = \kappa \neq \boldsymbol{0}$), Bartlett factor scores can still be computed by Eq. (3). This result is certainly important in the current context of structural equation modeling, in which factor means can be assumed to be nonzero in many applications. Appendix A.1 gives a proof of this result.

4 Illustrations

With the derived general formulas in Eqs. (18) and (21) for computing residual and leverage M-distances, this section shows how outlier and leverage point detection and residual diagnosis could be done in practical applications. A simulated data set with $N = 100$ is drawn from the model shown in Fig. 1a. The distribution of the data is multivariate normal. The SAS/IML software (SAS Institute Inc. 2012) was used to generate the data. Analysis results and graphical output were produced by the CALIS procedure of SAS/STAT software (SAS Institute Inc. 2012). Appendix A.2 shows the SAS program code for the simulation and the analysis.

Detection of Outliers and Leverage Points. To detect model outliers, one must first set a detection criterion. Under multivariate normality, the residual M-distance is

Table 2 The ten observations with largest residual M-distances

		Diagnostics	
Case number	Residual (M-distance)	Outlier	Leverage
13	3.02244	*	
5	2.97928	*	
93	2.91068	*	
78	2.86228	*	*
63	2.47793	*	
44	2.37628		
88	2.24721		
11	2.23010		
48	2.20710		
66	2.14201		

* Alpha-level = 0.05 is used.

approximately χ-distributed with degrees of freedom $(p - m)$, where p is the number of $\boldsymbol{y}$ variables and m is the number of exogenous latent factors in the reduced factor model [Eq. (10)]. Therefore, the detection criterion can be set at a certain "extreme" upper tail-value in the χ-distribution. Such a detection criterion can be defined by the usual notion of α-level (at the upper tail only). For example, the model in Fig. 1a has three endogenous observed variables and one factor to estimate. The degrees of freedom (df) is 2. Suppose that a 0.05 α-level is desirable, one can first find the upper 0.05 tail-value of the chi-square distribution with $df = 2$. This tail-value is 5.992. The square-root of this tail-value is 2.448, which will then be used as the criterion for outlier detection. Observations with residual M-distances [Eq. (18)] greater than 2.448 are judged to be model outliers by the criterion. Similarly, the detection criterion for leverage points is also set by specifying an appropriate α-level, say, 0.05, at the upper tail of the χ-distribution. Notice that, however, for leverage point detection the degrees of freedom (df) of the reference chi-distribution is the number of exogenous variables (excluding error terms) in the model. Because there are two exogenous non-error variables in Fig. 1a, the detection criterion value for leverage M-distance [Eq. (21)] is also 2.448 for the current example.

Table 2 shows the numerical results of outlier diagnosis. The ten observations with the largest residual M-distances [Eq. (18)] are shown and ordered. Observations 13, 5, 93, 78, and 63 are diagnosed as outliers. In addition to being an outlier, Observation 78 is also marked as a leverage point. Table 3 shows the numerical results of leverage points. The ten observations with the largest leverage M-distances [Eq. (21)] are shown and ordered. Observations 33, 71, 95, 78, and 53 are diagnosed as leverage points, with Observation 78 also being marked as an outlier. These results (detection of five outliers and five leverage points) are expected because the criteria have been set at the 0.05 α-level and the simulated data set ($N = 100$) was generated from a correctly specified model.

Figure 2 shows the residual by leverage plot for the current example. The residual by leverage plot is a popular graphical technique for showing outliers and leverage points in the context of regression analysis. With the uses of residual and leverage M-distances, this example can also make use of such a well-established graphical

Table 3 The ten observations with largest leverage M-distances

		Diagnostics	
Case number	Leverage (M-distance)	Leverage	Outlier
33	2.83947	*	
71	2.72600	*	
95	2.61350	*	
78	2.55818	*	*
53	2.55109	*	
29	2.41610		
65	2.31782		
24	2.30883		
50	2.11795		
68	2.08888		

* Alpha-level = 0.05 is used.

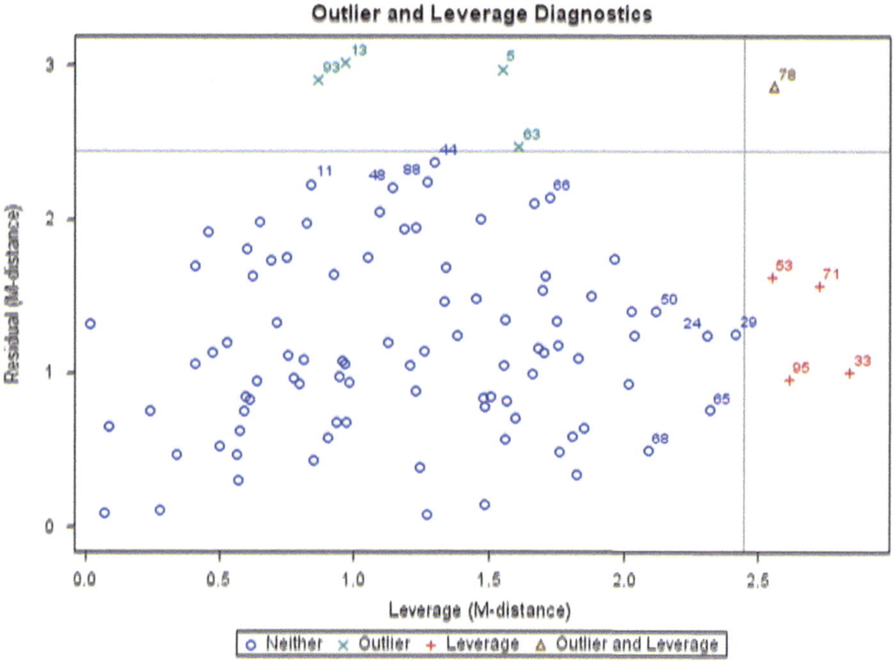

Fig. 2 Residual by leverage plot

technique. In fact, it would be more accurate to call Fig. 2 the residual M-distance by leverage M-distance plot. Calling it residual by leverage plot also makes perfect sense because the interpretations are actually the same as that in regression analysis.

Essentially, this residual by leverage plot shows the same outlier and leverage point diagnoses as that of Tables 2 and 3. However, the graphical plot shows an overall picture of the distribution of outliers and leverage points in a single display. As discussed in Yuan and Zhong (2008) and elsewhere, leverage points themselves

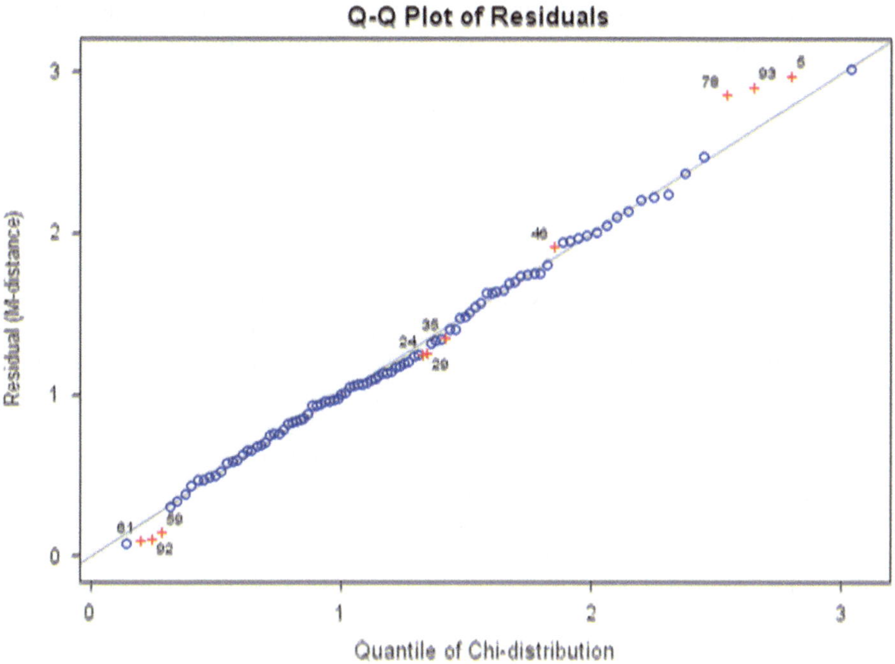

Fig. 3 Q–Q plot of residual M-distances

are not bad at all for model estimation unless they are also outliers. In the current example, only Observation 78 is classified both as an outlier and a leverage point, as shown in the upper-right region of the plot in Fig. 2.

Residual Diagnostics Based on Residual M-Distance. In regression analysis, the so-called Q–Q plot examines whether the empirical distribution of the residuals departs from the theoretical distribution. Significant departures might imply the model being considered is not adequate for the data. In general structural equation modeling, however, residuals are multi-dimensional and the corresponding Q–Q plot must be based on an overall measure of residuals. The residual M-distance measure [Eq. (18)] can serve such a purpose. Unlike the traditional residuals that can be positive and negative, residual M-distances are always positive. Also, the reference theoretical distribution for residual M-distances is the chi-distribution rather than the normal distribution in regression analysis. Figure 3 shows the Q–Q plot for the simulated data. The residual M-distances are plotted against their theoretical quantiles of the chi-distribution. Ideally, all observations should fall closely onto the line with slope = 1 for this simulated data set. Observations that are marked with the "+" signs (and with their observation numbers labeled) are those observations that show greatest departures from the theoretical distribution. Even though it is known that all data were generated from the true model, due to sampling fluctuation Fig. 3 still shows that some residual M-distances deviate significantly from the theoretical quantiles (for example, Observations 78, 93, and 5). More discussions on identifying outliers using the Q–Q plot are given in Yuan and Hayashi (2010).

5 Conclusion

In this paper, general formulas for computing Bartlett factor scores and the corresponding residuals are derived for general structural equation model. The derived results also lead to general formulas for computing residual and leverage M-distances, which play important roles in case-level (observation-level) residual diagnostics in general structural equation modeling. Along the line, some interesting properties of Bartlett factor scores are also discussed. Finally, a preceding section illustrates how these derived formulas are used in applications.

The current results can also be applied to robust estimation of structural equation models. The residual M-distance defined in Eq. (18) can be transformed into weights by some weighting functions in the context of robust estimation, as shown in Yuan and Hayashi (2010). The idea is that outlying observations with large residual M-distances are downweighted during the estimation of the model parameters. Residual M-distances are computed repeatedly during the iterative steps of estimation until a converged solution is found. The current results could broaden the application scope of the robust estimation scheme proposed by Yuan and Hayashi (2010). For example, robust estimation based on Eq. (18) and the weighting scheme proposed by Yuan and Hayashi (2010) have been implemented successfully in the CALIS procedure of the SAS/STAT software (2012) for general structural equation modeling. See Appendix A.2 for an example program.

If outlier and leverage detection is based on the robust estimation results of structural equation models, then it resembles to the "unmasking" technique in regression diagnostics (Rousseeuw and van Zomeren 1990). Masking effects refer to the situation where true model outliers (leverage points) could not be detected if there are multiple outliers (leverage points) present in the data. The reason is that the effect of a single outlier can be strong enough so that residuals (leverage points) corresponding to other outliers (leverage points) are not significant anymore. However, with the use of robust estimation, the influence of outliers has already been downweighted during the estimation. Consequently, the masking effects would be minimized at the later stage when outlier (leverage point) detection is performed. To a certain degree, the derived formula for Bartlett factor scores and other related ones in the current paper can advance the use of the unmasking technique in structural equation modeling (see Appendix A.2 for an example code in SAS). Hopefully, more and more useful regression diagnostic techniques could be adapted to the field of structural equation modeling.

A.1 Computing Bartlett Factor Scores with Nonzero κ for Factor Means

This appendix shows that the computation of Bartlett factor scores of the factor model in Eq. (3) will not be affected by the assumption of nonzero factor means κ for factors $\boldsymbol{f}$.

Now, assume in Eq. (1) that

$$\mathscr{E}\boldsymbol{f} = \kappa \neq \boldsymbol{0} \tag{A1}$$

Equation (1) is rewritten in the following form:

$$\begin{aligned} \boldsymbol{y} &= \nu + \Lambda(\boldsymbol{f} - \kappa + \kappa) + \boldsymbol{e} \\ &= \boldsymbol{\nu}^* + \Lambda \boldsymbol{f}^* + \boldsymbol{e} \end{aligned} \tag{A2}$$

where $\nu^* = \nu + \Lambda\kappa$ and $\boldsymbol{f}^* = (\boldsymbol{f} - \kappa)$. Because Eq. (A2) still has the same form as the original factor model in Eq. (1) (with $\mathscr{E}\boldsymbol{f}^* = \boldsymbol{0}$), Bartlett's formula for computing factor scores in Eq. (3) can be applied to the factor system in Eq. (A2). That is,

$$\begin{aligned} \widehat{\boldsymbol{f}^*} &= \left(\Lambda'\Theta^{-1}\Lambda\right)^{-1}\Lambda'\Theta^{-1}(\boldsymbol{y} - \boldsymbol{\nu}^*) \\ &= \left(\Lambda'\Theta^{-1}\Lambda\right)^{-1}\Lambda'\Theta^{-1}(\boldsymbol{y} - \nu) - \left(\Lambda'\Theta^{-1}\Lambda\right)^{-1}\Lambda'\Theta^{-1}\Lambda\kappa \\ &= \left(\Lambda'\Theta^{-1}\Lambda\right)^{-1}\Lambda'\Theta^{-1}(\boldsymbol{y} - \nu) - \kappa \end{aligned} \tag{A3}$$

Equation (A3) can then be written as:

$$\widehat{\boldsymbol{f}^*} + \kappa = \left(\Lambda'\Theta^{-1}\Lambda\right)^{-1}\Lambda'\Theta^{-1}(\boldsymbol{y} - \nu) \tag{A4}$$

Because $\boldsymbol{f} = (\boldsymbol{f}^* + \kappa)$ is just a translation of factor space with a fixed vector parameter in κ, by using Eq. (A4) Bartlett factor scores $\widehat{\boldsymbol{f}}$ for the original factors can be estimated equivalently by:

$$\widehat{\boldsymbol{f}} = \widehat{\boldsymbol{f}^*} + \kappa = \left(\Lambda'\Theta^{-1}\Lambda\right)^{-1}\Lambda'\Theta^{-1}(\boldsymbol{y} - \nu) \tag{A5}$$

Therefore, Eq. (A5) shows that Bartlett factor scores is computed the same way as Eq. (3), even if nonzero factor means κ is assumed for factors $\boldsymbol{f}$.

A.2 SAS Program for Generating Simulated Data and Model Fitting

```
/* Simulated Data */
proc iml;
   call randseed(111);
   mean     = {0, 5, 0, 0, 0};
   cov      = diag({1, 3, .6, .7, .6});
   cov[1,2] = .5;
   cov[2,1] = .5;
   N        = 100;
   exog     = randnormal(N, Mean, Cov);
   /* rows: x y1-y3; columns: xi, x, e1, e2, e3 */
   lambda = {0  1  0  0  0 ,
             1 .3  1  0  0 ,
            .7 .2  0  1  0 ,
            .6  0  0  0  1 };
   data    = exog*lambda';
   varname = {"x" "y1" "y2" "y3"};
   create sim_data from data [colname=varname];
   append from data;
   close sim_data;
quit;

/* Detection of outliers and leverage points */
ods graphics on;
proc calis residual alphalev=.05 alphaout=.05
plots=all;
   path
     kxi ===> y1-y3,
       x ===> y1-y2;
   pvar kxi = 1.;
run;
ods graphics off;
```

```
/* Robust estimation */
proc calis robust;
   path
      kxi ===> y1-y3,
        x ===> y1-y2;
   pvar kxi = 1.;
run;
/* Robust estimation with Unmasking in outlier and
leverage point detection*/
ods graphics on;
proc calis residual robust plots=all;
   path
      kxi ===> y1-y3,
        x ===> y1-y2;
   pvar kxi = 1.;
run;
ods graphics off;
```

References

Bartlett, M. S. (1937). The statistical conception of mental factors. *British Journal of Psychology, 28*, 97–104.

Johnson, R. A., & Wichern, D. W. (2007). *Applied multivariate statistical analysis* (6th ed.). NJ: Prentice Hall.

Lawley, D. N., & Maxwell, A. E. (1971). *Factor analysis as a statistical method*. New York: Macmillan.

Rousseeuw, P. J., & van Zomeren, B. C. (1990). Unmasking multivariate outliers and leverage points (with discussion). *Journal of the American Statistical Association, 85*, 633–651.

SAS Institute Inc. (2012). *SAS/STAT 12.1 User's Guide*. Cary, NC: Author.

Yuan, K. H., & Hayashi, K. (2010). Fitting data to model: Structural equation modeling diagnosis using two scatter plots. *Psychological Methods, 15*, 335–351.

Yuan, K. H., & Zhong, X. (2008). Outliers, leverage observations and influential cases in factor analysis: Minimizing their effect using robust procedure. *Sociological Methodology, 38*, 329–368.

A Scalable EM Algorithm for Hawkes Processes

Peter F. Halpin

1 Introduction

Halpin and De Boeck (2013) considered the time series analysis of bivariate event data in the context of dyadic interaction. They proposed the use of point processes (e.g., Daley and Vere-Jones 2003), and in particular Hawkes processes (Hawkes 1971; Hawkes and Oakes 1974), as way to capture the temporal dependence between the actions of two individuals. Here an action is treated as an *occurrence*, which is a discrete event that is viewed as having negligible duration relative to the period of observation. Occurrences may be contrasted with events that are viewed as extended in time (e.g., states, regimes). Examples of occurrences during the course of a conversation include specific types of statements (e.g., criticism, questions, lies) or nonverbal behaviors (e.g., laughter, facial expressions, gestures). Point processes are especially well suited to cases where human interaction is mediated by technology (e.g., text-messaging, emailing, chatting, tweeting), because such interactions are naturally parsed as series of time-stamped events. We can also view interaction more broadly, including, say, a student's interactions with an intelligent tutor, or a gamer's interactions with a virtual agent. The fundamental idea is to represent an interaction as a series of discrete, instantaneous actions. The theory of point processes then provides a general statistical framework for modelling the timing of those actions—how their probability changes in continuous time, how this depends on previous actions, and how the actions of two or more people may be coordinated in time.

The approach to estimation taken by Halpin and De Boeck (2013) was based on the so-called branching structure representation of the Hawkes process, which they showed to be amenable to the EM algorithm (see also Veen and Schoenberg 2008).

P.F. Halpin (✉)
New York University, 246 Greene Street, Office 316E, New York, NY 10003-6677, USA
e-mail: peter.halpin@nyu.edu; https://files.nyu.edu/pfh3/public

R.E. Millsap et al. (eds.), *New Developments in Quantitative Psychology*,
Springer Proceedings in Mathematics & Statistics 66, DOI 10.1007/978-1-4614-9348-8_26,

Unfortunately, the runtime of the algorithm grows quadratically in the number of observations, making its application to large data sets impractical. The present paper provides a modification of the original algorithm that substantially improves its runtime. The modification reduces the number of computations in the algorithm by tolerating a specified degree of rounding error, and this results in linear growth for many applications.

The next section outlines the Hawkes process in sufficient detail for this paper to be self-contained and gives an intuitive description of the problem to be addressed. The subsequent section presents the modification to the EM algorithm and illustrates some cases where this yields linear growth. The final section uses data simulation to arrive at a magnitude of rounding error that has a negligible effect on parameter recovery.

2 The Hawkes Process

Under mild conditions, a point process can be uniquely defined in terms of its conditional intensity function (CIF). The main reason for specifying a point process in terms of its CIF is that this leads directly to an expression for its likelihood. A general form for the CIF is

$$\lambda(t) = \lim_{\Delta \downarrow 0} \frac{E(M\{[t, t+\Delta)\} \mid H_t)}{\Delta} \tag{1}$$

where $M\{(a,b)\}$ is random counting measure representing the number of events (i.e., isolated points) falling in the interval (a,b), $E(M\{(a,b)\})$ is the expected value, and H_t is the σ-algebra generated by the time points t_k, $k \in \mathbb{N}$, occurring before time $t \in \mathbb{R}+$ (see Daley and Vere-Jones 2003). In this paper it is assumed that the probability of multiple events occurring simultaneously is negligible, in which case M is said to be orderly. Then for fixed t and sufficiently small values of Δ, $\lambda(t)\Delta$ is an approximation to the bernoulli probability of an event occurring in the interval $[t, t+\Delta)$, conditional on all of the events happening before time t. In applications, this means that we are concerned with modelling the probability of an event in continuous time, conditional on previous events.

Point processes extend immediately to the multivariate case. $M\{(a,b)\}$ is then vector-valued and each univariate margin gives the number of a different type of event occurring in the time period (a,b). Although Halpin and De Boeck (2013) considered a bivariate model, this paper focusses on the univariate case since the problem to be addressed can be most simply explained in that situation.

The CIF of the Hawkes process can be specified as a linear causal filter:

$$\lambda(t) = \mu + \int_0^t \phi(t-s)\, dM(s). \tag{2}$$

The interpretation of Eq. (2) is unpacked in the following three points.

1. The parameter $\mu > 0$ is baseline, which can be a function of time but is here treated as a constant.
2. The response function $\phi(u)$ governs how the process depends on its past. Hawkes processes require the following three assumptions:

$$\phi(u) \geq 0,\ u \geq 0; \qquad \phi(u) = 0,\ u < 0; \qquad \int_0^\infty \phi(u)du \leq 1.$$

   Together these assumptions imply that

$$\phi(u) = \alpha \times f(u;\xi) \tag{3}$$

   where $0 \leq \alpha \leq 1$ and $f(u;\xi)$ is a probability density function on $\mathbb{R}+$ with parameter ξ. Equation (3) presents a convenient method for parametrizing ϕ, with some common choices for $f(u;\xi)$ being the exponential (e.g., Ogata 1988; Truccolo et al. 2005), the two-parameter gamma (Halpin and De Boeck 2013), and the power law distribution (Barabási 2005; Crane and Sornette 2008). Under this parameterization, α is referred to as the intensity parameter and $f(u;\xi)$ the response kernel.
3. In the case that M is orderly, $dM(u) = M[u+\Delta)$ is representable as a series of right-shifted Dirac delta functions and the integral reduces to a sum over all events in $[0,t]$, yielding

$$\int \phi(t-s)\, dM(s) = \sum_{t_j<t} \phi(t-t_j). \tag{4}$$

   Thus each new time point is associated with a response function describing how that time point affects the future of the process. Under the assumptions of the Hawkes process, each new time point increases the probability of further events occurring in the immediate future (i.e., $\phi(u)$ is non-negative). The summation shows that the effect of multiple time points on the probability of further events is cumulative. For these reasons, Hawkes processes are often referred to as self-exciting; the occurrence of one event increases the probability of further events, whose occurrence in turn increases the probability of even more events. In terms of applications this means that Hawkes processes are appropriate for modelling clustering, which occurs when periods of high event frequency are separated by periods of relative inactivity. It has been argued that such a phenomenon is quite general in human dynamics (e.g. Barabási 2005; Kalman et al. 2006). An intuitive example is "chatting" or text-messaging. Here a conversation consists of bursts of messages sent from both users, and different chat sessions are separated by a relatively low frequency of messages. Other plausible examples from the dyadic context include turn taking in conversation (e.g., Sacks et al. 1974) and affective reciprocity (e.g., Gottman 1994).

As noted, the CIF leads directly to an expression for the log-likelihood (see Daley and Vere-Jones 2003):

$$l(\theta \mid X) = \sum_k \ln(\lambda(t_k)) - \int_0^T \lambda(s)ds \tag{5}$$

where $[0,T]$ is the observation period, $X = t_1, t_2, \ldots t_N$ denotes the observed event times, and θ contains the parameters of the model. Substitution of Eqs. (2) through (4) into Eq. (5) shows that the log-likelihood of the Hawkes process contains the logarithm of a weighted sum of density functions. A similar situation occurs in finite mixture modelling (e.g., McLachlan and Peel 2000) and nonlinear regression (e.g., Seber and Wild 2003), where it is known to lead to numerical optimization problems related to ill-conditioning of and multiple roots in the likelihood function. In the present case the problem is aggravated by the fact that the number of densities appearing in the likelihood increases with the number of observations, which is shown in Eq. (4). It is important to note that the number of model parameters does not grow with the number of time points; the densities are simply right-shifted. In general, if there are a total of N observed events, then there are a total of $N(N-1)/2$ response functions appearing in the summation in Eq. (5). This is the source of the quadratic growth of the optimization problem, which is the issue to be dealt with in this paper.

The quadratic growth is especially problematic because the EM algorithm proposed by Halpin and De Boeck (2013) requires the use of multiple starting values. This means that even moderately sized data sets cannot be estimated in a reasonable amount of time. For example, an actual runtime of over 24 h was recorded for a problem with $N \approx 1{,}500$ events and 50 starting values (implemented in the *C* language on a machine with 2 GHz of processing speed). Because one of the most exciting potential applications of Hawkes processes is to "big data" collected via computer-mediated communication (e.g., email, twitter), it is important to have an estimation approach that is feasible for large samples. The following section outlines how that can be accomplished.

3 Reducing Runtime by Introducing Rounding Error

This section outlines the original EM algorithm suggested by Halpin and De Boeck (2013) and then considers how to reduce its runtime. The algorithm is based on an alternative representation of the Hawkes process, which is referred to as its branching structure. In terms of the EM algorithm, the branching structure provides the complete data representation of the model, whereas the causal filter in Eq. (2) is the incomplete data representation. Taking this approach, the logarithm of the sum of densities in Eq. (5) is replaced by the sum of their logarithms, which results in better conditioning of the numerical optimization problem and was shown to perform satisfactorily with relatively small data sets ($N \approx 400$). Although the considerations of this section could also be made for Eq. (5), the focus is on the EM approach.

The branching structure representation of the Hawkes process is in terms of a cluster Poisson process. It was first proposed by Hawkes and Oakes (1974), who proved it to be equivalent to the representation given in the foregoing section, thereby establishing the existence and uniqueness of the process. The branching structure has also found more intuitive applications. For example, in ecology it is used to describe the growth of wildlife populations in terms of subsequent generations of offspring due to each immigrant (e.g., Rasmussen 2011). In the context of disease control, it is interpreted as the number of people contaminated by each subsequent carrier (e.g., Daley and Vere-Jones 2003). Veen and Schoenberg (2008) were the first to consider the branching structure as a strategy for obtaining maximum likelihood estimates (MLEs) of a Hawkes process.

For the present purpose, the effect of the branching structure is to decompose the Hawkes process into N independent Poisson processes whose rate functions are given by the response functions in Eq. 3. These processes govern the number of "offspring" of each event. There is also an additional Poisson process governing the number of "immigrant" events; this process has a rate function given by the baseline parameter μ. Importantly, each event t_k is assumed to be due to one and only one of these independent Poisson processes: either one centered at its parent, t_j, with $t_j < t_k$, or the baseline process. Consequently, if we knew which process each event belonged to, estimation would reduce to that for a collection of independent Poisson processes. It is therefore natural to introduce a missing variable that describes the specific process to which each event t_k belongs and proceed by means of the EM algorithm. As with other applications of the EM algorithm, the missing data need not correspond to the hypothesized data generating process; it can be treated merely as a tool for obtaining MLEs.

The following notation is employed to set up the algorithm. Let $Z = (Z_1, Z_2, \cdots, Z_N)$ denote the missing data. If an event t_k is an offspring of event t_j, $t_j < t_k$, this is denoted by setting $Z_k = j$. If an even t_k is an immigrant, then $Z_k = 0$. Also let $\phi_j(u)$ denote the response functions governing each Poisson process, where it is understood that $\phi_0(u) = \mu$. For $j > 0$, these response functions are identical to those introduced in Eq. (3) above, with the subscript serving to make explicit the centering event t_j.

Letting $l(\theta \mid X, Z)$ denote the complete data log-likelihood, Halpin and De Boeck (2013) showed that

$$\begin{aligned} Q(\theta) &= E_{Z|X,\theta}\, l(\theta \mid X, Z) \\ &= \sum_{j=0}^{N} \left(\sum_{k>j} \ln(\phi_j(t_k - t_j)) \times \text{Prob}(Z_k = j \mid X, \theta) - \int_0^T \phi_j(T - t_j) \right) \end{aligned} \tag{6}$$

where

$$\text{Prob}(Z_k = j \mid X, \theta) = \frac{\phi_j(t_k - t_j)}{\sum_{r<k} \phi_r(t_k - t_r)}. \tag{7}$$

Equations (6) and (7) provide the necessary components of an EM algorithm for the Hawkes process. Equation (7) is readily computed on the E step. On the M step these probabilities are treated as fixed and entered into Eq. (6). Using this approach, Halpin and De Boeck (2013) provided closed form solutions for the baseline parameter μ and the intensity parameter α. However, in order to obtain the parameters of the response kernel, it is necessary to numerically optimize the Q function. This is the computationally expensive part of the algorithm.

Since the sum over $k > j$ is the source of the quadratic growth of the Q function, let's first consider how this can be reduced. Recall that for $j > 0$, $\phi_j(u) = \alpha \times f(u;\xi)$ is just a weighted density on $\mathbb{R}+$. For usual choices of the response kernel, $f(u;\xi) \to 0$ as u becomes large (i.e., response functions typically have a right tail that asymptotes at zero). Intuitively, this means that when $t_k - t_j$ is large, the contribution of $\phi_j(t_k - t_j)$ to Eq. (6) will be negligible.

In order to make this idea more formal, consider the sets

$$W_j = \{k : f(t_k - t_j; \xi) > w\}.$$

If w denotes some specified degree of rounding error, then W_j contains the indices of all time points for which the response function $\phi_j(u)$ is greater than the rounding error. In other words, W_j denotes the non-negligible time points for process j.

Next consider the consequences of replacing the sum over $k > j$ with the sum over $k \in W_j$ in Eq. (6). This substitution will be referred to as the modified Q function and denoted $\tilde{Q}$. Letting $|W|$ denote the average of the cardinalities of the W_j then $|W| \times N$ densities appear in the sum over $k \in W_j$. $|W|$ is referred to as the linear growth factor of $\tilde{Q}$. The relative efficiency of $\tilde{Q}$ over Q may be expressed as

$$R = 1 - \frac{|W| \times N}{N(N-1)/2} = 1 - \frac{2|W|}{N-1}$$

where $1 \geq R \geq 0$ is scaled so that values closer to 1 denote better efficiency of $\tilde{Q}$. Clearly, the improvement comes down to how much smaller $|W|$ is than N. The exact value of $|W|$ depends on several factors including (a) ξ, which is updated throughout the optimization process, (b) w, which can be determined by the researcher, and (c) the actual observations t_k, which are fixed. This makes it difficult to obtain analytical results on $|W|$. However, Table 1 provides evidence that it does not grow with N.

The table was produced by simulating data using the inverse method (see Daley and Vere-Jones 2003). The causal filter in Eq. (2) was used for simulation, not the branching structure. Three different sample sizes ($N = 500, 1500$, and 5000) were simulated from each of three different models. Model 1 and Model 2 used exponential response functions, with Model 1 having moderate intensity ($\alpha = .4$) and Model 2 having high intensity ($\alpha = .8$). This means that the data from Model 2

Table 1 Growth of the $\tilde{Q}$ function in number of time points (simulated data)

	$N = 500$	$N = 1{,}500$	$N = 5{,}000$
Model 1	6.665	6.589	6.632
Model 2	19.870	23.609	25.083
Model 3	28.226	24.0133	23.567

Note: N is number of simulated time points and the table entries are the linear growth factor, $|W|$, of the modified Q function, $\tilde{Q}$, computed using the true parameter values. $|W| \times N$ gives the number of computations required for $\tilde{Q}$ and $1 - 2|W|/(N-1)$ gives the efficiency of $\tilde{Q}$ relative to the original Q function proposed by Halpin and De Boeck (2013). The models are described in the text

showed a much higher degree of clustering (i.e., a larger number of events occurring in close proximity to one another). Model 3 is also high intensity ($\alpha = .8$) but used a two-parameter gamma kernel with shape parameter set to .5. The result is heavier-tailed response functions, which have been reported in various applications to human communication data (e.g., Barabási 2005; Crane and Sornette 2008; Halpin and De Boeck 2013). The choices of the intensity parameter are intended to reflect its possible range rather than realistic values; I have not seen intensity estimates greater than .5 in real data applications. For each simulated data set, $\tilde{Q}$ was computed using the true parameter values and $w = 1 \times 10^{-10}$.

The main point to be taken from Table 1 is that the values of $|W|$ did not increase with N and therefore the rate of growth of $\tilde{Q}$ was linear. The exact rate of linear growth depended on the parameters of the data generating model, with more clustered data showing faster growth. However, even at extraordinarily high intensities and even at the smallest sample size, the growth rate was much smaller than $(N-1)/2$. Based on these results, it reasonable to conclude that $\tilde{Q}$ is more efficient to compute than Q, even in circumstances where the advantage is minimized. It should be emphasized that in general the improvement in performance will depend on the type of response kernel, with kernels that asymptote more quickly showing better improvements.

This section has only focussed on the computation of the Q function, but entirely similar remarks can be made about the computation of Eq. (7) on the E step, and about the computation of Eq. (5). We have not yet addressed how the rounding error w affects the MLEs produced by the EM algorithm. That is the topic of the next section.

4 Effect of Rounding Error on the EM Algorithm

This section considers how the use of $\tilde{Q}$ affects convergence and parameter recovery. Data were again simulated using the inverse method with the incomplete data model (Eq. (2)). The data generating model used a two-parameter gamma density as the response kernel. The parameters of the data generating model are stated in Table 3 and were based on the real data example reported in Halpin and De Boeck (2013).

Table 2 Effect of rounding error on log-likelihoods (simulated data)

	$w = 0$	$w = 1 \times 10^{-10}$	$w = 1 \times 10^{-5}$	$w = 1 \times 10^{-3}$
Mean	100	99.966	113.163	652.114
SD	100	100.014	99.268	284.921

Note: Table entries are means and standard deviations (SD) of differences between log-likelihoods of the estimated models and the log-likelihoods computed using the true values. The means and standard deviations are reported as percentages of the values for $w = 0$ (i.e., percentages of the intrinsic estimation error). The MLEs were obtained using the EM algorithm described by Halpin and De Boeck (2013) with the modified $\tilde{Q}$ function and the indicated levels of rounding error, w

A total of $n = 250$ data sets of $N = 500$ time points were generated from the model. For each data set, the EM algorithm described in Halpin and De Boeck (2013) was implemented using $\tilde{Q}$ in place of Q. The starting values for the estimation algorithm were obtained by randomly disturbing the data generating values, which avoided the need for multiple starting values. Convergence was evaluated using the incomplete data log-likelihood (Eq. (5)). The convergence criterion was an absolute difference of less than 1×10^{-5} on subsequent M steps.

The simulation compared the rounding errors $w = 0,\ 1 \times 10^{-10},\ 1 \times 10^{-5},\ 1 \times 10^{-3}$. Because a rounding error of 0 is not possible in practice, this was implemented using $w = 2.22 \times 10^{-16}$, which is the smallest double precision number representable in most modern computers. Therefore the value $w = 0$ represents the amount of error that is intrinsic to the specific realization of the estimation process (i.e., with the given sample size, convergence criterion, etc.). The remaining values of w represent the introduction of rounding error for computation efficiency.

Let's first consider the role of rounding error in the convergence of the algorithm. Figure 1 shows the relationship between the log-likelihoods evaluated at the MLEs and the log-likelihoods evaluated at the data generating parameters. The relation is quite similar for the three smallest values of w, but is appreciably worse for the largest value. It is important to note that even for $w = 0$, the relationship is not perfect. The amount of additional error introduced by the two middle values of w is not perceptible in the figure.

Table 2 provides a closer look at the log-likelihoods. It reports the mean and standard deviation for the differences between the log-likelihoods of the estimated models and the log-likelihoods computed using the true values. The table entries are reported as percentages of the difference between the log-likelihoods of $w = 0$ and of the true values (i.e., as percentages of the intrinsic estimation error). If $w > 0$ did not affect the convergence of the EM algorithm, all values in the table would be 100. Based on the table we can conclude that all values of $w > 0$ introduced additional error into the convergence of the EM algorithm. For $w = 1 \times 10^{-10}$ this was less than .1 % of the intrinsic estimation error.

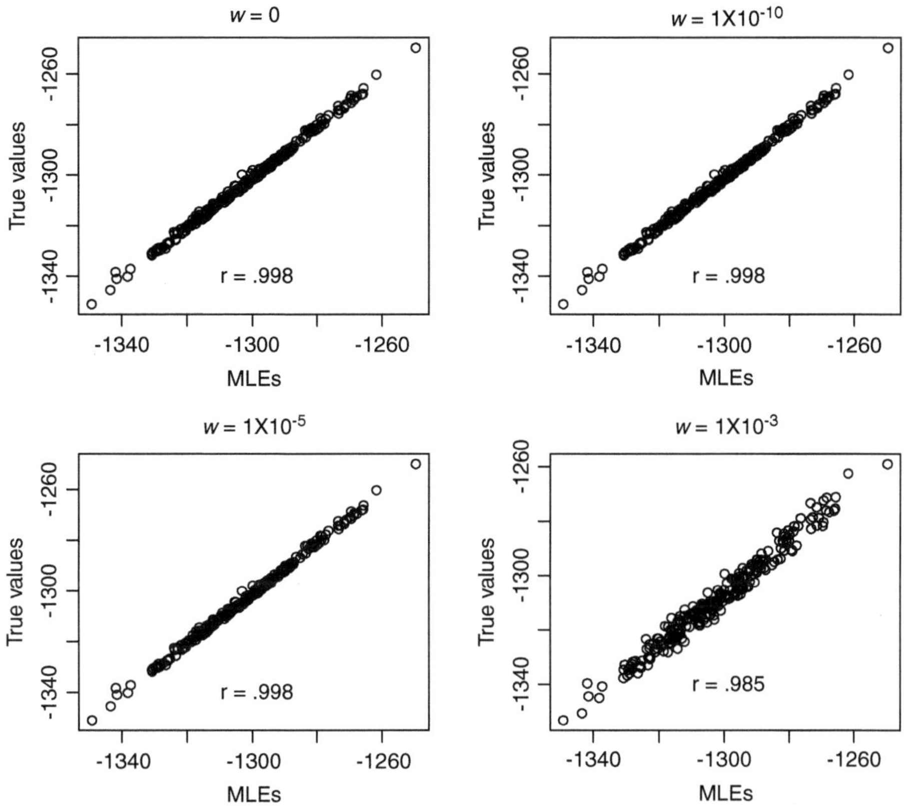

Fig. 1 Relation of log-likelihoods at convergence with log-likelihoods computed using the data generating values (simulated data). The model was estimated using the EM algorithm described by Halpin and De Boeck (2013) with the modified $\tilde{Q}$ function and the indicated levels of rounding error, w

Turning now to address parameter recovery, Table 3 reports the bias and error of the MLEs for each level of w. The entries are reported as percentages of the data generating parameters. It can be seen that bias and error were very similar for the lowest two values of w, but for larger values of w there is increased bias and reduced error. Figure 2 shows the distribution of estimates of the gamma response kernels for $w = 0$ and $w = 1 \times 10^{-10}$.

Based on this simulation it may be concluded that there is little to distinguish the results obtained using a rounding error of $w = 1 \times 10^{-10}$ from the intrinsic error in the algorithm (i.e., $w = 0$). On the other hand, $w \leq 1 \times 10^{-5}$ has a relatively large influence both on the convergence of the algorithm and on the bias and error of the resulting parameter estimates.

Table 3 Effect of rounding error on parameter recovery (simulated data)

	μ	α	κ	β
True values	.1	.45	.6	10
$w = 0$	2.289	−2.662	2.782	−0.4757
	(12.707)	(14.282)	(11.812)	(49.986)
$w = 1 \times 10^{-10}$	2.266	−2.634	2.775	−0.2537
	(12.725)	(14.315)	(11.824)	(50.664)
$w = 1 \times 10^{-5}$	4.458	−5.475	5.7890	−19.507
	(10.857)	(11.592)	(11.215)	(22.937)
$w = 1 \times 10^{-3}$	29.083	−35.617	28.390	−78.925
	(9.969)	(8.786)	(17.114)	(3.618)

Note: Table entries are bias (error) of maximum likelihood estimates (MLEs) as percentages of the true values. μ denotes the baseline parameter and α the intensity parameter; κ is the shape parameter of the two-parameter gamma response kernel, and β its scale parameter. MLEs were obtained using the EM algorithm described by Halpin and De Boeck (2013) with the modified $\tilde{Q}$ function and the indicated levels of rounding error, w

5 Conclusions

The number of computations required by the EM algorithm proposed by Halpin and De Boeck (2013) grows quadratically in the number of observed events, making its application to large data sets infeasible. This paper has shown that the runtime of the algorithm can be reduced by introducing rounding error into the computation of the Q function (i.e., the objective function of the M step of the EM algorithm). In three applications involving response functions with right tails asymptoting at zero, this was shown to result in linear growth. The consequences for convergence of the algorithm and parameter recovery were also considered. A rounding error of 1×10^{-10} was found to have negligible effects compared to the intrinsic error of the algorithm, but larger values were not. While more research can be done to optimize the rounding error for specific applications of the algorithm, it can be concluded that the approach presented here provides an acceptable compromise between runtime and computational accuracy, resulting in scalable maximum likelihood estimation of Hawkes processes.

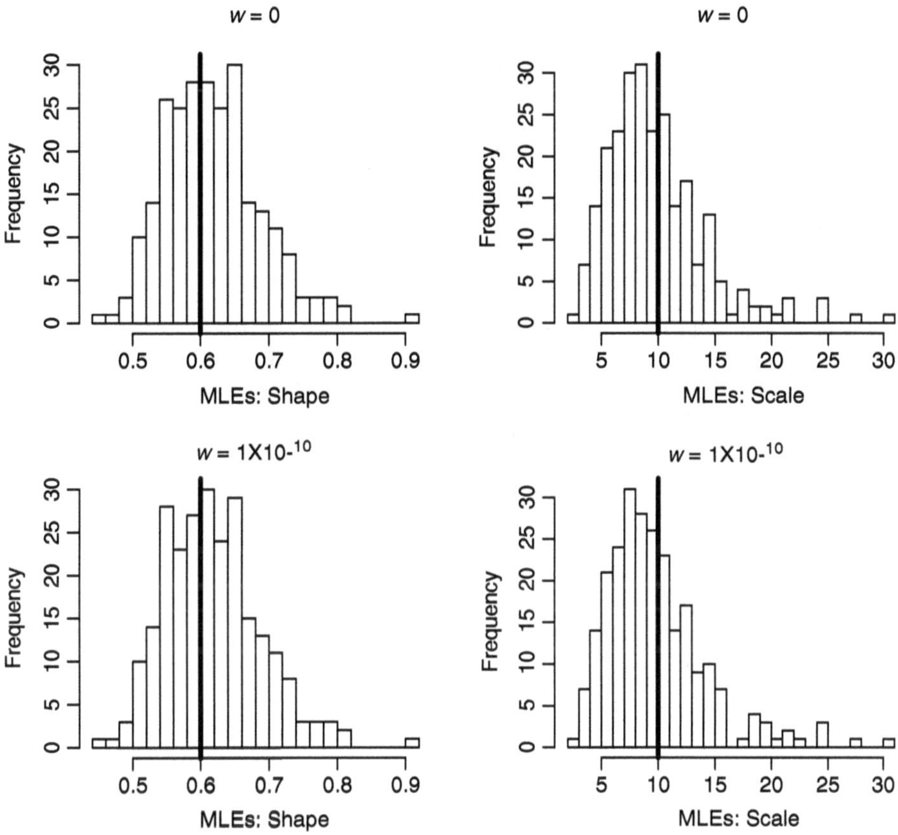

Fig. 2 Histograms of maximum likelihood estimates (MLEs) of the two-parameter gamma density kernel (simulated data). *Bold vertical line* indicates the value of the data generating parameters. MLEs were obtained using the EM algorithm described by Halpin and De Boeck (2013) with the modified $\tilde{Q}$ function and the indicated levels of rounding error, w

References

Barabási, A. L. (2005). The origin of bursts and heavy tails in human dynamics. *Nature, 435*, 207–211.

Crane, R., & Sornette, D. (2008). Robust dynamic classes revealed by measuring the response function of a social system. *Proceedings of the National Academy of Sciences, 105*, 15649–15653.

Daley, D. J., & Vere-Jones, D. (2003). *An introduction to the theory of point processes: Elementary theory and methods* (2nd ed., Vol. 1). New York: Springer.

Gottman, J. M. (1994). *Why marriages succeed or fail.* New York: Simon and Schuster.

Halpin, P. F., & De Boeck, P. (2013). Modelling dyadic interaction with Hawkes process. *Psychometrika, 78*, 793–814. doi:10.1007/s11336-013-9329-1.

Hawkes, A. G. (1971). Spectra of some self-exciting and mutually exciting point processes. *Biometrika, 58*, 83–90.

Hawkes, A. G., & Oakes, D. (1974). A cluster representation of a self-exciting process. *Journal of Applied Probability, 11*, 493–503.
Kalman, Y. M., David, G., & Rafaeli, D. R. R. S. (2006). Pauses and response latencies: A chronemic analysis of asynchronous cmc. *Journal of Computer-Mediated Communication, 12*, 1–23.
McLachlan, G. J., & Peel, D. (2000). *Finite mixture models*. New York: Wiley.
Ogata, Y. (1988). Statistical models for earthquake occurrences and residual analysis for point processes. *Journal of the American Statistical Association, 83*, 9–27.
Rasmussen, J. G. (2011). Bayesian inference for Hawkes' processes. *Methodology and Computing in Applied Probability*. doi:10.1007/s11009-011-9272-5.
Sacks, H., Schegloff, E. A., & Jefferson, G. (1974). A simplest systematics for the organization of turn-taking for conversation. *Language, 50*, 696–735.
Seber, G. A. F., & Wild, C. J. (2003). *Non-linear regression* (2nd ed.). Hoboken, NJ: Wiley.
Truccolo, W., Eden, U. T., Fellows, M. R., Donoghue, J. P., & Brown, E. N. (2005). A point process framework for relating neural spiking activity to spiking history, neural ensemble, and e extrinsic covariate effects. *Journal of Neurophysiology, 93*, 1074–1089.
Veen, A., & Schoenberg, F. P. (2008). Estimation of space-time branching process models in seismology using an EM-type algorithm. *Journal of the American Statistical Association, 103*, 614–624.

Estimating the Latent Trait Distribution with Loglinear Smoothing Models

Jodi M. Casabianca and Brian W. Junker

1 Introduction

This chapter is concerned with the specification of the latent trait distribution for purposes of numerical integration in the marginal maximum likelihood (MML) estimation of item parameters (Bock and Aitkin 1981; Bock and Lieberman 1970). Poor quality of specification of the latent trait distribution is linked to poor quality item parameter estimates (Boulet 1996; Casabianca et al. 2010; Stone 1992; Swaminathan and Gifford 1983; Woods and Lin 2009; Woods and Thissen 2006; Yamamoto and Muraki 1991). The current standard practice for specifying the latent trait distribution is to assume a fixed (standard) normal distribution. A popular alternative is to estimate the distribution (Bock and Aitkin 1981; Mislevy and Bock 1985). Since these standards were implemented, some alternatives were introduced (e.g., Woods and Lin 2009; Woods and Thissen 2006; Xu and Jia 2011), but none have replaced what is still considered standard practice.

In this chapter we place the current and standard specifications for the latent trait distribution into a framework defined by the family of loglinear smoothing (LLS) models, where the weights at each point in the distribution are the object of the smoothing. LLS models have a long history in psychometrics, and not only for smoothing observed test score distributions before test equating (Holland and Thayer 1987, 1998, 2000). Smoothing of the latent distribution is not a new concept for multidimensional discrete latent trait models either (Heinen 1996; Haberman

J.M. Casabianca (✉)
Department of Statistics, Carnegie Mellon University, 8119 Wean Hall,
5000 Forbes Avenue, Pittsburgh, PA 15213, USA
e-mail: jodicasa@andrew.cmu.edu

B.W. Junker
Department of Statistics, Carnegie Mellon University, 232 Baker Hall,
5000 Forbes Avenue, Pittsburgh, PA 15224, USA
e-mail: brian@stat.cmu.edu

R.E. Millsap et al. (eds.), *New Developments in Quantitative Psychology*,
Springer Proceedings in Mathematics & Statistics 66, DOI 10.1007/978-1-4614-9348-8_27,

et al. 2008; Rost and von Davier 1995, Chap. 14; Xu and von Davier 2008; von Davier 2005). Casabianca (2011), Casabianca and Lewis (2012), and Casabianca et al. (2010) demonstrate the usefulness of LLS in the unidimensional IRT context. Our purpose in this paper is to propose a theoretical generalization of this approach and connect it to extant treatments of the latent trait distribution.

The chapter is organized as follows. Section 2 introduces the notation needed to discuss the latent trait distribution; Sect. 3 integrates some pertinent discussions of the latent trait distribution for MML from the literature, mainly Mislevy (1984) and Heinen (1996); Sect. 4 provides a very brief introduction to LLS for latent distributions; Sect. 5 describes how LLS framework connects the various specifications of the distribution; Sect. 6 focuses on the importance of the smoothing aspect and how this relates to the bias–variance tradeoff; Sect. 7 provides results from a simulation study; lastly, Sect. 8 describes some future work and concluding statements.

2 Notation

Let n_l be the number of test takers with response pattern l ($l=1,\ldots,L$) and $\sum_{l=1}^{L} n_l = N$, $\mathbf{x}_l$ the vector of item response patterns, which gives the item responses for k items ($i=1,\ldots,k$) for response pattern l such that $x_{1l}, x_{2l}, \ldots, x_{kl}$, $P(x_{il}|\ \theta;\varphi)$ an IRT model specifying the conditional probability of obtaining a score x_{il} for item i from response pattern l given θ and a vector of item parameters φ (e.g., for a 3PL model: discrimination, difficulty, and guessing, $\varphi' = [\alpha'\ \beta'\ \gamma']$), and $g(\theta)$ the density for the latent trait distribution.

Any discrete approximation to the continuous density $g(\theta)$ can be characterized by a set of Q discrete points $T_1,\ldots,T_Q$ on the θ scale, together with weights $W(T_q)$. Because, for fixed Q, this setup cannot perfectly approximate a continuous density $g(\theta)$, it is common instead to consider the discrete density $g(\theta^*)$, with random variable θ^* taking values $T_1,\ldots,T_Q$ with probabilities $p_1,\ldots,p_q$. In the remainder of this paper we only consider the discrete density $g(\theta^*)$, which can be sufficiently approximated by the T_q, $W(T_q)$ setup.

The discretization and consequent summation eliminates the need for integration over $d\theta$. MML finds parameters φ and weights $W(T_q)$ to maximize

$$\ln L = \sum_{l=1}^{L} n_l \ln\left[L(\mathbf{x}_l)\right] \cong \sum_{l=1}^{L} n_l \ln\left\{ \sum_{q=1}^{Q} \left[\prod_{i=1}^{k} P\left(x_{il}\left|T_q\right.\right) \right] W\left(T_q\right) \right\}. \tag{1}$$

Note that since the density $g(\theta)$ is unobserved and therefore considered missing, Bock and Aitkin (1981) used the expectation-maximization (EM) algorithm (Dempster et al. 1977) to implement MML estimation of item parameters using discrete weights $W(T_q)$.

3 Extant Taxonomies for the Latent Trait Distribution

Mislevy (1984) discussed four approaches to treating $g(\theta)$, or equivalently, specifying $W(T_q)$, in MML. First, a normal solution for the latent trait distribution is specified by integrating over a continuous normal distribution (Bock and Lieberman 1970), or with Gauss–Hermite quadrature with fixed points and weights (Bock and Aitkin 1981). The normal solution appears in commercial IRT software as normal (symmetric) weights over fixed points where the same points are maintained throughout the solution of the likelihood equations. Second, in a nonparametric solution, a discrete distribution on a set of points approximates $g(\theta)$—the points and/or weights of the distribution are estimated without assuming a parametric or distributional form (Bock and Aitkin 1981; Laird 1978). The third and fourth approaches are less popular: a beta-binomial distribution and a resolution of mixed normal components (useful in a multidimensional context) (Mislevy 1984).

Heinen (1996) captured the true generality of the latent distribution by a classification of estimation methods in the context of discrete latent trait models. His taxonomy organizes MML estimation methods into parametric, [partially] semiparametric, and fully semiparametric; these labels assume a parametric item response function (IRF). For example, his *parametric* estimation uses a parametric form for the distribution (with or without specified parameter values), and points and weights remain fixed throughout the estimation procedure. The [partially] *semiparametric* method estimates distributional weights, and points are prespecified. Lastly, the *fully semiparametric* method estimates both points and weights, which is frequently the case when estimating (ordered) latent class models and less frequently the case when estimating IRT models. The two latter cases are "semi" parametric[1] since the model for the distribution is nonparametric and the model for the IRF is parametric. Note that Mislevy's normal and nonparametric solutions are analogous to Heinen's parametric and [partially] semiparametric estimation methods, respectively.

In the next section we provide a brief description of LLS in order to set up the structure and notation for the LLS framework for estimating latent distributions.

4 A Brief Primer on LLS

LLS estimates the probabilities p_q from the contingency table $n = (n_1, \ldots, n_Q)$ of observations of each value of θ^*, $T_1, T_2, \ldots, T_Q$, using the polynomial loglinear model

$$\log_e(p_q) = \beta_0 + \sum_{m=1}^{M} \beta_m T_q^m, \tag{2}$$

[1]Note that in the present paper, we label estimation methods based on the model for the latent distribution only; while it is acknowledged that the parametric form of the item response function may change, it will be restricted to having a parametric form throughout this discussion.

where T_q^m is the mth power of T_q, and the coefficients $\beta^t = (\beta_1, \beta_2, \ldots, \beta_M)$ and intercept β_0 are to be estimated from the observed counts $n = (n_1, \ldots, n_Q)$. Note that β_0 is a normalizing constant forcing the sum of the p_q to be 1.

The degree of smoothness (or actually "roughness") in LLS is determined by the highest power M of T_q in (2). For $M = 0$ (i.e., not including T_q in the model at all) LLS maximally smoothes the p_q estimating them as a uniform distribution. For M sufficiently large, the loglinear model in (2) is saturated and LLS estimates the p_q as the natural method of moments estimators, n_q/N; indeed for $M = Q - 1$, the polynomial on the right hand side of (2) will be an interpolating polynomial for the $\log(p_q)'s$.

The main feature of LLS is that it matches sample moments of the observed distribution. The maximum likelihood estimates from the model in (2), $\widehat{\beta}$, force the estimated probabilities to satisfy moment-matching conditions put forth by the model specification M and the observed distribution (Holland and Thayer 1987, 1998, 2000). That is, the $\widehat{\beta}$, satisfy the property that

$$\sum_q T_q^m \widehat{p}_q = \sum_q T_q^m (n_q/N), \quad m = 1, \ldots, M.$$

In other words, the sample moments of θ^* match the theoretical moments under the fitted model.

When M is small, few moments are matched, and fitting (2) provides more smoothing. When M is large, more moments are matched and fitting (2) provides less smoothing. Once the parameters are estimated, the estimated probabilities are computed and considered the weights $W(T_q)$ that characterize the smooth fitted distribution in the form of a histogram. The next section demonstrates how LLS with latent variables can accommodate some standard approaches to specifying $g(\theta^*)$.

5 LLS Framework for Estimating the Latent Trait Distribution

This section details the connection between LLS models with latent variables to the standard approaches for estimating distributions to characterize $g(\theta^*)$ (Casabianca 2011; Casabianca and Lewis 2012; Casabianca et al. 2010). Table 1 provides the LLS framework for estimating the latent trait distribution; for each method, the table lists the parameters estimated in order to specify $W(T_q)$, and the analogous LLS model. In order to associate the weights of the latent trait distribution to the probabilities determined by LLS, we denote the probability at location T_q by $W(T_q)$ instead of p_q as in the traditional LLS notation.

Table 1 LLS framework for methods of specifying the latent trait distribution

Method	What is estimated?	Number of parameters estimated	LLS analogue
Standard normal	–	0	$M = 2$
Normal	μ, σ^2	2	$M = 2$
LLS smooth	β	M	$2 < M < Q - 1$
Nonparametric	$W(T_q)$	$Q - 1$	$M = Q - 1$

Note: The standard normal approach is equivalent to a 2-moment LLS model with $\beta_1 = 0$ and $\beta_2 = -0.5$

5.1 Connections: LLS and the (Standard) Normal Distribution

Noting the normal distribution is a two parameter model, we begin with a basic smoothing model with $M = 2$ given by

$$\log_e [W(T_q)] = \beta_0 + \beta_1 T_q^1 + \beta_2 T_q^2. \tag{3}$$

If a quantity proportional to a normal density was inserted for $W(T_q)$ in (3) such that $W(T_q) = K \exp\left(-\frac{1}{2} \cdot \frac{(T_q - \mu)^2}{\sigma^2}\right)$ then:

$$\log [W(T_q)] = \log K - \frac{1}{2} \frac{(T_q - \mu)^2}{\sigma^2},$$

$$\log [W(T_q)] = \log K - \frac{T_q^2}{2\sigma^2} - \frac{T_q \mu}{\sigma^2} - \frac{\mu^2}{2\sigma^2},$$

$$\log [W(T_q)] = \left(\log K - \frac{\mu^2}{2\sigma^2}\right) + \left(-\frac{\mu}{\sigma^2}\right) T_q + \left(-\frac{1}{2\sigma^2}\right) T_q^2$$

and based on the form of (3), $\beta_1 = -\frac{\mu}{\sigma^2}$ and $\beta_2 = -\frac{1}{2\sigma^2}$.

Following from this are the moments of θ^* : $\mu = -\beta_1 \cdot \sigma^2 = \frac{\beta_1}{2\beta_2}$. and $\sigma^2 = \frac{-1}{2\beta_2}$. If $\mu = 0$ and $\sigma^2 = 1$, then $\beta_1 = 0$ and $\beta_2 = -0.5$, and the resultant probabilities (which must be scaled to sum to one) characterize a symmetric histogram or a discretized normal distribution. Depending on how the IRT scale is fixed, a normalizing of this distribution limits the moments of $\widehat{\theta}^*$ to characterize a standard normal. If the scale is fixed using the item parameters, the estimated moments of $\widehat{\theta}^*$ reflect the parameters of the latent trait distribution.

This relationship is implicitly acknowledged by many psychometricians and to the authors' knowledge has never been shown explicitly in an effort to point to a framework of models for θ^*. It is important to note that for computational reasons the recovered distribution will not precisely match a normal; as in any estimation procedure there is estimation error in the fitting process.

5.2 Connections: LLS and Nonparametric Estimation

A nonparametric model fully estimates the weights $W(T_q)$ of $g(\theta^*)$ from the data without constraints (with the exception that $\sum_{q=1}^{Q} \widehat{W}(T_q) = 1$; Bock and Aitkin 1981; Mislevy and Bock 1985). The sufficient statistic $N_q = \sum_{l=1}^{L} n_l P^{(j)}\left(T = T_q \middle| \mathbf{x}_l\right)$ is computed in the E-step of the EM algorithm for the MML estimation of item parameters. This quantity, which is a function of the posterior probability of trait level q given response pattern l, is subsequently used in the M-step to estimate item parameters; however, it is also used to compute the $W(T_q)$.

A saturated LLS model (where $M = Q - 1$) can exactly reproduce $W(T_q)$. The matrix equation $\log(\mathbf{p}) = \mathbf{T}\boldsymbol{\beta}$ defines a system of Q linear equations for the saturated LLS model with fixed locations. Here there are Q known values for the fixed distribution locations taken to powers 1, 2, …, $Q-1$ making $\mathbf{T}$ a square $Q \times Q$ (where $Q = M + 1$) matrix,

$$T = \begin{bmatrix} 1 & T_1^1 & T_1^2 & \cdots & T_1^{Q-1} \\ 1 & T_2^1 & T_2^2 & \cdots & T_2^{Q-1} \\ \vdots & \vdots & \vdots & \ddots & \vdots \\ 1 & T_Q^1 & T_Q^2 & \cdots & T_Q^{Q-1} \end{bmatrix},$$

$\boldsymbol{\beta}^t = (\beta_0, \beta_1, \beta_2, \ldots, \beta_{Q-1})$ are $M = Q - 1$ unknown model parameters plus a constant β_0, and $\mathbf{p}^t = (\log[W(T_1)], \log[W(T_2)], \ldots, \log[W(T_Q)])$ are Q unknown values for the probabilities for the discrete set of point locations for the distribution. If we consider this equation written as a linear combination of the columns of $\mathbf{T}$ such that

$$\begin{bmatrix} \log[W(T_1)] \\ \log[W(T_2)] \\ \vdots \\ \log[W(T_Q)] \end{bmatrix} = \beta_0 \begin{bmatrix} 1 \\ 1 \\ \vdots \\ 1 \end{bmatrix} + \beta_1 \begin{bmatrix} T_1 \\ T_2 \\ \vdots \\ T_Q \end{bmatrix} + \beta_2 \begin{bmatrix} T_1^2 \\ T_2^2 \\ \vdots \\ T_Q^2 \end{bmatrix} + \cdots + \beta_{Q-1} \begin{bmatrix} T_1^{Q-1} \\ T_2^{Q-1} \\ \vdots \\ T_Q^{Q-1} \end{bmatrix}$$

$$= \begin{bmatrix} \beta_0 + \beta_1 T_1 + \cdots + \beta_{Q-1} T_1^{Q-1} \\ \beta_0 + \beta_1 T_2 + \cdots + \beta_{Q-1} T_2^{Q-1} \\ \vdots \quad \vdots \quad \vdots \quad \vdots \\ \beta_0 + \beta_1 T_Q + \cdots + \beta_{Q-1} T_Q^{Q-1} \end{bmatrix},$$

it is easy to see that **T** is full rank ($r_{\mathbf{T}} = Q$) and invertible and therefore $\log(\mathbf{p}) = \mathbf{T}\beta$ is a determined system with a unique solution.

Depending on the number of items, k, and the number of support points, Q, this system may be nonlinear but can be approximated locally by a linear function (based on Taylor approximations) and solved with a number of approaches. Holland and Thayer (1987) give details on how to solve for β for when $\mathbf{p}$ is known. However, because the distributional parameters of $g(\theta^*)$ are unknown in the IRT context, we solve for β within an EM algorithm where values for $\mathbf{p}$ are obtained in the E-step and values for β are estimated in the M-step (see Casabianca 2011; Casabianca and Lewis 2012). The β estimated in the M-step are used to solve for fitted frequencies, which then become the updated weights used in the next iteration of the EM algorithm.

6 Smoothing and the Bias–Variance Tradeoff

We demonstrated how LLS can exactly reproduce the nonparametric model, but what is the advantage? The importance of LLS becomes apparent when actually smoothing or matching $M < Q - 1$ moments. Consider the family of smoothing models, which match M moments to the distribution. The advantage is that LLS will characterize a good representation of $g(\theta^*)$ but require fewer estimated parameters. The degree of the advantage depends on M and Q. If we thought of the bias–variance tradeoff on a continuum, LLS allows us to be in an optimal place on that continuum. As we increase M (or the number of estimated parameters), we will reduce bias, but also increase the variance. Smoothing permits us to find a model that well represents the original distribution, but at a lower cost. This is true with the nonparametric model (as described) as well as models where both point locations T_q and weights $W(T_q)$ are estimated, and models where the number of points Q, the point locations T_q, and the weights $W(T_q)$ are estimated. Thus far in our framework we have worked out the generalizations for the nonparametric model estimating $W(T_q)$; the generalizations for these other two nonparametric models are in progress, however, note that LLS has already been applied to such models in the literature (Haberman et al. 2008; Rost and von Davier 1995; Xu and von Davier 2008; von Davier 2005).

We simulated 50 3PL item responses from a bimodal latent trait distribution (depicted in Fig. 1 as the continuous bimodal curve on each plot) and performed a series of item calibrations using the LLSEM[2] software with a fixed standard normal distribution, the nonparametric model, and LLS specifications for the latent trait distribution. Figure 1 shows the estimated discrete distributions for $g(\theta^*)$ in order of increasing complexity from left to right: the discretized standard normal

[2]LLSEM: *LogLinear Smoothing Expectation Maximization* (Casabianca and Lewis 2011) is a software available upon request by Jodi M. Casabianca (jodicasa@andrew.cmu.edu).

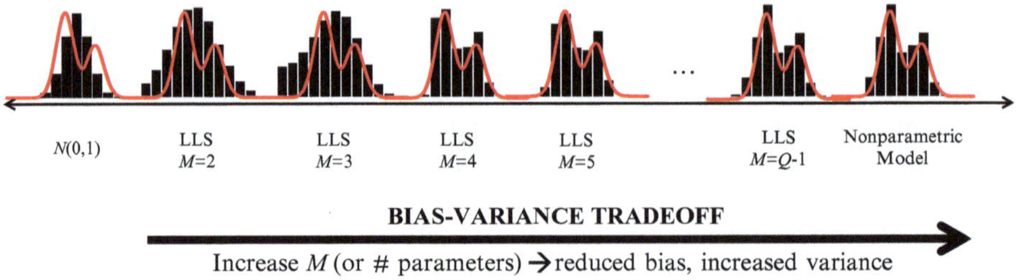

Fig. 1 The bias–variance tradeoff continuum as it pertains to the estimation of latent distributions with LLS models

distribution, distributions from the 2-, 3-, 4-, and 5-moment LLS models, and then distributions from the saturated LLS model ($M = Q - 1$) and the nonparametric model. Starting with the rightmost distribution, one can see that the true latent distribution is nicely captured by the nonparametric model, which is based on direct estimation using $N_q = \sum_{l=1}^{L} n_l P^{(j)}\left(T = T_q \middle| \mathbf{x}_l\right)$. One should also notice the saturated LLS model to the left of it, which is exactly the same. Depending on the number of support points Q for the latent distribution, the number of estimated parameters for these two options might be 10 (default in BILOG is $Q = 10$; Zimowski et al. 2003) or 40 (as is standard practice in many operational calibrations) or even 120 (used in item parameter recovery simulation studies; Woods and Lin 2009; Woods and Thissen 2006). Large Q presents estimation and identifiability issues when using it with a complex parametric form for the IRF (Haberman 2005); simply put, it behooves the modeler to select a parsimonious model for $g(\theta^*)$.

Now with parsimony and Q in mind, direct your attention to the distributions estimated with the LLS models. The $M = 2$ distribution will simply be a discretized normal, $M = 3$ will capture skew, $M = 4$ will capture skew and kurtosis, and so on. The $M = 4$ and $M = 5$ distributions are very similar to the $M = Q - 1$ and nonparametric distributions; the fit might even be better for the smoothing models, especially with the larger mode. What would be the advantage of using the 5-moment LLS model? With $Q = 10$, there would not be a huge difference; the 5-moment LLS model estimates 5 β parameters and the nonparametric model estimates 9 weights. However, with $Q = 40$ there are still only 5 β parameters estimated with LLS and 39 weights estimated with the nonparametric model. With $Q = 120$, which is an unusual level of Q but appears in the literature, there are 5 parameters estimated with LLS and 119 with the nonparametric model. Clearly, there is the opportunity for a much more parsimonious model with LLS, with lower standard errors, as long as not much bias is introduced.

It is also important to get the shape of the θ distribution right, rather than just estimating or assuming a discretized normal distribution for $g(\theta^*)$. One example of the importance is the impact on item parameter estimation. For item calibration, testing companies often use the normal distribution assumption (i.e., the fixed discretized normal). Research shows that when the true latent trait distribution is nonnormal (bimodal, skewed, etc.) there is bias in item parameter estimates when assuming the distribution is normal (Boulet 1996; Casabianca et al. 2010; Stone 1992; Swaminathan and Gifford 1983; Woods and Lin 2009; Woods and Thissen 2006; Yamamoto and Muraki 1991).

7 Item Parameter Recovery Simulation Results

The simulated results in the previous section were an excerpt from a simulation study that evaluated 3PL item parameter recovery under a true normal, negatively skewed, and bimodal distribution with three different treatments of $g(\theta^*)$ and $Q = 11$ (Casabianca and Lewis 2012). Results from this study show that the maximum absolute differences[3] in true versus estimated ICCs for 50 items were only negligibly different when the true distribution is normal. However, consistent with the literature on this topic, there were differences under nonnormal conditions. With a negatively skewed latent trait distribution (skewness $= -1.5$), the method yielding the least error (smallest of the maximum absolute differences) was the 4-moment LLS model (0.046). Assuming a normal distribution yielded approximately double the amount of error in ICCs (0.089). The nonparametric approach was comparable (0.053) but still technically yielded larger errors than LLS. The 4-moment LLS model also yielded the least error (0.045) under the bimodal latent trait distribution condition (as shown in Fig. 1). The maximum absolute difference from assuming a normal distribution was 0.01 higher, and the nonparametric model was only 0.003 higher. In both nonnormal cases, the amount of error from LLS models converged to the amount of error from the nonparametric model as the number of moments M increased.

It should be noted that these results are specific to the collection of items used in our simulation and the degree of nonnormality modeled for the true latent trait distributions. In addition, the small differences in error between the LLS models and the nonparametric model indicate that even with a relatively small degree of nonnormality, there is still an advantage to using a more parsimonious model and furthermore, the advantage may be greater with a larger degree of nonnormality or under more complex models with additional estimated parameters.

[3]The maximum absolute difference between the estimated item characteristic curves (ICCs) and the true ICCs was used to assess overall recovery of item parameters. That is, the absolute difference between the ICC using estimated item parameters and the ICC using the true item parameters was computed for each item across the Q quadrature points. Within condition, item, and replication, the maximum of these absolute differences (over the Q quadrature points) was determined. The mean of the absolute maximum difference was taken across the 50 items, and the mean was also taken across replications.

8 Future Work and Summary

In this chapter, we placed two standard approaches for specifying the latent trait distribution into a framework defined by the family of LLS models. For a normal distribution, this is just a LLS with two moments ($M = 2$). However, under a model that estimates the distribution, LLS allows the estimation of a more parsimonious model while still capturing any important nonnormal characteristics of the distribution. Depending on Q this is hugely important in reducing the number of estimated parameters.

Our theoretical generalization of LLS to extant treatments of the latent trait distribution is incomplete. As Heinen (1996) described, there are two other approaches to specifying the latent distribution: (1) estimating point locations and weights and (2) estimating Q, locations and weights. These models specify distributions for discrete latent trait models, or ordered latent class models. Clearly, there will be more estimated parameters with these models, specifically, $2Q - 1$ and $2Q$, respectively. LLS has already been used with these more complex models (Haberman et al. 2008; Rost and von Davier 1995; Xu and von Davier 2008; von Davier 2005). We foresee the theoretical advantage to LLS to be greater with these more complex models, such as multidimensional IRT models, where additional research with nonnormal latent variable distributions is needed (Cai 2010); however, both the theoretical component and empirical studies investigating the actual payoff are needed.

In addition to extending the LLS framework, we intend to compare this approach with recent contributions by Woods and colleagues which involve splines for estimating the latent trait distribution (Woods and Lin 2009; Woods and Thissen 2006).

References

Bock, R. D., & Aitkin, M. (1981). MML estimation of item parameters: Application of an EM algorithm. *Psychometrika, 46*, 443–459.

Bock, R. D., & Lieberman, M. (1970). Fitting a response model for *n* dichotomously scored items. *Psychometrika, 35*, 179–197.

Boulet, J. R. (1996). *The effect of nonnormal ability distributions on IRT parameter estimation using full-information and limited-information methods (IRT, nonlinear factor analysis).* Dissertation abstracts online, University of Ottawa, Canada.

Cai, L. (2010). A two-tier full-information item factor analysis model with applications. *Psychometrika, 75*, 581–612.

Casabianca, J. M. (2011). *Loglinear smoothing for the latent trait distribution: A two-tiered evaluation* (Doctoral Dissertation). ProQuest Dissertations and Theses (Accession Order No. AAT 3474125).

Casabianca, J. M., & Lewis, C. (2011). *LLSEM: A computer program for loglinear smoothing in an expectation maximization algorithm* (Unpublished software). Bronx, NY

Casabianca, J. M., & Lewis, C. (2012). *Loglinear smoothing for the latent trait distribution in the marginal maximum likelihood estimation of 3PL item parameters* (Unpublished manuscript).

Casabianca, J. M., Xu, X., Jia, Y., & Lewis, C. (2010). Estimation of item parameters when the underlying latent trait distribution of test takers is nonnormal. In *Annual meeting of the National Council for Measurement in Education*, Denver, Colorado.

Dempster, A., Laird, N., & Rubin, D. (1977). Maximum likelihood from incomplete data via the EM algorithm. *Journal of the Royal Statistical Society, Series B, 39*, 1–38.

Haberman, S. J. (2005). *Identifiability of parameters in item response models with unconstrained ability distributions* (Research Report 05-24). Princeton, NJ: Educational Testing Service.

Haberman, S. J., von Davier, M., & Lee, Y. H. (2008). *Comparison of multidimensional item response models: Multivariate normal ability distributions versus multivariate polytomous distributions* (Research Report 08-45). Princeton, NJ: Educational Testing Service.

Heinen, T. (1996). *Latent class and discrete latent trait models*. Thousand Oaks, CA: Sage.

Holland, P. W., & Thayer, D. T. (1987). *Notes on the use of log-linear models for fitting discrete probability distributions* (Research Report 87-31). Princeton, NJ: Educational Testing Service.

Holland, P. W., & Thayer, D. T. (1998). *Univariate and bivariate loglinear models for discrete test score distributions* (Research Report 98-1). Princeton, NJ: Educational Testing Service.

Holland, P. W., & Thayer, D. T. (2000). Univariate and bivariate loglinear models for discrete test score distributions. *Journal of Educational and Behavioral Statistics, 25*, 133–183.

Laird, N. M. (1978). Nonparametric likelihood estimation of a mixing distribution. *Journal of American Statistical Association, 73*, 805–811.

Mislevy, R. J. (1984). Estimating latent distributions. *Psychometrika, 49*, 359–381.

Mislevy, R. J., & Bock, R. D. (1985). Implementation of the EM Algorithm in the estimation of item parameters: The BILOG computer program. In D. J. Weiss (Ed.), *Proceedings of the 1982 IRT and computerized adaptive testing conference* (pp. 189–202). Minneapolis: University of Minnesota, Department of Psychology, Computerized Adaptive Testing Laboratory.

Rost, J., & von Davier, M. (1995). Mixture distribution Rasch models. In G. H. Fischer & I. W. Molenaar (Eds.), *Rasch models: Foundations, recent developments, and applications* (pp. 257–268). New York, NY: Springer Verlag.

Stone, C. A. (1992). Recovery of MML estimates in the two-parameter logistic response model: An evaluation of MULTILOG. *Applied Psychological Measurement, 16*, 1–16.

Swaminathan, H., & Gifford, J. (1983). Estimation of parameters in the three-parameter latent trait model. In D. J. Weiss (Ed.), *New horizons in testing: Latent trait test theory and computerized adaptive testing* (pp. 13–30). New York: Academic.

von Davier, M. (2005). *A general diagnostic model applied to language testing data* (Research Report 05-16). Princeton, NJ: Educational Testing Service.

Woods, C. M., & Lin, N. (2009). IRT with estimation of the latent density using Davidian curves. *Applied Psychological Measurement, 33*, 102–117.

Woods, C. M., & Thissen, D. (2006). IRT with estimation of the latent population distribution using spline-based densities. *Psychometrika, 71*, 281–301.

Xu, X., & Jia, Y. (2011). *The sensitivity of parameter estimates to the latent ability distribution* (Research Report 11-40). Princeton, NJ: Educational Testing Service.

Xu, X., & von Davier, M. (2008). *Fitting the structured general diagnostic model to NAEP data* (Research Report 08-27). Princeton, NJ: Educational Testing Service.

Yamamoto, K., & Muraki, E. (1991, April). *Non-linear transformation of IRT scale to account for the effect of nonnormal ability distribution on the item parameter estimation*. Paper presented at the annual meeting of the American Educational Research Association, Chicago, IL.

Zimowski, M. F., Muraki, E., Mislevy, R. J., & Bock, R. D. (2003). *BILOG-MG 3 for windows: Multiple-group IRT analysis and test maintenance for binary items [Computer software]*. Lincolnwood, IL: Scientific Software International, Inc.

From Modeling Long-Term Growth to Short-Term Fluctuations: Differential Equation Modeling Is the Language of Change

Pascal R. Deboeck, Jody S. Nicholson, C.S. Bergeman, and Kristopher J. Preacher

1 Introduction

Language is an integral part of expressing ideas, so much so that the statistical language(s) we understand may affect our ability to formulate ideas. One's initial statistics class consists of exposure to a new language; familiar words take on new meaning, mathematical symbols are used to abbreviate entire paragraphs, and you even learn a little Greek. Learning other dialects, for example structural equation modeling (SEM) diagrams, expands one's ability to posit and understand statistical models. The numerous simultaneous regressions occurring in many SEM diagrams would be difficult to understand as a list of equations, but these equations become readily accessible when expressed in the language of SEM diagrams. The representation of regression in diagram form allows for the formulation and understanding of new ideas. Differential equations, and their component derivatives,

P.R. Deboeck (✉)
Department of Psychology, University of Kansas, 1415 Jayhawk Blvd., Lawrence, KS 66049, USA
e-mail: pascal@ku.edu

J.S. Nicholson
Department of Psychology, University of North Florida, 1 UNF Drive, Jacksonville, FL 32224, USA
e-mail: jody.nicholson@unf.edu

C.S. Bergeman
Department of Psychology, University of Notre Dame, 122A Haggar Hall, Notre Dame, IN 46556, USA
e-mail: cbergema@nd.edu

K.J. Preacher
Psychology & Human Development, Vanderbilt University, PMB 552, 230 Appleton Place, Nashville, TN 37203, USA
e-mail: kris.preacher@vanderbilt.edu

R.E. Millsap et al. (eds.), *New Developments in Quantitative Psychology*, Springer Proceedings in Mathematics & Statistics 66, DOI 10.1007/978-1-4614-9348-8_28,

constitute a language that is less often used in the social sciences; the few clear exceptions like the Hessian matrix and calculation of the minima or maxima of functions are in the vernacular of relatively few social scientists. Like learning the language of SEM, learning the language of derivatives has the potential to change the way we understand models with which we are familiar, and opens us to new ways of formulating ideas.

In this chapter we present the idea that differential equation modeling is the language of change. The meaning in this statement is twofold. In the literal sense derivatives express the change in variables with respect to each other; differential equation models—models that include derivatives—are models that express the relations between the states of variables and how variables are changing. Derivatives and differential equations provide a language that gives a framework for precisely describing change. But this approach also provides a different way of understanding many of the models of change that are currently being used in research; by providing a unifying framework, differential equations have the potential to help in identifying models that have been overlooked and therefore can identify unexplored questions. By providing a means to alter how questions about change are being asked, differential equation models constitute a language that could lead to changes in the kinds of research being done.

This chapter begins by considering differential equations and derivatives in the context of something familiar—ordinary linear regression. As the new language is introduced, the chapter expands into other familiar models including hierarchical linear models (HLMs) and latent growth curve models (LGCMs). These sections introduce the derivative language framework as literally being a language for describing change. We then consider the application of derivatives to the modeling of intraindividual observations. The language framework is used to extend the idea of differential equation modeling as the language of change so as to introduce methods and models that are likely to be unfamiliar to many readers. Three differential equation models will be presented, each of which provides cutting edge questions that can be addressed using social science data.

2 Regression

Whether made explicit or not, early in statistics classes students are introduced to the idea that mathematics can be used to address whether one variable is related to another, and more specifically that the change in one variable can be related to changes in another variable. This idea often begins with the case of relating central tendency to group membership (i.e., t-tests), but becomes more general with the introduction of ordinary linear regression. This idea gets a formal mathematical representation,

$$y = \beta_0 + \beta_1 x + \epsilon, \tag{1}$$

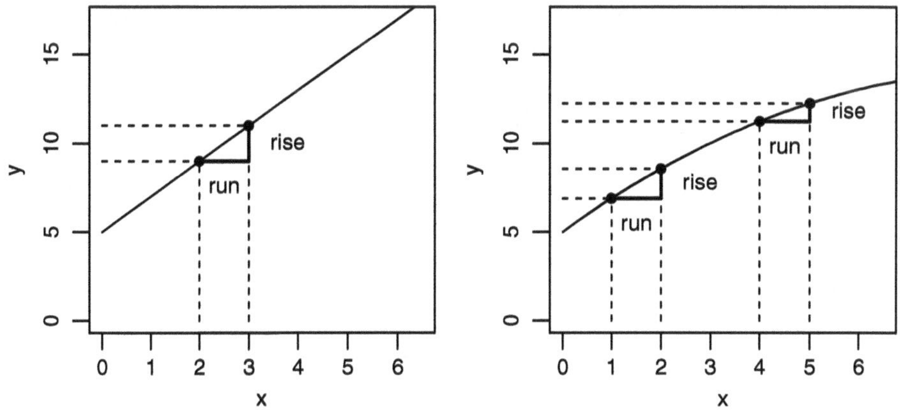

Fig. 1 The figure (*left*) depicts a trajectory with a constant first derivative, and consequently a second derivative equal to zero. The figure (*right*) depicts a trajectory where there is a change in the first derivative with respect to time; that is, the second derivative is nonzero

where β_0 represents the value of a variable y when $x = 0$, β_1 expresses how changes in a variable x are related to changes in y, and ϵ represents error. This seemingly simple equation allows for significant amounts of statistical language to be taught, including keywords like *intercept* and *slope*, *statistic* and *parameter*. Interpretation of β_0 and β_1 also becomes an important exercise, at which point figures such as Fig. 1 (left) may be used. In Fig. 1 it has been assumed that we are working with the equation $y = 5 + 2x$, and therefore $\beta_0 = 5$ is the value of y when $x = 0$. A series of points (joined with a line) can then be drawn, substituting values $x = 1, 2, 3 \ldots$ and solving for y. Earlier in your education, you may have been given a line and asked: "what is the rise over the run?" Said another way, this question asks how much of a change in y coincides with a specific amount of change in x (one unit); that is, what is β_1?

"Rise over run" can be equivalently expressed as "the change in y with respect to the change in x." In mathematics this is frequently expressed as $\frac{dy}{dx}$; this is the *first derivative* of y with respect to x. Instead of writing β_1 it would be equally appropriate to write

$$y = y_0 + \left(\frac{dy}{dx}\right)x + \epsilon, \tag{2}$$

where y_0 is the *zeroth derivative* which is the value of y at $x = 0$. This form of the regression equation, in the authors' experience, seems to appear rarely in introductory statistics texts. One likely reason is that Eq. (2) may be perceived as more complex than Eq. (1), even though these equations are equivalent. Another reason may be that the equivalence of β_1 and $\frac{dy}{dx}$ is thought to be commonly understood, so stating this explicitly in equations is considered unnecessary.

Whatever the reason, by not being explicit that β_1 is a derivative, useful language has been set aside. Consider the quadratic model,

$$y = \beta_0 + \beta_1 x + \beta_2 x^2 + \epsilon. \tag{3}$$

In presentations of this model, it is not unusual to hear that β_2 is difficult to directly interpret; so much so that efforts have been undertaken to reparameterize β_0, β_1, and β_2 so as to make the parameters more readily interpretable (Cudeck and du Toit 2002). Making the derivatives explicit, Eq. (3) is equivalent to

$$y = y_0 + \left(\frac{dy}{dx}\right) x + \frac{1}{2}\left(\frac{d^2y}{dx^2}\right) x^2 + \epsilon. \tag{4}$$

β_2 in itself is difficult to understand, but twice this quantity is equal to the *second derivative*, $\frac{d^2y}{dx^2}$. The second derivative expresses how the first derivative $\frac{dy}{dx}$ is changing with respect to changes in x. That is, twice the quadratic parameter β_2 conveys precisely how quickly the slope (first derivative) is changing for every unit change in x.

A person's score y based on Eq. (4) depends on three things: (a) the score at $x = 0$, that is, the zeroth derivative, (b) the rate at which scores change with respect to x (slope or first derivative) at $x = 0$, and (c) how the slope changes with respect to x (second derivative). If x represents time and y position, derivatives can be discussed drawing on the common experience of traveling in a vehicle. The zeroth derivative is the position, or *level* in the case of a construct, at some point in time. The first derivative, or change in position with respect to time, represents *velocity* (speed in a particular direction). The second derivative, or change in velocity with respect to time, corresponds to *acceleration* (positive or negative).

Early introduction of derivative language has the potential to provide a unifying framework for understanding many models of change. Extending Eq. (4) to include predictors of the estimated derivatives (parameters), as is often done in Hierarchical Linear Modeling (HLM) or Multilevel Modeling (MLM), the language of derivatives gives another way to understand the hypotheses being tested. Consider the equations

$$y_{ti} = \beta_{0i} + \beta_{1i} T_{ti} + \beta_{2i} T_{ti}^2 + \epsilon_{ti} \tag{5}$$

$$\begin{aligned}
\beta_{0i} &= \gamma_{00} + \gamma_{01} Z_i + u_{0i} \\
\beta_{1i} &= \gamma_{10} + \gamma_{11} Z_i + u_{1i} \\
\beta_{2i} &= \gamma_{20} + \gamma_{21} Z_i + u_{2i},
\end{aligned}$$

where the dependent variable y_{ti} is measured at multiple times t for each individual i. The effect of the predictor *time* (T) allows for a linear relationship (β_{1i}) with time and the possibility that the slope (β_{1i} at $T = 0$) may change with respect to time

(β_{2i}). Furthermore, each individual may have a different β_0, β_1, and/or β_2; it is hypothesized that individual differences in these parameters are related to a person's trait Z_i.

Rewriting the equations expressed in Eq. (5) using derivative notation

$$y_{0i} = \gamma_{00} + \gamma_{01} Z_i + u_{0i} \tag{6}$$

$$\left(\frac{dy}{dT}\right)_i = \gamma_{10} + \gamma_{11} Z_i + u_{1i} \tag{7}$$

$$\frac{1}{2}\left(\frac{d^2y}{dT^2}\right)_i = \gamma_{20} + \gamma_{21} Z_i + u_{2i}. \tag{8}$$

These equations express that in HLM/MLM one is examining the relations between the level (zeroth derivative) of a trait Z and derivatives expressing different aspects of how the dependent variable y is changing with respect to time T. In Eq. (6), γ_{01} posits a relation[1] between the zeroth derivative of the dependent variable y and the trait Z. In Eq. (7), γ_{11} relates the first derivative of the dependent variable to the trait. Finally, in Eq. (8), γ_{21} relates the second derivative of y to the trait. These three equations ask qualitatively different questions. The first asks whether Z is related to the level of y at $T = 0$; that is, a *level–level* relation. The second asks whether Z is related to the velocity of y at $T = 0$; that is, a *level–velocity* relation. The third asks whether Z is related to changes in velocity; that is, a *level–acceleration* relation.

Equations (5) and (6) through (8) show HLM/MLM as a series of differential equations. Looking at these equations, and considering the relations between level, velocity, and acceleration gives another way to understand this model in terms of level–level questions (Eq. (6)), level–velocity questions (Eq. (7)), and level–acceleration questions (Eq. (8)). Examining other models, and the relationships between derivatives that are being modeled, provides a way to organize the similarities and differences across a wide range of models of change. In the next section we examine the LGCM, which can relate both similar and different pairs of derivatives relative to HLM and therefore ask both similar and different questions about change. The decision to use one over the other should be driven by constraints such as the structure of the data collected, for example HLMs/MLMs can handle individuals with variations in sampling interval more readily than LGCMs; conversely, LGCMs can handle multiple dependent variables simultaneously. The decision to use one over the other should not be driven by the perception that these models are necessarily addressing different questions, as in some cases the questions being asked are very similar.

---

[1]This relation could be expanded to indicate that parameters such as γ_{11} express the change in an individual's first derivative $d\left(\frac{dy}{dT}\right)_i$ (numerator) divided by the change in the trait dZ_i.

3 Latent Growth Curve Model

We posit an example where we consider the effect of Stress on Negative Affect measured across the last 4 weeks of a semester in a hypothetical sample of undergraduate students. A LGCM is posited, as in Fig. 2, such that changes in stress result in changes to negative affect; a unidirectional relationship from stress to negative affect has been posited only to simplify discussion and is not based on theory. Typically the latent variables would be labeled "Intercept," "Slope," and "Quadratic," and the paths to the observed variables would all be fixed such that the latent variables would correspond to the names they were given. It may not be clear, however, what a quadratic–quadratic relationship implies. In Fig. 2, therefore, the labels have been changed to "Level," "Velocity," and "Acceleration" to reflect that the zeroth, first, and second derivatives, with respect to time, are being estimated; to accomplish this, only the loadings of the quadratic factor are changed, and these are merely multiplied by 1/2 as in Eq. (4).

There are many possible paths that could be drawn from stress to negative affect (paths A through I). Some of these paths are familiar, such as paths A, B, and C which ask level–level, level–velocity, and level–acceleration questions as in HLM.

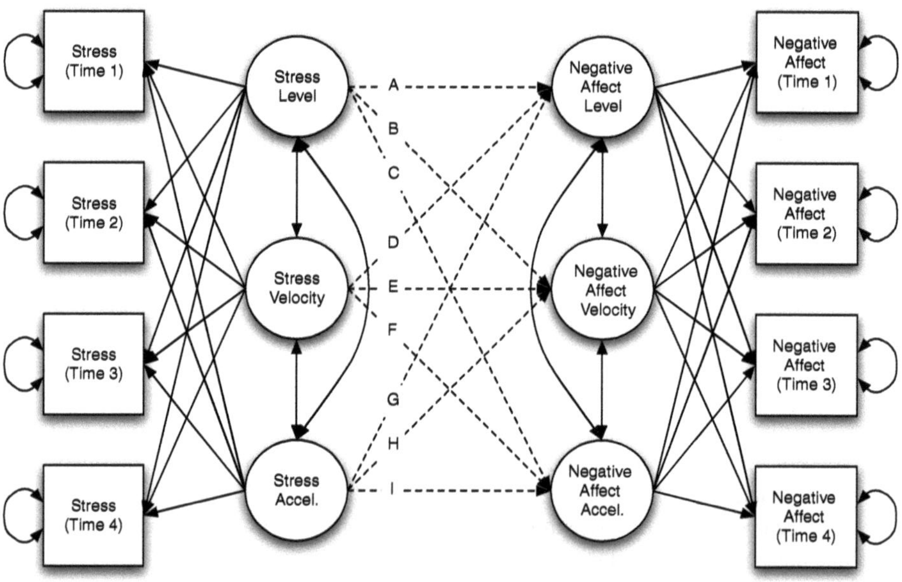

Fig. 2 A latent growth curve model which, with slightly modified fixed paths, expresses the level, velocity, and acceleration in stress and negative affect as latent variables. Many possible relationships between the stress and negative affect derivatives could be considered (paths A through I). It should be noted that causal interpretations of this model may not make sense, depending on how time has been coded. When Time = 1 is used as the initial time, paths D and G suggest that later changes over the four observations could alter one's initial level of Negative Affect (i.e., time travel)

LGCM allows for questions similar to HLM to be addressed, but also a multitude of additional questions (paths D through I). What then is meant when one states that stress and negative affect are related? Should we posit all paths?

When changed to level, velocity, and acceleration, it may be possible to argue that there are only a few paths that are of theoretical interest. First one must consider the dependent variable (negative affect): Do we wish to predict a person's level of negative affect at $T = 0$? Do we wish to predict a person's velocity at $T = 0$? or Do we wish to predict whether a person's trajectory of negative affect is changing—what traits are related to a person departing from their initial trajectory? The third question is one about the acceleration in negative affect (second derivative; paths C, F, and I). Turning to the predictor, what is it about stress that is related to changes in the velocity of negative affect (i.e., acceleration)? Is one's level of stress related to changes in the velocity of negative affect? Or, is it that increases in stress are related to changes in the velocity of negative affect? Or, is it the fact that one's stress is not just increasing, but increasing at a faster rate, that is related to changes in the velocity of negative affect? These three questions are qualitatively different, and the presence of any one relation does not necessarily imply anything about the presence or lack of the other two relations.

The question "Is stress related to negative affect?" is too simple, as even limiting ourselves to a unidirectional case implies nine possible relations as in Fig. 2 (paths A through I), or even more if one considers higher order derivatives. Even narrowing our interest to what is related to a change in the velocity of negative affect, there are still multiple possibilities to consider (paths C, F, and I), each of which addresses a qualitatively different question. What is it that most directly causes one's negative affect trajectory to curve (accelerate) in a negative direction—is it the specific level of one's stress, the fact that one's stress has been increasing for several weeks, or that one's stress level is increasing at a faster and faster rate? Whatever one's response, the language of derivatives allows us to more clearly highlight the questions addressed by the LGCM (as opposed to considering quadratic–quadratic relations). The common language between this section and the previous section also highlights that LGCM has the potential to address many of the questions addressed by HLM (see Bauer 2003; MacCallum et al. 1997).

4 Derivative Language Framework

In this chapter we have introduced the language of derivatives in a manner intended for a broad audience, and without requiring an introduction to calculus. Just the realization that many common models contain parameters that express the change in one variable with respect to another (derivatives), and labeling them as level, velocity, and acceleration, has the potential to provide researchers a novel language framework for understanding a variety of models. There are at least four consequences of adopting the language of differential equations and derivatives.

Table 1 Summary of derivatives related in several common methods for the analysis of change

		Construct 2		
		y	dy/dt	d^2y/dt^2
	x	Correlation[a]		
		Ordinary Regression[a]		
		SEM[a]		
		HLM/MLM		
		LGCM		
		GLLA/GOLD/LDE		
Construct 1	dx/dt	HLM/MLM		
		LGCM	LGCM/PPM	
		LCS	LCS	
		LPM/CLPM		
		GLLA/GOLD/LDE	GLLA/GOLD/LDE	
	d^2x/dt^2	HLM/MLM[b]		
		LGCM[b]	LGCM[b]	LGCM[b]
		LCS[b]	LCS[b]	LCS[b]
		GLLA/GOLD/LDE	GLLA/GOLD/LDE	GLLA/GOLD/LDE

SEM structural equation modeling, *HLM/MLM* Hierarchical Linear Modeling/Multilevel Modeling, *PPM* Parallel Process Modeling, *LGCM* latent growth curve modeling, *LCS* Latent Change Scores, *LPM/CLPM* lagged panel modeling/cross-lagged panel modeling, *GLLA/GOLD/LDE* Generalized Local Linear Approximation, Generalized Orthogonal Local Derivatives, Latent Differential Equations

[a]Many, but not all applications

[b]Applications corresponding to this relationship are unusual

First, by thinking about the possible ways derivatives can be related—level–acceleration relations, velocity–velocity relations, level–level relations, etc.—there is a relatively limited number of combinations that are possible (nine, unless higher order derivatives are considered). Rather than continue to present students an ever-increasing number of models and methods for describing change, a matrix of derivative relations could be introduced (e.g., Table 1). Each method/model would fall into one or more of the finite number of combinations. The differences between all methods/models that allow for level–acceleration questions to be addressed could then be compared and contrasted. From the authors' perspective, some of the key differences are the kind of data to which a particular method/model is typically applied, and the time scale over which derivatives are being estimated (Deboeck et al. submitted).

Second, using this language framework allows for the presentation of a theory–method Rosetta stone as in Table 2. Using level, velocity, and acceleration would allow researchers to be much more specific with regard to theories of change. But as these words are directly related to the zeroth, first, and second derivatives, the mathematical interpretation of these words is very precise. The challenging endeavor of translating theory into mathematics can then be made much more precise. Moreover, in areas where theory is rich, use of this language may drive the development of new, more appropriate models.

Table 2 Summary of several equivalent ways to express the zeroth through second derivatives

Characteristic of scores	Derivative	Name	Graphical depiction	Notation
Score at some time	0th	Level	Single point	y
Rate at which level is changing	1st	Velocity	Straight line	dy/dt
Rate at which velocity is changing	2nd	Acceleration	Curved line	d^2y/dt^2

Third, this framework would allow for more detailed and accurate interpretation of results. Putting into words the differences between Eqs. (6) through (8), or paths A through I in Fig. 2, may be challenging. By highlighting that the parameters and latent variables can take on names associated with change—level, velocity, acceleration—may allow the hypotheses being tested to be more readily put into words.

Fourth, this new framework provides a structure that allows for the understanding of new methodology relative to well-known models. The following section introduces three differential equations that can be used to model the complex, nonlinear changes in studies of intraindividual variability. These models will be introduced relative to the more familiar LGCM. In introducing these newer methods, we highlight some new questions that become accessible using the derivative language framework.

5 Modeling Intraindividual Observations

The collection of repeated, intraindividual measurements on psychological and behavioral variables presents a new challenge for modeling. To provide an example of these challenges, we take as a motivating example daily measurements of positive and negative affect from the Notre Dame Study of Health & Well-being. Figure 3 shows estimates of positive affect measured over time, representing a sample of everyday positive affect (i.e., not following any particular stressor). One way to model these data would be to consider an HLM or LGCM, which would give some impression of the overall trajectory. This trajectory might be related to changes in season, or other macrotemporal changes occurring in the participants' lives but not directly related to the daily regulation of emotions. Moreover, HLM, LGCM, and many other models designate the variation around the overall trajectory as error, when in fact it might be the case that characteristics of this variability are related to important differences between individuals, such as resiliency.

As introduced in the previous section, and depicted in Fig. 4a, the latent variables of an LGCM can be used to estimate the *level* at $T = 0$, the *velocity* at $T = 0$, and the *acceleration* across a series of observations. This model is closely related to Latent Differential Equation Modeling (LDE; Boker et al. 2004), a method for modeling the rich, complex nonlinearity of intraindividual variability. Despite the differences the names may convey, these methods have many similarities: both can estimate the same derivatives and allow for the same relations between derivatives

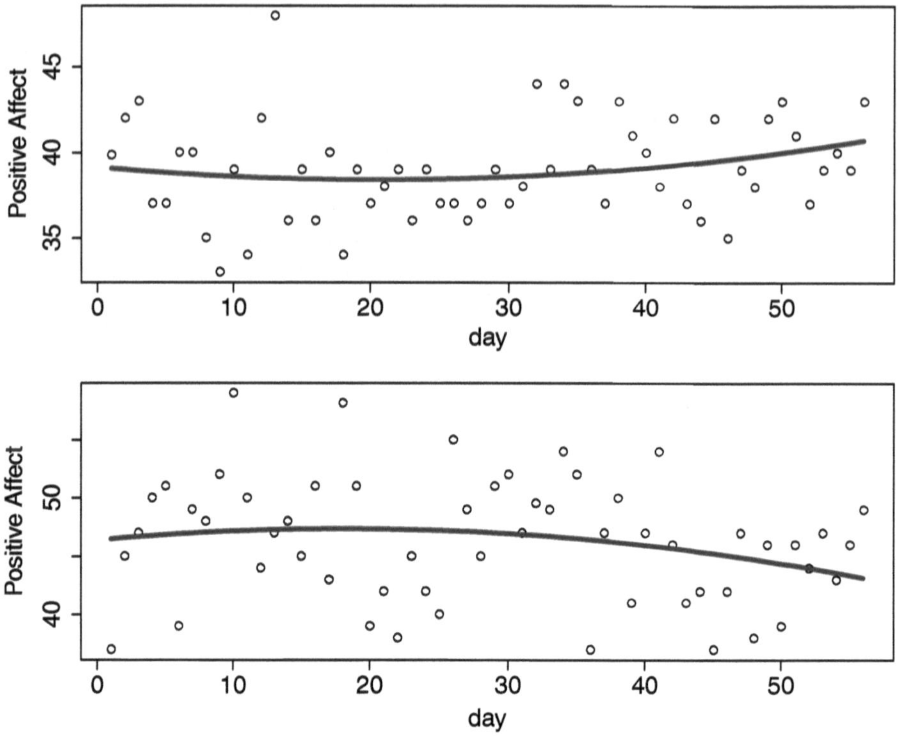

Fig. 3 Plots of positive affect measured over the course of 56 days. The plots contain the data from two different older adults. The *gray lines* are based on the estimated values of individual-specific quadratic regression models. Positive affect was measured using the PANAS (Watson et al. 1988) administered to older adults in paper and pencil daily diary self-report

to be examined (e.g., level–acceleration relations). The key difference between the two methods is the time scale over which they are applied; rather than estimate derivatives over the entire period of observations as in Fig. 4a, LDE estimates derivatives over the course of just a few observations as in Fig. 4b. The model in Fig. 4b may appear an impossible model to fit, but this is not the case once the data are reorganized into what is called an *embedded matrix*. In a manner akin to the depiction in Fig. 4c, one can rearrange data such that each row of a matrix consists of a subset of a longer time series. For example, given a time series $y = y_1, y_2, y_3, \ldots, y_t$ one can create an embedded matrix

$$\begin{bmatrix} y_1 & y_2 & y_3 & y_4 \\ y_2 & y_3 & y_4 & y_5 \\ y_3 & y_4 & y_5 & y_6 \\ \vdots & \vdots & \vdots & \vdots \\ y_{t-3} & y_{t-2} & y_{t-1} & y_t \end{bmatrix} \tag{9}$$

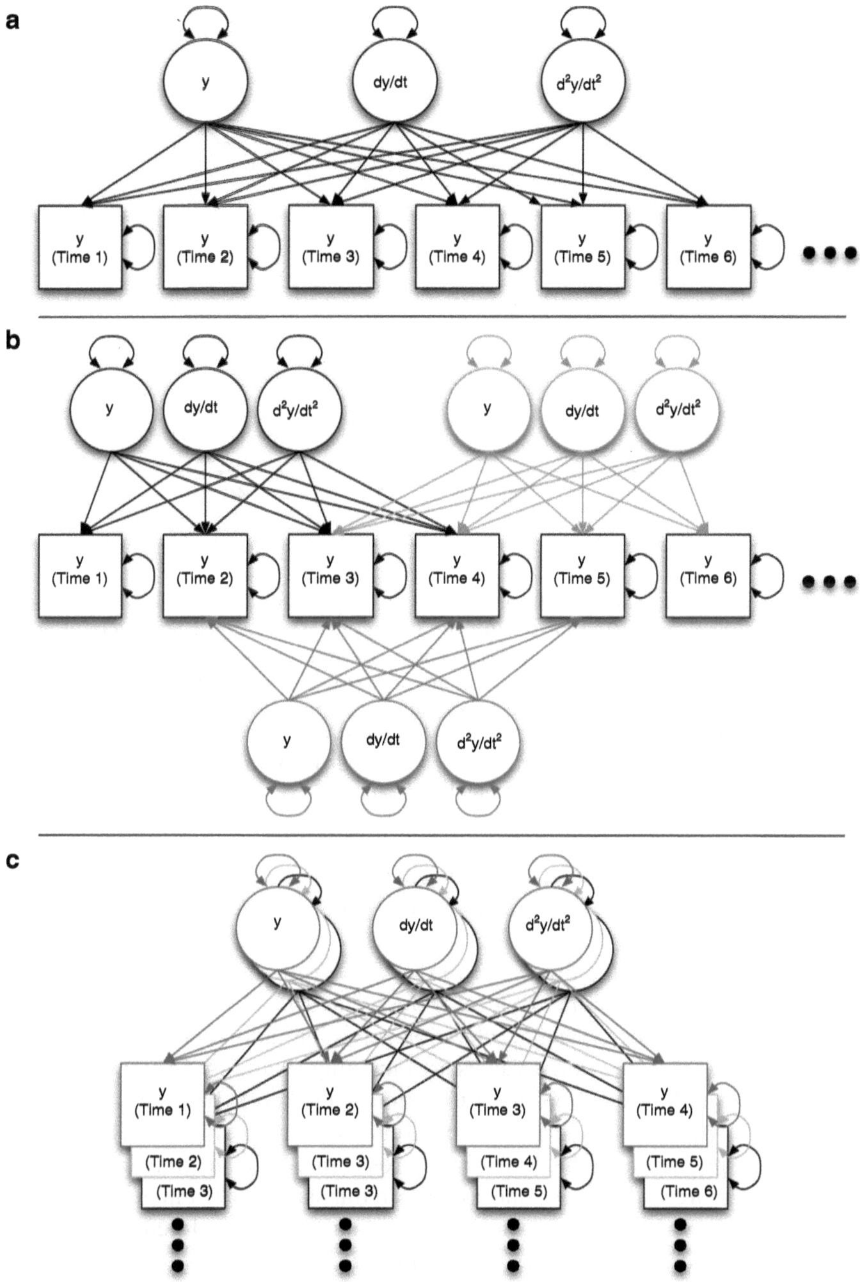

Fig. 4 Three differing versions of a latent growth curve model. (**a**) The LGCM can be applied to entire time series, providing a single estimate of the derivatives. (**b**) Many small LGCMs can be applied to a time series to generate estimates of derivatives at many different times across the series. (**c**) A revisualization of model (**b**) where the small LGCMs have been stacked. This both aids in estimation and allows one to think about the creation of an embedded data matrix which involves arranging data much as the observed variables have been stacked in this figure

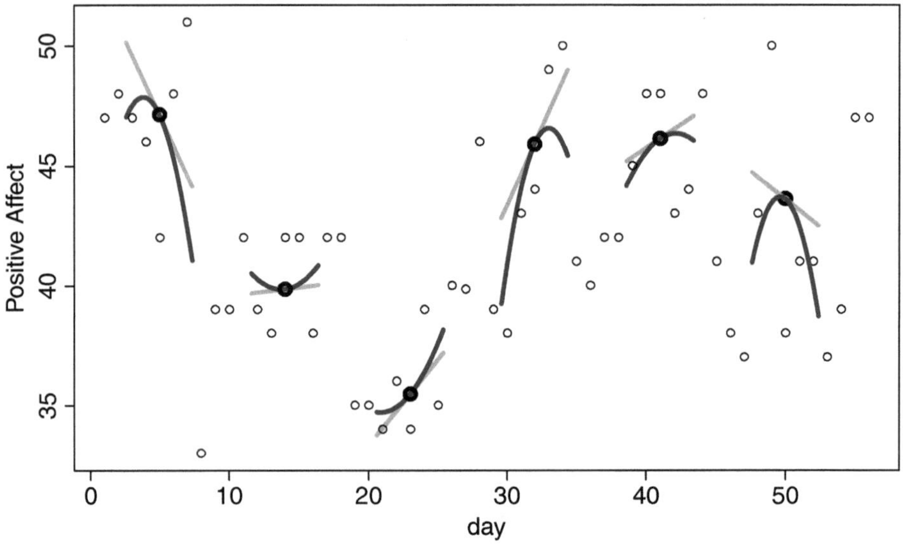

Fig. 5 By applying the latent growth curve model to short series of observations (*small circles*), the level (*bold, larger circles*), velocity (*straight, light gray lines*), and acceleration (*curved, dark gray lines*) can be estimated at many different times across a time series. The *gray acceleration lines* have been drawn such that they represent the slope that is expected at some time before/after the point at which the estimate was created; for example, for the estimate at day 23, the acceleration is such that a velocity of nearly zero would be estimated for day 20–21, and a relatively steep positive slope would be estimated for day 25–26. Confidence intervals exist for the derivative estimates, but have not been displayed to simplify the figure

where the first three rows of the matrix match the observed variable labels in Fig. 4c. Readers interested in more specifics about applying LDE are referred to Boker et al. (2004) and Deboeck (2011).

What does changing the time scale of derivative estimation buy us? In a LGCM we would have single estimates of level, velocity, and acceleration. In LDE we have estimates of level, velocity, and acceleration across an individual's time series, and therefore can observe how these values are changing, as in Fig. 5. In this figure, the observations (small circles) are used to estimate the level (bold circles), velocity (straight, light gray lines), and acceleration (curved, dark gray lines). The challenge lies in finding predictors of the derivatives across time. If the language of derivatives is applied to theoretical models, one could then translate theory into testable models to address research questions. Alternatively, data can be explored by examining predictors of different derivatives. As with the LGCM presented earlier, there are many possible derivative relations that could be considered (Fig. 2). Being precise as to how the level, velocity, and acceleration of variables affect each other over the span of a few days, however, is largely unexplored territory for many fields of study.

The following sections introduce three differential equation models. The models can be implemented in a variety of ways, including LDE (Boker et al. 2004),

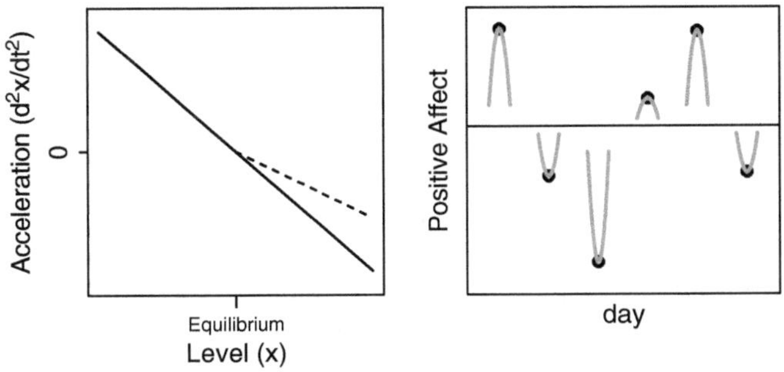

Fig. 6 A linear regression of level on acceleration (*solid line, left*) describes a model that implies that as one's level on a construct (*circles, right*) gets far from equilibrium (*horizontal line, right*) there is an acceleration (*gray curves, right*) in the direction of the equilibrium. As regressing level on acceleration is a linear relationship (*solid line, left*), one can borrow ideas from linear regression; for example, using piecewise regression one could allow the level–acceleration relation to be different when one is above equilibrium compared to when one is below equilibrium (*solid line* below equilibrium, *dashed line* above equilibrium)

Generalized Orthogonal Linear Derivative Estimates (Deboeck 2010), the Exact Discrete Model (Oud and Jansen 2000; Voelkle et al. 2012) and Generalized Local Linear Approximation (Boker et al. 2008; Boker and Nesselroade 2002). Through the three models that we present, we explore a few ideas of how relating derivatives may give some insight into certain processes. These models have not been applied in a wide range of contexts, so for many areas of the social sciences these are examples of how differential equations can provide a language to address new questions about change.

5.1 Model 1

The first model considers only a single variable—positive affect. As with the LGCM, we focus on the questions: What leads to changes in the trajectory of positive affect? and What is related to positive affect acceleration? But now these questions are being considered in the context of having made multiple derivative estimates over a time series as in Fig. 5. One way to model these data would be to posit additional variables, the derivatives of which might explain positive affect acceleration. Another option is to consider how the level, velocity, and acceleration estimates of positive affect might be related to each other.

For example, consider the linear relation (solid line) that has been drawn between the acceleration and level of positive affect in Fig. 6 (left). The interpretation of this relation is interesting, as when the level of positive affect is high there is negative acceleration; conversely, when positive affect is low, there is positive acceleration. This is depicted in another way in Fig. 6 (right). Such a relation would suggest that if one were near some average or typical level of positive affect (horizontal line) there might not be much change. But if one develops a high value of positive affect, negative acceleration is expected; the slope is changing so that the upward trajectory is not maintained, and eventually a negative trajectory will occur. The inverse is true for a low positive affect score.

This is one possible model of homeostasis or self-regulation. There is a typical state, or *equilibrium*, around which affect is expected to vary. Moreover, when affect is displaced far from equilibrium in either direction, there is a relation with an acceleration in the opposite direction, suggesting a change in slopes that would result in changes towards equilibrium. This model does not specify the mechanisms that lead to self-regulation, but it may be useful for characterizing how quickly individuals move towards and away from equilibrium; that is, do the gray acceleration curves in Fig. 6 (right) have a very steep or very shallow u-shape? The relationship in Fig. 6 can be written as the differential equation

$$\frac{d^2x}{dt^2} = \beta x + \epsilon, \tag{10}$$

which expresses that the second derivative (acceleration) is related to the zeroth derivative (level) times β plus error ϵ. The relationship β—which expresses how changes in the level of the self-regulating variable are related to changes in the acceleration of the same variable—is related to how quickly people return to, and move away from, their equilibrium state. For examples of papers implementing this model, see Bisconti et al. (2006), Boker and Laurenceau (2005), Montpetit et al. (2010), and Nicholson et al. (2011).

As the relationship in Fig. 6 and Eq. (10) consists of a linear regression, one can draw on familiarity with regression to inform how this model could be modified for different contexts. For example, the present model assumes the same relationship between acceleration and level regardless of whether one is above or below one's equilibrium. Perhaps it is expected that the level–acceleration relation above equilibrium is different than when it is below equilibrium; the rate at which one returns to equilibrium differs above and below one's equilibrium (see Fig. 6, left). This would correspond to a different slope above and below equilibrium, as depicted with the solid line below equilibrium and the dashed line above equilibrium. One could allow for the differing slopes using piecewise regression, using the equation

$$\frac{d^2x}{dt^2} = \beta_1 x + \beta_2 x_2 + \epsilon. \tag{11}$$

where x_2 is coded to be zero for negative values of x, and x_2 would be equal to x for positive values of x.

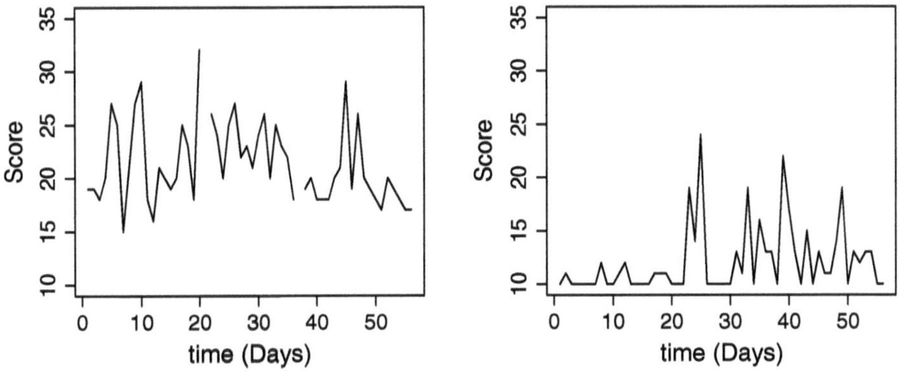

Fig. 7 Simulated plots of differing types of trajectories observed when measuring negative affect in a sample of older adults

5.2 *Model 2*

Models of self-regulation may be reasonable first approximations in many contexts; as in any domain, however, application of these models will require refinement. Figure 7 shows plots that are not atypical of what is observed when examining negative affect in older adults (Ram 2011). Some of the data patterns might be reasonably characterized using a model of self-regulation; there appears to be some equilibrium state around which an individual varies (Fig. 7, left). It is not unusual, however, to also observe patterns such as in Fig. 7 (right). In this figure, there appears to be a floor effect. Initially, one may expect this is due to a measurement problem, which could be solved by including items that would be more commonly endorsed. Attempts to take such a step, however, appear to mitigate but do not fully alleviate the presence of floor effects (Deboeck and Bergeman 2013). When examining negative affect, there appears to be a large proportion of individuals who do not follow a self-regulation-like model, but rather appear to register very low levels of negative affect that on occasion will increase in response to events.

One idea that has been proposed for modeling these data is the differential equation model

$$\frac{dx}{dt} = \beta x + \epsilon, \tag{12}$$

where the slope between days (first derivative) is related to the level of negative affect plus error (Deboeck and Bergeman 2013). Unlike other models, the errors in this model are assumed to consist of only positive values; for example, ϵ could follow a gamma distribution. If the errors are all positive, and the values of x are all positive, the value of β is required to be negative, otherwise scores would be required to monotonically increase for the duration of the study.

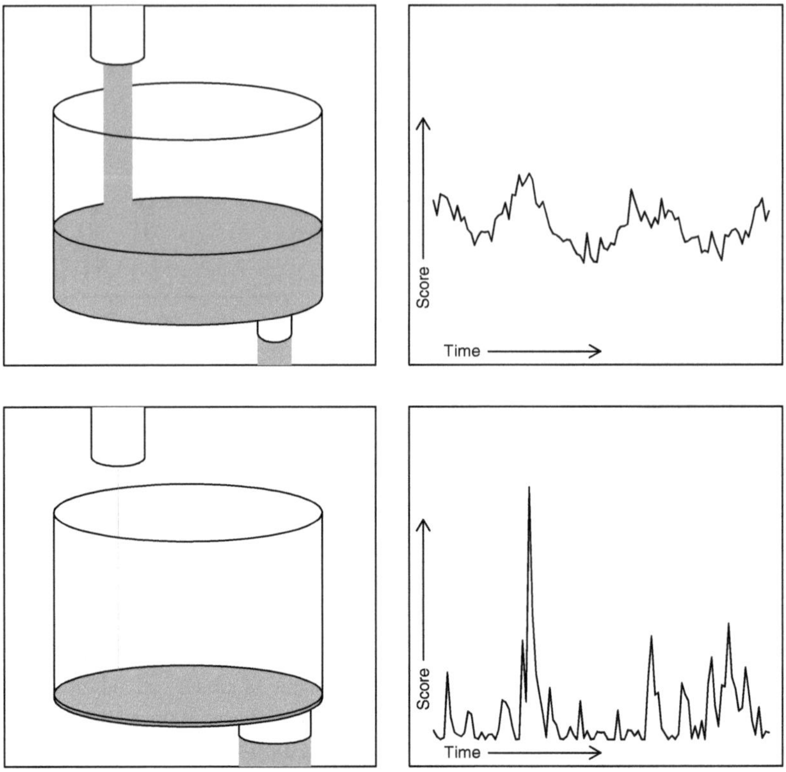

Fig. 8 Examples of the trajectories (*right column*) that occur from recording the height of the liquid in a simulation of two reservoirs (*left column*). In the reservoir in the *top row*, the rate of liquid (*gray*) inflow and outflow are approximately balanced; in this case, the reservoir always has liquid, although its level fluctuates around an equilibrium-like value. In the reservoir in the *bottom row*, the outflow is faster than the inflow; consequently, the trajectory often approaches the minimum value (empty reservoir) except when a large input event occurs

A metaphor for the behavior of this model is that of a reservoir, as in Fig. 8 (left column). The negative affect reported on any given day corresponds to the height (level) of the liquid in this reservoir. Above the reservoir is a pipe that adds liquid to the reservoir, increasing the height of the liquid; the added liquid corresponds to any events perceived as increasing one's negative affect. There is also a pipe at the bottom of the reservoir that allows the liquid to flow out of the reservoir; this corresponds to one's ability to dissipate negative affect.

When the input (inflow) and dissipation (outflow) rates are approximately balanced, the trajectory appears very much like someone who is self-regulating (Fig. 8, top row). If one's dissipation rate is larger than the rate of input, however,

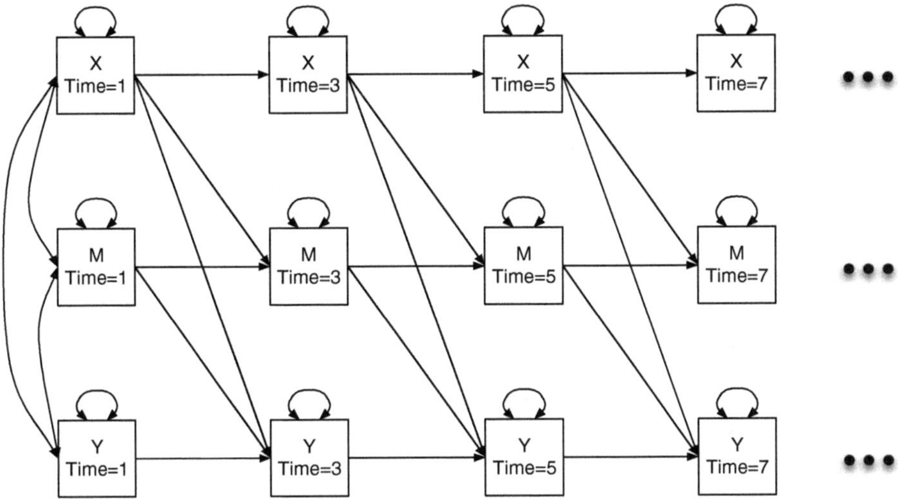

Fig. 9 A cross-lagged panel model

there is a tendency for floor effects to occur (Fig. 8, bottom row).[2] This model is one example of when a single differential equation can produce time series that appear qualitatively different, or time series with differing distributions for the dependent variable. Such models may be useful for identifying important parameters for characterizing intraindividual variability. Initially, it will be important to show how the average perceived input and dissipation parameters differentially relate to traits in the literature, but eventually these parameters may help to parse out similarities and differences between traits as well as identify traits that have been overlooked.

5.3 *Model 3*

The presentation of Models 1 and 2 has focused on new questions related to characterizing intraindividual variability and the relationship between different levels of the same variable that can be addressed using differential equations. The language of differential equations also has the potential to give new insight into old problems. The cross-lagged panel model (CLPM) in Fig. 9 has often been used in applications of longitudinal mediation. The ability to make a causal inference with this model is often stronger, although arguably not complete, because of the

[2]Videos demonstrating the evolution of these systems have been posted on the web site of the first author.

ability to test the directionality of relations such as X_t to M_{t+1} versus M_t to X_{t+1}. One limitation of drawing inferences with the CLPM is that inferences are limited to the specific lag at which data are collected (Cole and Maxwell 2003; Gollob and Reichardt 1987, 1991). Consequently, how to go about collecting data such that one selects the "correct" lag becomes a thorny issue, as the "correct" lag for one effect may not be the "correct" lag for another effect, and differing lags may be required for variables to reach their maximal influence (Cole and Maxwell 2003).

The CLPM is a discrete time model, as time is only implicitly considered through the order of the observations, but never explicitly considered through the specification of the time between observations (Voelkle et al. 2012). An alternative way of modeling data similar to the CLPM is by specifying a differential equation model that describes the underlying process that is generating the data. With such a model it would be possible to estimate the expected value of each variable at all times across the duration of the study, as time is explicitly considered in such a model. The expected values of the variables are calculated by integrating the differential equation model from some time t to some later time $t+\delta$.

One differential equation model that has been implemented frequently across many literatures is the model

$$\frac{dx}{dt} = Ax + \epsilon, \tag{13}$$

where the key difference with respect to Eq. (12) is that the errors are no longer all positive. Rather, ϵ is usually replaced with a continuous-time process that generates independent, normally distributed observations when integrated over some period of time (see Voelkle et al. 2012, for details). While Eqs. (12) and (13) appear very similar, the change in the distribution of the stochastic errors ϵ results in very different interpretations of β and A; while β addresses only the decay to zero, A is related to both increases and decreases that return the system to its steady state (see Deboeck and Boker in press, for examples and more details). The model in Eq. (13) can be rewritten in matrix form:

$$\frac{d\mathbf{X}}{dt} = \mathbf{AX} + \epsilon, \tag{14}$$

so as to allow it to be fit to more than one variable at a time, as in the CLPM in Fig. 9.

One advantage to using a differential equation model in this context is that the estimated parameters (e.g., $\mathbf{A}$) are independent of lag; that is, they do not depend on the spacing between repeated observations. Moreover, these parameters can be used to solve for the expected model parameters for differing lags; the lags for which one solves are not limited to those measured in one's data, although one should be cautious about examining lags that extrapolate beyond one's data. Figure 10 shows an example of the results that can be produced using differential equation models (Deboeck and Preacher 2013); the values of the lines, for any particular lag, can be

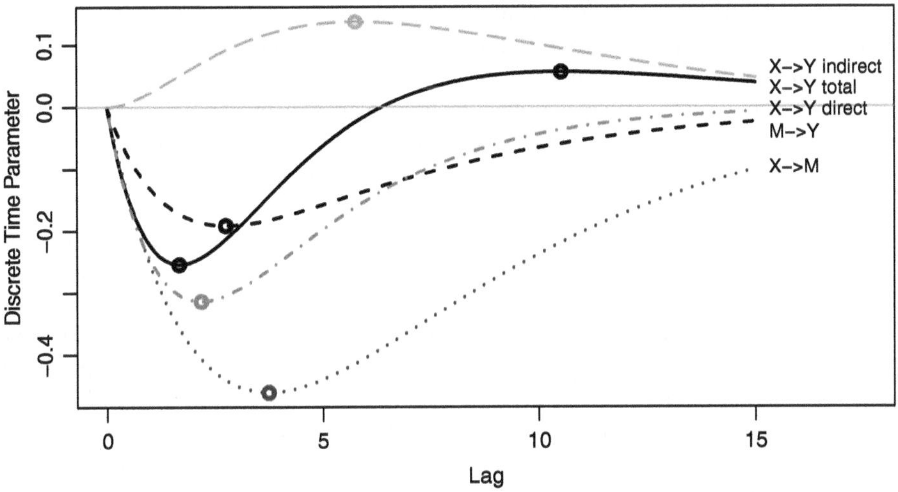

Fig. 10 Estimates based on differential equation model parameters of how the cross-lagged panel values (Discrete Time Parameters) change as a function of lag. The values of the lines, for any particular lag, can be interpreted as the parameters that would be expected if the cross-lagged panel model in Fig. 9 were fit to data with that particular lag. The maximal and minimal points have been marked with a *circle*, and the name of each effect is indicated on the *right*. The X to Y total effect represents the sum of the direct and indirect effects of X on Y

interpreted as the parameters that would be expected if the CLPM in Fig. 9 were fit to data with that particular lag assuming Eq. (14). Consequently, this figure shows how the discrete-time CLPM paths would be expected to change if data with differing lags were analyzed. While in a CLPM the results are typically presented for a single lag, corresponding to a single vertical slice through Fig. 10, with the differential equation model there is the potential to estimate relationships for many possible lags.

6 Concluding Remarks

In this chapter, the language of derivatives was introduced, and it was demonstrated how this language could be applied to familiar models to facilitate the appropriate application of these models to research questions related to change (e.g., HLM and LGCM). By using the language in Tables 1 and 2, precision in the specification of theories about change can be improved, methodology can be more easily identified, and accuracy of interpretation of results can be ensured. Perhaps most encouraging, this language framework also provides a structure within which new methods and models of change can be introduced, thus creating the potential to open new ways of formulating questions and ideas, such as those related to the analysis of intraindividual variability. Three models were explored to highlight some of the ways that dynamic, nonlinear, intraindividual variability can be characterized, and how these models have the potential to shed new light on old problems such as the dependency of results on sampling rate.

Curriculum used to train researchers on how to analyze research questions related to change already integrates some of the concepts presented in this chapter. Unfortunately, derivatives and differential equations are seldom presented in introductory texts, perhaps under the guise of simplifying the presentation of statistics. We propose this is a disservice to researchers as derivatives provide an appropriate framework to analyze change. Without training in the language of differential equation models, an incoherent framework may be presented for the different analytic approaches available for testing similar models. Without the Rosetta stone of derivatives, it is more difficult for researchers to integrate different approaches and systematically and effectively match their research question about change to the correct model. Rather than learning what makes models different, this approach first identifies the types of derivative relations present, and subsequently identifies key differences between models with differing names (i.e., LGCM versus LDE).

Differential equations have the potential to change the way we think about change, subsequently impacting the research questions asked and consequently the models fit. This is especially warranted given the increased focus on intraindividual variability that is occurring in many fields. Future decades promise to bring more application of statistics to individual lives, whether through personalized medicine, ecological momentary interventions, or other means. Learning the language of derivatives opens the floodgates to characterizing the rich complexity of intraindividual variability with interesting parameters that may be informative of unobserved processes. As with all languages, fluency takes practice; but fluency also provides a perspective, understanding, and beauty that is nearly unobtainable through translation.

References

Bauer, D. J. (2003). Estimating multilevel linear models as structural equation models. *Journal of Educational and Behavioral Statistics, 28*, 135–167.

Bisconti, T. L., Bergeman, C. S., & Boker, S. M. (2006). Social support as a predictor of variability: An examination of the adjustment trajectories of recent widows. *Psychology and Aging, 21*(3), 590–599.

Boker, S. M., & Laurenceau, J. P. (2005). Dynamical systems modeling: An application to the regulation of intimacy and disclosure in marriage. In T. A. Walls & J. L. Schafer (Eds.), *Models for intensive longitudinal data* (pp. 195–218). Oxford: Oxford University Press.

Boker, S. M., Leibenluft, E., Deboeck, P. R., Virk, G., & Postolache, T. T. (2008). Mood oscillations and coupling between mood and weather in patients with rapid cycling bipolar disorder. *International Journal of Child Health and Human Development, 1*(2), 181–202.

Boker, S. M., Neale, M. C., & Rausch, J. R. (2004). Latent differential equation modeling with multivariate multi-occasion indicators. In K. V. Montfort, J. Oud, & A. Satorra (Eds.), *Recent developments on structural equation models: Theory and applications* (pp. 151–174). Amsterdam: Kluwer.

Boker, S. M., & Nesselroade, J. R. (2002). A method for modeling the intrinsic dynamics of intraindividual variability: Recovering the parameters of simulated oscillators in multi-wave panel data. *Multivariate Behavioral Research, 37*(1), 127–160.

Cole, D. A., & Maxwell, S. E. (2003). Testing mediational models with longitudinal data: Questions and tips in the use of structural equation modeling. *Journal of Abnormal Psychology, 112*, 558–577.

Cudeck, R., & du Toit, S. H. C. (2002). A version of quadratic regression with interpretable parameters. *Multivariate Behavioral Research, 37*(4), 501–519.

Deboeck, P. R. (2010). Estimating dynamical systems, derivative estimation hints from Sir Ronald A. Fisher. *Multivariate Behavioral Research, 43*(4), 725–745.

Deboeck, P. R. (2011). Modeling nonlinear dynamics. In M. R. Mehl & T. S. Conner (Eds.), *The handbook of research methods for studying daily life* (pp. 440–458). New York: Guilford Press.

Deboeck, P. R., & Bergeman, C. S. (2013). The reservoir model: A differential equation model of psychological capacity. *Psychological Methods, 18*(2), 237–256.

Deboeck, P. R., & Boker, S. M. (in press). Analysis of dynamic systems: The modeling of change and variability. In S. Henly (Ed.), *International handbook of advanced quantitative methods in nursing research.* New York: Routledge.

Deboeck, P. R., Nicholson, J. S., Kouros, C. D., & Little, T. D. (submitted). Interfacing theory and method: Derivatives as the developmental Rosetta stone. *International Journal of Behavioral Development.*

Deboeck, P. R., & Preacher, K. J. (2013). No need to be discrete: A method for continuous time mediation analysis. Under review.

Gollob, H. F., & Reichardt, C. S. (1987). Taking account of time lags in causal models. *Child Development, 58*, 80–92.

Gollob, H. F., & Reichardt, C. S. (1991). Interpreting and estimating indirect effects assuming time lags really matter. In L. M. Collins & J. L. Horn (Eds.), *Best methods for the analysis of change: Recent advances, unanswered questions, future directions* (pp. 243–259). Washington, DC: American Psychological Association.

MacCallum, R. C., Kim, C., Malarkey, W. B., & Kiecolt-Glaser, J. K. (1997). Studying multivariate change using multilevel models and latent curve models. *Multivariate Behavioral Research, 32*, 215–253.

Montpetit, M. A., Bergeman, C. S., Deboeck, P. R., Tiberio, S. S., & Boker, S. M. (2010). Resilience-as-process: Negative affect, stress, and coupled dynamical systems. *Psychology and Aging, 25*(3), 631–640.

Nicholson, J. S., Deboeck, P. R., Farris, J. R., Boker, S. M., & Borkowski, J. G. (2011). Maternal depressive symptomatology and child behavior: A dynamical system with simultaneous bi-directional coupling. *Developmental Psychology, 47*(5), 1312–1323.

Oud, J. H. L., & Jansen, R. A. R. G. (2000). Continuous time state space modeling of panel data by means of SEM. *Psychometrika, 65*, 199–215.

Ram, N. (2011). *Analyzing large-scale ema data from a person-specific perspective: Pushing intraindividual variability into a real time world.* Presented at the Center for Research Methods and Data Analysis, University of Kansas, Lawrence, Kansas.

Voelkle, M. C., Oud, J. H. L., Davidov, E., & Schmidt, P. (2012). An SEM approach to continuous time modeling of panel data: Relating authoritarianism and anomia. *Psychological Methods, 17*, 176–192.

Watson, D., Clark, L. A., & Tellegan, A. (1988). Development and validation of brief measures of positive and negative affect: The PANAS scales. *Journal of Personality and Social Psychology, 54*, 1063–1070.

Evaluating Scales for Ordinal Assessment in Clinical and Medical Psychology

Wilco H.M. Emons and Paulette C. Flore

1 Introduction

Personality and psychosocial indicators such as quality of life, distress, anxiety, and social inhibition are increasingly being used as predictors of poor prognosis in medicine, and as outcome measures in counseling and psychotherapy. These indicators are often assessed by means of multiple item self-report questionnaires. Examples include the Hospital Anxiety and Depression Scale (Zigmond and Snaith 1983), the Outcome Questionnaire 45 (Lambert and Finch 1999) and the DS14 (Denollet 2005). Practitioners use the total score to decide whether a patient should receive counseling, has an elevated risk of poor prognosis, or has an improved health condition during treatment. For these purposes, the obtained total score must at least be an ordinal indicator of the intended attribute of measurement. In general, ordinal assessment often suffices in clinical and medical applications as they allow a categorization of persons into diagnostic groups and may reveal within-person changes during treatment. Hence, to determine whether a scale has sound psychometric quality amounts to evaluating whether the scale's total scores provide a reliable and valid rank ordering of persons on the intended attribute and whether the ranking is precise enough for reliable individual decision-making.

Nonparametric item-response theory (NIRT; Sijtsma 2005) offers a psychometric framework for constructing ordinal scales for person measurement. A distinctive feature of item-response theory (IRT) models is the definition of the item-response

W.H.M. Emons (✉) • P.C. Flore
Department of Methodology and Statistics, Tilburg School of Social and Behavioral Sciences, Tilburg University, PO Box 90153, 5000 LE Tilburg, The Netherlands
e-mail: w.h.m.emons@tilburguniversity.edu; p.c.flore@tilburguniversity.edu

R.E. Millsap et al. (eds.), *New Developments in Quantitative Psychology*, Springer Proceedings in Mathematics & Statistics 66, DOI 10.1007/978-1-4614-9348-8_29,

function, which describes the relationship between the latent attribute of interest and the probability of responding in a particular answer category. Parametric IRT models define this relationship by a mathematical function, such as a logistic function or the normal ogive. NIRT models, however, only impose monotone order restrictions on the item-response functions, without constraining the function to a particular parametric shape. NIRT models are thus more general than their parametric counterparts. The practical importance of NIRT models is that if the items in the scale satisfy the NIRT assumptions, it is reasonable to conceive total scores as ordinal measurements of the latent attribute (Sijtsma 2005; Van der Ark 2005). NIRT models are therefore particularly useful for analyzing ordinal measurement properties of clinical scales and outcome questionnaires (Meijer and Baneke 2004; Sijtsma et al. 2008; Waller and Reise 2010).

Popular NIRT approaches are exploratory in nature as they rely on summarized patterns in the data. A typical NIRT analysis estimates the item-response functions from the data by means of nonparametric regression techniques, such as binning (Sijtsma and Molenaar 2002) and kernel smoothing (Ramsay 1991). Based on graphical inspection, supported by statistical tests, one has to verify whether observed patterns agree with expectations under the NIRT model. If they do, the data support the hypothesis that the items constitute an ordinal scale. A confirmatory NIRT analysis may involve the use of a statistical model such as ordered latent class models (OR-LCMs; Croon 1991). OR-LCMs provide a full parameterization of the NIRT assumptions. Like parametric IRT models, the OR-LCM serves as a null hypothesis that can be tested in sample data. OR-LCMs thus maintain the flexibility of NIRT models but additionally offer a profound statistical framework for analyzing the psychometric properties of presumed ordinal scales (Van Onna 2004; Vermunt 2001).

Despite the promising possibilities of OR-LCMs for analyzing ordinal scales, two important practical issues remain neglected. First, in practice researchers often rely only on relative fit measures for selecting the best fitting model. However, the model with relatively the best fit may still have poor absolute fit. Hence, model selection should be based on both relative and absolute fit information. In our view, absolute fit assessment receives too little attention both in the psychometric literature and in applications. Second, OR-LCMs only provide a sparse (probabilistic) summary of the data and many of the scale properties of primary interest, such as total-score reliability, cannot be directly read from the fitted model. We believe that there is a need for more practice-oriented ways to meaningfully summarize the measurement properties that follow from the fitted model. The goal of the present chapter is to present a number of tools for testing absolute fit of OR-LCMs and to show how to use the OR-LCMs to gauge total-score reliability and measurement precision for ordinal person measurement.

2 Background

2.1 *OR-LCM for Likert-Type Items*

The OR-LCM discussed in this chapter belongs to the family of graded response models (GRM; Hemker et al. 1997). We assume that we have item-response data collected by means of Likert-type items. Let J be the number of items and X_j ($j = 1, \ldots, J$) be the item-score variable with realizations $x_j = 0, \ldots, M$. Hence, the number of answer categories per item equals $M + 1$. Latent attribute variables (e.g., anxiety, depression) are assumed to be unidimensional and denoted by θ. The OR-LCM divides the population into Q ordered latent classes of increasing θ levels; that is, $\theta_q < \theta_{q+1}$ and q (=1, …, Q) indexing the latent classes. Proportional class sizes are denoted by $P(\theta_q)$ such that $\sum_{q=1}^{Q} P(\theta_q) = 1$. The item scores are assumed to be independent within classes; this is the assumption of local independence. Item responses are related to θ_q by means of M cumulative response functions; that is, $P(X_j \geq x_j | \theta_q)$, $x_j = 1, \ldots, M$. Throughout this chapter, we use shorthand notation $\pi_{jx_j}(\theta_q)$ for the cumulative response probabilities $P(X_j \geq x_j | \theta_q)$, and we may note that $\pi_{j0}(\theta_q) = 1$ by definition. The graded response OR-LCM constrains the cumulative response probabilities between classes as follows:

$$\pi_{jx_j}(\theta_q) \leq \pi_{jx_j}(\theta_{q+1}).$$

The sum of the M cumulative response probabilities defines the class-specific item-mean score function (ISF); that is, $E\left(X_j \middle| \theta_q\right) = \sum_{x_j=1}^{M} \pi_{jx_j}(\theta_q)$. LatentGOLD 4.5 (Vermunt and Magidson 2005) was used to obtain maximum likelihood estimates of the class sizes $P(\theta_q)$ and the parameters $\pi_{jx_j}(\theta_q)$.

2.2 *Model-Fit Assessment*

To draw valid conclusions from the OR-LCM one has to ascertain that the model adequately fits the data for the application envisaged. For this purpose, most often researchers rely on information criteria, such as the Akaike Information Criterion 3 (AIC3) and the Bayesian Information Criterion (BIC). These are measures of relative fit and using them as the only criteria for model selection does not guarantee that the selected model is able to accurately reproduce the structure of the data at hand. To avoid that wrong conclusions are drawn from a poor fitting model, additional evidence of absolute fit should be included in the process of model selection. In the present chapter we evaluated absolute model fit by evaluating the agreement between model predictions and observed data at the item-pair, the item, and total-score level.

2.3 Psychometric Implications for Person Measurement

Once it is found that the postulated OR-LCM adequately fits the data, one can use the estimated parameters to evaluate the properties of the scale for person measurement. Examples include total-score reliability and item discrimination. In the present chapter, we focus on evaluating the scale's quality for screening and diagnosis, which are typical testing goals in the clinical and medical context. Assume persons are classified into one of two diagnostic categories (e.g., non-clinical versus clinical group), where the categories are defined by a fixed cut-off score. One of the test properties of interest concerns the reliability with which persons are ranked below or above the clinical cut-off point. For this purpose, Emons et al. (2007) introduced the concept of *certainty level*, which is defined as the proportion in which a person would be correctly classified in the hypothetical event of infinitely many independent replications of the test. They argued that for high-stakes decisions researchers want to have certainty levels of 0.9 or higher, whereas for low-stakes decisions certainty levels of 0.7 are deemed acceptable. The scale's classification consistency (*CC*) is defined as the proportion of persons in a population for whom the desired minimum certainty level is reached and it ideally should be high. The *CC* shows for how many respondents in the target population the test is able to come to a sufficiently reliable decision. This is important information because decision errors may have serious consequences, not only from the perspective of the person being tested but also from the perspective of the organization and clinician. We may add that the average certainty level in the population may be acceptable (say >0.80), but that still a non-negligible proportion of the respondents may be classified with a certainty that is deemed too low given the application envisaged. This raises concerns about the appropriateness of the scale in the target population. Because in practice persons cannot be repeatedly tested, information about certainty levels and *CC* has to be inferred from measurement models like the OR-LCM or the true-score model in classical test theory (e.g., Crocker and Algina 1986; Kruyen et al. 2013).

3 A Simulated Data Example

3.1 Data

Because we also wanted to illustrate the accuracy with which the OR-LCM recovers the true *CC* values, we used simulated data so we can compare model-based estimates with known true (population) values. In particular, data were simulated for a seven-item test, each item having five ordered answer categories. One thousand θ values were randomly drawn from two normal distributions, each with variance 1, but with means of 0 ($n = 600$) and 1 ($n = 400$), respectively. This results in a latent variable distribution that was positively skewed, which is typical for clinical

Table 1 Model-selection statistics AIC3 and BIC, proportional reduction in L^2, and proportion of classification errors, for OR-LCMs for seven OR-LCMs

Q	No. par.	BIC	AIC3	Prop. red in L^{2a}	Class. errors
1	28	21,563.0	21,453.4		
2	36	19,398.7	19,258.0	0.27	0.040
3	44	18,797.9	18,626.0	0.47	0.074
4	52	18,672.0	18,468.8	0.56	0.125
5	60	18,666.0	18,431.5	0.59	0.168
6	68	18,709.5	18,443.7	0.60	0.245
7	73	18,735.5	18,450.2	0.60	0.300

Note: Q = number of classes; no. par. = number of parameters in the model
[a]Prop. red in L^2 = proportional reduction in L^2 with respect to 1-class OR-LCM

attributes (Reise and Waller 2009). To generate realistic item responses, we used the parametric GRM (Samejima 1969) and parameter values from the social inhibition scale of the DS14 (Denollet 2005), which were obtained in a sample of cardiac patients (Emons et al. 2012, p. 215).

3.2 *Fitting the Model and Model-Fit Assessment*

Nine OR-LCMs were fitted to the simulated data set, starting with the one-class model and adding one latent class at the time; thus the number of classes (Q) ranged from 1 through 9. Table 1 shows for $Q = 1$–7 the BIC and AIC3, proportional reduction in the likelihood statistic (L^2), and the proportion of classification errors (Vermunt and Magidson 2005). The BIC and AIC3 both supported the 5-class OR-LCM. Considerable L^2 reductions were found going from $Q = 1$ to 5 classes (up to 59%), and then the reduction leveled off. To find further support for the final model, we inspected the absolute fit in three ways.

Pairwise Item-Fit Analysis. First, we inspected model fit at the item-pair level using the residual associations between all item pairs. The pairwise residual between two items is defined as the difference between the expected (or model-based reproduced) association under the postulated OR-LCM and the observed pairwise association in the sample. If the model fits the data well, bivariate residuals should be close to 0. To stay within the NIRT framework, we used scalability coefficient H_{ij} as the measure of association between two items i and j (Sijtsma and Molenaar 2002, Chap. 7), but other (ordinal) association measures such as Spearman's ρ and Kendall's τ can be applied as well. The reproduced coefficient H_{ij} was obtained from the weighted sum of the class-specific bivariate item-score distributions, where the weights are the class sizes $P(\theta_q)$. The class-specific bivariate distributions

Table 2 Unstandardized (below diagonal) and standardized (above diagonal) residual H_{ij} coefficients under the 4-class OR-LCM

	1	2	3	4	5	6	7
1		0.79	1.13	0.26	0.15	1.15	1.05
2	0.02		0.81	0.52	1.45	−0.67	−1.76
3	0.03	0.02		1.27	0.52	0.42	0.63
4	0.01	0.01	0.03		−0.07	1.08	0.72
5	0.00	0.04	0.01	0.00		0.10	1.05
6	0.03	−0.02	0.01	0.03	0.00		1.50
7	0.02	−0.02	0.01	0.05	0.02	0.03	

followed directly from the local independence assumption. Sample values for H_{ij} and corresponding standard errors were obtained using the R-package Mokken (Van der Ark 2012). The residual association was the expected H_{ij} value minus the observed H_{ij} value. Dividing the residuals by the standard error gave the standardized residuals. Absolute standardized values larger than 1.96 indicated significant differences between the model-based expected value and the observed value (two-tailed test, 5% significance level).

Inspection of the bivariate residuals for each of the nine fitted OR-LCMs suggested that four classes were enough to accurately describe pairwise associations. The residual H_{ij} coefficients under the 4-class OR-LCM are given in Table 2 (unstandardized values are displayed below diagonal, standardized above the diagonal). All values were close to 0 and none of the residuals was significant at the 5% level, which indicates adequate fit.

Item-Level Fit Analysis. Second, we graphically compared discrepancies between observed and model-based expected ISFs to assess absolute fit at the item level (i.e., the fitted model serves as the null hypothesis). However, when ISF are obtained using the estimated latent group membership, the uncertainty with which persons are assigned to latent classes must be taken into account (e.g., Stone 2003). Ignoring this uncertainty may produce spurious discrepancies and, as a result, lead to false rejection of items (Drasgow et al. 1995). In the framework of OR-LCMs, uncertainty in the ability estimates is reflected in the posterior distribution of class membership. This posterior distribution can be estimated from the sample using the cross-tabulation of modal and (posterior) probabilistic class assignments (Vermunt and Magidson 2005, p. 63). Table 3 gives an example for the 5-class OR-LCM; the diagonal elements represent the expected frequencies of correct classifications, the off-diagonal elements represent the expected classification errors.

The estimated ISFs under the postulated Q-class OR-LCM were obtained as follows. Let $f(s|\theta_q)$ be the posterior distribution of estimated class membership s ($s = 1, \ldots, Q$) for the population of persons in latent class q. The sample estimate of distribution $f(s|\theta_q)$ is given by the row percentages of the probabilistic (rows) by modal (columns) classification table. The estimated ISF under the fitted OR-LCM is given by

$$\widehat{E}\left(X_j\middle|\theta_q\right) = \sum_{s=1}^{Q}\left[f\left(s\middle|\theta_q\right)\sum_{x_j=1}^{M}\pi_{jx_j}\left(\theta_q = s\right)\right],\quad (q = 1,\ldots,Q).$$

Table 3 Cross-classification of modal and probabilistic latent class assignments of persons for the 5-class OR-LMC

	Modal assignment					
Prob. assign.	Class 1	Class 2	Class 3	Class 4	Class 5	Total
Class 1	154.194	20.984	0.011	0.000	0.000	175.188
Class 2	19.787	232.884	29.652	0.033	0.000	282.356
Class 3	0.019	31.082	265.497	21.893	0.025	318.516
Class 4	0.000	0.050	27.816	128.167	7.855	163.888
Class 5	0.000	0.000	0.024	8.907	51.120	60.052
Total	174.000	285.000	323.000	159.000	59.000	1,000.000

Note: Prob. assign. = probabilistic assignment

Following Drasgow et al. (1995) observed ISFs were estimated as follows. Let $\mathbf{x}_v^{-j}$ be the item-score vector of person v (=1,...,N) without item j and x_{vj} the person's response to item j. Furthermore, let $P(\theta_q = s|\mathbf{x}_v^{-j})$ be the corresponding posterior probability of being a member of class s for person v, given observed $\mathbf{x}_v^{-j}$. The observed ISF equals

$$O\left(X_j\middle|\theta_q\right) = \frac{\sum_{v=1}^{N} x_{vj} P\left(\theta_q = s\middle|\mathbf{x}_v^{-j}\right)}{\sum_{v=1}^{N} P\left(\theta_q = s\middle|\mathbf{x}_v^{-j}\right)}, \qquad (q = 1,\ldots,Q).$$

Substantial differences between $\widehat{E}\left(X_j\middle|\theta_q\right)$ and $O(X_j|\theta_q)$ indicated item misfit. Figure 1 gives the item-fit plots for two items for the 7-class OR-LCM, showing small differences between the observed (solid) and estimated (dashed line) ISFs. This result indicates adequate fit. Similar item-fit results were found for all other items.

Test-Level Fit Analysis. Third, we graphically inspected discrepancies between the observed and the expected total-score distribution under the fitted models. The expected total-score distributions were obtained as follows. Let X_+ be the total-score variable with realizations X_+ (=0, ..., JM), and let $f_{\widehat{E}}\left(X_+\middle|\theta_q\right)$ be the expected discrete sum-score distribution in class q under the postulated OR-LCM. For polytomous items, $f_{\widehat{E}}\left(X_+\middle|\theta_q\right)$ is a generalized multinomial distribution (e.g., Thissen et al. 1995). The model-based expected (marginal) sum-score distribution equals $f_{\widehat{E}}(X_+) = \sum_{q=1}^{Q} P(\theta_q) f\left(X_+\middle|\theta_q\right)$.

Figure 2 shows the observed (dots) and the expected distributions (solid line) for the 5-class (upper panel) and 7-class (lower panel) OR-LCM. Under the 5-class model, the function $f_{\widehat{E}}(X_+)$ already approximated the observed X_+ distribution quite well, but showed some irregularities at the lower range of the X_+ scale. The 7-class OR-LCM produced an $f_{\widehat{E}}(X_+)$ that runs more smoothly through the observed distribution at lower X_+ ranges. To evaluate the accuracy of $f_{\widehat{E}}(X_+)$, we also imposed the true X_+ distribution (dashed line) that results from the θ values

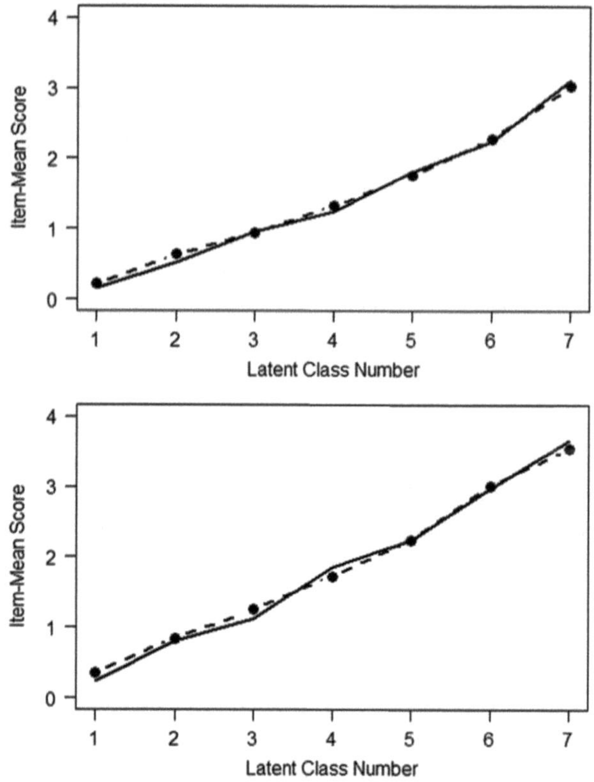

Fig. 1 Expected (*dashed lines*) and observed (*solid lines*) ISF for item 1 (*upper panel*) and item 5 (*lower panel*), under the 7-class OR-LCM

used for generating the data. It can be seen that the estimate $f_{\widehat{E}}(X_+)$ was quite accurate. Bootstrapped confidence envelopes can be added to reflect sampling error and to test the significance of sample discrepancies (e.g., De Cock et al. 2011).

3.3 Psychometric Implications: Classification Consistency

Our simulated data example was based on the social inhibition scale of the DS14. In practice, a cut-off value of $X_+ = 10$ is used for this scale to identify persons who have a so-called *distressed personality*, referred to as Type D personality (Denollet 2005). If these data were used to evaluate the suitability of the scale for assessing Type D personality, the question is how consistent are persons classified into one of two categories of distressed personality. This question is addressed by means of two *CC* indices. Index $CC_{90}(+)$ denotes the proportion of persons with a true score (i.e., the error-free score) at or above the cut-off point for whom the certainty level exceeds 0.90. Likewise, index $CC_{90}(-)$ denotes the proportion of persons with a true score below the cut-off point for whom the certainty level exceeds 0.90. Similar expressions are used for *CC*s at the 0.70 certainty level. We may add that

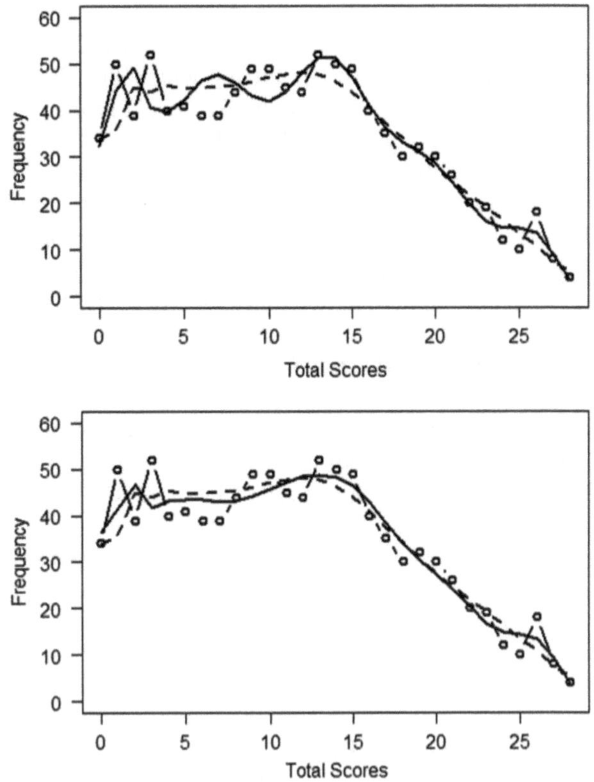

Fig. 2 Observed (*dotted lines*), the OR-LCM estimated total-score distribution (*solid lines*), and true-score (*dashed line*) frequency distribution, for the 5-class model (*upper panel*) and the 7-class model (*lower panel*)

indices $CC_{90}(+)$ and $CC_{90}(-)$ relate to the well-known concepts of *sensitivity* and *specificity*, respectively. In the context of screening for diseases, sensitivity indicates the proportion of patients the test correctly classifies as being ill, whereas specificity is the proportion of patient correctly classified as being healthy. The concept of classification consistency is different because it summarizes the certainty levels, which are measures of sensitivity and specificity defined at the person level. For example, a $CC_{90}(+)$ of 0.77 means that for 77% of the persons in the clinical population the sensitivity of the test is at least 0.90. Because tests can have high sensitivity, but low specificity, both aspects need to be studied separately (Kruyen et al. 2013).

To explain how *CCs* were estimated, we use some concepts from CTT. Let $f(X_+|T=t)$ denote the distribution of total score X_+ for persons whose true score (denoted T) equals t. This distribution is known as the propensity distribution (Lord and Novick 1968, pp. 29–30) and by definition its mean equals t. Because we have polytomous items, the propensity distribution is again a generalized multinomial distribution (Emons et al. 2007; Thissen et al. 1995). The area under the propensity distribution to the left or to the right of the cut-off score indicates the probability of a correct classification (certainty level) given t. For example, for persons having a true score t in excess of the clinical cut-off point 10, the certainty of a correct classification is given by $f(X_+ \geq 10|T = t)$. $CC+$ is the relative frequency of t-scores above the cut-off point for which the certainty level exceeds the desired minimum. The $CC-$ is obtained likewise for the true scores below the cut-off point, where the certainty level is defined as $(X_+ < 10|T = t)$.

From the above, it follows that for estimating the CCs we need to have the conditional item-response probabilities given t and the relative weights for each t. For practical reasons, we only considered the propensity distributions and weights at $t = 0, 1, 2 \ldots, \max(X_+)$. The true-score weights are obtained from expected total-score distribution under the postulated Q-class OR-LCM; that is, weights are given by $f_{\hat{E}}(X_+ = t)$. The item-response probabilities given t also have to be obtained from the OR-LCM. However, the OR-LCM only gives the class-specific item-response probabilities $\pi_{jx_j}(\theta_q)$ for the Q-classes, whereas we need them conditional on the true score. Therefore, we used a weighted sum of $\pi_{jx_j}(\theta_q)$ s between adjacent classes to obtain conditional response probabilities given t. This was done as follows. Let Π_q be the matrix of item-response probabilities in class q, where the rows correspond to the items and columns to the response options; that is, the mth column of the jth row gives the class-specific probability of responding in category m of item j. Furthermore, let $E(X_+|\theta_q)$ be the expected total score within class q, which follows from item-response probabilities in Π_q. We also introduce two matrices defining the item-response probabilities for $t = 0$ and $t = JM$. In particular, let Π_0 be a matrix with probabilities equal to 1 in the first column and 0s elsewhere; and Π_{Q+1} a matrix with 1s in the last column and 0s elsewhere. The expected total scores resulting from Π_0 and Π_{Q+1} are 0 and JM, respectively.

Now, suppose we want to have the estimated propensity distribution for $t = 5$. Because $E(X_+|\theta_q)$ is monotonically increasing with q, we can determine the two classes, q and w, satisfying the inequality $E(X_+|\theta_q) < 5 \leq E(X_+|\theta_w)$. The item-response probability matrix corresponding to $t = 5$, denoted $\Pi_{t=5}$, is then obtained as a weighted sum of Π_q and Π_w, where the weight is chosen such that the expected total score for the weighted matrix $\Pi_{t=5}$ equals 5. This means that persons having $t = 5$ are conceived as a mixture of classes q and s. The propensity distribution, $f(X_+|t = 5)$, results from the response probabilities defined by $\Pi_{t=5}$. This procedure was repeated for all true-score levels $t = 0, 1, 2, \ldots, T, \ldots, JM$ and the result is a set of $JM + 1$ (i.e., 29 in our example) propensity distributions.

Table 4 gives the estimated base rate and CCs for minimum certainty levels of 0.70 and 0.90, for both the 5-class and the 7-class OR-LCM. The 5-class model was included for comparison purposes. Inspection of the results showed that the 5-class and 7-class models produced slightly different results. The proportion of persons above the cut-off (i.e., base rate) is estimated to be 0.57. About 70% of all persons would be consistently classified with a certainty of at least 0.90, and 90% with a certainty of at least 0.70. Comparison of the CC estimates with those obtained from the true generating θ values showed that OR-LCM based CC estimates were quite accurate.

Table 4 True and estimated base rate and classification consistency at certainty levels of 0.70 and 0.90 for the 5-class and 7-class OR-LCM

Statistic	True value	OR-LCM estimate	
		$Q=5$	$Q=7$
Base rate (≥ 10)	0.55	0.57	0.57
$CC_{70}(-)$	0.87	0.90	0.90
$CC_{70}(+)$	0.88	0.84	0.92
$CC_{90}(-)$	0.64	0.69	0.70
$CC_{90}(+)$	0.68	0.67	0.67

4 Discussion

This chapter elaborated on the use of OR-LCMs for analyzing ordinal measurement properties of total scores obtained from Likert-type items. An important practical issue is model fit, which may be acceptable at the item-pair level, but may be inadequate at the item or total-score level. For example, we found that few classes were enough to adequately model the item-pair associations, even though the data were generated for a continuous latent variable. However, additional classes were needed to obtain a model that was able to reproduce the total-score distribution sufficiently precise. Therefore, to obtain sound inferences from the fitted OR-LCM, absolute model fit needs to be examined at the different levels in the data. In real applications, the level at which model fit has to be examined depends on the specific goals for which the model is used. For example, when the model is used to study dimensionality and scalability of a set of items, all one need is a model that can accurately describe the bivariate item associations. For this purpose, absolute model-fit is established if the model is able to adequately reproduce the bivariate inter-item associations. A few classes may then be sufficient (see also Van Onna 2004) even when the number of classes is too small to adequately reproduce the data structure at other levels, such as the total-score distribution. However, if the model is used to evaluate reliability and classification consistency, absolute fit at the level of the items and total scores has to be established as well. This may result in more classes than needed in applications where only the fit at the level of item pairs is concerned. We may add that if misfit persists after continuing adding classes, it means that one or more NIRT assumptions are violated. This may be a reason to remove some of the items or to split the scale into subscales.

The OR-LCM used in this study assumed unidimensionality, which means that the total score X_+ meaningfully orders persons on one underlying dimension. Although unidimensional measurement is worth pursuing, clinical scales with proven predictive validity often measure a hierarchically structured attribute that subsumes a mixture of related lower-level attributes (Gustafsson and Åberg-Bengtsson 2010). As a result, clinical scales are rarely strictly unidimensional. The pattern of local dependencies as shown in the residual H_{ij} matrix may reveal the presence of lower-level facets within an attribute hierarchy. However, as long as the local dependencies are within certain limits (say, $|H_{ij}| < 0.05$) and acceptable fit is found at the item and total-score level, one can have enough confidence in the total scores as unidimensional ordinal measures of the general attribute. Future research may focus on the use of OR-LCM as an exploratory tool for assessing an attribute hierarchy, for example, as a precursor to a confirmatory bifactor analysis (Reise et al. 2007).

To evaluate a scale's reliability, researchers commonly rely on group-level estimates such as coefficient alpha. A common rule is that for individual decision-making, reliability at least needs to be 0.7 (low-stakes decisions) or 0.9 (high-stakes decisions). However, one cannot infer from total-score reliability statistics whether individual measurements are precise enough for the application envisaged (Sijtsma 2009). In this chapter, we used OR-LCM for modeling measurement errors at the person level by deriving propensity distributions conditional on integer-valued true scores. This approach facilitates several conceptualizations of local measurement precision, including conditional standard errors of measurement (Feldt et al. 1985) for single and difference scores. Future research may further explore the usefulness of OR-LCMs for analyzing measurement precision at the individual level.

References

Crocker, L., & Algina, J. (1986). *Introduction to classical and modern test theory*. New York: Holt, Rinehart & Winston.

Croon, M. A. (1991). Investigating Mokken scalability of dichotomous items by means of ordinal latent class models. *British Journal of Mathematical and Statistical Psychology, 44*, 315–331.

De Cock, E. S. A., Emons, W. H. M., Nefs, G., Pop, V. J. M., & Pouwer, F. (2011). Dimensionality and scale properties of the Edinburgh Depression Scale (EDS) in patients with Type 2 diabetes mellitus: the DiaDDzoB study. *BMC Psychiatry, 11*, 141.

Denollet, J. (2005). DS14: Standard assessment of negative affectivity, social inhibition, and Type D personality. *Psychosomatic Medicine, 67*, 89–97.

Drasgow, F., Levine, M. V., Tsien, S., Williams, B., & Mead, A. (1995). Fitting polychotomous item response theory models to multiple choice tests. *Applied Psychological Measurement, 19*, 143–165.

Emons, W. H. M., Mols, F., Pelle, A. J. M., Smolderen, K. G. E., & Denollet, J. (2012). Type D assessment in patients with chronic heart failure and peripheral arterial disease: Evaluation of the Experimental DS(3) Scale using Item Response Theory. *Journal of Personality Assessment, 94*, 210–219.

Emons, W. H. M., Sijtsma, K., & Meijer, R. R. (2007). On the consistency of individual classification using short scales. *Psychological Methods, 12*, 105–120.

Feldt, L. S., Steffen, M., & Gupta, N. C. (1985). A comparison of five methods for estimating the standard error of measurement at specific score levels. *Applied Psychological Measurement, 4*, 351–361.

Gustafsson, J.-E., & Åberg-Bengtsson, L. (2010). Unidimensionality and interpretability of psychological instruments. In S. S. Embretson (Ed.), *Measuring psychological constructs: Advances in model-based approaches*. Washington, DC: American Psychological Association.

Hemker, B. T., Sijtsma, K., Molenaar, I. W., & Junker, B. W. (1997). Stochastic ordering using the latent trait and the sum score in polytomous IRT models. *Psychometrika, 62*, 331–347.

Kruyen, P. M., Emons, W. H. M., & Sijtsma, K. (2013). Shortening the S-STAI: Consequences for research and clinical practice. *Journal of Psychosomatic Research, 75*, 167–172.

Lambert, M. J., & Finch, A. E. (1999). *The Outcome Questionnaire*. Mahwah, NJ: Lawrence Erlbaum Associates Publishers.

Lord, F. M., & Novick, M. R. (1968). *Statistical theories of mental test scores*. Reading, MA: Addison-Wesley.
Meijer, R. R., & Baneke, J. J. (2004). Analyzing psychopathology items: A case for nonparametric item response theory modeling. *Psychological Methods, 9*, 354–368.
Ramsay, J. O. (1991). Kernel smoothing approaches to nonparametric item characteristic curve estimation. *Psychometrika, 56*, 611–630.
Reise, S. P., Morizot, J., & Hays, R. D. (2007). The role of the bifactor model in resolving dimensionality issues in health outcomes measures. *Quality of Life Research, 16*, 19–31.
Reise, S. P., & Waller, N. G. (2009). Item response theory and clinical measurement. *Annual Review of Clinical Psychology, 5*, 27–48.
Samejima, F. (1969). Estimation of latent ability using a response pattern of graded scores. In *Psychometric monograph* (Vol. 17). Richmond, VA: Psychometric Society. Retrieved from: http://www.psychometrika.org/journal/online/MN17.pdf
Sijtsma, K. (2005). Nonparametric item response theory models. *Encyclopedia of Social Measurement, 2*, 875–882.
Sijtsma, K. (2009). Correcting fallacies in validity, reliability and classification. *International Journal of Testing, 9*, 167–194.
Sijtsma, K., Emons, W. H. M., Bouwmeester, S., Nyklicek, I., & Roorda, L. D. (2008). Nonparametric IRT analysis of quality of life scales and its application to the World Health Organization Quality of Life Scale (WHOQoL-Bref). *Quality of Life Research, 17*, 275–290.
Sijtsma, K., & Molenaar, I. W. (2002). *Introduction to nonparametric item response theory*. Thousand Oaks, CA: Sage.
Stone, C. A. (2003). Empirical power and Type I error rates for an IRT fit statistic that considers the precision of ability estimates. *Educational and Psychological Measurement, 63*, 566–583.
Thissen, D., Pommerich, M., Billeau, K., & Williams, V. S. L. (1995). Item response theory for scores on test including polytomous items with ordered responses. *Applied Psychological Measurement, 19*, 39–49.
Van der Ark, L. A. (2005). Stochastic ordering of the latent trait by the sum score under various polytomous IRT models. *Psychometrika, 70*, 283–304.
Van der Ark, L. A. (2012). New Developments in Mokken Scale analysis in R. *Journal of Statistical Software*, *48*. Retrieved from http://www.jstatsoft.org/
Van Onna, M. J. H. (2004). *Ordered latent class models in nonparametric item response theory* (Doctoral dissertation). University of Groningen, The Netherlands. Retrieved from http://dissertations.ub.rug.nl/faculties/gmw/2004/m.j.h.van.onna/
Vermunt, J. K. (2001). The use of restricted latent class models for defining and testing nonparametric and parametric IRT models. *Applied Psychological Measurement, 25*, 283–294.
Vermunt, J. K., & Magidson, J. (2005). *Technical guide for LatentGOLD 4.5. Basic and advanced.* Belmont, MA: Statistical Innovations.
Waller, N. G., & Reise, S. P. (2010). Measuring psychopathology with nonstandard item-response theory models: Fitting the four-parameter model to the Minnesota Multiphasic Personality Inventory. In S. E. Embretson (Ed.), *Measuring psychological constructs: Advances in model-based approaches* (pp. 147–173). Washington, DC: American Psychological Association.
Zigmond, A. S., & Snaith, R. P. (1983). The Hospital Anxiety and Depression Scale. *Acta Psychiatrica Scandinavica, 67*, 361–370.

Differentiating Response Styles and Construct-Related Responses: A New IRT Approach Using Bifactor and Second-Order Models

Matthias von Davier and Lale Khorramdel

1 Introduction

The problem of construct-irrelevant preferences for response options or response styles (RS) in psychological assessment when rating scales or Likert scales are used has been known for a long time (Nunnally 1967). RS are defined as respondents' tendencies to respond in a systematic way independently of the item content (Paulhus 1991; Rost 2004) and are assumed to be largely stable individual characteristics not only within single questionnaire administrations (Nunnally 1967; Javaras and Ripley 2007) but across longitudinal survey data (Weijters et al. 2010). If respondents show certain RS when responding to a questionnaire, their test score does not reflect a fair measurement of personality. Thus, the presupposition that respondents' answers are based on the substantive meaning of the items is not met (Harzing 2006).

There are different kinds of response styles depending on the number of response categories. The current paper addresses the problem of the extreme response style (ERS) and the midpoint response style (MRS) using a five-point rating scale. ERS describes the tendency to choose the extreme response categories (in a rating scale with more than three response options) but not as expression of a very high or low intensity of the measured construct. MRS describes the tendency to choose the midpoint of the scale, if a middle category is provided, in order to avoid decisions rather than as an expression of an average degree of the variable being measured.

M. von Davier (✉)
Division of Research and Development, Educational Testing Service,
Rosedale Road, T-198, Princeton, NJ 08541, USA
e-mail: mvondavier@ets.org

L. Khorramdel
Division of Psychological Assessment and Applied Psychometrics, Faculty of Psychology,
University of Vienna, Liebiggasse 5, Vienna 1010, Austria
e-mail: lale.khorramdel@univie.ac.at

R.E. Millsap et al. (eds.), *New Developments in Quantitative Psychology*,
Springer Proceedings in Mathematics & Statistics 66, DOI 10.1007/978-1-4614-9348-8_30,

Response styles can affect the dimensionality of the measurement (Chun et al. 1974; Rost 2004) and the validity of survey data (Baumgartner and Steenkamp 2001; De Jong et al. 2008; Dolnicar and Grun 2009; Morren et al. 2012; Weijters et al. 2008) and thus are especially a problem in cross-cultural studies (Chun et al. 1974; Morren et al. 2012) or large-scale assessments (Buckley 2009; Bolt and Newton 2011) as differences in group means become uninterpretable (Chun et al. 1974; Harzing 2006; Morren et al. 2012).

Gender differences were found (De Jong et al. 2008; Weijters et al. 2010) as well as cultural or ethnic differences in the employment of different response styles (Bachman and O'Malley 1984; Chen et al. 1995; De Jong et al. 2008; Dolnicar and Grun 2009; Hamamura et al. 2008; Harzing 2006; Hui and Triandis 1989; Johnson et al. 2005; van Herk et al. 2004; Weijters et al. 2010). Correcting data for RS was shown to provide meaningful research and equivalent measurements with regard to cross-cultural data (Morren et al. 2012; Rammstedt et al. 2013) and other group comparisons such as with respondents with different educational levels (Rammstedt et al. 2010).

Reducing response styles in rating data by simply constraining the response categories to a dichotomous format with "agree" and "disagree" as the only response options leads to disadvantages. First, the information about the intensity of attitudes is lost. Second, a dichotomous response format was found to provoke reactance as respondents do not have the possibility to describe themselves in a sufficiently fine-grained way (resulting in atypical or arbitrary responses that do not describe the subjects' true character; Karner 2002) and might lead to higher faking tendencies or impression management (Khorramdel and Kubinger 2006).

In order to retain multicategory response formats, a variety of approaches has been developed trying to measure response styles and control for their effect. Some approaches are using simple frequency counts (e.g., the number of extreme responses to account for ERS) or the standard deviation of item scores within a respondent (Baumgartner and Steenkamp 2001; Buckley 2009). Such approaches are not as computationally intensive as more complex approaches but need heterogeneous items that are nearly uncorrelated. Such items are not always easy to find, and this may negatively influence the measurement's validity (Bolt and Newton 2011). Moreover, these approaches do not account for the influence of the substantive trait.

There is the possibility that some respondents might, for example, show a construct-unrelated ERS when choosing extreme response categories of a rating scale, while others give construct-related responses by choosing the same categories. Therefore, simple frequency counts cannot be assumed to be clear measures of response styles without looking into how differences in these individual frequencies relate to the target of measurement — the constructs of traits the questionnaire was developed to measure. Therefore, other approaches focused on item response theory (IRT), which provides the possibility to estimate item parameters (characteristics of items) and person parameters (trait level of respondents) that both can interact with response styles (Bolt and Johnson 2009; De Jong et al. 2008).

The most recent IRT approach to test and correct for response styles is proposed by Böckenholt (2012). The attempt is to separate RS from trait-related responses by decomposing the response process in ordinal rating scales into different sequential subprocesses using binary pseudo items (BPIs). This generates a set of BPI responses for each original ordinal item response.

Example for the decomposition into BPIs: A four-point rating scale, for example, (0–1–2–3) could be decomposed into BPIs which account only for the extreme responses (responses to 0 and 3 would be scored as 1, responses to 1 and 2 would be scored as 0), or into BPIs which account only for the moderate responses (responses to 1 and 2 would be scored as 1, responses to 0 and 3 would be scored as 0). Note that this is just an example to explain the decomposition in BPIs; this is not the decomposition used by Böckenholt (2012).

These single BPIs are then examined with simple-structure multidimensional IRT (MIRT) models. Thus, the observed responses in rating data can be viewed as result of multiple latent responses.

Simple-structure MIRT models actually postulate that there is a response process controlled by different latent variables at different stages that leads to the observed choices modeled as difference between respondents' ability and item difficulty. The advantage of this approach is that the hypotheses about the dimensionality of BPIs or response subprocesses can be tested. In other words, it is first tested if unidimensional RS exist in the data — that is, the score used for measuring RS is a distinct measurement for RS (items are loading on one factor only) — before data are corrected for (putative) RS. Moreover, this approach provides a data structure that is easy to handle and results in estimates of latent variables with a clear-cut interpretation.

Meisner and Böckenholt (2011) used a similar approach and decomposed responses to a questionnaire with one personality scale (personal need for structure) obtained from a six-point rating scale (coded from 0 to 5) into four response subprocesses or BPIs: one BPI type to account for clear-cut decisions (scored 1 if the categories 0, 1, 4, or 5 are chosen, 0 otherwise), two BPI types to account for the direction of the responses towards the trait (one BPI scored 1 if the category 3 is chosen, 0 or missing value otherwise; second BPI scored 1 if the category 4 or 5 is chosen, 0 or missing value otherwise), as well as one BPI type to account for extreme ratings (scored 1 if the category 0 or 5 is chosen, 0 or missing value otherwise). Then nonlinear mixed-effects IRT models (specifying generalized hierarchical models with items as fixed and respondents as random effects) were applied to the BPIs. Results showed a superior model fit of a four-dimensional IRT model (to account for the four response subprocesses: BPIs were related to four factors by type) compared to a unidimensional partial credit model (where all BPIs were related to one general factor only).

Expanding on this approach (using multiscale questionnaires), Khorramdel and von Davier (in press) investigated ERS and MRS by decomposing the data from a five-point rating scale. In contrast to Meisner and Böckenholt (2011), who investigated responses to a questionnaire with only one personality scale and multidimensional RS factors, they examined responses to a questionnaire with five personality scales with the opportunity to model unidimensional RS factors. The latter approach was compared to the approach with multidimensional RS factors and was shown to provide more detailed information about the dimensionality of RS measures. Furthermore, it could be shown that ERS and MRS measures are not always unidimensional but may be confounded with trait-related responses (c.f. Bolt and Johnson 2009; Bolt and Newton 2011; Johnson and Bolt 2010). The current paper addresses this problem by applying IRT models which allow items to have loadings on both an RS factor and a specific personality factor. These models are described in more detail below.

1.1 Aims of the Current Study

The current study addresses the conjecture that BPIs defined in the approach of Böckenholt (2012) may measure a mixture of RS and construct-related sources of variance. In a prior study Khorramdel and von Davier (in press) were able to show that simple-structure IRT models may not be sufficient to disambiguate between RS and construct-related variance. Some of the BPIs seemed to measure not only response styles but also (at least to some part) construct-relevant responses. Therefore, models are needed that allow items to measure both and enable researchers to assess the degree to which RS and trait variance mix in these binary response style indicators. In the present study, we propose using bifactor and second-order multidimensional IRT models to model RS factors if simple-structure IRT (Böckenholt 2012) and MIRT (Khorramdel and von Davier under review) approaches fail to show distinct measures of RS. A detailed description of the IRT models which were applied in the current study is given below.

We analyzed the data of two different questionnaires. Both are based on the five factor model (FFM) of personality (McCrae and Costa 1987), also called the Big Five, comprising the scales of agreeableness, emotional stability (or neuroticism), conscientiousness, extraversion, and openness. In both questionnaires, a Likert type scale with five response options was used. The rating data were decomposed into three different BPIs: one to measure ERS, one to measure MRS, and one to measure construct-related responses with regard to psychological personality constructs.

The aim is to provide an approach which enables researchers to test and correct their rating data for RS in order to obtain fair trait measures (e.g., assessments of personality). A score corrected for RS would be a score that uses only those response categories which are not influenced by response styles. In other words, only particular response categories are used to calculate the test score (after the data have been proofed to be biased by response styles).

2 Method

We applied unidimensional and multidimensional IRT (MIRT) models to the BPIs, which were constructed by decomposing the rating scale response data into multiple binary response subprocesses. Each test taker's responses are assumed to be driven by three latent variables per scale, the target of measurement (trait-related responses), the tendency to use extreme responses, and the tendency to choose the middle category (undecided responses). Because the FFM consists of five scales, there are five targets of measurement, and at a maximum twice as many variables that describe the two RS per scale. Because prior research indicates that RS are consistent behavioral patterns, we assumed for most models that ERS and MRS are best represented by a variable where each describes RS as a unidimensional factor across the five personality scales. Similar to Khorramdel and von Davier (under review), BPIs are modeled as unidimensional as well as multidimensional factors to measure ERS and MRS.

All IRT models were estimated by applying the mixture general diagnostic modeling framework (MGDM; von Davier 2008, 2010) using the software *mdltm* (von Davier 2005) for multidimensional discrete latent traits models. The software provides marginal maximum likelihood (MML) estimates obtained using customary expectation-maximization (EM) methods, with optional acceleration. It offers the possibility to estimate MIRT models based on the Rasch model and two-parameter logistic (2PL) model.

2.1 Simple-Structure Unidimensional and Multidimensional IRT Models

In a first step, we estimated simple-structure unidimensional and multidimensional IRT models which are based on the *two-parameter logistic model* (2PL model; Birnbaum 1968), a generalization of the Rasch model or one-parameter logistic (1PL) model (Rasch 1960). In contrast to the 1PL-Rasch model — which postulates that the probability for response x to item i for respondent v (or for answering towards a trait) depends on only two parameters, the item parameter β_i (difficulty of endorsement) and the person parameter θ_v (respondent's trait level) — the 2PL model postulates an additional item discrimination parameter α_i. For unidimensional scales, the model equation is defined as:

$$\mathrm{P}\ (\mathrm{x}\,|\,\theta_v, \beta_i\,, \alpha_i) = \frac{\exp(\alpha_i\,(\theta_v - \beta_i))}{1 + \exp(\alpha_i\,(\theta_v - \beta_i))} \tag{1}$$

The discrimination parameter α_i describes how well an item discriminates between examinees with different trait levels, independently of the difficulty of an item.

In MIRT models, the Rasch model or the 2PL model can be specified for multiple scales. It is assumed that the Rasch model or the 2PL model holds, with the qualifying condition that it holds with a different person parameter for each of a set of distinguishable subsets (scales) of items (von Davier et al. 2007). For the case of a multidimensional 2PL model with between-item multidimensionality (each item loads on only one scale), the probability of response x to item i (with $x = 1, \ldots, m_i$) in scale k by respondent v can be defined as:

$$\mathrm{P}\ (\mathrm{x}=1\,|\,\theta_{\mathrm{v}},\beta_i\ ,\alpha_i)=\frac{\exp\left(\alpha_i\left(x\theta_{vk}-\beta_{ix}\right)\right)}{1+\sum_{y=1}^{m_i}\exp\left(\alpha_i\left(y\theta_{vk}-\beta_{iy}\right)\right)} \tag{2}$$

2.2 *Bifactor and Second-Order Models*

In a second step, the bifactor model, which is a hierarchical IRT model, and the second-order model, which is a higher-order IRT model, were applied to the rating data. Both models account for items that are nested at more than one level. Hierarchical models with proportionality constraints on the loadings are equivalent to higher-order models (cf. Rijmen 2009, 2011; Yung et al. 1999).

In the *bifactor model* for binary data (Gibbons and Hedeker 1992), each item measures a general dimension and one out of K specific dimensions. The general dimension represents the latent variable of central interest and accounts for the covariance among all items. The specific dimensions are integrated to account for additional dependencies (unique coherency) among particular groups of items. Statistical independence is assumed between all responses that are conditionally dependent on the general dimension and the specific dimensions. The latent variables typically are assumed to be normally distributed. The model equation for binary data can be denoted as follows:

$$P\left(y\middle|\theta\right)=\prod_{i=1}^{I}P\left(y_{i(k)}\middle|\theta_g,\theta_k\right) \tag{3}$$

with y as vector of all binary scored responses, $y_{i(k)}$ as response on item i ($i = 1, \ldots, I$) in dimension k ($k = 1, \ldots, K$), θ_k as dimension-specific variable, and θ_g as general latent variable which is common to all items with $\theta = (\theta_g, \theta_1, \ldots, \theta_k, \ldots, \theta_K)$.

$\pi_i = (y_{i(k)} = 1\,|\,\theta_g, \theta_k)$ is related to a linear function of the latent variables through a (probit or logit) link function $g(\cdot)$:

$$g\left(\pi_i\right)=\alpha_{ig}\theta_g+\alpha_{ik}\theta_k+\beta_i \tag{4}$$

with β_i as intercept parameter for item i, and α_{ig} and α_{ik} as slopes or loadings of item i on the general and specific latent variables. When α_{ig} and α_{ik} are assumed to be known, a *one-parameter bifactor model* is obtained. A *three-parameter bifactor*

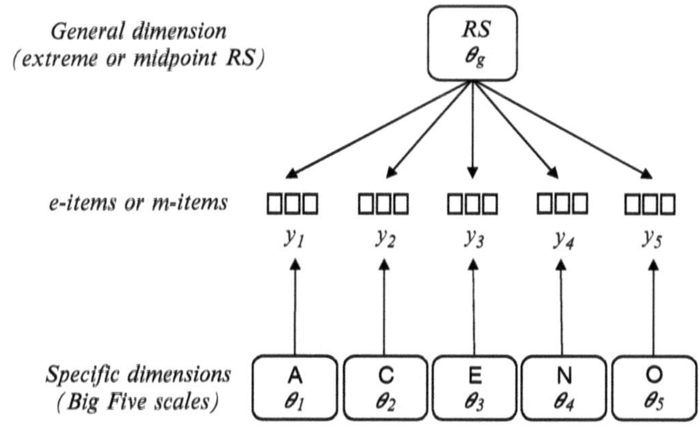

Fig. 1 Illustration of a bifactor model for *e*-items or *m*-items with regard to the Big Five scales (note: *arrows* represent conditional dependencies)

model is obtained if an additional guessing parameter is incorporated into the expression of π_i. Figure 1 shows an illustration of a bifactor model for the RS scores examined in the current study.

The *second-order model* — formally equivalent to the testlet model described by Bradlow et al. (1999) and Wainer et al. (2007) for discrete observed variables (cf. Rijmen 2009, 2011) — contains a general dimension and specific dimensions like the bifactor model. In contrast to the bifactor model, items do not directly depend on the general dimension but rather on their respective specific dimensions. The specific dimensions in turn depend on the general dimension and are assumed to be conditionally independent (the general dimension is assumed to account for all relations between the specific dimensions). Often, a standard normal distribution is assumed for the latent variables. The model equation for binary data can be denoted as follows:

$$g(\pi_i) = \alpha_{ik}\theta_k + \beta_i \tag{5}$$

$$\theta_k = \alpha_{kg}\theta_g + \xi_k \tag{6}$$

where α_{kg} accounts for the extent to which the specific dimension θ_k is explained by the general dimension θ_g, with ξ_k as the part of θ_k that is unique. All ξ_k are assumed to be statistically independent from each other and from θ_g. Equations (5) and (6) can be combined as follows:

$$g(\pi_i) = \alpha_{ik}\alpha_{kg}\theta_g + \alpha_{ik}\xi_k + \beta_i \tag{7}$$

Equation (7) shows that the second-order model is a restricted bifactor model, where the loadings on the specific dimensions are proportional to the loadings on the

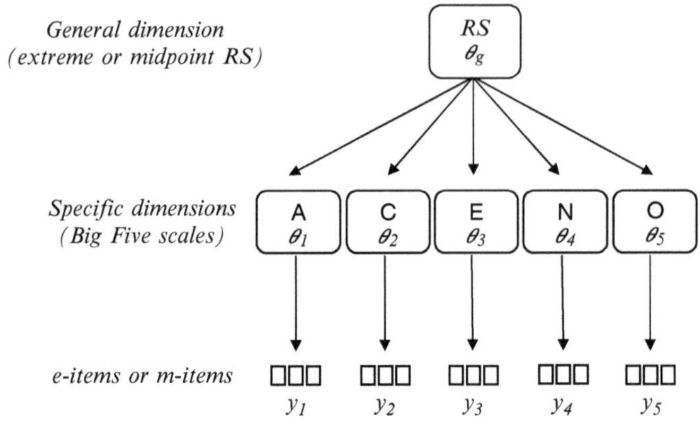

Fig. 2 Illustration of a second-order model for *e*-items or *m*-items with regard to the Big Five scales (note: *arrows* represent conditional dependencies)

general dimension within each testlet. Figure 2 shows an illustration of a second-order model for the RS scores examined in the current study.

2.3 Description of the Datasets (Samples and Instruments)

German sample and NEO-FFI instrument: The data which were used to test the current approach come from 11,697 respondents of the nonclinical German norm sample of the NEO Five-Factor Inventory (NEO-FFI; Borkenau and Ostendorf 2008). More than half of the test takers were female (64 %) and the mean age was 29.9 years. The NEO-FFI is a personality questionnaire which measures the Big Five personality dimensions and consists of 60 items, each rated on a five-point scale (1 = strong disagreement, 2 = disagreement, 3 = neutral, 4 = agreement, 5 = strong agreement). The Big Five dimensions comprise the following scales: agreeableness (e.g., "I try to be friendly towards everyone"), conscientiousness (e.g., "I always keep my things tidy and clean"), extraversion (e.g., "I love being around lots of people"), neuroticism (e.g., "I get worried easily"), and openness to experience (e.g., "I am very interested in philosophical discussions"). Each scale consists of 12 items. The Cronbach's alpha reliabilities of the NEO-FFI scales estimated using the current German dataset (based on the scores with regard to the five-point Likert scale) range from 0.70 to 0.86 (agreeableness: 0.70; conscientiousness: 0.83; extraversion: 0.79; neuroticism: 0.86; openness to experience: 0.74).

U.S. sample and International Personality Item Pool (IPIP) instrument: The findings obtained from the German NEO-FFI sample were validated on the sample used in the study of Khorramdel and von Davier (in press). The data come from 2,026 U.S. students with different ethnical background, who responded to an FFM questionnaire based on the IPIP (Goldberg et al. 2006) which, similar to the NEO-

FFI, measures the Big Five personality dimensions. More than half of the sample consists of females (60.6 %), and the mean age is 22.58 years. The IPIP consists of 50 items, each rated on a five-point Likert-type scale (1 = very inaccurate, 2 = moderately inaccurate, 3 = neither inaccurate nor accurate, 4 = moderately accurate, 5 = very accurate) and measures the dimensions of agreeableness (e.g., "I am not interested in other people's problems"), conscientiousness (e.g., "I pay attention to details"), extraversion (e.g., "I feel comfortable around people"), emotional stability (e.g., "I get stressed out easily"), and intellect-imagination (e.g., "I am full of ideas"), each with ten items. The Cronbach's alpha reliabilities of the IPIP scales were estimated using the current U.S. dataset range from 0.77 to 0.86 (agreeableness: 0.79; conscientiousness: 0.79; extraversion: 0.86; emotional stability: 0.84; intellect/imagination: 0.77). The items are publicly available at the IPIP website (http://ipip.ori.org/ipip/).

2.4 *Procedure and Design (BPIs)*

The data were prepared in a way that missing responses were coded with the number 9, and negatively worded items were recoded (27 items) so that endorsement on the recoded negative items and the positively phrased items all indicate higher levels of the trait. Then the five-category responses to the items were decomposed based on a decision tree (see Fig. 3) that assumes three sequential response subprocesses similar to Khorramdel and von Davier (in press): (1) the first response process constitutes the decision if a response towards the trait, positive or negative, will be given (clear-cut decision) or if the respondent is undecided and therefore chooses the scale midpoint; (2) the second response process, in the case of a clear-cut decision, constitutes the decision if there is a positive or negative response; (3) the third response process accounts for the intensity of the decision made in the second response process (extreme versus nonextreme trait loading).

Based on this multinomial processing tree, every questionnaire item (of the NEO-FFI and IPIP) was recoded into three different kinds of BPIs (see Table 1): one considering extreme positive and negative responses (BPI *e*), one accounting for responses to the middle category (BPI *m*), and one considering only positive (extreme and nonextreme) responses (BPI *d*).

The score composed out of BPIs *e* (*e*-score) constitutes a possible measure for ERS (where extreme positive and negative responses are weighted equally), and the score composed of BPIs *m* (*m*-score) a possible measure for MRS. Scale-wise scores based on BPIs *d* in turn aim to model the construct-relevant responses (actual trait level) for each of the five personality dimensions (or scales) that are not biased by RS tendencies. Note that the question whether *e*-items and *m*-items are measures of RS while *d*-items are construct-relevant measures can be examined using the above-mentioned IRT models. If the middle category was chosen (BPI $m = 1$), BPIs *e* and *d* receive a missing value code. If the original item response to the rating scale was missing, all BPIs (*e*, *m*, and *d*) received a missing value code.

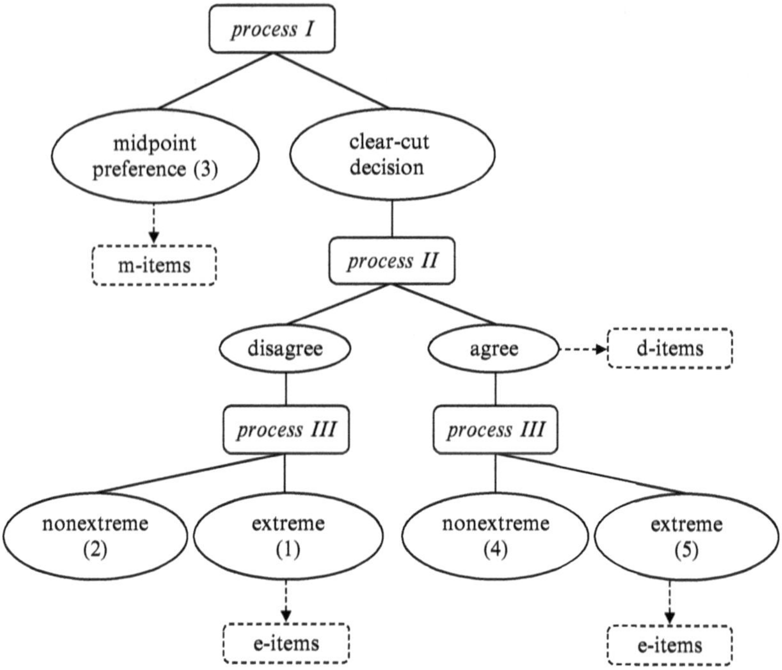

Fig. 3 Multinomial processing tree for a five-point rating scale to illustrate possible response processes according to ERS and MRS

Table 1 Example for coding binary pseudo items (BPIs)

Original NEO-FFI item (five-point rating scale)	BPI *e* (extreme responses)	BPI *m* (midpoint responses)	BPI *d* (trait responses)
1	1	0	0
2	0	0	0
3	–	1	–
4	0	0	1
5	1	0	1

The reason that responses to the middle category were coded as missing values (instead of 0) with regard to BPIs *e* and *d* is that this will produce an incomplete contingency table in which quasi-independence (Goodman 1994; Gail 1972; Fienberg 1970) may hold. This is not to say that independence will hold, but rather that, with the coding as given in Table 1, there is no implied dependency between BPIs *e*, *d*, and *m*.

In the case of a rating scale with only four response categories, the table would be a complete two-by-two table with no zero frequencies (see the two-by-two table defined by the cells with gray underground within the larger structure in Table 2).

Table 2 Incomplete contingency table for category probabilities for a five-point rating scale

		moderate	*extreme*	*midpoint*	
		0	*1*		
negative	*0*	P(1)	P(0)	0	P(p=0)
positive	*1*	P(3)	P(4)	0	P(p=1)
midpoint		0	0	P(2)	P(m=1)
		P(e=0)	P(e=1)	P(m=1)	

However, the additional fifth category together with the coding from Table 1 leads to an incomplete table with probabilities that are a priori zero (as, for example, it is not possible to observe both an extreme response and a midpoint response when using this coding).

As a consequence, the cells in this contingency table with missing responses jointly determine the BPIs e, d, and m without imposing implied dependencies. This allows us to use the three BPIs e, d, and m as indicators that relate to three different latent variables without the need to model implied dependencies (as there are none) between the three BPIs using specific (testlet) factors or similar to account for local dependencies. Therefore, a three-dimensional simple-structure MIRT model, with one dimension for each of the item types e, d, and m, can be used to analyze unidimensional scales based on this recoding of Likert type items. For multidimensional personality questionnaires such as the various Big Five instruments, a range of models will be introduced in the next section.

2.5 Hypotheses

If RS exist in the rating data, we expect that the IRT scales based on BPIs e and BPIs m, respectively, are measurements of ERS and MRS cutting across the five personality scales rather than measures that apply separately to each of the five NEO-FFI subscales. Therefore, we assume that in the case of distinct measurements of RS — that is, BPIs e and m are measuring RS only — one-dimensional simple-structure IRT models (where BPIs are modeled to load on one factor only) would fit these items across the five subscales better than five-dimensional simple-structure IRT models (where BPIs are modeled to load on the five personality dimensions). Moreover, we would expect substantial correlations between the five scales based on BPIs e and BPIs m, indicating high consistency across the scales.

However, if this is not the case, as items have loadings on both RS and the five personality dimensions, we assume that a bifactor IRT model or a higher-order IRT model can indicate whether BPIs e and BPIs m are indicators of either RS or personality dimensions. The corresponding RS would then be defined as the general factor and the five personality dimensions as specific factors. In the case of items with higher loadings on RS, most variance should be explained by the general (RS) factor. In the case of items with higher loadings on their respective specific factors (Big Five dimensions), the general factor should explain less variance than each of the specific factors.

Moreover, if BPIs *e* and BPIs *m* are indicators of RS (shown by simple-structure models or hierarchical/higher-order models), the binary *d*-based scores which are (almost) not affected by ERS and MRS should be a better measurement of the five personality dimensions than the original score using all five response categories. More specifically, we assume that correlations between the five scales based on BPIs *d* should be lower compared to scale intercorrelations based on the original score. However, if it turns out that BPIs *d* are better fitted by a five-dimensional than a one-dimensional simple-structure model, this would show that the five subscales based on BPIs *d* are an adequate measurement for the five personality dimensions.

3 Results

To investigate whether BPIs *e* (extreme responses) and BPIs *m* (midpoint responses) are measurements of RS, and whether BPIs *d* are rather a measurement of the Big Five personality dimensions, we estimated the following IRT models using the *NEO-FFI dataset* (*German sample*):

1. Simple-structure IRT and MIRT models with either unidimensional or multidimensional RS factors (cf. Khorramdel and von Davier in press):
   (a) First, three-dimensional, five-dimensional, and seven-dimensional IRT models with multidimensional RS factors were compared to one another: a three-dimensional model was calculated to examine the three different kinds of response processes or scores (*e*-items were assigned to one factor of ERS, *m*-items were assigned to one factor of MRS, and *d*-items were assigned to one factor); a five-dimensional model was calculated to account for the Big Five dimensions (all BPI types were assigned to the five personality factors); a seven-dimensional model was calculated to account for the Big Five dimensions, as well as for ERS and MRS (*e*-items were assigned to one factor of ERS, *m*-items were assigned to one factor of MRS, and *d*-items were assigned to the five personality factors).
   (b) Second, one-dimensional, and five-dimensional IRT models with unidimensional RS factors were estimated separately for each BPI type and compared to one another: In the one-dimensional model, BPIs were assigned to one factor only, while in the five-dimensional models, BPIs were assigned to the five personality factors.
2. Moreover, bifactor models and second-order models with unidimensional RS factors were estimated separately for each BPI type: these models were calculated to account for items with loadings on ERS or MRS as well as on one of the

Big Five personality dimensions. In both models, the Big Five dimensions were defined as specific factors, while ERS and MRS were defined as general factor. All BPIs were assigned to one general factor (ERS according to *e*-items and MRS according to *m*-items) as well as to their respective specific factors so that every item had two loadings.

3. Finally, we show how to correct the data for RS to obtain fair scores for the five personality dimensions: BPIs *d* were scored by omitting midpoint and extreme negative responses, and by using equally weighted extreme and nonextreme positive responses (both responses were coded with 1). The dimensionality of these BPIs was tested by comparing a five-dimensional (simple structure) model (all BPIs were assigned to the five personality factors, respectively) to a one-dimensional model (all BPIs were assigned to one factor only). Moreover, a bifactor and second-order model were estimated as well and compared to the five-dimensional model.

For model evaluation, the Akaike Information Criterion (AIC; Akaike 1974) and the Bayesian Information Criterion (BIC; Schwarz 1978) were used. Both AIC and BIC use the maximum likelihood value (L) of a model, the number of estimated model parameters (k), and the sample size. While the number of model parameters in the AIC is weighted with 2 ($\text{AIC} = -2\log L + 2k$), the BIC uses the logarithm of the sample size (N) as weight ($\text{BIC} = -2\log L + (\log N)k$) thus penalizing overparameterization more than the AIC as soon as $\text{Log(N)} > 2$.

3.1 Simple-Structure IRT and MIRT Models

3.1.1 IRT Models with Multidimensional RS Factors

To examine if there are response styles in the rating data which can be differentiated from personality traits, we estimated three-dimensional, five-dimensional, and seven-dimensional IRT models (all based on the 2PL model) and compared them to one another. We assigned BPIs by type (*e*, *m*, *d*) to the dimensions in the three-dimensional model, while in the five-dimensional model, all BPI types were assigned to the five personality factors. For the seven-dimensional model, we assigned BPIs of type *d* to the five personality traits, but BPIs *e* and *m* to a sixth and seventh (RS) factor, respectively.

Results show that the seven-dimensional model fits the data best. While the three-dimensional model (AIC = 257,970.67; BIC = 259,671.66) fits the data better than the five-dimensional model (AIC = 265,681.48; BIC = 267,421.77), the seven-dimensional model (AIC = 253,446.90; BIC = 255,209.64) fits the data better than the three-dimensional model. Thus, it can be assumed that BPIs *d* are measuring the five personality dimensions, and that BPIs *e* and *m* are measuring ERS and MRS. Detailed results are given in Table 3.

Table 3 Results of the three-dimensional, five-dimensional, and seven-dimensional simple-structure IRT models with multidimensional RS factors, including all BPI types (180 items in total) — *NEO-FFI dataset* (*German sample*)

All five scales, items: *e*, *d*, *m*	Seven-dimensional model	Five-dimensional model	Three-dimensional model
AIC index	253,446.90	265,681.48	257,970.67
BIC index	255,209.64	267,421.77	259,671.66
Log-penalty (model based, per item)	0.499	0.523	0.508

3.1.2 IRT Models with Unidimensional RS Factors

As the analysis with multidimensional RS factors shows that RS can be found in the decomposed rating data, further analysis at the BPI level with unidimensional RS factors was computed. Khorramdel and von Davier (in press) showed that analysis with unidimensional RS factors and multidimensional trait factors provide more information about the dimensionality of RS, and thus, provide more information with regard to the correction for RS (or finding an optimal trait score). Therefore, we estimated one-dimensional IRT models where either BPIs *e* or *m* were assigned to one (RS) factor, and five-dimensional IRT models where BPIs *e* or *m* were assigned to the five personality dimensions (all models were based on the 2PL model).

Comparing the results of the one-dimensional models with those of the five-dimensional models discloses that both BPIs *e* and *m* are not unidimensional measures of RS, as the five-dimensional models (*e*-items: AIC = 546,422.36, BIC = 547,380.08; *m*-items: AIC = 663,508.70; BIC = 664,466.42) fit the data better than the one-dimensional models (*e*-items: AIC = 553,234.01, BIC = 554,132.79; *m*-items: AIC = 666,969.17; BIC = 667,867.96). Detailed model-fit statistics are given in Table 4.

Still, it cannot be assumed that BPIs *e* and *m* are pure measures of the five personality traits because the differences between the model fit indexes (AIC, BIC) of the five-dimensional and one-dimensional models are not large, and the analysis with multidimensional RS factors (including all BPI types) showed that the seven-dimensional model fitted the data better than a five-dimensional model (see Table 3). Moreover, the intercorrelations between the five personality scales based on BPIs *e* and BPIs *m* (obtained from the five-dimensional models with unidimensional RS factors) are considerably higher than the intercorrelations of the five scales based on BPIs *d* or based on the original NEO-FFI items (where all five ordinal response categories are used to score test takers' responses: 0–1–2–3–4). Table 5 shows all scale intercorrelations based on BPIs and original NEO-FFI items.

As scores with lower intercorrelations represent more suitable measures of different scales or dimensions (the lower the intercorrelations are, the more justified it is to score different test items to separate scales), it must be assumed that BPIs *e* and *m* are not suitable measures of the five personality scales. With regard to these

Table 4 Results of the one-dimensional and five-dimensional simple-structure IRT models with unidimensional RS factors, and the bifactor and second-order models separately for each BPI type (60 items each) — *NEO-FFI dataset (German sample)*

	Five-dimensional model	One-dimensional model	Bifactor model	Second-order model
All five scales, e-items				
AIC index	546,422.36	553,234.01	542,792.26	544,970.46
BIC index	547,380.08	554,132.79	544,074.13	545,920.81
Log-penalty (model based, per item)	0.488	0.494	0.484	0.486
All five scales, m-items				
AIC index	663,508.70	666,969.17	661,288.93	663,597.44
BIC index	664,466.42	667,867.96	662,570.80	664,510.96
Log-penalty (model based, per item)	0.473	0.476	0.472	0.473
All five scales, d-items				
AIC index	506,963.78	552,898.86	507,570.29	509,986.36
BIC index	507,921.50	553,797.64	508,852.16	510,899.87
Log-penalty (model based, per item)	0.452	0.493	0.453	0.455

higher-scale intercorrelations and the better fit of the seven-dimensional model, we hypothesize that the BPIs *e* and *m* do measure both RS and trait-related responses. To test if this hypothesis is true, bifactor and second-order IRT models were applied to BPIs *e* and BPIs *m*. Note that the ERS measure based on BPIs *e* and the MRS measure based on BPIs *m* also show rather high IRT-based (marginal) reliabilities (Sireci et al. 1991; Wainer et al. 2007, p. 76) obtained from the one-dimensional model: 0.851 and 0.774.

3.2 *Bifactor and Second-Order IRT Models*

To examine if BPIs *e* and *m* have loadings on RS and personality dimensions, we computed bifactor IRT models and second-order IRT models (all based on the 2PL model), which allow items to load on two dimensions at the same time. BPIs were assigned to the five personality factors and one RS factor (see an illustration in Table 6). In the bifactor model, the general dimension (ERS factor or MRS factor) reflects the covariance among items (overlap across all items), while the independent specific dimensions (five personality factors) reflect the unique coherency among particular groups of items. Items depend directly on the general dimension (see Fig. 1). The second-order model items do not depend directly on the general dimension but rather on their respective specific (conditionally independent) dimensions, and the specific dimensions in turn depend on the general dimension.

Table 5 Intercorrelations of the score distributions of the Big Five dimensions according to the five-dimensional simple-structure IRT model for BPIs *e* (extreme responses), BPIs *m* (midpoint responses), BPIs *d* (construct-related responses), and for the original NEO-FFI items (original five-point Likert scale) — *NEO-FFI dataset* (*German sample*)

	Agreeableness	Conscientiousness	Extraversion	Neuroticism
e-items (extreme)				
Agreeableness				
Conscientiousness	0.617			
Extraversion	0.618	0.540		
Neuroticism	0.590	0.571	0.601	
Openness	0.541	0.477	0.551	0.512
m-items (midpoint)				
Agreeableness				
Conscientiousness	0.428			
Extraversion	0.463	0.445		
Emotional stability	0.428	0.435	0.471	
Openness	0.322	0.280	0.331	0.337
d-items (trait)				
Agreeableness				
Conscientiousness	0.149			
Extraversion	0.198	0.197		
Neuroticism	−0.147	−0.320	−0.479	
Openness	0.057	−0.111	0.114	0.024
Original NEO-FFI items (five-point rating scale)				
Agreeableness				
Conscientiousness	0.205			
Extraversion	0.315	0.198		
Neuroticism	−0.146	−0.319	−0.516	
Openness	0.084	−0.090	0.128	0.048

The general dimension is assumed to account for all relations between the specific dimensions (see Fig. 2).

Results (see Table 4) show that a bifactor IRT model fits BPIs *e* and BPIs *m* better (*e*-items: AIC = 542,792.26, BIC = 544,074.13; *m*-items: AIC = 661,288.93, BIC = 662,570.80) than a five-dimensional simple-structure IRT model (*e*-items: AIC = 546,422.36, BIC = 547,380.08; *m*-items: AIC = 663,508.70, BIC = 664, 466.42), and better than a second-order IRT model (*e*-items: AIC = 544,970.46, BIC = 545,920.81; *m*-items: AIC = 663,597.44, BIC = 664,510.96).

Table 7 gives an overview of how much variance is explained by each factor with regard to the bifactor model and (for complete information) the second-order model. For BPIs *e*, most variance is explained by the general (ERS) factor (ERS: 0.906, agreeableness: 0.393, conscientiousness: 0.711, extraversion: 0.516, neuroticism: 0.621, openness: 0.585), indicating they are mainly indicators of ERS. However, this does not pertain for BPIs *m*: the general (MRS) factor does not explain most of the variance. The specific factors, compared to the general (MRS) factor, explain about the same amount of variance (MRS: 0.297, agreeableness: 0.250, conscientiousness:

Table 6 Example of a data matrix for a bifactor or second-order IRT model for BPIs *e* and *m*, in the case of five questionnaire items which are decomposed in 15 BPIs — NEO-FFI dataset (*German sample*)

Item	RS factor	Agreeable ness	Conscien tiousness	Extra version	Emotional stability	Intellect/ imagination
Bifactor or second-order IRT model for **e-items**						
e-1	**1**	**1**	0	0	0	0
e-2	**1**	0	**1**	0	0	0
e-3	**1**	0	0	**1**	0	0
e-4	**1**	0	0	0	**1**	0
e-5	**1**	0	0	0	0	**1**
Bifactor or second-order IRT model for **m-items**						
m-1	**1**	**1**	0	0	0	0
m-2	**1**	0	**1**	0	0	0
m-3	**1**	0	0	**1**	0	0
m-4	**1**	0	0	0	**1**	0
m-5	**1**	0	0	0	0	**1**

Table 7 Variances (SD^2) of the estimated specific factors (Big Five dimensions) and the general factor (ERS factor for *e-items*, MRS factor for *m-items*, and undefined factor for *d-items*) according to the bifactor model and the second-order model — *NEO-FFI dataset* (*German sample*)

	Agreeable ness	Conscien tiousness	Extra version	Neuroticism	Openness	ERS/MRS
Bifactor model						
e-items, SD^2	0.393	0.711	0.516	0.621	0.585	0.906
m-items, SD^2	0.25	0.381	0.305	0.315	0.467	0.297
d-items, SD^2	1.553	2.680	3.799	1.844	1.874	0.101
Second-order model						
e-items, SD^2	0.440	0.634	0.456	0.541	0.741	0.855
m-items, SD^2	0.203	0.350	0.171	0.261	0.923	0.321
d-items, SD^2	0.569	1.326	7.334	26.670	2.126	0.156

0.381, extraversion: 0.305, neuroticism: 0.315, openness: 0.467). This indicates that the *m* BPIs are less (compared to the e items) influenced by RS and are a mixed measure of RS and the five personality variables (the same picture is shown in the second-order model; see Table 7).

3.3 *Correcting the Trait Scores for RS*

Our hypothesis was that if the data include ERS and MRS BPIs *d* (only extreme and nonextreme responses, weighted equally with 1), they might be a better measurement of the five personality scales than the original scored NEO-FFI items (all five response categories are used for scoring the personality dimensions) as they are not biased by ERS and MRS. To test if this the case, we calculated the following analysis:

1. We tested if BPIs *d* are measuring five factors and not one (BPI type based) factor. Therefore, we computed a five-dimensional model (BPIs were assigned to the five personality factors) and a one-dimensional model (BPIs were assigned to one factor only) based on BPIs *d* and compared them to each other (again, models were based on the 2PL model). A bifactor model and a second-order model (based on the 2PL model) with a general factor in addition to the five trait factors were computed as well and compared to the five-dimensional model.
2. We computed intercorrelations among the five personality scales based on BPIs *d*, and compared them to the scale intercorrelations based on the original NEO-FFI items (where all five ordinal response options are scored).

Results (see Table 4) show that BPIs *d* are better fitted with the five-dimensional model (AIC = 506,963.78, BIC = 507,921.50) than the one-dimensional model (AIC = 552,898.86, BIC = 553,797.64). The five-dimensional model also fits the data better than a bifactor model (AIC = 507,570.29, BIC = 508,852.16) or a second-order model (AIC = 509,986.36, BIC = 510,899.87). According to the variances explained by each factor (see Table 7), it can be seen that the general factor in the bifactor model and second-order model, respectively, explains the least variance in the data based on BPIs *d* compared to the variances explained by the five personality factors. Hence, the dimensionality of BPIs *d* seems to apply to the five personality dimensions. In addition, the scale intercorrelations based on BPIs d are slightly lower than the scale intercorrelations based on the original NEO-FFI items (see Table 5). Overall, it can be assumed that BPIs *d* are a more appropriate measure for the five personality dimensions than the original scored NEO-FFI items, which seem to be biased by RS.

3.4 *Validation of the Current Approach on a Second Dataset*

To validate the current approach of differentiating RS from trait-related responses by applying bifactor and second-order IRT models on BPIs, we used the *IPIP dataset* (*U.S. sample*) of a prior study by Khorramdel and von Davier (in press). The results of the simple-structure IRT models with multidimensional and unidimensional RS factors are similar to the results reported for the NEO-FFI dataset. BPIs *e*, *m*, and *d* were best described by a seven-dimensional model than a three-dimensional or five-dimensional model (including all BPI types). But analysis with unidimensional RS factors could show that BPIs *e* and *m* were each better fitted with a five-dimensional model than a one-dimensional model. While a better model fit of the one-dimensional model for BPIs *e* could be obtained after exclusion of only one misfitting item (with regard to a graphical item check; cf. Khorramdel and von Davier in press), 11 of 50 items had to be excluded from the analysis in order to

Table 8 Results of the one-dimensional and five-dimensional simple-structure IRT models with unidimensional RS factors, and the bifactor and second-order models separately for BPIs *e* and *m* (50 items each) — *IPIP dataset* (*U.S. sample*)

	Five-dimensional model	One-dimensional model	Bifactor model	Second-order model
All five scales, e-items				
AIC index	81,133.78	82,521.52	80,606.16	80,814.61
BIC index	81,723. 22	83,094.13	81,414.55	81,645.46
Log-penalty (model based, per item)	0.532	0.542	0.528	0.530
All five scales, m-items				
AIC index	100,885.44	101,129.70	100,464.48	100,684.18
BIC index	101,502.96	101,702.31	101,272.87	101,520.64
Log-penalty (model based, per item)	0.497	0.498	0.495	0.496

Table 9 Variances (SD^2) of the estimated specific factors (Big Five dimensions) and the general factor (ERS factor for *e-items*, MRS factor for *m-items*) according to the bifactor model — *IPIP dataset* (*U.S. sample*)

	Agreeable ness	Conscien tiousness	Extra version	Neuroticism	Openness	ERS/MRS
Bifactor model						
e-items, SD^2	1.595	0.778	0.961	1.290	0.858	2.076
m-items, SD^2	1.441	0.504	0.682	0.675	0.886	0.977

get a slightly better model fit of the one-dimensional model for BPIs *m* (but only with regard to the BIC index; the AIC index was still showing a better fit of the five-dimensional model).

Therefore, it was assumed that BPIs (especially BPIs m) are measuring not only RS but also (in part) trait-related responses. See the detailed results of all analyses in Khorramdel and von Davier (in press) and partly in Table 8.

In the current paper, a bifactor model and a second-order model were computed to better examine the dimensionality of BPIs *e* and *m*. Again, the results are similar to those of the NEO-FFI dataset: The bifactor model fits BPIs *e* and BPIs *m* better (*e*-items: AIC = 80,606.16, BIC = 81,414.55; *m*-items: AIC = 100,464.48, BIC = 101,272.87) than the five-dimensional model (*e*-items: AIC = 81,105.88, BIC = 81,723.40; *m*-items: AIC = 100,882.03, BIC = 101,499.55) and better than the second-order model (*e*-items: AIC = 80,814.61, BIC = 81,645.46; *m*-items: AIC = 100,684.18, BIC = 101,520.64). See the detailed information about the model fits in Table 8.

Furthermore, it is shown that the general factor (ERS) with regard to the bifactor model for BPIs *e* explains more variance than each of the five personality factors, while this is not true for the general factor (MRS) with regard to BPIs *m*. The MRS factor explains the second most variance, while the factor for agreeableness explains most variance. See the variances for each factor in Table 9.

4 Discussion

This paper introduces an approach to test and correct rating data for ERS, MRS if they are not unidimensional but mixed with trait-related responses (for example, because some test takers show RS while others do not). Response styles (RS) are differentiated from trait-related responses by using multidimensional bifactor and second-order IRT models. The aim is to find measures of personality which are unaffected by RS and can provide fair comparisons with regard to individual differences. Based on an approach of Böckenholt (2012), ordinal rating data are decomposed into BPIs which represent different sequential (nested) response processes. These reflect potential cognitive thought processes used by a test taker to a rating scale category. The advantage of such BPIs is that different response processes (trait-related responses and RS) can be scored and tested separately.

In the current study, rating data from the German version of the NEO-FFI personality questionnaire (Borkenau and Ostendorf 2008) using a five-point Likert-type scale are decomposed into single response processes. According to the number of response categories (five), it is hypothesized that ERS and MRS might occur. Therefore, the data are decomposed into three different BPIs: BPIs *e* (accounting for extreme positive and negative responses), BPIs *m* (accounting for midpoint responses) and BPIs *d* (trait-related responses: equally weighted extreme and nonextreme positive responses directed towards the measured trait). To examine if the different BPIs are measures of RS (*e*-items and *m*-items) and unbiased trait-related responses (*d*-items), different unidimensional and multidimensional IRT analyses were conducted. The different BPIs were modeled as multidimensional RS factors as described by Böckenholt (2012), and as unidimensional RS factors as described by Khorramdel and von Davier (in press). In addition to simple-structure IRT models, more complex models were computed as well: bifactor and second-order IRT models, which allow items to have loadings on both RS and trait factors, and which show how much variance is explained by each factor.

4.1 The Dimensionality of ERS and MRS Measures

The analyses with multidimensional and unidimensional RS factors using simple-structure IRT models show that RS can be assumed to exist in the data, but that it cannot be differentiated from trait-related responses straightforwardly. The *e*-items and *m*-items cannot be defined as pure RS measures, nor can they be seen as pure measures of the five personality traits. They are measuring both RS and trait-related responses.

4.2 Differentiating Between Trait-Related Responses and RS

To be able to differentiate RS from construct- or trait-related responses with regard to ERS and MRS, bifactor and second-order IRT models were applied to the BPIs, which allow items to have loadings on two factors at the same time. Results show that the bifactor model fits BPIs *e* and *m* best compared to the simple-structure models and the second-order model. Hence, hypothesis that these BPIs measure RS and trait-related responses is confirmed.

Importantly, the bifactor model discloses the variances explained by each factor. Thus, it shows to which extent the data are biased by RS. While the ERS factor clearly explained more variance than each of the five personality factors, the MRS factor did not and is therefore not a distinct RS measure.

4.3 Correcting Rating Data for RS

To correct data for ERS and MRS, we used a score which does not account for midpoint or extreme negative responses, and where extreme and nonextreme positive responses are equally weighted (both responses are coded with 1) — BPIs *d*. Results of the simple-structure IRT analysis could show that the BPIs *d* were rather multidimensional (five-dimensional) personality measures than unidimensional measures. Moreover, scale intercorrelations of the personality scales based on BPIs *d* are lower than scale intercorrelations based on the original (ordinal scored) NEO-FFI items.

Furthermore, a bifactor and a second-order model for the *d*-items showed no better model fit than the simple-structure IRT model, and more variance is explained by the five personality factors than by an additional general factor with regard to the bifactor and the second-order model. Therefore, it can be assumed that the binary coded *d*-items are not biased by RS and are a more adequate measurement of the five personality dimensions than the original scored NEO-FFI items with regard to the current data.

4.4 Validation of the Current Approach (Bifactor Model)

To validate the current approach, a bifactor model was estimated for the dataset (U.S. sample) of the prior study of Khorramdel and von Davier (in press), which comes from an FFM questionnaire (IPIP) as well using a five-point Likert scale. The results reflect those of the NEO-FFI dataset: A bifactor model fits BPIs *e* and *m* better than a simple-structure IRT model, and the bifactor model also shows superior model fit compared to a second-order model. Again, the MRS measure with BPIs *m* is not distinct.

4.5 *Summary of the Findings*

In summary, we were able to show that the current approach — a combination of Böckenholt's approach (2012), the extended approach of Khorramdel and von Davier (in press), and the application of multidimensional bifactor IRT models — can be used to identify RS in rating data, to achieve a better differentiation between RS and trait-related responses, and to correct for RS in order to provide less biased personality assessments.

In both studies (NEO-FFI and IPIP datasets), ERS and MRS are not purely unidimensional as both item types seem to have additional trait loadings. But both RS measurements show high IRT-based (marginal) reliabilities (in both studies). A bifactor model that accounts for RS and trait loadings for each item shows the best model fit, and demonstrates that ERS as a general factor explains more variance than the trait measures as specific factors. Thus, our hypothesis is supported that BPIs e are a measurement for ERS rather than for the five personality dimensions.

4.6 *Limitations and Implications for Further Research*

The demonstrated results are restricted to a five-point Likert scale and to instruments which are measuring the Big Five personality dimensions. Further research is needed using other rating scales and other questionnaires. Our problem in finding a distinct measure for MRS does not imply that the use of a middle category in rating scales is without problems, or that no MRS exists in the data (the latter would require a better fit of the five-dimensional model than of the bifactor model, which was not the case). Thus, the measurement of RS with BPIs should be further investigated, especially with regard to MRS. Moreover, the investigation of other scoring methods or types of RS (e.g., acquiescence) would be interesting as well.

Acknowledgments The work reported in this paper was carried out while the second author was a visiting scholar at Educational Testing Service (ETS, Princeton). The opinions expressed in this paper are those of the authors, not of ETS. We are grateful to Peter Borkenau (Martin-Luther-University in Halle-Wittenberg, Germany) and Fritz Ostendorf (University Bielefeld, Germany), who supported our work by providing norm sample of the German version of the NEO-FFI. Our sincere thanks go to Ulf Böckenholt (Northwestern University, Kellogg School of Management, USA) for providing the idea of response process decomposition into BPIs, and to Patrick Kyllonen and Richard Roberts (Center for Academic and Workplace Readiness and Success, ETS, USA) for providing the data of the U.S. sample for the validation of the current approach.

References

Akaike, H. (1974). A new look at the statistical model identification. *IEEE Transactions on Automatic Control, 19*, 716–723.

Bachman, J. G., & O'Malley, P. M. (1984). Yea-saying, nay-saying, and going to extremes: Black–White differences in response styles. *Public Opinion Quarterly, 48*, 491–509.

Baumgartner, H., & Steenkamp, J.-B. E. M. (2001). Response styles in marketing research: A cross-national investigation. *Journal of Marketing Research, 38*, 143–156.

Birnbaum, A. (1968). Some latent trait models and their use in inferring an examinee's ability. In F. M. Lord & M. R. Novick (Eds.), *Statistical theories of mental test scores*. Reading, MA: Addison-Wesley.

Böckenholt, U. (2012). Modeling multiple response processes in judgment and choice. *Psychological Methods, 17*, 665–678.

Bolt, D. M., & Johnson, T. R. (2009). Addressing score bias and differential item functioning due to individual differences in response style. *Applied Psychological Measurement, 33*, 335–352.

Bolt, D. M., & Newton, J. R. (2011). Multiscale measurement of extreme response style. *Educational and Psychological Measurement, 71*, 814–833.

Borkenau, P. & Ostendorf, F. (2008). NEO-FFI - NEO-Fünf-Faktoren-Inventar nach Costa und McCrae [NEO-FFI -NEO-Five-Factor-Inventory following Costa and McCrae]. Handanweisung.(2. Aufl.). Göttingen: Hogrefe.

Bradlow, E. T., Wainer, H., & Wang, X. (1999). A Bayesian random effects model for testlets. *Psychometrika, 64*, 153–168.

Buckley, J. (2009, June). Cross-national response styles in international educational assessments: Evidence from PISA 2006. In *NCES conference on the Program for International Student Assessment: What we can learn from PISA*, Washington, DC. Retrieved from http://edsurveys.rti.org/PISA/

Chen, C., Lee, S. Y., & Stevenson, H. W. (1995). Response style and cross-cultural comparisons of rating scales among East Asian and North American students. *Psychological Science, 6*, 170–175.

Chun, K.-T., Campbell, J. B., & Yoo, J. H. (1974). Extreme response style in cross-cultural research: A reminder. *Journal of Cross-Cultural Psychology, 5*, 465–480.

De Jong, M. G., Steenkamp, J.-B. E. M., Fox, J.-P., & Baumgartner, H. (2008). Using item response theory to measure extreme response style in marketing research: A global investigation. *Journal of Marketing Research, 45*, 104–115.

Dolnicar, S., & Grun, B. (2009). Response style contamination of student evaluation data. *Journal of Marketing Education, 31*, 160–172.

Fienberg, S. E. (1970). Quasi-independence and maximum likelihood estimation in incomplete contingency tables. *Journal of the American Statistical Association, 65*, 1610–1616.

Gail, M. H. (1972). Mixed quasi-independent models for categorical data. *Biometrics, 28*, 703–712.

Gibbons, R. D., & Hedeker, D. (1992). Full-information item bi-factor analysis. *Psychometrika, 57*, 423–436.

Goldberg, L. R., Johnson, J. A., Eber, H. W., Hogan, R., Ashton, M. C., Cloninger, C. R., et al. (2006). The International Personality Item Pool and the future of public-domain personality measures. *Journal of Research in Personality, 40*, 84–96.

Goodman, L. A. (1994). On quasi-independence and quasi-dependence in contingency tables, with special reference to ordinal triangular contingency tables. *Journal of the American Statistical Association, 89*, 1059–1063.

Hamamura, T., Heine, S. J., & Paulhus, D. L. (2008). Cultural differences in response styles: The role of dialectical thinking. *Personality and Individual differences, 44*, 932–942.

Harzing, A.-W. (2006). Response styles in cross-national survey research: A 26-country study. *International Journal of Crosscultural Management, 6*, 243–266.

Hui, C. H., & Triandis, H. C. (1989). Effects of culture and response format on extreme response style. *Journal of Cross-Cultural Psychology, 20*, 296–309.

Javaras, K. N., & Ripley, B. D. (2007). An "unfolding" latent variable model for Likert attitude data: Drawing inferences adjusted for response style. *Journal of the American Statistical Association, 102*, 454–463.

Johnson, T. R., & Bolt, D. M. (2010). On the use of factor-analytic multinomial logit item response models to account for individual differences in response style. *Journal of Educational and Behavioral Statistics, 35*, 92–114.

Johnson, T., Kulesa, P., Cho, Y. I., & Shavitt, S. (2005). The relation between culture and response styles: Evidence from 19 countries. *Journal of Cross-Cultural Psychology, 36*, 264–277.

Karner, T. (2002). The volunteer effect of answering personality questionnaires. *Psychologische Beiträge* (latterly: *Psychological Test and Assessment Modeling*), *44*, 42–49.

Khorramdel, L., & Kubinger, K. D. (2006). The effect of speediness on personality questionnaires: An experiment on applicants within a job recruiting procedure. *Psychology Science* (latterly: *Psychological Test and Assessment Modeling*), *48*, 378–397.

Khorramdel, L., & von Davier, M. (in press). Measuring response styles across the Big Five: A multi-scale extension of an approach using multinomial processing trees. *Multivariate Behavioral Research.*

McCrae, R. R., & Costa, P. T. (1987). Validation of the five-factor model of personality across instruments and observers. *Journal of Personality and Social Psychology, 52*, 81–90.

Meisner, T., & Böckenholt, U. (2011, September 21–23). *IRT-Analyse von Traitausprägung und Antwortstilen in Ratingdaten (IRT-analysis of trait degree and response styles in rating data).* Presentation at the Fachgruppentagung Methoden & Evaluation (Conference on Methods & Evaluation), University of Bamberg.

Morren, M., Gelissen, J., & Vermunt, J. (2012). The impact of controlling for extreme responding on measurement equivalence in cross-cultural research. *Methodology, 8*, 159–170.

Nunnally, J. (1967). *Psychometric theory*. New York, NY: McGraw-Hill.

Paulhus, D. L. (1991). Measurement and control of response bias. In J. P. Robinson, P. R. Shaver, & L. S. Wrightsman (Eds.), *Measures of personality and social psychological attitudes* (pp. 17–59). San Diego, CA: Academic.

Rammstedt, B., Goldberg, L. R., & Borg, I. (2010). The measurement equivalence of big-five factor markers for persons with different levels of education. *Journal of Research in Personality, 44*, 53–61.

Rammstedt, B., Kemper, C. J., & Borg, I. (2013). Correcting Big Five personality measurements for acquiescence: An 18-country cross-cultural study. *European Journal of Personality, 27*, 71–81.

Rasch, G. (1960). *Probabilistic models for some intelligence and attainment tests*. Copenhagen: Nielsen & Lydiche (Expanded Edition, Chicago, University of Chicago Press, 1980).

Rijmen, F. (2009). *Three multidimensional models for testlet-based tests: Formal relations and an empirical comparison*. Educational Testing Service (ETS) Research Report No. RR-09-37, Princeton, NJ.

Rijmen, F. (2011). Hierarchical factor item response theory models for PIRLS: Capturing clustering effects at multiple levels. *IERI Monograph Series: Issues and Methodologies in Large-Scale Assessments, 4*, 59–74.

Rost, J. (2004). *Lehrbuch Testtheorie – Testkonstruktion [Textbook test theory – Test construction]* (2nd ed.). Bern: Huber.

Schwarz, G. (1978). Estimating the dimension of a model. *Annals of Statistics, 6*, 461–464.

Sireci, S. G., Thissen, D., & Wainer, H. (1991). On the reliability of testlet-based tests. *Journal of Educational Measurement, 28*, 237–247.

van Herk, H., Poortinga, Y. H., & Verhallen, T. M. M. (2004). Response styles in rating scales: Evidence of method bias in data from six EU countries. *Journal of Cross-Cultural Psychology, 35*, 346–360.

von Davier, M. (2005). *A general diagnostic model applied to language testing data* (Research Report No. RR-05-16). Princeton, NJ: Educational Testing Service.

von Davier, M. (2008). The mixture general diagnostic model. In G. R. Hancock & K. M. Samuelson (Eds.), *Advances in latent variable mixture models*. Charlotte, NC: Information Age Publishing.

von Davier, M. (2010). Hierarchical mixtures of diagnostic models. *Psychological Test and Assessment Modeling, 52*, 8–28.

von Davier, M., Rost, R., & Carstensen, C. H. (2007). Introduction: Extending the Rasch model. In M. von Davier & C. H. Carstensen (Eds.), *Multivariate and mixture distribution Rasch models: Extensions and applications* (pp. 1–12). New York: Springer.

Wainer, H., Bradlow, E. T., & Wang, X. (2007). *Testlet response theory and its applications*. New York, NY: Cambridge University Press.

Weijters, B., Geuens, M., & Schillewaert, N. (2010). The stability of individual response styles. *Psychological Methods, 15*, 96–110.

Weijters, B., Schillewaert, N., & Geuens, M. (2008). Assessing response styles across modes of data collection. *Journal of the Academy of Marketing Science, 36*, 409–422.

Yung, Y.-F., Thissen, D., & McLeod, L. D. (1999). On the relationship between the higher-order factor model and the hierarchical factor model. *Psychometrika, 64*, 113–128.

Gender DIF in Reading Tests: A Synthesis of Research

Hongli Li, C. Vincent Hunter, and T.C. Oshima

1 Introduction

Many studies have investigated gender differences in reading from a range of perspectives. A general trend is that female students perform slightly better in reading than male students (Chiu and McBride-Chang 2006; Mullis et al. 1993). Neuroimaging studies suggest that male and female students have different patterns of functioning activation during reading (Pugh et al. 1996; Shaywitz et al. 1995). It has also been found that male and female students use different reading strategies (Thompson 1987) and that they benefit from different types of reading instruction (Johnston et al. 2009). Another finding is that, compared with male students, female students have a more positive attitude toward reading (McKenna et al. 1995; Sainsbury and Schagen 2004). Female students have also been found to read more often than males do (Hall and Coles 1999; Mullis et al. 2007). Furthermore, it is generally reported that male students have poorer attention during literacy lessons as compared with female students (Logan et al., as cited in Logan and Johnston 2009).

However, females' advantage at the item level may or may not exist, when their overall reading ability is controlled for. This can be interpreted as whether an item shows differential item functioning (DIF) between gender groups. DIF occurs when examinees from different groups show different probabilities of success on an item after being matched on the underlying ability the test is intended to measure (Camilli and Shepard 1994). A large number of gender-related DIF studies have been conducted with reading tests. However, we do not yet have an overall picture of gender DIF in reading tests, and the reasons for the existence of gender DIF are not fully understood. In addition to simply identifying the existence and the direction

H. Li (✉) • C.V. Hunter • T.C. Oshima
Department of Educational Policy Studies, Georgia State University, P.O. Box 3977, Atlanta, GA 30303, USA
e-mail: hli24@gsu.edu; chunter1@student.gsu.edu; oshima@gsu.edu

R.E. Millsap et al. (eds.), *New Developments in Quantitative Psychology*, Springer Proceedings in Mathematics & Statistics 66, DOI 10.1007/978-1-4614-9348-8_31,

of DIF, two primary reasons often motivate researchers to explore the sources for DIF. The first is that this information would help test developers plan appropriately during test development to make tests as DIF-free and as fair as possible. The second reason is that understanding the nature of group differences (Ferne and Rupp 2007; Gierl 2005; Shimizu and Zumbo 2005) would inform instructional changes that may ameliorate the differences.

The purpose of this study is to synthesize gender-related DIF in reading tests. Two main questions are asked: First, what is the average proportion of items identified as exhibiting gender DIF in reading tests, and is there any pattern involved? Second, what characteristics are prevalent in items and in tests exhibiting gender DIF? The results of the study will provide useful information regarding gender DIF in reading tests and the possible reasons behind such differences. It is expected that these results will have important implications for the assessment and instruction of reading skills.

2 Literature Review

2.1 DIF Methods

DIF is a widely used technique for item bias detection. However, items showing DIF are not necessarily biased. Item bias occurs when examinees in one group are less likely to answer an item correctly than examinees in another group because of some characteristics of the test item or testing situation that are irrelevant to the test purpose. Therefore, DIF is regarded as a necessary but not sufficient condition for item bias (Zumbo 1999). There are two types of DIF: uniform and nonuniform (Mellenbergh 1982). Uniform DIF exists when the statistical relationship between item response and group membership is constant for all levels of the matching ability variable. An item may consistently favor one group over another regardless of the underlying ability being tested. Nonuniform DIF exists when this statistical relationship is not the same for all the matching ability levels. One group may have a relative advantage at one end of the ability level, whereas the other group may have a relative advantage at the other end of the ability level.

A variety of statistical procedures for detecting DIF have been developed. The following gives a brief overview of four major DIF methods: Mantel–Haenszel (M–H), logistic regression, item response theory-likelihood ratio (IRT-LR), and the SIBTEST method. Mantel and Haenszel (1959) developed a model of relative risk given a set of possible risk factors. This method uses a non-iterative 2×2 contingency table. The expected value of any cell in the table can be tested as a χ^2 with one degree of freedom, calculated as the ratio of a squared deviation from the expected value of the cell to its variance, where the variance is defined as the marginal totals divided by the squared total times the total minus 1. Holland and Thayer (1988) generalized the Mantel–Haenszel (M–H) χ^2 procedure to education, substituting ability level for risk factor. They noted that the overall significance test proposed by Mantel and Haenszel is a common odds ratio that exists on a scale of 0 to ∞ with 1 being the null hypothesis of no DIF. The Mantel–Haenszel method is easy to implement and detects uniform, but not nonuniform, DIF (Swaminathan and Rogers 1990).

The logistic regression method (Swaminathan and Rogers 1990) models the probability of a correct response to an item as a function of the observed total score X, group membership G, and the interaction between X and G. To test for significance of DIF, there is a natural three-step hierarchy in regard to the entry of predictor variables as follows (Zumbo 1999). In Model 1, the conditioning variable X (i.e., the total score) is entered; in Model 2, the grouping variable G is entered; and in Model 3, the interaction term $X \times G$ is entered. Changes in the -2loglikelihood among the three models are compared so as to determine the existence of uniform DIF, nonuniform DIF, and/or both (Camilli and Shepard 1994; Hambleton et al. 1991).

The IRT-LR (Thissen et al. 1988) is based on testing the differences between IRT parameters for the reference and focal groups. It begins with the null hypothesis that there is no difference in the parameters (trace lines) for each group. Using a set of anchor items combined with the studied items, the IRT-LR method fits simultaneously the focal and reference groups to each of two models: an unconstrained model, in which all parameters are allowed to vary freely, and a constrained model, in which one or more of the parameters are constrained to be equal across the study groups (Pae 2012). Typically, the -2loglikelihood values of the models are compared to determine the existence of DIF.

SIBTEST is an implementation of the standardization approach, which is built on Shealy and Stout's (1993) multi-dimensional IRT model of differential functioning. It is a non-parametric, multi-dimensional IRT model to detect DIF at both the item and the test levels. The model holds that two classes of abilities affect scores: target ability, which is intentionally measured, and nuisance determinants, which are inadvertently measured. DIF comes from nuisance determinants having different levels of prevalence in different examinee groups. SIBTEST uses an internal set of test items that do not exhibit DIF as the matching criterion. This method requires a valid sub-test score and a studied sub-test score. Simulation studies (Shealy and Stout 1993; Zhou et al. 2006) have shown that SIBTEST has acceptable levels of Type 1 errors and has power comparable to the Mantel–Haenszel test.

For a DIF evaluation method to be informative, a measure of the magnitude (effect size) of DIF present is needed (Roussos and Stout 1996). For example, the SIBTEST DIF index (β) and the M–H index (Δ) do not have a mathematical equivalence. However, they do have a very strong correlation and can be approximately equated (Roussos and Stout 1996). Based on research (Dorans and Holland 1993; Jodoin and Gierl 2001; Roussos and Stout 1996; Zwick and Ercikan 1989), ETS proposes three categories of DIF magnitude: A (trivial), B (moderate), and C (large). For the Mantel–Haenszel test, DIF magnitude belongs to category A if $\left|\widehat{\Delta}\right| < 1$, category B if $1 \le \left|\widehat{\Delta}\right| < 1.5$, and category C if $\left|\widehat{\Delta}\right| \ge 1.5$ (Zieky 1993).

For SIBTEST, DIF magnitude belongs to category A if $\left|\widehat{\beta}\right| < 0.059$, category B if $0.059 \leq \left|\widehat{\beta}\right| < 0.088$, and category C if $\left|\widehat{\beta}\right| \geq 0.088$. Furthermore, for the logistic regression method, DIF magnitude belongs to category A if $R^2 < 0.035$, category B if $0.035 \leq R^2 < 0.07$, and category C if $R^2 \geq 0.07$. However, there is no complete agreement about this category separation (Zhang and French 2010), and it is unclear how DIF magnitude determined using other methods, such as IRT-LR, may be mapped on this scheme. When two different methods are on different metrics, they do not have a formal mathematical equivalence. Therefore, this classification can be used as a guideline but not as an exact transformation equation.

2.2 Gender-Related DIF in Reading

Researchers are motivated to examine the potential sources of DIF. However, this determination is a complex process, and the results of this effort have not been fruitful (Ryan and Bachman 1992). Because of the varying contexts in which DIF appears, Birjandi and Amini (2007) speculated that "item format, content, and type, along with word or sentence-level complexities and ambiguities were recognized as possible sources of bias in items flagged as DIF" (pp. 157–158).

The first possible source of DIF investigated is item content. Many researchers have noted that items with technical and/or science content tend to favor males, whereas items with content related to the arts and humanities or nontechnical science tend to favor females (Birjandi and Amini 2007; Doolittle and Welch 1989; Durand and Park 2007; Gibson 1998; Karami 2011; Lawrence et al. 1988). Similarly, for items whose content is about a traditionally gendered activity or occupation, the ones describing male activities tend to favor males, whereas the ones describing female activities tend to favor females (Dorans and Kulick 1983; Takala and Kaftandjieva 2000). Items from informational passages favor males, whereas items from narrative passages favor females (Lawrence et al. 1988). Items dealing with the concrete and practical tend to favor males, whereas items dealing with the abstract tend to favor females (Birjandi and Amini 2007; Carlton and Harris 1992). Additionally, items requiring logical inference favor males regardless of item content (Karami 2011; Pae 2004).

Item format or type has also been frequently found to be associated with gender DIF. According to Pae (2012), cloze items that require contextual information to answer the items tend to favor males over females more frequently. Multiple-choice items (including True/False/Not Given) tend to favor males, as do sentence-completion items (Birjandi and Amini 2007; Lin and Wu 2003; Ryan and Bachman 1992). Items related to summary completion and flowcharts tend to favor females (Birjandi and Amini 2007; Ryan and Bachman 1992). Pae (2012), while seeing item type and item content as both possible sources of gender DIF, indicates that item type is a more influential source than item content.

Another possible source of DIF, reported in the literature, is the examinee's attitude toward the test item, that is, the level of comfort or interest the examinee has toward the item. The more interest that an examinee has in the content of an item the more likely he or she is to perform well on it (Chavez, as cited in Brantmeier 2001). Where males and females have a wide gap in their respective interest in the content of an item, DIF is more likely to occur (Bügel and Buunk 1996). For example, Pae (2012) found that examinee interest in the subject explains a significant proportion of male–female DIF on test items.

Among DIF studies of reading tests, many research studies focused on DIF caused by examinees' different native languages (e.g., Abbott 2007; Bae and Bachman 1998; Bügel and Buunk 1996; Kim and Jang 2009; Stephenson et al. 2004). Therefore, it is necessary to investigate the possible relationship between gender DIF and the test-takers' native languages, which can be generally grouped into native speakers of English and nonnative speakers of English. In addition, test stakes is another important test characteristic. Tests can be defined as high stakes or low stakes when an examinee's test results produce significant or nonsignificant personal consequences, respectively, for that examinee (Wise 2006). Examinees' motivation to succeed varies accordingly, with more effort expended for high stakes tests (DeMars 2000; Jacob 2002; O'Neil et al. 1995; Wise et al. 2006). Because of the potential relationship between test stakes and gender difference (DeMars 2000), test stakes will also be considered in the current study.

3 Methods

The first step of this study was to collect studies on gender DIF in reading tests. The second was to select studies that met the inclusion criteria. Then important characteristics of the items and the tests in each study were coded. Finally, the results of each study were quantitatively synthesized. The following describes the procedure in detail.

3.1 Selecting the Studies

For the purpose of the current synthesis, the following criteria were used to select the studies to be included:

1. Eligible studies must include gender-related DIF analyses of reading tests.
2. Studies must provide sufficient information regarding item-level gender-DIF.
3. Only studies published in English are included.

In addition, to avoid the file-drawer problem, which is the tendency for only studies that produce significant effects to be published formally (Glass 1976; Lipsey and Wilson 2001), we considered a very broad range of studies, such that all published and unpublished studies were considered, including journal articles, technical reports, conference presentations, conference proceedings, theses, and dissertations.

Several strategies were used to search for eligible studies. First, using the combination of the keywords "DIF" "gender" and "reading," we searched well-known online databases (e.g., ERIC, ProQuest, Dissertation Abstracts International, Social Sciences Abstracts, and the Social Sciences Citation Index). Second, we searched major journals in educational measurement and language assessment to check for potentially relevant articles. Third, we searched the web sites of major testing companies and organizations, such as ETS, ACT, the College Board, Pearson, CTB/McGraw-Hill, Cambridge Michigan Language Assessments, the National Council on Measurement in Education (NCME) annual meeting program, and the American Educational Research Association (AERA) Division D annual meeting program. Finally, we reviewed references in the eligible studies and added those that we had not already found in our original search.

A total of 180 articles and reports were collected as a result of this initial search, as described above. However, after screening each article using the inclusion criteria, we determined that only 18 articles provided sufficient and unique information for this study. Table 1 summarizes these 18 studies. One major reason for excluding some studies is that they did not report item-level DIF. For example, Geske and Ozola (2010) conducted a DIF study using the IEA PIRLS 2006 data for Latvia; however, they did not present information regarding how many or which items exhibited DIF. Other studies were excluded because they used the same dataset. For example, three articles—Karami (2011), Rezaee and Shabani (2010), and Salehi and Tayebi (2011)—studied the University of Tehran English Proficiency Test, an entrance exam for PhD programs at the University of Tehran, using the same dataset. We decided to include only one study—Salehi and Tayebi (2011)—in order to ensure that each included study would provide unique information.

3.2 Coding Procedure

We coded item-level DIF information and other important item characteristics and test characteristics. To ensure coding reliability, two of the authors first coded each study independently and then convened to discuss any discrepancies. Table 2 lists the coded variables and the coding scheme. As indicated in the previous literature review section, there is a lack of universal criteria on DIF magnitude across different methods. In addition, some studies did not provide sufficient item-level DIF magnitude information. We, therefore, used a rough dichotomous variable to indicate the presence of DIF instead of continuous coding, which would have indicated the magnitude of any DIF present. Other DIF-related information includes whether the DIF item favors males or females and whether it is uniform or nonuniform. Item type and item scoring information were also coded. The topic of the item was not coded because the studies did not provide sufficient information on this point.

Table 1 Studies included

Study name	Test studied	DIF method used
Birjandi and Amini (2007)	International English Language Testing System (IELTS)	IRT-LR
Carlton and Harris (1992)	Scholastic Aptitude Test (SAT)	Mantel–Haenszel
Dorans and Kulick (1983)	Scholastic Aptitude Test (SAT)	Standardization
Durand and Park (2007)	Kanda English Placement Test (KEPT)	Mantel–Haenszel
Gibson (1998)	Armed Services Vocational Aptitude Battery (ASVAB)	Mantel–Haenszel
Gierl (2005)	High School Exit Exam	SIBTEST
Hauser and Kingsbury (2004)	National Curriculum Test 2008	IRT-LR
Kline (2004)	Test of Workplace Essential Skills (TOWES)	IRT-LR
Lawrence et al. (1988)	Scholastic Aptitude Test (SAT)	Standardization
Lin and Wu (2003)	English Proficiency Test (EPT)	SIBTEST
Pae (2004)	Korean National Entrance Exam for Colleges and Universities[a]	IRT-LR
Pae (2012)	Korean College Scholastic Aptitude Test (KCSAT)	IRT-LR
Pae and Park (2006)	Korean College Scholastic Aptitude Test (KCSAT)	IRT-LR
Park et al. (2005)	Korean College Scholastic Aptitude Test (KCSAT)	Mantel–Haenszel
Ross and Okabe (2006)	University Admissions Test of English as a Foreign Language (EFL)	Mantel–Haenszel
Ryan and Bachman (1992)	Test of English as a Foreign Language (TOEFL)/First Certificate of English (FCE)	Mantel–Haenszel
Salehi and Tayebi (2011)	University of Tehran English Proficiency Test (UTEPT)	Logistic regression
Twist and Sainsbury (2009)	National Curriculum Test 2008	Absolute mean difference[b]

[a]The Korean National Entrance Exam for Colleges and Universities was later called the KCSAT
[b]Twist and Sainsbury conducted t-tests between males' and females' performance on each item while controlling for their overall reading performance

Three test characteristics were coded. First, test length, which was indicated by the number of items on the test. Tests were found to range from 15 items (Gibson 1998) to 80 items (Birjandi and Amini 2007). Second, test stakes were mainly judged by whether the test had significant personal effects for the examinees, such as university admission (Salehi and Tayebi 2011; Wise 2006). For example, the Korean College Scholastic Aptitude Test (KCSAT), which is used to determine whether the examinees can be admitted to a university in Korea, is a high stakes test (Pae and Park 2006). On the other hand, the Kanda English Placement Test (KEPT), which is used to place students in different classes to receive appropriate instruction, was

Table 2 Variables and coding

	Variables	Coding
Item	DIF method	1 if IRT-LR 2 if logistic regression 3 if Mantel-Haenszel 4 if SIBTEST 5 if Standardization 6 if absolute mean difference
	DIF existence	1 if the item is determined as showing DIF, 0 if not
	Uniform or nonuniform	0 if nonuniform DIF, 1 if uniform DIF
	Favoring male or female	0 if favoring male, 1 if favoring female
	Item type	0 if multiple choice, 1 if constructed response items
	Item scoring	0 if dichotomous, 1 if polytomous
Test	Test length	Number of items on the test
	Test stakes	1 if high stakes, 0 if not
	Second language test	1 if test is for English as a second language speakers, 0 if not

not regarded as a high stakes test. The third test characteristic is whether the test is designed for native English speakers or for speakers of English as a second language (ESL). A second language test, such as the First Certificate in English (FCE; Ryan and Bachman 1992), is intended to assess the reading proficiency of examinees in a language other than their native language. Reading tests such as the Scholastic Aptitude Test-Verbal (SAT-V) are intended to be primarily used with native speakers of the test language.

3.3 Analysis Procedure

The coding data from these articles (1,210 items from 18 studies) were entered into SPSS software. Descriptive statistics, such as percentages and means, were produced to provide an overall picture of the gender DIF pattern in the included studies. Then correlation and cross-tab statistics were provided in order to describe any possible relationships between gender DIF and the item and test characteristics.

4 Results

4.1 Percentage of DIF Items

As shown in Table 3, 1,210 items from 18 gender DIF studies were collected. Six different DIF methods were used in the studies, with the most common ones being IRT-LR and M–H. The percentage of DIF items was 23.3% across the 18 studies,

Table 3 DIF methods used in the studies

DIF methods	Number of studies	Number of items	Percentage of DIF items
IRT-LR	6	541	28.1
M–H	6	432	18.9
Standardization	2	125	1.6
Logistic regression	1	35	2.9
Absolute mean difference	1	34	2.9
SIBTEST	2	52	3.8
Total	18	1,210	23.3

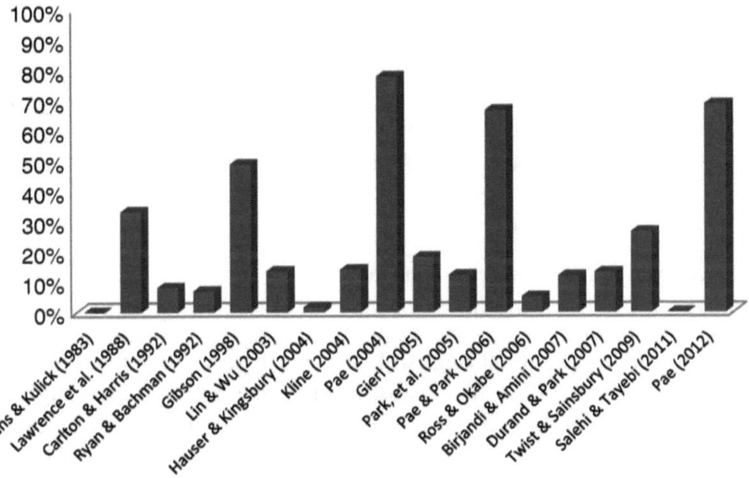

Fig. 1 Percentage of DIF items across individual studies

which indicates that in general almost one fourth of the items on a reading test may be detected as exhibiting gender DIF. The average percentage of DIF items for studies using IRT-LR was 28.1%, which is higher than the average percentage of DIF items for studies using M–H (18.9%).

Figure 1 shows the percentage of DIF items for each study. There is a large variation in the percentage of DIF items among the 18 studies. The study having the highest percentage of DIF items is Pae (2004): 77.78%, followed by Pae (2012): 68.6%, and Pae and Park (2006): 66.7%. All three of these studies used IRT-LR to detect DIF in the Korean College Scholastic Aptitude Test (KCSAT), and it should be noted that Pae is the sole author of the first two of these studies and the first author of the third. The percentage of DIF items was zero in both Dorans and Kulick (1983) and Salehi and Tayebi (2011).

Figure 2 lists the percentage of DIF items according to the kind of test being used. It is notable that the test having the highest percentage of DIF items is the KCSAT, which was studied in all three articles for which Pae is either the sole or the first author. When the KCSAT is not considered, the other second language

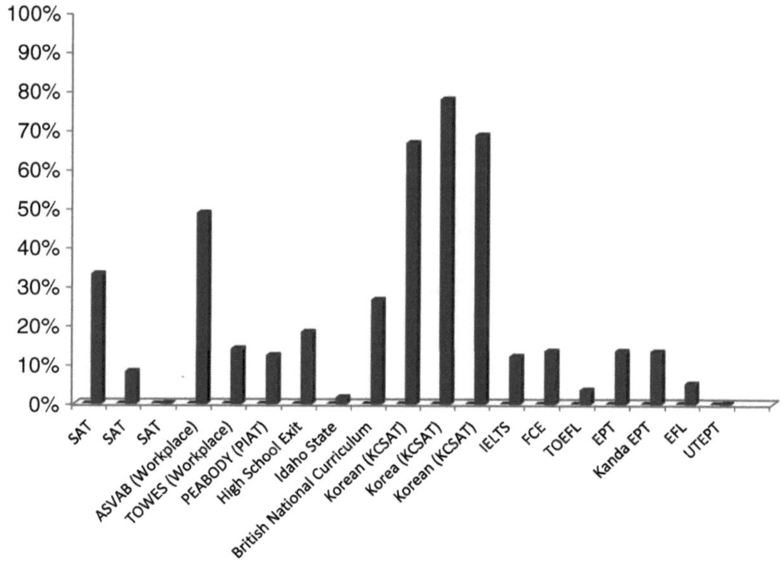

Fig. 2 Percentages of DIF items across tests studied

tests, such as the International English Language Testing System (IELTS), the First Certificate in English (FCE), the Test of English as a Foreign Language (TOEFL), and the University of Tehran English Proficiency Test (UTEPT), seem to have lower percentages of DIF items overall. In addition, in order to capture any trends in regard to the percentage of DIF items over time, we also graphed the percentage of DIF items in each study across time periods (Fig. 3). However, no trend could be identified.

Furthermore, we calculated the percentages of DIF items favoring males or females (Table 4). In terms of all 18 studies, half the DIF items favored males while half favored females. For studies using IRT-LR, about 53.5% of the DIF items favored males and 46.7% favored females. Similarly, for studies using M–H, 43.8% of the DIF items favored males and 56.3% favored females. A chi-square association test showed no significant association between the percentage of DIF items favoring males or females and the DIF method ($\chi^2 = 1.605$, df = 1, $p > 0.05$).

Unfortunately, many of the studies did not report whether the detected DIF was uniform or nonuniform. Also, the M–H method is unable to identify nonuniform DIF. For studies using IRT-LR, about 23.5% of the DIF items showed uniform DIF, whereas 28.8% of the DIF items showed nonuniform DIF. Overall, the information available in the included studies regarding uniform and nonuniform DIF is limited. Therefore, in the present study, we are not able to provide accurate patterns regarding whether uniform or nonuniform gender DIF is more prevalent in reading tests.

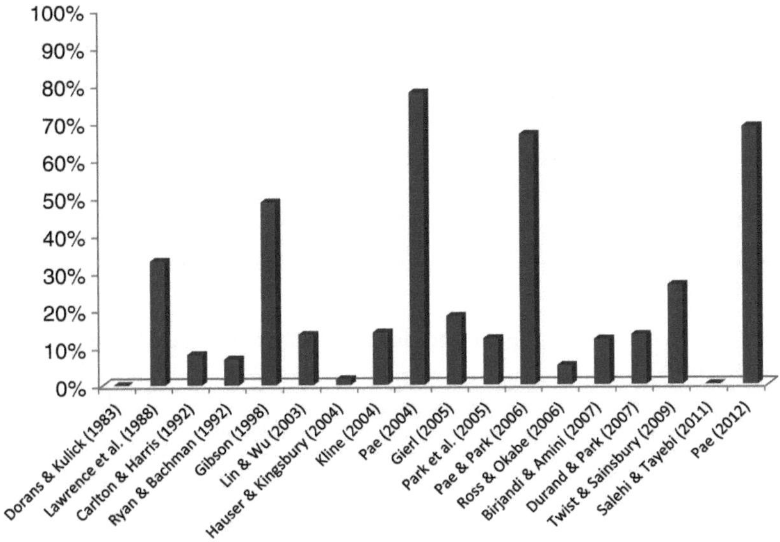

Fig. 3 Percentage of DIF items across time period

Table 4 Percentage of DIF items favoring males and percentage of DIF items favoring females

Gender	All studies (%)	Studies using IRT-LR (%)	Studies using M–H (%)
Favoring male	49.3	53.5	43.8
Favoring female	50.7	46.7	56.3

4.2 *Relationships Between DIF Existence and Item and Test Characteristics*

The respective relationships between DIF and item type and between DIF and item scoring are of theoretical interest. However, among the 1,210 items from the 18 studies, 1,176 items were multiple-choice and dichotomously coded. Due to insufficient variation to study the relationship between DIF existence and item type and the relationship between DIF existence and item scoring, we only examined the relationship between DIF existence and test length using point-biserial correlation. For all 18 studies, the correlation coefficient −0.145 is statistically significant ($p < 0.001$), which shows that items from shorter tests are more likely to show gender DIF than are items from longer tests. A similar pattern exists for studies using IRT-LR ($r = -0.468, p < 0.001$) and for studies using M–H ($r = -0.304, p < 0.001$), respectively.

Table 5 summarizes the relationship between DIF existence and test stakes. When all the studies are considered, the odds ratio is 1.59. This ratio indicates that the odds for an item from a high stakes test to show DIF are 1.59 times the odds for an item

Table 5 Relationship between DIF and test stakes

	Test stakes	With DIF	No DIF	$\chi^2_{(1)}$	Odds ratio
All studies	High	188	517	10.675***	1.590
	Not high	94	411		
Studies using IRT-LR	High	139	192	81.527***	10.971
	Not high	13	197		
Studies using M–H	High	16	198	36.936***	0.183
	Not high	64	145		

***$p < 0.001$

Table 6 Relationship between DIF existence and whether the test is administered to ESL speakers or to native speakers

	Tests	With DIF	No DIF	$\chi^2_{(1)}$	Odds ratio
All studies	ESL speakers Native English speakers	152130	346582	24.657***	0.508
Studies using IRT-LR	ESL speakers Native English speakers	13913	192197	81.527***	0.091
Studies using M–H	ESL speakers Native English speakers	971	93250	8.921**	2.935

**$p < 0.01$; ***$p < 0.001$

from a low stakes test. A similar pattern exists when only studies using IRT-LR are considered. That is, the odds ratio is 10.971, which indicates that the odds for an item from a high stakes test to show DIF are over 10 times the odds for an item from a low stakes test. However, when only studies using M–H are considered, the result is the opposite: the odds ratio of 0.183 indicates that the odds for an item from a high stakes test showing DIF are only 0.183 times the odds for an item from a low stakes test.

Table 6 summarizes the relationship between DIF existence and whether the test is for ESL speakers or native English speakers. When all the studies are considered, the odds ratio is 0.508. This ratio indicates that the odds for an item from tests for ESL speakers to show DIF are 0.508 times the odds for an item from tests for native English speakers. A similar pattern exists when only studies using IRT-LR are considered. That is, the odds ratio is 0.091, which indicates that the odds for an item from tests for ESL speakers to show DIF are 0.091 times the odds for an item from tests for native English speakers. However, when only studies using M–H are considered, the result is the opposite. The odds ratio of 2.935 indicates that the odds for an item from tests for ESL speakers to show DIF are 2.935 times the odds for an item from tests for native English speakers.

5 Discussion

5.1 Percentage of DIF Items

In this study, based on 1,210 items from 18 articles, the percentage of gender-related DIF items is 23.3%. This number is much smaller than what Zhang and French (2010) found in their study regarding gender DIF in math. Synthesizing 615 items from 14 studies, Zhang and French found that about 46% of the items were identified as not showing DIF, 23% of them were identified as showing moderate DIF, and 31% as showing large DIF. Based on the current study and the synthesis conducted by Zhang and French, it seems that the proportion of gender-related DIF items is lower in reading tests than in math tests.

The present study also shows that half of the DIF items favor males and half favor females. This pattern generally holds true across all the DIF methods used. For example, studies using IRT-LR showed about 53% of the DIF items favoring males and 47% of the DIF items favoring females; studies using M–H also showed DIF items approximately evenly favoring each gender but with a reverse twist: 44% favoring males and 56% favoring females. Zhang and French, however, reported that overall 60% of the math DIF items favor males and 40% favor females. Based on the present study and the synthesis conducted by Zhang and French, we would speculate that it is probably easier to develop DIF-free items in reading than in math. We were not able to determine whether there were any patterns regarding nonuniform or uniform DIF. The findings are inconclusive because studies using the M–H method cannot detect nonuniform DIF, and also some studies using the other methods did not report whether the detected DIF were uniform or nonuniform.

Another important finding is the large variation in the percentage of DIF items among the 18 studies, which ranges from 0 to 77.88%. For example, the study having the highest percentage of DIF item is 77.78% (Pae 2004), followed by 68.6% (Pae 2012), and 66.7% (Pae and Park 2006). All three of these studies examined gender DIF in the KCSAT test using IRT-LR, and all three used chi-square difference tests to determine the existence of DIF. It is not clear whether the KCSAT truly has many DIF items or the DIF procedure used in these three studies tends to inflate the Type 1 error. It would be very helpful to replicate those studies with other DIF detection methods.

We did not detect any obvious trends regarding whether the percentage of DIF items changes over time by referencing the chart in Fig. 3. However, it is important to note that the unclear trend observed in this study is probably due to the involvement of too many factors at the same time, such as different tests being studied, the different methods being used, and the limited samples included. For a clearer trend and a more definite conclusion, it would be meaningful to track the percentage of DIF items in a single test, such as the SAT, preferably with the same DIF method and criterion.

5.2 *Relationship Between DIF Existence and Item and Test Characteristics*

Although item type is a very important characteristic, as indicated in the literature, among the 1,210 items from 18 studies, 1,176 items were multiple-choice and dichotomously coded. Therefore, we were not able to examine how DIF existence might be related to item type. Similarly, item content information was often not provided in the studies reviewed, and we were not able to study the relationship between item content and DIF existence, though the previous literature has indicated that item content is a potentially important source of gender DIF in reading.

The only clear relationship we found was that items from shorter tests are more likely to show DIF. A point-biserial correlation between test length and number of DIF items found a significant negative relationship. Shorter tests tended to have more DIF items than longer tests regardless of the DIF analysis method used. Noteworthy in this regard is that studies using either IRT-LR or M–H have medium-sized correlations (−0.468 and −0.304, respectively).

Based on all 18 studies, it seems that high stakes tests generally have more DIF items than low stakes tests. In studies using IRT-LR, this pattern holds true; however, in studies using M–H, this pattern is reversed with low stakes tests having more DIF items. Furthermore, tests developed for ESL learners are less likely to contain DIF items than tests developed for native speakers of English. While studies using IRT-LR show this pattern, in studies using M–H, tests developed for ESL learners are more likely to show DIF. To summarize, the relationship between DIF existence and test stakes and the relationship between DIF existence and whether tests are developed for ESL learners are inconclusive.

6 Conclusion, Limitations, and Further Study

To summarize, this study provides a synthesis of gender-related DIF studies in reading tests. Based on 1,210 items from 18 articles, the study shows that 23.3% of the items in reading tests show gender DIF. There is a large variation in the percentage of items determined as showing DIF across studies, ranging from 0% (Dorans and Kulick 1983) to 77.78% (Pae 2004). Also, studies using IRT-LR methods report a higher percentage of DIF items than studies using M–H. Among the DIF items, about half favor males and half favor females, and this pattern holds true for studies using IRT-LR and for those using M–H. Furthermore, items from shorter tests are more likely to be determined as having DIF than items from longer tests. Other potential DIF patterns seem to depend on the DIF methods and the tests. For example, for studies using IRT-LR, tests developed for ESL learners are less likely to contain DIF items than tests developed for native speakers of English; however, the opposite pattern is found for studies using M–H. This inverse relationship needs further investigation to determine what is occurring. Another possible cause of these differences, which should be considered in follow-up studies, is how the studies constructed the set of presumably DIF-free anchor items. In some studies, anchor items consist of all items other than the studied item, whereas in other studies the anchor items consist of a set of items which have been previously identified as being DIF-free. The different methods can potentially produce very different outcomes.

The present study does not report averaged DIF magnitude (or effect sizes). Despite the fact that ETS proposes a three-category DIF effect size scheme, there is much disagreement on how accurately we can align effect sizes from different DIF methods to the same metric (DeMars 2011). Also many studies did not provide any item-level DIF effect size information. Therefore, we had to use a rougher classification of whether the item did or did not show DIF. Most of these decisions were based on the hypothesis testing in the original articles. Another challenge for this study was the insufficient DIF-related information reported in the articles. This restricted us from examining meaningful research questions such as how item content is related to gender DIF in reading tests. A more standardized procedure needs to be adopted regarding how to report DIF studies.

Finally, this study is limited in that it only provides primarily descriptive information. The 1,210 items from the 18 studies involve a nesting structure, such that items (level 1) are nested in studies (level 2). A multi-level regression analysis would have provided more informative inferences regarding how item characteristics and test characteristics simultaneously influence the existence of gender DIF in reading tests. This kind of analysis would also show how the variance of DIF existence is partitioned between studies and within studies. However, preliminary analyses indicate that the results of such a multi-level analysis would not have been reliable due to the small level-2 sample size in this study. Should more qualified studies be collected in the future, a multi-level regression analysis will be used.

References[1]

Abbott, M. L. (2007). A confirmatory approach to differential item functioning on an ESL reading assessment. *Language Testing, 24*, 7–36.

Bae, J., & Bachman, L. F. (1998). A latent variable approach to listening and reading: Testing factorial invariance across two groups of children in the Korean/English two-way immersion. *Language Testing, 15*, 380–414.

*Birjandi, P., & Amini, M. (2007). Differential item functioning (test bias) analysis paradigm across manifest and latent examinee groups (on the construct validity of IELTS) [special issue]. *Journal of Human Sciences, 55*, 1–20.

Brantmeier, C. (2001). Second language reading research on passage content and gender: Challenges for the intermediate-level curriculum. *Foreign Language Annals, 34*, 325–333.

Bügel, K., & Buunk, B. P. (1996). Sex differences in foreign language text comprehension: The role of interests and prior knowledge. *The Modern Language Journal, 80*, 15–31.

[1]References marked with an asterisk indicate studies included in the synthesis.

Camilli, G., & Shepard, L. A. (1994). *Methods for identifying biased test items*. Thousand Oaks, CA: Sage.

*Carlton, S. T., & Harris, A. M. (1992). *Characteristics associated with differential item functioning on the Scholastic Aptitude Test: Gender and majority/minority group comparisons* (ETS Research Report, 92-64). Princeton, NJ: Educational Testing Service.

Chiu, M. M., & McBride-Chang, C. (2006). Gender, context, and reading: A comparison of students in 43 countries. *Scientific Studies of Reading, 10*, 331–362.

DeMars, C. E. (2000). Test stakes and item format interactions. *Applied Measurement in Education, 13*, 55–77.

DeMars, C. E. (2011). An analytic comparison of effect sizes for differential item functioning. *Applied Measurement in Education, 24*, 189–209.

Doolittle, A., & Welch, C. (1989). *Gender differences in performance on a college-level achievement test* (ACT Research Report Series 89-9). Iowa City, IA: ACT.

Dorans, N. J., & Holland, P. W. (1993). DIF detection and description: Mantel-Haenszel and standardization. In P. W. Holland & H. Wainer (Eds.), *Differential item functioning* (pp. 35–66). Hillsdale, NJ: Erlbaum.

*Dorans, N. J., & Kulick, E. (1983). *Assessing unexpected differential item performance on female candidates on SAT and TSWE forms administered in December 1977: An application of the standardization approach* (ETS Research Report RR 83-9). Princeton, NJ: Educational Testing Service.

*Durand, J., & Park, S. (2007). A study of gender- and academic major-based differential item functioning (DIF) in KEPT 2006, Mexico. *Studies in Linguistics and Language Teaching, 19*, 55–85. Retrieved from http://www.kandagaigo.ac.jp/kuis/about/bulletin/jp/019/pdf/jeffrey_siwon.pdf

Ferne, T., & Rupp, A. A. (2007). A synthesis of 15 years of research on DIF in language testing: Methodological advances, challenges, and recommendations. *Language Assessment Quarterly, 4*, 113–148.

Geske, A., & Ozola, A. (2010, July). *Differential item functioning in the aspect of gender differences in reading literacy*. Paper presented at the IEA International Research Conference, Gothenburg, Sweden. Retrieved from http://www.iea.nl/fileadmin/user_upload/IRC/IRC_2010/Papers/IRC2010_Geske_Ozola.pdf

*Gibson, S. G. (1998). *Gender and ethnicity-based differential item functioning on the armed services vocational aptitude battery* (Unpublished doctoral dissertation). Virginia Polytechnic Institute and State University, Blacksburg, VA.

*Gierl, M. J. (2005). Using dimensionality-based DIF analyses to identify and interpret constructs that elicit group differences. *Educational Measurement: Issues and Practice, 24*(1), 3–14.

Glass, G. V. (1976). Primary, secondary, and meta-analysis of research. *Educational Researcher, 5*, 3–8.

Hall, C., & Coles, M. (1999). *Children's reading choices*. London/New York: Routledge.

Hambleton, R., Swaminathan, H., & Rogers, H. (1991). *Fundamentals of item response theory*. Newbury Park, CA: Sage.

*Hauser, C., & Kingsbury, G. (2004, January). *Differential item functioning and differential test functioning in the "Idaho Standards Achievement Tests" for spring 2003* (ERIC Document Reproduction Service No. ED491249). Portland, OR: Northwest Evaluation Association.

Holland, P., & Thayer, D. (1988). Differential item performance and the Mantel-Haenszel procedure. In H. Wainer & H. I. Braun (Eds.), *Test validity* (pp. 129–145). Hillsdale, NJ: Erlbaum.

Jacob, B. A. (2002). *The impact of high-stakes testing on student achievement: Evidence from Chicago*. Unpublished manuscript, Harvard University. Retrieved November 10, 2012 from http://www.terry.uga.edu/~mustard/courses/e4250/Jacob-testing.pdf

Jodoin, G. M., & Gierl, M. J. (2001). Evaluating type I error and power rates using an effect size measure with the logistic regression procedure for DIF detection. *Applied Measurement in Education, 14*, 329–349.

Johnston, R. S., Watson, J. E., & Logan, S. (2009). Enhancing word reading, spelling and reading comprehension skills with synthetic phonics teaching: Studies in Scotland and England. In C. Wood & V. Connelly (Eds.), *Contemporary perspectives on reading and spelling*. London: Routledge.

Karami, H. (2011). Detecting gender bias in a language proficiency test. *International Journal of Language Studies, 5*(2), 27–38. Retrieved October 18, 2011 from http://www.ijls.net/volumes/volume5issue2/karami1.pdf

Kim, Y.-H., & Jang, E. E. (2009). Differential functioning of reading subskills on the OSSLT for L1 and ELL students: A multidimensionality model-based DBF/DIF approach. *Language Learning, 59*, 825–865.

*Kline, T. J. B. (2004). Gender and language differences on the test of workplace essential skills: Using overall mean scores and item-level differential item functioning analyses. *Educational and Psychological Measurement, 64*, 549–559.

*Lawrence, I. M., Curley, W. E., & McHale, F. J. (1988). *Differential item functioning for males and females on SAT-Verbal reading subscore items* (College Board Report No. 88-4). New York, NY: The College Board.

*Lin, J., & Wu, F. (2003, April). *Differential performance by gender in foreign language testing*. Paper presented at the meeting of the National Council on Measurement in Education (NCME), Chicago, IL. Retrieved August 25, 2011 from http://www2.education.ualberta.ca/educ/psych/crame/files/ncmepaper.pdf

Lipsey, M. W., & Wilson, D. B. (2001). *Practical meta-analysis*. Thousand Oaks, CA: Sage.

Logan, S., & Johnston, R. (2009). Gender differences in reading ability and attitudes: Examining where these differences lie. *Journal of Research in Reading, 32*, 199–214.

Mantel, N., & Haenszel, W. (1959). Statistical aspects of the analysis of data from retrospective studies of disease. *Journal of the National Cancer Institute, 22*(4), 719–748.

McKenna, M. C., Kear, D. J., & Ellsworth, R. A. (1995). Children's attitudes towards reading: A national survey. *Reading Research Quarterly, 30*, 934–956.

Mellenbergh, G. J. (1982). Contingency table models for assessing item bias. *Journal of Educational Statistics, 7*, 105–108.

Mullis, I., Campbell, J., & Farstrup, A. (1993). *NAEP 1992: Reading report card for the nation and the states*. Washington, DC: U.S. Department of Education.

Mullis, I. V. S., Martin, M. O., Kennedy, A. M., & Foy, P. (2007). *PIRLS 2006 international report: IEA's progress in international reading literacy study in primary schools in 40 countries*. Chestnut Hill, MA: TIMSS and PIRLS International Study Center, Lynch School of Education, Boston College.

O'Neil, H. F., Jr., Sugrue, B., & Baker, E. L. (1995). Effects of motivational interventions on the National Assessment of Educational Progress mathematics performance. *Educational Assessment, 3*, 135–157.

*Pae, T. I. (2004). Gender effect on reading comprehension with Korean EFL learners. *System, 32*, 265–281.

*Pae, T. I. (2012). Causes of gender DIF on an EFL language test: A multiple data analysis over nine years. *Language Testing, 29*, 533–554.

*Pae, T. I., & Park, G. P. (2006). Examining the relationship between differential item functioning and differential test functioning. *Language Testing, 23*, 475–496.

*Park, H., Pearson, P. D., & Reckase, M. D. (2005). Assessing the effect of cohort, gender, and race on differential item functioning (DIF) in an adaptive test designed for multi-age groups. *Reading Psychology: An International Quarterly, 26*, 81–101.

Pugh, K. R., Shaywitz, B. A., Shaywitz, S. E., Constable, R. T., Skudlarski, P., Fulbright, R. K., et al. (1996). Cerebral organization of component processes in reading. *Brain, 119*, 1221–1238.

Rezaee, A. A., & Shabani, E. (2010). Gender differential item functioning analysis of the University of Tehran English Proficiency Test. *Pazhuhesh-E Zabanha-Ye Khareji, 56*, 89–108.

*Ross, S. J., & Okabe, J. (2006). The subjective and objective interface of bias detection on language tests. *International Journal of Testing, 6*, 229–253.

Roussos, L., & Stout, W. (1996). Simulation studies of the effects of small sample size and studied item parameters on SIBTEST and Mantel-Haenszel type I error performance. *Journal of Educational Measurement, 33*, 215–230.

*Ryan, K., & Bachman, L. (1992). Differential item functioning on two tests of EFL proficiency. *Language Testing, 9*, 12–29.

Sainsbury, M., & Schagen, I. (2004). Attitudes to reading at ages nine and eleven. *Journal of Research in Reading, 27*, 373–386.

*Salehi, M., & Tayebi, A. (2011, October). *Differential item functioning in terms of gender in the reading comprehension sub-test of a high-stakes test*. Paper presented at the meeting of the East Coast Organization of Language Testers (ECOLT), Washington, D.C.

Shaywitz, B. A., Shaywitz, S. E., Pugh, K. R., Constable, R. T., Skudlarski, P., Fulbright, R. K., et al. (1995). Sex differences in the functional organization of the brain for language. *Nature, 373*, 607–609.

Shealy, R., & Stout, W. (1993). An item response theory model for test bias and differential test functioning. In P. Holland & H. Wainer (Eds.), *Differential item functioning* (pp. 123–135). Hillsdale, NJ: Erlbaum.

Shimizu, Y., & Zumbo, B. D. (2005). Logistic regression for differential item functioning: A primer. *Japan Language Testing Association Journal, 7*, 110–124.

Stephenson, A., Jiao, H., & Wall, N. (2004, April). *A performance comparison of native and non-native speakers of English on an English language proficiency test*. Paper presented at the American Educational Research Association Annual Meeting, San Diego, CA.

Swaminathan, H., & Rogers, H. J. (1990). Detecting differential item functioning using logistic regression procedures. *Journal of Educational Measurement, 27*, 361–370.

Takala, S., & Kaftandjieva, F. (2000). Test fairness: A DIF analysis of an L2 vocabulary test. *Language Testing, 117*, 323–340.

Thissen, D., Steinberg, L., & Wainer, H. (1988). Use of item response theory in the study of group differences in trace lines. In H. Wainer & H. I. Braun (Eds.), *Test validity* (pp. 147–169). Hillsdale, NJ: Erlbaum.

Thompson, I. (1987). Memory in language learning. In A. Wenden & J. Rubin (Eds.), *Learner strategies in language learning* (pp. 43–56). Englewood Cliffs, NJ: Prentice Hall International Ltd.

*Twist, L., & Sainsbury, M. (2009). Girl friendly? Investigating the gender gap in national reading tests at age 11. *Educational Research, 51*, 283–297.

Wise, S. L. (2006). An investigation of the differential effort received by items on a low-stakes computer-based test. *Applied Measurement in Education, 19*, 95–114.

Wise, S. L., Bhola, D. S., & Yang, S. T. (2006). Taking the time to improve the validity of low-stakes tests: The effort-monitoring CBT. *Educational Measurement: Issues and Practice, 25*, 21–30.

Zhang, M., & French, B. F. (2010, May). *Gender related differential item functioning in mathematics tests: A meta-analysis*. Paper presented at the Annual Meeting of the American Educational Research Association, Denver, CO.

Zhou, J., Gierl, M., & Tan, X. (2006). *Evaluating the performance of SIBTEST and MULTISIB using different matching criteria*. Paper presented at the annual meeting of the National Council on Measurement in Education. San Diego, CA. Retrieved March18, 2008 from http://www.education.ualberta.ca/educ/psych/crame/files/ncme06_JZ.pdf

Zieky, M. (1993). History and development of DIF. In P. W. Holland & H. Wainer (Eds.), *Differential item functioning* (pp. 337–347). Hillsdale, NJ: Erlbaum.

Zumbo, B. D. (1999, April). *A handbook on the theory and methods of differential item functioning (DIF): Logistic regression modeling as a unitary framework for binary and Likert-type (ordinal) item scores*. Ottawa, ON: Directorate of Human Resources Research and Evaluation, Department of National Defense. Retrieved September 10, 2012 from http://www.educ.ubc.ca/faculty/zumbo/DIF/handbook.pdf

Zwick, R., & Ercikan, K. (1989). Analysis of differential item functioning in the NAEP history assessment. *Journal of Educational Measurement, 26*, 55–66.

MIX
Papier aus verantwortungsvollen Quellen
Paper from responsible sources
FSC® C105338

If you have any concerns about our products,
you can contact us on
ProductSafety@springernature.com

In case Publisher is established outside the EU,
the EU authorized representative is:
Springer Nature Customer Service Center GmbH
Europaplatz 3, 69115 Heidelberg, Germany

Printed by Libri Plureos GmbH
in Hamburg, Germany